The
MASTER

Yasin T. al-Jibouri

اللهم آرزقنا شفاعة الحسين

Paperback: 561 pages
Publisher: Yasin Publications
Date of publication: January 17, 2015
Language: English
ISBN-13: 978-1507611234
ISBN-10: 1507611234

Yasin Publications
P.O. Box 338
8253-A Backlick Rd.
Newington, VA 22122

Website: www.yasinpublications.org
Email: info@yasinpublications.org

YasinPublications.org

اللّٰهُمَّ صَلِّ عَلىٰ مُحَمَّدٍ وَآلِ مُحَمَّد

السلام على الشيب الخضيب، السلام على الخد التريب
السلام على البدن السليب ، السلام على الثغر المقروع بالقضيب
السلام على الرأس المرفوع، السلام على الاجسام العارية في الفلوات
السلام على المرمل بالدماء، السلام على المهتوك الخباء
السلام على خامس أصحاب الكساء، السلام على غريب الغرباء
السلام على شهيد الشهداء، السلام على قتيل الأدعياء
السلام على ساكن كربلاء، السلام على من بكته ملائكة السماء
و رحمة الله و بركاته

O Allāh! Bless Muhammed and the progeny of Muhammed

Peace with the blood-drenched gray hair. Peace with the dust-covered cheek. Peace with the maraudered body. Peace with the mouth beaten with the iron bar. Peace with the head raised [atop a spear]. Peace with the bodies exposed in the plains. Peace with the one covered with blood. Peace with the one whose privacy was violated. Peace with the fifth of the Fellows of the Covering Sheet. Peace with the stranger of all strangers. Peace with the martyr of all martyrs. Peace with the one killed by the da'is. Peace with the one who resides in Kerbalā. Peace with the one mourned by the angels of the heavens. Peace with you, O Father of Abdullāh…

Shrine of Imam al-Abbas عليه السلام
which faces that of his brother, Imam al-Hussain عليه السلام

اللهم أرزقنا شفاعةَ الحُسَين

THE LARGEST GATHERING ON EARTH

Millions continue their march towards Kerbala for the Arba`een

**OVER TWENTY MILLION PEOPLE
GATHER IN KERBALA, IRAQ, ON
DECEMBER 13, 2014,
TO COMMEMMORATE THE "ARBA`EEN"
OF IMAM AL-HUSSAIN...**

Read more in this book's Conclusion

CONTENTS

TREE LAMENTS AND BLEEDS ON *ĀSHŪRA*

In Qazween city, Iran there is an old tree which for so long has been wailing and lamenting the martyrdom of Imām Hussain (ع). Its branches bleed warm blood on the 10th Muharram, i.e. Āshūra, when the Imām was martyred, and it keeps doing so till the 11th night of Muharram. The faithful residing in Qazween and surrounding areas gather there and commemorate Āshūra.

■ الشجرة الدامية قبيل الفجر حيث يبدأ لونها يميل إلى الحمرة

Bleeding tree shortly before dawn when its color starts changing to red

■ آثار الدم الحسيني على الشجرة المعجزة بعد شروق الشمس

Marks of Hussaini blood visibly appear on the miracle tree after sunrise

The faithful take blood specimens to show others

In the Name of Allāh, the most Gracious, the most Merciful

PREFACE

This is an edited version of my book titled Kerbala and Beyod: An Epic of Immortal Heroism which was published by Authorhouse of Bloomington, Indiana, U.S.A., on August 26, 2011 (ISBN 978-1-4634-2074-1 softcover, 978-1-4634-2070-3 hardcover which I think Authorhouse no longer publishes and 978-1-4670-2613-0 electronic edition). The number of pages of the said edition is 714 which makes it the largest book I have so far written, and it pleases me to tell you that Amazon, the world's largest bookseller, is marketing it all over the world, including in China where most people do not really care for religion.

Initially, this Preface was intended to introduce the reader to the author, but I, the author, suggest that if you really are curious about who Yasin T. al-Jibouri really is, you can send an email to this address and request the list of books which this guy has so far written, edited or translated: info@yasinpublications.org and you will receive a PDF file containing basic details and many front cover images of 78 of my works.

It is also my pleasure to inform you that Harvard University, the most prestigious university in the United States, formed a team of professors and scholars who set up a "Pluralism Project" one of the tasks of which was to research the presence of Islam and Muslims in America, and my name is mentioned in it twice. The team took more than two decades to gather, verify and compare information which it finally posted on the Internet under the title "Islam in America" and

you can review if Online if you click on this Link:
http://www.pluralism.org/religion/islam/timeline/america   which   I
think is the best research available on this subject.

One fact I am very keen about introducing to the reader is the
following:

In 1975, I received instructions to facilitate the entry to the United
States of the very first representative of the then Grand Ayatullah
Abul-Qasim al-Khoei, may Allāh reward him, in North America,
namely Shaikh Muhammed Sarwar of Quetta, Pakistan. Due to my
sponsorship through my then organization, the Islamic Society of
Georgia, Inc., Shaikh Sarwar did, indeed, arrive at the U.S. on
January 25, 1976; a few days later, the Shaikh became my roommate
in a very poor section of Atlanta, Georgia. A few months later, the
Shaikh moved from Atlanta to New York where there has been a
much larger Shī'a population.

I was surprised not to see Sarwar's name in the report referred to
above by Harvard University, so I wrote it a letter with facts and
figures in the hope its future reports will be more precise and
complete, and I then expanded my letter to several pages in which I
commented on that report. You can get a copy of my comment, too,
if you ask for it.

This much should suffice the kind reader who can find out more
about me if he runs a Google search on the Internet or visits
Amazon's wep site: www.amazon.com then keys my name in the
search box.

I have included many Arabic poems in this book for Arabic speaking
readers, especially those living abroad, and I hope they will enjoy
reading them and shed plenty of tears for the trials and tribulations
through which Imam al-Hussain عليه السلام and his family and supporters
went. I hope that these tears will wash away their sins and mine,
Allahomma Aameen, Wassalamo Alaikom.

Yasin T. al-Jibouri
December 15, 2014

Thousands of worshippers at the Shrine of Imam Ali عليه السلام, al-Najaf al-Ashraf, Iraq. Below: Interior of Shrine

PROLOGUE

ETERNAL STRUGGLE BETWEEN RIGHT AND WRONG

This is a tale of an ongoing struggle between right and wrong, truth and falsehood, piety and impiety, worldliness and spirituality. Such struggles take place in our life each and every day on different scales. Other religions, too, have immortalized the struggle between right and wrong: the struggle of Rama against Ravana, the contest between Moses, peace be with him, and Pharaoh, the challenge of Abraham, peace be with him, to Nimrud, the contest of Jesus Christ, peace be with him, against Herod... All these are examples of the contest, the struggle, the ongoing war, between right and wrong, truth and falsehood. Falsehood appears to the eyes of most people as being very strong, armed with material power. It has the authority of the ruling government, of the veto at the "U.N. Security Council," of the awe of military might, the carriers and the cruise missiles, the satellites and the spy planes, the lackeys and the stooges, the silver and the gold, and the numerical superiority... Its ostentatious grandeur and splendor cannot be denied, nor can its glittering crowns, thrones studded with gems, palaces and dazzling swords... And the truth! The humble truth! The meek and weak truth! It appears helpless, handicapped, powerless... But the truth possesses the vigor of faith, the reliance on the Almighty, and the precious asset of spiritual power. These armaments of the truth are so powerful, they smash the head of falsehood, reducing its splendor and grandeur to dust. Truth, in the end, triumphs, achieving success so splendidly that the world is awe-stricken... Such is the epic of heroism recorded on the pages of history not with the ink of the writers but with the blood of the martyrs. Such is each and every epic of heroism... Such is the epic of martyrdom of Imām al-Hussain (ع).

Interior of Imam al-Hussain's Tomb. Below: Shrine of Imam al-Abbas عليه السلام

In the Name of Allāh, the Most Gracious, the Most Merciful

INTRODUCTION

This book contains a brief yet documented narrative of an incident that took place in Kerbalā', Iraq, in 61 A.H. (After Hijra, or Hegira)/680 A.D. It has stamped the history of the Muslim nation ever since, and it will continue to do so till the reappearance of the Awaited One, the Mahdi from among the offspring of Prophet Muhammed ﷺ. It refers to a revolution against tyranny and oppression led by Imām al-Hussain عليه السلام son of Imām Ali ibn [son of] Abū [father of] Talib عليه السلام and grandson of Prophet Muhammed ﷺ. The confrontation left a lone male survivor from Imām al-Hussain's camp: Imām al-Hussain's son Ali, titled "as-Sajjād," the one who quite often prostrates to Allāh, and also "Zain al-Ābidīn," the best of worshippers of Allāh. He later became the fourth in the series of the Twelve Infallible Imāms عليه السلام. His offspring migrated to north Africa where they founded the Fatimide caliphate that lasted from 296 - 566 A.H./909 - 1171 A.D. Having conquered Egypt in 358 A.H./969 A.D., they built Cairo in order to make it their capital and founded in the next year the al-Azhar mosque and university. The latter was founded by caliph "al-Muizz li Deenillah," Abū Tameem Maadd ibn al-Mansur who was born in 319 A.H./931 A.D. and died in 365 A.H./975 A.D.; he ruled from 341 A.H./953 A.D. till his death.

The bloody confrontation between Hussain's tiny group of family members and supports and the huge army raised according to orders issued by the ruler of his time, namely Yazid "son" of Mu'awiyah, which is referred to in history books as the Taff Battle, started on the first day of Muharram, 61 A.H./October 4, 680 A.D. and ended ten days later with the barbaric killing of Imām al-Hussain ؏ and all males with him—with the exception of his ailing son referred to above, namely Ali—, including his infant Abdullāh, who was six months old and who was shot with an arrow in the neck. Imām al-Hussain ؏ was pleading to those folks to give Abdullāh some water to drink. Imām al-Hussain ؏ and his small band were not permitted to the end to have access to the water of the Euphrates that lied a short distance from their camp. This reveals the extent of cruelty of those who fought Imām al-Hussain ؏ and his small band of supporters, the brave defender of principles and the reformer of the nation that he was, the man whom the Prophet on many occasions praised and honoured as one of the Masters of the Youths of Paradise, the other Master being his older brother Hassan ؏. Imām al-Hussain's body was trampled under the hoofs of the soldiers' horses and his head was cut off, placed on top of a spear and paraded before his women and children, who were all tied and chained as captives and conveyed in the most cruel manner the entire distance from Kerbalā', as the Taff area came to be called, to Damascus, Syria, seat of the Umayyad tyrant Yazid "son" of Mu'awiyah ibn Abū Sufyan. The heads of the other heroes who fought on Imām al-Hussain's side were also cut off and paraded in the same manner as trophies although Islam does not permit the mutilation of anyone's body, be he a Muslim or a non-Muslim. Little did those killers care to know about Islam, and the same can be said about those who refrain from condemning them and who, thus, share in the burden of sins those killers shall bear on the Day of Judgment.

The primary sources of this book are: *Maqtal al-Hussain* by Abdul-Razzaq al-Musawi al-Muqarram, and *Tarikh al-Umam wal Muluk* by Abū Ja'far Muhammed ibn Jarar at-Tabari (better known as *Tarikh at-Tabari*). Several secondary references, in Arabic and English, have been consulted and are cited in elaborate footnotes.

It is hoped that this book will open the eyes of new Muslim converts in the West in general and here in the U.S. in particular so that they may see the other side of the coin. Most of them were not taught

Islamic history because, in most likelihood, it would indict their mentors. It is also hoped that such converts will realize the pitfalls of little knowledge which is surely a dangerous thing.

There is a story behind every book. This one is no exception. As of the date of writing this Introduction (Shawwal 1419 A.H./February 1999), Northern Virginia Muslims who love and revere Imām Hussain عليه السلام do not have a place of their own where they can assemble to commemorate the Kerbalā' tragedy, the greatest of all; therefore, they have to meet here and there, mostly at homes and apartments of their brethren who can accommodate them. The most prominent of such dedicated brethren have been: Hamzah ash-Shawwaf (nicknamed Abū Muhammed-Ali), Abdul-Muhsin as-Sa'igh (Abū Abdul-Aziz), and Ahmed al-Haddad (Abū Abdullāh). These brethren have always opened their homes and hearts to all those who cherish the memory of Imām Hussain عليه السلام and of all other Imāms belonging to the Prophet's Progeny, "Ahl al-Bayt," peace and blessings of Allāh be upon all of them. During the past commemoration (Muharram 1419/May 1998), an Azari brother named Salashour who runs a rug store tried his best to make us feel at home, permitting us to use the premises of his business for the first ten days of the month of Muharram. It was there and then that another very dedicated brother named Ja'far Madan suggested that I write a few pages in English about the martyrdom of Imām Hussain عليه السلام in order to circulate them on the Internet. Alhamdu-Lillah, both I and he did what we promised. Then Br. Madan asked me whether I would consider turning those few pages into a book for the American and European readers. We liked the idea. You see, a good word, a wise suggestion, is like a seed; if it finds the right soil, it will shoot roots and sprout, and soon a seed becomes a tree bearing fruit, and the fruit carry seeds that will eventually be sowed, and they, too, will set roots, sprout and bear fruit..., and so on. May the Almighty bless and reward our dear brother Ja'far Madan for his suggestion, and may He bless all other dedicated brethren like him. May He forever guide our steps to what He loves and prefers, *Allāhomma AAameen.*

As the Dedication suggests, the publication of this book has been made possible by the generosity of a number of such dedicated lovers of Imām al-Hussain (ع), and of his Ahl al-Bayt (ع), and who reside in metropolitan Washington, D.C., and elsewhere. The author apologizes if some of the photographs are not of good quality. May the Almighty reward all those who brought this book to light and who circulate it and help others benefit from it with the very best of His rewards in the life of this world and in the hereafter, *Allāhomma Āmeen.*

WHAT SOME NON-MUSLIMS HAVE SAID ABOUT IMAM AL-HUSSAIN

Edward G. Brown, professor of Arabic and oriental studies at the University of Cambridge, praises Imam Hussain in his book, "A Literary History of Persia" (London 1999) thus:

"... a reminder of the blood-stained field of Kerbela, where the grandson of the Apostle of God fell at length, tortured by thirst and surrounded by the bodies of his murdered kinsmen, has been at anytime since then sufficient to evoke, even in the most lukewarm and heedless, the deepest emotions, the most frantic grief, and an exaltation of spirit before which pain, danger and death shrink to unconsidered trifles."

According to the great poet Rabindranath Tagore, Hussain's sacrifice indicates spiritual liberation. He writes:

"In order to keep alive justice and truth, instead of an army or weapons, success can be achieved by sacrificing lives, exactly what Imam Hussain did."

Thomas Carlyle, a Scottish historian and essayist, explains:

"The best lesson which we get from the tragedy of Karbala is that Hussain and his companions were rigid believers in God. They illustrated that the numerical superiority does not count when it comes to the truth and the falsehood. The victory of Hussain, despite his minority, marvels me!"

Charles Dickens, English novelist, writes:

"If Hussain had fought to quench his worldly desires...then I do not understand why his sister, wife, and children accompanied him. It stands to reason therefore, that he sacrificed purely for Islam."

Antoine Bara, Lebanese writer and the author of "Christian Ideology, said:

"No battle in the modern and past history of mankind has earned more sympathy and admiration as well as provided more lessons than the martyrdom of Husayn in the battle of Karbala."

Dr. K. Sheldrake writes:
"Of that gallant band, male and female knew that the enemy forces around were implacable, and were not only ready to fight, but to kill. Denied even water for the children, they remained parched under the burning sun and scorching sands, yet not one faltered for a moment. Hussain marched with his little company, not to glory, not to power of wealth, but to a supreme sacrifice, and every member bravely faced the greatest odds without flinching."

Dr. Radha Krishnan writes:
"Though Imam Hussain gave his life years ago, but his indestructible soul rules the hearts of people even today."

Mahatma Gandhi's first Salt march was inspired by Imam Hussain's non violent resistance to the tyranny of Yazid. Gandhi is said to have studied the history of Islam and Imam Hussain, and was of the opinion that Islam represented not the legacy of a sword but of sacrifices of saints like Imam Hussain. Mahatma Gandhi writes:
"My faith is that the progress of Islam does not depend on the use of sword by its believers, but the result of the supreme sacrifice of Hussain, the great saint."

Jawaharlal Nehru considered Karbala to represent humanities strength and determination. He writes:
"Imam Hussain's sacrifice is for all groups and communities, an example of the path of righteousness."

Dr. Rajendra Prasad says:
"The sacrifice of Imam Hussain is not limited to one country, or nation, but it is the hereditary state of the brotherhood of all mankind."

Dr. Radha Krishnan writes:
"Though Imam Hussain gave his life almost 1300 years ago, but his indestructible soul rules the hearts of people even today."

24

Swami Shankaracharya describes:
"It is Hussain's sacrifice that has kept Islam alive or else in this world there would be no one left to take Islam's name."

Mrs. Sarojini Naidu writes:
"I congratulate the Muslims that from among them, Hussain, a great human being was born, who is reverted and honored totally by all communities."

Simon Ockley, Professor of Arabic at the University of Cambridge, writes the following in his book *The History of Saracens:*
"Then Hussain mounted his horse, and took the Koran and laid it before him, and, coming up to the people, invited them to the performances of their duty: adding, 'O God, thou art my confidence in every trouble, and my hope in all adversity!'... He next reminded them of his excellencies, the nobility of his birth, the greatness of his power, and his high descent, and said, 'Consider with yourselves whether or not such a man as I am is not better than you; I who am the son of your prophet's daughter, besides whom there is no other upon the face of the earth. Ali was my father; Jaafar and Hamza, the chief of the martyrs, were both my uncles; and the apostle of God, upon whom be peace, said both of me and my brother, that we were the chief of the youth of paradise. If you will believe me, what I say is true, for by God, I never told a lie in earnest since I had my understanding; for God hates a lie. If you do not believe me, ask the companions of the apostle of God [here he named them], and they will tell you the same. Let me go back to what I have.' They asked, 'What hindered him from being ruled by the rest of his relations.' He answered, 'God forbid that I should set my hand to the resignation of my right after a slavish manner. I have recourse to God from every tyrant that doth not believe in the day of account."

Ignaz Goldziher, the famous Hungarian orientalist scholar, writes the following in his book *Introduction to Islamic Theology and Law:*
"Ever since the black day of Karbala, the history of this family ... has been a continuous series of sufferings and persecutions. These are narrated in poetry and prose, in a richly cultivated literature of martyrologies - a Shia specialty - and form the theme of Shi'i

gatherings in the first third of the month of Muharram, whose tenth day (Ashura) is kept as the anniversary of the tragedy at Karbala. Scenes of that tragedy are also presented on this day of commemoration in dramatic form (ta'ziya). 'Our feast days are our assemblies of mourning.' So concludes a poem by a prince of Shi'i disposition recalling the many mihan of the Prophet's family. Weeping and lamentation over the evils and persecutions suffered by the 'Alid family, and mourning for its martyrs: these are things from which loyal supporters of the cause cannot cease. 'More touching than the tears of the Shi'is' has even become an Arabic proverb."

Edward Gibbon, considered as the greatest British historian of his time, writes the following in *The Decline and Fall of the Roman Empire:*
"In a distant age and climate the tragic scene of the death of Hussain will awaken the sympathy of the coldest reader."

Peter J. Chelkowski, Professor of Middle Eastern Studies, New York University, writes:
"Hussain accepted and set out from Mecca with his family and an entourage of about seventy followers. But on the plain of Kerbela they were caught in an ambush set by the ... caliph, Yazid. Though defeat was certain, Hussain refused to pay homage to him. Surrounded by a great enemy force, Hussain and his company existed without water for ten days in the burning desert of Kerbela. Finally Hussain, the adults and some male children of his family and his companions were cut to bits by the arrows and swords of Yazid's army; his women and remaining children were taken as captives to Yazid in Damascus. The renowned historian Abu Reyhan al-Biruni states; "... then fire was set to their camp and the bodies were trampled by the hoofs of the horses; nobody in the history of the human kind has seen such atrocities."

Reynold Alleyne Nicholson, in *A Literary History of the Arabs,* Sir Thomas Adams, Professor of Arabic at the University of Cambridge, write:
"Husayn fell, pierced by an arrow, and his brave followers were cut down beside him to the last man. Muhammadan tradition, which with rare exceptions is uniformly hostile to the Umayyad dynasty,

26

regards Husayn as a martyr and Yazid as his murderer."

Shrine of Imam Hussain عليه السلام (above) at dusk and that of his brother, al-Abbas عليه السلام (below)

In the Name of Allāh, the most Gracious, the most Merciful

SACRED *AHADITH* IN HONOR OF
IMAM AL-HUSSAIN عليه السلام

أحاديث نبوية شريفة عن فضل الامام الحسين عليه السلام

اللّهمّ صَلِّ عَلى مُحَمَّدٍ وآلِ مُحَمَّد

In the Name of Allah, the most Gracious, the most Merciful

Since there are many editions of the references cited in these *ahādith* because of being printed in various countries and at different times, volume and page numbers have been removed. In instances where the reference is not mentioned at all, it is due to the *hadith* being cited in more than one source.

نظر النبي صلى الله عليه وآله إلى الحسين بن علي عليهما السلام و هو مقبل، فأجلسه في حجره وقال
إن لقتل الحسين حرارةً في قلوب المؤمنين لا تبرد أبداً ثم قال عليه السلام بأبي قتيل كل عبرةٍ قيل
وما قتيل كل عبرةٍ يا ابن رسول الله قال: لا يذكره مؤمنٌ إلا بكى.

The Prophet ﷺ looked at al-Hussain son of Ali عليه السلام as young al-Hussain was approaching, so he seated him in his lap and said, "The killing of al-Hussain shall have a flame in the hearts of the believers that shall never be put out." Then he said, "By the life of my father, he is the victim who is mourned by every teardrop." When he ﷺ was requested to explain what he meant, he ﷺ said, "Whenever a believer remembers him, he becomes tearful."

رسول الله صلى الله عليه وآله يقول: يأتي قومٌ في آخر الزمان يزورون قبر ابني الحسين ــــ عليه السلام، فمن زاره فكأنما زارني، ومن زارني فكأنما زار الله سبحانه، ألا ومن زار الحسين ــــ عليه السلام فكأنما زار الله في عرشه.

The Messenger of Allāh ﷺ has said, "At later times, some people will come to visit the gravesite of my son, al-Hussain عليه السلام. Anyone who visits it will be as though he visited me, and whoever visits me, it is as though he visits Allāh, Praise is all due to Him. Whoever visits [the gravesite of] al-Hussain, it is as though he visits Allāh in His Throne."

رسول الله عليه افضل الصلاة والسلام قال: أحبّ الأعمال إلى الله تعالى زيارةُ قبر الحسين عليه السلام، وأفضل الأعمال عند الله إدخال السرور على المؤمن، وأقرب ما يكون العبد إلى الله تعالى وهو ساجد بـــــــــــاك.

The Messenger of Allāh ﷺ has said, "The best of deeds with Allāh is visiting the gravesite of al-Hussain ؏; the best of deeds with Allāh is pleasing a Muslim, and the closest to Allāh a servant gets is when he tearfully prostrates."

قال سلام الله عليه : ان البكاء والجزع مكروه للعبد في كل ما جزع ما خلا البكاء والجزع على الحسين بن علي عليهما السلام فإنه فيه مأجور .

He ﷺ has said, "If a servant of the Almighty weeps and laments because of anything which anyone hates, it is not a commendable act save in mourning al-Hussain son of Ali ؏, for in this case it is rewardable.

عن سلمان الفارسي رضي الله عنه أن الحسين عليه السلام كان على فخذ رسول الله صلى الله عليه وآله، وكان يقبّله ويقول : " أنت السيّد ابن السيّد أبو السادة، أنت الإمام ابن الإمام أبو الأئمة، أنت الحجّة ابن الحجّة أبو الحجج تسعة من صلبك، وتاسعهم قائمهم " .

Salman the Persian ؓ is quoted as having said that al-Hussain ؏ was sitting on the thigh of the Messenger of Allāh ﷺ who was kissing him and saying, "You are the Sayyid (master), the son of the Sayyid and the father of the Sayyids; you are the Imām, the son of the Imām, the father of Imāms; you are the Hujja, the son of the Hujja and the father of seven Hujjas from your loins the ninth of whom is their Qa'im."

قال رسول الله: مَنْ أتى الحسين عليه السلام عارفاً بحقّه كتبه الله وأعلى علّيين.

The Messenger of Allāh ﷺ has said, "One who visits [the gravesite of] al-Hussain, knowing his worth, will be written down by Allāh in the highest of rungs."

وفي منتهى الآمال: يروي ابن طاووس عن حذيفة أنّه قال: سمعت الحسين بن عليّ، عليهما السلام، يقول: "والله ليجتمعنّ على قتلي طغاة بني أمية، يقدمهم عمر بن سعد"، وذلك في حياة النبي (صلى الله عليه وآله)، فقلت له: أبأك بهذا رسول الله؟ فقال: لا، فأتيتُ النبي صلى الله عليه وآله فأخبرته

فقال: "علمي علمُه، وعلمُه علمي."

In the reference *Muntaha al-Āmāl*, Ibn Tawoos quotes Huthaifah as saying that he heard al-Hussain ibn Ali عليه السلام as saying, "By Allāh, the tyrants of Banu Umayyah shall join ranks to kill them [i.e. to kill both al-Hassan and al-Hussain عليه السلام]; in their vanguard will be Omer ibn Sa`d."

قال رسول الله: إنّ فاطمة عليها السلام تحضر لزوّار قبر ابنها الحسين عليه السلام فتستغفر لهم ذنوبهم.

The Messenger of Allāh ﷺ has said that Fātima عليها السلام would be present for those who visit the grave of her son, al-Hussain عليه السلام, in order to plead to the Almighty for the forgiveness of their sins.

روى سلمان، رضي الله عنه، أنه سمع رسول الله صلى الله عليه وآله يقول في الحسن والحسين عليهم السلام: "اللهم إني أحبهما، فأحبّهما، وأحبُّ مَن أحبّهما."

Salman ![] narrated saying that he heard the Messenger of Allāh ![] as saying the following about al-Hassan and al-Hussain ![]: "O Lord! I love them both; so, do love them and love all those who love them!"

وروى سلمان أيضاً عن الرسول الأعظم صلى الله عليه وآله انه قال: "من احب الحسن والحسين أحبته، ومن أحبّته أحبّه الله، ومن أحبّه الله عز وجل أدخله الجنة، ومن أبغضهما أبغضته، ومن أبغضته أبغضه الله، ومن أبغضه الله خلّده في النّار."

Salman has also quoted the greatest Prophet ![] as saying, " I love whomsoever loves al-Hassan and al-Hussain ![]; whomsoever I love is loved by Allāh, and whomsoever is loved by Allāh, the most Exalted One, the most Great, He will permit him to enter Paradise. Whoever hates them I hate; whoever I hate is hated by Allāh, and whosoever is hated by Allāh will be lodged by Him in the fire forever."

وعن ابن مسعود انه قال: كان النبي صلى الله عليه وآله يصلي فجاء الحسن والحسين عليهما السلام فارتدفاه، فلما رفع رأسه أخذهما أخذاً رفيقاً فلما عاد عادا، فلما انصرف اجلس هذا على فخذه الأيمن وهذا على فخذه الأيسر، ثم قال: "مَن أحبني فليحب هذين" وقال ايظاً صلى الله عليه وآله: "إنّ ابنيّ هذين ريحانتاي من الدنيا."

Ibn Mas'ud is quoted as having said that the Prophet ﷺ was once praying, so al-Hassan and al-Hussain عليهما السلام came and climbed over him. When he ﷺ raised his head, he took them both down gently. When he ﷺ resumed his prayer, they, too, resumed. Once he ﷺ finished his prayers, he ﷺ seated one on his right thigh and the other on the left then said, "Anyone who loves you must love these two." He ﷺ also said, "These sons of mine are my two fragrant flowers in this world."

وفي بحار الانوار في وصية النبي صلى الله عليه وآله اوصى الإمام علي عليه السلام برعاية سبطيه، وكان ذلك

قبل موته بثلاثة ايام، فقد قال له : سلام الله عليك أبا الريحانتين ــ، اوصيكَ بريحانتيَّ من الدنيا ،

عن قليل ينهدّ ركناك، والله خليفتي عليك، فلمّا قبض رسول الله صلى الله عليه وآله قال علي عليه

السلام: هذا أحد ركني الذي قال لي رسول الله صلى الله عليه وآله؛ فلما ماتت فاطمة عليها السلام، قال

علي عليه السلام : هذا الركن الثاني الذي قال لي رسول الله صلى الله عليه وآله. "

In *Bihār al-Anwār*, while discussing the will of the Prophet ﷺ to Imām Ali عليه السلام, the Imām عليه السلام willed that both grandsons of the Prophet ﷺ be looked after. This was three days before his death (martyrdom). He (Prophet ﷺ) said to him, "Peace with you, O Father of the two flowers! I commend you to look after both my two flowers in the life of this world, for soon both your corners will collapse. Allāh watches over you after me." When the Prophet ﷺ passed away, Ali عليه السلام said, "This is one of the two corners which the Messenger of Allāh ﷺ has mentioned to me." When Fātima ﵊ passed away, Ali ﵇ said, "This is the second corner which the Messenger of Allāh ﷺ told me about."

قال رسول الله: "حُسين مصباحُ هدى وسفينةُ نجاة."

The Messenger of Allāh ﷺ has said, "Al-Hussain is the lantern of guidance and the ark of salvation."

قال النبي صلى الله عليه وآله: ألا وإنّ الحسين عليه السلام باب من أبواب الجنّة، من عانده حرم الله عليه ريح الجنّة.

The Prophet ﷺ has said, "Al-Hussain is one of the gates of Paradise; whoever opposes him will be deprived by Allāh of the aroma of Paradise."

روي في فردوس الأخبار وبحار الأنوار ومناقب ابن شهر آشوب وإرشاد المفيد وكشف الغمة: عن يعلى بن مرّة قال رسول الله، صلى الله عليه وآله، حسين منّي وأنا من حسين؛ أحبّ الله من أحبّ حُسيناً، حسين سِبطٌ من الأسباط.

In these references: *Firdaws al-Akhbar, Bihār al-Anwār,* Ibn Shahr Āshūb's *Manāqib,* al-Mufid's *Irshad* and *Kashf al-Ghumma,* it is stated that Ya`li ibn Murrah has said that the Messenger of Allāh ﷺ said, "Hussain is of me, and I am of Hussain; Allāh loves whoever loves Hussain;

35

Hussain is one of the grandsons [of the Prophet of Islam ﷺ]."

وفي كامل الزيارات والبحار ووسائل الشيعة وجامع الأحاديث : عن أبي عبد الله عليه السلام قال : أحبّ الأعمال إلى الله تعالى زيارةُ قبر الحسين ــــ عليه السلام ــــ ، وأفضل الأعمال عند الله إدخال السرور على المؤمن ، وأقرب ما يكون العبد إلى الله تعالى وهو ساجد باك .

In these references: *Kāmil al-Ziyārāt*, *Bihār al-Anwār*, *Wasā'il al-Shi`a* and *Jāmi` al-Ahādith*, Abu Abdullāh [Imām Ja`far al-Sadiq عليه السلام] is quoted as having said, "The deed that pleases Allāh Almighty the most is visiting the gravesite of al-Hussain; the best of deeds with Allāh is pleasing a believer, and the closest to Allāh Almighty a servant is when he is prostrating, tearful."

وفي المستدرك وبحار الأنوار : عن حماد بن إسحاق الأنصاري عن ابن سنان عن ابن محمد ، عليه السلام ، قال : نظر النبي ، صلى الله عليه وآله ، إلى الحسين ــــ بن علي عليهما السلام وهو مقبل فأجلسه في حجره وقال : إن لقتل الحسين حرارةً في قلوب المؤمنين لا تبرُدُ أبداً ؛ ثم قال عليه السلام بأبي قتيل كل عبرة ؛ قيل : وما قتيل كل عبرة يا ابن رسول الله ؟ قال : لا يذكره مؤمن إلا بكى .

In *Al-Mustadrak `ala al-Sahihain* and in *Bihār al-Anwār*, Hammad ibn Ishaq al-Ansari quotes Ibn Sinan quoting [Imām Ali] ibn Muhammed [al-Hadi عليه السلام] as saying that the Prophet ﷺ looked at al-Hussain ibn Ali عليه السلام as young al-Hussain was approaching, so he placed him in his lap and said, "The killing of al-Hussain leaves a flame in the hearts of the faithful that will never cool down." Then he said, "By my father, he is the one who is killed and is behind every teardrop." When the Imām was asked to explain, he said, "No believer remembers him without shedding tears."

وفي كامل الزيارت وبحار الأنوار: عن بشير الدّهان، عن أبي عبد الله، عليه السلام، قال: يا بشير! ان مَن زار قبر الحسين عليه السلام عارفاً بحقّه كان كمن زار الله في عرشه.

In Kāmil al-Ziyārāt and Bihār al-Anwār, Basheer, the [cooking] oil seller, quotes Abu Abdullāh ﷺ as saying, "O Basheer! One who visits the gravesite of al-Hussain knowing his worth is like one who visits Allāh in His `Arsh."

وفي نور العين في المشي إلى زيارة قبر الحسين عليه السلام وفضل زيارة الحسين عليه السلام: عن الحسن بن علي عليهم السلام، قال: كُنّا مع أمير المؤمنين عليه السلام، أنا وحارث الأعور، قال: سمعتُ رسولَ الله، صلى الله عليه وآله، يقول: يأتي قومٌ في آخر الزمان يزورون قبر ابني الحسين عليه السلام، فمن زاره فكأنّما زارني، و من زارني فكأنّما زار الله سبحانه، ألا ومن زار الحسين عليه السلام فكأنّما زار الله في عرشه.

In *Noor al-Uyoon*, where the subject of walking the distance to the gravesite of al-Hussain, peace with him and the distinction enjoyed by visiting [the gravesite of al-Hussain ﷺ] is discussed, [Imām] al-Hassan ibn Ali ﷺ is quoted as having said, "We were in the company of [my father] the Commander of the Faithful ﷺ, I and al-Harith, the one-eyed, who said, 'I heard the Messenger of Allāh saying, 'There will be people at the later time who will visit the gravesite of my son, al-Hussain. Whoever visits him is as though he visits me, and whoever visits me is as though he visits Allāh, the most Praised One. Indeed, whoever visits al-Hussain is as though he visits Allāh in His `Arsh.'"

وفي كامل الزيارات وبحار الأنوار : عن الحسن بن علي بن أبي حمزة ، عن أبيه ، عن أبي عبد الله عليه السلام قال : سمعته يقول : ان البكاء والجزع مكروه للعبد في كل ما جزع ما خلا البكاء والجزع على الحسين بن علي عليهما السلام فإنه فيه مأجور.

In *Kāmil al-Ziyārāt* and *Bihār al-Anwār*, al-Hassan ibn Ali ibn Abu Hamzah quotes his father citing Abu Abdullāh ﷺ as saying that it is hateful for a servant of Allāh to weep and to grieve on account of something which he hated having taking place save when it comes to al-Hussain ibn Ali ﷺ, for in this case he will be rewarded."

وفي مناقب ابن شهر اشوب ومنتهى الآمال : عن سلمان الفارسي رضي الله عنه أن الحسين عليه السلام كان على فخذ رسول الله صلى الله عليه وآله ، وكان يقبّله ويقول : " أنت السيّد ابن السيّد أبو السادة ، أنت الإمام ابن الإمام أبو الأئمة ، أنت الحجّة ابن الحجّة أبو الحجج تسعة من صلبك ، وتاسعهم قائمهم."

In the book titled *Manāqib* by Ibn Shahr Āshūb and also in *Muntaha al-A`māl*, Salman al-Farisi ﷺ is quoted as having said that al-Hussain ﷺ was once sitting on the thigh of the Messenger of Allāh ﷺ who was kissing him and saying, "You are the Sayyid (master), the son of the Sayyid and the father of Sayyids... You are the Imām, the son of the Imām and the father of the Imāms... You are the Hujjah, the son of the Hujjah and the father of nine Hujjas from your loins whose ninth is their Qa'im [al-Mahdi]."

وفي كامل الزيارات وثواب الأعمال وبحار الأنوار والمستدرك والوسائل : عن أبي عبد الله عليه السلام قال : من أتى الحسين عليه السلام عارفاً بحقه كتبه الله في أعلى عليّين .

In *Kāmil al-Ziyārāt*, *Thawab al-A`mal*, *Bihār al-Anwār*, *Al-Mustadrak* and *Al-Wasā'il* [*Wasā'il al-Shi`a*], Abu Abdullāh عليه السلام is quoted as having said, "Whoever visits [the gravesite of] al-Hussain knowing his worth will be written down by Allāh as being among those who occupy the highest `Illiyyeen rung."

وفي كامل الزيارات وبحار الأنوار والمستدرك والوسائل ونور العين وجامع الأحاديث : عن علي بن ميمون الصائغ ، عن أبي عبد الله عليه السلام قال : يا علي ، بلغني أنّ قوماً من شيعتنا يمرّ بأحدهم السنة والسنتان لا يزورون الحسين عليه السلام ! قلت : جعلت فداك ، إني أعرف أناساً كثيرة بهذه الصفة ، قال : أما والله لعظم أخطأوا ، وعن ثواب الله زاغوا ، وعن جوار محمد صلى الله عليه وآله تباعدوا ، إلى أن قال : قلت : فإن أخرج عنه رجلاً فيجوز ذلك ؟ قال : نعم ، وخروجه بنفسه أعظم أجراً وخيراً له عند ربه ؛ يراه ربه ساهر الليل له تعب النهار ، بنظر الله إليه نظرة توجب له الفردوس الأعلى مع محمد وأهل بيته عليهم السلام ، فتنافسوا في ذلك وكونوا من أهله .

In *Kāmil al-Ziyārāt*, *Bihār al-Anwār*, *Al-Wasā'il*, *Al-Mustadrak*, *Noor al-`Uyoon* and *Jāmi` al-Ahādith*, Ali ibn

Maymoon, the goldsmith, quotes Abu Abdullāh ﷺ as saying to him, "O Ali, it has come to my knowledge that some of our followers (Shi`as) spend a year or two without visiting [the gravesite of] al-Hussain!" Ali ﷺ said, "May I be sacrificed for your sake! I know many people to be like that." He ﷺ said, "By Allāh, it is to their own misfortune that they thus err, shunning the rewards of Allāh, keeping themselves distant from the neighborhood of Muhammed..." Then Ali asked the Imām ﷺ, "If someone sends someone else to do so on his behalf, will it be accepted?" The Imām ﷺ said, "Yes, it will be, but his own going there in person is much more rewardable and is better for him with his Lord; he will be seen by his Lord as spending the night in adoration, working hard during the day, as Allāh casts at him a look that necessitates the highest Paradise for him in the company of Muhammed and his Ahlul-Bayt ﷺ. So, you all should compete with each other in doing so and in being worthy of so doing."

وفي منتهى الآمال : يروي ابن طاوس عن حذيفة أنه قال : سمعت الحسين بن علي عليهما السلام يقول : "

والله ليجتمعنّ على قتلي طغاة بني اميّة، يقدمهم عمر بن سعد " ، وذلك في حياة النبي (صلى الله عليه وآله) ،

فقلتُ له : أنبأك بهذا رسولُ الله ؟ فقال : لا ، فأتيتُ النبي ، صلى الله عليه وآله ، فأخبرته فقال : "

علمي علمه وعلمه علمي ."

In *Muntaha al-Āmāl*, Ibn Tawoos narrates from Huthayfah saying that he heard al-Hussain ibn Ali ﷺ saying, "By Allāh, the tyrants of Banu Umayyah will join ranks to kill me in the vanguard of whom Omer ibn Sa`d is." This took place during the lifetime of the Prophet ﷺ. I, therefore, said to him, "Were you informed of this by the Messenger of Allāh ﷺ?" He answered in the negative, so I [Huthayfah] went to the Prophet ﷺ and informed him of it, whereupon he said, "My knowledge is his knowledge, and his knowledge is mine."

وفي كامل الزيارات والبحار والمستدرك وجامع الأحاديث: عن داود بن كثير، عن أبي عبد الله عليه السلام

قال: إنَّ فاطمة عليها السلام بنت محمد صلى الله عليه وآله تحضر لزوّار قبر ابنها الحسين عليه

السلام فتستغفر لهم ذنوبهم.

In *Kāmil al-Ziyārāt*, *Bihār al-Anwār*, *Al-Mustadrak* and *Jāmi` al-Ahādith*, Dawud ibn Katheer quotes Abu Abdullāh ﷺ as saying that [the soul of] Fātima ﷺ daughter of Prophet Muhammed ﷺ is present to witness those who visit [the gravesite of] her son, al-Hussain ﷺ, and she pleads to the Almighty to forgive their sins.

وفي من لا يحضره الفقيه واما لي الصدوق والبحار والمناقب: عن محمد بن مسلم عن أبي جعفر عليه السلام

قال: مُرُوا شيعتنا بزيارة الحسين ابن علي عليه السلام فإن زيارته تدفع الهدم والغرق والحرق وأكل

السبع، وزيارته مفترضة على من أقرّ للحسين عليه السلام بالإمامة من الله عزّ وجلّ.

In *Man la Yahdhuruhu al-Faqih*, al-Saduq's *Āmāli*, *Bihār al-Anwār* and *Al-Manāqib*, Muhammed ibn Muslim quotes [Imām] Ja`far al-Sadiq ﷺ as saying, "Order our followers (Shi`as) to visit [the gravesite of] al-Hussain son of Ali ﷺ, for such a visit prevents demolition [of one's home], drowning, burning and falling prey to a wild beast, and such a visit is obligatory on anyone who recognizes al-

Hussain عليه السلام as an Imām appointed by Allāh, the most Exalted One, the most Sublime."

روي في البحار وكنز جامع الفوائد : قال رجل للحسين ــ عليه السلام : إن فيك كبراً؛ فقال عليه السلام : كل الكبر لله وحده ، ولا يكون في غيره ، قال تعالى ــ : ﴿وَلِلَّهِ الْعِزَّةُ وَلِرَسُولِهِ وَلِلْمُؤْمِنِينَ﴾ .

It is narrated in both *Bihār al-Anwār* and *Kanz Jami' al-Fawa'id* that a man said to al-Hussain عليه السلام, "You look old." He عليه السلام, thereupon said, "Only Allāh is timeless and none else is; the Almighty has said, 'Dignity belongs to Allāh, His Messenger and the believers.'"

روي انه لما اخبر النبي صلى الله عليه وآله وسلم فاطمة ابنته بقتل ولدها الحسين ــ عليهم أفضل الصلاة والسلام وما يجري عليه من الحزن بكت فاطمة عليها السلام بكاء شديدا وقالت : يا أبه ، متى يكون ذلك ؟ فقال النبي صلى الله عليه وآله وسلم : يا فاطمة ، ان نساء امتي يكون على نساء أهل بيتي ، ورجالهم يكون على رجال أهل بيتي ، ويجدد ون العزاء جيلا بعد جيل وفي كل سنة ، فإذا كان يوم القيامة تشفعين انت للنساء وأنا اشفع للرجال ، وكل من بكى منهم على مصاب الحسين ــ أخذنا بيده و أدخلناه الجنة . يا فاطمة ! كل عين ــ باكية يوم القيامة الا عين ــ بكت على مصاب الحسين ــ فإنها ﴿ضَاحِكَةٌ مُسْتَبْشِرَةٌ﴾ بنعيم الجنة .

It has been narrated that when the Prophet صلى الله عليه وآله وسلم informed his daughter, Fātima عليها السلام, that her son, al-Hussain عليه السلام, would be killed, narrating the calamities through which he would pass, Fātima عليها السلام wept profusely and said, "Father! When will all this take place?" The Prophet صلى الله عليه وآله وسلم said, "O

Fātima! My nation's women shall weep over the women of my household, and their men shall weep over the men of my household and renew their mourning one generation after another, every year. So, when the Judgment Day comes, you shall intercede for the women and I shall intercede for the men, and we shall take whoever from among them who weeps over the agony of al-Hussain by the hand and escort him into Paradise. O Fātima! Every eye shall be weeping on the Judgment Day save an eye that wept over the calamity that would befall al-Hussain, for it shall be 'smiling, optimistic' in expectation of the felicity of Paradise."

عن هارون بن خارجة قال: سمعتُ أبا عبد الله (عليه السلام) يقول: " وكّل الله بقبر الحسين (عليه السلام) أربعة آلاف مَلَك، شُعْث غُبْر، يبكونه إلى يوم القيامة، فمن زاره عارفاً بحقه شيعوه حتى يبلغوه مأمنه، وإن مرض عادوه غدوة وعشية، وإن مات شهدوا جنازته واستغفروا له إلى يوم القيامة.

Harun ibn Kharijah is quoted as having said that he heard Abu Abdullāh [Imām Ja`far al-Sadiq عليه السلام] as saying, "Allāh commissioned four thousand angels to be in charge of al-Hussain's gravesite. Their hair is untidy, their faces are dust-covered, and they weep over him up to the Judgment Day. When someone visits him, knowing his worth, they would escort him until he reaches his place of safety. If he falls sick, they would visit him, and if he dies, they would be present when his coffin is bidden farewell, and they would seek Allāh's forgiveness for him up to the Judgment Day."

43

وفي كامل الزيارات و البحار والوسائل وجامع الأحاديث : عن أبي بكر الحضرمي ، عن أبي جعفر عليه
السلام قال : سمعته يقول : من أراد أن يعلم أنّه من أهل الجنّة، فليعرض حبّنا على قلبه؛ فإن قبله فهو
مؤمن، ومن كان لنا محبّاً فليرغب في زيارة قبر الحسين عليه السلام ، فمن كان للحسين عليه
السلام زوّاراً عرفناه بالحبّ لنا أهل البيت وكان من أهل الجنّة، ومن لم يكن للحسين عليه السلام
زوّاراً كان ناقص الإيمان.

In *Kāmil al-Ziyārāt*, *Bihār al-Anwār*, *Al-Wasā'il* and *Jāmi`
al-Ahādith*, Abu Bakr al-Hadhrami quotes [Imām] Abu
Ja`far [al-Baqir ﷺ] as saying, "If anyone wants to find
out if he will be among the residents of Paradise, let him
offer loving us before his heart: If his heart accepts it, he is
a believer. And if one loves us, let him desire to visit the
gravesite of al-Hussain ﷺ. Anyone who visits al-Hussain
ﷺ, we will recognize him through his love for us, we
Ahlul-Bayt, and he will be among the people of Paradise.
And if one never visits [the gravesite of] al-Hussain, peace
with him, his belief will be deficient."

عن أبي عبد الله عليه السلام قال: ما من شهيد إلا وهو يحب لو أنّ الحسين بن علي عليه السلام
حيّ حتى يدخلوا الجنّة معه.

Abu Abdullāh ﷺ is quoted as having said, "Every martyr
loves that al-Hussain son of Ali ﷺ were alive so they
would enter Paradise together."

روى عن خالد الربعي قال: حدثني من سمع كعبا يقول: أول من لعن قاتل الحسين بن علي عليه السلام

إبراهيم خليل الرحمن عليه السلام ثم لعنه عيسى عليه السلام وأكثر من قول: يا بني إسرائيل العنوا قاتله، و

إن أدركتم أيامه فلا تجلسوا عنه، فإن الشهيد معه كالشهيد مع الأنبياء، مقبل غير مدبر، وكأني أنظر

إلى بقعته، وما من نبي إلا وقد زار كربلاء ووقف عليها، وقال: إنك لبقعة كثيرة الخير فيك يدفن القمر

الأزهر.

It has been narrated about Khalid al-Rab`i saying that he was told by someone who heard Ka`b saying that the first person who cursed the killer of al-Hussain son of Ali عليه السلام was (Prophet) Ibrahim (Abraham), the Friend of Allāh. Then he was cursed by Jesus عليه السلام who quite often used to say, "O Children of Israel! Curse his killer, and if you live to see him, do not be too reluctant to support him, for one who becomes a martyr in his company will be like one who was martyred in the company of the prophets, advancing not retreating. It is as though I see his spot visited by every prophet who visits Kerbala and stand at it to say, 'You are a spot with plenty of goodness in you. The shining moon shall be buried in you'."

روى سلمان رضي الله عنه أنه سمع رسول الله صلى الله عليه وآله يقول في الحسن والحسين عليهما

السلام: "اللهم إني أحبهما فأحبهما وأحب من أحبهما."

Salman رضي الله عنه has narrated saying that he heard the Messenger of Allāh صلى الله عليه وسلم saying the following about al-Hassan and al-Hussain عليهما: "Lord! I love them, so, I plead to You to love them, too, and to love everyone who loves them."

ورى سلمان ايضاً عن الرسول الأعظم صلى الله عليه وآله انه قال : " مَنْ أَحَبَّ الحسنَ والحسينَ أحبَّتُه ، ومَنْ أَحبَبتُهُ أَحَبَّهُ اللهُ ، ومَنْ أَحَبَّهُ اللهُ عزَّ وجلَّ أَدخلَهُ الجنةَ ، ومَنْ أبغضَهُما أبغضتُه ، ومَنْ أبغضتُه أبغضــــــــــــهُ اللهُ ، ومـــــــنْ أبغضـــــــهُ اللهُ خلَّـــــــــدهُ فِي النـــــــــارِ . "

Salman ﷺ has also narrated about the greatest Prophet ﷺ saying, "One who loves al-Hassan and al-Hussain I love him, and whomsoever I love is loved by Allāh, and if one is loved by Allāh, the most Exalted One, the most Great, He will permit him into Paradise. And I hate anyone who hates them, and whomsoever I hate is hated by Allāh, and one who is hated by Allāh will be hurled by Allāh into the fire of hell forever."

وعن ابن مسعود انه قال : كان النبي صلى الله عليه وآله يصلي فجاء الحسنُ والحسينُ عليهما السلام فارتدفاه ، فلما رفع رأسَه أخذهُما أخذاً رفيقاً فلما عاد عادا ، فلما انصرف اجلس هذا على فخذه الأيمن وهذا على فخذه الأيسر ، ثم قال : " مَنْ أحبَّني فليحبَّ هذيْن " ، وقال ايضاً صلى الله عليه وآله : " إنَّ ابنــــــيَّ هـــــــذيْن ريحانتــــــايَ مـــــــنَ الــــــدنيا . "

Ibn Mas`ud is quoted as having said that the Messenger of Allāh ﷺ was once performing his prayers when al-Hassan and al-Hussain ﷺ came. They climbed on his back. When he raised his head, he gently took them down, and when he resumed, they, too, resumed their climbing. When he finished his prayers, he seated one of them on his right thigh and the other on the left then said, "Anyone who loves me must love both of these." He ﷺ also said, "These sons of mine are my two fragrant flowers in this life."

وفي البحار إن النبي صلى الله عليه وآله كان جالساً فأقبل الحسن والحسين عليهما السلام، فلمّا رآهما النبي صلى الله عليه وآله قام لهما واستبطأ بلوغهما إليه، فاستقبلهما وحملهما على كتفيه، وقال صلى الله عليه وآله: "نِعْمَ المطيُّ مطيكما، ونِعْمَ الركبانِ أنتما، وأبوكما خيرٌ منكما. "

In *Bihār al-Anwār*, it is recorded that the Prophet ﷺ was once sitting when al-Hassan and al-Hussain ﵇ [who were then children] approached. When the Prophet ﷺ saw them, he stood up for them and waited until they reached him, whereupon he welcomed and carried them on his shoulders saying, "Great is the one who is carrying them, and great are you, the ones whom he carries, while your father is even greater than both of you."

وروي في بحار الأنوار ومناقب آل أبي طالب انه عند ما علمت سيدة نساء العالمين عليها السلام لقاء أبيها بربه عز وجل قريب أتت بابنيها الحسن والحسين عليهما السلام، فقالت: يا رسول الله، هذان إبناك، فورّثهما شيئاً، فقال صلى الله عليه وآله: أمّا الحسن، فإنَّ لهُ هيبتي و سؤددي، وأنتَ الحسين فإنَّ لهُ شجاعتي وجودي،

In both *Bihār al-Anwār* and *Manāqib Āl Abi Talib*, it is narrated that when the Chief Lady of the Women of the World ﵙ came to know that her father ﷺ was about to meet his Lord, the most Exalted One, the most Great, she brought her sons, al-Hassan and al-Hussain عليهما, and said, "O Messenger of Allāh! Here are both your sons; so, do let them inherit something from you." He ﷺ, whereupon, said, "As for al-Hassan, he shall inherit my prestigious status and loftiness. As for al-Hussain, for him I leave my courage and generosity."

وفي بحار الانوار في وصية النبي صلى الله عليه وآله اوصى الإمام علي عليه السلام برعاية سبطيه، وكان ذلك

قبل موته بثلاث ايام، فقد قال له: سلام الله عليك أبا الريحانتين، أوصيك بريحانتيّ من الدنيا،

عن قليل ينهدّ ركناك، والله خليفتي عليك، فلمّا قبض رسول الله صلى الله عليه وآله قال عليّ عليه

السلام: هذا أحد ركني الذي قال لي رسول الله صلى الله عليه وآله؛ فلما ماتت فاطمة عليها السلام،

قال علي عليه السلام: هذا الركن الثاني الذي قال لي رسول الله صلى الله عليه وآله.

In *Bihār al-Anwār*, where the will of the Prophet ﷺ to Imām Ali عليه السلام is discussed and in which he commended him to look after both his grandsons, three days before his demise, he [the Prophet ﷺ] said to him, "May the peace of Allāh be with you, O father of both fragrant flowers! I commend you to look after my two fragrant flowers of this life, for soon both of your corners shall collapse, and Allāh shall oversee you after my demise." When the Messenger of Allāh ﷺ passed away, Ali said, "This is one of my two corners about which the Messenger of Allāh had told me." When Fātima عليها السلام passed away, Ali عليه السلام said, "This is the second corner about which the Messenger of Allāh had told me."

روي في مثير الأحزان عن لوعة النبي صلى الله عليه وآله عند ما حضر الإمام الحسين عليه السلام
عند جدّه الرسول صلى الله عليه وآله حينما كان يعاني آلام المرض ويقترب من لحظات الاحتضار ، فلما رآه
ضمّه إلى صدره وجعل يقول صلى الله عليه وآله : "ما لي وليزيد ؟! لا بارك الله فيه ." ثمّ غشي عليه
طويلاً ، فلمّا أفاق أخذ يوسع الحسين تقبيلاً وعيناه تفيضان بالدموع ، و هو يقول : "أما
إنّ لي ولقاتلك موقفاً بين يدي الله عزّ وجلّ."

It is narrated in *Mutheer al-Ahzan* how the Prophet ﷺ felt
so agonized when Imām al-Hussain عليه السلام came to him as he
was suffering from the pain of sickness and as he was
about to draw his last breath. The Prophet ﷺ hugged him
and kept saying, "What do I have to do with Yazid?! May
Allāh never bless him." He ﷺ then went into a deep
swoon. Upon recovering, he kept kissing al-Hussain عليه السلام,
as his eyes were overflowing with tears, while saying,
"Indeed, there will be a stance for me and for your killer
before Allāh, the most Exalted One, the most Great."

وفي مقتل الحسين للخوارزمي انه في اللحظات الأخيرة من عمره الشريف صلى الله عليه وآله
ألقى السبطان عليهما السلام بأنفسهما عليه وهما يذرفان الدموع والنبي صلى الله عليه وآله يوسعهما تقبيلاً
، فأراد أبوهما أمير المؤمنين عليه السلام أن ينحّيهما عنه فأبى صلى الله عليه وآله وقال له : "دعهما
يتزوّدا منّي وأتزوّد منهما فستصيبهما بعدي أثرة" . ثم التفت صلى الله عليه وآله إلى عوّده (الذين أتوا
لعيادته) فقال لهم : قد خلّفتُ فيكم كتابَ الله و عترتي أهلَ بيتي ، فالمضيّع لكتاب الله كالمضيّع

لسـنتي، والمضـيع لسـنتي كالمضـيع لعترتي، إنهمـا الـزن يفترقـا حتـي يـردا علـي الحـوض.

In al-Khawarizmi's book titled *Maqtal al-Hussain*, it is recorded that during the very last moments of his sacred life, the Prophet ﷺ fell on both his grandsons as they were shedding their tears and kissed them so many times. Their father, the Commander of the Faithful عليه‌السلام, wanted to take them away from him, but he ﷺ refused to part with them and said to him, "Let them enjoy my presence and I enjoy theirs, for they shall have, after my demise, a calamitous event." Then he turned to those who were visiting him and said, "I have left among you the Book of Allāh and my `Itra, my Ahlul-Bayt; one who loses the Book of Allāh will be akin to the one who loses my Sunnah, and the one who loses my Sunnah will be akin to that who loses my `Itra; they both shall never part from each other until they meet me at the Kawthar Pool."

وفي مناقب ابن شهر اشوب : والبحار روي انه وجد على ظهر الحسين عليه السلام يوم الطف اثر فسألوا زين العابدين عليه السلام عنه فقال: هذا مما كان ينقل الجراب على ظهره إلى منازل الأرامل واليتـــــــامى والمســـــــاكين.

In Shahr Āshūb's *Manāqib* book and in *Bihār al-Anwār*, it is narrated that on the Taff [Battle] Day, a mark was noticed on al-Hussain's back, so they asked Zain al-`Ābidin about it. He said, "This mark was caused by his carrying sacks on his back to the houses of widows, orphans and the poor."

وفي عيون أخبار الرضا عليه السلام : عن الحسين ـــ عليهما السلام قال : دخلت على رسول الله صلى

الله عليه وآله وعنده أُبيّ بن كعب ، فقال رسول الله صلى الله عليه وآله : مرحباً بك يا أبا عبد الله ، يا زين

السماوات والأرضين ـــ ، فقال أُبيّ : وكيف يكون يا رسول الله زين السماوات والأرض أحدٌ غيرُك ؟

فقال : يا أُبيّ ، والذي بعثني بالحقّ نبيّاً ، إنّ الحسين ـــ بن عليّ ، عليهما السلام ، في السماء أكبر منه في

الأرض ، وإنه لمكتوبٌ عن يمين ـــ عرش الله : "حُسين ـــ مصباحُ هدى وسفينةُ نجاة ."

In `Uyoon Akhbār al-Ridha, al-Hussain ﷺ is quoted as having said that he once went to see [his grandfather] the Messenger of Allāh ﷺ when Ubayy ibn Ka`b[1] was with him. The Messenger of Allah ﷺ said, "Welcome, Abu Abdullah, the adornment of the heavens and of the earth!" Ubayy said, "How can anyone other than yourself, O Messenger of Allah, be the adornment of the heavens and the earth?" He ﷺ said, "O Ubayy! By the One Who sent

---

1 There are two men by this name whose biographies are recorded in Volume One of Ibn al-Atheer's encyclopedia titled *Usd al-Ghaba* أُسْدُ الغابة, and it seems to me that he is the second one whose biography starts on page 69 of the said Volume and continues up to page 71. His date of birth is unknown, and there is a good deal of difference of opinion about his year of death which may be the Hijri year 23 or 19 or 20 or 32. Ibn al-Atheer quotes [the *sahabi* and narrator of traditions Abdullāh] Ibn Omer as saying that this *sahabi* died during the government of [Abdullāh's father] Omer ibn al-Khattab without giving a specific date. I searched for more information about him and found a page detailing his biography in the Internet's Wikipedia where there are two suggested years of death: 22 A.H./642-43 A.D. and 29 A.H./649 A.D. The Link to that Wikipedia page is: http://en.wikipedia.org/wiki/Ubay_ibn_Ka'b.

me with the truth as a Prophet, al-Hussain son of Ali, peace with them both, is in the heavens greater than he is on earth, and it is written on the right of the `Arsh of Allah that Hussain is the lantern of guidance and the ark of salvation."

وفي علل الشرايع والكافي والمناقب : عن الأمام جعفر بن محمد الصادق عليه السلام : كان رسول الله صلى

الله عليه وآله في كل يوم يأتي الحسين عليه السلام فيضع لسانه في فمه فيمصّه، حتى يروى، فأنبت الله

عز وجل لحمه من لحم رسول الله صلى الله عليه وآله، ولم يرضع من فاطمة عليها السلام ولا من غيرها لبناً

قط . وإن الرسول صلى الله عليه وآله فعل ذلك أربعين يوماً وليلة ، فنبت لحمه من لحم رسول الله

صلى الله عليه وآله .

In `Ilal al-Shara'i`, Al-Kafi and Al-Manāqib, Imām Ja`far al-Sadiq son of Imām Muhammed al-Baqir عليه‌السلام is quoted as having said that the Messenger of Allāh ﷺ used to go every day to [newborn] al-Hussain عليه‌السلام and put his tongue in his mouth, so he would suck it until he was satisfied, whereupon Allāh, the most Exalted One, the most Great, caused Hussain's flesh to grow from the flesh of the Messenger of Allāh ﷺ, and Hussain عليه‌السلام never had milk from Fātima عليها‌السلام or anyone else at all. The Imām عليه‌السلام added saying that the Messenger of Allāh ﷺ did so for forty days and nights, so his [Hussain's] flesh grew out of that of the Messenger of Allāh ﷺ.

وفي المائة منقبة في مناقب النبي حيث قال النبي صلّى الله عليه وآله: ألا وإنّ الحسين عليه السلام بابٌ من أبواب الجنّة، مَن عانده حَرَّمَ الله عليه ريح الجنّة.

In a book recounting one hundred feats of the Prophet ﷺ, the Messenger of Allāh ﷺ is quoted as having said, "Indeed, al-Hussain, peace with him, is one of the gates of Paradise; whoever opposes him will be prohibited by Allāh from even smelling the aroma of Paradise."

وفي كامل الزيارات وبحار الأنوار و مستدرك الوسائل وجامع أحاديث الشيعة: عن جويرية بن العلاء، عن بعض أصحابنا، قال في حديث: من سرّه أن ينظرَ إلى الله يومَ القيامة وتهونُ عليه سكرةُ الموت وهول المطلع فليُكثر من زيارة قبر الحسين عليه السلام؛ فإنّ زيارة الحسين عليه السلام زيارةُ الرسول، صلّى الله عليه وآله.

In *Kāmil al-Ziyārāt*, *Bihār al-Anwār*, *Mustadrak al-Wasā'il* and *Jami` Ahadith al-Shi`a*, Juwayriyyah son of al-`Alā' quotes some of our narrators as saying in one *hadith* that [the Prophet ﷺ said,] "Anyone who is pleased by looking forward to meeting Allāh on the Judgment Day, that the stupor of death will be easy for him and so will leaving the grave, he should visit the gravesite of al-Hussain, peace with him, for visiting [the gravesite of] al-Hussain is [like] visiting the Messenger of Allāh."

وفي الكافي، وتهذيب الأحكام، وكامل الزيارات، وبحار الأنوار، والوسائل، ونور العين: عن جعفر بن ابراهيم الحضرميّ، عن سعد بن سعد، قال سألت أبا الحسن عليه السلام عن الطين؟ قال

فقال : أكلُ الطينِ حرامٌ مثلُ الدمِ ولحمِ الخنزيرِ ، إلا طينَ قبرِ الحسينِ عليه السلام ، فإنَّ فيه شفاءً من كلِّ داءٍ ، وأمناً من كلِّ خوفٍ.

In *Al-Kafi*, *Tahtheeb al-Ahkam*, *Kāmil al-Ziyārāt*, *Bihār al-Anwār*, *Al-Wasā'il* [*Wasā'il Al-Shi`a*] and *Noor al-`Uyoon*, Ja`far ibn Ibrahim al-Hadhrami quotes Sa`d ibn Sa`d as saying that he once asked the father of al-Hassan [Imām Ali ﷺ] about clay. He said, "Ingesting clay is prohibitive just as in the case of eating blood and the meat of swine with the exception of the clay of al-Hussain's grave, for it heals from every ailment and is safety against every fear."

وفي كامل الزيارات وبحار الأنوار والوسائل ونور العين : عن أبي أسامة ، قال : سمعتُ أبا عبد الله عليه السلام يقول : من أراد أن يكون في جوار نبيه صلى الله عليه وآله وجوار عليٍّ وفاطمة عليهما السلام فلا يدع زيارة الحسين بن عليٍّ عليهما السلام.

In *Kāmil al-Ziyārāt*, *Bihār al-Anwār* and *Noor al-`Uyoon*, Abu Usamah is quoted as having said that he heard Abu Abdullāh ﷺ as saying, "If one wishes to be in the neighborhood of his Prophet ﷺ and in that of Ali and Fātima ﷺ he must not abandon visiting [the gravesite of] al-Hussain son of Ali ﷺ."

كان الحسين يوماً في حجر النبي صلى الله عليه وآله و هو يلاعبه ويضاحكه ، فقالت عائشة : يا رسول الله ، ما أشد إعجابك بهذا الصبي فقال لها ويلك ، وكيف لا أحبه ولا أعجب به وهو ثمرة فؤادي وقرة

عيني؟ اما ازا امتي ستقتله؛ فمن زاره بعد وفاته كتب الله له حجة من حجحي. قالت: يارسول الله،

حجة من حججك؟! قال نعم، وحجتين من حجحي؛ قالت: يا رسول الله، حجتين من

حججك؟! قال: نعم، واربعة. قال: فلم تزل تزاده ويزيد ويضعف حتى بلغ تسعين حجة من

حجج رسول الله صلى الله عليه وآله بأعمارها (أي: مع كل حجة عمرة.)

In *Muntaha al-Āmāl*, Imām al-Sadiq is quoted as having said that al-Hussain son of Ali ﷺ was one day in the lap of the Prophet ﷺ who was playing and laughing with him, so `Āisha said, "O Messenger of Allāh! How fond you are of this child!" He ﷺ, therefore, said to her, "Woe on you! Why should I not love him and admire him since he is the fruit of my heart and the apple of my eyes? My nation shall kill him; so, whoever visits him [his grave] after his demise, Allāh will write down for him the rewards of one of the times when I performed the pilgrimage." `Āisha asked him, "O Messenger of Allāh! The rewards of one of your pilgrimages?!" He ﷺ said, "Yes; the rewards of two." She asked him, "O Messenger of Allāh! The rewards of two of your pilgrimages?!" He ﷺ said, "Yes; the rewards of four." He kept doubling the figure until the final number reached 90 of the pilgrimages of the Prophet ﷺ together with the `Omra of each as well.

عن الحسين بن محمد قال: قال أبو الحسن موسى (عليه السلام):

"أدنى ما يثاب به زائر أبي عبد الله (عليه السلام) بشط الفرات، إذا عرف حقه وحرمته وولايته،

أن يغفر له ما تقدم من ذنبه وما تأخر."

Al-Hussain ibn Muhammed has said that the father of al-Hassan, Mousa [son of Ja`far ﷺ], has said, "The minimum reward earned by one who visits [the gravesite of] the father of Abdullāh [Imām al-Hussain whose infant son, Abdullāh, was shot and killed with an arrow as his father was pleading those brutes for water for him] at the Euphrates River bank, if he knows his rights, sanctity and authority, that Allāh forgives the sins he has committed and those he will commit."

عـن محمـد بـن مسـلم، عـن أبـي جعفـر (عليـه السـلام) قـال :

" مروا شيعتنا بزيارة قبر الحسين (عليه السلام) ... فإن إتيانه يزيد في الرزق، ويمد في العمر، ويـدفع مـدافع السـوء ، وإتيانـه مفـترض علـى كـل مـؤمن يقـر لـه بالإمامـة مـن الله. "

Muhammed ibn Muslim has quoted the father of Ja`far [Imām al-Baqir ﷺ] as saying, "Order our Shi`as to visit the gravesite of al-Hussain, for visiting it increase's one's sustenance, extends one's lifespan and repels all evils, and visiting it is incumbent on every believer who recognizes that he was appointed by Allāh as the Imām."

عـن الإمـام الصـادق عليـه السـلام قـال :

" إن أيـام زائـري الحسـين بـن علـي (عليـه السـلام) لا تعـد مـن آجـالهم. "

Imām al-Sadiq ﷺ has said, "The days spent by those who visit [the gravesite of] al-Hussain son of Ali are not counted from their decreed lifespans."

عن أبي عبد الله (عليه السلام) قال :

"موضع قبر أبي عبد الله الحسين (عليه السلام) منذ يوم دفن فيه روضة من رياض الجنة."

Abu Abdullāh ﷺ has said, "The site where Abu Abdullāh al-Hussain is buried, since the day he was buried in it, remains to be one of the Gardens of Paradise."

عن أبي عبد الله (عليه السلام) قال : قال الحسين بن علي (عليهما السلام) : "أنا قتيل العَبرة؛ قُتلتُ مكروباً، وحقيقٌ على الله أن لا يأتيني مكروبٌ إلا ردَّهُ وقلبه إلى أهله مسرورا."

Abu Abdullāh [Imam al-Sādiq ﷺ] has said that al-Hussain ibn Ali ﷺ had said to him, "I am the one killing whom draws tears; I was killed with hardship, and Allāh has undertaken on Himself that any distressed person who visits me [my gravesite] will be sent back by Allāh to his family pleased."

PART I

HUSSAIN AND HIS FOES, MARTYRDOM

ABŪ SUFYAN

Abū Sufyan was a wealthy and influential man who belonged to the Banu Umayyah clan of the once pagan tribe of Quraish of Mecca, Hijaz, that fought the spread of Islam relentlessly during the time of the Prophet of Islam (ﷺ). He was contemporary to the Prophet of Islam (ﷺ) whom he fought vigorously. His date of birth is unknown, but he died in 31 A.H./652 A.D. "Abū Sufyan" is his *kunya*, surname; his name is Sakhr ibn Harb ibn Umayyah. He is father of Mu'awiyah and grandfather of Yazid.

Abū Sufyan led pagan Quraish in its many wars against Prophet Muhammed (ﷺ) and his small band of supporters, making alliances with other pagan tribes and with the Jews of Medīna against the new rising power of Islam. He kept leading one battle after another till the fall of Mecca to the Muslims in 630 A.D. It was then that he had to either accept the Islamic faith or face a sure death for all the mischief he had committed against the Muslims, so he preferred to live in hypocrisy as a "Muslim," though only in name, rather than accept death. He was the most cunning man in all of Arabia and one of its aristocrats and men of might and means. He saw Islam as the harbinger of the waning of his own personal power and prestige and those of his tribe, Quraish, not to mention the decline of his faith, paganism, and the pre-Islamic way of life to which he and his likes were very much accustomed, the life of promiscuity, lewdness and debauchery, with all the wine, women and wealth aristocrats like him very much enjoyed. His likes are present throughout the Islamic lands in our time and in every time and clime... This has always been so, and it shall unfortunately remain so...

MU'AWIYAH AND YAZID

Mu'awiyah son of Abū Sufyan was born out of wedlock in 602 A.D. during the *jahiliyya*, the time of ignorance, the period that preceded Islam. His mother, Maysun, was one of his father's slave-girls. Maysan had a sexual intercourse with one of Mu'awiyah's slaves and conceived Yazid by him. Mu'awiyah, in total disregard for Islamic or traditional Arab traditions, claimed Yazid as his son. A testimony to this fact is the well-documented tradition of the Prophet (ﷺ) wherein he said, "The murderer of my [grand]son al-Hussain is a bastard." This tradition is quoted on p. 156, Vol. 1, of Kanz al-Ummal of al-Muttaqi al-Hindi. The stigma of being a bastard applies actually not only to Yazid but also to both Shimr ibn Thul-Jawshan and Ubaydullāh ibn Sa'd, the accomplices about  whom the reader will read later; all of these men were born out of wedlock.

Mu'awiyah played a major role in distorting the Islamic creed by paying writers to tailor design "traditions" to serve his interests and support his deviated views. He installed himself as ruler of Syria in 40 A.H./661 A.D. and ruled for twenty long years till his death at the age of seventy-eight. Shortly before his death, which took place in the month of Rajab of 60 A.H./May of 680 A.D., he managed to secure the oath of allegiance to his corrupt and immoral son Yazid as his successor. He did so by intimidation once and once by buying loyalty and favours, spending in the process huge sums of money that belonged to the Muslims. The weak-minded majority of the Muslims of his time swore allegiance to him. This proves that the majority does not necessarily have to be right. Imām al-Hussain (ع), together with a small band of devotees to the cause of truth, refused to bow their heads to the oppressive forces, hence this tale of heroism.

Mu'awiyah declared himself "caliph" in Syria when he was 59 years old and assumed authority by sheer force. He was not elected, nor was he requested to take charge. He did not hide this fact; rather, he bragged about it once when he addressed the Kufians saying, "O people of Kūfa! Do you think that I fought you in order that you may establish prayers or give zakat or perform the pilgrimage?! I know that you do pray, pay zakat and perform the pilgrimage. Indeed, I fought you in order to take command over you with contempt, and Allāh has given me that against your wishes. Rest assured that whoever killed any of us will himself be killed. And the treaty between us of amnesty is under my feet."[1]

Mu'awiyah's rule was terror in the whole Muslim land. Such terrorism was spread by many convoys sent to various regions. Historians have narrated saying that Muawiyh summoned Sufyan ibn 'Awf al-Ghamidi, one of the commanders of his army, and said to him, "This army is under your command. Proceed along the Euphrates River till you reach Heet. Any resistance you meet on your way should be crushed, and then you should proceed to invade Anbar. After that, penetrate deeply into Mada'in. O Sufyan! These invasions will frighten the Iraqis and please those who like us. Such campaigns will attract frightened people to our side. Kill whoever holds different views from ours; loot their villages and demolish their homes. Indeed, fighting them against their livelihood and taking their wealth away is similar to killing them but is more

---

[1]Ibn Abul-Hadid, *Sharh Nahjul-Balagha* شرح نهج البلاغة, Vol. 16, p. 15.

painful to their hearts."[1]

Another of his commanders, namely Bishr ibn Arta'ah, was summoned and ordered to proceed to Hijaz and Yemen with these instructions issued by Mu'awiyah: "Proceed to Medīna and expel its people. Meanwhile, people in your way, who are not from our camp, should be terrorized. When you enter Medīna, let it appear as if you are going to kill them. Make it appear that your aim is to exterminate them. Then pardon them. Terrorize the people around Mecca and Medīna and scatter them around."[2]

During Mu'awiyah's reign, basic human rights were denied, not simply violated. No one was free to express his views. Government spies were paid to terrorize the public, assisting the army and the police in sparing no opportunity to crush the people and to silence their dissent. There are some documents which reveal Mu'awiyah's instructions to his governors to do just that. For instance, the following letter was addressed to all judges: "Do not accept the testimony of Ali's followers (Shī'as) or of his descendants in (your) courts." Another letter stated: "If you have evidence that someone likes Ali and his family, omit his name from the recipients of rations stipulated from the *zakat* funds." Another letter said, "Punish whoever is suspected of following Ali and demolish his house."[3] Such was the situation during the government of Mu'awiyah, Yazid's infamous father. Historians who were recording these waves of terror described them as unprecedented in history. People were so frightened, they did not mind being called atheists, thieves, etc., but not followers of Imām Ali ibn Abū Talib (ع), Prophet Muhammed's right hand, confidant and son-in-law.

Another aspect of the government of Mu'awiyah was the racist discrimination between Arabs and non-Arabs. Although they were

---

[1] *Ibid.*, Vol. 2, p. 86.

[2] *Ibid.*

[3] *Ibid.*

supposed to have embraced Islam which tolerates no racism in its teachings, non-Arabs were forced to pay *khiraj* and *jizya* taxes that are levied from non-Muslims living under the protection of Muslims and enjoying certain privileges, including the exemption from the military service. A non-Arab soldier fighting in the state's army used to receive bare subsistence from the rations. Once, a dispute flared up between an Arab and a non-Arab and both were brought to court. The judge, namely Abdullāh ibn amir, heard the non-Arab saying to his Arab opponent, "May Allāh not permit people of your kind (i.e. Arabs) to multiply." The Arab answered him by saying, "O Allāh! I invoke You to multiply their (non-Arabs') population among us!" People present there and then were bewildered to hear such a plea, so they asked him, "How do you pray for this man's people to multiply while he prays for yours to be diminished?!" The Arab opponent said, "Yes, indeed, I do so! They clean our streets and make shoes for our animals, and they weave our clothes!"

Imām al-Hussain's older brother, Imām al-Hassan (ع), was elected in Medīna on the 21st of the month of Ramadan, 40 A.H./January 28, 661 A.D. as the caliph, but his caliphate did not last long due to the terrorism promoted by Mu'awiyah who either intimidated, killed, or bribed the most distinguished men upon whom Imām al-Hassan (ع) depended to run the affairs of the government. Finally, Mu'awiyah pushed Imām al-Hassan (ع) out of power after signing a treaty with him the terms of which were, indeed, honourable and fair, had they only been implemented. Finding his men too weak or too reluctant to fight Mu'awiyah, Imām al-Hassan (ع) had no alternative except to sign the said treaty with a man whom he knew very well to be the most hypocritical of all and the most untrustworthy. Since there are too many ignorant folks who dare to blaspheme and cast doubt about the integrity of Imām al-Hassan (ع), we have to review the terms of that treaty and leave the reader to draw his own conclusion; those terms, in brief, were:

1) **Mu'awiyah shall rule according to the Holy Qur'ān and the Sunnah of the Prophet (ص) in the territories under his control.**
2) **Mu'awiyah shall have no right to nominate his successor.**
3) **All people in Syria, Iraq, Hizaj and Yemen shall lead their**

lives safely and securely.

4) The lives and properties of the followers (Shī'as) of Imām Ali ibn Abū Talib (ع), wherever they may be, shall remain safe and secure.

5) Mu'awiyah shall not try, openly or secretly, to harm or to kill Imām al-Hassan (ع) son of Imām Ali ibn Abū Talib (ع), his brother Imām al-Hussain (ع), or any other member of the family of the Prophet (ص), nor shall they be threatened or terrorized.

6) The abusive language, the cursing of Imām Ali (ع) during prayer services (ordered by Mu'awiyah and continued after his death for a long period of time) at the Grand Mosque of Damascus shall be stopped.

Mu'awiyah had ordered all Imāms who led congregational prayers not to descend from their pulpits before cursing Ali (ع), a practice which they labeled as "Sunnah." It is documented that one such Imām forgot once to curse Ali (ع), whereupon people shouted at him that he had violated the Sunnah. Those who prayed at home and who forgot to curse Ali (ع) after their prayers felt obligated to repeat them, being convinced that such cursing was an integral part of the compulsory prayers without which they would not be accepted by Allāh... Such abominable blasphemy continued from the year when Othman was killed, that is, 35 A.H./656 A.D. till it was terminated by orders of the only righteous Umayyad caliph, namely Omer ibn Abdul-Aziz, one year after his becoming caliph, that is, in 100 A.H../718 A.D., for a total of 62 years. Historians say that the public actually did not stop cursing Ali (ع) even then but continued to do so for at least 18 more years, extending the total to 80 years... Omer ibn Abdul-Aziz was killed in 101 A.H./719 A.D. after having ruled for only two years and five months because he was fair and just and, most importantly, because he was sympathetic to the Prophet's family (Ahl al-Bayt); peace and blessings of Allāh be with him.

Shortly after concluding the said treaty, Mu'awiyah lured Imām al-Hassan's wife, Juda daughter of al-Ash'ath ibn Qays, into poisoning her husband with the promise that he would marry her off to his son and heir apparent Yazid. Juda killed her husband who died on Safar 28, 50 A.H./March 30, 670 A.D. She was cursed by the Almighty with an embarrassing ailment for which nobody could find any cure. Mu'awiyah, as expected, did not fulfill his promise.

Having succeeded in getting Imām al-Hassan (ع), Imām al-Hussain's older brother, killed, Mu'awiyah sent letters to one of his Umayyad relatives, namely Marwan ibn al-Hakam, a cousin of Othman ibn Affan and bearer of his seal, a seal which he used quite often for his own gains and even without the knowledge of the aging caliph, instructing him to obtain the oath of allegiance for his son Yazid as his (Mu'awiyah's) successor. By the way, the Umayyads succeeded in making this same Marwan caliph in 64 A.H./683 A.D., and his government lasted for seventeen months till it ended in 65 A.H./684-85 A.D. when he died at the age of 63 and was buried in Damascus. Marwan, accordingly, delivered a speech following the prayers and concluded it by saying, "The commander of the faithful (meaning Mu'awiyah) is of the view that he chooses his son Yazid to succeed him as your ruler following in the footsteps of Abū Bakr and Omer ibn al-Khattab..." He was at that moment interrupted by Abdul-Rahman son of first caliph Abū Bakr. "Nay!," Abdul-Rahman ibn Abū Bakr shouted, "You mean in the footsteps of Kisra (Khosro, emperor of Persia) and Caesar (emperor of Rome)! Neither Abū Bakr nor Omer appointed their sons or relatives as their successors...!"

In 51 A.H./671 A.D., Mu'awiyah performed the pilgrimage then went to Medīna where he called to his presence Abdullāh son of second caliph Omer ibn al-Khattab. His father, Omer , succeeded Abū Bakr as the caliph in 13 A.H./634 A.D.; he remained caliph for ten years till he was killed by a Persian slave in the month of Thul-Hijja, 23 A.H./November 644 A.D. He was succeeded by Othman ibn Affan who ruled for eleven years (till 35 A.H./656 A.D.). Mu'awiyah said to Abdullāh ibn Omer, "O son of Omer ! You used to tell me that you never liked to sleep one night without knowing who your Imām (here the word means "ruler") is, and I warn you against spreading the seeds of dissension among the Muslims or corrupting their views." Abdullāh praised Allāh then said, "There were other caliphs before you who had sons who were not inferior to yours, yet they did not decide to do what you have decided to do regarding your son. Rather, they let the Muslims make their own choice. You warn me against dissension, and I am not an advocate of dissension. I am just one of the Muslims, and if they are unanimous regarding an issue, I will then add my voice to theirs." Having said so, Abdullāh left. Then Muhammed, son of first caliph Abū Bakr, referred to above, was presented before Mu'awiyah. The latter started his rhetoric but Abdul-Rahman interrupted him by saying, "All you want to say is that you wish we obey your son after obeying Allāh, and this, by Allāh, we will never do. And, by Allāh, we shall settle this issue by mutual consultation among the Muslims; otherwise, we will treat you as you were treated at the dawn of Islam...!" Then he, too, stood up and left.

Yazid son of Mu'awiyah was born in 17 A.H./645 A.D. and inherited his father's post in 60 A.H./680 A.D. He ruled for only three years and one month then died in mid-Rab'iul-Awwal of 64 A.H./December 14, 683 A.D. at the young age of 38. He was a playboy, a drunkard, and a man who used to enjoy seeing animals fight. He used to play with animals. Monkeys were dressed in gold-embroidered multi-colored clothes and trained to dance for him, and he had salaried "officials" to look after his animal collection. Such collection included monkeys and race dogs. He was fond of gambling and wine drinking, and he demonstrated disrespect towards the Mosque of the Prophet (ص) and towards the Ka'ba itself, causing very serious damages to its structure as the reader will come to know in a later part of this book. He forced women to take their veils off and killed thousands of innocent people and encouraged the rape of women, girls, and children during the uprisings that took place in Hijaz, particularly in the Harra incident, details of which will follow. In short, Yazid did not have one iota of respect for Islamic tenets or moral ethics. Strange enough, there are some ignorant Muslims who sing his praise, justify and defend his barbaric conduct...

This much gives the reader an idea about what type of persons Abū Sufyan, Mu'awiyah, and Yazid were. Now let us review the brief biography of their opponents.

ALI, HUSSAIN'S FATHER

Imām al-Hussain's father, Ali (ع), needs no introduction, but for the

66

benefit of those who do not know much about him, we would like to state the following:

Ali was born in May of 600 A.D. inside the Ka'ba, the holiest of all holy places in Islam, the cubic symbol of "Allāh's House" in Mecca, Hijaz, northern part of today's Saudi Arabia, the only country in the world named after its ruling dynasty! No other human being was ever born in the holiest of holies besides him. Ali (ع) was raised and cared for by his cousin Muhammed (ص), the Messenger of Allāh, who wished to return the favor Ali's father had done him when he was a child. You see, when Muhammed (ص) was orphaned, Ali's father, Abū Talib, took him in his custody and raised him, so Muhammed (ص) wanted to return the favor especially after seeing how Abū Talib's trade business was not doing well in his old age. Muhammed (ص)'s upbringing of Ali (ع) polished the lad's personality and prepared him to play a major role in the dissemination of the Islamic creed. He was the first male to believe in Muhammed (ص) and to offer prayers with him. The second was another young man who was also raised and cared for by Muhammed (ص), namely Zaid ibn Harithah who later commanded the army of the Muslims during the Battle of Mu'ta of 629 A.D., and so did his son Usamah in 632 A.D., both proving their military ability, insight and wisdom. The third to embrace the Islamic faith was Muhammed's longtime friend Abū Bakr.

When pagan Meccans wanted to assassinate Muhammed (ص) in 622 A.D., Ali (ع) slept in his (Muhammed's) bed, offering his life as a sacrifice to save his, while the Prophet succeeded in leaving his house safely even under the nose of the infidels, having recited the first eight verses of Sūrat Yasin (Chapter 36 of the Holy Qur'ān) and thrown a handful of dust before their eyes. They could not see him leave. Muhammed (ص) safely reached Quba, a suburb of Medīna where he camped and waited for Ali (ع) to rejoin him. He did not want to enter Medīna triumphantly without Ali (ع). After a few days, Ali (ع) walked all alone the entire distance from Mecca to Medīna, about 250 Arabian miles, arriving there with swollen and lacerated feet, bleeding and fatigued.

Ali (ع) defended Islam in the Battle of Badr (624 A.D.) and married

Fātima, the Prophet's only surviving offspring, in the same year. He also fought in the Battle of Uhud in the next year, in the Battle of Moat (Khandaq) in 627 A.D., in the Battle of Khayber (against the Jews of Medīna) in 628 A.D., and took part in the Conquest of Mecca in 630 A.D. He also fought in the Battle of Hunain in the same year. On Thul-Hijjah 18, 10 A.H., corresponding to March 19, 632 A.D., and according to divine orders which Muhammed (ص) had received from his Lord in the form of Qur'ānic verse No. 67 of Sūrat al-Ma'ida (Chapter 5), the Prophet of Islam delivered a speech at a place between Mecca and Medīna known as Ghadīr Khumm in the Juhfa valley wherein he enumerated some of Ali's merits and informed the huge crowd of an estimated 132,000 pilgrims who had accompanied him during his last pilgrimage, the Farewell Pilgrimage, that just as they had accepted him as the Prophet, they were bound to accept Ali (ع) as "Ameerul-Mu'mineen," Commander of the Faithful, title of one who rules the Muslims as the supreme political leader and, at the same time, as the highest religious authority. Details of and references to this historic event are recorded, with the entire original Arabic text (23 pages) of the Prophet's historic sermon, are in my book titled *Ghadīr Khumm: Where Islam was Perfected*.

Because of the numerous battles in which Ali (ع) participated and the number of those whom he killed, he was not popular with those who considered blood relations more important than earning the Pleasure of the Almighty; therefore, only a few months after that date did some people promote Abū Bakr, a wealthy Meccan and a very successful businessman, to the post of "Ameerul-Mu'mineen." This took place in 11 A.H./632 A.D. He ruled for two years and a half, dying on a Tuesday, 13 A.H./634 A.D. at the age of 63... They promoted Abū Bakr to be "Ameerul-Mo'minnen" instead of Ali (ع), forgetting or pretending to forget what they had heard from and pledged to the Prophet (ص) only two months and nine days ago at Ghadīr Khumm. This took place immediately after the Prophet's demise on Safar 28, 11 A.H./May 28, 632 A.D. (By the way, like all lunar Hijri years, the solar calendar year 632 of the Christian Era coincided with both the 10th and the 11th Hijri years.)

Imām Ali (ع) did not receive any significant recognition during the reign of the first three caliphs, and even his wife's property, Fadak, was confiscated; thus, his family was deprived of a good source of income. Abū Bakr ordered the confiscation in 632 A.D. The only just and fair Umayyad ruler, namely the last one, Omer ibn Abdul-Aziz, returned Fadak to Fātima's offspring in 718 A.D., 86 years after its confiscation with profound apologies. When Ali (ع) was elected as caliph in 36 A.H./657 A.D., tribalism and racism were as rampant as they used to be during the pre-Islamic era. Islam's teachings were either forgotten or distorted. In Syria, Mu'awiyah ibn Abū Sufyan had declared himself "caliph" and was buying people's conscience and loyalty. He was, once more, raising one army after another to fight Ali (ع) just as his father Abū Sufyan had raised one army after another to fight Muhammed (ص), causing tens of thousands of Muslims to be killed in the process. Most of Ali's time was spent in defending law and order; he hardly had time to rest and to improve the conditions which he knew were in need of improvement because of the injustices of past regimes that did not protect the Islamic creed from liars and fabricators of traditions, indirectly assisting in the distortion of the Sunnah.

Caliph Ali (ع) had to fight the Battle of Jamal (Camel), which broke out at the end of Rab'i II 36 A.H./June 28, 632 A.D., the forces of dissent which had been herded and led by Aisha daughter of the same Abū Bakr mentioned above and one of the Prophet's wives. She was then nineteen years old and was riding a huge camel named Askar, hence the name of the battle: Harb al-Jamal, battle of the camel. She kept urging her men to fight Ali (ع) and his men. It was the first time that Muslims killed Muslims, and such killing has been going on ever since. Look at Afghanistan, Algeria, Iraq and Iran (during the 1980s when more than a million Muslim lives were lost), and remember the civil wars in Lebanon, Somalia, Yemen, and elsewhere... History repeats itself. Those who do not learn from the mistakes of past generations are doomed, condemned and destined to repeat them, rest assured. Aisha accused Ali (ع) of having collaborated with those who had killed her Umayyad relative Othman ibn Affan who became caliph in 24 A.H./645 A.D. and ruled till he was killed in 35 A.H./656 A.D. when he was 89. Ali (ع), in fact, had sent both of his sons, Imām al-Hassan (ع) and Imām al-Hussain (ع) (the latter being the hero of this brief report), to defend

Othman who was placed by the angry protesters under virtual house arrest and his mansion was twice subjected to a siege. Water and food supplies were blocked from reaching him. Ali (ع) used to get water and food smuggled to Othman's mansion during the night passed on from one person to another from one flat rooftop to another till they reached Othman's mansion. The public outrage stemmed from Othman's mismanagement of public funds and preference of his own relatives over all others for top government jobs even when such relatives were not fit at all to occupy any government post. He himself lived in luxury unseen before, getting mansions built for him and for his wife, and silk clothes and exotic perfumes were being imported especially for him and for her. His wife, Na'ila daughter of al-Qarafisah, used to wear so much jewelry that people could hear the jingle from a distance! Such should not be the conduct of successors of Prophets. While defending Othman, Imām al-Hassan (ع) received a wound on his forehead. But the huge number of the angry crowd finally assaulted Othman's mansion and dealt him blows with their swords, killing him instantly. It was the first time Muslims killed their caliph. Na'ila tried to defend her husband with her bare hands, getting four of her fingers cut off. She sent those fingers together with the copy of the Holy Qur'ān which Othman was reciting when he was killed and which was stained with his blood to Mu'awiyah in Damascus to use them to excite people and to urge them to seek revenge for Othman's murder.

Aisha, ironically, was one of those who had urged the Muslims to kill Othman, making her historic statement which we would like to quote here in its original Arabic text verbatim: أقتلوا نعثلا فقد كفر "Uqtulu Na'thalan faqad kafar," that is, "Kill Na'thal, for he has committed apostasy." Na'thal was a contemporary Jew famous for his untidy and too long beard; hence, Aisha was comparing Othman with a Jew. She, in fact, was trying to get either Talhah ibn Ubaydullāh, her cousin who aspired to marry her after the demise of the Prophet (ص), something which Islam prohibited, or az-Zubair ibn al-Awwam, son of her older sister Asma' daughter of Abū Bakr, become caliph instead of Ali (ع). Az-Zubair ibn al-Awwam did, in fact, succeed in declaring himself as the caliph after rebelling against the Umayyads as the reader will come to know in the chapter dealing with the Harra incident. Aisha disliked Ali (ع) very much despite all the praise lavished on him by her husband, the Messenger of Allāh (ﷺ), and although he did not do anything to warrant such an attitude.

There is no room here to detail all the grievances the Muslims raised against their caliph, Othman, in addition to the above, for these would fill an entire volume, and books have, in fact, been already written about this subject. One such book is titled الفتنة الكبرى *Al-Fitnatul-Kubra* (the greatest dissension) by the renown Egyptian scholar Dr. Taha Hussain (winner of a Nobel prize for literature) and published in Cairo, Egypt, a book which the author may have modelled after at-Tabari's book bearing the exact title and dealing with the same theme. One of the best references written about the Battle of the Camel is al-Mas'ūdi's famous book مروج الذهب *Muraj at-Thahab*. Ali (ﷺ) won the battle; 13,000 men from aisha's camp and 5,000 from Ali's were killed, according to p. 177, Vol. 5, of *Muraj at-Thahab*. The heaviest casualty was the loss of thousands who knew the entire text of the Holy Qur'ān by heart and whose knowledge, during that critical time, was crucial. The Prophet of Islam has said: موت العالم موت العالم "Mawt al-aalim mawt al-aalam," that is, "The death of a scholar spells the death of the world." What is the world without scholars? It is darkness without light, trees without fruit, river without water... Islam very much encourages scholarship and reveres scholars, writers, intellectuals, researchers, scientists, etc.

After the Battle of Camel, Ali (ﷺ) had to fight the Battle of Siffeen (40 A.H./661 A.D.) against the army of Mu'awiyah ibn Abū Sufyan, Yazid's father. Shortly after that, and in the same year, and to be exact on the 19th of the month of Ramadan, 40 A.H./January 29, 661 A.D., Ali (ﷺ) was killed by Ibn Muljim al-Muradi, one of the Kharijites, those who were fed-up with certain Muslim caliphs and with some of the latter's un-Islamic practices. These Kharijites had been crushed by Ali (ﷺ) in the Battle of Nahrawan, which started on Safar 6, 38 A.H./July 17, 658 A.D., but their remnants scattered thereafter throughout the Islamic lands. When he was killed, Ali (ﷺ) was leading the morning prayers at Kūfa's grand mosque. Ali (ﷺ) was the embodiment of everything Islam stands for. Even his name, Ali (ﷺ), is derived from "Al-Aliyy," one of the Amighty's ninety-nine Attributes known as Asma' Allāh al-Husna, Allāh's most beautiful names. Scholars of tafsir, exegesis of the Holy Qur'ān, have identified numerous Qur'ānic verses praising Ali (ع) and his fāmily, his Ahl al-Bayt أهل البيت. The most widely known of such verses is No. 33 of Chapter 33 of the Holy Qur'ān (Ayat at-Tathir, Sūrat al-Ahzab).

This much should suffice the reader to form an idea about Imām al-Hussain's father, so let us now discuss the hero of our story.

قال رسول الله (ص): "حسين مني و أنا من حسين؛ أحب الله من أحب حسينا"

The Messenger of Allāh (ص) has said, "Hussain is of me, and I am of Hussain; Allāh loves whoever loves Hussain."

السَّلام عَلَى الْحُسَيْن ، وَعَلَى عَلِيِّ بْنِ الْحُسَيْنِ ، وَعَلَى أَوْلادِ الْحُسَيْنِ وَعَلَى أَصْحَابِ الْحُسَيْنِ

Peace with al-Hussain, with Ali son of al-Hussain, with the offspring of al-Hussain and with the companions of al-Hussain

---

IMĀM HUSSAIN SON OF IMĀM ALI (ع)

Imām al-Hussain (ع), the Master of Martyrs and the hero of this brief history review, was the greatest spiritual leader of his time in the entire world of Islam. He was an Imām, the brother of an Imām, and the son of an Imām. None in history ever enjoyed such merits. All religious authorities admitted his moral, spiritual and religious superiority over everyone else. They admitted that if there was an individual fit for the spiritual and religious vicegerency of the Holy prophet of Islam (ع), Imām al-Hussain (ع) was the person best suited for it. Imām al-Hussain (ع) was born in Medīna on the 15th of the month of Ramadan, 3 A.H./March 1, 625 A.D. and was named " al-Hussain" which means "Junior al-Hassan," since his older brother is named " al-Hassan." Ali (ع) chose to name both his sons after Shabar and Shubayr, sons of prophet Aaron, older brother of Prophet Moses, peace be with both of them. Even during his childhood, Imām al-Hussain (ع) was known for his brilliance, piety, and lofty upbringing. His grandfather, the Prophet of Islam, surrounded him with his affection and taught him a great deal, making him the custodian of Allāh's knowledge, and so did Imām al-Hussain's mother, Fātima (ع), the Head of all the Women of the World, and so did his father Imām Ali (ع) whom the Prophet (ص) took as a "brother" when he joined the Ansār and the Muhajirun with the bond of brotherhood following his historic migration from Mecca to Medīna. The Prophet (ص), who never uttered a word out of favoritism or in response to an emotional outburst, called Imām al-Hussain (ع) and his older brother Imām al-Hassan (ع) "Masters of the Youths of Paradise;" all the residents of Paradise are young.

Page of the Holy Qur'ān handwritten by Imām al-Hussain (ع)

Imām al-Hussain's life and status in the Islamic history are formidable. Fātima (ع), his mother, was the dearest daughter of her father (ع). At-Tirmithi cited Usamah ibn Zaid ibn Harithah (referred to above) saying that the Prophet (ص) had said, "The dearest member of my family to me is Fātima." She was declared by the Prophet as the Head of all the Women of the world. She and her husband were members of the family who were distinguished for their qualities and services to Islam. They are role models for all Muslim men and women. Their role was an extension of the Prophet's role in leading the great cultural transformation from the darkness of an infidel culture to the light of Islam, the beacon of guidance and the guarantor of happiness in this life and in the one to come.

Historians recorded the birth of Imām al-Hussain (ع) as an exciting event for the Muslims of Medīna and especially for the Prophet of Allāh (ع). The Muslims congratulated each other for the new child whom the Prophet considered as his own son. The Prophet once declared, "Hussain is of me, and I am of Hussain. O Allāh! Be pleased with whoever pleases al-Hussain!" This testimony was not accidental, nor was it the result of emotional expressions. This declaration came from a responsible wise leader, the Prophet of Allāh, who would never commit a mistake during the performance of his Prophetic mission. It is easy to understand the first part of this weighty statement: " al-Hussain is of me," for surely Imām al-Hussain (ع) was of the Prophet's own lineage through his daughter Fāṭima.(ع). But what about the other half, that of "and I am of al-Hussain"? How could the grandfather be of his grandson? If you consider this statement in the light of the role Imām al-Hussain (ع) played in Islam's history, you will understand what the Prophet meant. He simply meant to say, "And my Message is to be continued through al-Hussain's martyrdom." The Prophet, in this statement, was delivering an important message and foretelling people of who would act as the fountainheads of Islamic guidance and who would guard his divine message in the future. Emotions and sentiments are not loose in a Muslim's life but are controlled by Islamic concepts and principles. There is always a criterion for "like" and "dislike" which evolves from the deeply rooted Islamic concepts. Although Abū Lahab was an uncle of the Prophet (ص), his infidelity made him cursed till the Day of Judgment. The same applied to another uncle, Abū Jahal. The Prophet of Allāh made another statement which leaves no doubt about Imām Imām al-Hassan's and Imām al-Hussain's roles. As indicated above, he (ع) said, " al-Hassan and al-Hussain are the masters of the youths of Paradise." This was presented as a credential to the Muslim nation so that it would uphold their leadership.

At a certain time, the Muslims in Medīna realized and appreciated the Islamic message's glory and sweet tasting fruits, so they intended to reward the Prophet (ص) for his efforts in guiding them out of the darkness of jahiliyya and into the light of Islam. The gift they presented to the Prophet (ص) was some gold which they had collected. The Prophet's answer came not from him personally but, rather, from his Lord on his behalf in the text of the following Qur'ānic verses which were revealed during this very incident:

Say (O Muhammed !): "No reward do I ask you for this (conveying of the Message) except that you be kind to those of my kin." (Qur'ān, 23:42)

Muhammed Jawad Maghniyyah, author of تفسير الكاشف *Tafsir al-Kashif*[1], narrates saying that when this verse was revealed, people asked the Prophet (ص), "O Messenger of Allāh! Who are these of your kin for whom respect is made obligatory on us by this verse?" The Prophet (ص) answered, "They are Ali, Fātima, and their two sons." However, this did not imply disrespect for other members of his kinsfolk or companions. Looking objectively at the message of this verse, it will indicate to you, first of all, reluctance to accept material rewards. If a reward is not suitable, it cannot, and it must not, be accepted. Hence, the verse was enjoining respect for specific people, not because they are only the Prophet's relatives. But the real reason behind this respect was to safeguard the Islamic message. The role these holy personalities played in the Islamic history required such respect in order to enable them to perform their duties.

Al-Hakim quoted Au Sa'd al-Khudri saying that the Prophet (ص) once said, "One who dislikes us, we Ahl al-Bayt [ع] (family of Prophet Muhammed [ص]), Allāh shall hurl him into the fire of Hell." This implies that those who dislike the Islamic conduct and way of life as personified by these individuals, through their exemplary conduct, shall receive the Almighty's condemnation and shall taste of His torment.

Jābir ibn Abdullāh al-Ansāri[2], a maternal relative and one of the greatest of all companions of Prophet Muhammed (ص), narrated

---

[1] The fourth edition of this famous 7-volume *tafsīr* adorns our library and it was published in Beirut, Lebanon, in Thul-Qi'da 1410 A.H./June 1990 A.D. by Dar al-Ilm lil Malayeen (P.O. Box 1085, Beirut, Lebanon).

[2] Jābir ibn Abdullāh al-Ansāri is a maternal relative and one of the greatest *sahabis* of Prophet Muhammed (ص), a first-class traditionist and a most zealous supporter of Imām Ali ibn Abū Talib (ع). When the Prophet (ص) migrated from Mecca to Medīna in 622 A.D., he was hosted by Jābir for one week. According to *Al-Isti'ab*, Jābir died at the age of 94 in 74 A.H./693 A.D. (some say in 77 and others in 78 A.H./696 or 697 A.D. respectively), and his funeral prayers were led by Aban ibn Othman, then governor of Medīna. He was the very last to die from among the Prophet's closest companions.

75

once saying that in a speech delivered immediately following the performance of his last pilgrimage, the Farewell Pilgrimage referred to above, the Prophet (ﺹ) said, "O people! I am leaving among you the Book of Allāh and my Itrat (Progeny) for your guidance. So long as you hold fast to them both (at the same time), surely you will never stray." This tradition was narrated not only by Jābir but also by at least twenty other eyewitnesses who heard it in person and who participated in that same pilgrimage, and their statements are recorded in numerous references. Such statements were transmitted by chains of trusted narrators of hadīth. In his renown book Sahīh, Muslim cites some of them. In another tradition transmitted by Abū Tharr al-Ghifāri, the Prophet (ﺹ) is quoted as saying, "O people! Let my family act among you like the head of the body, and like the eyes of the head among you." These traditions are impressive in many respects. First, they were narrated by different sources of different inclinations; this adds to their credibility. Second, the same content indicates their consistency, underscoring their authenticity.

Imām al-Hussain (ﻉ) was one member of the family of the Prophet (ﺹ). He was brought up in the Prophetic guidance where he received the direct attention of the Prophet (ﺹ). The ideal atmosphere where he had grown up with his grandfather, father, mother, and elder brother, was the highest level ever attained. Thus, he acquired wisdom and learned generosity, bravery, piety while attaining the highest knowledge. He occupied outstanding posts during his father's caliphate. During the terror and corruption which swept the Muslim world at the hands of the Umayyad dynasty that ruled the Islamic world (from 661 - 750 A.D.) with an iron fist, he was the sole hope of the Muslims to restore the Islamic laws and to thus bring them prosperity, peace, and happiness in both worlds.

Having seen how his older brother Imām al-Hassan (ﻉ) was betrayed by his friends and poisoned by his foes, Imām al-Hussain (ﻉ) remained in seclusion from the public for ten years, feeling helpless against the tide of Umayyad corruption and tyranny. Gradually, people realized that none could save them from such tyranny except Imām al-Hussain (ﻉ) himself, so they kept appealing to him to lead them against the Umayyads, and he kept ignoring their pleas due to his knowledge that he could not rely on them to remain steadfast on the battlefield against Mu'awiyah's mighty Syrian army, being convinced that they would betray him just as they had betrayed his older brother and his father. They did exactly so as you will see...

Most of the pleas came from the people of Kūfa, Iraq, mostly Shī'as who were subjected to untold atrocities by Kūfa's then governor (appointed on behalf of the central Umayyad government in Damascus) Muhammed ibn al-Ash'ath and the top men who supported him and his Umayyad superiors, namely Shurayh, Kūfa's judge, a typical preacher of the rulers, by the rulers, and for the rulers, a man who was issuing verdicts according not to the teachings of the Holy Qur'ān and the Sunnah but to please the Umayyads who were paying his salary and showering him and his likes with gifts from time to time, and Omer ibn Sa'd. The letters those Kufians sent to Imām al-Hussain (ع) numbered ten to twelve thousand, and many of them threatened Imām al-Hussain (ع) of questioning him before the Almighty on the Day of Judgment as to: "Why did you not respond to the people who sought your assistance to put an end to tyranny and oppression?" Imām al-Hussain (ع) had to oblige despite all the odds against him. He, in fact, knew fully well that he was marching to his death, having already been informed of his martyrdom in the land of Kerbalā' by none other than his holy grandfather who even named his killer. He was informed of his women and children taken captive and of the time and day when he would be martyred. Everything was already decreed, and Imām al-Hussain (ع) had no choice except to fulfil a decree by sacrificing himself and all the dear ones with him for the sake of Islam. We only wish here to unveil the startling aspects of the revolution's message which is often neglected in its traditional commemoration.

Confronting all the details of this momentous event, we have to answer many pressing questions such as: Why did this revolution take place? What were its implications and procedures? And what were its conclusive results? The answers may provide a guiding light so that we may form our conclusions. The following account is based on the most popular and trustworthy authorities on the subject.

To understand Imām al-Hussain's personality and the collective culture of the society, a summary of Islam's view of life is necessary.

ISLAM'S MESSAGE TO HUMANITY

Islam is a way of life. It gives reasons and sets a purpose for living. We were not placed on earth by accident or without a purpose. Everything in life has a purpose; every being has a role to play; every inanimate object serves an end. Islam elevates the spirit while satisfying the material needs...

Islam considers man as God's vicegerent on earth. This status is a lofty and weighty one, but it is also critical: the requirements must be met, the conditions must be satisfied; the mission must be accomplished. Thus, man is in an envied position and, consequently, his acts and norms of conduct are expected to conform with the high level he is to occupy.

The Islamic concepts and laws are inseparable parts of the Islamic ideology; milk is inseparable from water. They make up the practical expression of Islam in society and in life as a whole. These concepts and laws are essentially to harmonize people's relationships with each other, with other beings, with nature and the environment and, above all, with the Creator.

The basic Islamic outlook of this life is one of an introductory course; the real life is the one to come, not this one. This worldly life is a prelude to another eternal one; therefore, this world is a preparatory stage for people in order to attain the spiritual level which permits them to enter Paradise. It is a microcosm of the real eternal macrocosm. The other side of the picture is the horror of Hell for people who misuse or abuse the power placed at their disposal. Hence, success and failure are not measured by the known criteria of this world, by, say, materialistic supremacy, wealth and power. The Islamic criteria differ from the materialistic ones; they account for the life hereafter; they take into consideration the next phase of our existence. Death is not the end of everything; it is the beginning of real life. To die is to wake up from a brief dream. To please Allāh is the sublime goal which surpasses all other wishes and desires, or so should it be. This by no account means that we should neglect acquiring materialistic supremacy, wealth and riches, by legitimate means; it only means that we must put such supremacy, or such wealth, in its rightful place: to serve man and to please Allāh. What a noble concept! It is with pleasing Allāh and with His support that Muslims seek materialistic supremacy. Alas! The Muslims now do not have any materialistic supremacy at all. Their natural resources are being sold for less than it costs to produce them; their countries are supermarkets for goods manufactured by those who despise them and look down upon them; their leaders can hardly agree on one common cause, and their nations have no say about who should rule them and who should not, and they are robbed of their freedom of expression, worship, and movement. Turkey, for example, used to be the center of the Islamic world and the source of its pride and glory. Now its ruling juntas, supported by non-Muslim and anti-Islamic "superpowers," by Zionists and imperialists, are fighting Islam with all their might and means. The same can be said about the rulers of many other countries who are Muslims only in name. The Muslims are now prisoners in their own homes. They are the underdogs of the world. Gone are the days of their supremacy and glory and shall never return unless and until they regret and return to their creed and practice it as it should be.

ORIGINS OF DEVIATION

How did Mu'awiyah ascend to the post of ruler of the Muslims, and how did he dare to claim succession to the Prophet (ص), the irreligious, liar, cheating, cunning and conniving man that he was? What happened to the Muslim world? Why was it silent at seeing the assumption of power by an ignoble person like Yazid? Indeed, it is astonishing to witness the indifference and irresponsibility demonstrated by the vast majority of Muslims. One is tempted to say that such indifference is present even in our own time. Our time, in fact, can best be described as the neo-*jahiliyya*. There are already too many Yazids but no al-Hussain to come to the rescue. Islamic values and ideals were as if totally alien to the society. What happened to the dynamic forces that had awakened the world and shaken it like never before? The Prophet's voice had not yet died away regarding the responsibility of the Muslims. He once said, "One who sees a cruel governor violating Allāh's laws, breaking His covenant, acting in contrast to the tradition of the Prophet, committing mischief and intruding upon peoples' rights, without trying to change that governor through his action, or speech, Allāh will then reserve a suitable place for him in Hell."

We all may wonder about the causes of deviation which led to this deplorable state of affairs. We know for sure that Islam is a perfect and practical religion, a complete way of life. Islam, no doubt, assured us of guiding us to a secure and prosperous life. The question of deficiency in the Islamic message, however, if there is such deficiency at all, or in the way it was conducted by the Prophet (ﷺ), has no place here. The only possible shortcomings, therefore, are confined to the subsequent status of the Muslims, to their way of handling their affairs, and to their conformity to the Islamic laws besides the "natural" obstacles encountered in the sequence of events. Following is the major cause that contributed to the deplorable status quo of the Muslims of the time and is still contributing to that of our own and will continue to do so till the end of time.

FALSIFICATION OF *HADĪTH* AND DISTORTION OF THE *SUNNA*

The worst mischief upon which Mu'awiyah embarked was the fabrication of hadīth, traditions detailing what the Prophet of Islam (ع) said or did. Hadīth is one of the two sources of Islam's legislative system, the Shari'a. Selecting Imām Ali (ع) as his lifetime's adversary, Mu'awiyah soon found out that his cause was hopeless. Ali's merits were very well recognized by every Muslim while Mu'awiyah's family and dismal conduct were the objects of their contempt. Mu'awiyah's past record was dark and shameful whereas that of Ali (ع) was glorious and shining, full of heroism in defense of Islam.

In order to sustain his campaign and raise the status of his likes, Mu'awiyah had to attract the remnant of some companions of the Prophet (ﷺ) whose characters were known as weak and who had a genuine interest in this world and in its vanishing riches. He

80

employed them to fabricate traditions custom-designed to his own tailoring. This trend of fabricating hadīth constituted a grave danger to the integrity of the Islamic tenets. Hadīth is second in importance to the Holy Qur'ān. It was very important to ward off such a danger. To expose such a trend to the Muslims at large was very vital, pivotal, of the highest priority. It would be accomplished by exposing and disgracing those who embarked upon committing and nurturing such a terrible mischief. Imām al-Hussain's revolution broke out in order to undertake this very task.

Let us now review a few samples of fabricated traditions[1].

Abū Hurayra is supposed to have quoted the Prophet (ص) as saying, "Allāh has trusted three persons for His revelation: Myself, Gabriel and Mu'awiyah." We wonder what Allāh was doing for the revelation when Mu'awiyah was in the camp of the infidels. This quotation is cited by Ibn Asakir, Ibn Uday, Muhammed ibn Aa'ith, Muhammed ibn Abd al-Samarqandi, Muhammed ibn Mubarak al-Suri and al-Khateeb al-Baghdadi who all quote Abū Hurayra saying, "سمعت رسول الله يقول: ان الله ائتمن على وحيه ثلاثة أنا و جبرائيل و معاوية". Imagine! He even puts his name before that of arch-angel Gabriel! *Astaghfirullāh!*

According to al-Khateeb al-Baghdadi, Abū Hurayra claimed, " ناول النبي معاوية سهما فقال: خذ هذا السهم حتى تلقاني به في الجنة!" The Prophet (ص) gave Mu'awiyah an arrow then said to him, "Take this arrow until we meet in Paradise." What a lucky arrow to enter Paradise! Let us stop here to discuss this man, Abū Hurayra, who may have had the lion's share in distorting the Prophet's Sunnah especially when we come to know that he was quoted by a host of *tabi'in* who

---

[1]For more information about this man, Abū Hurayra, refer to *Shī'as are the Ahl as-Sunnah*, a book written in Arabic by Dr. Muhammed at-Tijani as-Samawi and translated into English by myself. It is available for sale from Vantage Press, Inc., 516 West 34th Street, New York, N.Y. 10001, or you may order it through the Internet's worldwide web: www.amazon.com. Its title in the said web is "Shī'as are the Ahl as-Sunnah."

in turn are quoted by hundreds others who in turn are quoted by thousands others..., and so on and so forth. This is why his name is in the forefront of narrators of *hadīth*.

There is no agreement about what Abū Hurayra's name was, nor when he was born or when he died. He is said as having died in 59 A.H./678 A.D., and some say that his name was Abdul-Rahman ibn Sakhr al-Azdi, while others say it was Umair ibn amir ibn Abd Thish-Shari ibn Taraf. But it is agreed upon that he belonged to the Yemenite tribe of Daws ibn Adnan and that his mother's name was Umaima daughter of Safeeh ibn al-Harith ibn Shabi ibn Abū Sa'd; she, too, belonged to the Daws tribe. It is said that the Prophet (ص) nicknamed him "Abū Hurayra" after a kitten to which he was attached. He accepted Islam in 7 A.H./628-9 A.D. immediately after the Battle of Khaybar, and he was then more than thirty years old. He was one of those indigent Muslims who had no house to live in, so they were lodged at the Suffa, a row of rooms adjacent to the Prophet's mosque at Medīna. These residents used to receive the charity doled out to them by other Muslims. He used to see the Prophet (ص) mostly when it was time to eat. He missed most of the battles in defense of Islam waged after that date although he was young and healthy and capable of serving in the army.

What is the meaning of his title "Abū Hurayra", man of the kitten? Ibn Qutaybah al-Dainuri quotes Abū Hurayra on p. 93 of his book titled *Al-Ma'arif* المعارف as saying, "... و كنيت بأبي هريرة بهرة صغيرة كنت ألعب بها" "... And I was called 'Abū Hurayra' because of a small kitten I used to play with." In his *Tabaqat* book, Ibn Sa'd quotes Abū Hurayra as saying, " كنت أرعى غنما و كانت لي هرة صغيرة فكنت اذا كان الليل وضعتها في شجرة فاذا أصبحت أخذتها فلعبت بها فكنونى أبا هريرة" "I used to tend to a herd, and I had a small kitten. When it was night time, I would place her on a tree. When it was morning, I would take her and play with her, so I was called 'Abū Hurayra' [man of the small kitten]."

The time Abū Hurayra spent in the company of the Prophet (ص), that is to say, on and off, is by the most generous estimates three years, yet this man narrated more traditions of the Prophet (ص) than anyone else in history. The total number of "traditions" which he attributed to the Prophet (ص) reached the astronomical figure of

5,374 of which only 326 are quoted by al-Bukhari, the most famous compiler of hadīth, and who endorses no more than 93 of them! Muslim, another compiler of hadīth, endorses only 89 of Abū Hurayray's alleged ahadīth. These facts and figures are stated in the famous classic reference titled Siyar Alam an-Nubala' by at-Thahbi. Compare this unrealistic figure of 5,374 "traditions" attributed to the Prophet (ﷺ) and compiled during less than three years with the 586 traditions compiled by Ali ibn Abū Talib (ع), the Prophet's cousin and son-in-law who was raised by the Prophet (ﷺ) since his birth in 600 A.D. and who followed the Prophet (ﷺ) like his shadow for 32 years. Compare it with the figure of 142 traditions narrated by Abū Bakr, one of the closest companions and a longtime friend of the Prophet (ﷺ) and one of the earliest to embrace Islam. Compare it with the figure of 537 traditions narrated by the second caliph Omer ibn al-Khattab and with the 146 traditions narrated by Othman ibn Affan, keeping in mind that all these men knew how to read and write whereas Abū Hurayra was illiterate; he could neither read nor write...

The Umayyads found in Abū Hurayra the right man to fabricate as many "traditions" as they needed to support their un-Islamic practices and then attribute them to the Prophet (ﷺ), hence the existence of such a huge number of traditions filling the books of the Sunnah. And the Umayyads rewarded Abū Hurayra very generously. When he came from Yemen to Hijaz, Abū Hurayra had only one single piece of striped cloth to cover his private parts. When Mu'awiyah employed Abū Hurayra to work in the factories producing custom-designed "traditions," he rewarded him by appointing him as the governor of Medīna. He also married him off to a lady of prestige for whom Abū Hurayra used to work as a servant and built him al-Aqeeq mansion. Who was that lady?

She was Bisra daughter of Ghazwan ibn Jābir ibn Wahab of Banu Mazin, sister of Prince Utbah ibn Ghazwan, an ally of Banu Abd Shams, the man who was appointed by Omer ibn al-Khattab as governor of Basra. Utbah ibn Ghazwan was a famous *sahabi* and a hero of Islam, and he died during the time of Omer ibn al-Khattab. The Umayyads married Abū Hurayra off to Utbah's sister, Bisra, a number of years after the death of her famous brother. He used to work for Bisra as a servant. Ibn Hajar al-Asqalani mentions Bisra in the first setion of his famous work *Al-Isaba fi Akhbar al-Sahāba* and says the following about Bisra, " ثم النبوي العهد في استأجرته قد كانت و "She تزوجها بعد ذلك لما كان مروان يستخلفه في امرة المدينة على عهد معاوية used to let him work for her during the time of the Prophet, then he married her after that when Marwan [ibn al-Hakam] used to let him be in charge of Medīna during the time of Mu'awiyah." In his *Tabaqat*, Ibn Sa'd quotes Abū Hurayra as saying the following about his wife, Bisra, " ...رجلي عقبة و بطني طعام على غزوان ابنة من نفسي أكريت فكانت تكلفني أن أركب قائما، و أورد حافيا، فلما كان بعد ذلك زوجنيها الله فكلفتها أن تركب قائمة و أن تورد حافية!! " I placed myself at the service of the daughter of Ghazwan in exchange for food for my stomach and for something to wear on my feet... She used to order me to ride while serving her and to approach her barefoot to serve her. After that,

Night view of the Prophet's Mosque in Medīna, Saudi Arabia

Allāh made her my wife, so I ordered her to ride as she served me and to approach me barefoot!!" Thus, Abū Hurayra "got even" with the unfortunate lady!

Abū Hurayra found himself during the Umayyads' reign of terror

and oppression a man of wealth and influence, owning slaves and having servants. Prior to that, Omer ibn al-Khattab appointed him as governor of Bahrain for about two years during which Abū Hurayra amassed a huge wealth, so much so that people complained about him to Omer who called him to account for it. Finding his excuse too petty to accept, Omer deposed him. Omer also questioned him about the unrealistically abundant traditions which he was attributing to the Prophet (ص), hitting him with his cane and reprimanding him for forging traditions and even threatening to expel him from the Muslim lands. All these details and more can be reviewed in famous references such as: Ar-Riyad an-Nadira الرياض النضرة by at-Tabari, in Vol. 4 of the original Arabic text of al-Bukhari's *Sahīh*, where the author quotes Abū Hurayra talking about himself, in Abū Hurayra by the Egyptian scholar Mahmoud Abū Rayyah, in سير أعلام النبلاء *Siyar Alam an-Nubala'* by at-Thahbi, in شرح نهج البلاغة *Sharh Nahjul-Balāgha* by Ibn Abul-Hadad, in البداية و النهاية *Al-Bidaya wal Nihaya* by Ibn Katheer, in طبقات الفقهاء *Tabaqat al-Fuqaha* by Ibn Sa'd (also famous as Tabaqat Ibn Sa'd), in تأريخ الأمم و الملوك *Tarikh al-Umam wal Muluk* by at-Tabari, in تاريخ الخلفاء *Tarikh al-Khulafa* by as-Sayyuti, in فتح الباري *Fath al-Bari* by Ibn Hajar al-Asqalani, in المستدرك *Al-Mustadrak* by al-Hakim, and in numerous other references. Yet some Muslims label Abū Hurayra as "Islam's narrator," propagating for his fabrications without first studying them in the light of the Qur'ān and going as far as invoking the Almighty to be pleased with him....

Abdullāh ibn Omer (ibn al-Khattab), too, claimed that the Prophet said, "You will see greed after me and things with which you will disagree." People, he went on, asked, "O Messenger of Allāh! What do you order us to do then?" The Prophet, Abdullāh continued, said, "Give the governor what is his and plead to Allāh for yours." Islam, true Islam, never condones toleration of unjust rulers. Another fabricated tradition is also by Abdullāh ibn Omer who quoted the Prophet (ص) saying, "Put up with whatever conduct you do not like of your rulers because if you abandon the جماعة Jama'a (group) even the distance of one foot and then die, you will die as unbelievers." Surely many despots ruling the Muslim world nowadays can appreciate such "traditions" and will not hesitate to publicize for them and be generous to those who promote them; they would give

85

them generous salaries and build them mansions... Such fabricated "traditions" are not only in total contrast with the Qur'ān and the Sunnah as well as with other verified traditions, they invite the Muslims to be the slaves of their rulers. This is exactly what Mu'awiyah wanted, and this is exactly what so-called "Muslim" rulers like him want in our day and time... Unfortunately for the Muslims and fortunately for their enemies, there are quite a few "Muslim" rulers like this Mu'awiyah. This is why there is poverty, ignorance, dictatorship, injustice, oppression and subjugation to the enemies of Islam throughout the Muslim world nowadays.

YAZID APPOINTED AS SUPREME RULER

Yazid's grandfather, Abū Sufyan, advised and managed the infidel's campaigns against Islam till the conquest of Mecca, as stated above. His wife Hind (mother of Mu'awiyah and grandmother of Yazid) tried to chew the liver of Hamzah, uncle of the Prophet (ص), because of her burning hatred and cannibalism. Mu'awiyah, too, was an active opponent of Islam. Indeed, Abū Sufyan's family was performing the strategic, financial and morale boosting in the infidel's campaign against the Muslims for many years. Their efforts, wealth and diplomacy formed a great obstacle in the way of spreading Islam.

Time had lapsed and Mecca was suddenly besieged with the considerably large forces of the Muslims. The unbelievers in Mecca were stunned at seeing the Muslim fighters who had caught them by surprise, thanks to the shrewd military tactics of the Prophet (ص). Thus, the infidels, including Abū Sufyan, had no choice except to abandon their arrogance and to accept Allāh's sovereignty, or so did most of them pretend. Mu'awiyah was then 28 years old. Having seen how his father "accepted" Islam, though reluctantly, he fled for Bahrain where he wrote his father a very nasty letter reprimanding him for his "conversion." It is not clear when Mu'awiyah brought himself to profess adherence to the Islamic creed. During this incident, i.e. the fall of Mecca to the Muslims, which was accomplished on a Friday, the 20th of the month of Ramadan, 8 A.H., corresponding to January 14, 630 A.D., less than two years before the Prophet's demise, historians recorded some peculiar stories about Abū Sufyan's family; however, there is one thing certain: They accepted Islam unwillingly, and they were treated in a special way on that account. For instance, they were given more than their share of the treasury in order to gain their hearts and win them over to Islam. But whether this generosity had any effect in producing any change at all in their attitude is quite another story. Indeed, subsequent events revealed the fact that no change at all had taken place in their way of thinking.

Yazid was brought up in such a family whose atmosphere was electrified with emotions of its dead who fought Islam and who were killed mostly during Islam's first major battle, that of Badr which broke out on a Friday, the 17th of the month of Ramadan, 2 A.H., corresponding to March 16, 624 A.D. and to which the Holy Qur'ān refers in 8:5-11. Seventy prominent pagan Quraishites were killed in it, half of them at the hands of Imām al-Hussain's father Ali ibn Abū Talib (ع). That, by the way, was Ali's first battle; he was 24 years old. Among the Umayyads who were killed in it were: Utbah, father-in-law of Yazid's father Mu'awiyah, Utbah's son al-Walid ibn al-Mugharah (father of the famous military leader Khalid ibn al-Walid), and Shaybah, Utbah's brother. Al-Walid ibn al-Mugharah is cursed in the Holy Qur'ān in 74:11-30 (Sūrat al-Muddaththir). Utbah is father of Hind, mother of Yazid, who tried to chew the liver of Hamzah, Prophet Muhammed's dear uncle and valiant defender of Islam. Add to this the fact that such family witnessed how those who had killed their kinsfolk received full honour, recognition, and respect by the entire community, not to mention the wasted wealth, the injured pride, and the loss of privileges which they used to enjoy during the pre-Islamic period known as the *jahiliyya*. Yet Yazid himself had some unique characteristics in the negative and adverse sense of the word in addition to what we recorded above. He was known as a playboy; he is on record as the first person ever to compose pornographic poetry. He described each and every part of his aunt's body for sensual excitement, doing so without being reprimanded by his father or mother or anyone else. Historians record his being seen drunk in public, his committing adultery, and his leading quite a corrupt life, a life which did not last for long, thank Allāh. In one of his poetic verses, Yazid stated, "The family of Hashim (the Prophet's clansmen) staged a play to get a kingdom. Actually, there was neither news from Allāh (*wahi*) received nor a revelation."

Clock Tower overlooking the Ka'ba Haram, Mecca, Saudi Arabia

Mu'awiyah was not ruling as an individual but was representing a way of thinking which differed in nature from everything Islam stands for. However, he was not satisfied to leave the ruling stage without making sure that it was properly looked after. His pragmatic and materialistic mind drove him to prepare for the crowning of his son, Yazid, as his successor. Mu'awiyah had made many pledges not to install Yazid when he saw the conditions at the time not conducive to such a plan because Muslims were still politically conscious and desired to see the restoration of the Islamic laws and values. Mu'awiyah, hence, had a difficult job at hand before leaving this world. He, in fact, tried his best to buy the allegiance for his son from his army's commanders, tribal chiefs and chieftains, and entire tribes as well as men of distinction and influence, spending huge sums of money in the process. But his efforts did not succeed with everyone. One of his failed attempts was when he wrote Imām al-Hussain (ع) soliciting his endorsement for his appointment of Yazid as the heir apparent to the throne. Imām al-Hussain's answer was a scathing criticism of all what Mu'awiyah and Yazid had committed. Mu'awiyah, therefore, forewarned his son Yazid to beware of Imām al-Hussain (ع).

Night view of the shrine of Ma'suma daughter of Imām ar-Ridha (ع) in Qum, Iran

Yazid eventually succeeded his father Mu'awiyah as the ruler. Yazid now spared no means to secure the submission for his unholy practices, oppression and aggression, from everyone. He knew very well that in reality, he had no legitimate right whatsoever to make claims or to issue demands. On the contrary, he was guilty of having committed many illegal and sacrilegious deeds for which he should

89

have been killed, had there anyone powerful enough to implement the Islamic code of justice.

Once in charge, Yazid took his father's advice regarding Imām al-Hussain (ﻉ) seriously. He wrote the then governor of Medīna, al-Walid ibn Utbah, ordering him to secure the oath of allegiance to him as the new ruler from everyone in general and from Imām al-Hussain (ﻉ), Abdullāh ibn Omer (son of second caliph Omer ibn al-Khattab), and Abdullāh ibn az-Zubair in particular, being the most prominent personalities. Yazid in an unmistakable language ordered al-Walid to secure such an oath for him by force if necessary, and that if Imām al-Hussain (ﻉ) refused, he should behead him and send his severed head to him in Damascus. But al-Walid's efforts were fruitless. Imām al-Hussain's reply was exact and direct; said he, "Ameer (Governor)! I belong to the Ahl al-Bayt (fāmily) of the Prophet. Allāh has consigned to and charged us with the Imāmate (spiritual and political leadership of the Muslims). Angels pay us visits. Yazid is a wicked sinner, a depraved reprobate, a wanton drunkard, a man who sheds blood unjustly, and a man who openly defies Allāh's commandments. A man like me will never yield his allegiance to a person like him."

THE NOBLE MOTIVES BEHIND IMĀM HUSSAIN'S REVOLUTION
Such motives were numerous. Some of them stemmed from the grievances of the general public, while others were ideological in nature and noble in objective. They may be summed up as follows:

1) The most urgent need was to stop the attempts to distort the Islamic concepts and code of conduct, particularly the falsification of hadīth as discussed above. This was of the utmost significance; it preoccupied the minds of responsible Muslims at the time. Such fabrication was quite rampant, epidemic in nature, festered by the funds available for those who rushed to please the Umayyads with their pens, those who did not hesitate to sell their religion for a trifling. Such fabrication was poisonous in effect, and it affected the lives of all Muslims, and it still does. It was giving the Umayyads a free hand to do whatever they desired of unfair and

90

unethical policies in dealing with their subjects. The mask of religion with which they used to hide their un-Islamic conduct was quite dangerous. In the long run, such danger would eventually change the pristine concepts introduced by Islam and substitute them with anything but Islam. Stripping such a mask and exposing the true picture of the Umayyads was the most urgent task of a revolutionary like Imām al-Hussain (ع).

2) The Umayyads considered the Islamic world as their own real estate property. The zakat and other Islamic taxes were levied, but nobody knew where the funds went. Large gifts were doled out from the state treasury (called in Islam bayt al-mal) to governors, government officials, tribal chiefs, army commanders, and officers who surpassed others in their cruelty and oppression... Large sums of money were spent on activities which Islam prohibits: racing, gambling, wines, slave women to entertain the high class and the people in power, etc.

3) The State's structure was built on un-Islamic premises. Quraish was born to rule; non-Arabs were second-class citizens who formed the base of the society's pyramid. That was the general social picture of the Islamic world under the Umayyad's rule. Anyone who dared to express an opinion which did not agree with that of the Umayyads had to be placed under house arrest if not altogether eliminated. His property would then be confiscated and his life would be at stake. He would live in fear for the rest of his miserable life. Nowadays, there are millions of Muslims who live under such conditions. You see, the Umayyads are not dead; they are very much alive and well...

The majority of Muslims were left on the brink of starvation while the ruling clique enjoyed the social and material privileges. It very much is like what one sees happening nowadays in many Muslim countries. Let us face it; most Muslims are nowadays the laughing stocks of the world; انا لله و انا اليه راجعون *Inna Lillah wa Inna Ilayhi Rajioon* (We belong to Allāh, and to Him shall we return).

4) The Muslims had apparently become accustomed to the un-Islamic rule of the Umayyads as time passed by. Their resistance gradually slackened, and some people began adjusting to the new realities. The revolutionary spirit of Islam began to disappear little by little from the Muslims' lives and thoughts. A new stimulant to their souls was necessary in order to bring life back to their misled souls and to restore the Islamic conduct and way of life to the society.

Interior gate to the shrine of Imām al-Hussain (ع)

THE REVOLUTION'S PROCESS

Having refused to swear the oath of allegiance to Yazid, Imām al-Hussain (ع) realized that his stay in Medīna was becoming impossible, unsafe; therefore, he decided to bid farewell to it. Bidding his people and friends to get ready for the journey, he went at night to the tomb of his grandfather Prophet Muhammed (ص). Approaching the grave, he greeted him then said, "Assalamo Alaikom, O Messenger of Allāh! I am the son of the beloved portion of your heart Fātima. Grandfather! You yourself had bequeathed to our Umma (nation) urging them to look after me and to take care of me, but they have neglected doing so and quite forgotten all of that."

He spent the entire night at the tomb occupied in prayer the entire period, returning after daybreak. He did the same in the following night. One of his prayers in that second night was:

Allāh! This is the resting-place of Your beloved Prophet Muhammed (ص) and I am his grandson. You know well the present situation in which I am, and You know what is in the innermost of my heart. I invoke You, Lord, to keep me by the grace of this holy place firmly steadfast in my pursuit of whatever meets Your Pleasure and the Pleasure of Your Prophet.

At-Tabari, Abū Mikhnaf and many other historians record saying that Imām al-Hussain (ع) saw his grandfather the Prophet (ص) in his vision at the end of that same second night calling unto him thus:

Come to me, O Hussain! Come to me going by and passing through the torturous stage of martyrdom and claim the right position reserved for you. The Lord, Allāh, will resurrect me, your parents, your elder brother (al-Hassan) and yourself at the same time and gather us all at the same place on the Day of Judgment.

Umm Salamah, the virtuous wife of Prophet Muhammed (ص), hurried to Imām al-Hussain (ع) as soon as she heard that he intended to depart from Medīna. She said to him, "Son! How will I be able to bear your journey to Iraq? I have heard your grandfather (the Prophet [ص]) saying, My son al-Hussain will be murdered on a tract of land people will call Kerbalā'.'" "By Allāh, mother," Imām al-Hussain (ع) answered, adding, "I know all that. I also know on what day I will be murdered, and the name of the man who will murder me. I know, too, the people who will inter my dead body and the members of my Ahl al-Bayt and friends who will meet their martyrdom along with me. If you desire, I will show you the exact spot of my grave." On Rajab 28, 60 A.D./May 7, 680 A.D., Imām al-Hussain (ع) left Medīna for good accompanied by 21 male children in addition to the ladies.

HUSSAIN IN MECCA

When Yazid came to know that al-Walid had allowed Imām al-Hussain (ع) and Abdullāh ibn az-Zubair to leave Medīna for Mecca without taking their oath of allegiance to him, he became very angry and immediately deposed al-Walid from his post and appointed Amr ibn Sa'd in his place. Amr, in turn, appointed Omer ibn az-Zubair as his chief executive officer. Omer began to harass and intimidate the supporters of Abdullāh ibn az-Zubair. The Imām (ع) understood that those were scaring tactics meant to convey the message that he would be next to harass and intimidate; therefore, he felt that it was not safe for him to stay even in Mecca. There, Imām al-Hussain (ع) received thousands of letters, mostly from the people of Kūfa, pleading to him to rescue them from the Umayyads' tyranny. According to the renown writer al-Balathiri, Imām al-Hussain (ع) received as many as six hundred letters in one day and a total of twelve thousands, all requesting the same. Among those who wrote him were these renown Kufians some of whom betrayed him then fought him: Shabth ibn Rab'i, Hijar ibn Abjar, Yazid ibn al-Harith, Izrah ibn Qays, Amr ibn al-Hajjaj, and Muhammed ibn Omayr ibn Utarid. First, Imām al-Hussain (ع) did not respond to any of these letters, then he wrote one letter which he entrusted to Hani ibn Hani as-Subayi and Sa'd ibn Abdullāh al-Hanafi wherein he said, *"In the Name of Allāh, the Most Benevolent, the Most Merciful. Hani and Sa'd brought me your letters, and they are the last to deliver such letters to me. I understand what you narrate, and the gist of most of your letters is: "We have no Imām; so, come to us, perhaps Allāh will gather us with you on the path of guidance and righteousness." I have sent you my brother and cousin and the confidant of my Ahl al-Bayt and ordered him to write me with regard to your conditions, views and intentions. So, if he writes me saying that your view is united with that of those of distinction and wisdom from among you and in agreement with what your messengers and letters state, I shall, by the Will of Allāh, come to you very soon. By my life, an Imām is one who acts upon the Book [of Allāh] and implements justice and follows the path of righteousness; he dedicates himself to follow Allāh's Commandments, and peace be with you."*

He handed his letter to his cousin Muslim ibn Aqeel saying, "I am dispatching you to the people of Kūfa, and Allāh shall deal with you as He pleases. I wish that I and you should be in the company of the martyrs; so, proceed with Allāh's blessing and help. Once you get there, stay with the most trustworthy of its people."

Muslim left Mecca on the fifteenth of the month of Ramadan,

corresponding to June 22, 680 A.D., via the Mecca-Medīna highway. He reached Medīna and went to the Mosque of the Prophet (ص), then he bade his family farewell after having hired two road guides from the tribe of Qays. One night the road guides were lost, and they became extremely thirsty, and it was very hot. They said to Muslim (ع) once they recognized some road marks, "Take yonder road and follow it, perhaps you will be saved." He, therefore, left them, following their advice. Both road guides died of thirst. He could not carry them because they were about to pass away. What those road guides had actually seen was not the road itself but some landmarks leading thereto. The distance between them and water was not known, and they were unable to ride on their own, nor could they ride with someone else. Had Muslim (ع) stayed with them, he, too, would have perished. The most urgent matter was to preserve precious lives and to continue the march till water could be reached, hence his decision to abandon them where they were. Muslim and those serving him barely survived till they reached the highway and the water source where they rested for a short while.

Muslim sent a letter to Imām al-Hussain (ع) with a messenger whom he hired from those who settled near that water source. He told him about the death of the road guides, about the hardship he underwent, and that he was staying at a narrow passage at Batn al-Khabt awaiting his instructions. The messenger met Imām al-Hussain (ع) at Mecca and delivered the letter to him. Al-Imām al-Hussain (ع) wrote him back ordering him to continue his march to Kūfa without any delay. Having read the letter, Muslim immediately resumed his trip and passed by a watering place belonging to the tribe of Tay. He Alighted there then departed. He saw a man shooting and killing a deer, so he took it as a sign of good omen: the killing of his foe.On the twenty-fifth of Shawwal, 60 A.H./July 27, 680 A.D., Muslim ibn Aqeel entered Kūfa and stayed with al-Mukhtar ibn Abū Ubayd ath-Thaqafiwho was highly respected among his people, a generous man, a man of ambition and daring, one well experienced and determined, and a formidable opponent of the enemies of Ahl al-Bayt, peace be with them. He was a man of great discretion especially with regard to the rules of the battle and the means of subduing the foe. He kept company with the Progeny of the most holy Prophet (ص), so he benefitted from their ethics and virtuous morals, and he sought their advice publicly and privately.

MUSLIM SWEARS OATH OF ALLEGIANCE FOR HUSSAIN

The Shī'as of Kūfa came in groups to meet Muslim as he stayed at al-Mukhtar's house, pledging to him their obedience. This increased his happiness and elation. When he read to them Imām al-Hussain's letter, Abis ibn Shibeeb ash-Shakiri stood and said, "I do not speak on behalf of the people, nor do I know what they conceal in their hearts, nor do I deceive you in their regard. By Allāh! I can tell you what I personally have decided to do. By Allāh! I shall respond to your call, and I shall fight your enemy. I shall defend you with my sword till I meet Allāh desiring nothing except what He has in store for me." Habib ibn Muzahir said, "You have briefly stated your intention, and by Allāh, the One and only Allāh, I feel exactly as you do." Sa'd ibn Abdullāh al-Hanafi made a similar statement. Other Shī'as came to swear the oath of allegiance to him till his *diwan* counted as many as eighteen thousand men. Some historians say that they were as many as twenty five thousand men. According to ash-Sha'bi, however, the number of those who swore allegiance to him reached forty thousand. It was then that Muslim wrote Imām al-Hussain (ع) a letter which he handed to Abis ibn Shibeeb ash-Shakiri informing him of the consensus among the people of Kūfa to obey him and to wait for his arrival. In it, he said, "A scout does not lie to his people. Eighteen thousand Kufians have already come to me; so, hurry and come here as soon as this letter reaches you." That was twenty-seven days before Muslim's martyrdom. The Kufians, too, added to it their own letter wherein they stated the following: "Hurry and come to us, O son of the Messenger of Allāh! A hundred thousand swords are in Kūfa on your side; so, do not tarry."

This angered a group of the Umayyads with vested interests. Among them were Omer bin Sa'd, son of the renown Sa'd ibn Abū Waqqas, Abdullāh ibn Muslim ibn Rabi'ah al-Hadrami, and Imarah ibn Uqbah ibn Abū Mueet. They wrote Yazid warning him of the arrival of Muslim ibn Aqeel and the rallying of the people of Kūfa behind him, adding that an-Numan ibn Basheer, governor of Kūfa, was not strong enough to stand in his [Aqeel's] way. Yazid deposed an-Numan ibn Basheer and appointed Ubaydullāh ibn Ziyad in his place. The new governor was a man very well known for his

96

ruthfulness. Yazid ordered Ubaydullāh ibn Ziyad to rush to Kūfa in the company of Muslim ibn Omer al-Bahili, al-Munthir ibn al-Jarad, and Abdullāh ibn al-Harith ibn Nawfal escorted by five hundred soldiers whom he hand-picked from among the people of Basra. Ibn Ziyad rushed to Kūfa, paying no attention to anyone who fell off his horse due to exhaustion even if he were one of his own closest friends. For example, when Shurayk ibn al-A'war fell on the way, and even when Abdullāh ibn al-Harith fell, thinking that Ibn Ziyad would slow down for their sake, Ibn Ziyad paid no attention to them, fearing that Imām al-Hussain (ع) might reach Kūfa before him. Whenever he passed by a checkpoint, its guards thought that he was Imām al-Hussain (ع), so they said, "Welcome, O son of the Messenger of Allāh!" He remained silent till he reached Kūfa via the Najaf highway. When he arrived, people welcomed him and said in one voice: "Welcome, O son of the Messenger of Allāh!" This only intensified his outrage. He continued his march till he reached the governor's mansion. An-Numan did not open the gate for him, and he spoke to him from the mansion's roof-top. Said he, "I shall not return the trust to you, O son of the Messenger of Allāh!" Ibn Ziyad said to him, "Open the gate, for your night has extended too long!" A man heard his voice and recognized him. He, therefore, said to the people, "He is Ibn Ziyad, by the Lord of the Ka'ba!" They, therefore, opened the gate for him then dispersed, going back home.

In the morning, Ibn Ziyad gathered people at the grand mosque. There, he delivered a speech warning them against mutiny and promising them generous rewards for conforming. Said he, "Anyone found to be sheltering one of those who scheme against the authority of the commander of the faithful [meaning Yazid] and who does not hand him over will be crucified on the door of his own house."

When Muslim ibn Aqeel came to know about Ibn Ziyad's speech and his explicit threats and having come to know about people's conditions, he feared being assassinated. He, therefore, left al-Mukhtar's house after the dark and went to the house of Hani ibn Urwah al-Mathhaji who was a very zealous Shī'a. He was also one of Kūfa's dignitaries, one of its qaris of the Holy Qur'ān, and the shaikh and chief of the Banu Murad. He could easily raise four thousand troops fully armed and eight thousand cavaliers. If he includes his tribe's allies from Kindah, the number would swell to thirty thousand. He was one of the closest friends of the Commander of the Faithful Imām Ali ibn Abū Talib (ع) on whose side he fought in all his three battles. He had seen and was honored by being a companion of the Prophet (ص). When he was later killed in defense of Imām al-Hussain (ع), he was more than ninety years old. Muslim ibn Aqeel stayed at the house of Shareek ibn Abdullāh al-A'war al-Harithi al-Hamadani al-Basri, one of the main supporters of the Commander of the Faithful, peace be with him, in Basra. He had participated in the Battle of Siffeen and fought side by side with the great *sahabi* Ammar ibn Yasir. Due to his distinction and prominence, Ubaydullāh ibn Ziyad appointed him as Governor of Kerman on behalf of Mu'awiyah. He used to be in contact with and in the company of Hani ibn Urwah.

The Shī'as kept meeting Muslim ibn Aqeel secretly at Hani's house without attracting the attention of Ibn Ziyad, admonishing each other to keep it to themselves. Ibn Ziyad, therefore, could not know where Muslim was. He called Maqil, his slave, to meet him. He gave him three thousand [dinars] and ordered him to meet the Shī'as and to tell them that he was a Syrian slave of Thul-Kila and that Allāh blessed him with loving Ahl al-Bayt of His Messenger (ع), that it came to his knowledge that one of the members of Ahl al-Bayt (ع) had come to that country, and that he had with him some money which he wanted to deliver to him. Maqil entered the grand mosque and saw Muslim ibn Awsajah al-Asadi offering his prayers. Having seen him finish his prayers, he came close to him and made the above claim to him. Muslim ibn Awsajah prayed Allāh to grant that man goodness and success. He then accompanied him to the place where Muslim ibn Aqeel was hiding. The spy delivered the money to Muslim and swore the oath of allegiance to him. The money was handed over to Abū Thumamah as-Saidi who was a far-sighted and a brave Shī'a dignitary appointed by Muslim to receive the funds and to buy thereby weapons. That man kept meeting Muslim every day. No secrets were kept from him, so he kept gathering intelligence and getting it to Ibn Ziyad in the evening.

HANI IBN URWAH

When the matter became clear to Ibn Ziyad, who by now knew that

98

Muslim was hiding at the house of Hani ibn Urwah, he had Asma' ibn Kharijah, Muhammed ibn al-Ash'ath and Amr ibn al-Hajjaj brought to him. He asked them why Hani had not been coming lately to visit him at his governor's mansion. They told him that it was due to his sickness, but he was not convinced especially since his informers had already told him that Hani used to sit at the door of his house every evening. These same men rode to Hani and asked him to meet the sultan, for "He cannot stand you staying away from him," they said, pressuring him till he yielded. Hani, therefore, rode his mule and went. As soon as Ibn Ziyad saw him, he said, "His feet, the feet of the treacherous one, have brought him to you." Then he turned to his judge Shurayh and cited verses about judges who rush to please their tyrannical rulers who appoint them in their positions rather than implement Islam's legislative system, the Sharaa. Ibn Ziyad turned to Hani and said, "You brought Aqeel's son to your house and gathered weapons for him, did you not?" Hani denied, and when their argument intensified, Ibn Ziyad ordered Maqil to be brought to him. Hani, hence, understood that that man was actually Ibn Ziyad's spy, so he said to Ibn Ziyad, "Your father had done me great favors, and I now wish to reward him. Why do you not listen to my good advice and safely depart for Syria with your family and wealth? Someone who is more worthy than you and your friend [meaning Yazid] of taking charge has come here." Ibn Ziyad said, "And under the foam is the pure sour cream."

Ibn Ziyad then said to him, "By Allāh! You will not stay out of my sight before you bring him to me." Hani said, "By Allāh! Had he been under my foot, I would not have lifted it!" Ibn Ziyad then spoke rudely to him and even threatened to kill him. Hani, therefore, said, "In that case, there will be plenty of swords around you," thinking that the tribesmen of Murad would protect him from Ibn Ziyad who then pulled Hani's braids, hitting his face with his sword, breaking his nose and scattering the flesh from his cheeks and forehead on his beard. He then jailed him at his mansion.

Amr ibn al-Hajjaj heard that Hani had been killed. Hani's wife Raw'a, who is well known as the mother of Yahya son of Hani, was the sister of Amr ibn al-Hajjaj. The latter, therefore, rode with a multitude from the tribe of Mathhaj, and they all surrounded the mansion. When Ibn Ziyad came to know about it, he ordered Shurayh, the judge, to see Hani and then to tell those horsemen that Hani was still alive. Shurayh narrates saying, "When Hani saw me, he said in a loud voice, O Muslims! Should ten persons enter here, you must come to my rescue!' Had Hameed ibn Abū Bakr al-Ahmari, the policeman, not been with me, I would have conveyed his message, but I had to simply say instead that Hani was still alive. Amr ibn al-Hajjaj then praised Allāh and went back accompanied by the other men."

MUSLIM'S UPRISING

When Muslim came to know about what had happened to Hani, he feared being assassinated; therefore, he rushed to rise before the time he had set with the people. He ordered Abdullāh ibn Hazim to call upon his men, who had then filled the houses surrounding him, to gather together. Four thousand men assembled. They were shouting Badr's call which was: "O Supported One! Annihilate them!"

Ubaydullāh ibn Amr ibn Aziz al-Kindi was placed in command of the Kindah and Rabi'ah quarters. "March ahead of me," said Muslim, "in command of the cavalry." Muslim ibn Awsajah al-Asadi was placed in command of Mathhaj and Banu Asad. "Take charge of the infantry," Muslim ordered him. Abū Thumamah as-Saidi was placed in charge of Tameem and Hamadan, whereas al-Abbas ibn Jadah al-Jadli was given the command of the Medīna troops.

They marched towards the governor's mansion. Ibn Ziyad fortified himself inside it, locking all its gates. He could not resist because there were only thirty policemen with him and twenty of his close men and slaves. But the substance from which the people of Kūfa were made was treachery; so, their standards kept disappearing till no more than three hundred men remained out of the original four thousand. Al-Ahnaf ibn Qays described them as a whore who demanded a different man every day.

When those inside the mansion called upon the people of Kūfa saying, "O Kufians! Fear Allāh and do not expose yourselves to Syrian cavaliers whose might you have already tasted and whom you have already tested on the battlefield," the remaining three hundred

100

dispersed, so much so that a man would come to his son, brother, or cousin and tell him to go home, and a wife would cling to her husband till he returned home.

Muslim offered the evening prayers at the [grand Kūfa] mosque accompanied by only thirty men. Then, when he went to Kindah's quarters, only three men accompanied him. He hardly proceeded for a short while before finding himself without anyone at all to show him the way. He alighted from his horse and cautiously traversed Kūfa's alleys not knowing where to go.

When people abandoned Muslim, their noise died down, and Ibn Ziyad could not hear the voice of any of their men. Ibn Ziyad ordered his bodyguards to inspect the mosque's courtyard to see whether there were any men lying in ambush. They, therefore, kept lowering their lanterns down its walls and lighting reeds then lowering them down with ropes till they reached the mosque's courtyard. They could not see anyone, so they informed Ibn Ziyad who ordered his caller to call people to assemble at the mosque. When they filled the mosque, he ascended the pulpit and said, "Aqeel's son has caused the dissension and disunity with which you all are familiar; so, there is no security henceforth to any man in whose house we find him. Anyone who captures him and brings him to us will be paid his blood money. O servants of Allāh! Fear Allāh and safeguard your obedience and oath of allegiance, and do not expose yourselves to peril."

Then he ordered al-Haseen ibn Tameem, chief of his police force, to search homes and highways, warning him that he would kill Muslim should he succeed in escaping from Kūfa.

Al-Haseen stationed his guards at highway crossroads and pursued the dignitaries who had supported Muslim, arresting Abdul-Ala ibn Yazid al-Kalbi and Imarah ibn Salkhab al-Azdi. He threw them in jail then killed them. Then he jailed a group of prominent leaders as a safeguarding measure against what they might do. Among them were al-Asbagh ibn Nubatah and al-Harith al-A'war al-Hamadani.

AL-MUKHTAR JAILED

When Muslim marched out, al-Mukhtar was at a village called Khatwaniyya. He came accompanied by his supporters raising a green standard while Abdullāh ibn al-Harith was raising a red one. Having planted his standard at the door of Amr ibn Hareeth's house, he said, "I want to stop Amr." It became obvious to them that both Muslim and Hani had been killed, and it was suggested to them that they would feel more secure in the company of Amr ibn Hareeth, and so they did. Ibn Hareeth testified that they had both avoided Muslim ibn Aqeel... Ibn Ziyad ordered them jailed after having reviled al-Mukhtar and hit his face with a lance, gouging one of his eyes. They remained in prison till Imām al-Hussain, peace be with him, was martyred.

Ibn Ziyad ordered Muhammed ibn al-Ash'ath, Shabth ibn Rab'i, al-Qaqa ibn Shawr at-Thuhli, Hijar ibn Abjar, Shimr Thul-Jawshan, and Amr ibn Hareeth to surrender and to discourage people from rebelling. A number of men who were controlled by fear responded positively to his call in addition to others who coveted rich rewards and were thus deceived, whereas those whose conscience was pure went underground, waiting for an opportunity to launch an attack on the camp of falsehood.

MUSLIM AT THE HOUSE OF TAW'A

Ibn Aqeel's feet took him to the quarters of Banu Jiblah who belonged to the tribe of Kindah. He stood at the door of a house of a freed bondmaid named Tawa who had a number of sons. She used to be the bondmaid of al-Ash'ath ibn Qays who freed her. Aseed al-Hadrami married her, and she gave birth to his son Bilal who was in the crowd when his mother was standing at the door waiting for him. Muslim requested her to give him some water, which she did. He then requested her to host him, telling her that he was a stranger in that land without a fāmily or a tribe, and that he belonged to a fāmily capable of intercession on the Day of Judgment, and that his name was Muslim ibn Aqeel. She took him to a room which was not the same one where her son used to sleep, and she served him some food. Her son was surprised to see her entering that room quite often, so he asked her about it. She refused to answer his question except after obtaining an oath from him to keep the matter to himself.

But in the morning he informed Ibn Ziyad of where Muslim had been hiding. Ibn Ziyad dispatched al-Ash'ath accompanied by seventy men who belonged to the Qays tribe in order to arrest him. Upon hearing the horses' hoofs ploughing the ground, Muslim realized that he was being pursued, so he hurried to finish a supplication which he was reciting following the morning prayers. Then he put on his battle gear and said to his hostess Tawa: "You have carried out your share of righteousness, and you have secured your share of the intercession of the Messenger of Allāh. Yesterday, I saw my uncle the Commander of the Faithful in a vision telling me that I was going to join him the next day."

He came out to face them raising his unsheathed sword as they assaulted the house, succeeding in repelling their attack. They repeated their attack, and again he repelled them, killing as many as forty-one of their men, and he was so strong that he would take hold of one man then hurl him on the rooftop.

Ibn al-Ash'ath sent a messenger to Ibn Ziyad requesting additional enforcements. The messenger came back to him carrying the latter's blame of his incompetence. He, therefore, sent him this message: "Do you think that you sent me to one of Kūfa's shopkeepers, or to a Nabatean from Heera?! Rather, you sent me to one of the swords of [Prophet] Muhammed ibn Abdullāh !" Ibn Ziyad then assisted him with additional soldiers.

Fighting intensified. Muslim and Bakeer ibn Hamran al-Ahmari exchanged blows. Bakeer struck Muslim on the mouth, cutting his upper lip, wounding the lower and breaking two of his lower teeth. Muslim fiercely struck him with one blow on his head and another on his shoulder muscle, almost splitting his stomach, killing him instantly.

Then they attacked him from the house's rooftop, hurling rocks at him. They kept burning reed bales then throwing them at him. He attacked them in the alley. His wounds were numerous; he bled extensively, so he supported his body on the side of the house. It was then that they assaulted him with arrows and stones. "Why do you hurl stones at me," he asked them, "as non-believers are stoned, the member of the household of the pure Prophet that I am? Do you not have any respect for the Messenger of Allāh with regard to one of his own descendants?" Ibn al-Ash'ath said to him, "Please do not get yourself killed while you are in my custody." Muslim asked him, "Shall I then be captured so long as I have some strength in me? No, by Allāh! This shall never be." Then he attacked Ibn al-Ash'ath who fled away before him. They attacked him from all directions. Thirst had taken its toll on him. A man stabbed him from the back, so he fell on the ground and was arrested.

Another account says that they dug a hole for him which they covered then fled before him, thus luring him to fall into it, then they arrested him. When they took his sword away from him, he wept. Amr ibn Ubaydullāh as-Salami was surprised to see him weep. A man without his weapon is helpless, defenseless and vulnerable.

MUSLIM MEETS IBN ZIYAD

Muslim ibn Aqeel was brought to Ibn Ziyad. At the entrance of the mansion he saw an urn containing cooled water. He asked to drink of it. Muslim ibn Amr al-Bahili said to him, "You shall not taste one drop of it till you taste of the *hameem* in the fire of hell." Muslim asked him, "Who are you?" He said, "I am one who knew the truth which you rejected, and who remained faithful to his imām as you betrayed him." Muslim ibn Aqeel said to him, "May your mother lose you! How hard-hearted and rude you are! You, son of Bahilah, are more worthy of tasting of the *hameem* (hell)." Having said so, he sat down, supporting his back on the mansion's wall.

Imarah ibn Uqbah ibn Abū [son of] Mu'eet sent a slave named Qays to give him water. Whenever Muslim was about to drink of it, the cup became full of his blood. In his third attempt to drink, the cup became full of his blood and both his front teeth fell in it, so he abandoned it saying, "Had it been prescribed in destiny for me to drink it, I would have drunk it."

Ibn Ziyad's guard came out to escort Muslim. Having entered Ibn Ziyad's room, Muslim did not greet him. The guard asked Muslim,

104

"Why did you not greet the *ameer* (ruler)?" "Shut your mouth," said Muslim, "he is not my *ameer*." It is also said that he said to Ibn Ziyad, "Peace be upon whoever followed the right guidance, feared the consequences in the hereafter, and obeyed the Exalted King," so Ibn Ziyad laughed and said, "Whether you greet me or not, you shall be killed." Muslim said, "If you kill me, someone worse than you had already killed someone much better than me. Besides, you shall never abandon committing murders, setting a bad example, thinking ill of others, or being mean; having the upper hand will be the doing of anyone else but you."

Ibn Ziyad said, "You disobeyed your imām, divided the Muslims, and sowed the seeds of dissension." Muslim said, "You have uttered falsehood. Rather, those who divided the Muslims are Mu'awiyah and his son Yazid. The seeds of dissension were sown by your father, and I wish Allāh will grant me to be martyred at the hand of the worst of His creation."

Then Muslim asked permission to convey his will to some of his people. He was granted permission, so he looked at those present there and saw Omer ibn Sa'd. "There is kinship between me and you," said he to him, "and I need a favor of you which you should oblige, and it is a secret between us." But he refused to listen to it, whereupon Ibn Ziyad said to him, "Do not hesitate to tend to your cousin's need." Omer stood with Muslim in a way that enabled Ibn Ziyad to see them both. Muslim conveyed his desire to him to sell his sword and shield and pay a debt in the amount of six hundred *dirhams* which he had borrowed since entering Kūfa, to ask Ibn Ziyad to give him his corpse to bury it, and to write al-Hussain to tell him what had happened to him. Omer ibn Sa'd stood up and walked to Ibn Ziyad to reveal the secret with which he had just been entrusted by Muslim! Ibn Ziyad said to Muslim, "A trustworthy person never betrays you, but you have placed your trust in a treacherous person."

Then Ibn Ziyad turned again to Muslim and said, "O son of Aqeel! You came to a united people and disunited them." Muslim said, "No, indeed, I did not come to do that, but the people of this country claimed that your father killed their best men, shed their blood, and

105

did what Kisra and Caesar do, so we came to them in order to enjoin justice, and to invite all to accept the judgment of the Book [of Allāh]." Ibn Ziyad said, "What do you have to do with all of that? Have we not been dealing with them with equity?" Muslim said, "Allāh knows that you are not telling the truth. You, in fact, kill when angry, out of enmity, and for mere suspicion." Ibn Ziyad then verbally abused him and abused Ali, Aqeel, and al-Hussain, whereupon Muslim said, "You and your father are more worthy of being thus abused; so, issue whatever decree you wish, you enemy of Allāh!"

It was then that Ibn Ziyad ordered a Syrian to go to the top of the mansion and to behead Muslim and throw both the head and the body to the ground. The Syrian took Muslim to the flat rooftop of the mansion as the latter kept repeating, "*Subhan-Allāh! La ilaha illa-Allāh! Allāhu Akbar!*" He also kept repeating, "O Allāh! Judge between us and the people who deceived, betrayed and lied to us," then he faced Medīna and saluted Imām al-Hussain (ع).

The Syrian struck Muslim's neck with his sword and threw his head and body to the ground and hurried down; he was very, very much startled. Ibn Ziyad asked him what was wrong with him. "The moment I killed him," said he, "I saw a black man with an extremely ugly face standing beside me biting his finger, so I was frightened." "Perhaps you lost your mind for a moment," said Ibn Ziyad.

Hani was taken to an area of the market place where sheep are sold; his arms were tied. He kept saying, "O Mathhaj! Any man from Mathhaj to help me this day?! O Mathhaj! Where has Mathhaj gone away from me?!" Having seen that there was none to respond to him, he somehow managed to get one of his arms out of the ropes and said, "Is there anyone who would hand me a stick, a knife, a rock, or even a bone so that a man may be able to defend himself?" Guards attacked him and tied him again. He was ordered to stretch his neck so that they might strike it with their swords. "I am not going to give it away to you so generously. I shall not assist you at the cost of my own life." A Turkish slave named Rasheed owned by Ubaydullāh ibn Ziyad struck him with his sword, but he missed. Hani said, "To Allāh is my return! O Allāh! To Your Mercy do I

106

come and to Your Pleasure!" Rasheed hit him again and killed him. This same slave was killed by Abdul-Rahman ibn al-Haseen al-Muradi after having seen him at the Khazar (Caspian Sea, also the Basque Sea, Tabarestan Sea, and Baku Sea, *bahr baku* in Arabic, an area where Islam reached in the early 9th century A.D.) in the company of Ubaydullāh.

Ibn Ziyad ordered the corpses of both Muslim and Hani to be tied with ropes from their feet and dragged in the market places. Then he crucified them upside-down at the garbage collection site then sent their severed heads to Yazid who displayed them at one of the streets of Damascus.

He, Ubaydullāh Ibn Ziyad, wrote Yazid saying,

"Praise to Allāh Who affected justice on behalf of the commander of the faithful and sufficed him for having to deal with his foes. I would like to inform the commander of the faithful, may Allāh bless him, that Muslim ibn Aqeel had sought refuge at the house of Hani ibn Urwah al-Muradi, that I assigned spies for them and let men infiltrate their assemblies and plotted against them till I forced them out. Allāh gave me the upper hand over them, so I killed them and sent you both of their heads with Hani ibn Abū Hayya al-Wadii al-Hamadani and az-Zubair ibn al-Arwah at-Tameemi who both are from among those who listen to and obey us; so, let the commander of the faithful ask them whatever he pleases, for there is knowledge with them, and there is truth, understanding, and piety. And peace be with you."

Yazid wrote Ibn Ziyad saying,

"You do not cease to be the source of my delight. You have behaved with strictness and assaulted with courage, maintaining your composure. You have done very well and testified to the correctness of my good impression of you. I invited your messengers and asked them and confided in them, and I found their views and merits just as you indicated; so, take good care of them. It has also come to my knowledge that al-Hussain ibn Ali has marched towards Iraq. You should, therefore, set up observation posts, prepare with arms, be cautious for mere suspicion. Kill anyone whom you suspect (of dissent). Your tenure is put to the test by this al-Hussain rather than by anyone else, so is your country and your own self as governor. The outcome will determine whether you will be freed or whether you will return to slavery; so, you have to either fight him or arrest and transport him to me."

Let us now leave Kūfa and its Kufian men of treachery and to al-Hussain in Mecca where he was performing the rites of the pilgrimage. As he was thus engaged, Yazid dispatched thirty men disguised as pilgrims with strict instructions to assassinate him. Commenting on this attempt to assassinate him, al-Hussain said, "Even if I were to bury myself in some hideout, they are sure to hunt me out and to try to force me to swear the oath of allegiance to Yazid. And if I refused, they would kill me and would not spare me without inflicting upon me the same torture as the Jews had done to Jesus." There were unsuccessful attempts to prevent him from leaving Mecca.

Imām al-Hussain (ع) did not mask his intentions and determination to fight the Umayyad regime of corruption. The speeches he delivered at Mecca were consistent with those he made elsewhere. So does his will which he wrote and entrusted to his brother Muhammed ibn al-Hanafiyya who stayed in Medīna when al-Hussain (ع) left it first for Mecca then for Kerbalā', Iraq. This said will was, in fact, a formal declaration of his holy revolution. He, peace be with him and upon his Ahl al-Bayt, wrote saying, "I am not campaigning because I am unwilling to accept righteousness, nor do I intend to do mischief or suppress people. Indeed, I have decided to seek to reform my grandfather's nation. I want to enjoin what is right and to forbid what is wrong. If people accept my call for righteousness, Allāh is the Master of the righteous people. Those who reject my call, I shall remain steadfast till Allāh passes His judgment; surely Allāh is the best of judges."

Imām al-Hussain's statements were aiming directly at stripping the "religious" mask behind which the Umayyads were hiding as they ruled the Muslim masses. He was introducing himself to people and explaining his message to the nation. In fact, the very personality of

Imām al-Hussain (ع) and his religious devotion and impeccable character were all beyond question or doubt. No wonder, then, that he shouldered such a tremendous task, one which many distinguished personalities were not able to shoulder or even to raise a finger and point at the oppressors.

Let us now follow the Imām on his journey to martyrdom and eternal bliss.

Imām al-Hussain (ع) left Mecca on Thul-Hijja 8, 60 A.H./September 12, 680 A.D. accompanied by his family members, slaves and Shī'as from among the people of Hijaz, Basra, and Kūfa who joined him when he was in Mecca. According to p. 91 of *Nafas al-Mahmum* by Shaikh Abbas al-Qummi, he gave each one of them ten dinars and a camel to carry his luggage.

The places (including water places and caravans' temporary tent lodges), cities and towns by which Imām al-Hussain (ع) passed on his way to Taff area, where the famous Taff Battle took place, were: as-Sifah, That Irq, al-Hajir, al-Khuzaymiyya, Zarood, at-Thalabiyya, ash-Shuqooq, Zubala, al-Aqaba, Sharif, al-Bayda, ar-Ruhayma, al-Qadisiyya, al-Uthayb, and Qasr Muqatil. At as-Sifah, Imām al-Hussain (ع) met the famous poet al-Farazdaq ibn Ghalib and asked him about the people whom he had left behind, since al-Farazdaq had come from the opposite direction and had been in Kūfa. Al-Farazdaq, as we are told on p. 218, Vol. 6, of at-Tabari's *Tarikh*, said, "Their hearts are with you; the swords are with Banu Umayyah, and Destiny descends from the heavens."

QASR MUQATIL

When the Imām reached Qasr Muqatil, a place not far from Kūfa, he found it like a beehive, full of men and horses with rows of pitched-up tents spread all over, far and wide. Ibn Ziyad had sent a detachment of 1,000 troops (very brave ones!) under the command of Hurr ibn Yazid ar-Riyahi to divert the Imām and his small band to a particular site chosen for them, and not to permit them to go anywhere except to Kūfa. At that time, when the Imām reached there, Hurr's army had become thirsty. Its water supply had been fully exhausted, and no water could be seen around for miles. On becoming aware of this, the Imām at once ordered his men to serve water to the thirsty enemy army and to their horses as well. When the time of noon prayers approached, the Imām admonished Hurr's army to give up fighting on the side of tyranny and falsehood adding, "But if you disapprove of us, and are willfully ignoring our claim and reneging from your pledge to support us, a proxy pledge that you expressed in your letters and through your messengers, well, in that case, it does not matter, for I am quite prepared to go back (where I had come from)." But orders had already been issued to Hurr to take the Imām in his custody. The Imām asked Hurr, "Why have you come here at all?" "In obedience to my imām (meaning Ubaydullāh ibn Ziyad, the governor)," answered Hurr. In obeying your imām," responded Imām al-Hussain (ع), "you have committed a great sin against Allāh," adding after a short while, "You have lost your all, ruined your life here as well as your life hereafter. You have kindled the fire of hell for your own self and kept it ready for you to be hurled therein on the Day of Judgment. As for your imām, Allāh has explicitly said in the Holy Qur'ān, And We made them imāms inviting them to the fire, and on the Day of Judgment, no help shall they find. In this world We made a curse to follow them, and on the Day of Judgment, they will be among the loathed and the despised' (Qur'ān, 28:41-42)."

Later on, another order to Hurr came from Ubaydullāh ibn Ziyad to confine the Imām and his companions to a water land waste at a distance of about 9 - 10 miles from Kūfa off the bank of the Euphrates river. This area, known as at-Taff, later came to be called "Kerbalā'." It is there that the historical battle which stamped and is still stamping the Islamic history and the conduct of all Muslims, took place. As a matter of fact, this battle was already predicted in the Old Testament in the following verse in Jeremiah 46:10:

> ... For this is the day of the Lord Allāh of hosts, a day of vengeance, that He may avenge him of his adversaries, and the sword shall devour, and it shall be satiated and made drunk with their blood, for the Lord Allāh of hosts has a sacrifice in the north country by the river Euphrates.

In his famous book titled الصواعق المحرقة *As-Sawaiq al-Muhriqa* ("the burning thunderbolts), Ibn Hajar al-Asqalani writes saying that when the Imām came to that place, he took a handful of its soil and, having smelt it, he declared, "By Allāh! This is the land of *karb* (affliction) and *bala'* (trial and tribulation)! Here the ladies of my *haram* will be taken prisoners! Here my children will be butchered and our men will be slain! Here Ahl al-Bayt of the Prophet (ﷺ) will be subjected to indignities! Here my beard will be stained with the blood of my head! And here our graves will be dug."

Historians contemporary to the Imām related that after coming to Kerbalā', the Imām purchased that lot from its owners for 60,000 dinars, although it was only four miles square, so that it would be the site of his and his family's and relatives' graves.

THE KUFIAN HOSTS

Different accounts of he full number of al-Hussain's camp range from seventy-two to a hundred fighters..., but how many were al-Hussain's foes?! Omer ibn Sa'd was dispatched to Kerbalā' to fight the Imām with 6,000 strong. Then Shabth ibn Rab'i went there to take charge of the largest fighting force of 24,000 men. The commanders' names and the numbers of their troops are here provided for the kind reader:

1. Omer ibn Sa'd	6,000
2. Shabth ibn Rab'i	24,000
3. Urwah ibn Qais	4,000
4. Sinan ibn Anas	4,000
5. Haseen ibn Nameer	9,000
6. Shimr ibn Thul-Jawshan	4,000
7. Mazar ibn Ruhaynah	3,000
8. Yazid ibn Rikab	2,000
9. Najr ibn KharShī'ah	2,000
10. Muhammed ibn al-Ash'ath	1,000
11. Abdullāh ibn Haseen	1,000
12. Khawli ibn Yazid al-Asbahi	1,000
13. Bakr ibn Kasab ibn Talhah	3,000
14. Hijr ibn Abjar	1,000
15. Hurr ibn Yazid ar-Riyahi	3,000

TOTAL: <u>**68,000**</u>

The reader can notice that some of these commanders had already
written al-Hussain (ع) inviting him to go to Kūfa so that they would
support him in putting an end to the tyranny of the Umayyads. The
details of how those men changed heart and the amounts of money
they received are too lengthy to include in this brief account.

EFFORTS TO SECURE WATER

The access to water was cut off on the seventh day of Muharram
and, before the evening of the eighth, the young, the children, and
the women grew extremely restless, being overcome by the pangs of
thirst. On the morning of the eighth, al-
Abbas son of Ali ibn Abū Talib, al-
Hussain's brother, who was appointed
by al-Hussain (ع) as commander-in-
chief of the tiny force, began digging
wells assisted by all loyal companions
and kinsmen of the Imām. They
succeeded in boring a well, but stones
were found instead of water. They soon
dug another, but no water was found in it. The Imām then requested
his brother al-Abbas to go to fetch water from the Euphrates. Al-
Abbas took thirty cavaliers and twenty footmen and twenty large-
size empty water-bags. After a fierce battle at the river's bank, they
succeeded in fetching water. Although they themselves were
extremely thirsty, they refused to drink before the others. Al-Abbas,
hence, was given the title of "Saqqah," the water-bearer, ever since.
When Omer ibn Sa'd came to know about this incident, he
reinforced the detachment sent to guard the Euphrates against al-
Hussain's people having access to the water. The total force
guarding the water now reached 800...! Ubaydullāh ibn Ziyad
himself sent a letter to Omer ibn Sa'd telling him that, "It is
necessary to take more precautions so that they (al-Hussain's folks)
may not be able to obtain a drop of water."

CONDITIONAL RESPITE GRANTED

Imām al-Hussain (ع) knew that war was unavoidable, so he asked
his foes to put off the fighting for one night since, he said, he wanted

112

to spend it praying to Allāh. It was grudgingly granted. On the other hand, the misery of the prevailing conditions at al-Hussain's camp due to the shortage of water caused by the water supply being intercepted could not be imagined. The only survivor of that tragedy, namely al-Hussain's ailing son Ali, said later on about their suffering, "We, all in all, were twenty children, and we were very thirsty and crying for water, gasping with thirst." It is also noteworthy that this same survivor's offspring and supporters later on established the Fatimide ruling dynasty in north Africa with its capital first at Qairawan, Tunisia, then at Cairo, Egypt. The Fatimide caliph al-Muizz li Deenillah founded Cairo and built its renown al-Azhar mosque and university.

ANOTHER CONFRONTATION AT WATERING PLACE
Burayr al-Hamadani, a loyal companion of Imām al-Hussain (ع), tried to fetch water, igniting a fierce battle at the river's bank. He and only three brave warriors had to face the entire 800-strong regiment guarding the watering place. The battle cries reached al-Hussain's camp, whereupon the Imām ordered a rescue mission. Water was miraculously brought in a single water-skin. All the children rushed to it, frantically trying to quench their thirst therewith. Crowding around it, some were pressing it to them, others falling upon it till, alas, suddenly the mouth of the water-skin flung open by the children's crowding upon it and all the water flowed out on the dusty floor. All the children loudly cried and lamented saying, "O Burayr! All the water you have brought us is gone!"

FIRM RESOLUTION
In the eve of the ninth of Muharram, Imām al-Hussain (ع) gathered

all his companions together and said to them, "Whoever remains with me will be killed tomorrow; so, consider this opportunity as Allāh-sent and take advantage of the darkness and go home to your villages." He then extinguished the light so that those who wanted to go away might not be too embarrassed when seen by others. al-Hussain's loyal companions burst out in inconsolable weeping and distressfully said to him, "Mawla (master)! Do not thus shame us before the Messenger of Allāh, before Ali and Fātima! With what face will we present ourselves to them on the Day of Judgment? Were we to desert you, may the wild beasts of the jungle tear us to pieces."

Having said so, the faithful companions drew their swords out of their scabbards. Then they threw the scabbards in the fire of a ditch dug to protect the tents of the ladies. Holding their naked swords, they offered humble supplications to the Almighty beseeching Him thus: "O Lord of the creation! We are passing through the sea of trouble and sorrow in obedience to Your Prophet (ص) and in defense of the religion. You are the Sustainer of our honor and reputation. You are our Lord and Master. Grant us the strength of will and the spirit of enduring patience and perseverance so that we may remain firm and give our all in Your Path."

LOVE AND DEVOTION

Al-Qasim son of Imām al-Hassan son of Ali ibn Abū Talib, nephew of Imām al-Hussain (ع), was a 13-year old lad. He sought audience with the Imām in order to inquire whether his name was on the list of martyrs. "Your name," answered al-Hussain (ع), "is also included in the list of martyrs. You will be killed, and so will my suckling baby Ali al-Asghar (Junior)." After a short while, the Imām continued saying, "I, too, will be killed, but Allāh will continue my lineage. How would the cruel oppressors succeed in putting an end to his [Ali Zain al-Ābidīn's] life when eight Imāms are to be born as his offspring?"

In a tent sat Umm Kulthum, sister of al-Abbas, watching her brother polishing his weapons. She wore a woe-begone face, and tears kept trickling down her cheeks. Suddenly al-Abbas happened to look up. Seeing her tears, he inquired, "Honoured sister, why are you

114

weeping?" "How could I help doing so," she replied, adding, "since I am an unlucky childless woman? Tomorrow, all the ladies will offer the lives of their sons for the Imām, whom shall I offer, having no son of my own?" Tears trickling down his cheeks, al-Abbas said, "Sister! From now on, I am your slave, and tomorrow you offer me, your slave, as a sacrifice for the Imām." Who else, dear reader, would call himself a slave of his sister besides al-Abbas? Such are the Ahl al-Bayt, and such are their manners.

`ĀSHŪRA

The author of صلاح النشأتين *Salah an-Nash'atayn* records saying that the tragic and historical battle culminated on a Friday, the tenth of Muharram, 61 A.H., corresponding to October 13, 680 A.D., a day known in Islamic history as `Āshūra. Imām al-Hussain (ع) delivered two sermons to the misled souls that surrounded him from all directions, trying to bring them back to their senses, but it was to no avail.

ثُمَّ دعا براحلته فركبها ، و نادى بصوت عالٍ يسمعه جلّهم : أيّها النّاس اسمعوا قَولي ، ولا تعجلوا حتّى أعظكم بما هو حقٌّ لكم عليّ ، وحتّى أعتذر إليكم من مَقدمي عليكم ، فإن قبلتم عذري وصدقتم قولي وأعطيتموني النّصف من أنفسكم ، كنتم بذلك أسعد ، ولم يكن لكم عليَّ سبيل . وإنْ لَم تقبلوا منّي العذر ولَم تعطوا النّصف من أنفسكم ، فأجمعوا أمركم و شركاءكم ثُمَّ لا يكن أمركم عليكم غمّة . ثُمَّ اقضوا إليَّ ولا تنظرون . إنَّ وليِّيَ الله الذي نزل الكتاب وهو يتولّى الصالحين. فلمّا سمعَت النّساء هذا منه صحنَ وبكينَ وارتفعت أصواتهُنَّ ، فأرسل إليهنَّ أخاه العبّاس وابنه عليّاً الأكبر وقال لهما : (سكّتاهُنَّ فلعمري ليكثرِ بكاؤهُنَّ. ولمّا سكتنَ ، حمد الله وأثنى عليه وصلّى على محمّد وعلى الملائكة والأنبياء وقال في ذلك ما لا يحصى ذكره ولَم يُسمع متكلّم قبله ولا بعده أبلغ منه في منطقه ، ثُمَّ قال : عباد الله ، اتقوا الله وكونوا من الدنيا على حذر ؛ فإنَّ الدنيا لَو بقيت على أحد أو بقي عليها أحد لكانت الأنبياء أحقَّ بالبقاء وأولى بالرضا وأرضى بالقضاء ، غير أنَّ الله خلق الدنيا للفناء ، فجديدها بالٍ ونعيمها مضمحل وسرورها مكفهر ، والمنزل تلعة والدار قلعة ، فتزوّدوا فإنَّ خير الزاد التقوى ، واتقوا الله لعلّكم تفلحون. أيّها النّاس إنَّ الله تعالى خلق الدنيا فجعلها دار فناء وزوال متصرفة بأهلها حالاً بعد حال ، فالمغرور من غرَّته دنيا والشقيُّ من فتنته ، فلا تغرَّنكم هذه الدنيا ، فإنَّها تقطع رجاء من ركن إليها وتُخيَّب طمع من طمع فيها . وأراكم قد اجتمعتم على أمر قد أسخطتم الله فيه عليكم وأعرض بوجهه الكريم عنكم وأحلَّ بكم نقمته ، فنعمَ الربُّ ربّنا وبئس العبيد أنتم ؛ أقررتم بالطاعة وآمنتم بالرسول محمّد (ص) ، ثُمَّ إنّكم زحفتم إلى ذريّته وعترته تريدون قتلهم ، لقد استحوذ عليكم الشيطان فأنساكم ذكر الله العظيم ، فتبّاً لكم ولِما تريدون . إنّا لله وإنّا إليه راجعون هؤلاء قوم كفروا بعد إيمانهم فبُعداً للقوم الظالمين. أيّها النّاس أنسبوني مَن أنا ثُمَّ ارجعوا إلى أنفسكم وعاتبوها وانظروا هل يحلّ لكم قتلي وانتهاك

115

حرمتي ؟ ألستُ ابن بنت نبيّكم وابن وصيّه وابن عمّه وأول المؤمنين بالله والمصدّق
لرسوله بما جاء من عند ربّه ؟ أوَ ليس حمزة سيّد الشهداء عمَ أبي ؟ أوَ ليس جعفر
الطيّار عمّي ، أوَ لَم يبلغكم قول رسول الله لي ولأخي : هذان سيّدا شباب أهل الجنّة ؟ فإنْ
صدّقتموني بما أقول وهو الحقّ ـ والله ما تعمّدتُ الكذب منذ علمتُ أنّ الله يمقت عليه أهله
ويضرّ به من اختلقه ـ وإن كذبتموني فإنّ فيكم مَن إن سألتموه عن ذلك أخبركم ، سلوا
جابر بن عبد الله الأنصاري ، وأبا سعيد الخدري ، وسهل بن سعد الساعدي ، وزيد بن
أرقم ، وأنس بن مالك يخبروكم أنّهم سمعوا هذه المقالة من رسول الله لي ولأخي ، أما
في هذا حاجز لكم عن سفك دمي ؟! فقال الشمر : هو يعبد الله على حرف إنْ كان يدري
ما يقول . فقال له حبيب بن مظاهر : والله إنّي أراك تعبد الله على سبعين حرفاً ، وأنا
أشهد أنّك صادق ما تدري ما يقول ، قد طبع الله على قلبك . ثَمَ قال الحسين (ع) : فإنْ
كنتم في شكّ من هذا القول ، أفتشكّون أنّي ابن بنت نبيّكم ، فوالله ما بين المشرق
والمغرب ابن بنت نبي غيري فيكم ولا في غيركم ، ويحكم اتطلبوني بقتيل منكم قتلته ؟!
أو مال لكم استهلكته ؟! أو بقصاص جراحة ؟! ، فأخذوا لا يكلّمونه ! فنادى : يا شبث بن
ربعي ، ويا حَجّار بن أبجر ، ويا قيس بن الأشعث ، ويا زيد بن الحارث : ألم تكتبوا إليَّ
أنْ اقدم قد أينعت الثمار واخضرّ الجناب ، وإنّما تقدم على جند لك مجنّدة ؟ فقالوا: لَم
نفعل . قال : سبحان الله ! بلى والله لقد فعلتم. ثَمَ قال : أيّها النّاس ، إذا كرهتموني
فدعوني أنصرف عنكم إلى مأمن من الأرض. فقال له قَيس بن الأشعث : أولا تنزل على
حكم بني عمّك ؟ فإنّهم لَن يروك إلاّ ما تُحبّ ولَن يصل إليك منهم مكروه . فقال الحسين
عليه السّلام : أنت أخو أخيك ، أتريد أن يطلبك بنو هاشم أكثر من دم مسلم بن عقيل ؟ لا
والله لا أعطيكم بيدي إعطاء الذليل ولا أفِرّ فِرار العبيد ، عباد الله إنّي عذتُ بربّي وربّكم
أنْ ترجمون ، أعوذ بربّي وربّكم من كلّ متكبّر لا يؤمن بيوم الحساب .(ثَمَ أناخ وأمر
عقبة بن سمعان فعقلها.

The dumb and stonehearted rogues were not affected by al-
Hussain's eloquent sermons. He asked them, "Am I not your
Prophet's grandson? Am I not the son of the Commander of the
Faithful, cousin of the Prophet and the first male to believe in the
divine message of Allāh? Is not Hamzah, the head of the martyrs,
my father's uncle? Is not the martyr Ja'far at-Tayyar my uncle? Did
the Prophet not reach your ears with words spoken in reference to
me and to my elder brother (al-Hassan), saying, These (al-Hassan
and al-Hussain (ع) are the masters of the youths of Paradise'?"

The renown historian at-Tabari and all other historians unanimously
record that when al-Hussain (ع) proceeded so far in his sermon, the
audience was moved against their wish, so much so that tears began
to flow from the eyes of friends and foes alike. It was only al-Hurr,
however, who was truly moved to the extent of stirring to action.

Slowly did he walk as he kept saying, "Allāh! I turn to You in repentance from the depth of my heart, so do forgive me and forgive my sinful misconduct towards the Prophet's beloved Ahl al-Bayt." Approaching the Imām with eyes streaming with tears, with his shield turned the other way and his spear turned upside-down, he knelt down and kept crawling on his knees till he reached the Imām and fell on his feet kissing them, begging for his forgiveness. Al-Hussain (ع) accepted his apologies and prayed for him. Meanwhile, al-Hurr's defection alarmed Omer ibn Sa'd, the commander-in-chief of the enemies of al-Hussain (ع) and of Allāh. He was afraid such defection might encourage other commanders of his army to do likewise. Calling his slave, who was bearing the standard, he put an arrow on the string of his bow and discharged it at al-Hussain (ع), signaling the beginning of the battle. Martyrs fell one after another, recording epics of heroism unlike any others in the entire history of the human race. Their names and deeds of heroism are recorded on the pages of history for all generations to come.

خطبة الحسين (ع) الثانية

ثُمّ إنّ الحسين (ع) ركب فرسه ، وأخذ مصحفاً ونشره على رأسه ، ووقف بإزاء القوم وقال : "يا قوم ، إنّ بيني وبينكم كتاب الله وسنّة جدّي رسول الله (ص) . ثُمّ استشهدهم عن نفسه المقدّسة وما عليه من سيف النّبي (ص) ولامته وعمامته فأجأبوه بالتصديق . فسألهم عمّا أخذهم على قتله ؟ قالوا : طاعةً للأمير عبيد الله بن زياد ، فقال عليه السّلام : "تبّاً لكم أيّتها الجماعة و ترحاً ، أحين استصرختمونا وآله ين فأصرخناكم موجفين ، سللتم علينا سيفاً لنا في أيمانكم وحششتم علينا ناراً اقتدحناها على عدوّنا وعدوّكم ، فأصبحتم إلباً لأعدائكم على أوليائكم ، بغير عدل أفشوه فيكم ولا أمل أصبح لكم فيهم . فهلاّ ـ لكم الويلات ! ـ تركتمونا والسّيف مشيم والجأش طامن والرأي لَما يستحصف ، ولكنْ أسرعتم إليها كطيرة الدبا وتداعيتم عليها كتهافت الفراش ، ثُمّ نقضتموها ، فسحقاً لكم يا عبيد الأمة وشذاذ الأحزاب ونبذة الكتاب ومحرّفي الكلم وعصبة الإثم ونفثة الشيطان ومطفئي السّنَن ! ويحكم أهوَلاء تعضدون وعنّا تتخاذلون ! أجل والله غدر فيكم قديم وشجت عليه أصولكم وتأزّرت فروعكم فكنتم أخبث ثمرة ، شجى للناظر وأكلة للغاصب ! ألا وإنّ الدَعيّ بن الدَعيّ قد ركز بين اثنتَين ؛ بين السّلة والذلّة ، وهيهات منّا الذلّة ، يأبي الله لنا ذلك ورسوله والمؤمنون وحجور طابت وطهرت وأنوف حميّة ونفوس أبيّة ، من أن نؤثر طاعة اللئام من مصارع الكرام ، ألا وإنّي زاحف بهذه الأُسرة على قلّة العدد وخذلان النّاصر .(ثُمّ أنشد أبيات فروة بن مُسيك المرادي. أما والله ، لا تلبثون بعدها إلاّ كريثما يركب الفرس ، حتّى تدور بكم دور الرحى وتقلق بكم قلق المحور ، عهدٌ عَهَده إليّ أبي عن جدّي رسول الله ، فاجمعوا أمركم وشركاءكم ، ثُمّ لا يكن أمركم عليكم غمّة ثُمّ اقضوا إليّ ولا تنظرون ، إنّي توكّلت على الله ربّي وربّكم ، ما من دابّة إلاّ

117

هو آخذ بناصيتها إنّ ربّي على صراط المستقيم. 2.) ثُمّ رفع يدَيه نحو السّماء وقال :
"اللهمّ ، احبس عنهم قطر السّماء ، وابعث عليهم سنين كسنيّ يوسف ، وسلّط عليهم
غلام ثقيف يسقيهم كأساً مصبرة ، فإنّهم كذبونا وخذلونا ، وأنت ربّنا عليك توكّلنا وإليك
المصير. 3.) والله لا يدع أحداً منهم إلاّ انتقم لي منه ، قتلةً بقتلة وضربةً بضربة ، وإنّه
لينتصر لي ولأهل بيتي وأشياعي .

THE FIRST LADY MARTYR

Wahab ibn Abū Wahab, a Christian, and his wife, also a Christian,
were married only a fortnight ago. Having witnessed what went on
between al-Hussain (ع) and his foes, they sympathized with al-
Hussain (ع) and embraced the Islamic creed at his hands. The words
of the Imām's sermons penetrated their hearts and found an echo.
Wahab's mother, still Christian, said to her son, "I will not be
pleased with you till you give your life away for the sake of al-
Hussain (ع)." Wahab charged at the enemies of Allāh like a lion, and
when a man from Kūfa severed his right arm, he transferred the
sword to the left and went on fighting as if nothing at all had
happened. Soon his left arm, too, was lopped off by a single stroke
of a sword, and the hero fell to the ground. His wife watched the
whole scene. She pleaded to the Imām thus as she darted towards his
enemies, "O Imām! Please do not ask me to go back! I prefer to die
fighting rather than to fall captive in the hands of Banu Umayyah!"
The Imām tried to dissuade her, explaining to her that fighting is not
mandated on women, but at seeing her husband martyred, she ran to
him and, putting his lifeless head in her lap, she began to wipe it
with her clothes. Soon a slave of Shimr ibn Thul-Jawshan put an end
to her life while she was thus engaged; may the Almighty shower
His blessings on her. It is unanimously agreed on by the historians
that she was the first lady martyred on that day. Wahab's mother
was very happy. She said, "Allāh! Thank You for saving my honour
through my son's martyrdom before the Imām." Then the old
Christian lady turned to the Kufians and said, "You wicked people! I
bear witness that the Christians in their churches and the
Zoroastrians in their fire houses are better people than you!" Saying
so, she seized a stout candle (or, according to other accounts, a tent
post) in her hand and fell upon the enemies, sending two of them to
hell. The Imām sent two of his companions to bring her back. When
she stood before him, he said to her, "O bondmaid of Allāh! Women
are not allowed to go to war. Sit down; I assure you that you and

118

your son will be with my grandfather in Paradise." Another martyr to be mentioned here, who was also Christian, is John, a slave of the great *sahabi* Abū Tharr al-Ghifāri, may Allāh be pleased with both of them. He had been for many years in the service of Abū Tharr, and although he was a very old man (according to some accounts, he was 90 years old), he fought al-Hussain's enemies till he was martyred.

AL-ABBAS IS MARTYRED

The story of the martyrdom of al-Abbas is a very sad one. Unfortunately, there is no room here to provide you with all its details due to the lack of space; therefore, we have to summarize it to you in a few words. Al-Abbas ventured to bring water to the wailing thirsty children. He individually had to face the eight hundred soldiers guarding the bank of the Euphrates against al-Hussain (ع) and his small band having access to it. He was al-Hussain's standard-bearer. Both his arms were severed, one after the other, and arrows made his body look like a porcupine. One of those arrows penetrated his right eye... When al-Hussain (ع) saw his brother fall like that, he wept profusely as he said, "Now I have become spineless..." When al-Hussain (ع) tried to carry him to his camp, al-Abbas pleaded to him not to do so since he could not stand hearing the cries of the thirsty children especially since he had promised to bring them some water. He hated to go back to them empty-handed. Al-Hussain (ع), therefore, honoured his last wish; al-Abbas breathed his last as his brother al-Hussain (ع) was holding to him...

MARTYRDOM OF THE IMĀM

The Imām was also very courageous, so much so that he had already been called "the lion of Banu Hashim." He had participated in the wars waged by his father, the Commander of the Faithful Ali ibn Abū Talib (ع), in defense of the creed against the hypocrites led by the Umayyads and against the Kharijites, proving his military ability and mastership of the art of war. Had the Muslims of today mastered this art, and had they been able to make their own weapons rather than import them from others, they would not have been forced to sell their God-given natural resources, especially oil, dirt cheap to

119

those who do not wish them any good. Had the rulers of the Muslim world learned how to get along with each other, they would have cooperated with each other for their own common good. Had the Muslims of the world implemented the commandments of their creed as strictly as they are supposed to, no unjust or tyrannical ruler would have ever ruled them... I think that such rulers, the likes of Yazid, are the main cause of the pathetic situation wherein the Muslims of the world find themselves at the present time, yet these rulers derive their strength from the weakness of their subjects; so, one problem is connected to the other...

Narrators of this incident record saying that there was hardly any place in al-Hussain's body that escaped a sword stroke or an arrow, and the same can be said about his horse as-Sahab which used to belong to Prophet Muhammed (ﷺ) who, shortly before breathing his last, gave it to his right hand, cousin, and son-in-law Ali ibn Abū Talib (ع). Al-Hussain's older brother, Imām al-Hassan (ع), inherited it; after his martyrdom, it became the property of Imām al-Hussain (ع). Having become too feeble to fight, he stood to rest. It was then that a man threw a stone at him, hitting his forehead and causing his blood to run down his face. He took his shirt to wipe his blood from his eyes just as another man shot him with a three-pronged arrow which pierced his chest and settled in his heart. He instantly said, "In the Name of Allāh, through Allāh, and on the creed of the Messenger of Allāh [do I die]." Raising his head to the heavens, he said, "Lord! You know that they are killing a man besides whom there is no other son of Your Prophet's daughter." As soon as he took the arrow out of his back, blood gushed forth like a drain pipe. He placed his hand on his wound and once his hand was filled with blood, he threw it above saying, "Make what has happened to me easy for me; it is being witnessed by Allāh." Not a single drop of that blood fell on the ground. Then he put it back a second time, and it was again filled with blood. This time he rubbed it on his face and beard as he said, "Thus shall I appear when I meet my Lord and my grandfather the Messenger of Allāh (ع), drenched in my blood. It is then that I shall say: O grandfather! So-and-so killed me.'"

Bleeding soon sapped his strength, so he sat down on the ground, feeling his head being too heavy. Malik ibn an-Nisr noticed his

120

condition, so he taunted him then dealt him a stroke with his sword on the head. Al-Hussain (ع) was wearing a burnoose which soon became full of blood. Al-Hussain (ع) said, "May you never be able to eat or drink with your right hand, and may Allāh gather you among the oppressors." Having said so, the dying Imām threw his burnoose away and put on a turban on top of his capuche cap.

Hani ibn Thabeet al-Hadrami has said, "I was standing with nine other men when al-Hussain (ع) was killed. It was then that I looked and saw one of the children from al-Hussain's family wearing a robe and a shirt, and he was wearing two ear-rings. He held a post from those buildings and stood startled looking right and left. A man came running. Having come close to that child, the man leaned from his horse and killed that child with his horse. When he was shamed for thus killing a helpless child, he revealed his last name..."

That child was Muhammed ibn Abū Sa'd ibn Aqeel ibn Abū Talib. His mother, dazed, stunned, and speechless, kept looking at him as the incident unfolded before her very eyes...

The enemies of Allāh waited for a short while then returned to al-Hussain (ع) whom they surrounded as he sat on the ground unable to stand. Abdullāh son of Imām al-Hassan (ع), grandson of the Prophet (ص), who was eleven years old, looked and saw how his uncle was being surrounded by those people, so he came running towards him. Zainab, al-Hussain's revered sister, wanted to restrain him but he managed to evade her and to reach his uncle. Bahr ibn Ka'b lowered his head to strike al-Hussain (ع), so the child shouted, "O son of the corrupt woman, are you going to strike my uncle?" The man dealt a blow from his sword which the child received with his hand, cutting it off. The child cried in agony, "O uncle!" Then he fell in the lap of al-Hussain (ع) who hugged him and said, "O son of my brother! Be patient with regard to what has befallen us, and consider it as goodness, for Allāh, the most Exalted, will make you join your righteous ancestors." Then he raised his hands and supplicated saying, "O Allāh! Let them enjoy themselves for some time then divide them and make them into parties, and do not let their rulers ever be pleased with them, for they invited us to support us, then they turned their backs to us and fought us."

121

Harmalah ibn Kahil shot the child with an arrow, killing him as he sat in his uncle's lap.

Al-Hussain (ع) remained lying on the ground for some time. Had those rogues wished to kill him, they could have done so, but each tribe relied on the other to do what it hated to do itself. Ash-Shimr shouted, "What are you standing like that for?! What do you expect the man to do since your arrows and spears have wounded him so heavily? Attack him!" Zarah ibn Shareek struck him on his left shoulder with his sword while al-Haseen shot him with an arrow which penetrated his mouth; another man struck him on the shoulder. Sinan ibn Anas stabbed him in his collar bone area of the chest then shot him with an arrow in the neck. Salih ibn Wahab stabbed him in the side...

قال هلال بن نافع: كنت واقفاً نحو الحسين وهو يجود بنفسه ، فوالله ما رأيت قتيلاً قطّ مضمّخاً بدمه أحسن منه وجهاً ولا أنور ، ولقد شغلني نور وجهه عن الفكرة في قتله . فاستقى في هذه الحال ماء فأبوا ان يسقوه . وقال له رجل : لا تذوق الماء حتّى ترد الحامية فتشرب من حميمها . فقال عليه السّلام : "أنا أرد الحامية ؟! وإنّما أرد على جدّي رسول الله وأسكن معه في داره في مقعد صدق عند مليك مقتدر وأشكو إليه ما ارتكبتم منّي وفعلتم بي). فغضبوا بأجمعهم حتّى كأنّ الله لَم يجعل في قلب أحدهم من الرحمة شيئاً.

Hilal ibn Nafi` has said, "I was standing in front of al-Hussain (ع) as he was drawing his last breath. Never did I ever see anyone whose face looked better or more glowing as he was stained with his own blood! In fact, the light emanating from his face distracted me altogether from the thought of killing him! As he was in such a condition, he asked for some water to drink, but they refused to give him any."

A man said to him, "You shall not taste of water till you reach hell from whose hot boiling water shall you drink." He, peace be with him said, "Am I the one who will reach it? Rather, I will reach my grandfather the Messenger of Allāh (ع) and reside with him in his abode of truth near an Omnipotent King, and I shall complain to him about what crimes you committed against me and what you have done to me." They all became very angry. It is as if Allāh did not

122

leave an iota of compassion in their hearts. When his condition worsened, al-Hussain (ع) raised his eyes to the heavens and said,

"O Allāh! Sublime You are, Great of Might, Omnipotent, Independent of all creation, greatly Proud, Capable of doing whatever You please, Forthcoming in mercy, True of Promise, Inclusive of Blessings, Clement, Near to those who invoke Him, Subduing His creation, Receptive to Repentance, Able, Overpowering, Appreciative when thanked, Remembering those who remember Him! Thee do I call upon out of my want, and Thee do I seek out of need! From Thee do I seek help when in fear and cry when depressed! Thine help do I seek in my weakness, and upon Thee do I rely! O Allāh! Judge between us and our people, for they deceived and betrayed us. They were treacherous to us, and they killed us although we are the *Itrat* of Your Prophet and the offspring of the one You love: Muhammed (ص) whom You chose for Your Message and entrusted with the revelation. Do find an ease for our affair and an exit, O most Merciful of all merciful ones! Grant me patience to bear Your destiny, O Lord! There is no Allāh but You! O Helper of those who seek help! I have no Allāh besides You, nor do I adore anyone but You! Grant me to persevere as I face Your decree, O Helper of the helpless, O Eternal One Who knows no end, O One Who brings the dead back to life, O One Who rewards every soul as it earned, do judge between me and them; surely You are the best of judges."

HUSSAIN'S HORSE

Al-Hussain's horse came circling around him, rubbing his head on his blood. It was then that Ibn Sa'd shouted, "The horse! Get the horse, for it is one of the horses of the Messenger of Allāh!" Horsemen surrounded that horse which kept kicking with its front legs, killing forty riders and ten horses. Ibn Sa'd then said, "Leave him and let us see what he does." Once he felt secure, the horse went back to al-Hussain (ع) to rub his head on the Imām's blood as he sniffed him. He was neighing very loudly. Imām Abū Ja'far al-Bāqir (ع) used to say that that horse was repeating these words: "Retribution! Retribution against a nation that killed the son of its Prophet's daughter!" The horse then went to the camp neighing likewise. When the women saw the horse without its rider and its saddle twisted, they went out, their hair spread out, beating their cheeks, their faces uncovered, screaming and wailing, feeling the humiliation after enjoying prestige, going in the direction of the place where al-Hussain (ع) had been killed.

Umm Kulthum, Zainab the wise, cried out, "O Muhammed! O father! O Ali! O Ja'far! O Hamzah! Here is al-Hussain in the open slain in Kerbalā'!" Then Zainab said, "I wish the heavens had fallen upon the earth! I wish the mountains had crushed the valley!" She was near al-Hussain (ع) when Omer ibn Sa'd came close to her flanked by some of his men. Al-Hussain (ع) was drawing his last breath. She cried out, "O Omer! Should Abū Abdullāh be killed as you look on?!" He turned his face away. His tears were flooding his beard. She said, "Woe unto you! Is there any Muslim man among you?" None answered her. Then Omer Ibn Sa'd shouted at people, "Alight and put him to rest!" Ash-Shimr was the first to do so. He kicked the Imām with his foot then sat on his chest and took hold of his holy beard. He dealt him twelve sword strokes. He then severed his sacred head...

AL-HUSSAIN MARAUDED
Those folks now took to maurauding the Imām: Ishāq ibn Hawayh took his shirt. Al-Akhnas ibn Murthid ibn Alqamah al-Hadrami took his turban. Al-Aswad ibn Khalid took his sandals. Jamee ibn al-Khalq al-Awdi, and some say a man from Tameem named al-Aswad ibn Hanzalah, took his sword.

Bajdal came. He saw the Imām (ع) wearing a ring covered with his blood. He cut his finger off and took the ring... Qays ibn al-Ash'ath took his velvet on which he since then used to sit, so he came to be called "Qays Qateefa." Qateefa is Arabic for velvet. His worn out garment was taken by Jaoonah ibn Hawiyyah al-Hadrami. His bow and outer garments were taken by ar-Raheel ibn Khaythamah al-Ju'fi and Hani ibn Shabeeb al-Hadrami and Jarar Ibn Mas'ūd al-Hadrami. A man among them wanted to take his underpants after all his other clothes had been taken away by others. This man said, "I wanted to take it off, but he had put his right hand on it which I could not lift; therefore, I severed his right hand... He then put his left hand on it which I also could not lift, so I severed it, too, and I

124

was about to bare him and take it off when I heard a rumbling like that of an earthquake, so I became frightened. I left him and fell into a swoon, a slumber. While I was unconscious, I saw the Prophet, Ali, Fātima, and al-Hassan, in a vision. Fātima was saying, O son! They killed you! May Allāh kill them!' He said to her, O mother! This sleeping man has severed my hands!' She then invoked Allāh's curse on me saying, May Allāh cut your hands and legs, and may He blind you and hurl you into the fire!' Indeed, I am now blind. My hands and legs have already been amputated, and nothing remains from her curse except the fire."

Interior of Imam al-Hussain's Shrine

اللهم ارزقنا شفاعة الحسين

FRONT COVER IMAGES OF PREVIOUS EDITIONS OF THIS BOOK:

KERBALA AND BEYOND

Author: Yasin T. Al-Jibouri

An Epic of
Immortal Heroism

Kerbala
and Beyond

Yasin T. al-Jibouri

128

PART II

A SUMMARY OF

POST-MARTYRDOM EVENTS

When al-Hussain (ﻉ) was martyred, people fell upon his luggage and belongings looting everything they could find in his tents[1], then they set the tents to fire. People raced to rob the ladies of the Messenger of Allāh (ﻉ). Daughters of Fātima az-Zahrā' (ﻉ) tearfully ran away, their hair uncovered[2]. Scarves were snatched, rings were pulled out of fingers, ear-rings were taken out, and so were ankle-rings[3]. A man took both ear-rings belonging to Umm Kulthum, riddling her ears in the process[4]. Another approached Fātima daughter of al-Hussain (ﻉ), taking her ankle-rings out. He was weeping as he committed his foul deed. "What is the matter with you?," she asked him. "How can I help weeping," he answered, "since I am looting the daughter of the

---

[1]Ibn al-Atheer, *At-Tarikh al-Kāmil*, Vol. 4, p. 32.

[2]at-Tabari, *Tarikh*, Vol. 6, p. 260.

[3]Ibn Nama, *Muthir al-Ahzan*, p. 40.

[4]Muhammed Jawad Shubbar, *Al-Dam'a as-Sakiba*, p. 348.

Messenger of Allāh?" She asked him to leave her alone. He said, "I am afraid if I do not take it, someone else will."[1]

Another man was seen driving the women with the butt of his spear, having robbed them of their coverings and jewelry as they sought refuge with one another. He was seen by the same Fātima. Having realized that she had seen him, he went towards her, and she fled away. He threw his spear at her; she fell headlong and fainted. When she recovered, she saw her aunt, Umm Kulthum, sitting at her head crying.[2]

A woman from the clan of Bakr ibn Wa'il, who was accompanied by her husband, saw the daughters of the Messenger of Allāh (ﷺ) in such a condition, so she cried out, "O offspring of Bakr ibn Wa'il! Do you permit the daughters of the Messenger of Allāh (ﷺ) to be robbed like that? There is no judgment except Allāh's! O how the Messenger of Allāh (ﷺ) should be avenged!" Her husband brought her back to his conveyance[3].

The rogues reached Ali son of al-Hussain (ﷺ) who was sick on his bed unable to stand up[4]. Some were saying, "Do not let any of them,

---

[1]as-Sadūq, *Aamali*, p. 99, *majlis* 31. at-Thahbi, *Siyar Alam an-Nubala'*, Vol. 3, p. 204.

[2]Mawla Hussain ibn Mawla Muhammed al-Jammi (known as the virtuous man of Jamm) *Riyad al-Masa'ib fil Mawaiz wal Tawarikh wal Siyar wal Masa'ib*, p. 341. al-Qazwini, *Tazallum az-Zahra'*, p. 130.

[3]Ibn Tawoos, namely Sayyid Ali ibn Musa ibn Ja'far, *Al-Luhuf fi Qatla at-Tufuf*, p. 74. Ibn Nama, *Muthir al-Ahzan*, p. 41.

[4]Reference to the sickness of Ali son of al-Hussain, as-Sajjād (ﷺ) is referred to by at-Tabari on p. 260, Vol. 6, of his *Tarikh*. It is also mentioned by Ibn al-Atheer on p. 33, Vol. 4, of his book *At-Tarikh al-Kāmil*, by Ibn Katheer on p. 188, Vol. 8, of his book *Al-Bidaya*, by al-Yafii on p. 133, Vol. 1, of his book *Mir'at al-Jinan*, by Shaikh al-Mufid in his book *Kitab Al-Irshad*, by Ibn Shahr Ashub on p. 225, Vol. 2, of his book *Manaqib*, by at-Tibrisi on p. 148 of his book *I'lam al-Wara bi A'lam al-Huda*, by Muhammed ibn Ahmed ibn Ali an-Nishapuri on p. 162 of his

young or old, alive." Others were saying, "Do not be rash in your

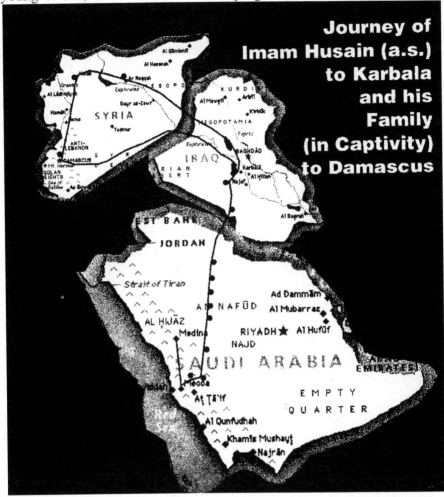

Journey of Imam Husain (a.s.) to Karbala and his Family (in Captivity) to Damascus

judgment till we consult the governor Amr ibn Sa'd."[1] Ash-Shimr unsheathed his sword with the intention to kill Ali. Hameed ibn Muslim said to him, "Glory to Allāh! Do you really kill children?!

book *Rawdat al-Waizeen*, and by al-Mas'udi on p. 140 of his book *Ithbat al-Wasiyya*.

[1] al-Qazwini, *Tazallum az-Zahra'*, p. 132.

He is only a sick lad!"[1] He said, "Ibn Ziyad ordered all al-Hussain's sons killed." Ibn Sa'd went to extremes to stop him[2] especially after having heard the wise lady Zainab daughter of the Commander of the Faithful (ع) saying, "You will not kill him before killing me first;" so, they left him alone[3].

Ibn Sa'd himself came to the ladies who burst in tears upon seeing him. He ordered the men to stay away from them. Those men had already taken all the ornaments those ladies had had and never returned any of them back. He assigned to a group of men the task of protecting them, then he returned to his tent.

THE STEED

Ibn Sa'd shouted, "Who volunteers to make sure that the chest and the back of al-Hussain (ع) are run over by the horses?" Ten men stood up.[4] Those miscreant "volunteers" were: Ishāq ibn Hawiyyah, al-Ahbash ibn Murshid ibn Alqamah ibn Salamah al-Hadrami, Hakeem ibn at-Tufayl as-Sinbisi, Amr ibn Sabeeh as-Saydawi, Raja' ibn Munqith al-Abdi, Salim ibn Khaythamah al-Ju'fi, Salih ibn Wahab al-Ju'fi, Wakhit ibn Ghanim, Hani ibn Thabeet al-Hadrami, and Aseed ibn Malik. They rode their horses and trampled upon the body of the fragrant flower of the Messenger of Allāh...

Ibn Ziyad ordered liberal awards to be given to them[5]. Al-Bayruni

---

[1] at-Tabari, *Tarikh*, Vol. 6, p. 260.

[2] Shaikh Abbas al-Qummi, *Nafas al-Mahmum*.

[3] al-Qarmani, *Tarikh*, p. 108.

[4] at-Tabari, *Tarikh*, Vol. 6, p. 161. Ibn al-Atheer, *At-Tarikh al-Kāmil*, Vol. 4, p. 33. al-Mas'udi, *Muraj at-Thahab*, Vol. 2, p. 91. al-Maqrazi, *Khutat*, Vol. 2, p. 288. Ibn Katheer, *Al-Bidaya*, Vol. 8, p. 189. al-Khamees, *Tarikh*, Vol. 3, p. 333. Shaikh al-Mufid, *Al-Irshad*. at-Tibrisi, *I'lam al-Wara bi A'lam al-Huda*, p. 888. Muhammed ibn Ahmed ibn Ali an-Nishapuri, *Rawdat al-Wa'izeen*, p. 662. Ibn Shahr Ashub, *Al-Manaqib*, Vol. 2, p. 224.

[5] Ibn Tawoos *Al-Luhuf*, p. 75. Ibn Nama, *Muthir al-Ahzan*, p. 41.

has said that they did to al-Hussain (ع) what no other nation had ever done to their most evil ones: killing with the sword or the spear, with stone throwing, and with horse trampling[1]. Some of those horses reached Egypt were their shoes were pulled out and fixed on doors as means of seeking blessings. This became a custom among them, so much so that many of them started making the like of those shoes and hanging them over the doors of their houses.[2]

THE SEVERED HEADS

Ibn Sa'd ordered the heads to be severed from their bodies. They were distributed to various tribes that used them as means to seek favor with Ibn Ziyad. The Kindah tribe took thirteen brought by their envoy Qays ibn al-Ash'ath. The Hawazin tribe brought twelve with their "man" Shimr ibn Thul-Jawshan. The Tameem tribe brought seventeen; the Banu Asad tribe brought sixteen; the Mathhaj tribe brought seven, and the other tribes brought the rest[3]. The tribe to which al-Hurr ar-Riyahi belonged refused to cut anyone's head or to let their horses trample on the Imām's body[4].

On the tenth day, Ibn Sa'd had already entrusted the head of Imām al-Hussain (ع) to Khawli ibn Yazid al-Asbahi and Hameed ibn Muslim al-Azdi. He entrusted the heads of the Imām's family members and those of his companions to ash-Shimr, Qays ibn al-Ash'ath and Amr ibn al-Hajjaj[5]. Khawli's house was one farasang from Kūfa. He hid the head from his Ansari wife whom he knew to be loyal to Ahl al-Bayt, peace be with them. But when she saw a

---

[1] *Al-Aathar al-Baqiya*, p. 329.

[2] al-Karakchi, *Kitab at-Taajjub*, p. 46.

[3] Ibn Tawoos *Al-Luhuf*, p. 81. Al-Ayni, *Umdat al-Qari fi Sharh al-Bukhari*, Vol. 7, p. 656, where the name of Urwah ibn Qays is included among them.

[4] Al-Hajj Shaikh Muhammed Baqir ibn Mawla Hassan al-Qa'ini al-Birjandi as-Safi, *Al-Kibrit al-Ahmar fi Shar'iat Ahl al-Minbar*.

[5] Shaikh al-Mufid, *Al-Irshad*.

light emanating from the bakery oven [where it was hidden], she was terrified. When she came closer, she heard the voices of al-Hussain's women mourning al-Hussain (ع) in the most somber way. She mentioned this to her husband then went out crying[1]. Since then, she never used any kohl nor any perfume out of her grief for al-Hussain (ع). She was called Ayoof[2].

In the morning, Khawli took the head to the governor's mansion. By then, Ibn Ziyad had returned from his camp at an-Nakheela. Khawli put the head in front of Ibn Ziyad as he recited these poetic verses:

إمـــلأ ركـــابي فِضّـــة أو ذهبـــا   إنّـــي قتلـــتُ الســـيّدَ المحجّبـــا

وخيـــرهم مـــن يـــذكرون النســـبا   قـــتلتُ خيـــرَ النـــاسِ أمّـــاً وأبـــا

فساء ابن زياد قوله أمام الجمع فقال له : إذا علمت إنّه كذلك فلِمَ قتلته ؟ والله لا نلت نّي شيئاً.

Fill my stirrup with silver or with gold:
I killed the master of every honor told,
Their best when they mention descent.
I killed the best of people, son of the best parent.

But these words, spoken in front of everyone, were met by Ibn Ziyad with outrage. "Since you knew that he was that honorable," said Ibn Ziyad, "why did you then take part in killing him? By Allāh, you will receive nothing from me at all."[3]

---

[1]Muhammed an-Nishapuri, *Rawdat ash-Shuhada'*. On p. 190, Vol. 8, Ibn Katheer says that his wife saw the light emanating from underneath the lid and stretching to the heavens as white birds kept hovering around it. He adds saying that his other wife, Nuwar daughter of Malik, said to him, "Have you brought the head of the son of the Messenger of Allah, peace of Allah and His blessings upon him and his family, here?! I shall never share a bed with you henceforth." She separated from him.

[2]al-Balathiri, *Ansab al-Ashraf*, Vol. 5, p. 238.

[3]According to p. 133, Vol. 1, of al-Yafi'i's book *Mir'at al-Jinan*, Ibn Ziyad was very angry with him, so he killed him, but the author does not

134

LEAVING KERBALĀ

When Ibn Sa'd sent the heads to Kūfa, he remained with the army till noon on the eleventh day [of Muharram]. He gathered those killed from his army and performed the funeral prayers for them then buried them, leaving the corpses of the Master of the Youths of Paradise (ع) and those of his Ahl al-Bayt (ع) and companions unwashed, unshrouded, and unburied[1], exposed to the wind and to the wild beasts of the desert.

After the time of *zawal*, Ibn Sa'd left for Kūfa with the women, the children, the bondmaids, and the surviving family members of al-

---

identify the name of the head bearer. On p. 213, Vol. 2, of *Al-Iqd al-Farid fi Marifat al-Qira'a wal Tajwad* of Sayyid Muhammed Ridha ibn Abul-Qasim ibn FathAllah ibn Nejm ad-Din al-Hussaini al-Kamali al-Asterbadi al-Hilli (died in 1346 A.H./1927 A.D.), the head bearer is identified as Khawli ibn Yazid al-Asbahi who was killed by Ibn Ziyad. Historians contend among themselves about who had brought the head and who had said the above verses. According to Ibn Jarir at-Tabari, who indicates so on p. 261, Vol. 6, of his *Tarikh*, and Ibn al-Atheer who states so on p. 33, Vol. 4, of his book *At-Tarikh al-Kāmil*, the poet was Sinan ibn Anas who recited them to Omer ibn Sa'd. On p. 144 of *Tathkirat al-Khawass* of Ibn al-Jawzi, the grandson, Omer said to him, "You are insane! Had Ibn Ziyad heard you, he would have killed you!" On p. 193, Vol. 1, of ash-Sharishi's *Maqamat*, the author says that the poet recited them to Ibn Ziyad. According to al-Irbili's *Kashf al-Ghumma* and al-Khawarizmi's p. 40, Vol. 2, of *Maqtal al-Hussain (ع)*, Bishr ibn Malik recited them to Ibn Ziyad. On p. 76 of Ibn Talhah's *Matalib as-Saool*, there is the addition of "... and whoever says his prayers in both Qiblas," whereupon Ibn Ziyad became very angry with him and had him beheaded. On p. 437 of *Riyad al-Musa'ib*, it is stated that ash-Shimr is the one who recited these verses. Since you know that ash-Shimr is al-Hussain's killer according to the text of the *ziyarat* of the sacred area and according to a host of historians, you likewise know that he must be the one who recited them. It is very unlikely that he kills him and lets someone else take the head and use it to seek favor with Ibn Ziyad. We have mentioned the story from Khawli only to follow in the footsteps of those who wrote about the Imām's martyrdom.

[1]al-Khawarizmi, *Maqtal al-Hussain (ع)*, Vol. 2, p. 39.

Hussain's companions. They included twenty women[1] whom they mounted on camels without saddles just as was the custom then with Turks or Romans taken captive although they belonged to the best of all prophets (ع). With them was as-Sajjād Ali ibn al-Hussain (ع) who was twenty-three years old[2]. He was placed on a lean camel without a saddle, and he was worn out by sickness[3]. His son [the later Imām] al-Bāqir[4], who was two years and a few months old[5], accompanied him. Among the children of Imām al-Hassan (ع) taken captive were: Zaid, Amr, and al-Hassan II. The latter was captured after he had killed seventeen men. He received eighteen wounds, and his right arm had been cut off. Asma' ibn Kharijah al-Fizari intervened to get him freed because his mother was also Fizari, so Ibn Sa'd left her husband take him[6]. With them was Uqbah ibn Saman, a slave of ar-Rubab, al-Hussain's wife. When Ibn Ziyad came to know that that man was ar-Rubab's slave, he released him. Ibn Ziyad was informed

---

[1]Shaikh Abbas al-Qummi, *Nafas al-Mahmum*, p. 204. On p. 234, Vol. 2, of an-Nawari's book *Mustadrak al-Wasa'il* (first edition), both Shaikh al-Mufid and Sayyid Ibn Tawoos cite Imām as-Sadiq (ع) saying that he, peace be with him, had prayed two *rek'ats* at al-Qā'im, a place on the highway leading to al-Ghari (Najaf), then said, "Here was the head of my grandfather al-Hussain (ع) placed when they went to Kerbala' then carried it to Ubaydullah ibn Ziyad." Then the Imām (ع) recited a supplication to be recited following the prayer saying, "This place is called al-Hananah."

[2]Mis'ab az-Zubairi, *Nasab Quraish*, p. 58.

[3]Ibn Tawoos, *Al-Iqbal*, p. 54.

[4]Muhammed Hassan ash-Shaban Kurdi al-Qazwini, *Riyad al-Ahzan*, p. 49. al-Mas'udi, *Ithbat al-Wasiyya*, p. 143.

[5]al-Mas'udi, *Ithbat al-Wasiyya*, p. 143 (Najaf edition). According to p. 203, Vol. 1, of Abul-Fida''s *Tarikh*, Vol. 1, p. 203, he was three years old.

[6]al-Majlisi, *Bihār al-Anwār*, Vol. 10, in the chapter discussing the offspring of Imām al-Hassan (ع). According to p. 28 of *Isaf ar-Raghibeen*, commenting on a footnote in *Nar al-Absar*, and also according to p. 8 of *Al-Luhuf* by Ibn Tawoos, he treated him at Kufa, and when he healed, he transported him to Medīna.

that al-Muraqqa' ibn Thumamah al-Asadi had scattered his arrows around then fled to his tribe where he sought and received protection, he ordered him to be banished to az-Zara[1].

The ladies pleaded to him thus: "For the love of Allāh! Please take us to those killed." When they saw how they had lost their limbs, how the spears had drank of their blood, and how the horses had

---

[1] at-Tabari, *Tarikh*, Vol. 6, p. 261. Ibn al-Atheer, *At-Tarikh al-Kāmil*, Vol. 4, p. 33. According to p. 367, Vol. 4, of Yaqut al-Hamawi's *Mu'jam al-Buldan*, az-Zara is a village in Bahrain, and there is another in West Tripoli as well as another in the upper Delta of the Nile. According to p. 692, Vol. 2, of al-Bikri's book *Al-Mu'jam mimma Istajam'*, it is a place in the Bahrain area where wars waged by an-Nu'man ibn al-Munthir, who was nicknamed al-Gharoor (the conceited one), battled al-Aswaris. It also is a city in Persia where a duel took place between al-Bara' ibn Malik and the city's satrap, al-Bara' killed the latter and cut his hand off. He took his belt and both his bracelets the value of which was thirty thousand dinars. Omer ibn al-Khattab took the *khums* of the loot, and that was the first time in the history of Islam that a loot was taxed by 1/5 and delivered to the caliph (whereas it was/is supposed to be given to the Prophet's descendants according to the injunctions of the Holy Qur'an). On p. 10, Vol. 4, of his book *At-Tarikh al-Kāmil*, Ibn al-Atheer says that Ibn Ziyad threatened to banish the people of Kufa [who refused to fight al-Hussain (ع)] to Oman's Zara. Also on p. 86, Vol. 8, where the events of the year 321 A.H./933 A.D. are discussed, it is stated that Ali ibn Yaleeq ordered Mu'awiyah and his son Yazid to be cursed from the pulpits in Baghdad, whereupon the Sunnis were outraged. There, al-Barbahari, a Hanbalite, used to stir trouble; he ran away from Ali ibn Yaleeq. The latter captured al-Barbahari's followers and shipped them in a boat to Oman. It appears from the latter account that Zara is a place in Oman. On p. 256 of al-Dainuri's book *Al-Akhbar at-Tiwal*, Ibn Ziyad banished al-Muraqqa to az-Zabada where the latter stayed till Yazid's death and Ibn Ziyad's flight to Syria. Al-Muraqqa, therefore, left it and went back to Kufa. On p. 9, Vol. 8, of *Nashwar al-Muhadara wa Akhbar al-Muthakara* by at-Tanakhi, the judge, namely Muhsin ibn Ali ibn Muhammed Abul-Fahm (329 - 384 A.H./941 - 994 A.D.), it is stated that Muhammed al-Muhallabi banished Muhammed ibn al-Hassan ibn Abdul-Aziz al-Hashimi to Oman in a boat because of something he had done which angered him.

trampled upon them, they screamed and beat their faces in anguish[1].
Zainab cried out,

يا محمّداه ! هذا حسين بالعراء ، مرمّل بالدماء ، مقطّع الأعضاء ، وبناتك سبايا ،
وذريّتك مقتّلة . فأبكت كلّ عدو وصديق

"O Muhammed! Here is al-Hussain in the desert covered with blood,
his limbs cut off! Here are your daughters taken captive and your
offspring slaughtered!" These words caused friends and foes alike to
weep[2], even the horses' tears ran on their hooves[3]. Then she put her
hands under his sacred body and lifted it as she supplicated saying,
"O Lord! Do accept this sacrifice from us[4]."

Sukayna[5] hugged the body of her father al-Hussain (ع) and kept

[1]Ibn Nama, *Muthir al-Ahzan*, p. 41. Ibn Tawoos, *Al-Luhuf*, p. 74. Al-
Khawarizmi, *Maqtal al-Hussain (ع)*, Vol. 2, p. 39. At-Turayhi, *Maqtal al-
Hussain (ع)*, p. 332.

[2]al-Maqrazi, *Khutat*, Vol. 2, p. 280. According to the authors of both
Maqtal al-Hussain (ع) and *Al-Luhuf*, the mourning was even on a much
larger scale.

[3]al-Khawarizmi, *Maqtal al-Hussain (ع)*, Vol. 2, p. 39. Shaikh LutfAllah
ibn al-Mawla Muhammed Jawad as-Safi al-Gulpaigani, *Al-Muntakhab al-
Athar fi Akhbar al-Imām at-Thani Ashar* (usually referred to as simply *Al-
Muntakhab*), p. 332.

[4]al-Birjandi as-Safi, *Al-Kibrit al-Ahmar*, Vol. 3, p. 13, citing *At-Tiraz al-
Muthahhab*.

[5]According to p. 163, Vol. 1, of an-Nawawi's *Tahthib al-Asma'*, p. 58,
Vol. 1, of Shaikh Muhammed Ali ibn Ghanim al-Qatari al-Biladi al-
Bahrani's book *Al-Kawakib al-Durriyya*, p. 160 of ash-Shiblinji's *Nar al-
Absar*, and Ibn Khallikan's *Wafiyyat al-Ayan*, where the author details her
biography, Sukayna daughter of al-Hussain (ع) died on a Thursday, Rabi' I
5, 117 A.H./April 8, 735 A.D. According to Abul-Hassan al-Amri's book
Al-Mujdi and to at-Tibrisi's book *Alam al-Wara bi Alam al-Huda*, p. 127,
where the biographies of the offspring of Imām al-Hassan (ع) are
discussed, and also according to p. 163, Vol. 12, of Abul-Faraj al-
Isfahani's book *Al-Aghani*, she married her cousin Abdullāh ibn al-Hassan

telling him how she had heard him saying,

شيعتي ما أنْ شربتم عَذْبَ ماء فاذكروني
أو سمـعتم بغريـب او شـهيد فانـدبوني

O my Shī'as! Whenever of water you drink
Never from mentioning my name should you shrink.
And whenever you are a stranger on a sojourn
Or see a martyr, me should you remember and mourn.[1]

Only a number of them could collectively remove her from his corpse, forcefully dragging her away.[2]

When Ali ibn al-Hussain (ع) looked at his slaughtered family, he felt greatly grieved and worried. When his sister Zainab al-Kubra read his face, she felt upset on his account and took to consoling him and admonishing him to be patient although even the mountains could not match him in his patience and fortitude. Among what she said to him is the following:

ما لي أراك تجود بنفسك يا بقيّة جدّي وأبي وإخوتي؟ فوالله إنّ هذا لعهد من الله إلى جدّك
وأبيك ، ولقد أخذ الله ميثاق أُناس لا تعرفهم فراعنة هذه الأرض ، وهم معروفون في أهل
السّماوات ، إنّهم يجمعون هذه الأعضاء المقطّعة والجسوم المضرّجة ، فيوارونها
وينصبون بهذا الطفّ علماً لقبر سيّد الشهداء لا يُدرس أثره ولا يُمحى رسمه على

ibn Ali ibn Abū Talib (ع) who was killed during the Battle of at-Taff. She did not bear any children by him. But the author *I'lam al-Wara bi A'lam al-Huda*, namely at-Tibrisi, says that he was killed before marrying her, and that during the Battle of at-Taff, she was a little more than ten years old, and that she was born before the the death [martyrdom] of her uncle Imām al-Hassan (ع). The statement in her honor made by the Master of Martyrs (ع), "Sukayna is overcome by deep contemplation upon Allah," as is recorded by as-Sabban in his book *Isaf ar-Raghibeen*, clearly outlines for us the status his daughter occupied in the sacred canons of Islam's *Shari'a*.

[1]These verses are recorded on p. 376 of the Indian edition of *Misbah al-Kaf'ami*.

[2]al-Qazwini, *Tazallum az-Zahra'*, p. 135.

كرور الليالي والأيّام ، وليجتهدنّ أئمّة الكفر وأشياع الضلال في محوه وتطميسه ، فلا
يزداد أثره إلاّ علوّاً.

"Why do I see you pleading for death, O the legacy of my grandfather, of my father and brothers? By Allāh, this is something which Allāh had divulged to your grandfather (ع) and to your father (ع). Allāh took a covenant from people whom you do not know, the mighty ones on this land, and who are known to the people of the heavens, that they would gather these severed parts and wounded corpses and bury them, then shall they set up on this Taff a banner for the grave of your father, the Master of Martyrs (ع), the traces of which shall never be obliterated, nor shall it ever be wiped out so long as there is day and night. And the leaders of apostasy and the promoters of misguidance shall try their best to obliterate and efface it, yet it shall get more and more lofty instead."[1]

Zajr ibn Qays came to them and shouted at them to leave as he kept whipping them. Others surrounded them and mounted them on camel humps.[2]

Zainab the wise rode her own she-camel. She recollected the days of lofty honor and inviolable prestige, guarded by fierce and honorable lions of Abdul-Muttalib's offspring. And she used to always be surrounded by servants who would not enter without her permission.

AT KŪFA

When the daughters of the Commander of the Faithful (ع) entered Kūfa, the city's residents gathered to see them, so Umm Kulthum shouted at them, "O people of Kūfa! Do not you have any sense of shame before Allāh and His Messenger so you look at the ladies of

[1]Shaikh Abul-Qasim Ja'far ibn Muhammed ibn Ja'far ibn Musa ibn Qawlawayh al-Qummi (died in 367 A.H./977 A.D.), *Kāmil az-Ziyarat*, p. 361, chapter 88, virtues of Kerbala' and merits of viziting the grave site of al-Hussain (ع).

[2]Radiyy ad-Din ibn Nabi al-Qazwini (died in 1134 A.H./1722 A.D.), *Tazallum az-Zahra'*, p. 177.

the Prophet?"[1]

One of Kūfa's women came to them and saw their condition for which even a most bitter enemy would feel sorry. She asked them what captives they were, and she was told: "We are captives belonging to the Progeny of Muhammed."[2] The people of Kūfa kept doling out dates, walnuts and bread to the children, whereupon Umm Kulthum, that is, Zainab al-Kubra, shouted at them that they were prohibited from accepting charity. She threw away what had been given to the children[3]. A poet once composed these lines addressing Imām Ali ibn Abū Talib (ﻉ):

O father of Hassan!
She overlooks and in the slumber she delights,
But only with her hand can Zainab now cover her face.
O father of Hassan!
Does this sight you please:
Each of your women chained, uncovered the face,
While Banu Harb's women in their chambers veiled with grace?
Does your side on the bed find comfort and ease,
While your daughters on the camels to Syria are brought?
Are you pleased when your wise ladies are exposed?
With lashes they are whipped when they cry, having no rest..
To the east they are once taken by the mean gangs, the worst,
And once towards the land of shame are taken, to the west.
None to protect them as they cross every plain,
None heeds their complaints when they complain.
Their voices were lost and their hearts squeezed,
Their breath by grief is almost snatched away
Amazed am I about one who thinks of fate
And wonders and upon it does he contemplate:

---

[1]Muhammed Jawad Shubbar, *Al-Dam'ah as-Sakibah*, p. 364.

[2]Ibn Nama, p. 84. *Al-Luhuf*, p. 81.

[3]ar-Rashti al-Ha'iri, *Asrar ash-Shahada*, p. 477. Al-Qazwini, *Tazallum az-Zahra'*, p. 150.

A fornicator leisurely turns about on his throne,
As al-Hussain on the ground is left, unburied, alone,
And his head is on a lance openly carried,
And with the crown is crowned the son of a whore.
For three days did Hussain stay unburied or more.
One's body is to cruel elements is left exposed
As the other covers his with silk and with gold.[1]

ZAINAB'S SPEECH

The daughter of the Commander of the Faithful (ع) explained to people Ibn Ziyad's villainy and meanness in a speech which she delivered to them. When she signaled to them to calm down, they did. They stood speechless and motionless, and even the bells of their animals stopped ringing. It was then that she, calm and composed and with courage reminiscent of that of her father Haider (ع) addressed them saying,

يقول الراوي : لمّا أومأت زينب ابنة علي (ع) إلى النّاس ، فسكنت الأنفاس والأجراس ، فعندها اندفعت بخطابها مع طمأنينة نفس وثبات جأش ، وشجاعة حيدريّة ، فقالت صلوات الله عليها: الحمد لله والصلاة على أبي محمّد وآله الطيّبين الأخيار .

أمّا بعد ، يا أهل الكوفة ، يا أهل الختل والغدر ، أتبكون ؟! فلا رقأت الدمعة ، ولا هدأت الرنّة ، إنّما مثلكم كمثّل التي نقضت غزلها من بعد قوّة أنكاثاً ، تتّخذون أيمانكم دخلاً بينكم ، ألا وهل فيكم إلاّ الصلف النطف والعجب والكذب والشنف وملق الإماء ، وغمز الأعداء؟! أو كمرعى على دمنة أو كقصّة على ملحودة، ألا بئس ما قدّمتْ لكم أنفسكم أنْ سخط الله عليكم ، وفي العذاب أنتم خالدون .

أتبكون وتنتحبون ؟! إي والله فابكوا كثيراً ، واضحكوا قليلاً ؛ فلقد ذهبتم بعارها وشنارها ، ولن ترحضوها بغسل بعدها أبداً ، وأنّى ترحضون قتْل سليل خاتم النبوّة ومعدن الرسالة ، ومدرة حجّتكم و منار محجّتكم ، وملاذ خيرتكم ومفزع نازلتكم ، وسيّد شباب أهل الجنّة ، ألا ساء ما تزرون .

فتعساً و نكساً وبُعداً لكم وسحقاً ، فلقد خاب السّعي وتبّت الأيدي ، وخسرت الصفقة ، وبؤتم بغضب من الله ورسوله ، وضُربت عليكم الذّلّة والمسكنة. ويلكم يا أهل الكوفة ،

---

[1] Excerpted from a poem in praise of al-Hussain (as) by Shaikh Hassoon al-Hilli who died in 1305 A.H./1888 A.D. as we are told on p. 155, Vol. 2, of *Shuara' al-Hilla*.

أتدرون أيَّ كبدٍ لرسول الله فريتم ؟ وأيَّ كريمةٍ له أبرزتم ؟ وأيَّ دمٍ له سفكتم ؟ وأيَّ حرمةٍ له انتهكتم ؟ لقد جئتم شيئاً إذاً ، تكاد السَّموات يتفطَّرن منه ، وتنشقّ الأرض ، وتخرّ الجبال هدّاً . ولقد أتيتم بها خرقاء شوهاء كطلاع الأرض وملء السَّماء .

أفعجبتم أنْ مطرت السَّماء دماً ولعذاب الآخرة أخزى وهم لا يُنصرون ، فلا يستخفنَّكم المهل ، فإنّه لا يحفزه البدار ، ولا يخاف فوت الثار ، وإنَّ ربّكم لَبالمرصاد.

All Praise is due to Allāh. Peace and blessings be upon my father Muhammed (ص) and upon his good and righteous Progeny (ع). May the resounding [of this calamity] never stops. Your similitude is one who unspins what is already spun out of the desire to violate [a trust]. You make religion a source of your income... Is there anyone among you who is not a boaster of what he does not have, a charger of debauchery, a conceited liar, a man of grudge without any justification, one submissive like bondmaids, an instigator, a pasture of what is not wholesome, one who recites a story to someone who is buried? Truly bad is that which your souls have committed. You have reaped the Wrath of Allāh, remaining in the chastisement for eternity. Do you really cry and sob? By Allāh, you should then cry a great deal and laugh very little, for you have earned nothing but shame and infamy, and you shall never be able to wash it away, and how could you do so? The descendant of the Bearer of the Last Message (ع), the very essence of the Message, the source of your security and the beacon of your guidance, the refuge of the righteous from among you, the one who saves you from calamity, the Master of the Youths of Paradise... is killed. O how horrible is the sin that you bear...! Miserable you are and renegades from the path of righteousness; may you be distanced and crushed. The effort is rendered futile, the toil is ruined, the deal is lost, and you earned nothing but Wrath from Allāh and His Messenger (ص). You are doomed with servitude and humiliation. Woe unto you, O Kūfians (Kūfans)! Do you know whose heart you have burned, what a "feat" you have labored, what blood you have shed, and what sanctity you have violated? You have done a most monstrous deed, something for which the heavens are about to split asunder and so is the earth, and for which the mountains crumble. You have done something most uncanny, most defaced, as much as the fill of the earth and of the sky. Do you wonder why the sky rains blood? Surely the torment of the hereafter is a greater chastisement, and they shall not be helped.

143

Let no respite elate you, for rushing does not speed it up, nor does it fear the loss of the opportunity for revenge. Your Lord is waiting in ambush for you.[1]

Imām as-Sajjād (ع) said to her, "That is enough, O aunt, for you are, Praise to Allāh, a learned lady whom none taught, one who comprehends without being made to do so."[2]

FĀTIMA DELIVERS A SPEECH

Fātima, al-Hussain's daughter[3], delivered a speech wherein she said,

---

[1]This speech is compiled from the writings of Shaikh at-Tusi in his *Aamali* as well as that of his son, from *Al-Luhuf*, Ibn Nama, Ibn Shahr Ashub, and from at-Tibrisi's book *Al-Ihtijaj*.

[2]at-Tibrisi, *Al-Ihtijaj*, p. 166 (Najaf's edition).

[3]Fatima daughter of al-Hussain (ع), peace be with him, was a great personality; she enjoyed a great status in the creed. Her father, the Master of Martyrs, testifies to this fact. When al-Hassan II approached him asking him for the hand of either of his two daughters, he, peace be with him, as we are told on p. 202 of *Nar al-Absar*, said to him, "I choose for you Fatima, for she, more than anyone else, is like my mother Fatima daughter of the Messenger of Allah (ع). As far as the creed is concerned, she stays awake all night long offering prayers, and the daytime she spends fasting. In beauty, she looks like the *huris* with large lovely eyes." On p. 442, Vol. 12, of Ibn Hajar's *Tahthib at-Tahthib*, she is said to have narrated *hadīth* from her father, brother Zain al-Ābidīn, aunt Zainab, Ibn Abbas, and Asma' daughter of Umays. Her sons Abdullāh, Ibrahim, al-Hussain (ع), and her daughter Umm Ja'far, offspring of al-Hassan II, quote her *hadīth*. Abul-Miqdam quotes her *hadīth* through his mother. Zuhayr ibn Mu'awiyah quotes her *hadīth* through his mother. On p. 425 of *Khulasat Tahtheeb al-Kamal*, it is stated that the authors of *sunan* books, including at-Tirmithi, Abū Dāwūd, and an-Nassa'i, have all quoted her *ahadīth*. So does the author of *Musnad Ali*. Ibn Majah al-Qazwini does likewise. Ibn Hajar al-Asqalani says, "She is mentioned in the book of funerals in Bukhari's *Sahīh*, and Ibn Haban holds her reliable, adding that she died in 110 A.H./729 A.D." So do both authors al-Yafii, on p. 234, Vol. 1, of his book *Mir'at al-Jinan*, and Ibn al-Imad on p. 39, Vol. 1, of his book *Shatharat*. Based on what Ibn Hajar says in his book *Tahthib at-Tahthib*, she must have lived for almost ninety years, placing her year of birth at

144

الحمد لله عدد الرمل والحصى ، وزنة العرش إلى الثرى ، أحمده وأؤمن به وأتوكّل عليه ، وأشهد أنْ لا إله إلاّ الله وحده لا شريك له وأنّ محمداً عبده ورسوله ، وأنّ أولاده ذُبحوا بشطّ الفرات ، من غير ذحل ولا ترات .

اللهمّ إنّي أعوذ بك أنْ أفتري عليك ، وأنْ أقول عليك خلاف ما أنزلت من أخذ العهود والوصيّة لعلي بن أبي طالب المغلوب حقّه ، المقتول من غير ذنب كما قُتل ولده بالأمس ، في بيت من بيوت الله تعالى ، فيه معشر مسلمة بألسنتهم ، تعساً لرؤوسهم ما دفعت عنه ضيماً في حياته ولا عند مماته ، حتّى قبضه الله تعالى إليه محمود النّقيبة طيّب العريكة ، معروف المناقب مشهور المذاهب ، لم تأخذه في الله سبحانه لَومة لائم ولا عذل عاذل ، هديته اللهمّ للإسلام صغيراً ، وحمدت مناقبه كبيراً ، ولم يزل ناصحاً لك ولرسولك ، زاهداً في الدنيا غير حريص عليها ، راغباً في الآخرة ، مجاهداً لك في سبيلك ، رضيته فاخترته وهديته إلى صراط مستقيم .

أمّا بعد، يا أهل الكوفة ، يا أهل المكر والغدر والخيلاء ، فإنّا أهل بيت ابتلانا الله بكم ، وابتلاكم بنا . فجعل بلاءنا حسناً ، وجعل علمه عندنا وفهمه لدينا ، فنحن عَيبة علمه ، ووعاء فهمه وحكمته ، وحجّته على الأرض في بلاده لعباده ، أكرمنا الله بكرامته ، وفضّلنا بنبيّه محمّد (صلّى الله عليه وآله) على كثير ممّن خلق الله تفضيلاً ، فكذّبتمونا وكفّرتمونا ، ورأيتم قتالنا حلالاً ، وأموالنا نهباً ، كأنّا أولاد ترك أو كابل ، كما قتلتم جدّنا بالأمس ، وسيوفكم تقطر من دمائنا أهل البيت لحقد متقدّم ، قرّت لذلك عيونكم ، وفرحت قلوبكم افتراءً على الله ومكراً مكرتم، والله خير الماكرين ، فلا تدعونّكم أنفسكم إلى الجذل بما أصبتم من دمائنا ، ونالت أيديكم من أموالنا ، فإنّ ما أصابنا من المصائب الجليلة ، والرزايا العظيمة في كتاب من قبل أن نبرأها ، إنّ ذلك على الله يسير ؛ لكيلا تأسوا على

---

about 30 A.H./651 A.D. Hence, she must have been almost thirty years old during the Battle of at-Taff. She died seven years before her sister Sukayna. On p. 35, Vol. 4, of Ibn al-Atheer's book *At-Tarikh al-Kāmil*, and also according to p. 267, Vol. 6, of at-Tabari's *Tarikh*, Fatima was older than her sister Sukayna. On p. 18 of *Tahqiq an-Nusra ila Maalim Dar al-Hijra* by Abū Bakr ibn Hussain ibn Omer al-Maraghi (d. 816 A.H./1414 A.D.), one of the signs of her lofty status with Allah is that when al-Walid ibn Abdul-Malik ordered to deposit the relics at the mosque, Fatima daughter of al-Hussain (ع) went out to al-Harra where she had a house built for her. Then she ordered a well to be dug up; a stone appeared in it, and she was informed of it. She made her ablution then sprinkled the leftover water on it. After that, it was not difficult at all to dig that well. People used to seek blessings through the use of its water, and they named it "Zamzam". On p. 474, Vol. 8, of Ibn Sa'd's *Tabaqat* (Sadir's edition), Fatima daughter of al-Hussain (ع) used to use knots on a string as her rosary beads.

ما فاتكم ولا تفرحوا بما آتاكم ، والله لا يحبّ كلّ مختال فخور .

تبّاً لكم فانظروا اللعنة والعذاب ، فكأنّ قد حلّ بكم وتواترت من السّماء نقمات ، فيسحتكم بعذاب ويذيق بعضكم بأس بعض ، ثمّ تخلدون في العذاب الأليم يوم القيامة ؛ بما ظلمتمونا ، ألا لعنة الله على الظالمين .

ويلكم ! أتدرون أيّة يد طاعنتنا منكم ؟ وأيّة نفس نزعت إلى قتالنا ؟ أم بأيّة رِجل مشيتم إلينا ؟ تبغون محاربتنا ، قست قلوبكم وغلظت أكبادكم وطبع الله على أفئدتكم ، وختم على سمعكم وبصركم وسوّل لكم الشيطان وأملى لكم ، وجعل على بصركم غشاوة فأنتم لا تهتدون .

تبّاً لكم يا أهل الكوفة ، أيّ ترات لرسول الله قِبلَكم ، وذحول له لديكم ؟ بما عندتم بأخيه علي بن أبي الطالب جدّي وبنيه وعترته الطيّبين الأخيار ، وافتخر بذلك مفتخركم:

نحــن قتلنـــا عليـــاً وبنـــي علــي	بـــــسيوف هنديّـــــة ورمـــــاح
وسبينا نساءهم سبي تـــرك	و نطحناهم فــــأيّ نطـــــاح

بفيكِ أيها القائل الكثكث والأثلب؛ افتخرت بقتل قوم زكّاهم الله وطهّرهم وأذهب عنهم الرجس، فأكضم وأقع كما أقعى أبوك فإنّما لكلّ امرىء ما اكتسبَ وما قدّمت يداه .

حسدتمونا، ويلاً لكم، على ما فضّلنا الله تعالى ، ذلك فضل الله يؤتيه مَن يشاء والله ذو الفضل العظيم . ومَن لَم يجعل الله له نوراً فما له من نور .

فارتفعت الأصوات بالبكاء والنّحيب وقالوا : حسبكِ يا ابنة الطاهرين فقد حرقت قلوبنا وأنضجت نحورنا وأضرمت أجوافنا ، فسكتت .

"All Praise is due to Allāh, as much as the number of the sands and of the stones, as much as the Arsh weighs up to the ground. I praise Him, believe in Him and rely upon Him. And I testify that there is no Allāh other than Allāh, the One and Only Allāh, there is no partner with Him, and that Muhammed is His servant and Messenger, and that his offspring have been slaughtered by the Euphrates river neither on account of blood revenge nor out of dispute over inheritance. Lord! I seek refuge with You against telling a lie about You and against saying anything contrary to what You have revealed of taking many a covenant regarding the vice-regency of Ali ibn Abū Talib (ع), the man whose right is confiscated, who was killed without having committed a sin, just as his son was only yesterday killed, at one of the houses of Allāh, the most Exalted One, at the hand of those who give Islam nothing but lip service. Destruction may afflict their heads that did not ward off from him any injustice as long as he lived nor at his death, till Allāh Almighty took his soul to Him while his essence was praised, his dealing with others was commendable, his merits were well known, and his beliefs well admitted by everyone. Never did he ever accept anyone's blame nor the criticism of any critic in doing what is right. Lord! You guided him to Islam even when he was a child and praised his virtues when he grew up. Never did he ever cease enjoining others to follow Your Path and that of Your Messenger (ﻉ). He always paid no heed to the riches of this world. He always desired the hereafter, a man who carried out jihad for Your Cause. With him were You pleased, so You chose him and guided him to a Straight Path. O people of Kūfa! O people of treachery, of betrayal and conceit! We are members of a Household tried on your account by Allāh, afflicted by you. He made our dealing with you good, and He entrusted His knowledge to us, and He bestowed upon us its comprehension; so, we are the bastion of His knowledge, understanding and wisdom, and His Arguments on the earth which He created for the good of His servants! Allāh bestowed upon us His blessings and greatly honored us with His Prophet, peace and blessings of Allāh be upon him and his Progeny, favoring us over many of those whom He created. Yet you called us liars and apostates, and in your eyes you deemed killing us as lawful, and so is looting our possessions, as if we were the offspring of the Turks or of Kabul, just as you killed our grandfather in the past. Your swords drip with our blood, the blood of Ahl al-Bayt, out of past animosity. Thus have your eyes been cooled, and thus have your hearts been elated, telling lies about Allāh and out of evil plans which you hatched, while Allāh is the very best of planners. So do not be carried away with your excitement because of our blood which you have spilled or our wealth which you have snatched, for what has befallen us is truly a great tragedy and a momentous calamity "In a Book even before We created them; surely this is easy for Allāh, so that you may not be grieved because of what you missed nor feel happy because of what you acquired, and Allāh does not love anyone who is conceited, boastful" (57:23). May you be ruined!

Expect to be cursed and to be tormented, for it seems as though it has already befallen you, and more and more signs of Wrath are on their way to you from the heavens till He makes you taste of the chastisement and make some of you taste of the might of others, then on the Day of Judgment shall you all remain for eternity in the painful torment on account of the injustice with which you have treated us; the curse of Allāh be upon the oppressors. Woe unto you! Do you know what hand you have stabbed, what soul found fighting us agreeable? Rather, by what feet did you walk towards us with the intention to fight us? Your hearts became hardened, and Allāh sealed your hearts, your hearing, and your vision, and Satan inspired to you and dictated, placing a veil over your eyes, so you can never be guided. Destruction is your lot, O people of Kūfa! What a legacy of the Prophet (ﷺ) is standing before you, and what blood revenge will he seek from you on account of your enmity towards his brother Ali ibn Abū Talib (ع), my grandfather, and towards his good and righteous offspring, yet you even brag about it saying,

We killed Ali and Ali's sons,
With Indian swords and spears
And we placed their women in captivity
Like the Turks! We crushed them with severity.

May stones and pebbles fill your mouths! You brag about killing people whom Allāh chose and whom He purified with a perfect purification and from whom He kept away all abomination. Suppress it, then, and squat just as your fathers did, for each will get the rewards of what he earns and will be punished for what he committed. You envied us, woe unto you, for what Allāh, the most Exalted One, favored and preferred us. Such is Allāh's favor: He bestows His favors upon whomsoever He pleases, and surely with Allāh are great favors. For whoever Allāh does not make a *noor*, he shall have no light at all."

Voices were raised with weeping and wailing, and they said to her, "Enough, enough, O daughter of the pure ones, for you have burnt our hearts and necks," so she took to silence.

148

AS-SAJJĀD DELIVERS A SPEECH

Ali ibn al-Hussain (ع) was brought on a lean camel. Chains were placed on his neck, and he was handcuffed. Both sides of his neck were bleeding. He was repeating these verses:

O nation of evil, may your quarter never tastes of water!
O nation that never honored in our regard our Grandfather!
Should we and the Messenger of Allāh meet
On the Judgment Day, how would you then plead?
On bare beasts of burden have you
Transported us, as if we never put up a creed for you!

He signaled to people to be silent. Once they were silent, he praised Allāh and glorified Him and saluted the Prophet (ص). Then he said,

أيّها النّاس ، مَن عرفني فقد عرفني ، ومَن لم يعرفني فأنا علي بن الحسين بن علي بن أبي طالب ، أنا ابن من انتُهكت حرمته ، وسُلبت نعمته وانتهب ماله ، وسُبي عياله ، أنا ابن المذبوح بشطّ الفرات من غير ذحل ولا ترات ، أنا ابن من قُتِل صبراً ، وكفى بذلك فخراً .

أيّها النّاس ناشدتكم الله هل تعلمون أنّكم كتبتم إلى أبي وخدعتموه وأعطيتموه من أنفسكم العهود والميثاق والبيعة ، وقاتلتموه ؟

فتبّاً لكم لِما قدّمتم لأنفسكم ، وسوأة لرأيكم ، بأيّة عين تنظرون إلى رسول الله ؟ إذ يقول لكم : قتلتم عترتي ، وانتهكتم حرمتي ، فلستم من أمّتي.

فارتفعت الأصوات بالبكاء وقالوا : هلكتم وما تعلمون .

ثمّ قال عليه السّلام : (رحم الله امرءاً قبِل نصيحتي ، وحفظ وصيّتي في الله وفي رسوله وأهل بيته ، فإنّ لنا في رسول الله أسوة حسنة.)

فقالوا بأجمعهم : نحن يابن رسول الله سامعون مطيعون حافظون لذمامك ، غير زاهدين فيك ، ولا راغبين عنك ، فمرنا بأمرك يرحمك الله ، فإنّا حرب لحربك ، وسِلم لسلمك ، نبرأ ممّن ظلمك وظلمنا .

فقال عليه السّلام: هيهات هيهات، أيّها الغدرة المكرة ، حِيل بينكم وبين شهوات أنفسكم ، تريدون أن تأتوا إليَّ كما أتيتم إلى أبي من قبل ؟ كلاّ وربّ الراقصات ، فإنّ الجرح لمّا يندمل ، قُتِل أبي بالأمس وأهل بيته ، ولم ينس ثكل رسول الله وثكل أبي وبني أبي ، إنّ وجده والله لبين لهاتي ومرارته بين حناجري وحلقي ، وغصّته تجري في فراش صدري:

فـبعين جـبّار الــسّما لــم يكـتـم	مـهلاً بـني حـرب فمـا قـد نالنـا
بالرسـل يقـدم حاسـرا عـن معصـمِ	فـكأنّني يـوم الحسـاب بأحمـد
وتـركتم الأسـياف تنطـف مـن دمـي	و يــقول ويلكـم هتكـتم حرمتـي

149

تــدرون أيّ دم أرقــتم فــي الثــرى أمْ أيّ خـــــود ســـــقْتُمْ فــي المغـــنم

أمـــن الـــعدالة صـــونكم فتيـــاتكم وحـــــرائري تسـبى كسـبي الـــديلم؟

والـــماء تـــورده يـــعافير الفـــلا و كـــبود أطـــفالي ظمــاء تضـــرم؟

تـــالله لـــو ظفـرت سـراة الكفـر فـي رهطـــي لمـــا ارتكبـــوا لـــذاك المعظـم

يـــا لــيت شــعر محمّـد مـا فـاتكم طـــعن الحنــاجر بعـد حــزّ الغلصــم

O people! Whoever recognizes me knows me, and whoever does
not, let me tell him that I am Ali son of al-Hussain (ع) ibn Ali ibn
Abū Talib (ع). I am the son of the man whose sanctity has been
violated, whose wealth has been plundered, whose children have
been seized. I am the son of the one who has been slaughtered by the
Euphrates neither out of blood revenge nor on account of an
inheritance. I am the son of the one killed in the worst manner. This
suffices me to be proud. O people! I plead to you in the Name of
Allāh: Do you not know that you wrote my father then deceived
him? Did you not grant him your covenant, your promise, and your
allegiance, then you fought him? May you be ruined for what you
have committed against your own souls, and out of your corrupt
views! Through what eyes will you look at the Messenger of Allāh
(ع) when he says to you, "You killed my Progeny, violated my
sanctity, so you do not belong to my nation"?

Loud cries rose, and they said to each other, "You have perished, yet
you are not aware of it." Then he, peace be with him, said, "May
Allāh have mercy on anyone who acts upon my advice, who
safeguards my legacy with regard to Allāh, His Messenger (ع), and
his Ahl al-Bayt (ع), for we have in the Messenger of Allāh (ع) a
good example of conduct to emulate." They all said, "We, O son of
the Messenger of Allāh, hear and we obey, and we shall safeguard
your trust. We shall not turn away from you, nor shall we disobey
you; so, order us, may Allāh have mercy on you, for we shall fight
when you fight, and we shall seek asylum when you do so; we
dissociate ourselves from whoever oppressed you and dealt unjustly

with you." He, peace be with him, said, "Far, far away it is from you to do so, O people of treachery and conniving! You are separated from what you desire. Do you want to come to me as you did to my father saying, No, by the Lord of all those [angels] that ascend and descend'?! The wound is yet to heal. My father was killed only yesterday, and so were his Ahl al-Bayt (ع), and the loss inflicted upon the Messenger of Allāh (ع), upon my father (ع), and upon my family is yet to be forgotten. Its pain, by Allāh, is between both of these [sides] and its bitterness is between my throat and palate. Its choke is resting in my very chest."[1]

THE BURIAL

Historians record saying that the Master of Martyrs (ع) set up a tent on the battlefield[2], ordering those killed from among his companions and Ahl al-Bayt (ع) to be carried to it. Whenever a fresh martyr was brought, he, peace be with him, would say, "You have been killed just as the prophets and the families of prophets are killed."[3] He did so to everyone with the exception of his brother al-Abbas, peace be with him, whom he left where he fell near the river bank of the Euphrates.

When Omer ibn Sa'd accompanied those whom he arrested of the custodians of the Message and left for Kūfa, he left behind those who were described by the Commander of the Faithful (ع) as the masters of martyrs in the life of this world and in the hereafter, an honor to which nobody ever preceded nor will anyone succeed them[4], lying on the sands incinerated by the sun and sought by the wild beasts of the desert.

---

[1] All these speeches are mentioned by Ibn Tawoos in his book *Al-Luhuf* and by Ibn Nama in his book *Muthir al-Ahzan*.

[2] at-Tabari, *Tarikh*, Vol. 6, p. 256. Ibn al-Atheer, *At-Tarikh al-Kāmil*, Vol. 4, p. 30. Al-Mufid, *Al-Irshad*.

[3] This is narrated on p. 211, Vol. 10, and p. 125, Vol. 13, of al-Majlisi's *Bihār al-Anwār* where an-Nu'mani's book *Al-Ghaiba* is cited.

[4] al-Qummi, *Kāmil az-Ziyarat*, p. 219.

Among them was the Master of the Youths of Paradise who was in a condition that would split the hardest of the stones, yet divine lights were emanating from his corpse, and sweet scents were surrounding him from all directions.

A man belonging to Banu Asad has narrated the following:

Once the army left, I came to the battlefield and saw light emanating from those corpses that were covered with blood and smelled sweet scents. I saw a terrifying lion walking between the amputated parts till he reached the embodiment of sanctity and the sacrifice of guidance. He rubbed himself on his blood and rubbed his body on his as he kept muttering and letting out a very strange sound. I was amazed. Never have I ever seen such a fierce lion abandon what would be for his likes nothing but a meal. I hid among the marshes and kept watching to see what else he would do. I was more amazed when midnight came. It was then that I saw candles with voices that filled the earth with painful cries and wailing.[1]

On the 13th day of Muharram, Zain al-Ābidīn (ع) came to bury his martyred father, peace be with him, since only an Imām buries another Imām.[2]

When as-Sajjād (ع) came to the place, he saw Banu Asad assembled around the slain not knowing what to do. They could not identify the corpses especially since their killers had separated the heads from the bodies. Had it been otherwise, they could have inquired about them with the families and the tribes of those slain. But he, peace be with him, informed them that it was his task to bury those pure bodies. He informed them of the names of the slain, identifying those who belonged to Banu Hashim from the rest. Crying and wailing rose, and tears filled the eyes of everyone present there and then. The ladies of Banu Asad loosened their hair in grief and beat

---

[1] al-Bahrani, *Madeenat al-Ma'ajiz*, p. 263, chapter 127.

[2] al-Mas'udi, *Ithbat al-Wasiyya*, p. 173.

their cheeks.

Imām Zain al-Ābidīn (ع) walked to his father's body, hugged it and wept loudly. Then he came to the grave-site and lifted a handful of its soil. A grave already dug appeared, and so did a pre-constructed shrine... He placed his hands under the Imām's back and said, "In the Name of Allāh, and according to the creed of the Messenger of Allāh. Allāh has said the truth, and so has His Messenger (ع). The will of Allāh be done; there is neither power nor might except in Allāh, the Great." Then he took it and went down without being assisted by anyone from among the Banu Asad to whom he said, "I have with me someone who will assist me." Once he laid it down in the grave, he put his cheek on his father's sacred neck and said, "Congratulations to the land that contains your pure body, for the world after you is dark whereas the hereafter in your light shall shine. As to the night, it is the harbinger of sleep, while grief remains forever, for Allāh shall choose for your Ahl al-Bayt (ع) your abode wherein you shall abide. From me to you is Salam, O son of the Messenger of Allāh, and the mercy of Allāh and His blessings."

On the grave he wrote: "This is the grave of al-Hussain son of Ali son of Abū Talib, the one whom they killed even as he was a thirsty stranger." Then he walked to the body of his uncle al-Abbas, peace be with him, and he saw him in a condition that had left the angels in the heavens' strata baffled and caused the *huris* to weep even as they were in the chambers of Paradise. He fell upon it kissing his sacred neck and saying, "May the world after you be obliterated, O moon of Banu Hashim, and peace from me to you, O martyr, and the mercy of Allāh and His blessings."

He dug a grave for him and took him down in it by himself just as he had done to the corpse of his martyred father (ع). He said to Banu Asad, "There is someone with me to help me."

Yes, he gave a piece of jewelry to Banu Asad as a token of appreciation for consoling him in burying the martyrs, and he assigned for them two places, ordering them to dig two pits in the first of which he buried those slain from Banu Hashim and in the second those slain from among the companions[1].

As regarding al-Hurr ar-Riyahi, his corpse was taken away by his tribe that buried it where it now stands. It is said that his mother was present then and there, and when she saw what was being done to the corpses, she carried her son's corpse somewhere else.[2]

The closest in proximity to the grave of al-Hussain (ع) from among the martyrs is his son Ali al-Akbar, peace be with him. In this regard, Imām as-Sādiq (ع) says to Hammad al-Basri, "The father of Abdullāh was killed a stranger away from home; he is mourned be whoever visits his grave-site, and whoever does not visit it grieves for him; whoever doe not see him is very depressed on account of being deprived of doing so, so he grieves; whoever sees the grave of his son at his feet in a desolate land, far away from his kinsfolk, invokes Allāh's mercy for him because of the fact that he was not supported when he called upon people to uphold righteousness, and because the renegades assisted one another against him till they

---

[1]See *Al-Kibrit al-Ahmar fi Shara'it Ahl al-Minbar* الكبريت الأحمر في شريعة أهل المنبر by the narrator Shaikh Muhammed Baqir son of Mawla Hassan al-Qa'ini al-Birjandi as-Safi, *Asrar ash-Shahada* by Sayyid Kadhim ibn Qasim ar-Rashti al-Ha'iri (died in 1259 A.H./1843 A.D.), and *Al-Iyqad*.

[2]Al-Hajj Shaikh Muhammed Baqir al-Birjandi as-Safi, *Al-Kibrit al-Ahmar fi Shara'it Ahl al-Minbar*. On p. 344 of his book *Al-Anwar an-Nu'maniyya*, Sayyid al-Jaza'iri cites testimonials to this statement. He, for example, details how [sultan] Isma'eel as-Safawi [founder of the Safavid dynasty; he lived from 904 - 930 A.H./1499 - 1524 A.D. and ruled Iran from 907 - 930 A.H./1502 - 1524 A.D.] dug up the place, whereupon he saw the deceased as though he had just been killed; there was a bandage on his head. Once he untied it in person, blood started pouring out, and the bleeding did not stop till he tied it back again. He built a dome above the grave and assigned an attendant for it. So, when an-Nawari, in his book *Al-Lulu wal Marjan*, denies that he had been buried, he did not support his denial with any evidence at all. On p. 37, Vol. 1, of *Tuhfat al-Alim*, Sayyid Ja'far Bahr al-Ulum states that Hamid-Allah al-Mustawfi has indicated in his book *Nuzhat al-Quloob* saying that there is in Kerbala' the grave of al-Hurr [ar-Riyahi] which is visited by people. He is al-Hurr's grandson up to 18 generations back.

154

killed him and did not have any respect for him, so much so that they exposed his corpse to the wild beasts and prohibited him from drinking of the water of the Euphrates of which the dogs drink. They disregarded their obligations in his respect towards the Messenger of Allāh (ع) who had enjoined them to be kind to him and to his Ahl al-Bayt (ع). He became abandoned in his grave, slain among his kinsfolk and Shī'as. In loneliness, being near his grave removes the pain of loneliness and so is his being distant from his grandfather (ع) and from the house which none could enter except those whose conviction of heart Allāh tested, and by those who recognize our rights. My father has told me that since he was killed, his place has never been empty of those who bless him from among the angels, the *jinns*, mankind, and even the wild beasts. Whoever visits it is envied and is rubbed for blessing, and looking at his grave is done in anticipation of earning goodness. Allāh boasts to the angels of those who visit it. As far as what such pilgrim receives from us, we invoke Allāh's mercy for him every morning and every evening. It has come to my knowledge that some Kūfians as well as others in Kūfa's outskirts pay it a visit in the eve of the middle of Shaban. They recite the Holy Qur'an; they narrate his story; they mourn him, and women eulogize him while others compose their own eulogies." Hammad said to the Imām (ع), "I have personally witnessed some of what you have described." The Imām, peace be with him, then said, "Praise to Allāh Who has made some people come to us, praise us, and mourn us, and praised is He for making our enemy shame them for doing so, threaten them, and describe what they do as ugly."[1]

AT THE GOVERNOR'S MANSION
Having returned from his camp at Nakheela, Ubaydullāh Ibn Ziyad went straight to his mansion[2]. The sacred head was brought to him,

---

[1]al-Qummi, *Kāmil az-Ziyar az-Ziyarat*, p. 325.at-Tibrisi, *Mazar al-Bihar*, p. 124, citing the previous reference.

[2]According to p. 142, Chapter 9, of at-Thaalibi's book *Lataif al-Maarif*, Abdul-Malik ibn Ameer al-Lakhmi has narrated saying, "I saw the head of al-Hussain (ع) ibn Ali ibn Abū Talib (ع) at the government mansion of Ubaydullah ibn Ziyad placed on a shield, and I saw the head of al-Mukhtar with Mis'ab ibn az-Zubair on another shield. I saw the head of Mis'ab in

and it was then that the walls started bleeding[1] and a fire broke out from one part of the mansion and made its way to the place where Ibn Ziyad was sitting[2]. He fled away from it and entered one of the mansion's rooms. The head spoke out in a loud voice that was heard by Ibn Ziyad as well as by those who were present there and then. It said, "Where do you flee to? If fire does not catch you in the life of this world, it shall be your abode in the hereafter." The head did not stop speaking till the fire was out. Everyone at the mansion was stunned; nothing like this had ever taken place before[3]. Yet Ibn Ziyad was not admonished by an incident such as that, so he ordered the captives to be brought to him. The ladies of the Messenger of Allāh (ﷺ) were brought to him, and they were in the most pathetic condition[4].

Al-Hussain's head was placed in front of him, so he kept hitting its mouth with a rod which he had in his hand for some time. Zaid ibn Arqam said, "Stop hitting these lips with your rod, for by Allāh, the One and Only Allāh, I saw the lips of the Messenger of Allāh (ﷺ) kissing them," then he broke into tears. Ibn Ziyad said to him, "May

---

front of Abdul-Malik ibn Marwan on yet another shield! When I told Abdul-Malik [ibn Marwan ibn al-Hakam] about that, he regarded it as a bad omen and left the place." The same is narrated by as-Sayyati on p. 139 of his book *Tarikh al-Khulafa'*, and by Sibt ibn al-Jawzi on p. 148 of his book *Tathkirat al-Khawass* (Iranian edition) by Ibn al-Jawzi, the grandson..

[1]Ibn Asakir, *Tarikh*, Vol. 4, p. 329. Ibn Hajar al-Asqalani, *As-Sawa'iq al-Muhriqa*, p. 116. *Thakha'ir al-Uqba*, p. 145. Ibn Tawoos, *Al-Malahim*, p. 128 (first edition).

[2]Ibn al-Atheer, *At-Tarikh al-Kāmil*, Vol. 4, p. 103. Ibn Hajar al-Asqalani, *Mujma az-Zawa'id*, Vol. 9, p. 196. Al-Khawarizmi, *Maqtal al-Hussain (ﷺ)*, Vol. 2, p. 87. At-Turayhi, *Al-Muntakhab*, p. 339 (Hayderi Press edition). Ibn Katheer, *Al-Bidaya*, Vol. 8, p. 286.

[3]*Sharh Qaseedat Abi Firas*, p. 149.

[4]Abul-Abbas Ahmed ibn Yusuf al-Qarmani, *Akhbar al-Duwal*, Vol. 1, p. 8.

Allāh cause you never to cease crying! By Allāh, had you not been an old man who lost his wits, I would have killed you." Zaid went out of the meeting place saying, "A slave is now a monarch ruling them, treating them as his property. O Arabs! Henceforth, you are the slaves! You have killed Fātima's son and granted authority to the son of Marjana who kills the best among you and permits the evil ones among you to be worshipped. You have accepted humiliation, so away with whoever accepts humiliation."[1]

Zainab daughter of the Commander of the Faithful (ع) kept a distance from the women as she remained disguised, but she could not disguise the prestige of being brought up in the lap of prophethood and in the glory of Imāmate, so she attracted Ibn Ziyad's attention. He inquired about her. He was told that she was Zainab, the wise lady, daughter of the Commander of the Faithful (ع). He wanted to tell her how rejoiced he was at what had happened. Said he, "Praise be to Allāh Who exposed you to shame, Who killed you and proved you liars." She, peace be with her, responded with: "Praise be to Allāh Who honored us by choosing Muhammed [from among us] as His Prophet and purified us with a perfect purification. Rather, only a debauchee is exposed to shame, and a sinner is proven to be a liar, and we are neither."

Ibn Ziyad asked her, "How have you seen what Allāh has done to your Ahl al-Bayt (ع)?" She, peace be with her, said, "I have seen Him treating them most beautifully. These are people to whom Allāh prescribed martyrdom, so they leaped from their beds welcoming it, and Allāh shall gather you and them, and you shall be questioned, and your opponents shall charge you[2]; so, you will then find out

[1]Ibn Hajar al-Asqalani, *As-Sawa'iq al-Muhriqa*, p. 118. At-Tabari, *Tarikh*, Vol. 6, p. 262. Ibn Katheer, *Al-Bidaya wal Nihaya*, Vol. 8, p. 190. Ibn Hajar al-Asqalani, *Mujma az-Zawa'id*, Vol. 9, p. 195. Ibn Asakir, *Tarikh*, Vol. 4, p. 340. These authors have expressed their disbelief of what he has said. The fact that he was blind does not necessarily render his statement inaccurate, for it is quite possible he had heard the same. Ibn Asakir's statement that Zaid was present then and there supports his.

[2]at-Tabari, *Tarikh*, Vol. 6, p. 262.

whose lot shall be the crack of hell, may your mother, O son of Marjana, lose you."[1]

This statement enraged Ibn Ziyad, and her words incinerated him with ire, especially since she said it before such a huge crowd. He, therefore, was about to kill her when Amr ibn Hareeth said to him, "She is only a woman; can she be held accountable for what she said? She cannot be blamed when she thus prattles."

Ibn Ziyad turned to her one more time and said, "Allāh has healed my heart by letting me seek revenge against your tyrant and against the rebels and mutineers from among his Ahl al-Bayt (ع)!" The wise lady calmed herself and said, "By my life! You have killed my middle-aged protector, persecuted my family, cut off my branch and pulled out my roots; so, if all of this heals your heart, then you are indeed healed."[2]

He then turned to Ali ibn al-Hussain (ع) whom he asked what his name was. "I am Ali son of al-Hussain (ع)," came the answer. Ibn Ziyad asked Ali, "Did not Allāh kill Ali (ع)?" As-Sajjād (ع) answered, "I used to have an older brother[3] also named Ali whom

---

[1]Ibn Tawoos *Al-Luhuf*, p. 90.

[2]Ibn al-Atheer, *At-Tarikh al-Kāmil*, Vol. 4, p. 33. Al-Khawarizmi, *Maqtal al-Hussain (ع)*, Vol. 2, p. 42. At-Tabari, *Tarikh*, Vol. 6, p. 263. Al-Mufid, *Al-Irshad*. At-Tibrisi, *I'lam al-Wara bi A'lam al-Huda*, p. 141. According to p. 145, Vol. 3, of *Kāmil al-Mibrad* (1347 A.H./1735 A.D. edition), Zainab daughter of Ali ibn Abū Talib (ع), the eldest of those taken captive to Ibn Ziyad, was quite eloquent, driving her argument against the latter home. Ibn Ziyad, therefore, said to her, "If you achieved your objective behind your oratory, your father was an orator and a poet." She said to him, "What would women do with poetry?" Ibn Ziyad, in fact, used to stutter, and he had a lisp; his speech had a heavy Persian accent.

[3]Such is the statement of Muhammed ibn Jarir at-Tabari in his book *Al-Muntakhab* in a footnote on p. 89, Vol. 12, of his *Tarikh*. So does Abul Faraj al-Isfahani on p. 49 of the Iranian edition of his book *Maqatil at-Talibiyeen*, and al-Dimyari in his book *Hayat al-Hayawan*, as well as at-Turayhi's book *Al-Muntakhab*, p. 238 (Hayderi Press edition). It is also

people killed." Ibn Ziyad responded by repeating his statement that it was Allāh who had killed him. As-Sajjād, therefore, said, "Allāh takes the souls away at the time of their death; none dies except with Allāh's permission." Ibn Ziyad did not appreciate him thus responding to his statement rather than remaining silent, so he ordered him to be killed, but his aunt, the wise lady Zainab, put her arms around him and said, "O Ibn Ziyad! Suffices you what you have shed of our blood..., have you really spared anyone other than this?[1] If you want to kill him, kill me with him as well." As-Sajjād (ع) said [to Ibn Ziyad], "Do you not know that we are used to being killed, and that martyrdom is one of Allāh's blessings upon us?"[2] Ibn Ziyad looked at both of them then said, "Leave him for her. Amazing is their tie of kinship; she wishes to be killed with him."[3]

Ar-Rubab, wife of Imām al-Hussain (ع), took the head and put it in her lap. She kissed it and composed poetry lines mourning

When it became clear to Ibn Ziyad that there were many people present who were voicing their resentment of what he had committed and how everyone was repeating what Zainab had said, he feared an uprising, so he ordered the police to jail the captives inside a house adjacent to the grand mosque[4]. Ibn Ziyad's doorman has said, "I was with them when he issued his order to jail them. I saw how the men and women assembled there weeping and beating their faces."[5] Zainab shouted at people saying, "Nobody should tend

---

indicated on p. 58 of Mis'ab az-Zubayhi's book *Nasab Quraish*.

[1]at-Tabari, *Tarikh*, Vol. 6, p. 263.

[2]Ibn Tawoos *Al-Luhuf*, p. 91. Al-Khawarizmi, *Maqtal al-Hussain (ع)*, Vol. 2, p. 13.

[3]Ibn al-Atheer, Vol. 4, p. 34.

[4]Ibn Tawoos *Al-Luhuf*, p. 91. Al-Khawarizmi, *Maqtal al-Hussain (ع)*, Vol. 2, p. 43.

[5]Muhammed an-Nishapuri, *Rawdat al-Waizeen*, p. 163.

to us except either a bondmaid, a freed bondmaid, or *umm wuld* أم
ولد[1], for they were taken captive just as we have been."[2] Only a
female captive is familiar with the pain and humiliation of captivity;
therefore, she would be sympathetic and would not rejoice nor enjoy
seeing them in captivity. This is undeniable.

Ibn Ziyad again called them to his presence. When they were
brought to him, their women saw al-Hussain's head in front of him
with its divine rays ascending from its curves to the depth of the
heavens. Ar-Rubab, al-Hussain's wife, could not check herself from
falling upon it and composed more poetry eulogizing him.

Hameed ibn Muslim has said, "Ibn Ziyad ordered to hold a
congregational prayer service. They assembled at the grand mosque.
Ibn Ziyad ascended the pulpit and said, All Praise is due to Allāh
Who manifested the truth and elevated those who act according to it
and Who granted victory to the commander of the faithful Yazid and
to his party, and Who killed the liar and the son of the liar Hussain
son of Ali and his Shī'as.'[3] Nobody among that crowd that had sunk
in misguidance objected to such a preposterous statement except
Abdullāh ibn Afeef al-Azdi and also one of the sons of Walibah al-
Ghamidi who both stood up and said to him, O son of Marjana! The
liar and the son of the liar is you and your father, and so is everyone
who accepts your authority and his son! O son of Marjana! Do you
really kill the offspring of the prophets and still talk about who is
truthful and who is a liar?!'[4] Ibn Ziyad asked who the speaker was.
Ibn Afeef answered by saying, I am the speaker, O enemy of Allāh!
Do you really kill the righteous offspring from whom Allāh removed
all abomination then claim that you are a follower of the Islamic
creed?! Oh! Is there anyone to help?! Where are the sons of the

---

[1]"Freed mother of son" means a bondmaid who bears sons by her master
and who is set free on that account but remains in his custody as his wife.

[2]Ibn Tawoos *Al-Luhuf*, p. 92. al-Bahrani, *Maqtal al-Awalim*, p. 130.

[3]Ibn al-Atheer, Vol. 1, p. 34.

[4]at-Tabari, *Tarikh*, Vol. 6, p. 263.

Muhajirun and the Ansar to seek revenge against your tyrant, the one who and whose father were both cursed by Muhammed (ص), the Messenger of the Lord of the Worlds.' Ibn Ziyad's anger now intensified. He ordered him to be brought to him. The police grabbed him.[1] It was then that Ibn Afeef shouted the slogan (*nakhwa* نخوة) used by the Azdis which was: يا مبرور! '*Ya Mabroor!*' This caused a large number of the Azdis present there to leap to his rescue and to forcibly free him from the police and take him safely home."

Abdul-Rahman ibn Makhnaf al-Azdi said to him, "Woe unto someone else other than you! You have surely condemned yourself and your tribe to destruction!"[2]

Ibn Ziyad ordered Jandab ibn Abdullāh al-Azdi, who was an old man, to be brought to him. He said to him, "O enemy of Allāh! Did you not fight on Abū Turab's side during the Battle of Siffeen?" The old man answered, "Yes, and I love him and am proud of him, while I despise you and your father especially after you have killed the grandson of the Prophet (ص) and his companions and the members of his family without fearing the One and Only Allāh, the Great Avenger." Ibn Ziyad said, "You have less feeling of shame than that blind man, and I seek nearness to Allāh through shedding your blood." Jandab said, "In that case, Allāh shall never bring you closer to Him." Ibn Ziyad, on a second thought, feared the might of the man's Azd tribe, so he left him alone saying, "He is only an old man who has lost his mind and his wits." He released him.[3]

AL-MUKHTAR ATH-THAQAFI
At the same time when Ibn Ziyad ordered the captives to be brought to his meeting place, he also ordered al-Mukhtar son of Abū Ubayd

---

[1]Ibn Tawoos *Al-Luhuf.*

[2]at-Tabari, *Tarikh*, Vol. 6, p. 263.

[3]Ibn Nama, *Muthir al-Ahzan*, p. 51. Al-Khawarizmi, *Maqtal al-Hussain (ع)*, Vol. 2, p. 55.Muhammed Hassan ash-Shaban Kurdi al-Qazwini, *Riyad al-Ahzan*, p. 52.

ath-Thaqafīto be brought to him, too. Al-Mukhtar had been in prison since the assassination of Muslim ibn Aqeel. When al-Mukhtar saw that horrific and most deplorable scene, he sighed loudly and an exchange of harsh words took place between him and Ibn Ziyad wherein the harshest words were al-Mukhtar's. Ibn Ziyad became burning with outrage and ordered him to be sent back to jail[1]. Some say that he whipped him, blinding one of his eyes.[2]

After the execution of Ibn Afeef, al-Mukhtar was released due to the interference of Abdullāh son of Omer ibn al-Khattab who asked Yazid to have him released. Yazid was the husband of al-Mukhtar's sister Safiyya daughter of Abū Ubayd at-Thaqafi. But Ibn Ziyad postponed carrying out Yazid's order for three days. Having ordered the execution of Ibn Afeef, Ibn Ziyad delivered a speech wherein he abused the Commander of the Faithful (ع), causing al-Mukhtar to denounce and to taunt him to his face saying, "You are the liar, O enemy of Allāh and enemy of His Messenger! Rather, Praise to Allāh Who dignified al-Hussain (ع) and his army with Paradise and with forgiveness just as He humiliated Yazid and his army with the fire and with shame." Ibn Ziyad hurled an iron bar at him that fractured his forehead, then he ordered him to be sent back to jail, but people reminded him that Omer ibn Sa'd was the husband of his sister while another brother-in-law was none other than Abdullāh ibn Omer [ibn al-Khattab]. They reminded him of his lofty lineage, so he changed his mind of having him killed, yet he insisted on sending him back to prison. For the second time did Abdullāh ibn Omer write Yazid who in turn wrote Ubaydullāh ibn Ziyad ordering him to release the man[3].

Al-Mukhtar incessantly kept after that informing the Shī'as of the

---

[1]*Riyad al-Ahzan*, p. 52.

[2]Ibn Rustah, *Al-Alaq an-Nafisa*, p. 224.

[3]al-Khawarizmi, *Maqtal al-Hussain (ع)*, Vol. 2, pp. 178-179. The author of *Riyad al-Ahzan*, namely Muhammed Hassan ash-Shaban Kurdi al-Qazwini, briefly narrates it on p. 58.

merits which he knew of the companions of the Commander of the Faithful (ع), of how he rose seeking revenge for al-Hussain (ع), and how he killed Ibn Ziyad and those who fought al-Hussain (ع).[1]

One incident he narrated was the following which he recollected about the time when he was in Ibn Ziyad's jail:

Abdullāh ibn al-Harith ibn Nawfal ibn Abdul-Muttalib and Maytham at-Tammar were two of his cell mates. Abdullāh ibn al-Harith asked for a piece of iron to remove the hair in certain parts of his body saying, "I do not feel secure against Ibn Ziyad killing me, and I do not want him to do so while there is unwanted hair on my body." Al-Mukhtar said to him, "By Allāh he shall not kill you, nor shall he kill me, nor shall you face except very little hardship before you become the governor of Basra!" Maytham heard their dialogue, so he said to al-Mukhtar, "You yourself will rise seeking revenge for al-Hussain's blood, and you shall kill the same man who wants us to be killed, and you shall trample on his cheeks with your very foot."[2] This came to be exactly as these men had said. Abdullāh ibn al-Harith was released from jail after Yazid's death and became the governor of Basra. After only one year, al-Mukhtar rose seeking revenge against the killers of al-Hussain (ع), killing Ibn Ziyad, Harmalah ibn Kahil, Shimr ibn Thul-Jawshan and a large number of the Kūfians who had betrayed al-Hussain (ع). As Ibn Nama al-Hilli tells us, he [and his army] killed eighteen thousand Kūfians, then almost ten thousand[3] of them fled away from him and sought refuge with Mus'ab ibn az-Zubair. Among them was Shabth ibn Rab'i who reached him riding a mule whose ears and tail he had cut off and who was wearing a torn outer garment and shouting, "Help! Lead us to fight this debauchee

---

[1]al-Majlisi, *Bihār al-Anwār*, Vol. 10, p. 284, citing Ibn Nama's book *Akhth at-Thar*.

[2]Ibn Abul-Hadid, *Sharh Nahj al-Balagha*, Vol. 1, p. 210 (Egyptian edition). Al-Majlisi, *Bihār al-Anwār*, Vol. 10, p. 284. Al-Mufid, *Al-Irshad*.

[3]Abū Hanifah al-Dainuri, namely Ahmed ibn Dāwūd (died in 281 A.H./894 A.D.), *Al-Akhbar at-Tiwal*, p. 295.

who demolished our homes and killed our honorable men!"[1]

THE SACRED HEAD SPEAKS

Since his early childhood, the martyred grandson of the Prophet (ص) remained an ally of the Qur'an. Thus were both he and his brother (ع), for they were the legacy of the Messenger of Allāh and his vicegerents. The greatest Prophet (ص) had stated that they and the Holy Qur'an would never part from one another till they would meet him at the Pool of Kawthar. Al-Hussain (ع), therefore, never ceased reciting the Qur'an all his life as he taught and cultivated others, when he was at home or when travelling. Even during his stand in the Battle of Taff, although surrounded by his foes, he used the Qur'an to argue with them and to explain his point of view to them. Thus was the son of the Messenger of Allāh (ع) marching towards his sacred objective energetically, so much so that now his sacred head kept reciting the Qur'an even as it stood atop a spear, perhaps someone among the people would be illuminated with the light of the truth. But this lamp-post of guidance did not see except people whose comprehension was limited, whose hearts were sealed, and whose ears were deafened: "Allāh sealed their hearts and hearing, and over their vision there is a veil" (Qur'an, 2:7).

Zaid ibn Arqam has said, "I was sitting in my room when they passed by, and I heard the head reciting this verse: Or do you think that the fellows of the cave and the inscription were of Our wonderful signs?' (Qur'an, 18:9). My hair stood up, and I said, By Allāh, O son of the Messenger of Allāh! Your head is much more amazing!"[2]

---

[1] at-Tabari, *Tarikh*, Vol. 7, p. 146.

[2] al-Mufid, *Al-Irshad. Al-Khasa'is al-Kubra*, Vol. 2, p. 125. On p. 362, Vol. 1, of *Sharh Nahj al-Balagha*, Ibn Abul-Hadid says, "Zaid ibn Arqam was one of those who deviated from the line of the Commander of the Faithful Ali, peace be with him. He was reluctant to testify that the Commander of the Faithful (ع) was appointed [by the Prophet] to take charge of the nation after him, so he (ع) condemned him with blindness. He, indeed, became blind till his death. According to Ibn al-Atheer, who indicates so on p. 24, Vol. 4, of his book *At-Tarikh al-Kāmil*, Ibn Ziyad ordered the head of al-Hussain (ع) to be paraded throughout Kufa. The

164

When the severed head was placed at the money changers' section of the bazaar, there was a great deal of commotion and noise of the dealers and customers. The Master of Martyrs (ع) wanted to attract the attention to him so that people would listen to his terse admonishment, so his severed head hawked quite loudly, thus turning all faces to it. Never did people hear a severed head hawking before the martyrdom of al-Hussain (ع). It then recited Sūrat al-Kahf from its beginning till it reached the verse saying, "They were youths who believed in their Lord, and We increased their guidance" (Qur'an, 18:13), "... and do not (O Lord!) increase the unjust aught but error" (Qur'an, 71:24).

The head was hung on a tree. People assembled around it looking at the dazzling light that emanated from it as it recited the verse saying, "And those who oppressed shall come to know what an end they shall meet" (Qur'an, 26:227)[1].

Hilal ibn Mu'awiyah has said, "I saw a man carrying the head of al-Hussain (ع) as it [the head] was saying, You separated between my head and my body, so may Allāh separate between your flesh and bones, and may He make you a Sign for those who stray from the Straight Path.' He, therefore, raised his whip and kept whipping the head till it ceased."[2]

Salamah ibn Kaheel heard the head reciting the following verse from the top of the spear where it had been placed: "Allāh shall suffice you for them, and He is the Hearing, the Knowing" (Qur'an, 2:137)[3].

Ibn Wakeedah says that he heard the head reciting Sūrat al-Kahf, so

---

same is stated by Ibn Katheer on p. 191, Vol. 8, of his book *Al-Bidaya*, and also by al-Maqrizi on p. 288, Vol. 2, of his *Khutat*.

[1]Ibn Shahr Ashub, Vol. 2, p. 188.

[2]*Sharh Qasidat Abi Firas*, p. 148.

[3]*Asrar ash-Shahada*, p. 488.

he was doubtful whether it was, indeed, the voice of the Imām (ع), whereupon he, peace be with him, stopped his recitation and turned to the man to say, "O son of Wakeedah! Do you not know that we, the Imāms, are living with our Lord receiving our sustenance?" He, therefore, decided to steal and bury the head. It was then that the glorious head spoke again to him saying, "O son of Wakeedah! There is no way to do that. Their shedding my blood is greater with Allāh than placing me on a spear; so, leave them alone, for they shall come to know when the collars are placed around their necks and when they are dragged with chains."[1] Al-Minhal ibn Amr has said, "I saw al-Hussain's head in Damascus atop a spear and in front of it stood a man; the head was reciting Sūrat al-Kahf. When the recitation came to the verse saying, Or do you think that the fellows of the cave and the inscription were of Our wonderful signs?' (Qur'an, 18:9) , the head spoke in an articulate tongue saying, More wonderous than the fellows of the cave is killing me and thus transporting me.'"[2]

When Yazid ordered the killing of a messenger sent by the then Roman [Byzantine] emperor who resented what Yazid had committed, the head loudly articulated these words: La hawla wala quwwata illa billah! (There is no power nor might except in Allāh)."[3]

AL-ASHDAQ
Ibn Jarar at-Tabari, the renown historian, narrates the following:

"Ibn Ziyad wanted to send Abdul-Malik ibn al-Harith as-Salami to Medīna in order to inform Amr ibn Sa'd al-Ashdaq[4] of the killing of

---

[1]*Sharh Qasidat Abi Firas*, p. 148.

[2]as-Sayyati, *Al-Khasa'is*, Vol. 2, p. 127.

[3]al-Bahrani, *Maqtal al-Awalim*, p. 151.

[4]According to p. 240, Vol. 5, of Nar ad-Din Abul-Hassan, namely Ibn Hajar al-Haythami's book *Mujma az-Zawa'id wa Manba al-Fawa'id*, and also according to p. 141 of *As-Sawa'iq al-Muhriqa*, Abū Hurayra is quoted as saying, "I have heard the Messenger of Allah, peace of Allah be upon

al-Hussain (ع), but he sought to be excused of such an undertaking, claiming to be sick. Al-Ashdaq refused to accept his excuse. Ibn Ziyad is described as very heavy-handed, nobody can tolerate his ire. He ordered the man to rush and to buy another she-camel if the one he was riding was not fast enough, and not to let anyone reach the destination before him. He, therefore, rushed to Medīna. A man from Quraish met him and asked him why he seemed to be in such a hurry. The answer rests with the governor,' was his answer. When Ibn Sa'd was informed of al-Hussain (ع) having been killed, he was very happily excited and was subdued with elation. He ordered a caller to announce it in the city's alleys, and before long, the cries and the wailings coming from the Hashemite ladies mourning the Master of the Youths of Paradise (ع) were heard like never before. These cries reached all the way to the house of al-Ashdaq who laughed and quoted a verse of poetry composed by Amr ibn Ma'di-Karb. He maliciously added saying, "A wailing noise like the one we raised when Othman was killed."[1] Then he turned to the grave of the Messenger of Allāh (ع) and again maliciously said, "Now we have gotten even with you, Messenger of Allāh, for what you did to us during the Battle of Badr." A number of men from the Ansar rebuked him with shame for having made such a statement.[2]

He ascended the pulpit and said, "O people! It is a blow for a blow, and a crushing for a crushing! A sermon followed another! This is sound wisdom, so no nathr can do any good. He condemned us as we praised him, cut off his ties with us though we did not, just as it was his habit, and just as it was ours, but what else can we do to a man who drew his sword with the intention to kill us other than to put an end to the danger to which he exposed us?"

---

him and his progeny, saying, One of the tyrants of Banu Umayyah shall have a nosebleed on my pulpit, and his blood will flow thereupon.'" Amr ibn Sa'd did, indeed, have a nosebleed as he was on the pulpit of the Messenger of Allah (ع), staining it with his blood.

[1]at-Tabari, *Tarikh*, Vol. 6, p. 368.

[2]Shaikh Abbas al-Qummi, *Nafas al-Mahmum*, p. 222. Ibn Abul-Hadid, *Sharh Nahjul Balagha*, Vol. 1, p. 361.

Abdullāh ibn as-Sa'ib stood up and said to him, "Had Fātima (ع) been alive, and had she seen al-Hussain's [severed] head, she would have wept for him." Amr ibn Sa'd rebuked him and said, "We are more worthy of Fātima than you: Her father was our uncle, her husband was our brother, his mother was our daughter. And had Fātima been alive, she would have cried but would not have blamed those who killed him in self-defense."[1]

Amr was very crude and uncouth, a man of legendary cruelty. He ordered Amr ibn az-Zubair ibn al-Awwam[2], head of the police force, after al-Hussain (ع) had been killed, to demolish all the houses of Banu Hashim [the Prophet's clansmen]. He did, oppressing them beyond limits... He also demolished the home of Ibn Mutee and beat people with cruelty. They fled from him and went to join Abdullāh ibn az-Zubair[3]. The reason why he was called "al-Ashdaq" [one whose jaws are twisted to the right or to the left] is due to the fact that his jaws were twisted after having gone to extremes in taunting Imām Ali ibn Abū Talib (ع)[4]. Allāh, therefore, punished him [in this life before the hereafter] in the worst manner. He was carried to Abdul-Malik ibn Marwan chained; after he profusely remonstrated with the latter, he was ordered to be killed[5].

---

[1] al-Bahrani, *Maqtal al-Awalim*, p. 131.

[2] According to p. 23, Vol. 4, of al-Balathiri's book *Ansab al-Ashraf*, the mother of Amr ibn az-Zubair was Ama daughter of Khalid ibn Sa'd ibn al-as. Her father was in command of an army which Amr ibn Sa'd al-Ashdaq dispatched to Mecca to fight Abdullāh ibn az-Zubair. Abdullāh's army captured Amr ibn az-Zubair, so Abdullāh ordered everyone who had suffered an injustice at his hand to whip him. The whipping led to his death.

[3] Abul-Faraj al-Isfahani, *Al-Aghani*, Vol. 4, p. 155.

[4] al-Mirzabani, *Mu'jam ash-Shuara'*, p. 231.

[5] Abū Hilal al-'Askari, *Jamharat al-Amthal*, p. 9 (Indian edition).

Escorted by a number of women from her kinsfolk, the daughter of Aqeel ibn Abū Talib went out to visit the grave of the Prophet (ص) where she threw herself on it, burst in tears then turned to the Muhajirun and the Ansar and came forth instantaneously with these verses:

What will you on the Judgment Day
To the Prophet stand and say?
Surely what you will hear will be true:
Those who betrayed his Progeny were you.
Were you present, or were you not there at all
And justice is combined in the Lord of all...?
You handed it over to those who are never fair
So your intercession with Allāh will go nowhere.
Though on the Taff Day absent was he,
Yet all the dead did your very eyes see.
You saw all those who did die,
So to Allāh you shall never come nigh.

All those present wept. There was no such weeping ever before[1]. Her sister Zainab kept mourning al-Hussain (ع) in the most somber manner.

ABDULLĀH IBN JA'FAR

Ibn Jarar at-Tabari has said that when the news of al-Hussain's martyrdom was announced, Abdullāh ibn Ja'far held a mourning majlis, so people came to him to offer their condolences. His slave Abul-Lislas[2] said to him, "This is what we got from al-Hussain (ع)!" He hurled his sandal at him as he said, "O son of the stinking woman! How dare you say something like that about al-Hussain (ع)?! By Allāh! Had I been with him, I would not have liked to part

---

[1]Shaikh at-Tusi, *Al-Amali*, p. 55. On p. 227, Vol. 2, of his book *Al-Manaqib*, Ibn Shahr Ashub says it was Asma' who had composed those verses.

[2]His name as stated on p. 194 of al-Irbili's book *Kashf al-Ghummah* was "Abul-Salasil," the man of the chains.

with him before being killed defending him. By Allāh! What consoles me is that both my sons were martyred in his defense together with my brother as well as my cousin who all stood firmly on his side." Then he turned to those in his presence and said, "Praise to Allāh! It surely is very heavy on my heart to see al-Hussain (ع) get killed, and that I could not defend him with my life, but both my sons have."[1]

THE CAPTIVES TAKEN TO SYRIA

Ibn Ziyad sent a messenger to Yazid to inform him that al-Hussain (ع) and those in his company were killed, that his children were in Kūfa, and that he was waiting for his orders as to what to do with them. In his answer, Yazid ordered him to send them together with the severed heads to him[2].

Ubaydullāh wrote something, tied it to a rock then hurled it inside the prison where the family of Muhammed (ص) was kept. In it he said, "Orders have been received from Yazid to take you to him on such-and-such a day. If you hear the *takbeer*, you should write your wills; otherwise, there is security." The post returned from Syria with the news that al-Hussain's family is being sent to Syria[3].

Ibn Ziyad ordered Zajr ibn Qays and Abū Burda ibn 'Awf al-Azdi as well as Tariq ibn Zabyan to head a band of Kūfians charged with carrying al-Hussain's severed head and of those killed with him to Yazid[4]. Another account says that Mujbir ibn Murrah ibn Khalid ibn

---

[1]at-Tabari, *Tarikh*, Vol. 6, p. 218.

[2]Ibn Tawoos *Al-Luhuf*, pp. 95-97.

[3]at-Tabari, *Tarikh*, Vol. 6, p. 266. On p. 96, at-Tabari states that Abū Bukrah was given one week by Bishr ibn Arta'ah to go to Mu'awiyah. He went back from Syria on the seventh day. On p. 74 of his book *Muthir al-Ahzan*, Ibn Nama says that Amirah was dispatched by Abdullāh ibn Omer to Yazid in order to get him to release al-Mukhtar at-Thaqafi. Yazid wrote a letter in this regard to Ubaydullah ibn Ziyad. Amirah brought him the letter to Kufa, crossing the distance from Syria to Kufa in eleven days.

[4]*Ibid.*, Vol. 6, p. 264. Ibn al-Atheer, Vol. 4, p. 34. *Al-Bidaya*, Vol. 8, p.

Qanab ibn Omer ibn Qays ibn al-Harth ibn Malik ibn Ubaydullāh ibn Khuzaymah ibn Lu'ayy did so[1].

They were trailed by Ali ibn al-Hussain (ع) with his hands tied to his neck in the company of his family[2] in a condition the sight of which would cause anyone's skin to shiver[3].

With them was Shimr ibn Thul-Jawshan, Mujfir ibn Thulabah al-a'idi[4], Shabth ibn Rab'i, Amr ibn al-Hajjas, in addition to other men. They were ordered to mount the heads on spears and to display them wherever they went[5]. They hurried till they caught up with them[6].

Ibn Lahee'ah is quoted as saying that he saw a man clinging to

---

191. Al-Khawarizmi. Al-Mufid, *Al-Irshad*. At-Tibrisi, *I'lam al-Wara bi A'lam al-Huda*, p. 149. Ibn Tawoos, *Al-Luhuf*, p. 97.

[1]Ibn al-Atheer (died in 630 A.H./1232 A.D.), *Al-Isaba fi Tamyeez as-Sahāba*, Vol. 3, p. 489, where Murrah's biography is discussed.

[2]at-Tabari, *Tarikh*, Vol. 6, p. 254. al-Maqrazi, *Khutat*, Vol. 2, p. 288.

[3]al-Qarmani, *Tarikh*, p. 108. Al-Yafii, *Mir'at al-Jinan*, Vol. 1, p. 134. In both references, it is stated that the daughters of Imām al-Hussain (ع) son of Ali ibn Abū Talib (ع) were taken into captivity, and Zain al-Ābidīn (ع) was with them, and that he was sick. They were driven as captives; may Allah be the Killer of those who did it. Only Ibn Taymiyyah differed from all other historians when he stated on p. 288 of his book *Minhaj al-I'tidal* saying that al-Hussain's women were taken to Medīna after he had been killed.

[4]On p. 165 of Ibn Hazm's book *Jamharat Ansab al-Arab*, it is stated that, "Among Banu aidah are: Mujfir ibn Murrah ibn Khalid ibn Aamir ibn Qaban ibn Amr ibn Qays ibn al-Harith ibn Malik ibn Ubayd ibn Khuzaymah ibn Lu'ayy, and he is the one who carried the head of al-Hussain (ع) son of Ali, peace be with both of them, to Syria."

[5]at-Turayhi, *Al-Muntakhab*, p. 339 (second edition).

[6]al-Mufid, *Al-Irshad*.

Ka'ba's curtains seeking refuge with his Lord and saying, "And I cannot see You doing that!" Ibn Lahee'ah took him aside and said to him, "You must be insane! Allāh is most Forgiving, most Merciful. Had your sins been as many as rain drops, He would still forgive you." He said to Ibn Lahee'ah, "Be informed that I was among those who carried al-Hussain's head to Syria. Whenever it was dark, we would put the head down, sit around it and drink wine. During one night, I and my fellows were guarding it when I saw lightning and creatures that surrounded the head. I was terrified and stunned and remained silent. I heard crying and wailing and someone saying, O Muhammed! Allāh ordered me to obey you; so, if you order me, I can cause an earthquake that will swallow these people just as it swallowed the people of Lot.' He said to him, O Gabriel! I shall call them to account on the Day of Judgment before my Lord, Glory to Him.' It was then that I screamed, O Messenger of Allāh! I plead to you for security!' He said to me, Be gone, for Allāh shall never forgive you.' So, do you still think that Allāh will forgive me?"[1]

At one stop on their journey, they put the purified head down; soon they saw an iron pen that came out of the wall and wrote the following in blood[2]:

---

[1] Ibn Tawoos *Al-Luhuf*, p. 98.

[2] Ibn Hajar al-Asqalani, *Mujma az-Zawa'id*, Vol. 9, p. 199. As-Sayyati, *Al-Khasa'is*, Vol. 2, p. 127. Ibn Asakir, *Tarikh*, Vol. 4, p. 342. Ibn Hajar al-Asqalani, *As-Sawa'iq al-Muhriqa*, p. 116. *Al-Kawakib al-Durriyya* by al-Qatari al-Biladi al-Bahrani, Vol. 1, p. 57. Ash-Shabrawi, *Al-Ithaf bi Hubbil-Ashraf*, p. 23. On p. 98 of his book *Al-Luhuf*, Ibn Tawoos attributes this statement to *Tarikh Baghdad* by Ibn an-Najjar. On p. 108 of his *Tarikh*, al-Qarmani says, "They reached a monastery on the highway where they stayed for the afternoon. They found the said line written on one of its walls." On p. 285, Vol. 2, of his *Khutat*, al-Maqrazi says, "This was written in the past, and nobody knows who said it." On p. 53 of his book *Muthir al-Ahzan*, Ibn Nama says, "Three hundred years before the Prophetic mission, there was some digging in the land of the [Byzantine] Romans, and this line was found inscribed in the *Musnad* on a rock, and the *Musnad* is the language of the offspring of Seth."

Does a nation that killed al-Hussain really hope for a way
His grandfather will intercede for them on the Judgment Day?

But they were not admonished by such a miracle, and blindness hurled them into the very deepest of all pits; surely Allāh, the most Exalted One, is the best of judges.

One farasang before reaching their destination, they placed the head on a rock; a drop of blood fell from it on the rock. Every year, that drop would boil on Ashura, and people would assemble there around it and hold mourning commemorations in honor of al-Hussain (ع). A great deal of wailing would be around it. This continued to take place till Abdul-Malik ibn Marwan ascended the throne in 65 A.H./684 A.D.. He ordered that rock to be removed. It was never seen after that, but the spot where that rock stood became the site of a dome built in its honor which they called "an-Nuqta" (the drop)[1].

Near the town of Hamat and among its orchards stood a mosque called "Masjid al-Hussain (ع)." People there say that they escorted the rock and the head of al-Hussain (ع) that bled all the way to Damascus[2].

---

[1]Shaikh Abbas al-Qummi, *Nafas al-Mahmum*, p. 228. It is stated on p. 23, Vol. 3, of *Nahr at-Thahab fi Tarikh Halab* that, "When al-Hussain's head was brought with the captives, they reached a mountain to the west of Aleppo. One drop of blood fell from the sacred head above which a mausoleum called Mashhad an-Nuqta [mausoleum of the drop] was erected." On p. 280, Vol. 3, it cites Yahya ibn Abū Tay's *Tarikh* recounting the names of those who constructed and renovated it. On p. 66 of the book titled *Al-Isharat ila Marifat az-Ziyarat* by Abul- al-Hassan Ali ibn Abū Bakr al-Harawi (who died in 611 A.H./1215 A.D.), it states that, "In the town of Nasibin, there is a mausoleum called "Mashhad an-Nuqta", a reference to a drop from al-Hussain's head. Also, there is at Suq an-Nashshabin a place called Mashhad ar-Ras where the head was hung when the captives were brought to Syria."

[2]The mentor and revered *muhaddith* Shaikh Abbas al-Qummi says the following in his book *Nafas al-Mahmum*, "I saw that stone on my way to the pilgrimage, and I heard the servants talking about it."

Near Aleppo there is a shrine known as "Masqat as-Saqt."[1] The reason why it was called so is that when the ladies of the Messenger of Allāh (ﷺ) were taken to that place, al-Hussain's wife had miscarried a son named Muhsin[2].

At some stops, the head was placed atop a spear next to a monk's monastery. During the night, the monk heard a great deal of *tasbeeh* and *tahleel*, and he saw a dazzling light emanating from it. He also heard a voice saying, "Peace be upon you, O father of Abdulah!" He was amazed and did not know what to make of it. In the morning, he asked people about that head and was told that it was the head of al-Hussain (ﷺ) ibn Ali ibn Abū Talib (ﷺ), son of Fātima (ﷺ) daughter of Prophet Muhammed (ﷺ). He said to them, "Woe unto you, people! True are the accounts that said that the heavens would rain blood." He asked their permission to kiss the head, but they refused till he paid them some money. He declared his *shahada* and embraced Islam through the blessing of the one who was beheaded just for

---

[1]On p. 173, Vol. 3, of *Mu'jam al-Buldan*, and on p. 128 of *Khareedat al-Ajaib*, it is referred to as "Mashhad at-Tarh." On p. 278, Vol. 2, of *Nahr at-Thahab*, it is calle "Mashhad al-Dakka." Mashhad at-Tarh is located to the west of Aleppo. In the *Tarikh* of Ibn Abū Tay is cited saying that "Mashhad at-Tarh" was built in the year 351 A.H./962 A.D. according to the order of Sayf al-Dawlah. Other historians have said that one of al-Hussain's wives had miscarried in that place when al-Hussain's children and the severed heads were brought with them. There used to be a useful mineral in that area, but when its residents felt elated upon seeing the captives, Zainab invoked Allah's curse against them; therefore, that mineral lost its useful qualities. Then the author goes on to document the history of its renovations.

[2]In the discussion of the subject of "Jawshan," on p. 173, Vol. 3, of his work *Mu'jam al-Buldan*, and also on p. 128 of *Khareedat al-Ajaib*, where reference to the Jawshan Mountain is made, it is stated that one of al-Hussain's family members taken captive asked some of those who worked there to give him bread and water. When they refused, he invoked Allah to curse them, thus condemning the labor of all laborers at that place to always be unprofitable.

supporting the divine call. When they left that place, they looked at the money the monk had given them and saw this verse inscribed on it: "And those who oppressed shall come to find how evil their end shall be" (Qur'an, 26:227)[1].

IN SYRIA

When they were near Damascus, Umm Kulthum sent a message to ash-Shimr asking him to let them enter the city from the least crowded highway, and to take the heads out so that people might be diverted by looking at them rather than looking at the women. He escorted them as they were in a condition from which skins shiver and senses quiver. Ash-Shimr instead ordered his men to take the captives for display before onlookers and to place the severed heads in their midst[2].

On the first day of Safar, they entered Damascus[3] and were stopped at the Clocks Gate[4]. People came out carrying drums and trumpets in

---

[1]Ibn al-Jawzi, the grandson, *Tathkirat al-Khawass*, p. 150.

[2]Ibn Tawoos *Al-Luhuf*, p. 99. Ibn Nama, *Muthir al-Ahzan*, p. 53. *Maqtal al-Awalim*, p. 145.

[3]Such is recorded on p. 331 of the offset edition of al-Bayrani's book *Al-Aathar al-Baqiya*, al-Bahai's book *At-Tarikh al-Kāmil*, p. 269 of *Musbah al-Kaf'ami*, and p. 15 of al-Fayd's book *Taqwim al-Muhsinin*. According to p. 266, Vol. 6, of at-Tabari's *Tarikh*, the time from their imprisonment till the post coming from Syria informing them of their arrival at Syria in the beginning of the month of Safar must have been a lengthy one except if birds had been used to carry such mail.

[4]According to p. 61, Vol. 2, of al-Khawarizmi's book *Maqtal al-Hussain (ع)*, they were brought to Damascus through Toma's Gate [Gate of St. Thomas]. This Gate, according to p. 109 of *Al-Maqasid*, was one of the ancient gates of Damascus. Abū Abdullāh Muhammed ibn Ali ibn Ibrahim, who is known as Ibn Shaddad and who died in 684 A.H./1286 A.D., says on p. 72, Vol. 3, of *Alaq al-Khateera*, "It was called the Clocks Gate because atop that gate there were clocks marking each hour of the day: small copper sparrows, a copper raven and a copper snake marked the timing: at the end of each hour, sparrows would come out, the raven would let a shriek out, and one (or more) stone would be dropped in the copper

175

excitement and jubilation. A man came close to Sukayna and asked her, "What captives are you all from?" She said, "We are captives belonging to the fāmily of Muhammed (ص)."[1]

Yazid was sitting at a surveillance outpost overlooking the mountain of Jerun. When he saw the captives with the heads planted atop the spears as their throng came close, a crow croaked; so he composed these lines:

تلـــك الــرؤوسُ علــى شـــفا جيـــرونِ   لمـــا بـــدت تلـــك الحمـــول و أشـــرقت

فقـــد اقتضـــيتُ مـــن الرســـولِ ديـــوني   نعـب الغـراب فقلـت: قَـل أو لا تَقُـلْ

When those conveyances drew nigh
And the heads on the edge of Jerun,
The crow croaked so said I:
Say whatever you wish to say
Or say nothing at all,
From the Messenger have I today
What he <u>owed me</u> he did repay.[2]

It is due to these verses that Ibn al-Jawzi and Abū Ya'li, the judge, as

---

washbowl [making it sound]."

[1] as-Saduq, *Al-Aamali*, p. 100, *majlis* No. 31. Al-Khawarizmi, *Maqtal al-Hussain (ع)*, Vol. 2, p.60.

[2] According to p. 161 of the offset Damascus edition of Ibn Hawqal's book *Sourat al-Ard*, there is none in the Islamic world better than it. It used to be a temple for the Sabaeans, then the Greeks used to worship in it, then the Jews as well as Pagan kings. The gate of this mosque is called Jayrun's Gate. It is over this gate that the head of John the Baptist (Yahya son of Zakariyya) was crucified. It was on this same Jayrun's Gate that the head of al-Hussain (ع) ibn Ali ibn Abū Talib (ع) was crucified in the same place where the head of John the Baptist was crucified. During the reign of al-Walid ibn Abdul-Malik, its walls were covered with marble. It seems that this is the same as the Umayyad Mosque.

well as at-Taftazani and Jalal as-Sayyuti permitted cursing Yazid and labelling him as *kafir*, apostate, unbeliever.[1]

Sahl ibn Sa'd as-Sa'idi came close to Sukayna daughter of al-Hussain (ﻉ) and asked her, "Is there anything I can do for you?" She asked him to pay the man who was carrying the head some money and to ask him in return to stay away from the women so that people would be distracted by looking at the head instead of looking at the women. Sahl did so[2].

An elderly man came near as-Sajjād and said, "Praise be to Allāh Who annihilated you and Who granted the governor the upper hand over you!" At such a juncture, the Imām poured of his own kindness over that poor [ignorant] man who was brainwashed by falsehood in order to bring him closer to the truth and to show him the path of guidance. Such are the Ahl al-Bayt (ﻉ): their light shines over those whom they know to be pure of heart and pure of essence and, as such, who are ready to receive guidance. He, peace be with him, asked the man, "Have you read the Qur'an, O *shaikh*?" The man answered as-Sajjād in the affirmative. "Have you read," continued as-Sajjād, "the verse saying, Say: I do not ask you for a reward for it [for conveying the Islamic Message to you] except that you treat my kinsfolk with kindness,' the verse saying, And give the [Prophet's] kinsfolk their due rights,' and the verse saying, And be informed that whatever you earn by way of booty, for Allāh belongs the fifth thereof and for the Messenger [of Allāh] and for the [Prophet's] kinsfolk'?" The man answered by saying, "Yes, I have read all of them." He (ﻉ) then said, "We, by Allāh, are the kinsfolk referred to in all these verses." Then the Imām (ﻉ) asked him whether he had

---

[1] al-Ālusi, *Ruh al-Ma'ani*, Vol. 26, p. 73, where the verse "So do you wish, if you take charge... etc." is explained. The author says, "He meant, when he said, I have taken back from the Messenger (ﻉ) what he owed me,' that he avenged the loss which he had suffered during the Battle of Badr at the hands of the Messenger of Allah when his grandfather Utbah, his uncle, and others were killed. This is nothing but obvious apostasy. Such was the similitude struck by Ibn az-Zubari before accepting Islam.

[2] al-Bahrani, *Maqtal al-Awalim*, p. 145.

read the verse saying, "Allāh only desires to remove all abomination from you, O Ahl al-Bayt, and purifies you with a perfect purification" (Qur'an, 33:33). "Yes" was the answer. As-Sajjād, peace be with him, said to him, "We are Ahl al-Bayt whom Allāh purified." "I ask you in the Name of Allāh," asked the man, "are you really them?" As-Sajjād, peace be with him, said, "By our grandfather the Messenger of Allāh, we are, without any doubt."

It was then that the elderly man fell on as-Sajjād's feet kissing them as he said, "I dissociate myself before Allāh from whoever killed you." He sought repentance of the Imām (ع) from whatever rude remarks he had earlier made. The encounter involving this elderly man reached Yazid who ordered him to be killed[1]...

Before being brought to Yazid's court, they were tied with ropes. The beginning of the rope was around the neck of Zain al-Ābidīn [Ali son of Imām al-Hussain (ع), also called as-Sajjād, the one who prostrates to Allāh quite often], then around the necks of Zainab, Umm Kulthum, up to all the daughters of the Messenger of Allāh (ع)... Whenever they slow down in their walking because of fatigue, they were whipped till they were brought face to face with Yazid who was then sitting on his throne. Ali ibn al-Hussain (ع) asked him, "What do you think the reaction of the Messenger of Allāh (ع) might have been had he seen us looking like this?" Everyone wept. Yazid ordered the ropes to be cut off.[2]

---

[1]Ibn Tawoos, *Al-Luhuf*, p. 100. According to p. 112, Vol. 4, of Ibn Katheer's *Tafsir*, p. 31, Vol. 25, of al-Ālusi's *Ruh al-Ma'ani*, and p. 61, Vol. 2, of al-Khawarizmi's book *Maqtal al-Hussain (ع)*, as-Sajjād (ع) had recited the verse invoking compassion (for the Prophet's family) to that old man who accepted it as a valid argument.

[2]al-Yafi'i, *Mir'at al-Jinan*, p. 341. On p. 35, Vol. 4, of his book *At-Tarikh al-Kāmil*, Ibn al-Atheer, as well as the author of *Muraj at-Thahab*, both indicate that when the head was brought to Yazid, the latter kept hitting it with a rod in his hand as he cited these verses by the poet al-Haseen ibn Humam:

> *Our people refused to be fair to us, so*
> *Swords in our hands bleeding did so,*

178

They were lined up on the stairs leading to the gate leading to the [Umayyad Grand] mosque as was their custom with all captives, and the sacred head was placed in front of Yazid who kept looking at the captives and reciting poetry verses extolling his foul deed and demonstrating his elation. Then he turned to an-Nu'man ibn Basheer and said, "Praise to Allāh Who killed him [al-Hussain (ع)]." An-Nu'man said, "Commander of the faithful Mu'awiyah used to hate killing him." Yazid said, "That was before he rebelled. Had he rebelled against the commander of the faithful, he would have killed him."[1]

Yazid turned to as-Sajjād (ع) and asked him, "How did you, Ali, see what Allāh did to your father al-Hussain (ع)?" "I saw," answered as-Sajjād (ع), "What Allāh, the One and Only Allāh, the most Exalted One, had decreed before creating the heavens and the earth." Yazid consulted those around him as to what to do with as-Sajjād (ع), and they advised him to kill him. Imām as-Sajjād Zain al-Ābidīn (ع)

Splitting the heads of men who are to us dear
Though they were to injustice and oppression more near.

On p. 313, Vol. 2, of *Al-Iqd al-Farid*, where Yazid's reign is discussed, the author says, "When the head was placed in front of him, Yazid cited what al-Haseen ibn al-Hamam al-Mazni had said." He quoted the second verse [in the above English text, the last couple]. Ibn Hajar al-Haythami, on p. 198, Vol. 9, of his book *Mujma az-Zawa'id wa Manba al-Fawa'id*, quotes only the second verse. On p. 61, Vol. 2, of his book *Maqtal al-Hussain (ع)*, al-Khawarizmi contents himself by simply saying that they stood on the steps of the mosque's gate. These verses are cited by al-Aamidi on p. 91 of his book *Al-Mu'talif wal-Mukhtalif*. Then he traces the lineage of the poet al-Haseen ibn Humam ibn Rabaah and cited three verses, including these couple, from a lengthy poem. On p. 151 of *Ash-Shi'r wash-Shu'ara'*, three verses are cited which include this couple. On p. 4 of *Al-Ashya wal Nada'ir*, where immortalized ancient poems and those composed during the time of *jahiliyya* are cited, only the second verse is quoted. On p. 120, Vol. 12, of the Sassi edition of Abul-Faraj al-Isfahani's voluminous book *Al-Aghani*, thirteen lines are quoted, including this couple.

[1] al-Khawarizmi, *Maqtal al-Hussain (ع)*, Vol. 2, p. 59.

said, "O Yazid! These men have advised you to do the opposite of what Pharaoh's courtiers had advised Pharaoh saying, Grant him and his brother a respite.' The *ad'iyaa* أدعياء (plural of *da'iy*, one who pretends to be Muslim) do not kill the prophets' sons and grandsons." This statement caused Yazid to lower his head and contemplate for a good while[1].

Among the dialogue that went on between both men is Yazid quoting this Qur'anic verse to Ali ibn al-Hussain (ع): "Whatever misfortune befalls you is due to what your hands commit" (Qur'an, 45:22). Ali ibn al-Hussain (ع) responded by saying, "This verse was not revealed in reference to us. What was revealed in reference to us was this verse: Whatever misfortune befalls the earth or your own selves is already in a Book even before we cause it to happen; this is easy for Allāh, so that you may not grieve about what you missed nor feel elated on account of what you receive' (Qur'an, 57:22)[2]. We do not grieve over what we missed nor feel elated on account of what we receive."[3] Yazid then cited the following verse by al-Fadl ibn al-Abbas ibn 'Utbah:

Wait, O cousins, wait, O masters, do not hurry!
Do not bring to surface what we did bury.[4]

As-Sajjād, peace be with him, sought permission to speak. "Yes," said Yazid, "provided you do not utter verbal attacks." He (ع) said,

---

[1]al-Mas'udi, *Ithbat al-Wasiyya*, p. 143 (Najafi edition).

[2]al-Kamali al-Istarbadi al-Hilli, *Al-Iqd al-Farid*, Vol. 2, p. 313. At-Tabari, *Tarikh*, Vol. 6, p. 267.

[3]Ali ibn Ibrahim, *Tafsir*, p. 603, where the Chapter of ash-Shura is discussed.

[4]ar-Raghib al-Isfahani, *Al-Muhadarat*, Vol. 1, p. 775, in a chapter about those who boast of antagonizing their kinsfolk. This is one of five verses by al-Fadl ibn al-Abbas ibn Utbah ibn Abū Lahab recorded by Abū Tammam in his book *Al-Hamasa*. Refer to p. 223, Vol. 1, of *Sharh at-Tabrizi*.

"I am now standing like one who ought not verbally attack anyone, but tell me: How do you think the Messenger of Allāh (ع) would have felt had he seen me looking like this?" Yazid ordered him to be untied.[1]

Yazid ordered the person who used to recite the Friday *khutba* (sermon) to ascend the pulpit and insult Ali and al-Hussain (ع), which he did. As-Sajjād (ع) shouted at him saying, "You have traded the pleasure of the creature for the Wrath of the Creator, so take your place in the fire [of hell]."[2]

He asked Yazid saying, "Do you permit me to ascend this pulpit to deliver a speech that will please Allāh Almighty and that will bring good rewards for these folks?" Yazid refused, but people kept pleading to him to yield, yet he was still relentless. His son Mu'awiyah II said to him, "Permit him; what harm can his words cause?" Yazid said, "These are people who have inherited knowledge and oratory[3] and spoon-fed with knowledge[4]." They kept pressuring him till he agreed.

The Imām said,

ورد في كتاب فتوح ابن اعثم ٥ / ٢٤٧ ، ومقتل الخوارزمي ٢ / ٦٩ : إنّ يزيد أمر الخطيب أن يرقى المنبر ، ويثني على معاوية ويزيد ، وينال من الإمام علي والإمام الحسين ، فصعد الخطيب المنبر ، فحمد الله وأثنى عليه ، وأكثر الوقيعة في علي والحسين ، وأطنب في تقريض معاوية ويزيد ، فصاح به علي بن الحسين : "ويلك أيها الخاطب ، اشتريت رضا المخلوق بسخط الخالق ؟ فتبوأ مقعدك من النار". ثمّ قال : (يا يزيد ائذن لي حتى أصعد هذه الأعواد ، فأتكلم بكلمات فيهن لله رضا ، ولهؤلاء الجالسين أجر وثواب) ، فأبى يزيد ، فقال الناس : يا أمير المؤمنين ائذن له ليصعد ، فلعلنا نسمع منه شيئاً ، فقال لهم : إن صعد المنبر هذا ، لم ينزل إلا بفضيحتي ، وفضيحة آل أبي سفيان ، فقالوا : وما قدر ما يحسن هذا ؟ فقال : إنّه من أهل بيت قد زقوا العلم زقا . ولم

---

[1] Ibn Nama, *Muthir al-Ahzan*, p. 54.

[2] Shaikh Abbas al-Qummi, *Nafas al-Mahmum*, p. 242.

[3] *Kāmil al-Bahai*.

[4] al-Qazwini, *Riyad al-Ahzan*, p. 148.

يزالوا به حتى أذن له بالصعود ، فصعد المنبر ، فحمد الله وأثنى عليه ، وقال) : أيها الناس ، أعطينا ستاً ، وفضلنا بسبع : أعطينا العلم ، والحلم ، والسماحة والفصاحة ، والشجاعة ، والمحبة في قلوب المؤمنين ، وفضلنا بأن منا النبي المختار محمد (صلى الله عليه وآله) ، ومنا الصدّيق ، ومنا الطيار ، ومنا أسد الله وأسد الرسول ، ومنا سيدة نساء العالمين فاطمة البتول ، ومنا سبطا هذه الأمّة ، وسيدا شباب أهل الجنة ، فمن عرفني فقد عرفني ، ومن لم يعرفني أنبأته بحسبي ونسبي : أنا ابن مكة ومنى ، أنا ابن زمزم والصفا ، أنا ابن من حمل الزكاة بأطراف الرداء ، أنا ابن خير من ائتزر وارتدى ، أنا ابن خير من انتعل واحتفى ، أنا ابن خير من طاف وسعى ، أنا ابن خير من حج ولبّى ، أنا ابن من حمل على البراق في الهواء ، أنا ابن من أسري به من المسجد الحرام إلى المسجد الأقصى ، فسبحان من أسرى ، أنا ابن من بلغ به جبرائيل إلى سدرة المنتهى ، أنا ابن من دنا فتدلى ، فكان قاب قوسين أو أدنى ، أنا ابن من صلّى بملائكة السماء ، أنا ابن من أوحى إليه الجليل ما أوحى ، أنا ابن محمد المصطفى ، أنا ابن من ضرب خراطيم الخلق ، حتى قالوا لا اله إلا الله ، أنا ابن من بايع البيعتين ، وصلّى القبلتين ، وقاتل ببدر وحنين ، ولم يكفر بالله طرفة عين ، يعسوب المسلمين ، وقاتل الناكثين والقاسطين والمارقين ، سمح سخي ، بهلول زكي ، ليث الحجاز ، وكبش العراق ، مكّي مدني ، أبطحي تهامي ، خيفى عقبي ، بدري أحدي ، شجري مهاجري ، أبو السبطين ، الحسن والحسين ، علي بن أبي طالب ، أنا ابن فاطمة الزهراء ، أنا ابن سيدة النساء ، أنا ابن بضعة الرسول).

قال : ولم يزل يقول : أنا أنا ، حتى ضج الناس بالبكاء والنحيب ، وخشي يزيد أن تكون فتنة ، فأمر المؤذّن يؤذّن ، فقطع عليه الكلام وسكت ، فلمّا قال المؤذّن : الله أكبر. قال علي بن الحسين : كبرت كبيراً لا يقاس ، ولا يدرك بالحواس ، ولا شيء أكبر من الله؛ فلمّا قال : أشهد أن لا اله إلا الله ، قال علي : (شهد بها شعري وبشري ، ولحمي ودمي ، ومخي وعظمي) ، فلمّا قال : أشهد أن محمداً رسول الله ، التفت علي من أعلا المنبر إلى يزيد ، وقال ، (يا يزيد محمد هذا جدّي أم جدّك ؟ فإن زعمت أنه جدّك فقد كذبت ، وان قلت أنه جدّي ، فلم قتلت عترته ؟) .

قال : وفرغ المؤذّن من الأذان والإقامة ، فتقدّم يزيد ، وصلّى الظهر ، فلمّا فرغ من صلاته ، أمر بعلي بن الحسين ، وأخواته وعماته (رضوان الله عليهم) ، ففرغ لهم دار فنزلوها ، وأقاموا أياماً يبكون ، وينوحون على الحسين (عليه السلام) .وبراءة الذمة...

All Praise is due to Allāh for Whom there is no beginning, the ever-Lasting for Whom there is no end, the First for Whom there is no starting point, the Last for Whom there is no ending point, the One Who remains after all beings no longer exist. He measured the nights and the days. He divided them into parts; so, Blessed is Allāh, the King, the all-Knowing... O people! We were granted six things and favored with seven: We were granted knowledge, clemency, leniency, fluency, courage, and love for us in the hearts of the believers. And we were favored by the fact that from among us came a Prophet, a Siddeeq, a Tayyar, a Lion of Allāh and of His Prophet

(ص), and both Masters of the Youths of Paradise from among this nation. O people! Whoever recognizes me knows me, and whoever does not recognize me, let me tell him who I am and to what family I belong: O people! I am the son of Mecca and Mina; I am the son of Zamzam and as-Safa; I am the son of the one who carried the *rukn* on his mantle; I am the son of the best man who ever put on clothes and who ever made *tawaf* and *sa'i*, of whoever offered the hajj and pronounced the *talbiya*. I am the son of the one who was transported on the *buraq* and who was taken by Gabriel to *sidrat al-muntaha*, so he was near his Lord like the throw of a bow or closer still. I am the son of the one who led the angels of the heavens in the prayers. I am the son to whom the Mighty One revealed what He revealed. I am the son of the one who defended the Messenger of Allāh (ﻉ) at Badr and Hunayn and never disbelieved in Allāh not even as much as the twinkling of an eye. I am the son of the best of the believers and of the heir of the prophets, of the leader of the Muslims and the noor of those who offer jihad and the killer of the renegades and those who deviated from the straight path and who scattered the *ahzab* and the most courageous one, the one with the firmest determination: such is the father of the grandsons of the Prophet (ص), al-Hassan and al-Hussain (ﻉ), such is Ali ibn Abū Talib (ﻉ). I am the son of Fātima az-Zahrā' (ﻉ), the Head of all Women, the son of Khadija al-Kubra. I am the son of the one with whose blood the sand mixed. I am the son of the one who was slaughtered at Kerbalā'. I am the son of the one for whom the jinns wept in the dark and for whom the birds in the air cried.

Having said this much, people's cries filled the place, and Yazid feared dissension, so he ordered the *mu'aththin* to call the *athan* for the prayers. The latter shouted: Allāhu Akbar! The Imām (ﻉ) said, Allāh is Greater, more Magnanimous, and more Kind than what I fear and of what I avoid." The prayer caller now shouted: *Ashhadu an la ilaha illa-Allāh!* He (ﻉ) said, "Yes, I testify with everyone who testifies that there is no Allāh besides Him nor any other Lord." The caller shouted: *Ashahadu anna Muhammedan rasool-Allāh!* The Imām (ﻉ) said to the prayer caller, "I ask you by Muhammed to stop here till I speak to this man," then he turned to Yazid and asked him, "Is this great Messenger of Allāh (ﻉ) your grandfather or mine? If you say that he is yours, everyone present here as well as all other

183

people will come to know that you are a liar, and if you say that he is mine, then why did you kill my father unjustly and oppressively and plundered his wealth and took his women captive? Woe unto you on the Day of Judgment when my grandfather will be your opponent."

Yazid yelled at the prayer caller to start the prayers immediately. A great deal of commotion now could be heard among the people. Some people prayed whereas others left.[1]

HUSSAIN'S SEVERED HEAD

Yazid ordered al-Hussain's head to be brought to him. He put it in a gold washbowl[2]. The women were behind him. Sukayna and Fātima stood and tried anxiously to steal a look at it as Yazid kept hiding it from them. When they did see it, they burst in tears[3]. He then permitted people to enter to see him[4]. Yazid took a rod and kept hitting al-Hussain's lips with it[5] saying, "A day for a day: this day is

---

[1]Shaikh Abbas al-Qummi, *Nafas al-Mahmum*, p. 242. This lengthy sermon is quoted on p. 69, Vol. 2, of al-Khawarizmi's book *Maqtal al-Hussain (ع)*.

[2]al-Yafii, *Mir'at al-Jinan*, Vol. 1, p. 135.

[3]Ibn al-Atheer, *At-Tarikh al-Kāmil*, Vol. 4, p. 35. Al-Haythami, *Mujma az-Zawa'id*, Vol. 9, p. 195. Ibn as-Sabbagh, *Al-Fusool al-Muhimmah*, p. 205.

[4]Ibn al-Atheer, *At-Tarikh al-Kāmil*, Vol. 4, p. 35.

[5]at-Tabari, *Tarikh*, Vol. 6, p. 267. Ibn al-Atheer, *At-Tarikh al-Kāmil*, Vol. 4, p. 35. Ibn al-Jawzi, the grandson, *Tathkirat al-Khawass*, p. 148. Ibn Hajar al-Asqalani, *As-Sawa'iq al-Muhriqa*, p. 116. Ibn Muflih al-Hanbali, *Fiqh al-Hanabilah*, Vol. 3, p. 549. Ibn Hajar al-Asqalani, *Mujma' az-Zawa'id*, Vol. 9, p. 195. Ibn as-Sabbagh, *Al-Fusool al-Muhimma*, p. 205. Al-Maqrazi, *Khutat*, Vol. 3, p. 289. Ibn Katheer, *Al-Bidaya*, Vol. 8, p. 192. Ash-Shareeshi, *Sharh Maqamat al-Harari*, Vol. 1, p. 193, at the end of the 10th *maqam*. Muhammed Abul-Fadl and Ali Muhammed al-Bijawi, *Ayyam al-Arab fil Islam*, p. 435. Ibn Shahr Ashub, *Al-Manaqib*, Vol. 2, p. 225. According to p. 23 of *Al-Ithaf bi Hubbil-Ashraf*, Yazid kept hitting al-Hussain's front teeth, and so is stated by al-Bayruni on p. 331 of the offset edition of his book *Al-Aathaar al-Baqiya*.

184

[in revenge] for Badr[1]." Then he cited these verses by al-Haseen ibn al-Humam:[2]

To be fair to us our folks never did dare,
So swords dripping with blood were to them fair;
We split the heads of men dear to us
For they severed their ties and did oppress.

Abū Barzah al-Aslami said, "I bear witness that I saw the Prophet (ص) kissing his lips and those of his brother al-Hassan (ع) and say to them: You are the masters of the youths of Paradise; may Allāh fight whoever fights you; may He curse him and prepare hell for him, and what an evil refuge it is!'" Yazid became angry and ordered him to be dragged out of his courtroom[3].

A [Christian] messenger sent by emperor Caesar was present there; he said to Yazid, "We have in some islands the hoof of the donkey

---

[1]Ibn Shahr Ashub, *Al-Manaqib*, Vol. 2, p. 226.

[2]Ibn al-Atheer, *At-Tarikh al-Kāmil*, Vol. 4, p. 35. Ibn as-Sabbagh, *Al-Fusool al-Muhimma*, p. 205. The first line, according to p. 135, Vol. 1, of al-Yafii's *Mir'at al-Jinan*, is:

We took to patience, so patience proved to be our will
Even as our swords kept severing hands and arms.

It is narrated by Sibt ibn al-Jawzi on p. 148 of his book *Tathkirat al-Khawass* with some variation in its wording. A host of historians have contented themselves by citing only the second verse. Among them is ash-Shareeshi who does so on p. 193, Vol. 1, of his book *Sharh Maqamat al-Harari*, so does al-Ālusi on p. 313, Vol. 2, of his book *Al-Iqd al-Farid*. So does Ibn Katheer on p. 197, Vol. 8, of his book *Al-Bidaya*, the mentor Shaikh al-Mufid in his book *Al-Irshad*, and so does Ibn Jarir at-Tabari on p. 267, Vol. 6, of his *Tarikh*, adding that the verse was composed by al-Haseen ibn al-Hamam al-Murri.

[3]Ibn Tawoos, *Al-Luhuf*, p. 102. The incident is abridged on p. 205 of *Al-Fusool al-Muhimma*, on p. 267, Vol. 6, of at-Tabari's *Tarikh*, and on p. 26, Vol. 2, of Ibn Shahr Ashub's book *Al-Manaqib*.

upon which Jesus rode, and we make a pilgrimage to it every year from all lands and offer nathr to it and hold it in as much regard as you hold your sacred books; so, I bear witness that you are wrongdoers."[1] This statement enraged Yazid who ordered him to be killed. The messenger stood up, walked to the head, kissed it and pronounced the kalima. At the moment when that messenger's head was cut off, everyone heard a loud and fluent voice saying, *La hawla wala quwwata illa billah!* (There is neither power nor might except in Allāh).[2]

The head was taken out of the court and hung for three days on the mansion's gate[3]. When Hind daughter of Amr ibn Suhayl, Yazid's wife, saw the head on her house's door[4] with divine light emanating from it, its blood still fresh and had not yet dried, and it was emitting a sweet fragrance[5], she entered Yazid's court without any veil crying, "The head of the daughter of the Messenger of Allāh (ﷺ) is on our door!" Yazid stood up, covered her and said, "Mourn him, O Hind, for he is the reason why Banu Hashim are grieving. [Ubaydullāh] Ibn Ziyad hastily killed him."[6]

Yazid ordered the heads to be hung on the gates and on the

---

[1] Ibn Hajar al-Asqalani, *As-Sawa'iq al-Muhriqa*, p. 119.

[2] al-Bahrani, *Maqtal al-Awalim*, p. 151. Ibn Nama, *Muthir al-Ahzan*. On p. 72, Vol. 2, of his book *Maqtal al-Hussain (ﷺ)*, al-Khawarizmi states the dialogue between the Christian and Yazid and how the first was killed, but he does not indicate that the most sacred head spoke.

[3] al-Maqrazi, *Al-Khutat*, Vol. 2, p. 289. *Al-Ithaf bi Hubbil-Ashraf*, p. 23. Al-Khawarizmi, *Maqtal al-Hussain (ﷺ)*, Vol. 2, p. 75. Ibn Katheer, *Al-Bidaya*, Vol. 8, p. 204. *Siyar Alam an-Nubala'*, Vol. 3, p. 216.

[4] al-Bahrani, *Maqtal al-Awalim*, p. 151. In the Introduction to this book, her father is introduced to the reader and so is her husband.

[5] al-Maqrazi, *Al-Khutat*, Vol. 2, p. 284.

[6] al-Khawarizmi, *Maqtal al-Hussain (ﷺ)*, Vol. 2, p. 74.

186

Umayyad Mosque, and his order was carried out[1].

Marwan [ibn al-Hakam] was very happy about al-Hussain (ع) being killed, so he composed poetry lines and kept hitting al-Hussain's face with a rod.

A SYRIAN ENCOUNTERS FĀTIMA

Historians record that a Syrian looked at Fātima daughter of Ali (ع)[2] then asked Yazid to give her to him to serve him. This daughter of the Commander of the Faithful (ع) was terrified; she clung to her sister Zainab and said, "Serve him?! How could I do that?!" Zainab said to her, "Do not be concerned; this shall never happen at all." Hearing her, Yazid said, "It could if I would!" She said to him, "Not unless you renege from our religion." He answered her by saying, "Those who reneged from the religion are your father and your brother." Zainab said, "By Allāh's religion and the religion of my grandfather do I swear that it was through my father and brother that you and your father received guidance, had you been a Muslim at all." He said to her, "You lie, you enemy of Allāh!" She, peace be with her, toned down her language and said to him, "You are an emir over the destiny of people; you oppressively taunt and subdue others."[3] The same Syrian man repeated his plea to Yazid who now rebuked him and said, "May Allāh grant you a fate that will put an end to you!"[4]

ZAINAB DELIVERS ANOTHER SPEECH

Both Ibn Nama and Ibn Tawoos[5] say that Zainab daughter of Ali ibn

---

[1]Shaikh Abbas al-Qummi, *Nafas al-Mahmum*, p. 247.

[2]at-Tabari, *Tarikh*, Vol. 6. Ibn Katheer, *Al-Bidaya*, Vol. 8, p. 194. As-Saduq, *Al-Aamali*, p. 100, *majlis* 31. Both Ibn Nama, on p. 54 of his *Muthir al-Ahzan*, and al-Khawarizmi, on p. 62, Vol. 2, of his *Maqtal al-Hussain (ع)*, say that she was Fatima daughter of al-Hussain (ع).

[3]Ibn al-Atheer, Vol. 4, p. 35.

[4]at-Tabari, *Tarikh*, Vol. 6, p. 265.

[5]This sermon is documented on p. 21 of *Balaghat an-Nisa* ' (Najafi

187

Abū Talib[1] (ع) heard Yazid quoting the following verses by Ibn az-Zu'bari[2]:

I wish my forefathers at Badr had witnessed
How the Khazraj are by the thorns annoyed,
They would have Glorified and Unified Allāh
Then they would make tahleel and say in elation:
"May your hands, O Yazid, never be paralyzed!"
We have killed the masters of their chiefs
And equated it with Badr, and it was so, indeed
Hashim played with the dominion so indeed,
No news came, nor was there a revelation revealed.
I do not belong to Khandaf if I do not
Seek revenge from Ahmed's children
For what he to us had done.

She reacted to these lines and said the following:

All Praise is due to Allāh, Lord of the Worlds. Allāh has blessed His Messenger and all His Messenger's Progeny. Allāh, Glory to Him, has said the truth when He said, "Then the end of those who committed evil was that they disbelieved in Allāh's Signs and they were ridiculing them." (Qur'an, 30:10) Do you, O Yazid, think that

---

edition), and on p. 64, Vol. 2, of al-Khawarizmi's book *Maqtal al-Hussain* (ع).

[1]In his book *Maqtal al-Hussain (ع)*, al-Khawarizmi identifies her mother as Fatima (ع) daughter of the Messenger of Allah (ص).

[2]These verses are attributed by Ibn Tawoos to Ibn al-Zu'bari, as he so states on p. 102 of his book *Al-Luhuf*, but they are not all his. Al-Khawarizmi on p. 66, Vol. 2, of his book *Maqtal al-Hussain (ع)*, Ibn Abul-Hadid on p. 383, Vol. 3, of his book *Sharh Nahjul Balagha* (first Egyptian edition), and Ibn Hisham in his *Seerat*, where he discusses the Battle of Uhud, all state sixteen lines which do not include except the first and the third lines mentioned by Ibn Tawoos. Al-Bayruni cites all of them on p. 331 of the offset edition of his book *Al-Aathaar al-Baqiya*, excluding the fourth line.

188

when you blocked all the avenues before us, so we were driven as captives, that we are light in the sight of Allāh and that you are superior to us? Or is it because you enjoy with Him a great status, so you look down at us and become arrogant, elated, when you see the world submissive to you and things are done as you want them, and when our authority and power became all yours? But wait! Have you forgotten that Allāh has said, "Do not regard those who disbelieved that We grant them good for themselves? We only give them a respite so that they may increase their sins, and for them there is a humiliating torment" (Qur'an, 3:178)? Is it fair, O son of *taleeqs*, that you keep your free as well as slave women in their chambers and at the same time drive the daughters of the Messenger of Allāh (ع) as captives with their veils removed and faces exposed, taken by their enemies from one land to another, being viewed by those at watering places as well as those who man your forts, with their faces exposed to the looks of everyone near or distant, lowly or honorable, having none of their protectors with them nor any of their men? But what can be expected from one [descended from those] whose mouths chewed the livers of the purified ones and whose flesh grows out of the blood of the martyrs? How can it be expected that one who looks at us with grudge and animosity, with hatred and malice, would not hate us, we Ahl al-Bayt (ع)? Besides you, without feeling any guilt or weighing heavily what you say, you recite saying,

Then they would make tahleel *and say in elation:*
"May your hands, O Yazid, never be paralyzed!"

How dare you hit the lips of Abū Abdullāh (ع), the Master of the Youths of Paradise? But why should you not do so, since you stirred a wound that almost healed, and since all mercy is removed from your heart, having shed the blood of the offspring of Muhammed, peace and blessings of Allāh be upon him and his Progeny, and the stars on earth from among the fāmily of Abdul-Muttalib? Then you cite your mentors as if you speak to them... Soon shall you be lodged with them, and soon shall you wish you were paralyzed and muted and never said what you said nor did what you did. O Allāh! Take what belongs to us out of his hands, seek revenge against all those who oppressed us, and let Your Wrath descend upon whoever shed our blood and killed our protectors! By Allāh! You have burnt only your own skin! You have cut only your own flesh! You shall come face to face with the Messenger of Allāh, peace of Allāh be upon him and his Progeny, bearing the burdens of the blood which you have shed, the blood of his offspring, and of his sanctities which you violated, the sanctities of his women, his kinsfolk, his flesh and blood, when Allāh gathers them together and seeks equity on their behalf. "And do not reckon those who are slain in the Way of Allāh as dead. Nay! They are living with their Lord, receiving their sustenance" (Qur'an, 3:169). Allāh suffices you as your Judge and Muhammed, peace and blessings of Allāh be upon him and his progeny, as your opponent, and Gabriel as your foe. All those who instigated you to do what you did and who put you in charge so that you might play havoc with the lives of the Muslims, how evil the end of the oppressors is and which of you shall have the worst place and will be the least protected? Although calamities have forced me to speak to you, I nevertheless see you small in my eyes and find your verbal attacks monstrous, and I regard your rebuke too much to bear, but these eyes are tearful, and the chests are filled with depression. What is even more strange is that the honored Party of Allāh is being killed by the *taleeq* party of Satan. Such hands are dripping with our blood; such mouths are feeding on our flesh, while those sacred and pure corpses are offered as food to the wild beasts of the desert and are dirtied by the brutes. If you regard us as your booty, you shall soon find us as your opponents, that will be when you find nothing but what your hands had committed, and your Lord never treats His servants unjustly. To Allāh is my complaint, and upon Him do I rely. So scheme whatever you wish to scheme, and carry out your plots, and intensify your efforts, for by Allāh, you shall never be able to obliterate our mention, nor will you ever be able to kill our inspiration, nor will your shame ever be washed away. Your view shall be proven futile, your days numbered, and your wealth wasted on the Day when the caller calls out, "The curse of Allāh be upon the oppressors" (Qur'an, 11:18). All Praise is due to Allāh, Lord of the Worlds, Who sealed the life of our early ones with happiness and forgiveness, and that of our last with martyrdom and mercy. We plead to Allāh to complete His rewards for them and grant them an increase and make succession good for us; He is the most Merciful, the most Compassionate. Allāh suffices us, and how great He is!

190

Yazid responded to her speech by quoting a couplet of poetry demonstrating his excitement. This should not surprise anyone. Anyone who is familiar with Yazid and with his misguidance cannot be surprised at all to hear him asking with a full mouth the Syrian jackals around him: "Do you know where Fātima's son came from, and what prompted him to do what he did and to fall into the pitfalls of what he committed?" They answered in the negative. Said he, "He claims that his father is better than my father, that his mother Fātima (ﻉ) daughter of the Messenger of Allāh (ﻉ) is better than mine, that his grandfather (ﻉ) is better than mine, and that he is more worthy than me of taking charge. As regarding his saying that his father is better than my father, my father had asked Allāh, the Great, the Sublime, to arbitrate between them, and people know best in whose favor He ruled. As regarding his saying that his mother is better than mine, by my life, Fātima (ﻉ), daughter of the Messenger of Allāh (ﻉ), is better than my mother. As regarding his saying that his grandfather (ﻉ) is better than my grandfather, by my life, nobody who believes in Allāh and in the Last Day can find anyone among us equal to the Messenger of Allāh (ﻉ). But he speaks with a little understanding of what he says and has not read the verse saying, Say: Lord! Owner of the domain! You grant authority to whomsoever You please, and you take the authority from whomsoever You please; You exalt whomsoever You please, and You abase whomsoever You please,' (Qur'an, 3:26) and he did not read the verse saying, Allāh grants His domain to whomsoever He pleases.' (Qur'an, 2:247)"[1].

AT THE HOUSE OF RUIN

The speech quoted above, which was delivered by Zainab, shook the very foundations of Yazid's court, and people started discussing with one another as to what extent they had been misled, and in what valley of abyss they had been hurled. Yazid had no choice except to get the women out of his court and to lodge them at a house of ruins which could not protect them against any heat or any cold. They

---

[1]at-Tabari, *Tarikh*, Vol. 6, p. 266. Ibn Katheer, *Al-Bidaya*, Vol. 8, p. 195.

remained there weeping and wailing, mourning al-Hussain (ع)[1] for three days[2].

One evening as-Sajjād (ع) went out for a walk. Al-Minhal ibn Omer met him and asked him, "How have you received the evening, O son of the Messenger of Allāh (ع)?" "We have received the evening," the Imām (ع) answered, "like the Israelites among the people of Pharaoh: they kill their sons and take their women captive. The Arabs brag before the non-Arabs saying that Muhammed (ص) was one of them, while Quraish boasts before the rest of the Arabs of Muhammed (ص) belonging to it. We, his Ahl al-Bayt (ع), are now homeless; so, to Allāh do we belong, and to Him shall we all return."[3] Al-Minhal is quoted as saying, "While he was thus talking to me, a woman came out after him and said, Where are you going, O best of successors?' He left me and hurried back to her. I inquired about her, and I was told that she was his aunt Zainab (ع)."[4]

BACK TO MEDĪNA
Yazid was very happy about killing al-Hussain (ع) and those with him as well as the capture of the ladies who descended from the Messenger of Allāh, peace of Allāh be upon him and his progeny[5].

---

[1]Ibn Tawoos *Al-Luhuf*, p. 207. as-Saduq, *Al-Aamali*, p. 101, *majlis* 31.

[2]al-Khawarizmi, *Maqtal al-Hussain (ع)*, Vol. 2, p. 34. This shed, or say jail, as stated on p. 146, Vol. 4, of al-Yunini's *Mir'at az-Zaman*, where the events of the year 681 A.H./1283 A.D. are discussed. Says he, "On the eleventh night of the month of Ramadan, the felt market in Damascus caught fire and was burnt in its entirety, and the fire engulfed the Booksellers' Bridge, the fountain square, and the cloth market known as Saq AsAllah, as well as the watering area of Jayrun. The fire reached the Ajam street in the midst of Jayrun, scorching the wall of the Omeri Mosque adjacent to the jail were Zain al-Ābidīn (ع) had been imprisoned."

[3]Ibn Nama, *Muthir al-Ahzan*, p. 58. Al-Khawarizmi, *Maqtal al-Hussain (ع)*, Vol. 2, p. 72.

[4]*Al-Anwar an-Numainiyya*, p. 340.

[5]as-Sayyati, *Tarikh al-Khulafa*, p. 139.

192

He was seen at his court looking very excited, being unaware of the fact that he was an atheist and an apostate as testified by his own citing of the poetry of az-Zu'bari quoted above to the extent that he denied that the Messenger of Allāh Muhammed (ص) had ever received any revelation. But when he was rebuked by more and more people, it gradually appeared to him how he had failed and erred in what he had committed: a sin the like of which had never been committed by anyone who belongs to the Islamic creed. It was then that he realized the implication of Mu'awiyah's will to him wherein he said, "The people of Iraq shall not leave al-Hussain (ع) till they pressure him to revolt. If he rebels against you, forgive him, for he was begotten in sacred wombs, and he enjoys a lofty status."[1]

His closest courtiers, and even his family members and women, stayed away from him. He heard the statements uttered by the most sacred severed head when he ordered the messenger of the Roman emperor to be killed: *La hawla wala quwwata illa billāh!* (There is neither power nor might except in Allāh).[2]

Yazid's most abominable crime and extreme cruelty were now being discussed at every gathering, and such discussions were finding an echo throughout Damascus. Yazid at that juncture had no choice except to shift the blame to the shoulder of Ubaydullāh ibn Ziyad in order to distance the taunting from him, but what is already established cannot be removed.

When he feared dissension and repercussions, he rushed to get as-Sajjād and the children out of Syria and to send them back home. He carried out their wishes, ordering an-Nu'man ibn Basheer and a number of other men with him to escort them to Medīna and to treat them with kindness[3].

---

[1]at-Tabari, *Tarikh*, Vol. 6, p. 180.

[2]al-Bahrani, *Maqtal al-Awalim*, p. 150.

[3]al-Mufid, *Al-Irshad*.

When they reached Iraq, they asked the road guide to take the highway leading to Kerbalā'. They reached the place where al-Hussain (ع) had been martyred. There, they found Jābir ibn Abdullāh al-Ansari accompanied by a group of Banu Hashim and some of the family members of the Messenger of Allāh (ص). They had all gone there to visit al-Hussain's grave. They met each other weeping and grieving, beating their cheeks. They stayed there mourning al-Hussain (ع)[1] for three days.[2]

Jābir ibn Abdullāh al-Ansari stood at the grave and burst in tears then thrice called out al-Hussain's name, then he said, "Why a loved one does not answer one who loves him?" But soon he answered his own query by saying, "How can he answer while his cheeks are torn and his head is separated from his body? Yet I testify that you are the son of the Seal of Prophets (ع), the son of the master of the faithful (ع), the son of the inseparable ally of piety, the descendant of guidance, the fifth of the fellows of the kisa', the son of the master of *naqeebs*, the one who was brought up in the lap of the pious, that you were raised on the milk of iman, that you were weaned with Islam, so you were good when you were alive, and you are so when dead. But the hearts of the faithful are not pleased with parting with you, nor do they have any doubt about goodness being yours. So peace of Allāh be upon you and His Pleasure. And I bear witness that you treaded the same path treaded before you by your brother [prophet] Zakariyya (Zacharias)."

Having said so, Jābir turned his head around the grave as he said, "Assalamo Alaikom, O souls that abide at al-Hussain's courtyard! I bear witness that you upheld the prayers and paid the *zakat*, enjoined what is right and prohibited what is wrong, struggled against the atheists and adored Allāh till death overtook you. By the One Who sent Muhammed, peace of Allāh be upon him and his Progeny, as His Prophet sent with the truth, I testify that we have a share in what

---

[1]Ibn Tawoos, *Al-Luhuf*, p. 112. Ibn Nama, *Muthir al-Ahzan*, p. 79 (old edition).

[2]Muhammed Hassan al-Qazwini, *Riyad al-Ahzan*, p. 157.

194

you have earned." Atiyyah al-'Awfi [his companion[1] who was leading him, since he, a maternal relative and one of the greatest sahabis of Prophet Muhammed (ﺹ), as indicated above in a footnote, was by then a blind old man] asked him, "How so when we did not descend upon a valley nor ascend a mountain, nor did we strike with a sword, whereas the heads of these people have been severed from their bodies, their sons have been orphaned and their wives widowed?" Jābir answered: "I heard the Messenger of Allāh (ﻉ) whom I very much love saying, One who loves a people will be lodged with them, and one who loves what some people do will have a share in [the rewards of] their deeds.' By the One Who sent Muhammed (ﺹ) as a Prophet with the truth, my intention and that of my companions is similar to that for which al-Hussain (ﻉ) and his companions were all killed."[2]

THE SEVERED HEAD REJOINS BODY

Once Zain al-Ābidīn (ﻉ) came to know of Yazid's consent, he asked him for the heads so that he could bury them. Yazid showed no hesitation to do so, ordering the heads, including those of Zain al-Ābidīn's family members, to be handed over to him. Zain al-Ābidīn reunited them with their respective bodies.

The list of writers of biographies who recorded his bringing the heads to Kerbalā' includes Shaikh Abbas al-Qummi, author of *Nafas al-Mahmum*, who discusses this issue on p. 253 of his book, and it is also discussed on p. 155 of *Riyad al-Ahzan* of Muhammed Hassan ash-Sha'ban Kurdi al-Qazwani.

As regarding al-Hussain's head, we read about it on p. 165 of al-Fattal's book *Rawdat al-Wa'izeen*, and on p. 85 of *Muthir al-Ahzan* by Ibn Nama al-Hilli. The latter reference is the one the Shī'as

---

[1]Some accounts say that Atiyyah was his slave.

[2]Abū Ja'far Muhammed ibn Abul-Qasim ibn Muhammed ibn Ali at-Tabari al-Āmili, *Bisharat al-Mustafa*, p. 89 (Hayderi Press edition). This author is one of the 5th century A.H./11th century A.D. scholars who were tutored by Shaikh at-Tusi's son.

consider as the most accurate as stated on p. 112 of *Al-Luhuf* by Ibn Tawoos. On p. 151 of at-Tibrisi's book *I'lam al-Wara bi A'lam al-Huda*, as well as on p. 154 of *Maqtal al-'Awalim*, as is the case with both *Riyad al-Musa'ib* and *Bihār al-Anwār*, the same view is the most famous among scholars. On p. 200, Vol. 2, of his book titled *Al-Manaqib*, Ibn Shahr Ashub says, "In some of his letters, al-Murtada has stated that al-Hussain's head was reunited with its body in Kerbalā'." At-Tusi has said that that incident was the basis for *ziyarat al-arba'een*. The author of *Bihār al-Anwār* cites *Al-Udad al-Qawiyya* by the brother of allama al-Hilli. On p. 67 of his book *Aja'ib al-Makhlooqat*, al-Qazwani indicates that it was on the twentieth of Safar that al-Hussain's head was returned to its body. Ash-Shabrawi says, "The head was returned to the body after forty days."[1] According to Ibn Hajar's book Sharh al-Bawsari's Hamziyya[2], forty days after his martyrdom, al-Hussain's head was returned [to its body]. Sabt ibn al-Jawzi has said, "It is most widely known that it [the head] was returned to Kerbalā' and buried with the body."[3] On p. 57, Vol. 1, of his book Al-Kawakib al-Durriyya, al-Qatari al-Biladi al-Bahrani records the consensus among Imāmite Shī'as that the head was returned to Kerbalā', and that this view was the one accepted by al-Qurtubi. He did not list his sources but attributed it to "some people of knowledge as well as eye witnesses," becoming evident to him that the head was, indeed, returned to Kerbalā'. Abul-Rayhan al-Bayruni states that it was on the twentieth of Safar that al-Hussain's head was reunited and buried with its body.[4]

Based on the above, any statements to the contrary should not be taken seriously especially those claiming that he was buried with his father (ع), a claim with which the scholars mentioned above are

---

[1]ash-Shabrawi, *Al-Ithaf bi Hubbil-Ashraf* الاتحاف بحب الأشراف, p. 12.

[2]"Hamziyya همزية" means a poem the rhyme of which ends with a *hamza* (ء).

[3]Ibn al-Jawzi, the grandson, *Tathkirat al-Khawass* تذكرة الخواص, p. 150.

[4]*Al-Athar al-Baqiya* الآثار الباقية, Vol. 1, p. 331.

196

familiar and which they all discard. Their rejection of such a claim proves that it cannot be relied upon especially since its *isnad* is not complete and its narrators are not famous.

THE ARBA'EEN

It is customary to pay tribute to a deceased person forty days after his death by doing acts of righteousness on his behalf, by eulogizing him and enumerating his merits. This is done at organized gatherings in order to keep his memory alive just when people's minds start to forget about him and their hearts start to ignore him. Thus, he remains alive in people's minds.

Both Abū Tharr al-Ghifāri and Ibn Abbas[1] quote the Prophet (ص) saying, "The earth mourns the death of a believer for forty mornings."[2] Zurarah quotes Abū Abdullāh Imām as-Sādiq (ع) saying, "The sky wept over al-Hussain (ع) for forty mornings with blood, while the earth wept over him for forty mornings with blackness. The sun wept over him for forty mornings with an eclipse and with redness, whereas the angels wept over him for forty mornings. No woman among us ever dyed with henna, nor used any oil, nor any kohl nor cohabited with her husband till the head of Ubaydullah ibn Ziyad was brought to us, and we are still grieving even after all of that."[3]

This is the basis of the ongoing custom of grieving for the deceased for forty days. On the 40th day, a special mourning ceremony is held at his grave-site attended by his relatives and friends. This custom is not confined to Muslims. Adherents of other creeds hold commemorative mourning ceremonies for their lost ones. Some gather at a church and conduct a special funeral prayer service. Jews

---

[1] His full name is: Abdullāh ibn Abbas ibn Abdul-Muttalib, a cousin of the Prophet of Islam (ص). He is known as the Islamic nation's scholar. The traditions of the Prophet which he reported fill the Sahīh books. He died in Ta'if in 68 A.H./687 A.D. after having lost his eye-sight.

[2] al-Majlisi, *Bihār al-Anwār*, Vol. 2, p. 679.

[3] an-Nawari, *Mustadrak al-Wasa'il*, p. 215, chapter 94.

renew their mourning service thirty days after one's death, nine months after one's death, and one year after one's death[1]. All of this is done in order to keep his memory alive and so that people may not forget his legacy and deeds if he is one of the great ones with merits and feats.

At any rate, a researcher does not find in the band described as reformers a man so well shrouded in feats of the most sublime meanings, one whose life, uprising, and the tragic way in which he was killed..., a divine call and lessons in reform, even social systems, ethics, and sacred morals..., other than the master of the youths of Paradise, the man who was martyred for his creed, for Islam, for harmony, the martyr for ethics and cultivation, namely al-Hussain (ع). He, more than anyone else, deserves to be remembered on various occasions. People ought to make a pilgrimage to his sacred grave-site on the anniversary of the passage of 40 days since the date of his martyrdom so that they may achieve such lofty objectives.

The reason why most people hold only the first such an anniversary is due to the fact that the merits of those men are limited and temporal, unlike those of the Master of Martyrs: his feats are endless, his virtues are countless. The study of his life and martyrdom keeps his memory alive, and so is the case whenever he is mentioned. To follow in his footsteps is needed by every generation. To hold an annual ceremony at his grave on the anniversary of his Arba'een brings his revolution back to memory. It also brings back to memory the cruelty committed by the Umayyads and their henchmen. No matter how hard an orator tries, or how well a poet presents his theme, new doors of virtue, which were closed before, will then be opened.

This is why it has been the custom of the Shī'as to bring back to memory on the Arba'een those events every year. The tradition wherein Imām al-Bāqir (ع) says that the heavens wept over al-

---

[1]*Nahr at-Thahab fi Tarikh Halab*, Vol. 1, pp. 63 and 267.

Hussain (ع) for forty mornings, rising red and setting red[1], hints to such a public custom.

So is the case with a statement made once by Imām al-Hassan al-'Askari (ع) wherein he said, "There are five marks for a believer: his fifty-one *rek'at* prayers, *ziyarat al-arba'een*, his audible recitation of the *basmala*, his wearing his ring on the right hand, and his rubbing his forehead with the dust."[2]

Such a statement leads us to the ongoing public custom being discussed. Holding a mourning ceremony for the Master of Martyrs and holding meetings in his memory are all done by those who are loyal to him and who follow him. There is no doubt that those who follow his path are the believers who recognize him as their Imām; so, one of the marks highlighting their *iman*, as well as their loyalty to the master of the youths of Paradise, the one who was killed as he stood to defend the divine Message, is to be present on the Arba'een anniversary at his sacred grave in order to hold a mourning ceremony for him and remember the tragedies that had befallen him and his companions and Ahl al-Bayt (ع).

To twist the meaning of *ziyarat al-arba'een* by saying that it means visiting the grave-sites of forty believers is simply indicative of twisted minds, an attempt at distortion, one which good taste resents. Moreover, it is without any foundation. Had the goal been to visit forty believers, the Imām (ع) would have used the term "*ziyarat arba'een [mu'mineen]*." The original wording indicates that ziyarat al-arba'een is one of the conditions enumerated in the hadīth cited above saying that it is one of the marks of one's iman and an indication of his loyalty to the Twelve Imāms (ع).

---

[1]al-Qummi, *Kāmil az-Ziyarat* كامل الزيارات, p. 90, Chapter 28.

[2]This is narrated by Shaikh at-Tusi on p. 17, Vol. 3, of his *Tahthib* تهذيب, in a chapter discussing the merits of visiting the grave-site of Imām al-Hussain (ع). In it, he quotes Imām "Abū Muhammed" al-Hassan al-'Askari, peace be with him. It is also narrated on p. 551 of the Indian edition of *Musbah al-Mutahajjid* مصباح المتهجد.

All the Imāms who descended from the Prophet (ﷺ) were the gates of salvation, the arks of mercy. Through them can a believer be distinguished from a non-believer. They all left this world after being killed as they stood to defend the divine Message, accepting the possibility of their being killed for the stand which they took in obedience to the Command of their Lord, Glory to Him, the One Who sent His *wahi* to their grandfather the Prophet (ﷺ). Father of Muhammed, al-Hassan (ع) son of the Commander of the Faithful Ali (ع), has pointed out to this fact saying, "The mission which we undertake is assigned to Twelve Imāms (ع) each one of whom is either to be killed or poisoned."

For all of these reasons, the Imāms from among the Prophet's Progeny (ع) found no alternative to attracting the attention to such a glorious revolution because it contains tragedies that would split the hardest of rocks. They knew that persistence in demonstrating the injustice dealt to al-Hussain (ع) would stir the emotions and attract the hearts of sympathizers. One who hears the tales of such horrible events will come to conclude that al-Hussain (ع) was a fair and just Imām who did not succumb to lowly things, that his Imāmate was inherited from his grandfather the Prophet (ﷺ) and from his father the *wasi* (ع), that whoever opposes him deviates from the path of equity. Whoever absorbs the fact that right was on al-Hussain's side and on that of his infallible offspring would be embracing their method and following their path.

This is why the Imāms (ع) did not urge the holding of mourning ceremonies for the Arba'een anniversary of any of them, not even for that of the Prophet of Islam (ع), so that it alone would be the memory of his tragedy that would make a strong case for safeguarding the link with the creed. Turning attention to it is more effective in keeping the cause of the Infallible Ones dear to all those who discuss it: "Keep our cause alive, and discuss our cause."

The kind reader, anyway, can easily see why *ziyarat al-arba'een* is an indication of one's iman when he gets to know similar indications to which the *hadīth* has referred.

The first of such marks, namely the 51-*rek'at* prayers, legislated during the night of the Prophet's *mi'raj*, and which, through the Prophet's intercession, were reduced to only five during the day and the night, are: seventeen *rek'at* for the morning, the noon and the afternoon, the sunset and the evening, and the *nafl* prayers timed with them, in addition to night's *nafl* prayers: they all make up thirty-four: eight before the noon-time prayers, eight before the after-noon prayers, four after sunset prayers, and two after the evening prayers regarded as one, and two before the morning prayers, and finally eleven *rek'at* for the night's nafl prayers. Add to them the *shaf* and *witr rek'at*, and you will come to a total of obligatory and optional prayers of fifty-one *rek'at*. This is applicable to the Shī'as only. Although they agree with the Shī'as with regard to the number of obligatory *rek'at*, the Sunnis differ when it comes to optional prayers. On p. 314, Vol. 1, of Ibn Humam al-Hanafi's book *Fath al-Qadeer*, they are: two *rek'at* before the *fajr* prayers, four before the noon prayers and two after that, four before the afternoon prayers, or just two *rek'at*, two more after the sunset prayers and four thereafter, or just two, making up twenty-three *rek'at*. They differ about the night's *nafl* prayers whether they ought to be eight, only two, or thirteen, or even more. Hence, the total of optional and compulsory *rek'at* will in no case be fifty-one; so, the fifty-one *rek'at* are relevant to Imāmite (Twelver) Shī'as only.

The second on the list of marks referred to in the said hadīth is the audible pronunciation of the *basmala*. Imāmites seek nearness to Allāh, the most Exalted One, by making it obligatory to pronounce it audibly in the audible prayers and voluntary in the inaudible ones, following the text of their Imāms (ع). In this regard, al-Fakhr ar-Razi says, "Shī'as are of the view that it is a Sunnah to audibly pronounce the *basmala* in the audible prayers as well as the inaudible ones, whereas the majority of faqihs differ from them. It is proven through tawatur that Ali ibn Abū Talib (ع) used to audibly pronounce the *basmala*. Anyone who follows Ali (ع) in as far as his creed is concerned will surely be on the right guidance by token of the *hadīth* saying, O Allāh! Let right be with Ali wherever he goes.'"[1] This

---

[1] *Mafatih al-Ghayb*, Vol. 1, p. 107.

statement of ar-Razi was not digested by Abul-Thana' al-Ālusi who followed it with his comment in which he said, "Had anyone acted upon all what they claim to be *mutawatir* (consecutively reported) from the Commander of the Faithful (ع), he will surely be an apostate; so, there is no alternative to believing in some and disbelieving in others. His claim that anyone who emulates Ali (ع) in as far as his creed is concerned will be on the right guidance of Islam is accepted without any discussion so long as we are sure that it is proven as having been said by Ali, peace be with him. Anything else besides that is steam."[1]

Shī'as are not harmed when al-Ālusi and others assault them especially since their feet are firm on the path of loyalty for the master of *wasis* (ع) to whom the Messenger of Allāh (ع) says, "O Ali! Nobody knows Allāh, the most Exalted One, (fully well) except I and you, and nobody knows me (full well) except Allāh and you, and nobody knows you (fully well) except Allāh and I."[2]

Sunnis have opted to do the opposite with regard to such a pronouncement. On p. 478, Vol. 1, of Ibn Qudamah's book *Al-Mughni*, and also on p. 204, Vol. 1, of *Badai' as-Sanai'* by al-Kasani, and also on p. 216, Vol. 1, of az-Zarqani's *Sharh* of Abul-Diya's *Mukhtasar* of Malik's *fiqh*, audible pronouncement is not a Sunnah in the prayers.

The third mark mentioned in the said hadīth, that is, wearing a ring in the right hand, is something practiced religiously by the Shī'as on account of the traditions they quote from their Imāms (ع). A multitude among the Sunnis disagrees with them. Ibn al-Hajjaj al-Maliki has said, "The Sunnah has recorded everything as abominable if handed by the left hand and everything *tahir* if handed by the right. In this sense, it is highly recommended to wear a ring in the left hand to be taken by the right one and then placed on the

---

[1] *Ruh al-Ma'ani*, Vol. 1, p. 47.

[2] *Al-Muhtadir*, p. 165.

202

left."[1] Ibn Hajar narrates saying that Malik hated to wear a ring on his right hand, believing it should be worn on the left[2]. Shaikh Isma'eel al-Barusawi has said the following in *Iqd al-Durr*: "Originally, it was a Sunnah to wear a ring on the right hand, but since this is the distinguishing mark of the people of *bid'as*, innovations, and of injustice, it became a Sunnah in our time to place the ring on a finger on the left hand."[3]

---

[1]*Al-Madkhal*, Vol. 1, p. 46, in a chapter dealing with the etiquette of entering mosques.

[2]*Al-Fatawa al-Fiqhiyya al-Kubra*, Vol. 1, p. 264, in a chapter dealing with what to wear.

[3]This is narrated by the authority Shaikh Abdul-Hussain Ahmed al-Amini an-Najafi in his 11-volume encyclopedia titled *Al-Ghadīr* quoting p. 142, Vol. 4, of the exegesis titled *Ruh al-Bayan*. This is not the first issue wherein Sunnis practice the opposite of what the Shī'as practice. On p. 137, Vol. 1, of Abū Ishāq ash-Sharazi's book *Al-Muhaththab*, on p. 47, Vol. 1, of al-Ghazali's book *Al-Wajeeza*, on p. 25 of an-Nawawi's *Al-Minhaj* as well as on p. 560, Vol. 1, of its *Sharh* by Ibn Hajar titled *Tuhfat al-Muhtaj fi Sharh al-Minhaj*, on p. 248, Vol. 4, of al-Ayni's book *Umdat al-Qari fi Sharh al-Bukhari*, on p. 681, Vol. 1, of Ibn Muflih's book *Al-Furoo*, and on p. 505, Vol. 2, of Ibn Qudamah's book *Al-Mughni*, planing graves is looked upon as a mark of innovators. On p. 88, Vol. 1, of ash-Sharani's book *Rahmat al-Ummah bi Ikhtilaf al-A'immah*, a book written as a comment on the exegesis titled *Al-Mizan* by 'allama Tabatabai, the author states the following: "It is a Sunnah to plane graves. But since it became a distinguishing mark for the Rafidis, it is better to do contrariwise." Among other issues wherein Sunnis do the opposite of what the Shī'as do is blessing the Prophet (ﷺ) and his progeny (ع). Some of them suggest its elimination altogether. For example, az-Zamakhshari states the following comment after being tried to explain verse 56 of Sūrat al-Ahzab (Chapter 33 of the Holy Qur'an) in his book *Al-Kashshaf*: "It is *makrooh* to bless the Prophet (ﷺ) because it causes one to be charged with being a Rafidi, especially since he [the Prophet {ﷺ}] has said, Do not stand where you may be prone to being charged.'" The same theme exists on p. 135, Vol. 11, of Ibn Hajar's book *Fath al-Bari*, in "Kitab al-Da'awat" (book of supplications), where the author tries to answer the question: "Should one bless anyone else besides the Prophet (ﷺ)?" Says he, "There is a disagreement with regard to blessing anyone besides the prophets although there is a consensus that it is permissive to greet the Living One.

The fourth mark mentioned in the said *hadīth* is the placing of the forehead on dust [or dry soil]. Its message is to demonstrate that during the *sajda*, the forehead has to be placed on the ground. Sunnis do not place their forehead on the ground. Abū Haneefa, Malik, and Ahmed are reported as having authorized the prostrating on turban coils[1], or on a piece of garment[2] worn by the person performing the prayers or any piece of cloth. Hanafis have authorized placing it on the palms if one feels grudgingly that he has no other choice[3]. They also permit prostrating on wheat and barley, on a bed, on the back of another person standing in front of you who is also performing the same prayers![4]

The objective behind such a reference is that it is highly commendable, when one prostrates to thank Allāh, to rub his forehead on the dust as a symbol of humility and to shun arrogance. An examination of the original text will show any discreet person that it is equally commendable to rub both sides of the face on it.

Rubbing the cheeks exists when reference is made to *sajdat ash-*

Some say it is permissive in its absolute application, while others say it is conditional because it has become a distinguishing mark of the Rafidis." Even in the manner of dressing do some Sunnis want to distinguish themselves from others: On p. 13, Vol. 5, of az-Zarqani's book *Sharh al-Mawahib as-Saniyya*, it is stated that, "Some scholars used to loosen their tassels from the left front side, and I have never read any text that a tassel should be loosened from the right side except in a weak *hadīth* narrated by at-Tabrani. Now since this has become a distinguishing mark of the Imāmites, it ought to be abandoned in order to avoid looking like them." Imagine! Notice the prejudice and the narrow-mindedness!

[1] ash-Sha'rani, *Al-Mizan*, Vol. 1, p. 138.

[2] al-Marghinani, *Al-Hidaya*, Vol. 1, p. 33.

[3] Abdul-Rahman al-Jazari, *Al-Fiqh ala al-Mathahib al-Arba'ah*, Vol. 1, p. 189.

[4] Ibn Najeem, *Al-Bahr ar-Ra'iq*, Vol. 1, p. 319.

Shukr[1], something whereby prophet Moses son of Imran [Amram] (ع) deserved to be drawn closer to the Almighty whenever he addressed Him silently [during the *munajat*][2]. Nobody contradicted the Imāmites with regard to such rubbing, be it on the forehead or on the cheeks. Sunnis never bound themselves to rub their foreheads on dust when they perform their prayers or when they perform *sajdat ash-Shukr*. This is so despite the fact that an-Nakh'i, Malik, and Abū Haneefa have all disliked to perform *sajdat ash-Shukr*, although the Hanbalis observe it[3], and so do the Shafi'is[4] whenever they receive a divine blessing or whenever a sign of Allāh's wrath is removed from them.

IN MEDĪNA

As-Sajjād (ع) had no choice except to leave Kerbalā' and set forth to Medīna (which used to be called Yathrib during the pre-Islamic era) after having stayed there for three days. It was too much for him to see how his aunts and the other women, as well as the children, were all crying day and night while visiting one grave after another. Bashir ibn Hathlam has said, "When we came close to Medīna, Ali ibn al-Hussain (ع) alighted and tied his she-camel then set up a tent where he lodged the women. He said to me, O Bashir! May Allāh have mercy on your father! He was a poet. Can you compose any of it at all?' I said, Yes, O son of the Messenger of Allāh! I, too, am a poet.' He (ع) said, Then enter Medīna and mourn the martyrdom of Abū Abdullāh (ع).' So I rode my horse and entered Medīna. When I came near the Mosque of the Prophet, peace and blessings of Allāh be upon him and his progeny, I cried loudly and recited these verses:

---

[1]Shaikh al-Mufid, *Al-Kafi ala Hamish Mir'at al-Uqool*, Vol. 3, p. 129. As-Saduq, *Al-Faqih*, p. 69. Shaikh at-Tusi, *At-Tahthib*, Vol. 1, p. 266, in a chapter dealing with what ought to be recited following the prayers.

[2]Shaikh as-Saduq, *Al-Faqih*, p. 69.

[3]Ibn Qudamah, *Al-Mughni*, Vol. 1, p. 626. Ibn Muflih, *Al-Furoo'*, Vol. 1, p. 382.

[4]*Kitab al-Umm*, Vol. 1, p. 116. Al-Mazni, *Al-Mukhtasar*, Vol. 1, p. 90. Al-Ghazali, *Al-Wajeeza*, Vol. 1, p. 32.

يــا أهــل يثــربَ لا مُقَــام لكـم بهــا   قَتــــل الحســـينُ فــــأدمعي مـــــدرارُ

الجســـم منـــه بكـــربلاء مضـــرّجٌ   والـــرأسُ منـــه علـــى القنــاةِ يُـــدارُ

O people of Yathrib! May you never stay therein!
Al-Hussain (ع) is killed, so my tears now rain,
His body is in Kerbalā covered with blood
While his head is on a spear displayed.

"Then I said, Here is Ali ibn al-Hussain (ع) accompanied by his aunts and sisters; they have all returned to you. I am his messenger to you to inform you of his place.' People went out in a hurry, including women who had never before left their chambers, all weeping and wailing. All those in Medīna were in tears. Nobody had ever seen such crying and wailing. They surrounded Ali, Zain al-Ābidīn (ع), to offer him their condolences. He came out of the tent with a handkerchief in his hand with which he was wiping his tears. Behind him was one of his slaves carrying a chair in which the Imām (ع) later sat, being overcome by grief. The cries of the mourners were loud. Everyone was weeping and wailing. Ali signaled to people to calm down. Once they stopped crying, he, peace be with him said,

All Praise is due to Allāh, Lord of the Worlds, the Most Gracious, the Most Merciful, the King of the Day of Judgment, Creator of all creation Who is Exalted in the high heavens, Who is so near, He hears even the silent speech. We praise Him on the grave events, on time's tragedies, on the pain inflicted by such tragedies, on the crushing of calamities, on the greatness of our catastrophe, on our great, monstrous, magnanimous and afflicting hardships. O people! Allāh, the most Exalted One, Praise to Him, has tried us with great trials and tribulations, with a tremendous loss suffered by the religion of Islam. The father of Abdullāh, al-Hussain (ع) and his family have been killed, and his women and children taken captive. They displayed his head in every land from the top of a spear... Such is the catastrophe similar to which there is none at all. O people! Which men among you are happy after him, or which heart is not grieved on his account? Which eye among you withholds its tears and is too miser with its tears? The seven great heavens wept over his killing; the seas wept with their waves, and so did the heavens with their corners and the earth with its expanse; so did the trees with their branches and the fish in the depths of the seas. So did the angels who are close to their Lord. So did all those in the heavens. O people! Which heart is not grieved by his killing? Which heart does not yearn for him? Which hearing hears such a calamity that has befallen Islam without becoming deaf? O people! We have become homeless, exiles, outcasts, shunned, distanced from all countries as though we were the offspring of the Turks or of Kabul without having committed a crime, nor an abomination, nor afflicted a calamity on Islam! Never did we ever hear such thing from our fathers of old. This is something new. By Allāh! Had the Prophet (ص) required them to fight us just as he had required them to be good to us, they would not have done to us any more than what they already have. So we belong to Allāh, and to Him is our return from this calamity, and what a great, painful, hard, cruel, and catastrophic calamity it is! To Allāh do we complain from what has happened to us, from the suffering we have endured, for He is the Omnipotent, the Vengeful.

السَّلام عَلَيْكَ يَا أَبَا عَبْدِ اللهِ وَعَلَى الأرواح الَّتي حَلَّتْ بِفِنائِكَ ، وَأناخَت بِرَحْلِكَ، عَلَيْكَ مِنّي سَلامُ اللهِ أَبَداً مَا بَقِيتُ وَبَقِيَ اللَّيْلُ وَالنَّهارُ ، وَلا جَعَلَهُ اللهُ آخِرَ العَهْدِ مِنّي لِزِيارَتِكُمْ أَهْلَ البَيتِ، السَّلام عَلَى الحُسَينِ ، وَعَلى عَلِيِّ بْنِ الحُسَينِ ، وَعَلى أوْلادِ الحُسَينِ ، وَعَلى أصْحابِ الحُسَينِ و رحمة اللهِ و بركاته.

Peace with you, O father of Abdullāh, and with the souls that landed in your courtyard! Allāh's Greeting to you from me forever, so long as there is night and day! May Allāh not make it the last time I greet you, O Ahl al-Bayt! Peace with al-Hussain, with Ali son of al-Hussain, with the offspring of al-Hussain, and with the companions of al-Hussain, the mercy of Allāh and His blessings.

"Sa'sa'ah ibn Sawhan al-Abdi, an invalid who could barely walk on his feet, stood up and apologized to the Imām (ع) for not rushing to help his family due to his handicap. He, peace be with him, responded to him by accepting his excuse, telling him that he thought well of him, thanked him and sought Allāh's mercy for his father. Then Zain al-Ābidīn (ع) entered Medīna accompanied by his family and children.[1]

---

[1]Ibn Tawoos, *Al-Luhuf*, p. 116.

Ibrahim ibn Talhah ibn Ubaydullāh came to the Imām (ع) and asked him, "Who won?" The Imām, peace be with him, answered, "When the time for prayers comes, and when the *athan* and *iqama* are called, you will know who the winner is."[1]

Zainab took both knobs of the mosque's door and cried out, "O grandfather! I mourn to you my brother al-Hussain (ع)!"

Sukayna cried out, "O grandfather! To you do I complain from what we have been through, for by Allāh, I never saw anyone more hard-hearted than Yazid, nor have I ever seen anyone, be he an apostate or a polytheist, more evil than him, more rough, or more cruel. He kept hitting my father's lips with his iron bar as he said, How did you find the battle, O al-Hussain (ع)?!'"[2]

The ladies who were born and grew up in the lap of Prophethood held a mourning ceremony for the Master of Martyrs (ع). They put on the most coarse of clothes; they shrouded themselves in black, and they kept weeping and wailing day and night as Imām as-Sajjād was cooking for them[3].

Once Imām Ja'far as-Sādiq (ع) said, "No lady who descended from Hashim used any dye, nor any oil, nor any kohl, for full five years; it was then that al-Mukhtar sent them the head of Ubaydullāh ibn Ziyad."[4]

As regarding ar-Rubab, she wept over [her husband] Abū Abdullāh (ع) till her eyes were no longer capable of producing any more tears. One of her bondmaids told her that using a particular type of herb

---

[1]Shaikh at-Tusi, *Al-Aamali*, p. 66.

[2]al-Qazwini, *Riyad al-Ahzan*, p. 163.

[3]al-Barqi, *Mahasin*, Vol. 2, p. 420, in a chapter dealing with providing food for a mourning ceremony.

[4]*Mustadrak al-Wasa'il*, Vol. 2, p. 215, chapter 94.

was tear stimulant, so she ordered it to be prepared for her in order to induce her tears[1].

Ali Zain al-Ābidīn (ع), the only surviving son of Imām al-Hussain (ع), stayed aloof from the public in order to avoid being involved in their disputes with one another and in order to dedicate his entire time to worshipping Allāh and mourning his father. He kept weeping day and night. One of his slaves said to him, "I fear for you lest you should perish." He (ع) said to him, "I only convey my complaints and my grief to Allāh, and I know from Allāh what you all do not know. Jacob was a prophet from whom Allāh caused one of his sons to be separated. He had twelve sons, and he knew that his son (Joseph) was still alive, yet he wept over him till he lost his eye sight. If you look at my father, my brothers, my uncles, and my friends, how they were slain all around me, tell me how can my grief ever end? Whenever I remember how Fātima's children were slaughtered, I cannot help crying. And whenever I look at my aunts and sisters, I remember how they were fleeing from one tent to another..."

To you, O Messenger of Allāh (ع), is our complaint from the way whereby your nation treated your pure offspring, from the oppression and persecution to which they were subjected, and all Praise is due to Allāh, Lord of the Worlds.

عُذْرًا، إِذَا انْقَطَعَ الْكَـلَامُ .. فَالرُّوح يَقْتُلَهَا الحَنِينْ ..

وَأَنَـا الْمُكَـبَـلُ بِـالهَـوى .. والحُـبُّ قَيْـدٌ لا يَلِيـنْ ..

هَيْهَـاتَ أَنْسَـى كَرْبَـلَاءَ .. وَأَنَـا بِـذِكْـرَاهـا سَجِـيـنْ ..

سَـأَظَـلُ أَذْكُـرُ كَرْبَـلَاءَ .. وَأَظَـلُ أَهْـتِـفُ: يَـاحُسَيـنْ

---

[1] al-Majlisi, *Bihār al-Anwār*, Vol. 10, p. 235, citing *Al-Kafi* of Shaikh al-Mufid.

1. **Prophet Muhammed:** He is Muhammed ibn (son of) Abdullāh ibn Abdul-Muttalib ibn Hashim ibn Abd Munaf ibn Qusayy ibn Kilab ibn Murrah ibn Ka`b ibn ibn Ghalib ibn Fahr ibn Malik ibn Nadar ibn Kinanah ibn Khuzaymah ibn Mudrikah ibn Ilyas ibn Mazar ibn Nazar ibn Ma`ad ibn Adnan ibn Isma`eel (Ishmael) ibn Ibrahim (Abraham), peace and blessings of Allāh be upon him, his progeny, and righteous ancestors, especially his great grandfathers Isma`eel and Ibrahim. **PROPHET'S FATHER:** Abdullāh ibn Abdul-Muttalib (545 - 570 A.D.). The Blessed Prophet's father, Abdullāh ibn Abdul-Muttalib, was born in 545 A.D., 25 years before the Year of the Elephant. Abū Tālib and az-Zubair were his brothers by the same father and mother. So were the girls, except Safiyya. When his father died, the Prophet of Allāh (ص) was two months old, though reports about this differ. Abdul-Mut,.t,.alib loved `Abdullāh immensely because he was the best of his children, the most chaste and the most noble among them. Once Abdul-Muttalib sent his son on business, and when the caravan passed by Yathrib (Medīna), Abdullāh died there. He was buried in the house of Arqam ibn Ibrāhim ibn Surāqah al-Adawi. **PROPHET'S FOSTER FATHER:** Al-Hārith son of Abd al-Uzza ibn Rifā`ah ibn Millān ibn Nāsirah ibn Fusayya ibn Nasr ibn Sa`d ibn Bakr ibn Hawāzin. **PROPHET'S FOSTER MOTHERS:** Thawbiyya; she was a bondmaid of Abū Lahab, the paternal uncle of the Messenger of Allāh (ص). She breast-fed him with the milk of her son Masruh. **Halima**, the Prophet's foster mother. She was the daughter of "Abū Thu'aib" Abdullāh ibn Shajnah ibn Jābir ibn Rizām ibn Nās,.irah ibn Sa`d ibn Bakr ibn Hawāzin al-Qaisi. She breast-fed the Messenger of Allāh (ص) with the milk of her son Abdullāh and reared him (ص) for four years (till the year 574 A.D.). **PROPHET'S CHILDREN:** 1) Ibrāhim, 2) Abdullāh; 3) al-Qāsim; 4) stepdaughter (some say daughter) Zainab (d. 629 A.D.); 5) stepdaughter (some say daughter) Ruqayya (d. 624 A.D.), 6) stepdaughter (some say daughter) Umm Kulthum (d. 630 A.D.); 7) the Prophet's daughter Fāt,.ima, peace be upon her and her progeny. For more details, refer to my book titled *Muhammed: Prophet and Messenger of Allāh.*

2. **Fātima (ع) Daughter of Muhammed (ص):** Fātima (615 – 632 A.D.), mother of the Imāms (ع), is the daughter of the Messenger of Allāh (ص) by his first wife, Khadija daughter of Khuwaylid, may the Almighty be pleased with her. Fātima was born in Mecca on a Friday, the 20th of Jumada II in the fifth year after the declaration of the Prophetic message which corresponds, according to the Christian calendar, to the year 615. She was only 18 and 75 days when she died in Medīna few days only (some say 75) after the death of her revered father (ص): The Prophet (ص) passed away on Safar 28/May 28 according to the Christian Gregorian calendar, or the 25th according to the Julian calendar, of the same year. Fātima passed away on the 14th of Jumada I of 11 A.H. which corresponded to August 7, 632 A.D. She was buried somewhere in the graveyard of Jannatul-Baqi' in Medīna in an unmarked grave. According to her will, her husband, Imām Ali (ع), did not leave any marks identifying her grave, and nobody knows where it is. According to Shī'ite Muslims, she was the only daughter of the Holy Prophet (ص).

Fātima has nine names/titles: Fātima فاطمة, al-Siddiqa الصديقة (the truthful one), al-Mubaraka المباركة (the blessed one), al-Tahira الطاهرة (the pure one), al-Zakiyya الزكية (the chaste one), al-Radhiayya الرضية (the grateful one), al-Mardhiyya المرضية (the one who shall be pleased [on Judgment Day]), al-Muhaddatha المحدثة (the one, other than the Prophet, to whom an angel speaks) and al-Zahra الزهراء (the splendid one).

The Prophet (ص) taught Fātima (ع) divine knowledge and endowed her with special intellectual brilliance, so much so that she realized the true meaning of faith, piety, and the reality of Islam. But Fātima (ع) also was a witness to sorrow and a life of anguish from the very beginning of her life. She constantly saw how her revered father was mistreated by the unbelievers and later how she herself fell a victim to the same Abūse, only this time by some "Muslims".

A number of chronicles quote her mother, Khadija, narrating the following about the birth of her revered daughter: "At the time of Fātima's birth, I sent for my neighboring Quraishite women to assist me. They flatly refused, saying that I had betrayed them by marrying and supporting Muhammed. I was perturbed for a while when, to my great surprise, I saw four strange tall women with halos around their faces approaching me. Finding me dismayed, one of them addressed me thus, 'O Khadija! I am Sarah, mother of Ishāq (Isaac). The other three are: Mary mother of Christ, Asiya daughter of Muzahim and Umm Kulthum sister of Moses. We have all been commanded by God to put our nursing knowledge at your disposal.' Saying this, all of them sat around me and rendered the services of midwifery till my daughter Fātima was born."

The motherly blessings and affection received by Fātima (ع) were only for five years after which Khadija left for her heavenly home. The Holy Prophet brought her up thereafter.

The Holy Prophet said: "Whoever injures (bodily or otherwise) Fātima, he injures me; and whoever injures me injures Allāh; and whoever injures Allāh practices unbelief. O Fātima! If your wrath is incurred, it incurs the wrath of Allāh; and if you are pleased, it makes Allāh pleased, too."

M.H. Shakir writes the following: "Fātima, the only daughter of the Holy Prophet of Islam, was born in Mecca on 20th of Jumada al-Thaniya 18 B.H. (Before Hijra). The good and noble lady Khadija and the Apostle of Allāh bestowed all their natural love, care and devotion on their lovable and only child, Fātima, who in her turn was extremely fond of her parents. The Princess of the House of the Prophet was very intelligent, accomplished and cheerful. Her speeches, poems and sayings serve as an index to her strength of character and nobility of mind. Her virtues gained her the title 'Our Lady of Light'. She was moderately tall, slender and endowed with great beauty which caused her to be called 'az-Zahra' (the Lady of Light)".

Fātima (ع) was called az-Zahra' because her light used to shine among those in the heavens. After arriving in Medīna, she was married to Ali in the first year of Hijra, and she gave birth to three sons. Her sons were: Hassan, Hussain, Masters of the youths of Paradise, and Muhsin. Muhsin never saw the light because he was aborted as his mother was behind her house door fending for herself

212

while rogues were trying to break into it and force her husband to swear the oath of allegiance to Abū Bakr. She had two daughters, Zainab, the heroine of Kerbalā, and Umm Kulthum. Her children are well-known for their piety, righteousness and generosity. Their strength of character and actions changed the course of history.

The Holy Prophet said فاطمة بضعة مني, "Fātima is part of me". He would go out to receive his daughter whenever she came from her husband's house. Every morning on his way to the Mosque, he would pass by Fātima's house and say, *"as-Salamu `alaykum ya Ahla Bay annnubuwwah wa ma`din arr-risala "* (Peace be with you, O Ahl al-Bayt (Household of the Prophet) and the Substance of the Message).

Fātima (ع) is famous and acknowledged as the "Sayyidatu nisa '1-`alamin" (Leader of all the women of the world for all times) because the Prophethood of Muhammad would not have been everlasting without her. The Prophet is the perfect example for men, but could not be so for women. For all the verses revealed in the Holy Qur'ān for women, Fātima is the perfect model, who translated every verse into action. In her lifetime, she was a complete woman, being Daughter, Wife and Mother at the same time.

Fātima inherited the genius and wisdom, the determination and will power, piety and sanctity, generosity and benevolence, devotion and worship of Allāh, self-sacrifice and hospitality, forbearance and patience, knowledge and nobility of disposition of her illustrious father, both in words and in actions. "I often witnessed my mother," says Imām Hussain, "absorbed in prayer from dusk to dawn." Her generosity and compassion for the poor was such that no destitute or beggar ever returned from her door empty-handed. She (ع) worked, dressed, ate and lived very simply. She was very generous; and none who came to her door ever went away empty handed. Many times she gave away all the food she had had, staying without any food at all. As a daughter, she loved her parents so much that she won their love and regard to such an extent that the Holy Prophet (ص) used to stand up whenever she came to him.

Marriage: When Fātima came of age, a number of hopefuls sought her hand in marriage. The Holy Prophet was awaiting the Divine order in this respect until Imām `Ali approached him and asked for her hand in marriage. The Holy Prophet came to Fātima (ع) and asked, "My daughter! Do you consent to be wedded to `Ali, as I am so commanded by Allāh?" Fātima (ع) thereupon bowed her head in modesty. Umm Salamah narrates the following: "Fātima's face Fātima bloomed with joy and her silence was so suggestive and conspicuous that the Holy Prophet stood up to shout: *Allāhu Akbar'* (Allāh is great)! Fātima's silence is her acceptance." On Friday, Thul Hijja 1, 2 A.H., which corresponded to May 25, 624 A.D. according to the Julian Christian calendar or to the 28th of May of the same year according to the Gregorian Christian calendar which is widely used in the text of this book, the marriage ceremony took place. All the Muhajirun (emigrants) and Ansār (supporters) of Medīna assembled in the mosque while Imām `Ali was seated before the Holy Prophet with all the ceremonious modesty of a bridegroom. The Holy Prophet first recited an eloquent sermon then declared: "I have been commanded by Allāh to get Fātima wedded to `Ali, and so I do hereby solemnize the matrimony between `Ali and Fātima on a dower of four hundred *mithqal* of silver." Then he asked Imām Ali, "Do you consent to it, O Ali? " "Yes, I do, O Holy Prophet of Allāh!" replied Imām Ali (ع). Then the Holy Prophet raised his hands and supplicated thus: "O Lord! Bless both of them, sanctify their progeny and grant them the keys of Your beneficence, Your treasures of wisdom and genius; and let them be a source of blessing and peace to my *umma.*" Her children; Imām Hassan, Imām Hussain, Zainab and Umm Kulthum, are well-known for their piety, righteousness and generosity. Their strength of character and actions changed the course of history and fortified Islam which otherwise would have been lost to mankind.

As a wife, she was very devoted. She never asked Ali for anything in her entire life. As a mother, she cared for and brought up wonderful children; they have left their marks on the pages of world history which time and the plots of enemies of Ahl al-Bayt (ع) will never be able to erase.

214

AFTER THE PROPHET'S DEMISE

قال ابن الجوزي (أبو الفرج عبد الرحمن بن أبي الحسن علي بن محمد القرشي التيمي البكري، الفقيه الحنبلي الحافظ المفسر الواعظ المؤرخ الأديب المعروف بابن الجوزي، رحمه الله رحمة واسعة، وأدخله فسيح جناته، فقيه حنبلي محدث ومؤرخ ومتكلم [510هـ/1116م-12 رمضان592 هـ] ولد وتوفي في بغداد) : روي عن علي (عليه السلام) قال: لما مات رسول الله (صلى الله عليه وآله وسلم) جاءت فاطمة (عليها السلام) فأخذت قبضة من تراب القبر فوضعته على عينيها، فبكت وأنشأت تقول:

يـــا ليتهـــا خرجـــت مـــع الزفـــرات	نفسـي علـى زفراتهـا محبوسـة
أبكـــي مخافـــة أن تطــول حيـــاتي	لا خيــرَ بعـدكَ فـي الحيـاةِ وإنمـا

Ibn al-Jawzi, namely Abul-Faraj Abdul-Rahman ibn Abul-Hassan Ali ibn Muhammed al-Qarashi (or Quraishi, of Quraish tribe) al-Taymi al-Bakri, was a Hanbali *faqih* who knew the Holy Qur'ān by heart, an orator, historian and a man of letters. He was born in Baghdad in 510 A.H./1117 A.D. and died there on the 12th of the month of Ramadan of 592 A.H. which coincided with August 16, 1196 A.D. according to the Gregorian Christian calendar or the 9th of the same month and year according to the Julian calendar. May the Almighty shower him with His broad mercy and admit him into His spacious Paradise. He quotes Imām Ali (ع) saying that when the Messenger of Allāh (ص) died, Fātima (ع) went to his gravesite, took a handful of its dust, put it on her eyes, wept and composed these verses of poetry:

My soul is confined with every sigh,
How I wish it departed as sighs depart.
No good is there in life after you so I
For fear my life will prolong do I cry.

PROPERTY OF FADAK:

The Prophet (ص) taught Fātima (ع) divine knowledge and endowed her with special intellectual brilliance, so much so that she realized the true meaning of faith, piety, and the reality of Islam. But Fātima (ع) also was a witness to sorrow and a life of anguish from the very beginning of her life. She constantly saw how her revered father was mistreated by the unbelievers and later how she herself fell a victim

215

to the same Abūse, only this time by some "Muslims". For more details about Fadak, refer to its proper place in this Glossary.

KHUTBA OF FĀTIMA ZAHRA (A.S.) DEMANDING FADAK

خطبـة فاطمـة الزهـراء بنت النبـي محمـد فـي مسجـد أبيهـا (ص) عنـد مطالبتهـا بفدك و ميراثها من أبيها:

روى عبد الله بن الحسن باسناده عن آبائه ، أنه لما أجمع أبوبكر وعمر على منع فاطمـة عليها السلام فدكا و بلغها ذلك لاثت خمارهـا على رأسها و اشتملت بجلبابها وأقبلت في لمة من حفدتها ونساء قومها تطأ ذيولها، ما تخرم مشيتها مشية رسول الله (ص)، حتـى دخلت على أبي بكر وهو في حشد من المهاجرين والأنصار وغيرهم فنيطت دونها ملاءة فجلست ثم أنت أنّةً أجهش القوم لها بالبكاء فأرتج المجلس ثم أمهلت هنيئة حتى إذا سكن نشيج القوم وهدأت فورتهم افتتحت الكلام بحمد الله و الثناء عليه والصلاة على رسوله فعاد القوم في بكائهم فلما أمسكوا عادت في كلامها فقالت عليها السلام:

الحمد لله على ما أنعم وله الشكر على مـا ألهم والثناء بمـا قدم من عمـوم نعـم ابتداها وسبوغ آلاء أسداها وتمام منن أولاها جم عن الإحصاء عددها ونأى عن الجزاء أمدها وتفاوت عن الإدراك أبدها وندبهم لاستزادتها بالشكر لاتصالها واستحمد إلى الخلائق بإجزالها وثنى بالندب إلى أمثالها وأشهد أن لا إله إلا الله وحده لا شريك لـه كلمـة جعل الإخلاص تأويلها وضمن القلوب موصولها وأنار في التفكر معقولها الممتنع من الأبصار رؤيته ومن الألسن صفته ومن الأوهام كيفيته ابتدع الأشياء لا من شيء كـان قبلها وأنشأها بلا احتذاء أمثلة امتثلها كونها بقدرته وذرأها بمشيته من غير حاجة منـه إلى تكوينها ولا فائدة له في تصويرها إلا تثبيتا لحكمته وتنبيها على طاعتـه وإظهارا لقدرتـه تعبدا لبريته وإعزازا لدعوته ثم جعل الثواب على طاعتـه ووضع العقاب على معصيته ذيادة لعباده منكرة من نقمته وحياشة لهم إلى جنته وأشهد أن أبي محمدا عبده ورسوله اختاره قبل أن أرسله وسماه قبل أن اجتباه واصطفاه قبل أن ابتعثه إذ الخلائق بالغيب مكنونـة وبستر الأهاويل مصونة وبنهاية العدم مقرونة علما من الله تعالى بمآيل الأمور وإحاطة بحوادث الدهور ومعرفة بمواقع الأمور ابتعثه الله إتمامـا لأمره وعزيمـة على إمضاء حكمه وإنفاذا لمقادير رحمته فرأى الأمم فرقا في أديانها عكفا على نيرانها عابدة لأوثانها منكرة لله مع عرفانها فأنار الله بأبي محمد ص ظلمها وكشف عن القلوب بهمها وجلى عن الأبصار غممها وقام في النـاس بالهدايـة فأنقذهم من الغوايـة وبصرهم من العمايـة وهداهم إلى الدين القويم ودعاهم إلى الطريق المستقيم ثم قبضه الله إليه قبض رأفة واختيار ورغبة وإيثار فمحمد (ص) من تعب هذه الدار في راحة قد حف بالملائكـة الأبرار ورضوان الرب الغفار ومجاورة الملك الجبار صلى الله على أبي نبيـه وأمينـه وخيرته من الخلق وصفيه والسلام عليه ورحمة الله وبركاته.

ثم التفتت إلى أهل المجلس وقالت : أنتم عباد الله نصب أمره ونهيه وحملة دينه ووحيه وأمناء الله على أنفسكم وبلغاءه إلى الأمم زعيم حق له فيكم وعهد قدمه إليكم وبقية استخلفها عليكم كتاب الله الناطق والقرآن الصادق والنور الساطع والضياء اللامع بينة

بصائره منكشفة سرائره منجلية ظواهره مغتبطة به أشياعه قائدا إلى الرضوان اتباعه مؤد إلى النجاة استماعه به تنال حجج الله المنورة وعزائمه المفسرة ومحارمه المحذرة وبيناته الجالية وبراهينه الكافية وفضائله المندوبة ورخصه الموهوبة وشرائعه المكتوبة فجعل الله الإيمان تطهيرا لكم من الشرك والصلاة تنزيها لكم عن الكبر والزكاة تزكية للنفس ونماء في الرزق والصيام تثبيتا للإخلاص والحج تشييدا للدين والعدل تنسيقا للقلوب وطاعتنا نظاما للملة وإمامتنا أمانا للفرقة والجهاد عزا للإسلام والصبر معونة على استيجاب الأجر والأمر بالمعروف مصلحة للعامة وبر الوالدين وقاية من السخط وصلة الأرحام منسأة في العمر ومنماة للعدد والقصاص حقنا للدماء والوفاء بالنذر تعريضا للمغفرة وتوفية المكاييل والموازين تغييرا للبخس والنهي عن شرب الخمر تنزيها عن الرجس واجتناب القذف حجابا عن اللعنة وترك السرقة إيجابا للعفة وحرم الله الشرك إخلاصا له بالربوبية فاتقوا الله حق تقاته ولا تموتن إلا وأنتم مسلمون وأطيعوا الله فيما أمركم به ونهاكم عنه فإنه إنما يخشى الله من عباده العلماء.

ثم قالت: أيها الناس اعلموا أني فاطمة و أبي محمد ص أقول عودا وبدوا ولا أقول ما أقول غلطا ولا أفعل ما أفعل شططا ، لَقَدْ جَاءَكُمْ رَسُولٌ مِنْ أَنْفُسِكُمْ عَزِيزٌ عَلَيْهِ مَا عَنِتُّمْ حَرِيصٌ عَلَيْكُمْ بِالْمُؤْمِنِينَ رَؤُوفٌ رَحِيمٌ ، فإن تعزوه وتعرفوه تجدوه أبي دون نسائكم وأخا ابن عمي دون رجالكم ، ولنعم المعزى إليه ص فبلغ الرسالة صادعا بالنذارة مائلا عن مدرجة المشركين ضاربا ثبجهم آخذا بأكظامهم داعيا إلى سبيل ربه بالحكمة والموعظة الحسنة يجف الأصنام وينكث الهام حتى انهزم الجمع وولوا الدبر حتى تفرى الليل عن صبحه وأسفر الحق عن محضه ونطق زعيم الدين وخرست شقاشق الشياطين وطاح وشيظ النفاق وانحلت عقد الكفر والشقاق وفهتم بكلمة الإخلاص في نفر من البيض الخماص وكنتم على شفا حفرة من النار مذقة الشارب ونهزة الطامع وقبسة العجلان وموطئ الأقدام تشربون الطرق وتقتاتون القد و الورق أذلة خاسئين تخافون أن يتخطفكم الناس من حولكم فأنقذكم الله تبارك وتعالى بمحمد ص بعد اللتيا واللتي وبعد أن مني ببهم الرجال وذؤبان العرب ومردة أهل الكتاب كلما أوقدوا نارا للحرب أطفأها الله أو نجم قرن الشيطان أو فغرت فاغرة من المشركين قذف أخاه في لهواتها فلا ينكفئ حتى يطأ جناحها بأخمصه ويخمد لهبها بسيفه مكدودا في ذات الله مجتهدا في أمر الله قريبا من رسول الله سيدا في أولياء الله مشمرا ناصحا مجدا كادحا لا تأخذه في الله لومة لائم وأنتم في رفاهية من العيش وادعون فاكهون آمنون تتربصون بنا الدوائر وتتوكفون الأخبار وتنكصون عند النزال وتفرون من القتال. فلما اختار الله لنبيه دار أنبيائه ومأوى أصفيائه ظهر فيكم حسكة النفاق وسمل جلباب الدين ونطق كاظم الغاوين ونبغ خامل الأقلين وهدر فنيق المبطلين فخطر في عرصاتكم وأطلع الشيطان رأسه من مغرزه هاتفا بكم فألفاكم لدعوته مستجيبين وللعزة فيه ملاحظين ثم استنهضكم فوجدكم خفافا وأحمشكم فألفاكم غضابا فوسمتم غير إبلكم ووردتم غير مشربكم هذا والعهد قريب والكلم رحيب والجرح لما يندمل والرسول لما يقبر ابتدارا زعمتم خوف الفتنة ألا في الفتنة سقطوا وإن جهنم لمحيطة بالكافرين فهيهات منكم وكيف بكم وأنى تؤفكون وكتاب الله بين أظهركم أموره ظاهرة وأحكامه زاهرة وأعلامه باهرة وزواجره لائحة وأوامره واضحة وقد خلفتموه وراء ظهوركم أرغبة عنه تريدون أم بغيره تحكمون بئس للظالمين بدلا ومن يبتغ غير الإسلام دينا فلن يقبل منه وهو في الآخرة من الخاسرين ثم لم تلبثوا إلا ريث أن تسكن

217

نفرتها ويسلس قيادها ثم أخذتم تورون وقدتها وتهيجون جمرتها وتستجيبون لهتاف الشيطان الغوي وإطفاء أنوار الدين الجلي وإهمال سنن النبي الصفي تشربون حسوا في ارتغاء وتمشون لأهله وولده والضراء في الخمرة ويصير منكم على مثل حز المدى ووخز السنان في الحشا وأنتم الآن تزعمون أن لا إرث لنا ، أ فحكم الجاهلية تبغون ومن أحسن من الله حكما لقوم يوقنون أفلا تعلمون ، بلى قد تجلى لكم كالشمس الضاحية أني ابنته أيها المسلمون أأغلب على إرثي يا ابن أبي قحافة أفي كتاب الله ترث أباك ولا أرث أبي لقد جئت شيئا فريا أفعلى عمد تركتم كتاب الله ونبذتموه وراء ظهوركم إذ يقول " :وَوَرِثَ سُلَيْمَانُ دَاوُدَ" وقال فيما اقتص من خبر يحيى بن زكريا إذ قال : "فَهَبْ لِي مِنْ لَدُنْكَ وَلِيًّا يَرِثُنِي وَ يَرِثُ مِنْ آلِ يَعْقُوبَ" وقال: " وَ أُولُوا الْأَرْحَامِ بَعْضُهُمْ أَوْلَى بِبَعْضٍ فِي كتاب اللَّهِ" وقال:"يُوصِيكُمُ اللَّهُ فِي أَوْلَادِكُمْ لِلذَّكَرِ مِثْلُ حَظِّ الْأُنْثَيَيْنِ "وقال: " إِنْ تَرَكَ خَيْرًا الْوَصِيَّةُ لِلْوَالِدَيْنِ وَ الْأَقْرَبِينَ بِالْمَعْرُوفِ حَقًّا عَلَى الْمُتَّقِينَ"، وزعمتم أن لا حظوة لي ولا إرث من أبي ولا رحم بيننا أفخصكم الله بآية أخرج أبي منها أم هل تقولون إن أهل ملتين لا يتوارثان أو لست أنا وأبي من أهل ملة واحدة أم أنتم أعلم بخصوص القرآن وعمومه من أبي وابن عمي فدونكها مخطومة مرحولة تلقاك يوم حشرك فنعم الحكم الله والزعيم محمد والموعد القيامة وعند الساعة يخسر المبطلون ولا ينفعكم إذ تندمون ولكل نبأ مستقر وسوف تعلمون من يأتيه عذاب يخزيه ويحل عليه عذاب مقيم.

ثم رمت بطرفها نحو الأنصار فقالت:

يا معشر النقيبة وأعضاد الملة وحضنة الإسلام، ما هذه الغميزة في حقي والسنة عن ظلامتي أما كان رسول الله أبي يقول المرء يحفظ في ولده سرعان ما أحدثتم وعجلان ذا إهالة ولكم طاقة بما أحاول وقوة على ما أطلب و أزاول أتقولون مات محمد (ص) فخطب جليل استوسع وهنه واستنهر فتقه وانفتق رتقه وأظلمت الأرض لغيبته وكسفت الشمس والقمر وانتثرت النجوم لمصيبته وأكدت الآمال وخشعت الجبال وأضيع الحريم وأزيلت الحرمة عند مماته، فتلك والله النازلة الكبرى والمصيبة العظمى لا مثلها نازلة ولا بائقة عاجلة أعلن بها كتاب الله جل ثناؤه في ممساكم ومصبحكم يهتف في أفنيتكم هتافا وصراخا وتلاوة وألحانا ولقبله ما حل بأنبياء الله ورسله حكم فصل وقضاء حتم "وَ مَا مُحَمَّدٌ إِلَّا رَسُولٌ قَدْ خَلَتْ مِنْ قَبْلِهِ الرُّسُلُ أَ فَإِنْ مَاتَ أَوْ قُتِلَ انْقَلَبْتُمْ عَلَى أَعْقَابِكُمْ وَ مَنْ يَنْقَلِبْ عَلَى عَقِبَيْهِ فَلَنْ يَضُرَّ اللَّهَ شَيْئًا وَ سَيَجْزِي اللَّهُ الشَّاكِرِينَ . "إيها بني قيله تراث أبي وأنتم بمرأى مني ومسمع ومنتدى ومجمع تلبسكم الدعوة أأهضم وتشملكم الخبرة وأنتم ذوو العدد والعدة والأداة والقوة وعندكم السلاح والجنة توافيكم الدعوة فلا تجيبون وتأتيكم الصرخة فلا تغيثون؟ أنتم موصوفون بالكفاح معروفون بالخير والصلاح والنخبة التي انتخبت والخيرة التي اختيرت لنا أهل البيت قاتلتم العرب وتحملتم الكد والتعب وناطحتم الأمم كافحتم البهم لا نبرح أو تبرحون نأمركم فتأتمرون حتى إذا دارت بنا رحى الإسلام ودر حلب الأيام وخضعت ثغرة الشرك وسكنت فورة الإفك وخمدت نيران الكفر وهدأت دعوة الهرج واستوسق نظام الدين فأنى حزتم بعد البيان وأسررتم بعد الإعلان ونكصتم بعد الإقدام وأشركتم بعد الإيمان؛بؤسا لقوم نكثوا أيمانهم من بعد عهدهم وهموا بإخراج الرسول وهم بدءوكم أول مرة أ تخشونهم فالله أحق أن تخشوه إن كنتم مؤمنين ألا و قد أرى أن قد أخلدتم إلى الخفض وأبعدتم من هو أحق بالبسط والقبض وخلوتم بالدعة ونجوتم بالضيق من السعة فمججتم ما وعيتم ودسعتم

218

الذي تسوغتم فإن تكفروا أنتم ومن في الأرض جميعا فإن الله لغني حميد ألا وقد قلت ما
قلت هذا على معرفة مني بالجذلة التي خامرتكم والغدرة التي استشعرتها قلوبكم ولكنها
فيضة النفس ونفثة الغيظ وخور القناة وبثة الصدر وتقدمة الحجة فدونكموها فاحتقبوها
دبرة الظهر نقبة الخف باقية العار موسومة بغضب الجبار وشنار الأبد موصولة بنار الله
الموقدة التي تطلع على الأفئدة ، فبعين الله ما تفعلون وسيعلم الذين ظلموا أي منقلب
ينقلبون وأنا ابنة نذير لكم بين يدي عذاب شديد فاعملوا إنا عاملون و انتظروا إنا
منتظرون.

Abullah son of Imām al-Hassan (ع) quotes his forefathers saying that
Abū Bakr and Omer decided to prevent Fātima (ع) from her Fadak
property. When she came to know about it, she put her veil on her
head, wrapped herself with her outer cloak and, accompanied by
some of her relatives and men of her folks, stepping on her gown,
her gait not differing from that of the Messenger of Allāh (ص), went
till she entered [the Mosque of the Prophet] where Abū Bakr was.

Abū Bakr was in the company of a crowd of the Muhajirun and
Ansār and others. A curtain was placed behind which she sat and
moaned. Hearing her thus moaning, everyone present burst in tears,
so much so that the meeting place shook. She waited for a moment
till the sobbing stopped and the fervor abated. She started her speech
by praising Allāh and lauding Him, sending blessings to His
Messenger, whereupon people resumed their cries. When they
stopped, she resumed her speech saying,

"Praise to Allāh for that which He bestowed (us). We thank and laud
Him for all that which He inspired and offered, for the Abūndant
boons which He initiated, the perfect grants which He presented.
Such boons are too many to compute, too vast to measure. Their
limit is too distant to grasp. He commended them (to His beings) so
they would gain more by being grateful for their continuity. He
ordained Himself praiseworthy by giving generously to His
creatures. I testify that there is no God but Allāh, the One without a
partner, a statement which sincere devotion is its interpretation, the
hearts guarantee its continuation, and in the minds and hearts is its
perpetuation. He is the One Who cannot be perceived with vision,
nor can He be described by tongues, nor can imagination
comprehend how He is. He originated things but not from anything
that existed before them, created them without pre-existing

examples. Rather, He created them with His might and spread them according to His will. He did so not for a need for which He created them, nor for a benefit (for Him) did He shape them, but to establish His wisdom, bring attention to His obedience, manifest His might, lead His creatures to humbly venerate Him and exalt His decrees. He then made the reward for obedience to Him and punishment for disobedience so as to protect His creatures from His Wrath and amass them into His Paradise.

"I also testify that my Father, Muhammed, is His servant and messenger whom He chose and prior to sending him when the [souls of all] beings were still concealed in that which was transcendental, protected from anything appalling, associated with termination and nonexistence. Allāh the Exalted One knew that which was to follow, comprehended that which would come to pass and realized the place of every event. Allāh sent him (Muhammed) to perfect His commands, a resolution to accomplish His decree, and an implementation of the dictates of His Mercy. So he (Muhammed) found nations differing in their creeds, obsessed by their fires [Zoroastrians], worshipping their idols [Pagans], and denying Allāh [atheists] despite their knowledge of Him. Therefore, Allāh illuminated their darkness with my Father, Muhammed, uncovered obscurity from their hearts, and cleared the clouds from their insights. He revealed guidance to the people. He delivered them from being led astray, taking them away from misguidance, showing them the right religion and inviting them to the Straight Path (*as-Sirat al-Mustaqeem*).

"Allāh then chose to recall him mercifully, with love and preference. So, Muhammed is now in comfort, released from the burden of this world, surrounded angels of devotion, satisfied with the Merciful Lord and with being near the powerful King. So, peace of Allāh with my Father, His Prophet, the trusted one, the one whom He chose from among His servants, His sincere friend, and peace and blessings of Allāh with him."

Fātima (ع) then turned to the crowd and said:

"Surely you (people) are Allāh's servants at His command and prohibition, bearers of His creed and revelation. You are the ones whom Allāh entrusted to fare with your own selves, His messengers to the nations. Amongst you does He have the right authority, a covenant which He brought forth to you and an legacy which He left to guard you: The eloquent Book of Allāh, the Qur'ān of the truth, the brilliant light, the shining beam. Its insights are indisputable, its secrets are revealed, its indications are manifest and those who follow it are surely blessed. (The Qur'ān) leads its adherents to righteousness. Listening (and acting upon) it leads to salvation. Through it are the enlightening divine arguments achieved, His manifest determination acquired, His prohibited decrees avoided, His manifest evidence recognized, His convincing proofs made apparent, His permissions granted and His laws written. So Allāh made belief (in Islam) a purification for you from polytheism. He made prayers an exaltation for you from conceit, Zakāt purification for the soul and a (cause of) growth in subsistence, fasting an implantation of devotion, pilgrimage a construction of the creed and justice (Adl) the harmony of the hearts. And He made obedience to us (Ahl al-Bayt) the management of the affairs of the nation and our leadership (Ahl al-Bayt) a safeguard from disunity. He made *jihad* (struggle) a way for strengthening Islam and patience a helping course for deserving (divine) rewards. He made commending what is right (Amr Bil Ma'ruf) a cause for public welfare, kindness to parents a safeguard from (His) wrath, the maintaining of close ties with one's kin a cause for a longer life and for multiplying the number of offspring, in-kind reprisal (*qisas* قصاص) to save lives, fulfillment of vows the earning of mercy, the completion of weights and measures a cause for avoiding neglecting the rights of others, forbidding drinking wines an exaltation from atrocity, avoiding slander a veil from curse, abandoning theft a reason for deserving chastity. Allāh has also prohibited polytheism so that one can devote himself to His Mastership. Therefore; Fear Allāh as He should be feared, and die not except in a state of Islam; Obey Allāh in that which He has commanded you to do and that which He has forbidden, for surely those truly fear among His servants, who have knowledge.'

"O People! Be informed that I am Fātima, and my father is Muhammad I say that repeatedly and initiate it continually; I say not what I say mistakenly, nor do I do what I do aimlessly. Now has come unto you an Apostle from amongst yourselves; It grieves him that you should perish; ardently anxious is he over you; To the believers he is most kind and merciful. Thus, if you identify and recognize him, you shall realize that he is my father and not the father of any of your women; the brother of my cousin (Ali (ع)) rather than any of your men. What an excellent identity he was, may the peace and blessings of Allāh be upon him and his descendants Thus, he propagated the Message, by coming out openly with the warning, and while inclined away from the path of the polytheists, (whom he) struck their strength and seized their throats, while he invited (all) to the way of his Lord with wisdom and beautiful preaching He destroyed idols, and defeated heroes, until their group fled and turned their backs. So night revealed its dawn; righteousness uncovered its genuineness; the voice of the religious authority spoke out loud; the evil discords were silenced; The crown of hypocrisy was diminished; the tightening of infidelity and desertion were untied, So you spoke the statement of devotion amongst a band of starved ones; and you were on the edge of a hole of fire;(you were) the drink of the thirsty one; the opportunity of the desiring one; the fire brand of him who passes in haste; the step for feet; you used to drink from the water gathered on roads; eat jerked meat. (Lady Fātima (ع) was stating their lowly situation before Islam) You were despised outcasts always in fear of abduction from those around you. Yet, Allāh rescued you through my father, Muhammad after much ado, and after he was confronted by mighty men, the Arab beasts, and the demons of the people of the Book Who, whenever they ignited the fire of war, Allāh extinguished it; and whenever the thorn of the devil appeared, or a mouth of the polytheists opened wide in defiance, he would strike its discords with his brother (Ali, (ع", who comes not back until he treads its wing with the sole of his feet, and extinguishes its flames with his sword. (Ali is) diligent in Allāh's affair, near to the Messenger of Allāh, A master among Allāh's worshippers, setting to work briskly, sincere in his advice, earnest and exerting himself (in service to Islam); While you were calm, gay, and feeling safe in your comfortable lives, waiting for us to meet disasters, awaiting the spread of news, you fell back during every battle, and took to your heels at times of fighting. Yet, When Allāh chose His Prophet from

222

the dwell of His prophets, and the abode of His sincere (servants); The thorns of hypocrisy appeared on you, the garment of faith became worn out, The misguided ignorant(s) spoke out, the sluggish ignorant came to the front and brayed. The he camel of the vain wiggled his tail in your courtyards and the your courtyards and the Devil stuck his head from its place of hiding and called upon you, he found you responsive to his invitation, and observing his deceits. He then aroused you and found you quick (to answer him), and invited you to wrath, therefore; you branded other than your camels and proceeded to other than your drinking places. Then while the era of the Prophet was still near, the gash was still wide, the scar had not yet healed, and the Messenger was not yet buried. A (quick) undertaking as you claimed, aimed at preventing discord (trial), Surely, they have fallen into trial already! And indeed Hell surrounds the unbelievers. How preposterous! What an idea! What a falsehood! For Allāh's Book is still amongst you, its affairs are apparent; its rules are manifest; its signs are dazzling; its restrictions are visible, and its commands are evident. Yet, indeed you have cast it behind your backs! What! Do you detest it? Or according to something else you wish to rule? Evil would be the exchange for the wrongdoers! And if anyone desires a religion other than Islam (submission to Allāh), it never will it be accepted from him; And in the hereafter, he will be in the ranks of those who have lost. Surely you have not waited until its stampede seized, and it became obedient. You then started arousing its flames, instigating its coal, complying with the call of the misled devil, quenching the light of the manifest religion, and extinguished the light of the sincere Prophet. You concealed sips on froth and proceeded towards his (the Prophet) kin and children in swamps and forests (meaning you plot against them in deceitful ways), but we are patient with you as if we are being notched with knives and stung by spearheads in our abdomens, Yet-now you claim that there is not inheritance for us! What! "Do they then seek after a judgment of (the Days of) ignorance? But How, for a people whose faith is assured, can give better judgment than Allāh? Don't you know? Yes, indeed it is obvious to you that I am his daughter. O Muslims! Will my inheritance be usurped? O son of Abū Quhafa! Where is it in the Book of Allāh that you inherit your father and I do not inherit mine? Surely you have come up with an unprecedented thing. Do you intentionally abandon the Book of Allāh and cast it behind your back? Do you not read where it says: And Solomon (Sulayman) inherited David (Dawood)'? And when it narrates the story of Zacharias and says: `So give me an heir as from thyself (One that) will inherit me, and inherit the posterity of Jacob (Yaqoob)' And: `But kindred by hood have prior rights against each other in the Book of Allāh' And: Allāh (thus) directs you as regards your children's (inheritance) to the male, a portion equal to that of two females' And, If he leaves any goods, that he make a bequest to parents and next of kin, according to reasonable usage; this is due from the pious ones.' You claim that I have no share! And that I do not inherit my father! What! Did Allāh reveal a (Qur'ānic) verse regarding you, from which He excluded my father? Or do you say: `These (Fātima and her father) are the people of two faiths, they do not inherit each other?!' Are we not, me and my father, a people adhering to one faith? Or is it that you have more knowledge about the specifications and generalizations of the Qur'ān than my father and my cousin (Imām Ali)? So, here you are! Take it! (Ready with) its nose rope and saddled! But if shall encounter you on the Day of Gathering; (thus) what a wonderful judge is Allāh, a claimant is Muhammad, and a day is the Day of Rising. At the time of the Hour shall the wrongdoers lose; and it shall not benefit you to regret (your actions) then! For every Message, there is a time limit; and soon shall ye know who will be inflicted with torture that will humiliate him, and who will be confronted by an everlasting punishment. (Fātima then turned towards the Ansār and said:) O you people of intellect! The strong supporters of the nation! And those who embraced Islam; What is this shortcoming in defending my right? And what is this slumber (while you see) injustice (being done toward me)? Did not the Messenger of Allāh, my father, used to say: A man is upheld (remembered) by his children'? O how quick have you violated (his orders)?! How soon have you plotted against us? But you still are capable (of helping me in) my attempt, and powerful (to help me) in that which I request and (in) my pursuit (of it). Or do you say: "Muhammad has perished;" Surely this is a great calamity; Its damage is excessive its injury is great, Its wound (is much too deep) to heal. The Earth became darkened with his departure; the stars eclipsed for his calamity; hopes were seized; mountains submitted; sanctity was violated, and holiness was

224

encroached upon after his death. Therefore, this, by Allāh, is the great affliction, and the grand calamity; there is not an affliction-which is the like of it; nor will there be a sudden misfortune (as surprising as this). The Book of Allāh-excellent in praising him-announced in the courtyards (of your houses) in the place where you spend your evenings and mornings; A call, A cry, A recitation, and (verses) in order. It had previously came upon His (Allāh's) Prophets and Messengers; (for it is) A decree final, and a predestination fulfilled: "Muhammad is not but an Apostle: Many were the apostles that passed away before him. If he died or was slain, will ye then turn back on your heels? If any did turn back on his heels, not the least harm will he do to Allāh; but Allāh (on the other hand) will swiftly reward those who (serve Him) with gratitude." O you people of reflection; will I be usurped the inheritance of my father while you hear and see me?! (And while) You are sitting and gathered around me? You hear my call, and are included in the (news of the) affair? (But) You are numerous and well equipped! (You have) the means and the power, and the weapons and the shields. Yet, the call reaches you but you do not answer; the cry comes to you but you do not come to help? (This) While you are characterized by struggle, known for goodness and welfare, the selected group (which was chosen), and the best ones chosen by the Messenger for us, Ahlul-Bayt. You fought the Arabs, bore with pain and exhaustion, struggled against the nations, and resisted their heroes. We were still, so were you in ordering you, and you in obeying us. So that Islam became triumphant, the accomplishment of the days came near, the fort of polytheism was subjected, the outburst of was subjected, the outburst of infidelity calmed down, and the system of religion was well-ordered. Thus, (why have you) become confused after clearness? Conceal matters after announcing them? Do you thus turn on your heels after daring, associating (others with Allāh) after believing? Will you not fight people who violated their oaths? Plotted to expel the Apostle and became aggressive by being the first (to assault) you? Do ye fear them? Nay, it is Allāh Whom you should more justly fear, if you believe! Now I see that you are inclined to easy living; having dismissed one who is more worthy of guardianship [referring to Ali (ع)]. You secluded yourselves with meekness and dismissed that which you accepted. Yet, if you show ingratitude, ye and all on earth together, yet, Allāh free of all wants, worthy of all praise. Surely I have said all that I have said with full knowledge that you intent to forsake me, and knowing the betrayal that your hearts sensed. But it is the state of soul, the effusion of fury, the dissemination of (what is) the chest and the presentation of the proof. Hence, Here it is! Bag it (leadership and) put it on the back of an ill she camel, which has a thin hump with everlasting grace, marked with the wrath of Allāh, and the blame of ever (which leads to) the Fire of (the wrath of Allāh kindled (to a blaze), that which doth mount (right) to the hearts; For, Allāh witnesses what you do, and soon will the unjust assailants know what vicissitudes their affairs will take! And I am the daughter of a warner (the Prophet) to you against a severe punishment. So, act and so will we, and wait, and we shall wait.'"

فأجابها أبو بكر وقال : يا بنت رسول الله لقد كان أبوك بالمؤمنين عطوفا كريما رءوفا رحيما وعلى الكافرين عذابا أليما وعقابا عظيما إن عزوناه وجدناه أباك دون النساء وأخا إلفك دون الأخلاء آثره على كل حميم وساعده في كل أمر جسيم لا يحبكم إلا سعيد ولا يبغضكم إلا شقي بعيد فأنتم عترة رسول الله الطيبون الخيرة المنتجبون على الخير أدلتنا وإلى الجنة مسالكنا. وأنت يا خيرة النساء وابنة خير الأنبياء صادقة في قولك سابقة في وفور عقلك غير مردودة عن حقك ولا مصدودة عن صدقك والله ما عدوت رأي رسول الله ولا عملت إلا بإذنه والرائد لا يكذب أهله وإني أشهد الله وكفى به شهيدا أني سمعت رسول الله (ص) يقول نحن معاشر الأنبياء لا نورث ذهبا و لا فضة و لا دارا و لا عقارا و إنما نورث الكتاب والحكمة والعلم والنبوة وما كان لنا من طعمة فلولي الأمر بعدنا أن يحكم فيه بحكمه وقد جعلنا ما حاولته في الكراع والسلاح يقاتل بها المسلمون ويجاهدون.

فقالت عليها السلام ، سبحان الله ما كان أبي رسول الله (ص) عن كتاب الله صادفا ولا لأحكامه مخالفا بل كان يتبع أثره ويقفو سوره؛ أفتجمعون إلى الغدر اعتلالا عليه بالزور وهذا بعد وفاته شبيه بما بغي له من الغوائل في حياته هذا كتاب الله حكما عدلا وناطقا فصلا يقول يَرِثُني وَ يَرِثُ مِنْ آلِ يَعْقُوبَ و يقول وَ وَرِثَ سُلَيْمانُ داوُدَ وبين عز وجل فيما وزع من الأقساط وشرع من الفرائض والميراث وأباح من حظ الذكران والإناث ما أزاح به علة المبطلين وأزال التظني والشبهات في الغابرين كلا بل سولت لكم أنفسكم أمرا فصبر جميل والله المستعان على ما تصفون . فقال أبو بكر: صدق الله ورسوله وصدقت ابنته معدن الحكمة وموطن الهدى والرحمة وركن الدين وعين الحجة لا أبعد صوابك ولا أنكر خطابك هؤلاء المسلمون بيني وبينك قلدوني ما تقلدت وباتفاق منهم أخذت ما أخذت غير مكابر ولا مستبد ولا مستأثر وهم بذلك شهود.

فالتفتت فاطمة عليها السلام إلى الناس و قالت:

معاشر المسلمين المسرعة إلى قيل الباطل المغضية على الفعل القبيح الخاسر أفلا
تتدبرون القرآن أم على قلوب أقفالها كلا بل ران على قلوبكم ما أسأتم من أعمالكم فأخذ
بسمعكم وأبصاركم ولبنس ما تأولتم وساء ما به أشرتم وشر ما منه اغتصبتم لتجدن
والله محمله ثقيلا وغبه وبيلا إذا كشف لكم الغطاء وبان بإورائه الضراء وبدا لكم من
ربكم ما لم تكونوا تحتسبون و خسر هنا لك المبطلون.

Abū Bakr responded to her by saying, "O daughter of the Messenger
of Allāh! Your father was always affectionate with the believers,
generous, kind and merciful, and towards the unbelievers was a
painful torment and a great punishment. Surely the Prophet is your
father, not anyone else's, the brother of your husband, not any other
man's; he surely preferred him over all his friends and (Ali)
supported him in every important matter, no one loves you save the
lucky and no one hates you save the wretched. You are the blessed
progeny of Allāh's Messenger, the chosen ones, our guides to
goodness our path to Paradise, and you-the best of women-and the
daughter of the best of prophets, truthful is your sayings, excelling in
reason. You shall not be driven back from your right... But I surely
heard your father saying: 'We the, group of prophets do not inherit,
nor are we inherited Yet, this is my situation and property, it is yours
(if you wish); it shall not be concealed from you, nor will it be stored
away from you. You are the Mistress of your father's nation, and the
blessed tree of your descendants. Your property shall not be usurped
against your will nor can your name be defamed. Your judgment
shall be executed in all that which I possess. This, do you think that I
violate your father's (will)?"

Fātima then refuted Abū Bakr's claim that the Prophet had stated that
prophets cannot be inherited, and said: "Glory be to Allāh!! Surely
Allāh's Messenger did not abandon Allāh's Book nor did he violate
His commands. Rather, he followed its decrees and adhered to its
chapters. So do you unite with treachery justifying your acts with
fabrications? Indeed this—after his departure—is similar to the
disasters which were plotted against him during his lifetime. But
behold! This is Allāh's Book, a just judge and a decisive speaker,
saying: 'One that will (truly) inherit Me, and inherit the posterity of
Yaqub,' (19:6) and 'And Sulaiman (Solomon) inherited Dawood
(David).' (27: 16) Thus, He (Glory be to Him) made clear that which
He made share of all heirs, decreed from the amounts of inheritance,

allowed for males and females, and eradicated all doubts and ambiguities (pertaining to this issue which existed with the) bygones. Nay! But your minds have made up a tale (that may pass) with you, but (for me) patience is most fitting against that which ye assert; it is Allāh (alone) whose help can be sought." It is apparent that Abū Bakr chanced the mode with which he addressed Lady Fātima (ع) after delivering her speech. Listen to his following speech; which is his reply to Fātima's just reported speech.

Abū Bakr said: "Surely Allāh and His Apostle are truthful, and so has his (the Prophet's) daughter told the truth. Surely you are the source of wisdom, the element of faith, and the sole authority. May Allāh not refute your righteous argument, nor invalidate your decisive speech. But these are the Muslims between us-who have entrusted me with leadership, and it was according to their satisfaction that 1 received what 1 have. I am not being arrogant, autocratic, or selfish, and they are my witnesses." Upon hearing Abū Bakr speak of the people's support for him, Lady Fātima Zahra (ع) turned towards them and said:

"O people, who rush towards uttering falsehood and are indifferent to disgraceful and losing actions! Do you not earnestly seek to reflect upon the Qur'ān, or are your hearts isolated with locks? But on your hearts is the stain of the evil, which you committed; it has seized your hearing and your sight, evil is that which you justified cursed is that which you reckoned, and wicked is what you have taken for an exchange! You shall, by Allāh, find bearing it (to be a great) burden, and its consequence disastrous. (That is) on the day when the cover is removed and appears to you what is behind it of wrath. When you will be confronted by Allāh with that which you could never have expected, there will perish, there and then, those who stood on falsehoods." Although parts of Abū Bakr's speeches cannot be verified with authentic evidence, and despite the fact that we have already mentioned part of the actual speech, which Abū Bakr delivered after Lady Fātima's arguments, it appears certain that Abū Bakr was finally persuaded to submit Fadak to her. Nevertheless, when Fātima was leaving Abū Bakr's house, Omer suddenly appeared and exclaimed: "What is it that you hold in your hand?"

228

Abū Bakr replied: 'A decree I have written for Fātima in which I assigned Fadak and her father's inheritance to her." Omer then said: "With what will you spend on the Muslims if the Arabs decide to fight you?!"

وفي سيرة الحلبي ج ٣ ص ٣٩١ -: أن عمر أخذ الكتاب فشقه.

According to p. 391, Vol. 3, of al-Halabi's *Seera* book, Omer [ibn al-Khattab] seized the decree and tore it to pieces…

ثم عطفت على قبر النبي و قالت :

قَـد كـانَ بَعـدكَ انبـاءٌ و هَنْبَثَـةٌ   لَـو كُنـتَ شـاهِدَها لـم تَكثُـرُ الخُطَـبُ

انّـا فقـدنـاكَ فَقْـدَ الأرضِ وابِلَهـا   و اختَـلَّ قومُـكَ فاشـهَدهُم فقـد نَكبـوا

و قـد رُزِينـا بمـا لـم يَـرزَه أحـدٌ   مِـنَ البَرِيَّـةِ لا عُجـمٌ و لا عُـرُبُ

سَـيَعْلَمُ المُتـوَلّي ظُلـمَ حامَتِنـا   يـومَ القِيامَـةِ أنّـى سَـوفَ يَنقَلِـبُ

ضاقَـت عليَّ بـلادي بَعـدما رَحُبَـتْ   و سِيمَ سِبطاكَ خَسفاً فيـه لـي نَصَبُ

و كُـلُّ أهـلٍ لَـهُ قُـربـى و مَنزِلَـةٌ   عنـد الالـهِ عَلـى الأدنـينَ مُقتَـرِبُ

أبـدتْ رجـالٌ لنـا نَجـوى صُـدُورِهُم   لَمَـا مَضَـيتَ و حالَـتْ دونَـكَ التُّـرُبُ

تَجَهَّمَتنـا رجـالٌ و آستَخَـفَّ بنـا   اذ غِبـتَ عنّـا، فـنحنُ اليـومَ نُغتَصَبُ

وكُنـتَ بـدراً و نُـوراً يُسـتَضاءُ بـه   عليـكَ يَنـزِلُ مِـنْ ذي العِـزَّةِ الكُتُـبُ

قـد كـانَ جِبريـلُ بالآياتِ يؤنِسُـنا   فقـد فُقِـدْتَ و كُـلُّ الخَيـرِ مُحتَجَـبُ

فليتَ قَبلَـكَ كـانَ المـوتُ صـادَفَنا   لَمَـا مَضَـيتَ و حالَـتْ دونَكَ الكُثُبُ

فَسَـوفَ نَبكيكَ مـا عِشـنا وما بَقِيَتْ   مِـنَ العُيـونِ بِتهمـالٍ لهـا سَـكَبُ

و قـد رُزينـا بـه مَحضـاً خَليقَتُـهُ   صافي الضَـرائب و الأعـراقِ و النَّسَـبُ

فأنـتَ خَيـرُ عبـادِ اللهِ كُلَّهُـمْ   و أصـدَقُ الناسِـحينَ الصِـدقَ و الكَـذِبُ

229

After you, reports and momentous chaotic events we found,
If you witnessed them, calamities would not abound.
We missed you as sorely as earth would miss its rain,
Your folks lost balance, see how from the creed they did refrain,
We, like no others, have suffered affliction,
Unlike all Arabs, or others from among Allāh's creation.
One who has oppressed us will come on Judgment Day
To know what fate will be awaiting him.
My homeland is now narrow after its great expanse indeed,
Both your grandsons have been wronged, so my heart is grieved,
Every family has relatives and a place
With the Almighty Who is close to those of grace,
Certain men what their chests hid did they to us reveal,
When you went, and now you from our sights did a grave conceal,
Men assaulted and slighted us, when you became far away
So, now what rightfully belongs to us is being taken away.
You were the moon, your light showed us what we should heed,
Messages from the Exalted One were to you revealed.
With the Verses did Gabriel make our day,
Now you are gone, every good thing is kept away.
How we wish in our direction death did the Almighty guide
Before you left us, and you did the dunes from us hide.
We shall cry over you so long as our tears can pour,
So long as floods of tears can withstand and endure.
We have been afflicted with tragedy on his account
One who is pure in peers, folks and lineage,
For you are the best of Allāh's creation and
Most truthful of those who only the truth defend.

ـ من أشار إلى خطبة الصديقة فاطمة (عليها السلام) أو روى شيئاً منها نذكر بعضاً منهم على سبيل المثال لا حصر، وهم كالتالي:

1 ـ الخليل بن أحمد الفراهيدي (ت ١٧٥ هـ) في كتاب العين: ٨ / ٣٢٣ في كلمة اللمَة، وقال: وفي الحديث جاءت فاطمة (عليها السلام) إلى أبي بكر في لُميمة من حفدتها ونساء قومها.

2 ـ جار الله محمد بن عمر الزمخشري (ت ٥٣٨ هـ).
في الفائق: ٣ / ٣٣١ في مادة اللمة أيضاً قال: وفي حديث فاطمة (عليها السلام): إنّها

خرجت في لمة من نسائها تتوطأ ذيلها، حتى دخلت على أبي بكر.

٣ ـ أبو الفرج عبد الرحمن بن علي بن الجوزي، (ت ٥٩٧ هـ.)

في غريب الحديث: ٢ / ٣٣٣ وقال: وفي الحديث: أنّ فاطمة (عليها السلام) خرجت في لمة من نسائها إلى أبي بكر فعاتبته. أي في جماعة ؛ وقيل: من الثلاث إلى العشر.

٤ ـ مجد الدين أبو السعادات ابن الأثير (ت ٦٠٦ هـ.)

في النهاية في غريب الحديث والأثر: ٤ / ٢٧٣ وقال: في حديث فاطمة (عليها السلام): إنّها خرجت في لمة من نسائها تتوطأ ذيلها، إلى أبي بكر فعاتبته.

٥ ـ أبو الفضل جمال الدين بن منظور (ت ٧١١ هـ).

في لسان العرب: ١٢ / ٥٤٨ وقال: وفي حديث فاطمة (عليها السلام): إنّها خرجت في لمة من نسائها تتوطأ ذيلها إلى أبي بكر فعاتبته. ذكرها في مادة لمم.

References to this speech by the Truthful One, Fātima, peace with her, including some who cited excerpts of it, include the following:

1. Al-Khalil ibn Ahmed al-Farahidi الخليل بن أحمد الفراهيدي (d. 175 A.H./792 A.D.) on p. 323, Vol. 8, of *Kitab al-Ayn*,
2. Jarallāh Muhammed ibn Omer al-Zamakhshari[1] الزمخشري (d. 538 A.H./1144 A.D.) on p. 331, Vol. 3, of *Al-Faiq*;
3. Abul-Faraj Abdul-Rahman ibn Ali ibn al-Jawzi ابن الجوزي (d. 597 A.H./1201 A.D.),
4. Majd ad-Deen Abū al-Sa'adat Ibn al-Atheer ابن الأثير (d. 606 A.H./1210 A.D.) on p. 273, Vol. 4 of his book titled *Al-Nihaya*,
5. Abul-Fadl Jamal ad-Deen ibn Manzour ابن منظور (d. 711 A.H./1312 A.D.) on p. 548, Vol. 12 (old edition) of his lexicon titled *Lisan al-Arab*.

FĀTIMA FURTHER OPPRESSED

Throughout her life, Fātima (ع) never spoke to those who had oppressed her and deprived her of her rightful claims. She kept her grief to herself. During her sickness which preceded her death, she requested that her oppressors should be kept away even from attending her funeral. Her ill-wishers even resorted to physical violence. Once the door of her house was pushed on her, and the child she was carrying was hurt and the baby-boy was stillborn. This incident took place, and it is very well documented by Shī'ite and Sunni historians and chroniclers, when Omer ibn al-Khattab was

---

[1] Refer to a footnote about al-Zamakhshari above.

urging, sometimes even beating, people to go to the Prophet's Mosque to swear allegiance to his friend, Abū Bark. Omer promoted Abū Bakr to the seat of "caliph", being the very first person to swear allegiance to him after being convinced that it would not be long before he, too, would occupy the same seat. Fātima's house was set on fire. Having been mistreated and stricken with grief, which crossed all limits of forbearance and endurance, she expressed her sorrows in an elegy which she composed to mourn her father the Holy Prophet (ص). In that elegy, she makes a particular reference to her woeful plight saying, after having taken a handful of earth from her father's grave, putting it on her eyes, crying and saying,

أن لا يشــمَ مــدى الزمــان غَواليــا؟   مـــاذا علــى مـــن شـــمَ تربـــةَ أحمـــدٍ

صُــبّت علــى الأيّــام صِــرنَ لياليــا   صُــبّت علــيَّ مصــائبٌ لــو أنّهــا

لا أختشــي ضـــيماً، و كـــان جماليـــا   قـــد كنـــتُ ذات حمـــى بظـــلِّ محمـــدٍ

ضَــيمي، و أدفـــعُ ظـــالمي بردائيـــا   فـــاليومَ أخشـــعُ للـــذليلِ وأتّقـــي

شــجناً علــى غصــنٍ، بكيـــتُ صبــاحيا   فـــإذا بَكَـــتْ قمريـــةَ فـــي ليلهـــا

و لأجعَلَـــنَّ الـــدمعَ فيـــكَ وشـــاحيا   فلأجعلَـــنَّ الحـــزنَ بعـــدكَ مؤنسـِــي

What blame should be on one who smells Ahmed's soil
That he shall never smell any precious person at all?
Calamities have been poured on me (like waters boil)
Were they poured on days, they would become nights.
In the shade of Muhammed, I enjoyed all protection
And he was my beauty, and I feared no oppression,

But now I surrender to the lowly and fear I am done
Injustice, pushing my oppressor with only my gown.
So, if a dove cries during its night, forlorn,
Out of grief on its twig, I cry in my morn.
So, I shall after you let grief be a companion for me,
And my tears that mourn you my cover they shall be.

On p. 218, Vol. 2, of al-Tabari's

Tarikh (Dar al-Amira for Printing, Publishing and Distribution, Beirut, Lebanon, 2005), it is stated that when Fātima could not get her inheritance, Fadak, from Abū Bakr, she boycotted him and never spoke to him till her death.

The death of the Apostle, affected her very much and she was very sad and grief-stricken and wept her heart out crying all the time. Unfortunately, after the death of the Prophet, the Government confiscated her famous land of Fadak. Fātima (ع) was pushed behind her home door (when they attacked Ali's house and took him away in order to force him to accept the caliphate of Abū Bakr), so the fetus she was carrying, namely Muhsin, was subsequently aborted. Omer ibn al-Khattab ordered his servant, Qunfath, to set her house on fire, an incident which is immortalized by verses of poetry composed by the famous Egyptian poet Hafiz Ibrahim which is reproduced here but without English translation. The author has preferred not to translate it in order not to hurt the feelings of his Sunni brethren, especially non-Arabs:

اللهم

كمـا سترت ذنوبنـا وعيوبنـا
في الدنيا
فاسترها يوم القيامـة
يوم الحسرة والندامة
يوم يرى كل إنسـان منـا
عمله أمامه

وَقَوْلَـــةٌ لِـ (عليٌّ) قَـالَهـا (عُمَـر)   مـا نَحْـزَنْ فيـهِ بَقـايـا مِـنْ مَآسِـيهـا

حَرَقْتُ دَارَكَ لا أُبَـالي عَلَيْـكَ بِهـا   إنْ لَـمْ نُبَـالـغْ وبِنْـتُ المُصْطَفى فيهـا

ومـا أتى دارَ وَحْيِ اللَّـهِ مُنْـتَـفِـضًـا   بـالنّـارِ سوعِدُها حَـرْقـاً يُغَطِّيهـا

قالـوا إنَّـهُ: (فاطِـمٌ) في الدَّارِ قـالَ: (وإنْ)   بِلَظْـةٍ أعْجَـزَتْ حَـتّى مُداريهـا

فَقَوْلَـةٌ أَفْصَحَتْ عَنْ دِينِ صاحِبِها   فَـلْ كـانَ بـالحَـقِّ أمْ بـالظُّلْمِ مُلْقِبهـا؟

وقِـلْ لِمَنْ عَدَّ هـذا القَـوْلَ مَكْرُمَـةً   للكَـرمـاتِ بِسَـهْمِ الإفْكِ تَرْمِيهـا

سائِـلْ (أبا حَفْصٍ) فَـلْ كـانَتْ مَقْولُتُـهُ   وفـقَ الشَّـريعَـةِ؟ أمْ حُكْمـاً تُنافِيهـا؟

أفي الكِتـابِ؟ وإذا القُـرآنُ شـاهِـدُةٍ   آبـاءَنـةَ أُمّهـا للكُفْـرِ تَنْمِيهـا

أمْ سُنَّةُ المُصْطَفى جـاءتْ بِهـا ولَـنـا   علِـمٌ بأسْـرارِها فَتقْصـاعُ بُحْبِيهـا

إنَّ الذي بهيَّـةً (الزَّفْـراءَ) حَرَمَتهـا   مـا كـانَ يوْمـاً لآيِ الـذِّكْـرِ تالِيهـا

أنِيـسَ قَـوْلِ رَسُـولِ اللَّـهِ: فاطِمَـةُ   بَقْسـي فيكُـمْ بـالفَضْـلِ يُصْفِيهـا

و(فـاطِـمٌ) بِضْـعَـةٌ مِنّي فَيؤلِـمُـني   مـا كـانَ يسـؤلُهـا يـا بِئْسَ مؤْذِيهـا

يا لَهْفِ (فـاطِـم) خَلْفَ البابِ إذ وَقَفَتْ   تَدْعـو أبـاهـا عسى يأتي فَيَحْمِيهـا

لِـمْ يَبْلُ جِسْمَكَ والأَحْكـامُ قَـدْ بَلِيَتْ   و(السّـامِري) بِحُكْـمِ الجَـوْرِ ماحِيهـا

قَـدْ كـانَ بَعْدَكَ أُنْبِـاءٌ وَهَنْبَثَـةٌ   لـوْ كُنْتَ شـاهِـدَهـا هـانَتْ دَواهِيهـا

قَتْلُ الجَنِيـنِ وكَسْرُ الضِّلْعِ أعْظَمُهـا؟   أمْ غُضْـبُ حَقّي وأفْـسَـولُ الأفِهـا؟

يا بـابَ (فاطِـم) ما لاقَيْـتَ مِنْ مِحَـنٍ   تُنْـجي الكِـرامَ ومـا زالَـتْ تُقـاسِيهـا

On p. 220, Vol. 2, of al-Tabari's *Tarikh* (Arabic text), it is stated that the Holy Prophet (ص) remained unburied for three days. His sacred body finally received the burial bath by his cousin and son-in-law, Fātima's husband Ali (ع). Besides Ali (ع), those who attended the burial of the Prophet (ص) were: al-Abbās ibn Abdul-Muttalib, his son al-Fadhl, Qutham ibn al-Abbās, Usamah ibn Zaid, and Shuqran, a freed slave of the Prophet (ص), according to the same page. According to Ibn Ishāq, Aws ibn Khawli, who had taken part in the Battle of Badr, earnestly requested Ali (ع) to let him assist in burying the Messenger of Allāh (ص) which the Commander of the Faithful accepted (ع).

The tragedy of her father's death and the unkindness of her father's followers, were too much for the good, gentle and sensitive lady and she breathed her last on Jumda I 14, 11 A.H., exactly seventy-five days after the death of her revered father, the Holy Prophet of Islam. Grieved about the way she was treated by certain "sahāba" of the Prophet (ص), the confiscation of her property, Fadak, the aborting of her son, Musin, and the confiscation of the right to caliphate from her husband, Ali, were all too much for her, so much so that they eventually put an end to her life when she was in the prime of her life at the age of eighteen, although historians provide different dates, and was buried in Jannatul-Baqi', Medīna.

FĀTIMA'S DEATH

On p. 218, Vol. 2, of al-Tabari's *Tarikh*, al-Tabari says,

فدفنها علي ليلا، و لم يؤذن بها أبا بكر

"Ali buried her at night, and Abū Bakr did not call the *athan* (to announce her death)."

Fātima (ع) did not survive more than seventy-five days after the demise of her father. She breathed her last on the 14th Jumdi I, 11 A.H. Before her demise, she told her will to her husband, Imām Ali (ع), thus:

1. O Ali, you will personally perform my funeral rites.
2. Those who have displeased me should not be allowed to attend my funeral.
3. My corpse should be carried to the graveyard at night.

Thus, Imām Ali (ع), in compliance with her will, performed all the funeral rites and accompanied exclusively by her relatives and sons carried her at night to Jannatu'l-Baqi ', where she was laid to rest and her wishes fulfilled.

Having buried her, in the darkness of the night, her husband, the Commander of the Faithful Ali (ع) composed these verses of poetry:

هذي قصيدة الامام علي بن ابي طالب عندما كان عند قبر فاطمة الزهراء (ع):

قبــر الحبيــب، فلــم يــردّ جوابــي؟	مــا لـي وقفت علــى القبــور مُسلمـاً
أنســيتَ بعــدي خلّــة الأحبــابِ؟	أحبيــبُ، مــا لــكَ لا تــردّ جوابنــا
و أنــا رهيــنُ جنــادلٍ و تُــرابِ؟	قــال الحبيــبُ: وكيـفَ لـي بجـوابِكُم

235

أ كَـلَّ الثُّـرابُ مَحاسِنِــي فَنَسِيتَكُـم　　وحُجِبتُ عَـن أهلـي وعَـن أتـرابـي

فَعَليـكُمْ مِنـي مِنـي السـلامُ تقطّعَـتْ　　منـي و منكُـم خُلّـة الأحبـابِ

Why did I stand at the graves to greet,
The tomb of the loved one, but it did not respond?
O loved one! Why do you not answer us?
Have you forgotten the friendship among loved ones?
The loved one said: How can I answer you
While I am held hostage by soil and stones?
Earth has eaten my beauties, so I forgot about you,
And I now am kept away from family and peers;
So, peace from me to you, the ties are now cut off
And so are the ties with loved ones.

On p. 136 of Dalaa'il al-Imāma دلائل الامامة, we are told that those who attended Fātima's burial in the darkness of the night were, besides her husband Ali (ع), none other than both her sons al-Hassan and al-Hussain (ع), her daughters Zainab and Umm Kulthum, her maid Fidda and Asmaa daughter of Umays. The author, as quoted on p. 92, Vol. 10 of the newly published edition of *Bihār al-Anwār*, adds the following:

و أصبح البقيع ليلة دفنت و فيه أربعون قبرا جددا، و ان المسلمين لما علموا وفاتها جاءوا الى البقيع فوجدوا فيه أربعين قبرا، فأشكل عليهم قبرها من سائر القبور، فضج الناس و لام بعضهم بعضا و قالوا: لم يخلف نبيكم فيكم الا بنتا واحدة تموت و تدفن و لم تحضروا وفاتها و الصلاة عليها و لا حتى تعرفوا قبرها.

ثم قال ولاة الأمر منهم: هاتم من نساء المسلمين من ينبش هذه القبور حتى نجدها فنصلي عليها و نزور قبرها. فبلغ ذلك أمير المؤمنين صلوات الله عليه، فخرج مغضبا قد احمرت عيناه و درت أوداجه و عليه قباه الأصفر الذي كان يلبسه في كل كريهة و هو متوكيء على سيفه ذي الفقار حتى ورد البقيع، فسار الى الناس النذير و قال: هذا علي بن أبي طالب قد أقبل كما ترونه يقسم بالله لئن حول من هذه القبور حجر ليضعن السيف على غابر الآخر.

فتلقاه عمر (بن الخطاب) و من معه من أصحابه و قال له: ما لك يا أبا الحسن؟ و الله لننبشن قبرها و لنصلين عليها. فضرب علي (ع) بيده الى جوامع ثوبه (يعني ثوب

236

عمر) فهزه، ثم ضرب به الأرض و قال: يا ابن السوداء! أما حقي (في الخلافة) فقد تركته مخافة أن يرتد الناس عن دينهم، و أما قبر فاطمة، فو الذي نفس علي بيده، لئن رمت و أصحابك شيئا من ذلك، لأسقين الأرض من دمائكم. فان شئت، فأعرض يا عمر.

فتلقاه أبو بكر فقال: يا أبا الحسن بحق رسول الله و بحق من (هو) فوق العرش الا خليت عنه، فانا غير فاعلين شيئا تكرهه. فتخلى عنه و تفرق الناس و لم يعودوا الى ذلك.

In the morning of the eve in which she (Fātima) was buried, al-Baqi' was found to have forty new graves. When the Muslims came to know about her death, they went to al-Baqi' where they found forty freshly built graves, so they were confused and could not identify her grave from among all of them. People fussed and blamed each other. They said, "Your Prophet left only one daughter among you. She dies and is buried while you do not attend her demise or perform the prayers for her or even know where her grave is."

Those in authority among them said, "Bring from among the Muslims' women those who would inter these graves till we find her, perform the prayers for her and visit her grave." The report reached the Commander of the Faithful, Allāh's blessings with him, so he came out furious, his eyes reddened, his veins swollen and wearing his yellow outer garment which he always put on whenever there was trouble, leaning on his sword, Thul-Fiqar, till he reached al-Baqi'. A warner rushed to people to warn them saying, "Here is Ali ibn Abū Tālib has come as you can see, swearing by Allāh that if anyone moves a brick of these graves, he will kill each and every one of them."

He was met by Omer [ibn al-Khattab] and some of his companions and said, "What is wrong with you, O father of al-Hassan?! By Allāh, we shall inter her grave, and we shall perform the [funeral] prayers for her." Ali (ع) took hold of Omer's garment, shook him and threw him on the ground and said, "O son of the black woman! As regarding my right [to succeed the Prophet as the caliph], I have abandoned it for fear people might revert from their religion. As for Fātima's grave, I swear by the One Who holds Ali's soul in His hands that if you and your fellows want to do any such thing, I shall let the earth drink of your blood, all of you; so, if you want, stay away from it, O Omer."

Abū Bakr met him and said, "O father of al-Hassan! By the right of the Messenger of Allāh (ص) and by the right of the One on the Arsh, leave him, for we shall not do anything which you dislike." Ali (ع) left Omer alone. People dispersed and did not make any further attempt. This incident shows the reader how Abū Bakr was blessed with a higher degree of wisdom than Omer.

هذه الابيات من قصيدة فاطمة سيدة نساء العالمين للمرحوم الشيخ محسن أبو الحب الكبير أهديها الى كل الفاطميات:

فإن قيلَ حوّا قلتُ: فاطمُ فخرُها	أو قــيلَ مــريمُ، قــلتُ فـاطمُ أفـضلُ
أفـــهل لحـــوّا والـــدِّ كـــمحمّدٍ	أم هَـل لمــريم مــثل فـاطم أشـبَلُ؟
كـــلّ لهـــا عــند الـولادةِ حـــالةَ	مــنها عــقولُ ذوي البــصائر تـذهلُ
هـــذي لنــخلتها التـجت فـتساقطتْ	رطــباً جـنيّاً، فـهي مــنه تأكــلُ
وضعتْ بـعيسى وهـي غـير مـروعةٍ	أنّــى وحـارسُها السّـريُّ الأبسَـلُ؟
وإلى الجدارِ وصفحةِ البـاب التجت	بــنت النّــبيّ فأسـقطت مــا تَـحْملُ
سَـقطتْ وأسْـقَطتْ الجـنينَ وحـولها	مــن كــلّ ذي حَـسَبٍ لنـيمٍ جَـحفَلُ
هـــذا يـــعتّفها و ذاك يـــدُعَها	و يـــردُها هـــذا و هـــذا يَــركُلُ
و أمـــامها أسـدُ الأسـودِ يـقودُهُ	بــالحبلِ قُـنفذٌ، هــل كـهذا مـعضلُ؟
و لـسوفَ تأتـي فـي القـيامةِ فـاطمْ	تشكـــو الـى ربِّ السـماءِ و تـــعولُ
و لتـــعرفنَّ جَـــنينَها و حـــنينَها	بشكــــايةٍ مـــنها السّـــما تـــتزلزلُ:
ربّـــاه مـيراثـــي و بـــعلي حـــقّه	غَـصَبوا، و أبـنائي جَـميعاً قَـتّلوا

Following are verses of poetry in honor of Fātima, Head of the Women of Mankind, composed by the late Shaikh Muhsin Abū al-Hubb Senior presented to all ladies who descended from Fātima:

238

When they mention Eve, I say that Fātima is her pride,
Or if Mary is mentioned, I say that Fātima is superior.
Can anyone underestimate a father such as Muhammed?
Or does Mary have a lion cub more brave than Fātima's?
Each had a status at her birth that puzzles sages' minds:
This to her date tree resorted, so of fresh ripe dates she ate,
Giving birth to Jesus without fright, how so when the guard
Is the most brave night sojourner?
And to the wall and the door's slab did this resort,
Prophet's daughter, so she aborted what she was bearing.
She fell, and her fetus [Muhsin] fell with her, surrounded by
Every one of a mean descent and lowly birth:
This rogue rebukes her, that one reprimands her,
This one dismisses her, that one even kicks her...
Though before her was the lion of lions being led
By the rope..., so, is there a greater calamity?
Fātima will come on the Judgment Day to complain
To the Lord of the Heavens, and she will wail,
And you will know who her fetus was, why she wails
Why she presents a complaint from which the heavens shake:
"Lord! My inheritance and my husband's right did they confiscate
"And, moreover, all my sons did they kill, O Lord!"

قصيدة للشاعر المسيحي عبد المسيح الأنطاكي يمدح فيها فاطمة الزهراء (ع) فالسيدة الزهراء (ع) قد شهد بفضلها المخالف والمؤالف لأنها سيدة نساء العالمين من الأولين والآخرين:

بنـتُ لحـواءَ تـدنو مـن معاليهـا	و إنهـا فـزّةٌ بـين النسـاءِ فـلا
و لا تُلالـــي إذا لاحـت كلاليهـا؟	ومَنْ يُشِعُّ شَعاعَ الشمسِ جبهتُها؟
مَـن بالمفـاخِر و العُليـا يُحاكيهـا؟	هـي الجـديرةُ بـالكُفءِ الكـريمِ لهـا
بنـاتِهـا، سُـنّةً تـأبى تعـدّيْها	والعُـربُ تطلـبُ أكفـاءَ تَـزّوجُهُمْ
عـاراً عليهـا لـدى الأقـرانِ يُخزيهـا	وكـلُ عقـدٍ بغيـر الكُـفءِ تحسَـبُهُ

239

ومـن مِــنَ العَــرَب العَرَبــاءِ كافيهـا؟   فمـن يليـقُ ببنـتِ المُصطفى حَسَبـاً؟

وهــي المصــاهرَةُ المسـعودُ مُلقَيَهـا؟   و مَـن يناسَـبُ طـه كــي يُصـاهَرهُ؟

سَـبْقُ الهدايـةِ مُــذ نـادى مناديهـا   غيـر العلـيّ حبيـبُ المصُـطفى و لــهُ

قَـريشُ مُنـذ بــرا البـاري ذراريهـا   فانــه بعـدَ طـه خيــرُ مـن ولـدَتْ

تلـك الحـروبُ التـي أمْسـى مُجَلّيهـا   و أنــه بطــلُ الإســلام تعرفــهُ

Here is a poem composed by the Christian poet Abdul-Maseeh al-Antaki (of Antioch city) in praise of Fātima al-Zahra (ع), for those who agree with our [religious] views and those who do not have all testified to Fātima's distinction: She is the Mistress of all Women of Mankind from the early generations to the very last:

Among women, hers is a unique birth:
No other daughter of Eve comes to her distinctions close.
One from whose forehead the sun's rays shine,
From her standing places glitter glows.
She is the peer of the honored one and only who
In his feats and supreme honors is her only match.
Arabs seek competent peers for daughters to marry
A tradition which they refuse to forgo.
Any marriage without a competent peer they regard
As a shame on them that debases them among peers.
Who can match in lineage the daughter of the Chosen one?
Who among the Arabs in honors matches her?
Who suits Taha (ص) to be his son-in-law,
A marriage tie that brings happiness to one who wins it
Other than Ali, the one loved by the Chosen One?
He accepted Guidance since the Messenger called for it.
Next to the Chosen One, he is the best of Quraish
Since the Almighty created its souls.
And he is the hero of Islam well known
By those wars that raised his status.

ما هو "مصحف فاطمة"؟

"وخلفت فاطمة عليها السلام مصحفاً، ما هو قرآن، ولكنه كلام من كلام الله، أنزله عليها، إملاء رسول الله، وخط على عليه السلام"(بحار الأنوار ج٢٦ ص٤١ رواية٧٣ باب١) ولذا سمّيت فاطمة، فهي مظهر فاطر السموات والأرض. وحيث أن الملك المرسل من قِبَله تعالى يحدّثها، سمّيت المحدّثة، كما مرّ أنه كان يخبرها عمّا سيحدث بعدها في ذريّتها من المصائب والبلايا، والأهم من ذلك ما ستكتسبه الذرية، من انتصارات عظيمة، ونجاح كبير في عصر الغيبة، ومن ثمّ ظهور ابنها المهدي المنتظر، عجل الله تعالى فرجه الشريف.

عليٌّ عليه السلام كاتبُ المصحف

أنّ الزهراء، سلام الله عليها، كانت تحسُّ بالملك، وتسمع صوته، ولم تكن تشاهده، فبمجرّد أن حصل ذلك، شكت إلى أمير المؤمنين علي، عليه السلام، حيث لم تكن تتوقّع هذا الأمر بهذه الصورة المستمرّة. اذن كان أمير المؤمنين علي، عليه السلام صاحب فكرة كتابة المصحف، حيث يسمع صوت روح الأمين، فيكتب كلّما يسمعه، إلى أن اجتمع في مصحف متكامل، وهو مصحف الزهراء عليها السلام. ولا يخفى عليك ، أنّه ليس من السهل كتابة ما يلقيه جبرئيل، بل كان ذلك ضمن العلوم الخاصّة الإلهيّة التي امتاز بها أمير المؤمنين، عليه السلام، فهو الذي كتب من قِبل ما أملاه رسول الله عليه، وهو الذي معَ القرآن الكريم في المصحف الشريف كما هو ثابت في محلّه.

محتوى المصحف

إنّ المصحف يشتمل على أمورٍ كثيرةٍ تتلخص في كلمةٍ واحدةٍ وهي: استيعابه لجميع الحوادث الخطيرة الآتية، خصوصاً ما سيواجه ذريّتها، من المصائب والبلايا، وأيضاً الانتصارات، ويشتمل على أسماء جميع الملوك والحكّام إلى يوم القيامة، كما ورد في الحديث: "ما من نبي و لا وصي ولا ملك إلا وفي مصحف فاطمة" (بحار الأنوار ج٤٧ ص٣٢ رواية٢٩ باب٤). ويحتوى على أمور ترجع إلى شخص رسول الله، صلى الله عليه وآله وسلم، وأيضاً يشتمل على وصيتها سلام الله عليها.

"ابن هاشم عن يحيى بن أبي عمران عن يونس عن رجل عن سليمان بن خالد قال : قال أبو عبد الله عليه السلام.. فإن فيه وصية فاطمة عليها السلام.."(بحار الأنوار ج٢٦ ص٤٣ رواية٧٦ باب١). ومن الطبيعي أنَّ الوصيّة تشتمل على أمور خاصّة، تتعلّق بحزنها عليها السلام، وبالمصائب الواردة عليها، من أعدائها، لينفّذها ابنها الإمام الثاني عشر المهدي المنتظر، عجّل الله تعالى فرجه الشريف، لأنّه هو الإمام مبسوط اليد، الذي به يملأ الله الأرض قسطاً وعدلاً، كما مُلئت ظلماً وجوراً.

الأئمّة عليهم السلام ومصحف فاطمة

كان الإمام الصادق عليه السلام، يؤكّد دائماً على علوم أهل البيت عليهم السلام، ففي الحديث أنّه كان يقول "أنَّ علمهم عليهم السلام غابر ومزبور ونكتٌ في القلوب ونقر في الأسماع" وأنّهم يمتلكون "الجفر الأحمر، والجفر الأبيض، ومصحف فاطمة، والجامعة" فهم عليهم السلام رغم ارتباطهم وسماعهم صوت الملائكة ورغم تبعيّتهم لمصحف الإمام عليٍّ الذي هو الجامعة المشتملة على جميع الأحكام حتى أرش الخدش، ورغم معرفتهم

241

بعلم الجفر الذي يشتمل على "علم ما يحتاج إليها الناس إلى يوم القيامة من حلال و حرام" إلاّ أنّهم كانوا يعتمدون في فهم الحوادث الخطيرة على مصحف فاطمة عليها السلام كما ورد في الحديث "فنحن نتبع ما فيها فلا نعدوها" حيث يشتمل على الحوادث الخارجية جميعاً. وأيضاً أسماء الملوك إلى يوم القيامة، ففي الحديث: "سئل عن محمد بن عبد الله بن الحسن فقال عليه السلام: ما من نبي ولا وصى ولا ملك إلاّ وهو في كتاب عندي. يعني مصحف فاطمة، والله ما لمحمد بن عبدالله فيه اسم" (بحار الأنوار ج٤٧ ص٣٢ رواية٢٩ باب٤).

لقد وصل المصحف إلى مستوى من الرفعة والسموّ بحيث صار مصدر سرورهم واستبشارهم، كما يستفاد من جملة قرت عينه في الحديث التالي: "عن فضيل بن عثمان عن الحذاء قال: قال لي أبو جعفر عليه السلام يا أبا عبيدة كان عنده سيف رسول الله صلى الله عليه وآله وسلم ودرعه ورايته المغلبة ومصحف فاطمة عليها السلام قرّت عينُه" (بحار الأنوار ج٢٦ ص٢١١ رواية٢٢ باب١٦).

هل مصحف فاطمة هو القرآن؟

إنّ الكثير من الناس كانوا ولا زالوا يتصوّرون أنّ المصحف يشتمل على الآيات القرآنية الشريفة، أو أنّ هناك قرآناً آخر عند الشيعة، كما يزعم بعضُ الجُهالِ من العامّة. ولكنّ الواقع هو خلاف ذلك، فإنّ المصحف لا يشتمل حتى على آية واحدة من آيات القرآن الكريم، كما هو المستفاد من الأحاديث الكثيرة، كما أنّه ليس من قبيل القرآن ولا يشبهه من ناحية المحتوى أصلاً، فهو من مقولةٍ أخرى، فأحاديثنا صريحةٌ في ذلك فقد ورد في حديث: "...عن على بن سعيد عن أبي عبد الله عليه السلام... ما فيه آيةٌ من القرآن" (بحار الأنوار ج٢٦ ص٤٢ رواية٧٤ باب١).

وفي أحاديث أخر: "...عن على بن الحسين عن أبى عبد الله عليه السلام .. عندنا مصحف فاطمة، أما والله ما فيه حرفٌ من القرآن"(بحار الأنوار ج٢٦ ص٤٦ رواية٨٤ باب١).

- "عبد الله بن جعفر عن موسى بن جعفر عن الوشاء عن أبي حمزة عن أبي عبد الله عليه السلام قال: مصحف فاطمة عليها السلام ما فيه شيء من كتاب الله.."(بحار الأنوار ج٢٦ ص٤٨ رواية٨٩ باب١).

- "عن عنبسة بن مصعب قال: كنا عند أبي عبد الله عليه السلام.. ومصحف فاطمة أما والله ما أزعم أنه قرآن"(بحار الأنوار ج٢٦ ص٣٣ رواية٥٠ باب١).

عند ملاحظة الأحاديث تعرف أنّ الشبهة كانت منتشرة في عصر الأئمة عليهم السلام، ولهذا نراهم يستنكرون بكلّ حزم وجدّ، ويتوسّلون بالقسم لنفي ذلك، غير أنّ هناك حديثا يدلّ على أنّ المصحف:

"فيه مثل قرآنكم هذا ثلاث مرات"(بحار الأنوار ج٢٦ ص٣٨ رواية٧٠ باب).

والظاهر أنّ المقصود هو من ناحية الكميّة وحجم المعلومات، لا من حيث المحتوى. ثُمّ لا يخفى عليك ما في كلمة قرآنكم من معانٍ فتأمّل جيّداً.

وأيضاً:

المستفاد من أحاديث كثيرة أنّ مصحف الزهراء عليها السلام ليس فيه شيء من الحلال

والحرام أصلاً، ومن تلك الأحاديث قوله عليه السلام: "أما إنَّه ليس من الحلال والحرام"(بحار الأنوار ج٢٦ ص٤٤ رواية٧٧ باب١).

WHAT IS FĀTIMA'S *MUSHAF*?

Fātima (ع) has left us a book behind her which is not a Qur'ān but speech of the Almighty revealed to her, dictated by the Messenger of Allāh (ص) and written down by Ali (ع), according to p. 41, Vol. 26 of *Bihār al-Anwār*. This is why she is named "Fātima": the one who manifests the speech of the Fatir (Creator) of the heavens and earth. Since the angel sent by Him speaks to her on behalf of the Almighty, she is called "muhaddatha المحدثة", one spoken to. Also, the angel used to tell her the calamities and afflictions that will happen after her death to her progeny and, more importantly, the gains such progeny will achieve, the great victories and success during the Time of Occultation then during the time when her descendant, al-Mahdi, the Awaited One, may the Almighty speed up his holy ease, reappears.

Ali (ع) was the scribe of this *mushaf*. Al-Zahra used to sense the presence of the angel and hear his voice, but she did not see him. When this took place, she complained about it to the Commander of the Faithful Ali (ع) because she did not expect the matter would thus continue taking place.

Ali (ع), then, was the one who thought about writing the *mushaf* down since he heard the voice of the trusted angels, so he would write down what he heard till a complete *mushaf* was gathered which is al-Zahra's *mushaf*, peace with her. You realize that it is not easy to write down what Gabriel was dictating; rather, this was among the special divine sciences which characterized the Commander of the Faithful (ع). He was the one who used to write down what the Messenger of Allāh (ص) used to dictate to him, and he was the one who compiled together the Holy Qur'ān as is confirmed.

MUSHAF'S CONTENTS

Fātima's *mushaf* (book) contains many matters which can be summarized thus: It absorbs all upcoming serious events, especially the calamities and afflictions her progeny would face as well as the victories. It contains names of all kings and rulers till Judgment Day, according to this tradition which is recorded on p. 32, Vol. 47, of *Bihār al-Anwār*: "There is no prophet or *wasi* or king except that he is mentioned in Fātima's *mushaf*." It also contains matters relevant to the person of the Messenger of Allāh (ص) as well as her own will (ع).

Ibn Hisham quotes Yahya ibn Abū Omran quoting other sources citing Abū Abdullāh (Imām Ja'far al-Sādiq [ع]) saying that it contains the will of Fātima (ع) as stated on p. 43, Vol. 26, of *Bihār al-Anwār*. Naturally, the said will contains personal matters relevant to her grief and the predicaments she had to go through which her enemies caused so her descendant, the 12ᵗʰ Imām, the Awaited Mahdi, may Allāh Almighty hasten his sacred ease, would carry it. This is so because the Mahdi is the one who will have the power to do so, who will be empowered by Allāh to fill the earth with justice and equity after having been filled with injustice and iniquity.

THE IMĀMS (ع) AND FĀTIMA'S *MUSHAF*

Imām Ja'far al-Sādiq (ع) used to always emphasize the significance of the sciences of Ahl al-Bayt (ع). In one tradition, he used to say, "Their knowledge, peace with them, transcends time, comprehended and recorded, effective in the hearts, having an impact on those who hear it," that they have الجفر الأحمر و الجفر الأبيض, the Red Wide Well (or pool) and the White one, Fātima's *mushaf* and al-Jami'a." The red and white wells or pools referred to above are connotations of what is prohibitive and permissible in Islam. As for al-Jami'a , it is a collection of writings by the Commander of the Faithful Ali (ع) who held them so precious, he attached them to his sword, Thul-Fiqar. The contents of this Jami'a were recorded on animal's skin and used to be inherited, as is the case with Fātima's book, by the immediate family of the Prophet (ص), the Ahl al-Bayt (ع), who were subjected to untold trials and tribulations, persecution, imprisonment, poisoning, beheading and a host of injustices because of which these precious writings are now lost. Ahl al-Bayt (ع) used to maintain connection with the angels and adhere to the contents of Imām Ali's book, the Jami'a which contained all judicial rulings, including the penalty for one slightly scratching someone else's cheek. Their knowledge included the "science of Jafr" which contains branches of knowledge relevant to what is permissible in Islam and what is not needed by people of all times till the Judgment Day. But they used to depend in understanding serious events on Fātima's book according to a tradition that says, "We follow its contents and do not go beyond them." Such contents include all external [beyond the Household of the Prophet {ص}] incidents as well as the names of kings till the Day of Judgment. One tradition states that Muhammed son of Abdullāh son of Imām al-Hassan (ع) was once asked and he said this in his answer: "The names of every prophet, *wasi*, king... is with me in a book," meaning Fātima's book, adding, "By Allāh! It does not contain any mention of [Prophet] Muhammed ibn Abdullāh," according to p. 32, Vol. 47, of *Bihār al-Anwār*.

This *mushaf* reached a high level of loftiness, so much so that it became a source of happiness and optimism as is concluded from the phrase "apple of his eyes" in the following tradition: "Fudhail ibn Othman quotes al-Haththa saying that Imām Abū Ja'far [al-Bāqir] (ع) said to him, 'O Abū Ubaidah! He used to have the sword of the Messenger of Allāh (ص), his shield, winning banner and Fātima's *mushaf*, the apple of his eyes," as indicated on p. 211, Vol. 26, of *Bihār al-Anwār*.

IS FĀTIMA'S MUSHAF THE HOLY QUR'ĀN?

Most people used to, and still do, imagine that this *mushaf* contains the sacred Qur'ānic verses, or that there is another Qur'ān the Shī'as have, as ignorant commoners claim. But the reality is contrary to this: This *mushaf* does not contain a single verse of the verses of the Holy Qur'ān, as is understood from many traditions. Also, it is not similar to the Qur'ān, nor is it like it from the standpoint of context at all. It tells quite a different tale. Traditions are clear in this regard: One tradition says, "... quoting Ali ibn Sa'eed citing Abū Abdullāh (ع), 'It does not contain any verse of the Qur'ān,'" according to p. 42, Vol. 26, of *Bihār al-Anwār*.

In another tradition, it is indicated that "... from Ali son of al-Hussain who quotes Abū Abdullāh (ع), 'We have Fātima's *mushaf*.

By Allāh! It does not contain a single syllable of the Qur'ān," as stated on p. 46, Vol. 26, of *Bihār al-Anwār*.

❖ Abdullāh ibn Ja'far quotes Mousa ibn Ja'far quoting al-Washa citing Abū Hamzah citing Abū Abdullāh (ع) saying, 'The *mushaf* of Fātima, peace with her, does not contain anything of the Book of Allāh,'" according to p. 48, Vol. 26, of *Bihār al-Anwār*.

❖ Anbasah ibn Mus'ab has said, "We were in the company of Abū Abdullāh (ع)... and Fātima's *mushaf*; by Allāh, he did not claim at all that it is a Qur'ān," as we read on p. 33, Vol. 26, of *Bihār al-Anwār*.

When examining these traditions, you will come to know that this confusion spread even during the time of the Imāms (ع); therefore, we find them strictly and seriously denouncing it, swearing about denying it. There is one tradition which indicates that this *mushaf* "contains three times the like of your Qur'ān," according to p. 38, Vol. 26, of *Bihār al-Anwār*. It is quite obvious the comparison is with regard to the quantity and size of information, not from that of context. You can conclude that from the phrase "your Qur'ān"; so, carefully ponder.

Many traditions conclude that the *mushaf* of al-Zahra (ع) does not contain anything about what is permissible and what is not; among such traditions is this statement (by Imām al-Sādiq, peace with him): "It is not about what is permissible and what is not," as stated on p. 44, Vol. 26, of *Bihār al-Anwār*.

The list of the other Infallible Fourteen (ع) is as follows:

3. Ali ibn Abū Tālib (ع)
4. Al-Hassan ibn Ali (ع)
5. Al-Hussain ibn Ali (ع)
6. Ali ibn al-Hussain (ع)
7. Muhammed ibn Ali al-Bāqir (ع)
8. Ja'far ibn Muhammed al-Sādiq (ع)
9. Mousa ibn Ja'far al-Kādhim (ع)

246

10. Ali ibn Mousa al-Ridha (ع)
11. Muhammed ibn Ali al-Taqi (ع)
12. Ali ibn Muhammed al-Naqi (ع)
13. al-Hassan ibn Ali al-Askari (ع)
14. Muhammed ibn al-Hassan al-Mahdi (ع).

The author of this book, his family and ancestors up to about 150 years back are followers of the Shī'a Ithna-Asheri faith. Earlier than that, his ancestors were Sunnis, and the conversion of his first ancestor took place in al-Kādhimiyya city following a bloody incident which shook him. Details of this incident and the persecution to which early Jibouri (author's tribesmen) Shī'as were exposed, as well as the prejudice the author received from Sunnis in Atlanta, Georgia, where he was studying for his higher degree, are all recorded in his Memoirs. These Memoirs are available for all to read on an Internet web page by clicking on this link: http://www.scribd.com/yasinaljibouri/, but if you cannot find or access it, just send an email to: info@yasinpublications.org and ask for it.

بســــــمرالله الرحمن الرحيـــم

PART III

THE REVOLUTION'S OUTCOME

What place does Imām al-Hussain's revolution occupy in Islamic history? Those who are not familiar with its motives "innocently" or ignorantly inquire about its results, outcomes, fruits, achievements, etc. Others have even questioned its wisdom, arguing that to challenge a mighty force like that of the Umayyads of the time was fatal, suicidal, futile.

The revolution's motives have already been discussed; therefore, a brief review of the changes brought about in its aftermath throughout the Muslim world is appropriate at this stage.

Murdering Imām al-Hussain (ع), grandson of the Messenger of Allāh (ع), produced great shock waves throughout the Islamic world due to its horrible nature, to the unprecedented cruelty with which he and his family members and companions were treated, to the fact that he and his family were forbidden from having access to water while dogs and pigs were drinking of it, to the fact that he and his family were recognized as the most prestigious people on the face of earth, securing the highest esteem and regard of the Muslims who still remembered some of the statements made by their Prophet (ص) in honor of al-Hassan and al-Hussain (ع) in particular and of Ahl al-Bayt (ع) in general. Muslims, as a result, loathed to associate

249

themselves with his murderers or with anyone who had a hand in that massacre, in effect performing an act of civil disobedience of their rulers. Many of them openly cursed his murderers, for who can call himself a Muslim and who does not curse the murderer of his Prophet's family? Thus, the revolution achieved the task of unveiling the Umayyad's un-Islamic character to the general public, leaving no doubt in anyone's mind about what kind of barbarians those Umayyads were.

The concepts which the Umayyads were promoting were now being questioned by everyone; they were for the first time being recognized for what they really were: a distortion of everything Islam stands for. This isolated the Umayyads and changed the public's attitude towards them and towards anything they said or did.

Imām al-Hussain's revolution set a living example as to what every Muslim should do in such situations. It had deeply penetrated people's hearts, producing a great pain and feeling of guilt at thus abandoning al-Hussain (ع) and leaving him to be slaughtered at the hands of Allāh's worst creatures without assisting him. Such feeling of shame grew greater and greater, transforming itself into sincere repentance and translating into open and massive popular revolutions against the Umayyads' regime of terror and, in the end, succeeding in putting an end to Yazid's authority and to that of his likes. Thus, al-Hussain's revolution prompted the public to shake the dust of neo-*jahiliyya* brought about by the Umayyads and to stir, in a dynamic movement, to action to demolish all its edifices and altars.

Now let us review some of these massive popular uprisings. Among the references the reader can review for more information are: at-Tabari's *Tarikh*, al-Mas'udi's *Muraj at-Thahab*, and Ibn Katheer's *Tarikh*.

The first of those revolutions took place in Mecca after the news of the barbaric way wherein Imām al-Hussain (ع) and his small band of supporters were butchered had reached the Meccans who started discussing them. It was led by Abdullāh bin az-Zubair and is known in history books as the Harra incident which, according to p. 374,

250

Vol. 4, of the Arabic text of at-Tabari's *Tarikh* (the issue consulted by the writer is dated 1409 A.H./1989 A.D. and is published by al-A'lami Establishment for Publications, P.O. Box 7120, Beirut, Lebanon), broke out on a Wednesday, Thul-Hijja 28, 63 A.H./August 31, 683 A.D.

THE HARRA INCIDENT

This incident started on a Wednesday, Thul-Hijja 28, 63 A.H./August 31, 683 A.D. and was led by Abdullāh ibn az-Zubair. Let us stop here to introduce the reader to this man although he is too well known to any average student of Islamic history.

His full name is Abdullāh ibn az-Zubair ibn al-Awwam. His mother was Asma', the oldest daughter of caliph Abū Bakr and older sister of Aisha, the youngest wife of Prophet Muhammed (ﺹ). He was born in 1 A.H. and died in 73 A.H. (622 - 692 A.D.) and participated in the Muslim invasions of Persia, Egypt and North Africa and sided with his maternal aunt, Aisha, during the Battle of the Camel against Imām Ali ibn Abū Talib (ﻉ). He lived most of his life in Medīna and rebelled against the government of Yazid ibn Mu'awiyah and against Umayyad rulers of Hijaz, declaring himself caliph. He extended his influence to Iraq after the Battle of Marj Rahit till al-Hajjaj ibn Yousuf at-Thaqafi[1] succeeded in putting an end to his reign,

---

[1] al-Hajjaj ibn Yusuf at-Thaqafi's cruelty and disrespect for Islamic tenets are matched only by those demonstrated by Yazid. His date of birth is unknown, but he died in 95 A.H./762 A.D. He was born at Ta'if, not far from Mecca, and was famous for his loyalty to the Umayyads. Marwan ibn al-Hakam, with whom the reader is already fāmiliar, placed him in command of an army he raised to subject Hijaz to the Umayyads' control, rewarding him for his success by appointing him as governor of Mecca and Medīna to which he later added Ta'if and Iraq. He founded the city of Wasit (located in Iraq midway between Basra and Kufa), where he died, and expanded the territory under the Umayyads' control. He also crushed the Kharijites. He was proverbial in his ruthlessness and love for shedding blood. His passion for shedding blood can be understood from the way he was born. Having just been born, he refused to take his mother's breast. It is said that Satan appeared in human form and said that the newborn had to be given the blood of animals to drink and to be fed with insects for four days. His cruelty towards those whom he jailed was unheard of. His

251

executing him in the most ruthless way by nailing him to the Ka'ba..

Abdullāh ibn az-Zubair delivered a sermon once wherein he strongly condemned those responsible for killing Imām al-Hussain (ع), his family and friends, describing Yazid as a shameless drunkard, a man who preferred to listen to songs rather than to the recitation of the Holy Qur'ān, who preferred wine drinking over fasting and the company of his hunting party to any majlis where the Qur'ān is explained. Amr ibn Sa'd ibn al-as was then governor of Mecca, and he was quite ruthless in dealing with Abdullāh ibn az-Zubair, keeping him under constant surveillance, sending spies to his meeting places and constantly harassing him. When Yazid heard about Ibn az-Zubair's denunciations, he pledged to have him chained, so he dispatched some of his men with a silver chain, ordering them to tie Ibn az-Zubair with it. His deputies passed by Medīna on their way to Mecca and met with Marwan ibn al-Hakam who joined them in their effort to arrest Ibn az-Zubair, but the party failed in carrying out its mission, and more and more people pledged to assist Ibn az-Zubair against Yazid.

Having come to know of such failure, Yazid called to his presence ten men from among the most prominent supporters of his bloody regime, and there are always those who support bloody regimes in every time and clime. He ordered these ten men to meet with Ibn az-Zubair to dissuade him from rebelling. But they, too, failed in their attempt due to the public support Ibn az-Zubair was enjoying. Yazid now resorted to deposing Mecca's governor Amr ibn Sa'd and appointing al-Walid ibn Utbah in his place, prompting Ibn az-Zubair to write Yazid to describe his newly appointed governor as an idiot who never listened to advice nor enjoyed any wisdom. Yazid deposed al-Walid ibn Utbah and replaced him with Othman ibn Muhammed ibn Abū Sufyan, a young man who knew absolutely

---

prisoners were fed with bread mixed with ashes. At the time of his death, may he be placed in the deepest depths of hell, he and his Umayyad mentors and their supporters, his prisoners numbered 33,000 men and women, 16,000 of whom were completely naked and left to sleep without any blanket or sheet covering whatsoever.

nothing about politics or diplomacy.

The first action the new governor undertook was dispatching a fact finding committee to Damascus to ascertain all the rumors about Yazid being a corrupt bastard, a man unfit to rule. Among the members of the mission were: Abdullāh ibn Hanzalah al-Ansāri[1], Abdullāh ibn Abū Amr al-Makhzumi, al-Munthir ibn az-Zubair, and a good number of the most prominent men of Hijaz. Yazid received them with open arms and showered them with money and presents, but when they returned, they cursed Yazid for his blasphemy and un-Islamic conduct and encouraged people to revolt against him, using the money they had received from him to finance the rebellion against him. While passing by Medīna, the residents heard the report of the members of this committee. They, therefore, deposed their governor, Othman ibn Muhammed, and elected Abdullāh ibn Hanzalah as their new governor.

When the Umayyads saw how the public turned against them, they sought refuge at the house of Marwan ibn al-Hakam, cousin of caliph Othman ibn Affan, where they were besieged. The siege was not lifted till those Umayyads solemnly swore not to take any measure against those who laid the siege against them and not to help Yazid in any way, a pledge which they did not keep, for Abū Sufyan, Mu'awiyah and Yazid were their mentors, and these men never honored a pledge.

When the rebellion reached such a point, Yazid realized that he had lost control over the people of Hijaz, and that only an army sent against them from Damascus would do the job. He, therefore, appointed a ruffian named Muslim ibn Uqbah al-Murri who was, at the time, quite advanced in age, to undertake such a task. Despite his age, Muslim agreed to shoulder the responsibility of quelling the rebellion. An army, hence, of twenty thousand strong set out from

---

[1]Abdullāh ibn Hanzalah belonged to the Ansar of the Aws tribe, and he was one of the most famous of the *tabi'een*, a man of legendary courage and fortitude. When the people of Medīna rebelled against Yazid, they chose him as their governor. He was killed during the Harra incident.

Damascus to quell the rebellion in Hijaz with clear orders from Yazid to "... invite the people to renounce their rebellion and to renew their pledge of loyalty [to Yazid]. Give them three days to consider doing so. If they persist in their defiance, let the soldiers have a free hand in the city for three days: Any money or weapons or food they lay their hands on is theirs. Once the three days are over, leave the people alone, and spare Ali son of al-Hussain (ع), and admonish everyone to be good to him and show respect to him, for he did not join the rebellion," as at-Tabari tells us.

Yazid's troops first attacked Medīna then Mecca. In Medīna, according to al-Mas'udi and al-Daynari, they demolished homes, raped women, girls and even children, plundered anything and everything they found in their way, committing untold atrocities justified only by those who follow Yazid and who do not curse or condemn him, hence they shall receive their share of the Almighty's condemnation on the Day of Judgment and shall be lodged in hell in the company of Yazid and his likes. In his renown Tarikh, Ibn Katheer tells us that as many as seven hundred men who knew the text of the Holy Qur'ān by heart, including three close *sahabis* of the Prophet (ﺹ), were killed in that incident which is referred to in the books of history as the Incident of the Harra, a reference to "Harrat Waqim" where Yazid's army first attacked. This place is named after a man belonging to the Amaliqa ("the giants") and is one of two Medīna suburbs bearing the same name: the eastern Harra, this same "Harrat Waqim," located on the eastern side of Medīna, and the western Harra, as we are told by Imām Shihabud-Deen Abū Abdullāh Yaqut ibn Abdullāh al-Hamawi ar-Rami al-Baghdadi, famous as Yaqut al-Hamawi, who describes several places each one of which is called "Harra," then he details Harrat Waqim and comments saying the following on pp. 287-288, Vol. 2, of his voluminous work *Mu'jam al-Buldan*:

It was at this Harra that the famous "Harra Incident" took place during the lifetime of Yazid son of Mu'awiyah in the year 63 A.H./683 A.D. The commander of the army, who had been appointed by Yazid, was Muslim ibn Uqbah al-Murri who, on account of his ugly action, was called "al-musrif" (the one who went to extremes in committing evil). He [Muslim] came to Harrat

254

Waqim and the people of Medīna went out to fight him. He vanquished them, killing three thousand and five hundred men from among the *mawali*, one thousand and four hundred from among the Ansār, but some say one thousand and seven hundred, and one thousand and three hundred men from among Quraish. His hosts entered Medīna. They confiscated wealth, arrested some people and raped women. Eight hundred women became pregnant and gave birth, and the offspring were called "the offspring of the Harra." Then he brought prominent personalities to swear the oath of allegiance to Yazid ibn Mu'awiyah and to declare that they were slaves of Yazid ibn Mu'awiyah. Anyone who refused was killed.

The people of Medīna had re-dug the moat (*khandaq*) which had been dug during the Battle of the Moat, preparations for which started at the beginning of the month of Shawwal, 5 A.H. (the end of February, 627 A.D.), according to the orders of the Prophet (ﷺ) and in response to a suggestion presented to him by the great *sahabi* Salman al-Farisi as they stood to defend themselves against a huge army raised by Abū Sufyan to fight them. They also tried to fortify their city with a bulwark.

Yazid's army succeeded in putting an end to the rebellion at a very high cost, but Abdullāh ibn az-Zubair survived unscathed. A number of highly respected *sahāba* and *tabi'een* as well as narrators of *hadīth* and Sunna were branded like animals as an additional insult.

WHAT HAPPENED IN MECCA?

Having finished with the people of Medīna, Muslim, the aging commander of Yazid's handpicked troops, marched to Mecca. On the way, he camped at a place called al-Mushallal. There, he felt that death was approaching him, so he called to his presence al-Haseen ibn Nameer as-Sukuni and said to him, "O son of the donkey's saddle! By Allāh, had I not felt that death was approaching me, I would never have given you command of this army. But the commander of the faithful (meaning Yazid) had put you second in command, and none can override his orders. Listen, therefore, carefully to my will, and do not listen to any man from Quraish at all. Do not stop the Syrians from slaughtering their foes, and do not stay for more than three days before putting an end to the reprobate

Ibn az-Zubair." This is sated by at-Tabari on p. 381, Vol. 4, of the Arabic text of his famous voluminous *Tarikh* where he provides details of this incident. Muslim died and was buried there. Once the Syrian army left al-Mushallal, people dug up his grave, took his corpse out and hanged it on a palm tree. When the army came to know about this incident, a detachment was sent to investigate and to kill those suspected of hanging the corpse which was buried again and soldiers were assigned to guard it at all times. These details and many more are stated on p. 251, Vol. 2, of al-Ya'qubi's *Tarikh*.

Catapults were installed around Mecca and in the vicinity of the Ka'ba, the holiest of holies in Islam. Fireballs were hurled and the Ka'ba was soon in flames... Its walls collapsed and were burnt, and its ceiling crumbled... According to pp. 71-72, Vol. 3, of al-Mas'udi's voluminous book *Muraj at-Thahab*, a thunderbolt hit the Syrian army on a Saturday, Rab'i I 27, 61 A.H./December 28, 680 A.D., only eleven days before Yazid's death, burning eleven of the attackers. Pleas to spare the Ka'ba went unheeded, and the fighting went beyond the three days' deadline put by Muslim. The fighting took place during the last days of the month of Muharram and continued through the entire month of Safar. When the news that Yazid had died reached Mecca, Ibn az-Zubair addressed the Syrians thus: "Your tyrant has just died; so, whoever among you wishes to join the people (in their rebellion) may do so or he may return to Syria." But the Syrians attacked him. The people of Mecca saw the extent of savagery of the Syrian army, so they collectively shielded Ibn az-Zubair and forced the army to retreat and to confine itself to its camp. Slowly the Syrians slipped out of their camp and joined the Umayyads in Mecca who sheltered them and transported them back to Syria in small groups, as we are told by at-Tabari who details these events on pp. 16-17, Vol. 7, of his *Tarikh*.

Abdullāh ibn az-Zubair declared himself as caliph and appointed a new governor for Mecca, and the people of Hijaz enjoyed a measure of self-rule till the year 72 A.H./692 A.D. when al-Hajjaj ibn Yousuf ath-Thaqafiwas ordered by the Umayyad "caliph" then, namely Abdul-Malik ibn Marwan, to bring the people of Hijaz back under his rule. It was in the month of Thul-Qida 72 A.H./March 692 A.D. that Mecca was attacked again (some of the war equipment used then included five catapults, predecessors of today's field artillery) and burnt again and its governor was deposed. A new governor loyal to the Umayyads was installed in his place, and he was a Syrian named Thu'labah who demonstrated utmost disregard and disrespect towards the Islamic tenets and towards the people of Hijaz while still claiming to be a Muslim!

Detailing the events of the year 73 A.H./692-93, at-Tabari, on p. 202, Vol. 7, of his *Tarikh*, narrates saying that when the Ka'ba was burnt, a dark cloud came from the direction of Jiddah roaring with lightning and thunder. It stood above the Ka'ba and poured its water on it and put the fire out. Then it went to the Abū Qubays mountain area where its lightning damaged one of the five catapults, killing four of the soldiers tending to it. Another lightning hit, killing forty other men. This incident is narrated by several other historians besides at-Tabari. It was not long before al-Hajjaj was able to arrest and behead Ibn az-Zubair whose severed head he sent to Damascus together with those of Abdullāh ibn Safwan, Imarah ibn Amr ibn Hazm and others. Those who carried the heads and displayed them on the way in Medīna were generously rewarded by Marwan ibn Abdul-Malik.

Not everyone supported the revolt led by Abdullāh ibn az-Zubair. The famous *sahabi* and cousin of the Prophet (ﷺ), Ibn Abbās, that is, Abdullāh ibn Abbās ibn Abdul-Muttalib, was among those who did not support Ibn az-Zubair, considering him as an opportunist. When Imām Hussain (ع) was in Mecca immediately after his departure from Medīna, and when the Meccans expressed their support for him, Abdullāh ibn az-Zubair isolated himself and did not show any support for the Imām (ع), considering him as a competitor for his own bid to power. When the Imām (ع) left Mecca, Abdullāh ibn az-Zubair felt relieved. Ibn Abbās composed poetry depicting such an attitude of Abdullāh ibn az-Zubair. The reader is already acquainted with Ibn Abbās in a footnote above. Since Aisha could not get Ibn az-Zubair, son of her sister Asma' daughter of caliph Abū Bakr, to become the caliph following the murder of her cousin, caliph Othman ibn Affan, Ibn az-Zubair now tried on his own to acquire the caliphate for himself, and he met with success though for a short while.

Having come to know that Abdullāh ibn Abbās refused to swear the oath of allegiance to Ibn az-Zubair, Yazid wrote him saying,

It has come to my knowledge that the atheist son of az-Zubair invited you to swear the oath of allegiance to him and to be obedient to him so that you might support him in his wrongdoing and share in his sins, and that you refused and kept your distance from him because Allāh made you aware of our rights, we family members of the Prophet; so, may He grant you the rewards due to those who maintain their ties of kinship, those who are true to their promise. No matter what I forget, I shall never forget how you always remained in contact with us, and how good the reward you have received, the one due to those who obey and who are honored by being relatives of the Messenger of Allāh. Look, then, after your people, and look at those whom the son of az-Zubair enchants with his words and promises and pull them away from him, for they will listen to you more than they will to him; they would hear you more than they would hear that renegade atheist, and peace be with you.

Ibn Abbās wrote Yazid back saying,

"I received your letter wherein you mentioned Ibn az-Zubair's invitation to me to swear the oath of allegiance to him, and that I refused due to recognizing your right. If that is the case [as you claim], I desire nothing but being kind to you. But Allāh knows best what I intend to do. And you wrote me urging me to encourage people to rally behind you and to discourage them from supporting Ibn az-Zubair... Nay! Neither pleasure nor happiness is here for you; may your mouth be filled with stones, for you are the one whose view is weak when you listened to your own whims and desires, and it is you who is at fault and who shall perish! And you wrote me urging me to hurry and to join my ties of kinship. Withhold your own, man, for I shall withhold from you my affection and my support. By my life, you do not give us of what is in your hand except very little while withholding a lot; may your father lose you! Do you think that I will really forget how you killed al-Hussain (ع) and the youths of Banu Abdul-Muttalib, the lanterns that shone in the dark, the stars of guidance, the lamp-posts of piety, and how your horses trampled upon their bodies according to your command, so they were left unburied, drenched in their blood on the desert without any shrouds, nor were they buried, with the wind blowing on them and the wolves invading them, and the heinas assaulting them till Allāh sent them people who do not have shirk running through their veins and who shrouded and buried them...? From me and from them come supplications to Allāh to torment you! No matter what I forget, I shall never forget how you let loose on them the *da'iyy* (pretender of following Islam) and the son of the *da'iyy*, the one begotten by that promiscuous whore, the one whose lineage is distant, whose father and mother are mean, the one because of whose adoption did your father earn shame, sin, humiliation and abasement in the life of this world and in the hereafter. This is so because the Messenger of Allāh (ع) said, "The son is begotten by wedlock, whereas for the prostitute there are stones." Your father claims that the son is out of wedlock, and it does not harm the prostitute, and he accepts him as his son just as he does his legitimate offspring! Your father killed the Sunnah with ignorance while deliberately bringing to life all misguidance. And no matter what I forget, I shall never forget how you chased al-Hussain (ع) out of the sanctuary of the Messenger of Allāh [Medīna] to that of Allāh Almighty [Mecca], and how you dispatched men to kill him there. You kept trying till you caused him to leave Mecca and to go to Kūfa pursued by your horsemen, with your soldiers roaring at him like lions, O enemy of Allāh, of His Messenger (ع), and of his Ahl al-Bayt (ع)! Then you wrote Marjana's son ordering him to face al-Hussain (ع) with his cavalry and infantry, with spears and swords. And you wrote him ordering him to be swift in attacking him and not to give him time to negotiate any settlement till you killed him and the youths of Banu Abdul-Muttalib who belong to Ahl al-Bayt (ع) with him, those from whom Allāh removed all abomination and whom He purified with a perfect purification. Such are we, unlike your own uncouth fathers, the livers of donkeys! You knew fully well that he was most prominent in the past and most cherished in the present, had he only sought refuge in Mecca and permitted bloodshed in its sanctuary. But he sought reconciliation, and he asked you to go back to your senses, yet you went after the few who were in his company and desired to eradicate his Ahl al-Bayt (ع) as if you were killing dynasties from Turkey or from Kabul! How do

259

you conceive me as being friendly to you, and how dare you ask me to support you?! You have killed my own brothers, and your sword is dripping with my blood, and you are the one whom I seek for revenge. So if Allāh wills, you shall not be able to shed my blood, nor shall you be faster than me in seeking revenge so you would be more swift in killing us just as the prophets are killed, considering their blood equal to that of others. But the promise is with Allāh, and Allāh suffices in supporting the wronged, and He seeks revenge for the oppressed. What is truly amazing is your own transporting the daughters of Abdul-Muttalib and their children to Syria. You see yourself as our vanquisher, and that you have the right to humiliate us, although through me and through them did Allāh bestow blessings upon you and upon your slave parents. By Allāh! You welcome the evening and the day in security indifferent to my wounds; so, let my own tongue wound you instead, and let my tying and untying not provoke you to argue. Allāh shall not give you a respite following your killing of the Progeny of the Messenger of Allāh (ع) except for a very short while before He takes you like a Mighty One, and He shall not take you out of the life of this world except as an abased and dejected sinner; so, enjoy your days, may you lose your father, as you please, for what you have committed has surely made you abased in the sight of Allāh."[1]

Ibn Abbās never swore the oath of allegiance to the tyrant Yazid till his death.

Following the revolt of Abdullāh ibn az-Zubair, other revolts erupted throughout the Islamic lands. One of them was the Revolt of the Tawwabeen (the penitents) which broke out in Kūfa in 65 A.H./684-85 A.D., then the revolt in 66 A.H./686 A.D. which was led by al-

---

[1]This text is compiled from the contents of p. 250, Vol. 7, of *Mujma az-Zawa'id* of Abū Bakr al-Haythami, p. 18, Vol. 4 (first edition), of al-Balathiri's book *Ansab al-Ashraf*, p. 77, Vol. 2, of al-Khawarizmi's great book *Maqtal al-Hussain (ع)*, p. 50, Vol. 4, and of Ibn Katheer's book *At-Tarikh al-Kāmil*, where the events of the year 64 A.H./684 A.D. are detailed, an account which agrees with what is recorded in al-Mas'udi's book *Muraj at-Thahab*.

Mukhtar who killed all those who had participated in killing al-Hussain (ع). The Alawites (Alawids) followed with revolts of their own, including that of the great martyr Zaid ibn Ali and his son Yahya and finally the revolt of the Abbāsides who put an end to the Umayyads' rule for good.

AL-HUSSAIN'S GRAVE

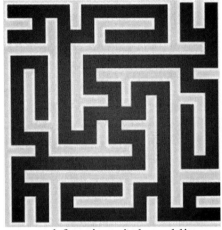

Anyone who is lucky enough to visit Imām Hussain's grave-site stands awe-stricken at the beauty of the magnificent shrine housing his tomb, a shrine which has been renovated time and over again all these centuries. It truly is a masterpiece of architecture, a jewel of art, and a pleasure to the eyes of the beholder. It also houses a grand center for theological studies. Yet many tyrants and fanatics tried to obliterate it and reduce it to rubble, while the Almighty has always been protecting it and getting it rebuilt and renovated. This is made partially possible through the generous donations of those who love the Imām (ع) and who seek nearness to Allāh by visiting the grave-site of one of His true servants, a man of honorable descent who sacrificed his life and family and everything he had for the sake of reawakening the Islamic world and getting it to refine Islam from the distortion introduced into it by the Umayyad tyrants and miscreants. Let us, therefore, stop here for a minute to review the history of the attempts aiming at obliterating Imām Hussain's grave and identify them, call them and shame them, condemn them and condemn those who do not condemn them. What is truly amazing is that all those who attacked this shrine claim to be Muslims who follow the Sunnah of the Messenger of Allāh (ع)!

In 236 A.H./850-51 A.D., the Abbāside caliph al-Mutawakkil Billah aimed at demolishing the shrine and all its attachments by razing it to the ground and planting the area where it stands. He hoped to prohibit anyone from visiting it or visiting any places held by Shī'as as sacred, threatening their pilgrims with stiff penalties. During his reign, which lasted from 232 - 247 A.H. (847 - 861 A.D.), he issued such orders four times. The first time such an attempt was made is dated 232 A.H./846 A.D. He was outraged because one of his singing concubines had gone to perform the pilgrimage to it during the month of Sha'ban of that year. The second attempt was four years later (in 236 A.H./850 A.D.). The third attempt took place in the next year, 237 A.H./850-51 A.D. The fourth attempt took place in 247 A.H./861 A.D., in the aftermath of which he himself was killed by his son, the later Abbāside caliph al-Muntasir, who was a pious and ascetic and sympathetic towards the family members (Ahl al-Bayt) of the Prophet (ص). All these attempts were carried out, according to al-Mutawakkil's orders, by a Jew named Ebrahim (Abram) who was nicknamed Deezaj, the dumb donkey. Yet despite all these attempts, the shrine kept standing again and again due to the zeal of those who believed in the message for which Imām Hussain (ع) sacrificed himself and all those who were dear and near to him.

Another demolition attempt was carried out by one Zabbah ibn Muhammed al-Asdi, a highway robber by profession, who, assisted by a number of Bedouin tribesmen, committed his foul act in 369 A.H./979-80 A.D. for which he was chased and punished by the Buwayhid ruler Izzud-Dawlah who put the shrine of Imām Hussain (ع) in Kerbalā' and that of his father Imām Ali (ع) in Najaf under his protection. This incident took place during the reign of the Abbāside ruler at-Ta'i Lillah.

In 407 A.H./1016 A.D., during the reign of the Abbāside ruler al-Qadir Billah, a mid-night fire engulfed the shrine, damaging the dome and the corridors. Some historians believe that it was not an accident but a deliberate sabotage. The said Abbāside ruler was siding with one Muslim sect against another, sowing the seeds of discord among various Islamic sects.

The most serious damage to the shrine was inflicted by the Wahhabis, followers of Muhammed ibn Abdul-Wahhab who invented an odd interpretation of Islam which does not respect the grave-sites of any holy person, including that of the Prophet of Islam

(ص). Since the Wahhabis have proven to be the most antagonistic[1] towards the followers of Ahl al-Bayt (ع), it is not out of place here to introduce the reader to their man, Muhammed ibn Abdul-Wahhab, while narrating the mischief he and his ignorant Bedouin zealots committed against the shrine of Imām Hussain (ع) in Kerbalā' and that of his father, Imām Ali (ع), in Najaf.

Muhammed ibn Abdul-Wahhab was born in 1115 A.H./1703 A.D. in the small town of Uyayna in Najd, the southern highland of Arabia's interior, and died in 1206 A.H./1791-92 A.D. He belonged to the tribe of Tamim. His father was a lawyer and a pious Muslim adhering to the Hanbalite sect founded by Imām Ahmed ibn Hanbal who, with the most rigid consistency, had advocated the principle of the exclusive validity of the *hadīth* as against the inclination among the older sects to make concessions to reason and commonsense, especially since Islam is the religion of commonsense. In Baghdad, Muhammed learned the jurisprudence of the Hanbali Sunni sect which remains to be predominant among the people of Najd and Hijaz: Whabbis constitute no more than 8% of the entire population of today's Saudi Arabia, the only country in the world named after its ruling clan. The reader has already come to know how much distortion exists in *hadīth* and can appreciate the danger of believing in each and every hadīth as though it were the inviolable and irrefutable gospel truth. He also studied jurisprudence at Mecca and Medīna where his mentors were admirers of Ibn Taymiyyah who, in the 7th Century A.H./the 14th Century A.D., had revived the teachings of Imām Ahmed ibn Hanbal. The founder of the sect, the last in the series of the four Sunni sects, namely Ahmed ibn Hanbal, was a theologian born in and died in Baghdad; the year of his birth is 164 A.H./780 A.D. and that of his death is 241 A.H./855 A.D.

Since his childhood, Muhammed ibn Abdul-Wahhab was influenced by the writings of Ibn Taymiyyah[2] and, therefore, looked askance at

---

[1]Such antagonism has proven to be bloody especially in India, Pakistan, Bangladesh and Afghanistan. Wahabbis also justify the killing of other Sunnis who do not subscribe to their beliefs as they have done in Iraq.

[2]Ibn Taymiyyah, mentor of Wahhabis and Takfiris, is Ahmed ibn Abdul-

many religious practices of the people of Najd (southern section of today's kingdom of the Wahhabi Al Saud clan). Such an influence convinced him that the dominant form of contemporary Islam, particularly among the Turks of his time, was permeated with abuses. He, therefore, sought to restore the original purity of the doctrine and of life in its restricted milieus. The facts that the Wahhabis are the minority of all Muslim minorities, and that the people of Najd and Hijaz are still predominantly Hanbalites who do not subscribe to Wahhabism by choice, prove that he did not achieve his objective and, most likely, such an objective will never be achieved despite all Saudi Arabia's petro-dollars and the abundance of those who solicit such dollars, the ruler-appointed preachers most of whom are Salafis.

Having joined his father, with whom he debated his personal views, Muhammed ibn Abdul-Wahhab caused a seriously violent confrontation to erupt from such an exchange of opposite views, for his father's views were consistent with mainstream Hanbali Muslim thought. He performed the pilgrimage for the first time, visiting Mecca and Medīna where he attended lectures on different branches of Islamic learning. His mentors included Abdullāh ibn Ibrahim ibn

---

Halim ibn Abdul-Salam ibn Abdullāh al-Khidr, "Taqiyy ad-Din ," "Abul-Abbās," a Hanbali scholar who was born in Harran (ancient Carrhae where Mudar Arabs lived, a town built by Harran brother of prophet Abraham [ع] from whom it derived its name), Iraq, in 661 A.H./1263 A.D. and died inside a Damascus, Syria, prison in 728 A.H./1328 A.D. He had his own radical and un-orthodox way of interpreting *hadīth* which was different from everyone else's, distinguishing him from all other scholars of jurisprudence. Those who adopt his views are called "Salafis," followers of the "salaf," the "pious" predecessors. He is on the record as the first person to disbelieve in intercession (*shafaa*). For more details, refer to the 463-page book titled *Ibn Taymiyyah* by Sa'ib Abdul-Hamid, published in Arabic in Qum, Islamic Republic of Iran, by the Ghadīr Center for Islamic Studies. There are many fanatical groups in India, Pakistan, Bangladesh and Afghanistan that adopt this "Salafi" ideology disseminated by government-sponsored Saudi mis-sionary activities and funded by petro-dollars.

Shrine of Imām Ali (ع) in Najaf, Iraq

Saif and Hayat as-Sindi, who both were admirers of Ibn Taymiyyah. They both rejected the principle of *taqlid* (imitation) which is commonly accepted by all four Sunni schools of jurisprudence as well as by Shī'a Muslims. These men's teachings had a great impact on Muhammed ibn Abdul-Wahhab who began to take a more aggressive attitude in preaching his views and, hence, he publicly expressed his denunciation of the sanctification of the holy precincts of the Prophet's shrine and of the shrines of any "saint." Then he went back home and decided to go to Basra, Iraq, on his way to Damascus, Syria. During his stay in Basra, he expressed the same views, whereupon its people kicked him out of the city. He almost died of thirst once, due to exhaustion and to the intensity of the heat in the desert, when he was on his way from Basra to the city of Zubair but was saved by a Zubairi man. Finding his provisions insufficient to travel to Damascus, Muhammed had to change his travel plan and to go to the (Saudi) al-Ahsa (or al-Hasa) province then to Huraymala, one of the cities of Najd, to which his father and the entire family had to move because of the public's denunciation

Prophet's Mosque in Medīna, Saudi Arabia, at dusk

of young Muhammed's views, reaching it in 1139 A.H./1726-27 A.D. By then, Muhammed's good and pious father had lost his job as *qadi* (judge) on account of his son's radical preaching. The denunciation continued till his father's death in 1153 A.H./1740 A.D.

His father's death emboldened him to express his thoughts more freely and consolidate his movement. His preaching found an echo among some of the people of his town, and his fame started on the rise, so much so that he was welcomed by the ruler of his home town Uyayna, namely Othman ibn Muammar Al Hamad, who offered him protection and appointed him as his personal assistant. In order to cement his ties with Othman, Muhammed ibn Abdul-Wahhab married Jawhara, Othman's aunt. Othman ordered his townsmen to observe the Wahhabi teachings, and Muhammed now felt strong

266

enough to demolish the monument erected on the burial site of Zaid ibn al-Khattab. But the new alliance between Muhammed ibn Abdul-Wahhab and Othman ibn Muammar Al Hamad disturbed the scholars of Najd who complained against the first to the emir (provincial governor) of the al-Ahsa province. The emir wrote Othman reprimanding and warning him of dire consequences for encouraging Muhammed ibn Abdul-Wahhab to revolt against the established authority and creed. Finding himself in a precarious situation and his job in jeopardy, Othman dismissed Muhammed ibn Abdul-Wahhab from his service and asked him to leave the town.

In 1160 A.H./1746-47 A.D., having been expelled from Uyayna, Muhammed ibn Abdul-Wahhab sought refuge in Dar'iyya, only six hours away from Uyayna, at the invitation of its ruler, Muhammed ibn Saud[1], ancestor of the Al Saud dynasty now ruling Saudi Arabia. Muhammed ibn Saud lived in a fortified settlement as chief of the Unayza clan. Soon, an alliance was forged between both men, each promising the other glory, fame, and riches for his support. The people of that town lived at the time in utter destitution, and something was needed to bring them relief. Muhammed ibn Saud rejected any veneration of the Prophet (ﺹ) or of other men of piety. It was there that Muhammed ibn Abdul-Wahhab stayed for more than two years. Both men felt that it was time to declare "jihad" against all those who rejected the new Wahhabi dogma, forming a small band of raiders mounted on horseback to invade various towns, kill and loot. The lives and property of all those who did not subscribe to the views of these two men were now in jeopardy for they were considered as guilty of being pagans fighting against whom is justified by the Qur'ān until they converted or extirpated. These raids extended far beyond Dar'iyya to include all of Najd and parts of Yemen, Hijaz, Syria and Iraq. In 1187 A.H./1773 A.D., the principality of Riyadh fell to them, marking a new era in the lucrative career of Muhammed ibn Abdul-Wahhab.

---

[1]The correct pronunciation of "Saud" is Sa'ood," but we will stick to the commonly used spelling of this word.

دار السيدة خديجة التي كانت منزل النبي (ص) و
مولد فاطمة الزهراء (ع) الواقعة في سوق الصاغة
في مكة هدمتها الحكمة السعودية عام ١٤١٣ هـ .

House (left of photo) of Lady Khadija, Prophet's wife, before the Wahhabi minority rulers of Saudi Arabia demolished it in 1413 A.H./1993 A.D. This is where Fatima, Prophet's only daughter, was born and where Gabriel used to bring the Almighty's messages to the Prophet.

During a short period of time, the destitutes of Dar'iyya found themselves wearing sumptuous clothes, carrying weapons decorated with gold and silver, eating meat, and baking wheat bread; in short, they found their dreams come true, going from rags to riches, thanks to those raids which continued till Muhammed ibn Abdul-Wahhab died in 1206 A.H./1791-92 A.D., leaving his band to carry out more and more raids and his form of "Wahhabism" embraced by the Al Saud clansmen who eventually ascended to power, due to the support they received from the British who used them to undermine the last Islamic power, the Ottoman Sultanate. Al Saud became the sole rulers of Najd and Hijaz, promoting and publicizing for Wahhabism by any and all means, spending in the process funds which belong to the Muslim masses, not to them.

After the death of Muhammed ibn Abdul-Wahhab, his band of raiders, under the leadership of the Al Saud dynasty, pursued their campaigns in the pretext of disseminating Wahhabism. In the years that followed Muhammed ibn Abdul-Wahhab's death, the Wahhabis gradually became burdensome to their neighbors. They pursued their northward advance; therefore, the Pasha of Baghdad found himself compelled to take defensive measures against them, having heard about their ruthlessness and disregard for the lives of all non-Wahhabis. He, therefore, led an army of about seven thousand Turks and twice did his army of mostly Arabs attacked them in their richest and most fertile oasis, that of al-Ahsa, in 1212 A.H./1797 A.D. but did not move on their capital, Dar'iyya, at once, as he should have, laying a siege for a month to the citadel of al-Ahsa. When Muhammed ibn Saud himself advanced against the Pasha, the latter did not dare to attack him but concluded a six-year peace treaty with him, a treaty for which the Wahhabis later demonstrated their disregard. By then, they had already set their eyes on plundering the shrine of Imām Hussain (ع) and all the valuable relics it contained.

On the anniversary of the historic Ghadīr Khumm incident, that is, Thul-Hijja 18, 1216 A.H./April 21, 1801 A.D.[1], Prince Saud mobilized an army of twenty thousand strong and invaded the holy city of Kerbalā'. First they laid a siege of the city then entered the city and brutally massacred its defenders, visitors and inhabitants, looting, burning, demolishing and wreaking havoc ... The city [Kerbalā'] fell into their hands. The magnificent domed building over the grave of Hussain was destroyed and enormous booty dragged off.[2]

---

[1]Other references consulted for this book indicate that the said attack was carried out on Thul-Hijja 14, 1215 A.H./April 28, 1801 A.D., but we are of the view that the above date is more accurate.

[2]Carl Brockelmann, ed., *History of the Islamic Peoples* (London, 1980), p.

More than five thousand Muslims were slaughtered. Then the Saudi prince turned to the Kerbalā' shrine itself; he and his men pulled gold slabs out of their places, stole chandeliers and Persian rugs and historical relics, plundering anything of value. This tragedy is immortalized by eulogies composed by poets from Kerbalā' and elsewhere. And the Wahhabis did not leave Kerbalā' alone after this massacre; rather, they continued for the next twelve years invading it, killing and looting, taking advantage of the administrative weakness of the aging Ottoman Sultanate responsible for protecting it. During those twelve years, more and more Bedouin tribes joined them for a "piece of the action." In 1218 A.H./1803 A.D., during the time of hajj (pilgrimage), the Wahhabis, led by Abdul-Aziz Al Saud, attacked Mecca, which surrendered to them after putting up a brief resistance. They looted whatever possessions the pilgrims had had. The governor of Mecca, Sharif Ghalib, fled to Jiddah which was shortly thereafter besieged, and the leader of the Syrian pilgrim caravan, Abd-Allāh Pasha of Damascus, had to leave Mecca, too. On Rajab 19, 1218 A.H./November 4, 1803, Abdul-Aziz Al Saud paid with his life for what he had committed; he was killed in Dar'iyya. His son, Saud ibn Abdul-Aziz Al Saud, lifted the siege of Jiddah and had Sharif Ghalib sent back to Mecca as his vassal in exchange for Jiddah's customs revenue.

In 1220 A.H./1805 and 1221 A.H./1806 A.D., Mecca and Medīna fell to the Wahhabis[1] respectively. The Wahhabis unleashed their wrath on both holy cities, committing untold atrocities and razing the cemetery, where many relatives and *sahāba* (companions) of the Prophet (ص) were buried, to the ground[2]. Having spread their

---

354.

[1]*Ibid.*

[2]The Wahhabis have carried out their campaigns against the burial grounds of the Prophet's family and companions well into the next century. For example, in 1343 A.H./1924 A.D., they demolished the grave-sites of many family members and companions (*sahāba*) of the Prophet (ص) against the wish and despite the denunciation of the adherents of all other Muslim sects world-wide. And in 1413 A.H./1993, they also

270

control over Riyadh, Jiddah, Mecca and Medīna, all of today's Saudi Arabia became practically under their control.

The next major invasion of the holy city of Kerbalā' by the Wahhabis took place on the 9th of the holy month of Ramadan of 1225 A.H., corresponding to October 8, 1810 A.D. It was then that both Kerbalā' and Najaf (where the magnificent shrine of Imām Ali ibn Abū Talib (ع) is located) were besieged. Roads were blocked, pilgrims were looted then massacred, and the shrines were attacked and damaged. The details of this second invasion were recorded by an eyewitness: Sayyid Muhammed Jawad al-Āmili, author of the famous book of jurisprudence titled *Miftah al-Karama* which was completed shortly after midnight on the very first day when the siege was laid. The writer recorded how terrified he and the other residents of Kerbalā' felt at seeing their city receiving a major attack from the Wahhabis. A large number of pilgrims were killed. Their number varies from one account to another, and the most realistic figure seems to be the one provided by Sayyid Muhammed Jawad al-Āmili who puts it at one hundred and fifty.

The Wahhabis no longer attack and demolish Imām Hussain's shrine, but they have been relentlessly attacking the creed of those who venerate him through a flood of books written and printed world-wide. They fund their writing, publication and circulation. They sometimes distribute them free of charge during the annual pilgrimage season while prohibiting all pilgrims from carrying or distributing any literature at all... During recent years, they have been beheading Shī'ite scholars wherever they can find them, destroying Shī'ite shrines, such as the famous 'Askari Shrine in Samarra, Iraq, which was bombed and destroyed in February of 2006 and in June of 2007; it houses the remains of both Imām Ali al-Hadi and Hassan al-'Askari, peace be with them, who descended from the immediate family of the Prophet of Islam, peace and

---

demolished the house of Khadija, wife of Prophet Muhammed (ص), as well as the house where the Prophet (ص) had been born, which stood approximately 50 meters northward from Khadija's house, turning both of them into public bathrooms...

blessings of the Almighty be with him and his progeny. Many other Shī'ite mosques and Hussainiyyas were bombed by the Wahhabis and are still targets of their mischief, yet these rogues will never be able to destroy Shī'ite Islam till the Resurrection Day. They have plenty of money, so they send their filthy money to Iraq to get the Muslims to kill each other, the Shī'ite to kill the Sunni and vice versa, thus making Satan the happiest being on earth, for nothing pleases this damned creature more than seeing Muslims at each other's throats. Such is the desire of all the enemies of Islam and Muslims. Actually, due to the barbarism of these fundamentalist Wahhabis, more and more Muslims are getting to be curious about Shī'ite Islam, so they study it and many of them end up eventually switching their sect from Sunni to Shī'ite Islam. There is no harm in a Sunni becoming Shī'ite or in a Shī'ite becoming Sunni: Islam is one tree stalk having two major branches. After all, religions of the world have sects, and people change the sect they follow according to their personal convictions and satisfaction. It happens every day, and nobody fusses about it. Thus, the Wahhabis' mischief is actually having the opposite result of what these fundamentalist fanatics, who have ruined the reputation of Islam and Muslims world-wide, anticipate.

PERFORMING *ZIYARAT* TO HUSSAIN'S SHRINE

When you visit a dignitary of a special social or political status, you are expected to follow a protocol of etiquette which you may have to learn from a secretary or a protocol specialist. Muslims believe that the soul never dies; it only travels from one stage of life to another. The Holy Qur'ān tells us that we should not consider those who die in defending His cause as dead; they are living though we are not aware of it; here is the Qur'ānic proof: "And do not reckon those who are slain in the Way of Allāh as dead. Nay! They are living with their Lord, receiving their sustenance" (Qur'ān, 3:169). So, when you visit Hussain's sacred shrine or greet it from a distance, wherever you may be in Allāh's spacious earth, you have to observe certain basic principles of etiquette such as having ablution and wearing clean clothes. There are many statements you can recite, but we have chosen this one which is known as "ziyarat warith," visiting the heir, the one who inherited the message and the knowledge of his pious predecessors. We would like to quote it here for you in its original Arabic text, then I will *Insha-Allāh* translate it for you:

السَّلامُ عَلَيْكَ يَا أَبَا عَبْدِ اللهِ وَعَلَى الأرواحِ الّتِي حَلَّتْ بِفِنَائِكَ ، وَأَنَاخَتْ بِرَحْلِكَ، عَلَيْكَ مِنِّي سَلامُ اللهِ أَبَداً مَا بَقِيتُ وَبَقِيَ اللَّيْلُ وَالنَّهَارُ ، وَلا جَعَلَهُ اللهُ آخِرَ العَهْدِ مِنِّي لِزِيَارَتِكُمْ أَهْلَ البَيتِ.

السَّلامُ عَلَى الحُسَيْنِ ، وَعَلَى عَلِيِّ بْنِ الحُسَيْنِ ، وَعَلَى أوْلادِ الحُسَيْنِ ، وَعَلَى أصْحابِ الحُسَينِ و رحمةُ اللهِ و بركاتَهُ. اللهم ارزقنا شفاعةَ الحسينِ.

زيارة الإمام الحسين (عليه السلام)

زيارة وارث

السَّلامُ عَلَيكَ يَا وَارِثَ آدَمَ صِفْوَةِ اللهِ السَّلامُ عَلَيكَ يَا وَارِثَ نوحٍ نَبِيِّ اللهِ السَّلامُ عَلَيكَ يَا وَارِثَ إِبْراهِيمَ خَليلِ اللهِ السَّلامُ عَلَيكَ يَا وَارِثَ موسى كَليمِ اللهِ السَّلامُ عَلَيكَ يَا وَارِثَ عيسى روحِ اللهِ السَّلامُ عَلَيكَ يَا وَارِثَ مُحَمَّدٍ حَبيبِ اللهِ عَلَيكَ يَا وَارِثَ أَميرِ المُؤْمِنينَ عَلَيهِ السَّلامُ السَّلامُ عَلَيكَ يا ابْنَ مُحَمَّدٍ المُصطَفى السَّلامُ عَلَيكَ يَا ابْنَ عَلِيٍّ المُرتَضى السَّلامُ عَلَيكَ يا ابْنَ فاطِمَةَ الزَّهراءِ السَّلامُ عَلَيكَ يا ابْنَ خَديجَةَ الكُبْرى السَّلامُ عَلَيكَ يا ثارَ اللهِ وَابْنَ ثارِهِ وَالوِتْرَ المَوْتورَ أَشْهَدُ أَنَّكَ قَدْ أَقَمْتَ الصَّلاةَ وَآتَيْتَ الزَّكاةَ وَأَمَرْتَ بِالمَعْروفِ وَنَهَيْتَ عَنِ المُنكَرِ وَأَطَعْتَ اللهَ وَرَسُولَهُ حَتّى أَتاكَ اليَقينُ فَلَعَنَ اللهُ أُمَّةً قَتَلَتكَ وَلَعَنَ اللهُ أُمَّةً ظَلَمَتكَ وَلَعَنَ اللهُ أُمَّةً سَمِعَتْ بِذلِكَ فَرَضِيَتْ بِهِ يا مَوْلايَ يا أَبا عَبدِ اللهِ أَشْهَدُ أَنَّكَ كُنْتَ نُوراً في الأَصْلابِ الشَّامِخَةِ وَالأَرحامِ المُطَهَّرَةِ لَمْ تُنَجِّسكَ الجاهِليَّةُ بِأَنجاسِها وَلَمْ تُلبِسكَ مِنْ مُدلَهِمّاتِ ثِيابِها وَأَشْهَدُ أَنَّكَ مِنْ دَعائِمِ الدّينِ وَأَركانِ المُؤْمِنينَ وَأَشْهَدُ أَنَّكَ الإمامُ البَرُّ التَّقيُّ الرَّضيُّ الزَّكِيُّ الهادي المَهْديُّ وَأَشْهَدُ أَنَّ الأَئِمَّةَ مِنْ وُلدِكَ كَلِمَةُ التَّقْوى وَأَعْلامُ الهُدى وَالعُرْوَةُ الوُثْقى وَالحُجَّةُ عَلى أَهلِ الدُّنْيا وَأُشْهِدُ اللهَ وَمَلائِكَتَهُ وَأَنْبِياءَهُ وَرُسُلَهُ أَنّي بِكُمْ

مُؤمِنٌ وبإيابِكُم مُوقِنٌ بِشَرائِعِ دِينِي وَخَواتِيمِ عَمَلِي وَقَلْبِي لِقَلْبِكُم
سِلْمٌ وَأَمْرِي لِأَمْرِكُم مُتَّبِعٌ صَلَواتُ اللهِ عَلَيْكُم وَعَلى أَرْواحِكُم وَعَلى
أَجْسادِكُم وَعَلى أَجْسامِكُم وَعَلى شاهِدِكُم وَعَلى غائِبِكُم وَعَلى
ظاهِرِكُم وَعَلى باطِنِكُم.

ثم انكَبّ على القبر وقبّله وقل : بِأَبِي أَنْتَ وَأُمِّي يا ابْنَ رَسُولِ اللهِ بِأَبِي
أَنْتَ وَأُمِّي يا أَبا عَبْدِ اللهِ لَقَدْ عَظُمَتِ الرَّزِيَّةُ وَجَلَّتِ الْمُصِيبَةُ بِكَ عَلَيْنا
وَعَلى جَمِيعِ أَهْلِ السَّماواتِ والأَرْضِ فَلَعَنَ اللهُ أُمَّةً أَسْرَجَتْ وَأَلْجَمَتْ
وَتَهَيَّأَتْ لِقِتالِكَ يا مَوْلايَ يا أَبا عَبْدِ اللهِ قَصَدْتُ حَرَمَكَ وَأَتَيْتُ إلى
مَشْهَدِكَ أَسْأَلُ اللهَ بِالشَّأْنِ الَّذِي لَكَ عِنْدَهُ وَبِالْمَحَلِّ الَّذِي لَكَ لَدَيْهِ أن
يُصَلِّيَ عَلى مُحَمَّدٍ وَآلِ مُحَمَّدٍ وأن يَجْعَلَنِي مَعَكُم في الدُّنيا والآخِرَةِ.

ثم قم فصلّ ركعتين عند الرّأس إقرأ فيها ما أحببت فإذا فرغت من صلاتِك
فقل:

اللَّهُمَّ إنِّي صَلَّيْتُ وَرَكَعْتُ وَسَجَدْتُ لَكَ وحْدَكَ لا شَرِيكَ لَكَ
لأَنَّ الصَّلاةَ والرُّكُوعَ والسُّجُودَ لا تَكُونُ إلَّا لَكَ لأنَّكَ أنْتَ اللهُ لا إلهَ
إلا أنْتَ اللَّهُمَّ صَلِّ على مُحَمَّدٍ وَآلِ مُحَمَّدٍ وَأَبْلِغْهُمْ عَنِّي أفضَلَ السَّلامِ
والتَّحِيَّةِ وارْدُدْ عَلَيَّ مِنْهُمُ السَّلامَ اللَّهُمَّ وَهاتانِ الرَّكْعَتانِ هَدِيَّةٌ مِنِّي إلى
مَوْلايَ الحُسَيْنِ بْنِ عَلِيٍّ عَلَيْهِما السَّلامُ اللَّهُمَّ صَلِّ على مُحَمَّدٍ وَعَلَيْهِ
وَتَقَبَّلْ مِنِّي واجِرِنِي على ذَلِكَ بِأَفْضَلِ أمَلِي وَرَجائِي فِيكَ وَفِي وَلِيِّكَ يا
وَلِيَّ الْمُؤْمِنِينَ.

السَّلامُ عَلَيْكَ يا أبا عَبْدِ اللهِ وَعَلى الأرواحِ الَّتِي حَلَّتْ بِفِنائِكَ ،
وأَناخَتْ بِرَحْلِكَ ، عَلَيْكَ مِنِّي سَلامُ اللهِ أبَداً ما بَقِيتُ وَبَقِيَ اللَّيْلُ
والنَّهارُ ، وَلا جَعَلَهُ اللهُ آخِرَ العَهْدِ مِنِّي لِزِيارَتِكُم أهْلَ البَيتِ

TRANSLATION:

Assalamo Alaikum, O heir of Adam, the one chosen by Allāh (as His vicegerent on earth)! *Assalamo Alaikum*, O heir of Noah, the prophet of Allāh! *Assalamo Alaikum*, O heir of Abraham, the Friend of Allāh! *Assalamo Alaikum*, O heir of Moses who spoke to Allāh! *Assalamo Alaikum*, O heir of Jesus, the Spirit of Allāh! *Assalamo Alaikum*, O heir of Muhammed, the one loved by Allāh! *Assalamo Alaikum*, O heir of the Commander of the Faithful, peace be with him! *Assalamo Alaikum*, O son of Muhammed, the chosen one! *Assalamo Alaikum*, O son of Ali, the one with whom Allāh and His Messenger are pleased! Assalamo Alaikum, O son of Fatima az-Zahra! Assalamo Alaikum, O son of Khadija al-Kubra! *Assalamo Alaikum*, O revolutionary for the cause of Allāh and the son of a revolutionary for the cause of Allāh, the oppressed one who is yet to receive redress and the son of an oppressed one who has not been redressed! I testify that you upheld the prayers, paid the *zakat*, enjoined what is right, prohibited what is wrong, and obeyed Allāh and His Messenger till death overtook you; so, the curse of Allāh be on a people who killed you, and the curse of Allāh be on a people who oppressed you, and the curse of Allāh be on those who heard about you being oppressed and were pleased thereby! O master! O father of Abdullāh! I testify that you were a light in the lofty loins and purified wombs: the *jahiliyya* never polluted you nor spread its garments over you! And I further testify that you are among the pillars of the creed and the corner-stones of the believers! And I further testify that you are the Imām who is kind, pious, pure, guiding to righteousness and is rightly guided, and I testify that the Imāms from among your offspring are the embodiment of piety and the flag-poles of guidance, the strong niche and the argument against the people of the world! And I further implore Allāh, His angels, prophets and messenger, to testify that I believe in you, being convinced that you shall return according to the tenets of my faith and the conclusions of my deeds, and that my heart is at ease with whatever pleases you, and my will is subservient to yours! The blessings of Allāh be upon you, upon your souls, upon your bodies, upon your being, upon those present from among you and those absent, upon what you reveal and what you conceal.

Having thus saluted the Imām, you should kiss the tomb then say the following:

By my parents (do I swear), O son of the Messenger of Allāh, by my parents (do I swear), O father of Abdullāh, that the calamity is great and the catastrophe magnanimous, and it has afflicted us and all the residents of the heavens and the earth, so may the curse of Allāh be upon a people that gathered their forces to fight you, O master, O father of Abdullāh! I have come to your sacred site and desired to be at your shrine, pleading to Allāh by the status which you enjoy with Him to bless Muhammed and the progeny of Muhammed and to permit me to be with you in the life of this world and in the life hereafter

After that you should perform two prostrations (rek'at) at the Imām's head, and you may recite in them whatever *suras* (Qur'ānic chapters) you wish. Once you have finished your prayers, you should recite the following:

O Allāh! I have performed my prayers, and I have knelt and prostrated to You, and only to You, the One and Only God, there is no partner with You, for the prayers, the kneeling and the prostrating cannot be to anyone but to You, since You are Allāh, there is no god but You! O Allāh! I plead to You to bless Muhammed and the progeny of Muhammed and to convey the best of my Salam to them and the best of salutation and, O Lord, do convey their own greeting to me! O Allāh! These two rek'at are a gift from me to my master al-Hussain son of Ali, peace be with both of them! O Allāh! Bless Muhammed and bless him, and do accept it from me and reward me for it with the best of what I anticipate, and my hope rests upon You, and upon Your servant, O Master of the believers!

278

CONCLUSION

Imām al-Hussain's revolution was not only for changing a government, as noble an objective as it was. Had it been so, it would have been wrong to call it a revolution. Imām al-Hussain ﷺ advocated a drastic change in the social order, in the economic and political structure, and he enjoined the refining of the Islamic concepts from foreign ideas that had crept into them. In other words, Imām al-Hussain ﷺ wanted to change the life of the Muslims for all time to come in conformity with the established Islamic laws and principles.

The site of Imam al-Hussain's Shrine is now also the hub of an intellectual and scholarly activity known as the hawza where people learn the teachings of Islam, particularly of the Holy Qur'an and *hadith*. Pilgrims visit this Shrine from all parts of the world, and the visit reaches its peak during what is known as the "Arba`een Ziyara." The word "ziyara" means literally a visit, but here it means paying homage to this great Imam who gave his all so the Islamic faith would return to the right track. As for the word "arba`een," it literally means "forty," but here it is the commemoration of the visit by returning surviving family members of Imam al-Hussain, mostly women and children, to the grave of the Imam forty days after his martyrdom.

During Saddam Hussein's regime, Shi`a Muslims were not free to practice their rituals and pay homage to their Imams, but this is now history. This year's Arba`een Ziyara has been amazing: Every Arba`een during past years witnessed the killing of some pilgrims at the hands of terrorists, Wahhabi fanatics who received military training at the hands of Wahhabi governments, such as that of Saudi Arabia, to kill non-Wahhabis in general and Shi`a Muslims in particular. This year, following military victories scored by the Iraqi forces that waged a war against these terrorists, there have been no pilgrims killed or wounded. The terrorists could only fire some mortar shells at Kerbala which injured some residents of the city, not the pilgrims.

There has been an improvement in the security situation in Iraq lately, and all types of Western news media in general and American media in particular have been claiming that this improvement is due to the air raids staged by the "coalition" of a number of Western countries led by the U.S. Do not believe this lie, dear reader; I now live in Iraq and I can assure you that up to this day, the fifteenth of December of 2014, 1,150 air raids staged by these allies have not had the slightest effect on the war on terrorism in three of Iraq's four troubled areas. These three regions are: Anbar, which covers one third of the entire area of Iraq, Salahuddin, birthplace of Saddam Hussein who was handpicked by the U.S. to rule Iraq and was supported by Saudi Arabia and the Gulf countries, and Diyala. No air cover was provided for Iraqis fighting the terrorists there. Despite that, there have been major victories by Iraqi troops supported by volunteers who enlisted following a fatwa, binding religious edict, issued by Iraq's supreme Shiite leader, Grand Ayatollah Sayyid Ali al-Sistni, which he issued on the 12th of Sha`ban of 1435 accordign to the Hijri calendar, the 11th of June of 2014, one day after governor of Mosul and his corrupt army and police leaders handed over the city of Mosul to the terrorists without any fighting, and thus do some people behave. Needless to say, the governor is Sunni.

The effect of this historic fatwa has been phenomenal, dealing a heavy blow to some Iraqi Sunnis who were dreaming of the return of the regime of Saddam Hussein to Iraq and to their supporters inside and outside the Arab world. An estimated half a million people are now enlisted in what is called , massive crowds which back military operations throughout the three governorates mentioned above.

Let us go back to the 1,150 air raids launched by military jets of the "coalition" led by the U.S. What have these raids been targeting? From my personal monitoring of the news media at home, Iraq, and abroad via satellite television stations worldwide, I assure you that these raids have had two objectives: 1) protecting the Kurds in northern Iraq who are viewed as beign similar to the Israelis in their ties to the West, and 2) targeting certain groups and civilian installations in Syria, such as the Nusra and the Khurasan terrorist

280

groups, and the Syrian oil wells which the terrorists seized and have been using to smuggle oil with help from Iraq's Kurds and from Turkish war mongers and profiteers.

The type of Islam, as we Shiite Muslims know it, calls for love and respect for all religions in the world: No Muslim should hate or harm a non-Muslim, or even one who has no faith at all. Instead, he must try to attract him with good manners and conduct. If a Sunni changes his School of Thought to the Shi`ite School, nobody should condemn him. Likewise, if a Shiite changes his School of Though to one of the four Schools, nobody should condemn or even ask him why. Everyone is eresponsible for his beliefs and actions. There have been tens of thousands of innocent people killed in Iraq at the hands of terrorists who claim falsely that they want to establish an Islamic state, and a number of Arab governments have been funding, training, supporting them and appluading their crimes. Who do you think is responsible for all of this bloodshed the victims of which have not only been Shiites but also many innocent Sunnis and non-Muslims? In my opinion, Ibn Taymiyyah, whose biography is briefly discussed in this book, is to blame since he was the first to introduce extremism and fanaticism into the Islamic faith and whose ideas influenced the founder of Wahhabism, namely Muhammed ibn Abdul-Wahhab, who is also discussed above. Sunnis and Shiites have been living throughout the Arab and Islamic world with each other in peace and harmony, and no Sunni beheaded a Shiite nor a Shiite beheaded Sunnis before the rise of Wahhabism which is encouraged and funded by the enemies of Islam, and we all know who they are.

Here below are some highlights of this year's Arba`een gathering:

The number of the Arba`een pilgrims this year are estimated by Iraqi government officials at over TWENTY MILLION people. Four and a half million pilgrims came from outside Iraq. Only from Iran, more than a million came, many of them on foot. The Iraqi Ports Authority arranged to transport many of them free of charge from the Abbadan Port to Basra by sea and from there to Kerbala by land.

Iraq's trains and airports have never been this busy. Pilgrim were exempted from visa fees or any other fees.

Everyone received, free of charge, full accommodation, foods, drinks, sleeping facilities, shower and other sanitary needs, complete health care, transportation and plenty of hospitality from the people of Iraq. Even tasty baklava was served to them, and mouth water kabab (kabob) and grilled chicken were served in addition to freshly baked bread, pastries, cookies, imported candies, rice and *qeema* (*kima* or *keema*), the last couple of items used to be the only food served to these pilgrims. Farmers brought their vegetables and fruits

Marchers proceed towards Kerbala on foot

and displayed them on the route used by the marchers, begging the latter to take as much as they wanted. Tea is served, too, everywhere because the weather is cold and even Turkish coffee. Some volunteers offered to massage fatigued pilgrims. You do not have to request anyone to give you a massage, you will be requested to receive one, as is the case with serving foods, drinks, pastries..., etc. A man insisted on washing the feet of pilgrims seeking the Pleasure of Allah.

Almost all religions of the world sent delegations to represent them during this multi-million man procession. On the next page is a photograph showing you one Christian delegation that participated in the procession.

A pregnant Iranian woman came walking the entire distance from Iran to Iraq and gave birth in Iraq to a baby girl whom she named "Zahraa", after Fatima al-Zahraa, peace with her, mother of Imam al-Hussain (as), which also, folks, happens to be the name of my own oldest daughter! Immediately after her delivery, she carried her infant and continued the march to Kerbala on foot........!!! At the Hilla Public Hospital in the governorate of Babylon, hospital doctors and nurses helped more than four hundred pregnant women deliver. Like their Iranian sister, they all carried their infants and kept marching towards Kerbala. Tell me if such religious fervor exists in any other faith, country or area of the world.

Imam al-Hussain belongs to all humanity, not to this "sect" or that…

One hundred thousand identification cards were passed on to parents accompanying their children as a precautionary measure against these children getting lost in the crowds.

Flags of foreign countries from which the pilgrims had come were raised during the procession, and the Iraqi news media gave these flags full television coverage.

The Kerbala Municipality distributed ONE MILLION garbage bags in order to keep the relatively small city of 1.7 million clean, getting rid of seventeen thousand tons of garbage.

Now, this question faces the reader: How many pilgrims visit the gravesite of Yazid, killer of Imam al-Hussain عليه السلام? How many people even know where it is?!

In our time and age, there are many Yazids ruling our Muslim world. This is why when the Muslim women were raped in Bosnia, massacred in Chechnya, Kashmir, Palestine, or southern Lebanon, very, very few Muslims stirred to action while the rest remained in their slumber, preferring to close their eyes rather than see the

284

horrors of what was happening to their brethren. Yes, there are many Yazids throughout our Islamic world, but there is no Hussain ﷺ to lead the revolution against them; so, the oppression and the inequity shall continue unabated, and the Muslims shall remain the underdogs of the world till they take Islam more seriously and defend its pristine tenets with all their might and means. Meanwhile, the suffering continues.., *Inna Lillah wa Inna Ilayahi Raji'oon* (We belong to Allāh, and to Him shall we return).

It is sincerely hoped that the discreet reader has benefitted from this book, that it has brought him closer to His Maker, the One Who created him for one and only reason: to worship Him, and only Him. It is hoped that this book has brought him closer to Him, to His last Prophet ﷺ, and to the Prophet's Ahl al-Bayt ﷺ and distanced himself from all those who do not denounce the murderers of Imām Hussain ﷺ, those who do not learn any lesson from his epic of heroism, who do not mourn his tragedy, who do not shed tears during the month of Muharram to commemorate this tragedy the like of which has never been recorded in history..., and unfortunately this description fits the majority of Muslims, for the majority is not always right. Seventy-two verses in the Holy Qur'ān condemn the majority. Let this be a lesson for all of us. Might and numerical superiority do not necessarily have to be right. In most instances, they are not.

For sure, whoever bases his belief in the Almighty on solid foundations will be the winner in this life and in the life to come, and the most solid of all foundations is one built on knowledge and conviction, not on ignorance, nor on taking things for granted, nor on hiding the truth or distorting it. This address is directed specifically to new Muslim converts in the West in general and in the U.S. in particular, those who have been taught to glorify certain sahāba and to forget about everyone else, to study the first few years of the dawn of Islam, and to forget about the rest. These converts should spare no time nor effort to study Islamic history and to find out who actually took Islam seriously and who did not, who shed the blood of innocent Muslims, including members of the Prophet's family, the very best of all families in the entire history of mankind, and altered the Sunnah to serve his own ambition.

One authentic *hadīth* says, "For everything there is a zakat, and the zakat of knowledge is its dissemination." The reader who reads this book ought not keep what he/she has learned to himself/herself but share it with others, believers or non-believers. It will then enhance the conviction of the believers and plant the seed of iman in the hearts of the unbelievers. Who knows? Maybe one day that seed will grow. It is the Almighty Who permits its growth, and He does so at the right time, the time which He chooses. Pass this book on to a relative or a friend. Translate it into another language. Let on-line computer services benefit from it. Make photocopies of some of its contents and distribute them to others. Write a dissertation or a thesis utilizing its text. Extract excerpts from it for inclusion in your newsletter or magazine, book or booklet. Or write one like it or better. All these options are yours; so, do not sit idle. Move to action, and let the Almighty use you as His tool for disseminating useful knowledge.

Do you, dear reader, think that you have a choice whether to disseminate the knowledge included in this book with others or not? If you think that you do, read the following statement of the great grandson of the Messenger of Allāh ﷺ, namely Imām Mūsa ibn Ja'far عليه السلام, who quotes his forefathers citing the Messenger of Allāh ﷺ saying,

One who reneges from his oath of allegiance, or who promotes what misleads people, or who hides some knowledge with him, or who confines some wealth with him unjustly, or who knowingly aids an oppressor in committing oppression while being fully aware of his oppression, is outside the folds of Islam.

This tradition is recorded on p. 67, Vol. 2, of al-Majlisi's *Bihār al-Anwār*. It clearly demonstrates that one who hides knowledge is on the same level with that who deliberately assists oppressors and tyrants. We, therefore, should spare no means to share what we know with others, with those who listen and who follow the best of what they listen to. Earn rewards by bringing the servants of Allāh closer to their Creator Who made and sustained them, Who will try them and place them either in His Paradise or in His hell. If acts of worship are based on shallow conviction, they are as good as nothing. Strengthen your brethren's conviction through this book. They will surely appreciate it and, above all, Allāh, too, will.

If the reader appreciates the time and effort exerted in writing this book, I, the author, kindly request him/her to recite Sūrat al-Fātiha for the soul of my father, the late qari al-Hajj Tu'mah Abbās al-Jibouri who died in 1991 of diabetes, medicines for which were not available because of the "economic sanctions" imposed on the people of Iraq by the tyrants of the world, and for the souls of all believing men and women, the living and the dead. If you do so, rest assured that your rewards will be with the Most Generous of all those who reward, with Allāh Almighty Who appreciates even the smallest of good deeds. Why do I request the kind reader to recite Sūrat al-Fātiha for my parents? Well, this is the least a son can do for his deceased father who worked very hard to raise him as a Muslim. My father was a *qari* of the Holy Qur'ān who refused to read any other book besides the Qur'ān as long as he lived, a man who never intentionally hurt anyone all his life. Not only will my father receive blessings when you recite Sūrat al-Fātiha for his soul, but you, too, dear reader, will get your rewards as well. How will you be rewarded? Well, read on! Here is a glimpse of what you will Insha-Allāh receive:

On p. 88, Vol. 1, of *Mujma' al-Bayan fi Tafsir al-Qur'ān*, at-Tibrisi cites a tradition through a chain of narrator wherein the Prophet of Islam is quoted as saying, "Whoever recites Sūrat al-Fātiha will be rewarded as though he had read two thirds of the Holy Qur'ān and will be (in addition to that) given rewards as though he gave charity to each and every believing man and woman." Just imagine how generous the Almighty is! Ubayy ibn Ka'b is cited in the same reference saying, "I once recited Sūrat al-Fātiha in the presence of the Messenger of Allāh, peace and blessings of Allāh be upon him and his progeny, who said to me, I swear by the One Who controls my life, Allāh never revealed any chapter in the Torah, the Gospel, the Psalms, or (even) in the Qur'ān like it. It is the mother of the

Book, and it is the seven oft-repeated verses. It is divided between Allāh and His servant, and His servant will get whatever he asks Him for.'" The Messenger of Allāh ﷺ said once to Jābir ibn Abdullāh al-Ansāri, one of his greatest sahāba, may Allāh be pleased with all his good *sahāba*, "O Jābir! Shall I teach you the merits of a Sura which Allāh revealed in His Book?" Jābir said, "Yes, O Messenger of Allāh! May both my parents be sacrificed for your sake! Please do!" The Messenger of Allāh ﷺ taught him Sūrat al-Hamd, the "Mother of the Book," then said to him, "Shall I tell you something about it?" "Yes, O Messenger of Allāh," Jābir responded, "May my father and mother be sacrificed for your sake!" The Messenger of Allāh ﷺ said, "It cures everything except death." Imām Ja'far as-Sādiq is quoted on the same page as saying, "Anyone who is not cured by the Book's Fātiha cannot be cured by anything else." Imām Ali ibn Abū Talib عليه السلام has said,

The Messenger of Allāh ﷺ has said, "Allāh, the Exalted One, the Sublime, said to me: (O Muhammed!) We have bestowed upon you seven oft-repeated verses and the Great Qur'ān (verse 87 of Sūrat al-Hijr); so, express your appreciation for it by reciting the Book's Fatih,.a,' thus comparing it to the entire Qur'ān." Sūrat al-Fātiha is the most precious of the treasures of the Arsh. Allāh specifically chose Muhammed ﷺ to be honoured by it without having done so to any of His prophets with the exception of prophet Sulayman (Solomon) who was granted (only this verse) of it: Bismillahir-Rahmanir-Rahim (verse 30 of Chapter 27, Sūrat an-Naml); don't you see how He narrates about Balqees[220] saying, "O Chiefs (of

---

[1]Balqees Queen of Saba' (Sheba) belonged to the Arab tribe of Himyar which for centuries has been residing in Yemen. Her people used to worship the sun and the moon and other stars, and some of the ruins of the temples she had built for them can still be seen in Saba'. Solomon (Sulayman), on the other hand, was headquartered in Jerusalem (Ur-o-Shalom, the city of peace, as it is called in Hebrew; the Arabs used to refer to it as Eilya). The place where Balqees met Sulayman, that is to say, his palace, had been built in the 10th century B.C. Reference to the grandeur of this palace exists in 27:44: its glass-covered floor was so smooth, Balqees thought she was in front of a lake. Damascus, a very ancient city not far from Jerusalem, had by then established a reputation for its glass

Yemen's tribes)! Surely an honourable letter has been delivered to me; it is from Solomon, and it is: In the Name of Allāh, the Beneficent, the Merciful..." (27:29-30)? So whoever recites it sincerely believing that he/she is following in the footsteps of Muhammed and his progeny, ābidīng by its injunctions, believing in its apparent as well as hidden meanings, Allāh will give him for each of its letters a good deed better than all this world and everything in it of wealth and good things. And whoever listens to someone reciting it will receive a third of the rewards the reciter receives; so, let each one of you accumulate of such available goodness, for it surely is a great gain. Do not let it pass you by, for then you will have a great sigh in your heart about it."[221]

Rewards of reciting Sūrat al-Fātiha are also recorded on p. 132 of *Thawab al-A'mal wa Iqab al-A'mal* ثواب الأعمال و عقاب الأعمال cited above. Abū Abdullāh Imām Ja'far as-Sādiq has said, "Whoever recites Sūrat al-Baqara and Sūrat al-Fātiha, they will both shade him like two clouds on the Day of Judgment. And if the reader wishes to read more about the merits of the Basmala (Bismillahir-Rahmānir-Rahīm), he is referred to pp. 70-71 of my book *Fast of the Month of Ramadan: Philosophy and Ahkam* published by Ansāriyan (P.O. Box 37185/187, Qum, Islamic Republic of Iran). As for the merits of Sūrat al-Fātiha, I would like to quote for you here what is published on pp. 71-73 of the same book:

At-Tibrisi, in his exegesis *Mujma'ul-Bayan fi Tafsir al-Qur'ān*, provides nine names for the first chapter of the Holy Qur'ān, namely Sūrat al-Fātiha: 1) al-Fātiha الفاتحة, the one that opens, for it is like a gate: when opened, it leads one to the Book of Allāh; 2) al-Hamd الحمد, the praise, for its verses are clearly praising the Almighty; 3)

---

industry. Damascus, in 940 B.C. (around the same period of time when Sulayman was ruling in Jerusalem) was the city capital of the Aramaeans, the nations that spoke Aramaic, mother-tongue of prophet Jesus Christ عليه السلام. This is why Syria used to be called Aram, the land of the Aramaens. Aramaic is still spoken in some part of Syria even today.

[2]at-Tabari, *Tarikh*, Vol. 1, p. 88.

Ummul-Kitāb أم الكتاب, the mother of the Book, for its status is superior to all other chapters of the Holy Qur'ān, or like the war standard: it is always in the forefront; 4) as-Sab' السبع, the seven verses, for it is comprised of seven verses and the only one whose verses are seven, and there is no room here to elaborate on the merits of the number 7 especially since most readers of this book are already aware of such merits; 5) al-Mathāni المثاني, the oft-repeated Chapter, for no other Chapter of the Holy Qur'ān is repeated as often as this one; 6) al-Kāfiya الكافية, the chapter that suffices and that has no substitute; you simply cannot replace its recitation with that of any other chapter of the Holy Qur'ān in the first two rek'ats of the prayers, whereas it can substitute others; 7) al-Asās الأساس, the basis or foundation or bed-rock, a connotation of its being the foundation upon which the Holy Qur'ān stands just as the Basmala ("Bismillahir-Rahmānir-Rahīm") is the foundation of the Fātiha; 8) ash-Shifā' الشفاء, the healing, due to the fact that the Messenger of Allāh (ص) has said that the Fātiha heals from all ailments except death, and 9) as-Salāt الصلاة, the prayers, or the basic requirement of the daily prayers, one without the recitation of which no prayer can be accepted. The Prophet has quoted the Almighty as saying, "The prayers have been divided between Me and My servant: one half for Me, and one for him;" so when one recites it and says, "Alhamdu lillahi Rabbil-Ālamīn," the Almighty says, "My servant has praised Me." And when he says, "Arrahmānir-Rahīm," the Almighty says, "My servant has lauded Me." And when he says, "Māliki Yawmid-Dīn," Allāh says, "My servant has exalted Me." And when he says, "Iyyaka Nabudu wa iyyaka nastaan," Allāh will say, "This is a covenant between Me and My servant, and My servant shall be granted the fulfillment of his pleas." Then if he finishes reciting the Fātiha to the end, Allāh will again confirm His promise by saying, "This is for [the benefit of] My servant, and My servant will be granted the answer to his wishes."

The Messenger of Allāh ﷺ is quoted by Abū Ali al-Fadl ibn al-Hassan ibn al-Fadl at-Tibrisi, may Allāh have mercy on his soul, saying that one who recites al-Fātih,.a will be regarded by the Almighty as though he recited two-thirds of the Holy Qur'ān and as though he gave by way of charity to each and every believing man and woman. "By the One in Whose hand my soul is," the Prophet ﷺ continues, "Allāh Almighty did not reveal in the Torah, the Gospel, or the Psalms any chapter like it; it is the Mother of the Book and as-Sab' al-Mathāni السبع المثاني (the oft-repeated seven verses), and it is divided between Allāh and His servant, and His servant shall get whatever he asks; it is the best Sura in the Book of the most Exalted One, and it is a healing from every ailment except poison, which is death." He is also quoted by al-Kaf'ami as saying, "He (Allāh) bestowed it upon me as His blessing, making it equivalent to the Holy Qur'ān, saying, And We have granted you as-Sab' al-Mathani and the Great Qur'ān (Sūrat al-Hijr, verse 87).' It is the most precious among the treasures of the Arsh." Indeed, Allāh, the most Sublime, has chosen Muhammed ﷺ alone to be honoured by it without doing so to any other Prophet or Messenger of His with the exception of Solomon (Solomon) who was granted the Basmala. One who recites it, being fully convinced of his following in the footsteps of Muhammed ﷺ and his Progeny ﷺ, adhering to its injunctions, believing in its outward and inward meanings, will be granted by Allāh for each of its letters a blessing better than what all there is in the world of wealth and good things, and whoever listens to someone reciting it will receive one third of the rewards due to its reciter.

There is no doubt that you, dear reader, know that it is very costly to print books, and philanthropists in the Muslim world are rare and endangered species. Once you find one, you will find out that he is willing to spend money on anything except on a book! This is very sad, very tragic, very shameful. Islam spread through a Book: the Holy Qur'ān. That was all the early generations of Muslims needed besides the presence of the Messenger of Allāh. But times have changed; we do not have the presence of the Messenger of Allāh in our midst to ask him whenever we need to know, and his Sunnah has suffered acutely of alteration, addition, deletion, custom-designing and tailoring to fit the needs of the powerful politicians of the times, so much so that it is now very hard to find the pristine truth among all the numerous different views and interpretations. This is why the reader has to spend more effort to get to know the truth; nobody is going to hand it to you on a golden platter. You have to work hard to acquire it. "Easy come, easy go." Yet readers who would like to earn a place in Paradise through their dissemination of Islamic knowledge, such as the knowledge included in this book, are very much needed and are advised in earnest to send their contributions to the Publisher of this book in order to help him print more copies of it and make them available to those who cannot afford to purchase them. Some readers erroneously surmise that book publishers are wealthy people who make a lot of money selling books, but, alas, this applies ONLY to non-Muslim publishers. After all, Allāh will judge our actions according to our intentions, and if you help promote a book seeking the Pleasure of Allāh, rest assured that you will be richly rewarded. It remains to see how strong you are against the temptations of Satan who will try his best, and his worst, to dissuade you from doing so. He very well knows that nothing in the world stands between him and corrupting the minds of Muslims more than accurate knowledge about Allāh and the men of Allāh. May Allāh Taala include us among the latter, *Allāhomma Aameen*.

May Allāh Ta'āla accept our humble effort; may He forgive our sins and shortcomings; may He take our hands and guide us to what He loves and prefers, *Allāhomma Aameen, Wassalāmo Alaikom wa Rahmatullāhi wa Barakātuh.*

ARABIC EULOGIES

It will be unfair to attempt to translate any of these great poems, they are simply too beautiful to be rendered into any other language.

مراثي سيد الشهداء الامام الحسين عليه السلام

من كتاب "مقتل الحسين" للمقرم

و مصادر أخرى

إنّ قضيّة سيّد الشهداء (عليه السّلام) بما اشتملت عليه من القساوة الشائنة كانت مثيرة للعواطف ، مرققةً للأفئدة ، فتذمّر منها حتّى مَن لم ينتحل دين الإسلام ؛ لذلك ازدلف الشعراء قديماً وحديثاً ، باللغة الفصحى والدارجة ، إلى ذكرها وتعريف الأجيال المتعاقبة بما جاء الأمويّون من استئصال شأفة آل الرسول (ص) فجاؤا بما فيه نجعة المرتاد .

ومن هؤلاء المناضلين لإحياء المذهب ، الحجّة آية الله الشيخ محمّد حسين كاشف الغطاء (نوّر الله ضريحه) فلقد جاء بمراثٍ كثيرة لها حُسن السّبك ودقّة المعنى وسلاسة النّظم ورقّة الانشاء ، آثرنا منها أربع قصائد ساطعة في رثاء السّبط الشهيد سيّد شباب أهل الجنّة (عليه السّلام):

1- قال رحمه الله :

فجرت بها محمرّة عبراتها	نفس أذابتها أسىً حسراتها
فتوقّدت بضلوعها جمراتها	وتذكّرت عهد المحصّب من منى
حنّت مطاياهم لها وحداتها	سارت وراءهم ترجع رنّة
ليلاً فردّت شمسه جبهاتها	طلعوا بيوم للوداع وقد غدا
بدراً فأطراف القنا هالاتها	وسروا بكلّ فتاة خدرٍ إنْ تكن
فجناتها دون الورى وجناتها	فخذوا احمرار خدودها بدمائنا

295

واستعطفوا باللين أعطافاً لها | فلقد أقمنَ قيامتي قاماتها

وعلى عذيب الريق بارق لؤلؤ | بالمنحنى من أضلعي قبساتها

لاثت على شهدية بخمارها | والخمر يشهد إنـه لـثـأَتها

لله يوم تلفّتت لـو أنـها | كانت لقتلى حبَّها لـفـتاتها

ثـملت بخمرة ريقها أعطافها | زهت بلؤلؤ ثغرها لثاتها

ومشت فخاطرت النَفوس كأنَّما | ماست بخطّار القنا خطراتها

ومن البليّة أنَّني أشكو لها | بلوى الضَّنا فتزيدني لحظاتها

وأبيت أسهر ليلتي وكأنَّما | قد وقَّرت في جنحها وفراتها

ومهى قنصت لصيدهنّ فعدت في | شرك الغرام وأفلتت ظبياتها

عجباً تفاد لـي الأسود مهابةً | وتقودني وأنا الأبيّ مهاتها

أنا من بعين المكرمات ضياؤها | لكن بعين الحاسدين قذاتها

إن أنكرتني مقلة عميا فلا | عجب فإنّي في سناني فقأتها

تعساً لدهر أصبحت أيّامه | والغدر نجح عداتها وعداتها

لا غرو أنْ تعتد بنوه الغدر | فالأبناء من آبائها عاداتها

ولقد وجدت ملاءة الدنيا خلت | من عفَّة ونجابة فملاتها

وأرى أخلّاني غداة خبرتهم | أعدى عدى شئت بنا غاراتها

كنت الحماة أظنّهم فكشفتهم | عن عقرب لسعت حشاي حماتها

وتعذَّهم نفسي الحياة لها وقد | دبّت إليها منهم حيّاتها

أسدت إليّ بكلّ سيّئة ومن | صفحى أقدَّر أنَّها حسناتها

قد ســوَّدتها اليـوم تـمويهاتهـا	ولـكم عـليهـا مـن يـد بيضاء لـي
عـرفت بـخبث الجـنس ماهيّاتهـا	إنْ فـصَّلت لـي الغدر أنواعـاً فقـد
نـبح الـكلاب عـليَّ أو أصـواتها	لـؤمت إسـاءتها فهانـت واستوى
لـولا خـساستها عـليَّ خـساتها	وتـكـرَّماً عـنهـا صـددت وإنّـي
عـن وطء كـلّ دنـيَّة لـوطاتها	ولـقـد دنـت شـأناً فـلـولا عفّتـي
تـجد المسـاغ قـذفن بـي لهواتهـا	وأنـا الـشجى في حلقها فلـو أنّهـا
قـذفت بـجمرة غيظهـا حصياتهـا	وتهـشَّ بـشراً إن حضرت فان أغب
الـورى شـرَّاً عـليَّ دهـاتها	كـم صـانعتني بالـدهاء وإنّـما أدهى
يـدها عـلى عيـني العمـى لـدراتها	لـكنْ جُبِلْـتُ على الوفاء فلَـو جنت
فـي طـاعـة الحـرِّ الكريم عصاتها	وأنـا الـعصيّ مـن الإبـا وخلائقـي
إلَّا لآل محمّـــــدٍ عبراتهـــا	عـوَّدتُ عـينيَّ الإبـاء فلـم تـسل
لـم أسـتطع دفعـاً لـها فشناتها	كـم غـارة لـك يـا زمـان شـننتها
للـحـرِّ غـير مـلمّة غـدراتها	وأرى الـلـيالي مـنك حُـلبى لَـم تلد
ذكـراً عـلـى أسـماعنا عـثراتها	تجرى لـها العبرات حمراً إنْ جرت
ورمـت بـنيهـا بـالـصروف بناتهـا	وودَدْت مـذ جـارت عـلـى أبنائهـا
وهُـمُ أنـمَّة عـدلها وقـضاتها	عـدلت بـآل محمّـدٍ فيمـا قـضت
ونـدىً تـميح صَـلاتها وصِـلاتها	الـمرشدون الـمرفدون فكـم هـدى
نـكباء صـوَّحت الـثَّرى نكباتها	والـمنعمون المطعمـون إذا انبـرت
لَـم تـجتمع بـسواهُم أشـتاتها	والـجامعون شـتات غـرِّ مناقب

297

يا غاية تقف العقول كليلة	عنها وإنْ ذهبت بها غاياتها
ياجذوة القدس التي ما أشرقت	شهب السّما لو لَم تكن لمعاتها
ياقبّة الشرف التي لو في الثَّرى	نُصبت سمت هام السّما شرفاتها
ياكعبة لله إنْ حجّت لها	الأملاك منه فعرشه ميقاتها
يانقطة الباء التي باءت لها	الكلمات وائتلفت بها ألفاتها
يا وحدة الحقِّ التي ما إنْ لها	ثانٍ ولكن ما انتهت كثراتها
يا وجهة الأحديَّة العليا التي	بالأحمديَّة تستنير جهاتها
يا عاقلي العشر العقول ومَن لها	السَّبع الطباق تحرَّكت سكناتها
أقسمتُ لو سِرَّ الحقيقة صورة	راحت وأنتم للورى مرآتها
أنتم مشئنته التي خلقت بها	الأشياء بل ذُرِئت بها ذرّاتها
وخزانة الأسرار بل خزَّانها	وزجاجة الأنوار بل مشكاتها
أنا في الورى قال لكم إنْ لَم أقل	ما لم تقله في المسيح غُلاتها
سفهاً لحلمي إن تطر بثباتي السف	هاء مذ طارت بها جهلاتها
أنا من شربت هناك أول درِّها	كأساً سرت بسرائري نشواتها
فاليوم لا أصحو وإن ذهبت بيَ	الأقوال أو شدَّت عليَّ رماتها
أو هل ترى يصحو صريع مدامة	ممّا به إن عنّفته صحاتها
أو هل يحول أخو الحجى عن رشده	ممّا تؤنِّبه عليه غواتها
بأبي وبي مَن هم أجلُّ عصابة	سارت تؤمَ بها العلا سرواتها
عطري الثياب سروا فقل في روضة	غبّ السّحاب سرت بها نسماتها

298

ركبٌ حجازيون عرّقت العلا	فيـهم ومِـسك ثنائهم شاماتها
تـحدو الحـداة بـذكرهم وكـأَنَّما	فتـقت لـطيمة تـاجر لـهواتها
ومطَوَّحين ولا غـناء لـهم سوى	هـزج الـتلاوة رتّـلت آيـاتها
وإلـى الـلقاء تـشوَّقاً أعطافها	مـهـزوزةً فكـأنَّها قنـواتها
خفّـت بـهم نـحو الـمنايا همَّة	ثـقلت على جيش العدى وطآتها
وبـعزمها مـن مـثل مـا بـأكفِّها	قـطع الـحديد تـأجَّجت لـهباتها
فكـأنَّ مـن عـزماتها أسـيافها	طـبعت ومـن أسـيافها عـزماتها
قـسم الحيا فيها فـمن مقصورة	الأيـدي وممـدودة قـسماتها
ومـلوك بـأسٍ في الحروب قبابها	قـبّ الـبطون ودسـتها صـهواتها
يـسطون فـي الجمِّ الغفير ضياغما	لكـنّما شجـر الـقنا أجـماتها
كـالليث أو كالغيث في يومي وغىً	ونـدىً غـدت هبـاتها وهبـاتها
حـتَّى إذا نـزلوا العـراق فأشرقت	أكـنافها وزهـت بـهم عرصـاتها
ضـربوا الـخيام بـكربلا وعلـيهم	قـد خـيَّمت بـبلائها كُـرُباتها
نـزلوا بـها فانصاع من شوك القنا	ولـظى الـهواجر مـاؤها ونباتهـا
وأتت بـنو حـرب تـروم ودون مـا	رامـت تـخرُّ مـن السَّـما طبقاتها
رامـت بـأن تعنـو لـها سـفهاً وهـل	تـعنو لـشرِّ عـبيدها سـاداتها
وتـسومها إمَّـا الخضوع أو الـردى	عـزاً وهـل غير الإبـاء سـماتها
فـأبوا وهـل مـن عـزَّة أو ذلَّـة	إلّا وهـم آبـاؤهـا وأبـاتهـا
وتـقحَموا لـيل الحـروب فأشرقت	بـوجـوههم وسـيوفهم ظـلماتها

لـلأسد فـي يـوم الـهياج شياتها	وبـدت عـلوج أمـيّة فتعرّضت
يـوم الـلـقـا بـعداتها عـاداتها	تـعدو لـهـا فـتميتها رعباً وذي
وتـفـرّ قـبل جـسومها هـاماتها	فتخرُّ بـعد قـلوبها أذقـانها
صـينت بـبذل نـفوسها فـتياتها	وبـأسـرة مـن آل أحـمد فـتية
راحـاتها قـد أتـرعت راحـاتها	يتضاحكون إلـى المنـون كأنّ فـي
فيـهم قيـان رجِّعت نـغماتها	وتـرى الـصّهيل مـع الـصّليل كأنّـه
فتـمايلت لعـنـاقها قامـاتها	وكأنّـما سـمر الـرماح معاطف
ضـمنت لـمى رشـفاتها شفراتها	وكـأنّـما بـيض الظّـبى بـيض الـدّمى
قـد خـضّبتها عـندماً كـاساتها	وكـأنّـما حـمر النّـصول أنامـل
دون الـشّـدائد نكّـصـاً شـدّاتها	ومـذ الـوغى شبّـت لظى وتقاعست
قـد أنـبتت شجر الـقنا حافاتها	وغـدت تـعوم مـن الحديد بلجّـة
نيـرانها لجـنـانهم جنّـاتها	خـلعوا لـها جنن الـدّروع ولاح مـن
الآجال تحـسب أنّـها عـاداتها	وتـزاحفوا يتنافـسون عـلى لقى
ولـها الـفوارس سـجّد هـاماتها	بأكـفّها عـوج الأسنّة ركّـع
وعـلت بـفردوس العلى درجاتهـا	حـتّى إذا وافـت حـقوق وفائهـا
وجـرى القضاء فنكّـصت راياتها	شـاء الإلـه فنكّـست أعلامها
مـن صمِّ شاهقة الـذرى هـضباتها	وهوت كما انهالت على وجه الثرى
لكـن تـزيد طلاقة قـسماتها	وغـدت تقسّم بـالظّبى أشلاؤها
تـمعت عـليه طـغامها وطغاتها	ثـمّ انـثنى فـرداً أبـو السّجاد فاجـ

حــرب جـيوش مـنيَّة حملاتهـا	غير أن يحمـل عزمـة عملت إلـى
وتـجول فـي أوسـاطهم سطواتهـا	تـلوي بـأولاهم عـلى أخـراهم
ديست عـلى أشـبالها غاباتهـا	يـحمي مـخيّمه فقل أسد الشَّرى
لـلــسانه وسنــانه كلــماتها	خطبَ العدى فـوق العـوادي خطبـةً
طعن الـسّنان فـلم تفته عتاتها	وعظ اللسان ومـذ عتوا عن أمره
سلـك الـقنا لـقلوبهم حـبّاتها	نـثر الـرؤوس بسيفه ونظمـن فـي
ردَّت ومــن أكــبادها عـذباتها	إن يـشرع الخرصان نحو مكردس
عـادت عـلى أرواحهـم قبضاتها	واذا هـوت بـالبيض قبضة كفّـه
ظـمأ تـطاير شعلة قـطعاتها	يـروي الثـرى بـدمائهم وحشاه من
صمَ الـصفا ذابـت عليـه صفاتها	لـو قـلبت مـن فـوق غلَّـة قلبه
مـاء لغلَّـة قـلبه قـطراتها	تـبكي الـسّماء لـه دماً أفـلا بكت
لـك والعدى بـك أنجحت طلباتها	وا حـرَّ قـلبي يـابن بنت محمَّـد
لـلنّاس بـعدك نِيلهـا وفراتهـا	مـنعتك مـن نيـل الفـرات فـلا هنا
وبـرأسك السّـامي تـشال قناتها	وعـلى الثنايـا منـك يلعب عودها
وجـسومكم فـوق الثَّـرى حلباتها	وبهم تـروح العاديـات وتغتـدي
تـدعو وعنهـا اليـوم أين سـراتها	ونسـاؤكم أسـرى سـرت بـسراتكم
صـرعى وتلـك على القنا هاماتها	هـاتيك في حـرِّ الهجير جسومها
للحـشر تنـشر فخرهم حـسناتها	بـأبي وبِي مـنهم محاسن في الثَّرى
راحـت ومـن أسـيافهم أقواتهـا	أقـوت معالم أنـسهم والـوحش كم

في كـربلا أبـناؤها وبـناتها	يـا هل تـرى مضراً درت مـاذا لقت
هـتكت لـها مـا بيـنهم خفراتها	خـفرت لـها أبـناء حرب ذمّة
تـهوى النّـجوم لـو أنّها جاراتها	جـارت على تلك المنيعـات التي
تنـتاشها أجلافـها وجـفاتها	حـتّى غـدت بـين الأرازل مغنمـا
أبرادهـا ولنـهبها أبيـاتها	فلـضربها أعـضادها ولـسلبها
والنّـوح ردّدت الشّجى لهواتهـا	وثـواكلٍ لـمّا دفعـن عـن البكـا
بـالدمع، أضـرمت السـما جذواتها	زفـراتها، لـو لَـم تكـن مـشفوعة
في الشمس تـصلى حرُّهـا أخواتهـا	وعـلى الأيـانق مـن بنـات محمّد
حتّـى لأنفـاس الـصّبا صفحاتها	أبـدى الـعدوَ لها وجوهـاً لـم تـبن
فتـجاب ضـرباً بالـسّياط شكاتها	ومـروعة فـي السّبي تـشكو بثُّهـا
قـعدت بـها عـن شـاوهم سبّاتها	قـامت تـسُب لـها الجـدود أرازل
راحـت وفـي أبـياتكم غاراتهـا	يـا غـيرة الـجبّار أنّـى والعـدى
فيهـا وعـزّة ربِّـه حـرماتها	يـا حـرمةً هُـتكت لعـزّة أحمـد
سـاروا بـها والـشامتون حماتهـا	أحـماة ديـن الله كـيف بـناتكم
حـرب بـشعث خيـولكم فلواتهـا	تطوي الفـلاة بـها ومـا ضـاقت على
عـزماتكم وهـي الحتـوف كفاتهـا	كفأت لكـم ظهر المجنّ فهـل سـوى
شـهب السّـماء وعرشهـا داراتهـا	وخـيامكم تـلك الـتي أوتـادها
أربابـها وحريـمكم ربّـاتها	بـالنّار أضـرمها الـعدوُ وأنـتُم
حـسرى تـقطِّع قلبهـا حـسراتها	فـرّت تـعادى في الفـلاة نوائحـاً

حتَّى إذا وقفـت علـى جثـث لكـم	طـالب عليهـا للظَّبى وقـفاتها
قـدحت لكـم زنـد العتـاب فلـم تجد	غيـر السِّـياط لـجنبها هفواتهـا
وسـرت علـى حـالٍ يحـقُّ لـشجوها	الأفـلاك لـو وقفـت لهـا حركاتهـا
حنّـت ولـولا زجـر زجـر مـا حـدت	أظعانهـا بسـوى الحنـين حداتهـا
يـا لوعة قعدت وقامـت فـي الحشا	خـرساء تـنطق بالشَّجى نفثاتهـا
قـعدت ولا تـنفكُّ أو أرزاؤكـم	بـقيام قـائمكم تُـصاب تراتهـا
فـانهض فدىً لـك أنفس كمنت بها	طـير الـشّجون كـأنَّها وكناتهـا
واحـصد رؤوسـهُم فكـم رأس لكـم	حـصدته بـعد ولـم يشبَّ شباتها
وأحـرق لهـم صنمي ضـلال وطِّدا	لـهم الأمـور فـأمكنت وثباتهـا
تـبعاً بـما ابتدعا فمـا مـن سـوأة	إلّا وفـي عنـقيهما تـبعاتهـا
وهـما الـلذان عليكُم قـد جـزءا	مـن لا يـداني نعـلكم جبهاتهـا
جـرَّا إليـكم كـلّ جـور نـالكم	مـن عـصبة فعـليهما لعناتهـا
فلرزئكم إن لـم أمـت حزنـاً فلي	نـفس أذابـتها أسـى زفـراتها
ولـقد نـشرت رثـاً لكـم وكأنَّ فـي	طـيِّ الـجوانح لـلقنا وخزاتهـا
وإليـكم مـن بـكر فكـري ثاكل	تـنعى فـتهتف بالنَّفوس نعاتهـا
مـنكم لـكم أهـديتها وبـرزئكم	آل النَّـبيِّ خـتمتها وبـدأتها
ولنـشاتي أنـشأتها ذخـراً لـكم	أفـهل أخـيب وفـيكم أنـشأتها؟
ولـمهجتي بـولاكم الحـسنى إذا	فـقدت غـداً بـصحيفتي حـسناتها
فـولاؤكم حـسبي وإنَّـي عبـدكم	فخـري وذخـري أن تـضق حلقاتها

وإلـيكم شكـواي مـن نفـس غـدت   تقــتادني لـلـسّوء إمــاراتها

وجـرائـم عـبّـت بـمـهلك لجّــة   تـرمي لـها بـنفوسها غفلاتهـا

وأنـا الـغـريق بهـا فهـل إلّا بكـم   لـلنّفس، يا سُـفُن النّجاة، نجاتهـا؟

وعليكم يـا رحمـة البـاري مـن التّـ   ـسـليم مـا سـارت بـه صلواتها

* * *

2- وقال أيضاً :

أقـوت فهـنَّ مـن الأنيـس خـلاءُ؟   دمـن محـت آيـاتها الأنـواءُ؟

درسـت فغـيّرها البلـى فكأنّمـا   طـارت بـشمل أنيـسها عنقـاء

يـا دار مقريّـة الـضيوف بـشاشة   وقـراي منـك الوجـد والبرحـاء

عـبقت بـتربك نـفحة مـسكيّة   وسقت ثـراك الديمـة الوطفـاء

عـهدي بـربعك آنسـأ بـك آهـلا   يعلوه مـنك البـشر والسّـراء

وثـرى ربـوعك للنّـواظر أثمـد   والـعقد حلـي ضيائك الحصبـاء

قـد كـان مجتمع الهـوى واليـوم في   عـرصاته تـتفرّق الأهـواءُ

أخـنى علـيه دهـره والـدهر لا   يـرجى لـه بـذوي الوفـاء وفـاء

أيـن الـذين بـبشرهم وبـنشرهم   يحيـا الرجـال وتأرج الأرجـاء

ضربوا بعرصـة كـربلا خيـامهم   فـأطلَّ كـرب فـوقها وبـلاء

لله أيّ رزيّـة فـي كـربلا   عظمت فهانـت دونهـا الأرزاء

يـوم بـه سـلّ ابن أحمد مرهفاً   لـفرنده بـدجى الـوغى لألاء

وفـدى شـريعة جـدّه بعصابة   تـفدى وقلَّ مـن الوجـود فـداء

صيد إذا ارتعد الكميَّ مهابة	ومشت إلى أكفائها الأكفاء
وعلا الغبار فأظلمت لولا سنا	جبهاتها وسيوفها الهيجاء
عشت العيون فليس إلا الطعنة	النجلا وإلا المقلة الخوصاء
زحفوا إلى ورد المنون تشوّقا	حتى كأنَّ مماتها الأحياء
عبست وجوه عداهم فتبسّموا	فرحاً وأظلمت الوغى فأضاؤوا
فلها قراع السَّمهري تسامر	وصليل وقع المرهفات غناء
بأبي لها من أن تشمَّ مذلَّة	أنف أشمَّ وهمَّة قعساء
يقتادهم للحرب أروع ماجد	صعب القياد على الأبا أبّاء
صحبته من عزماته هنديَّة	بيضاء أو يزنيَّة سمراء
تجري المنايا السَّود طوع يمينه	وتصرَّف الأقدار حيث تشاء
ذلَّت لعزمته القروم بموقف	عقَّت به آباءها الأبناء
بفرائص رعدت وهامات همت	مذ لاح بارق سيفه الوضّاء
ولئن تنكَّر في العجاج فطالما	شهدت بغرِّ فعاله الهيجاء
من أبيض نثر الرؤوس وأسمر	نُظِمتْ بسلك كعوبه الأحشاء
كره الحمام لقاءه في معرك	حسدتْ به أمواتها الأحياء
بأبي أبي الضيم سيم هوانه	فلواه عن ورد الهوان إباء
وتألَّبوا زمراً عليه تقودها	لقتاله الأحقاد والبغضاء
فسطا عليهم مفرداً فثنت له	تلك الجموع النَّظرة الشزراء
يا واحداً للشَّهب من عزماته	تسري لدَيه كتيبة شهباء

305

ضاقت بها سعة الفضاء على العدى ::: فتيقّنوا ما بالنّجاة رجاء

فغدت رؤوسهم تخرّ أمامهم ::: فوق الثّرى وجسومهنَّ وراء

تسع السيوف رقابهم ضرباً وبا ::: لأجسام منهم ضاقت البيداء

ما زال يفنيهم إلى أنْ كاد أنْ ::: يأتي على الإيجاد منه فناء

لكنّما طلب الإله لقاءه ::: وجرى بما قد شاء فيه قضاء

فهوى على غبرائها فتضعضعت ::: لهويه الغبراء والخضراء

وعلا السنان برأسه فالصعدة ::: السَّمراء فيها الطلعة الغرّاء

ومكفَّن وثيابه قصد القنا ::: ومغسّل وله المياه دماء

ظام تفطَّر قلبه ظمأ وبا ::: لحملات منه ترتوي الغبراء

تبكي السماء دماً له أفلا بكت ::: ماء لغلَّة قلبه الأنواء

وآ لهف قلبي يابن بنت محمّد ::: لك والعدى بك أدركوا ما شاؤا

فلخيلها أجسامكم ولنبلها ::: أكبادكم ولقضبها الأعضاء

وعلى رؤوس السمر منكم أرؤوس ::: شمس الضّحى لوجوهها حرباء

يابن النبيّ أقول فيك معزّيا ::: نفساً وعزَّ على الثكول عزاء

ما غضَّ من علياك سوء صنيعهم ::: شرفاً وإنْ عظم الذي قد جاؤا

إنْ تمس مغبرَّ الجبين معفَّراً ::: فعليك من نور النّبيّ بهاء

أو تبق فوق الأرض غير مغسَّل ::: فلك البسيطانُ: الثَّرى والماءُ

أو تغتدى عار فقد صنعت لكم ::: برد العلا الخطيّ لا صنعاء

أو تقض ظمآن الفؤاد فمِن دما ::: أعداك سيفك والرماح رواء

306

الثَّرى لفرشـن منـه لجسمك الأحشاء	فلو أنَّ أحـمد قـد رآك علـى
مـاء الـمدامع أمَّـك الزهـراء	أو بـالطّفوف رأت ظمـاك سقتك من
وقلـوبُ أبـناءِ الـنَّبيّ ظمـاءُ	يـا ليت لا عَـذُبَ الفـراتُ لـواردٍ
وتقـاسمت أحـشاءها أرزاء	كـم حـرَّة نـهب الـعدى أبياتهـا
بـسوى الـسِّياط لهـا يجاب دعـاء	تعدو وتـدعو بـالحماة ولـم يكن
عدو الـعوادي الجـرد والأعداء	تـعدو فـإنْ عـادت عليهـا بالـعدى
قد أرمضتـه في الثَّـرى الرمضاء	هـتفت تـثير كـفيلها وكـفيلها
بـهم علـى هـام الـسَّما البطحاء	يـا كعبـة البيت الحرام ومَن سمت
أسراء قوم هـم لكن طلقـاء	لله يـوم فـيه قـد أمسيتم
وسـروا بهـا في الأسر أنَّـى شـاؤا	حملوا لكم في الـسَّبي كـل مصونة
وتـرقّ إنْ نـاحت لهـا الورقـاء	ثكلى تـحنُّ لـشجوها عيس الفـلا
وغيـوثهـا إنْ عـمَّت الـبأساء	تـنعى لـيوث البـأس مـن فتيانها
وغـفوا ومـا فـي بأسهم إعفـاء	رقـدوا وليس بعزمهم مـن قـدرة
تـسيل الـعـبرة الـحمراء	تـبكيهم بـدم فقـل بالمهجة الحـرَّى
بـزفيـرها أنـفاسها الـصعداء	نـاحت فلمّـا غضّـضت مـن صوتها
نـاحـت ولـكن نـوحها أيمـاء	حنَّت ولـكنَّ الـحنين بكـى وقـد
الـصخر الأصمَّ ودونهـا الخنساء	وقسـت علـيهنَّ القـلوب فدونها
ولـهنَّ رجـع حـنينهنَّ حـداء	وحـدت بـهنَّ الـيعملات كلابهـا
غـلاً وأقـعد جـسمه الاعـياء	ومقـيّد قـام الـحديد بـمتنه

307

وسـرت بـه الـمهزولة العجفاءُ   رهـن الـضّنـا قـعدت بـه أسقامُه

مـا حـال مـن رقّـت لـه الأعداء؟   وغـدت تـرقّ على بليتـه العدى

وضمير غـيّب الله وهـو خفاء   لله سـر الله وهـو مـحجّب

فـي حكمها يـنقاد حيث يشاؤا   أنّـى اغتدى لـلكافرين غنيمـة

الأمـصار فـيه وترتمي الأحيـاء   عـالٍ على عـاري المطيِّ تقاذف

نـصب الـعيون وكلّـها عميـاء   طـوع الأكفِّ وكـلّهنّ لـئيمة

قـذفتهم الـدئماء والـدهماء   وهـو الذي لـو شاء أنْ يفنيهم

وأطـاعه الإصباح والإمـساء   وهَوَت لـه شُهُب السّماء بقوسها

وتـصاغرت فـي وقعـه الأرزاء   آل الـنّبيِّ لأن تعـاظم رزؤكـم

يـوم الـجزاء وأنـتم الخصماء   فـلأنتم يـا أيّـها الشفعاء في

تـنعى وقـد أودت بهـا البرحـاء   وإلـيكم مـن بكر فكري ثاكـل

إلّا بحـسن مـنكمُ الحـسنـاء   حسناء جاءت للعزاء ولـم تعد

***

3ـ وقال أيضاً:

ولا تـحملوا لـلبرق منّـأ ولا الـسّحب   خذوا الماء من عيني والنّار من قلبي

بـطوفان ذاك الـمدمع الـسّافح الغربِ   ولا تـحسبوا نـيران وجدى تنطفي

فـكم مدمع صبٍّ لـذي غلّة صبّ   ولا أنّ ذاك الـسّيل يـبرد غلَّتي

لغـانية عـفراء أو شـادن تـربِ   ولا أنّ ذاك الوجد مـنّي صبابة

لـواعج قـد جرّعني غصص الكربِ   نـفى عـن فؤادي كـلَّ لهوٍ وباطلٍ

308

كـأنّي على جمـر الغضا واضعاً جنبي	أبيت لها أطوي الضلوع على جوىً
أغصّ لـذكراهنّ بـالمنهل الـعـذبِ	رزايـاكـم يـا آل بـيـت مـحـمّـد
عليكم وقد فاضت دماكم على الـتّربِ	عـمى لـعيون لا تـفيض دمـوعها
لـحرب بـها قـد مـزّقتكم بنـو حربِ	وتعـساً لــقـلب لا يـمـزّقـه الأسـى
تطـير شـظاياها بـواحرتا قـلبي	فـوا حـرّتا قـلبي وتـلكم حشاشتي
الـبت عـلـى ديـن الـهداية ذولبِ	أنـسى وهل ينسى رزايـاكم التي
تـذادون ذود الخمص عن سائغ الشربِ	أنـساكم حـرّى الـقـلوب على الظَّمـا
تـطّلع كـالأقمار في الأنجم الشهبِ	أنـسى بـأطراف الـرماح رؤوسـكم
وماوطأت من موضع الطَّعن والضربِ	أنـسى طراد الخيل فوق جسومكم
سُـكبن وأحـرارا هُـتكن مـن الحجبِ	أنـسى دمـاء قـد سُـفِكْنَ وأدمـعـا
سُـلبن وأكـباداً أذبـن مـن الرعبِ	أنـسى بـيوتاً قـد نُـهبن ونسوة
تـروّع آل الله بالـضّرب والنّهبِ	أنـسى اقتحام الـظالمين بـيوتكم
سوى صبية فرّت مذعرة الـسّربِ	أنـسى اضطرام النّار فيها وما بها
على الهضب كنتم فيه أرسى من الهضبِ	أنـسى لـكم في عرصة الطَّف موقفاً
على قـلَّة الأنصار فادحة الخطبِ	تـشاطرتموا فيه رجالاً ونسوةً
ونسوتكم لــلأسر والـسّبى والسّلبِ	فأنتم بـه لــلقتل والـنَّبل والـقنا
عـلا نـدبها لكن على غوثها النّدبِ	إذا أوجبت أحشاءها وطأة العدى
على عضديها من سوار ومن قلبِ	وإنْ نـازعتها الـحلي فالسّوط كم له
بـراقع تعلوهنَّ حمراً مـن الضّربِ	وإنْ جـذبت عنها البراقع جـدِّدت

اذا بـثت الـشكوى عـن الـسّلب بالسّب	وان سلبت عنها المـقانع قـنّعت
ونـاحت فما الورقاء في الغصن الرطب	وثـاكلة حنّت فـما الـعيس في الفلا
تـشبّ وقد يخطي الحيا موضع الجّدب	تـروي الـثّرى بـالدمع والـقلب نـاره
لـكلّ حـشى مـا فـي حشاها مـن النّدب	وتـندب عـن شجوٍ فـتعطي بـندبها
وتصدع شكواها الرواسي من الخطب	وتـنعى فتشجي الصّمّ زينب إذ نعت
لـيوث وغى لـكن مـوسّدة الـتّرب	تـثير عـلى وجـه الـثّرى من حماتها
ونـشوانة الأعطاف لـكن بـلا شـرب	نـيام عـلى الأحـقاف لـكن بـلا كـرى
لـتعلم بـعد الـقوم عـن خطـة العتب	تطارحهم بـالـعتب شـجواً وإنّـها
وطـلّت ومـا طـالت إليهـا يـد النّصب	حموا خدرها حتّى أستبيحت دماؤهم
غدت نـهب أطـراف الأسنّة والقضب	ومـن دونـها أجـسامهم ورؤوسـهم
وأوتـاركم ضـاقت بهـا سعة الرحب	فـيا مـدركي الأوتـار حتّى مَ صبركم
قـعدتم وفـي أيـديكم قـائم العضب	ويـا طاعني صدر الـكتائب مـا لكم
وقد طحنتكم في الحروب رحى حَرب	ويا طاحني هـام العدى ما انتظاركم
وقـد ظـفرت مـن ليثكم ظفر الكلب	ويـا مزعجي أسد الشّرى ما قعودكم
فـيا غـيرة الـجبّار مـن غضب هبي	جبـار بـأيـدي الـظالمين دمـاؤكم
لآل رسول الله سيقت عـلى النّجب	فكـم غـرّة فـوق الـرماح وحـرّة
ومـسبيّة بـالحبل شـدّت إلـى مـسبي	وكـم مـن يـتيم مـوثق لـيتيمة
تـعالى فـأضحى قـاب قوسَين للربّ	بـني النّـسب الـوضّاح والحسب الذي
تطـاول بـالأنسـاب سيّارة الشّهب	إذا عـدّت الأنسـاب لـلفخر أو غدت

فمــا نـسبي إلّا انـتـسابي إلـيـكم   ومــا حــسبي إلّا بـأنّـكم حـسبي

4- وقال :

في الـقلب حـرّ جوى ذاك توهّجه   الـدمع يـطفيه والـذكرى تؤجّجه
أفدي الأولى للعلا أسرى بهم ظعن   وراء حــاد مــن الاقـدار يـزعجه
ركـب عـلى جـنّة المأوى معرّسه   لـكن عـلى مـحن البلوى معرّجه
مثل الحسين تضيق الأرض فيه فلا   يـدري إلـى أيـن مـأواه ومولجه
ويطلب الأمن بالبطحا وخوف بني   سـفيان يـقلقه عـنها ويـخرجه
وهـو الـذي شرّف البيت الحرام به   ولاح بـعد الـعمى لـلنّاس منهجه
يـا حـائراً لا وحـاشا نـور عزمته   بـمَن سواك الهدى قد شعّ مسرجه
وواسـع الـحلم والـدنيا تـضيق به   سـواك إن ضاق خطب من يفرّجه
ويـا مـليكاً رعـاياه عـليه طغت   وبالخـلافة بـاريـه مـتوجّه
يـا عـارياً قد كساه النّور ثوب سناً   زهـا بـصبغ الـدّم الـقاني مدبّجه
يـا ريَّ كـلّ ظـما واليوم قلبك من   حـرّ الظّما لـو يمسُّ الصخر ينضجه
يـا مـيّتاً بـات والـذاري يـكفّنه   والأرض بـالـتّرب كـافوراً تؤرّجه
ويـا مـسيح هدى للرأس منه على   الـرماح مـعراج قـدس راح يعرجه
ويـا كـليماً هوى فوق الثرى صعقا   لـكن مـحيّاه فـوق الـرمح أبلجه
ويـا مـغيث الـهدى كـم تـستغيث ولا   مـغيث نـحوك يـلويه تـحرّجه
فـأين جـدّك والأنـصار عنك ألا   هـبّت لـه أوسـه مـنهم وخزرجه

311

شـاكي الـسِّلاح لـدى الهيجا مدجِّجـه	وأيـن فـرسان عـدنان وكـلُّ فتـىً
يهـيجه لـك إذ تـدعو مـهيِّجه	وأيـن عـنك أبـوك المرتضى أفـلا
البـغي يـلجمه والـغيُّ يـسرجه	يـروك بـالطَّف فرداً بـين جمع عدى
بـالبيض والسُّمر زخـار مموِّجـه	تـخوض فـوق سفين الخيل بحر دم
يمـسي عـلى الأرض مغبَّراً مبلِّجـه	حـاشا لـوجهك يـا نـور النبـوَة أن
زهـا وصخـر بنـي صخـر يـشجِّجه	وللـجبين بـأنوار الإمـامة قـد
يـبقى ثـلاثاً على البوغـا مضرَّجـه	أعيذ جـسمك يـا روح النبيّ بـأن
أيـدي صـنائعه بـالفخر تنسجـه	عـار يحوك لـه الـذكر الجميـل ردى
والـثغر بـالعود مـقروع مـفلَّجـه	والـرأس بـالرمح مـرفوع مبلّجـه
عن الأُولـى صحَّ اسناداً مخرجـه	حـديث رزءٍ قـديم الأصل أخـرج إذ
ومثل ذا الفـرع ذاك الأصـل ينتجـه	تـالله مـا كـربلا لـو لا سـقيفتهم
مـن سقط محسن خلـف الباب منهجـه	وفـي الطَّفوف سقوط السِّبط منجدلا
بـباب دار ابنـة الـهادي تـأجِّجه	وبـالخيام ضـرام النَّار مـن حطبٍ
كـانت عـلى ذلك المنـوال تنسجـه	لـكنْ أُمـيَّة جـاءتكم بـأخبث مـا
قـبابه الـكور والأقـتاب هـودجه	سـرت بـنسوتكم للـشَّام فـي ظعن
عـلى عجـاف المطى بالسَّير مدلجـه	مـن كـلّ والـهة حـسرى يعنِّفها
زنـد بـأيدي الجفاة ابتـزَّ دملجـه	كم دحلج صاغه ضرب السِّياط على
تـرثى لـه ألـم الـبلوى وتنـشجـه	ولا كـفيل لـها غير العليـل سـرت
حـال مـن الـشجو لـفَّ الصبر مدرجه	تـشكو عـداها وتـنعى قومها فلها

ودمعها بـدم الأحـشاء تـمزجه	فـنعيها بـشجى الـشكوى تـؤلِّفه
تـزفُّر مـن شظايا القلب تخرجه	ويدخل الشّجو في الصخر الأصمّ لها
بـاباً مـن الـصبر لا ينفكُّ مرتجه	فـيا لأرزائكم سدَّت على جزعي
طـول الـعويل ولكن لـيس يثلجه	يـفرُّ قـلبي مـن حـرِّ الغليل إلى
مـراثياً لـه تـمسُّ الطـود تزعجه	أودُّ أنْ لا أزال الدهرأنـــشئها
لـكـن عـظيم رزايـاكم يـلجلجه	ومـقولي طـلقٌ فـي القول أعهده
فـي الـقلب حـرّ جوى ذاك توهُّجه	ولا يـزال عـلى طـول الزمـان لكم

للحجّة آية الله الشيخ محمّد حسين الاصفهاني (قُدّس سرُه):

عـن وجـه سـرِّ الـغيب والشّهادة	أسـفرَ صبح الـيُمن والـسّعادة
ونـسخة الأسـماء والـصفات	أسـفرَ عـن مـرآة غيب الـذّات
تـفصح عـن أسـمائه صـفاته	تعرب عن غيب الغيوب ذاتـه
بـالحقِّ والـصّدق بوحـهِ لانـق	يـنبِّئ عـن حقيقة الخلائق
فـي الـذات والـصّفات والأفعال	لـقد تـجلّى أعظـم المجالي
عـقل الـعقول الكُمَل العليَّة	روح الحـقيقة المـحمديَّة
مـفيض كـلّ شاهد وغائب	فـيضٌ مُقدَّسٌ عـن الـشوائب
بـل هـو عنـد أهلـه صبح الأزل	تَـنفَّس الـصّبح بنـور لـم يـزل
فـي نفس كـلِّ عـارف ربّـاني	وكيف وهـو الـنَّفَس الرحمـاني
بـه نظـام الـصُّحف المكرّمة	بـه قـوام الكلمـات المحكّمة
بـصورة جـامعة لـلكَلِم	تـنفَّس الـصُّبح بـسرِّ القِدم

313

محا عن الوجود رسم العدم	تنفّس الصُّبح بالاسم الأعظم
فلا ترى بعد النَّهار ليلا	بل فالقُ الإصباح قد تجلَّى
وأيَ نور فوق نور الطور؟!	فأصبح العلم ملاء النُّور
بل كلّ ما في الكون من ظهوره	ونار موسى قبَسٌ من نوره
به استبان كلّ اسم وصفة	أشرق بدرٌ من سماء المعرفة
والكلّ تحت ذلك الشعاع	به استنار عالم الإبداع
من ذرَة العرش إلى فوق الثرى	به استنار ما يُرى ولا يُرى
نور السَّماوات ونور الأرض	فهو بوجهه الرضي المرضي
بل جلّ أن تدركه الأبصار	أفلا توازي نوره الأنوار
قرَّة عين خاتم النبوَة	غرَّته بارقة الفتوَة
شارقة الشهامة البيضاء	تبدو على غرَّته الغرَّاء
دلائل الإعجاز والكرامة	بادية من آية الشهامة
تكاد تسبق القضا مشيئته	من فوق هامة السَّماء همَّته
إنَّ إلى ربك منتهاها	ما همَّة السَّماء من مداها
وفي الإبا نقطة باء البسملة	أمُّ الكتاب في علوِّ المنزلة
وفي محيطها له السِّيادة	تمَّت به دائرة الشهادة
سواه مركزاً لها ومحوراً	لو كشف الغطاء عنك لا ترى
أثبت نقطة من الحسين؟!	وهل ترى لملتقى القوسين
جلّ عن الأشباه والنظائر	فلا وربِّ هذه الدوائر

بـالمعجز البـاقي مـدى الأحقـاب	بشراك يـا فـاتحة الـكتاب
وسـرّ مـعنى لـفظة الجلالة	وآيـة الـتوحيد والـرسالة
فمـا أجـلّ شـأئه وأرفعـا	بـل هـو قـرآن وفرقـان معا
وهـو مـثال ذاتـه كـما هـي	هـو الـكتاب الـناطق الإلهـي
كـلّ نـقوش لـوحه المكنون	ونـشأة الاسـماء والـشؤون
كأنّـه طـوع بـنانه الـقلم	لا حـكم للقـضاء إلاّ مـا حكـم
كأنّـه واسطـة القـلادة	رابطـة المـراد بـالإرادة
ونـسخة اللاهـوت عينـاً وصفة	نـاطقة الـوجود عـين المعرفة
بـالقبض والبـسط علـى العبـاد	فـي يـده أزمـة الأيـادي
فـي الأمـر والخلـق ولا غـضاضة	بـل يـده الـعليا يـد الإفاضة
فغاية الآمـال فـي الحـسين	لـك الـهنا يـا سـيّد الكونين
مـن المـحمّديّة البيـضاء	وارث كـلّ الـمجد والـعلياء
كـلّ الـمعالي يـا لـه مـن شـرف	فـإنّه مـنك وأنـت مـنه فـي
روحـان فـي روح الكمـال اتحـدا	وفيه سـرّ الـكلّ فـي الـكلّ بـدا
لـه العروج فـي سـماوات الـملا	لـك العروج فـي الـسّماوات العلا
وسـهمه أقـصى المنـى مـن الفنـا	حـظك منتهـى الـشهود فـي دنا
مـنه بـناء قـصره الـمشيد	مـنك أسـاس العـدل والتوحيـد
قـام بـحمله الـثقيل كـاهله	مـنك لـواء الـدين وهـو حاملـه
أنـت لهـا المبدأ وهـو المنتهى	والـمكرمات والـمعالي كـلّها

لك الهنا يا صاحب الولاية ... بنعمة ليس لها نهاية

أنت من الوجود عين العين ... فكن قرير العين بالحسين

شبلك في القوّة والشجاعة ... نفسك في العزّة والمناعة

منطقك البليغ في البيان ... لسانك البديع في المعاني

طلعتك الغرّاء بالإشراق ... كالبدر في الأنفس والآفاق

صفاتك الغرّ له ميراث ... والمجد ما بين الورى تراث

لك الهنا يا غاية الإيجاد ... بمبدئ الخيرات والأيادي

وهو سفينة النّجاة في اللجج ... وبابها السّامي ومن لجّ ولج

سلطان إقليم الحفاظ والإبا ... مليك عرش الفخر أمّاً وأبا

رافع راية الهدى بمهجته ... كاشف ظلمة العمى ببهجته

به استقامت هذه الشريعة ... به علت أركانها الرفيعة

بنى المعالي بمعالي هممه ... ما اخضرّ عود الدّين إلاّ بدمه

بنفسه اشترى حياة الدّين ... فيا له من ثمن ثمين

أحيا معالم الهدى بروحه ... داوى جروح الدّين من جروحه

جفَّت رياض العلم بالسّموم ... لم يَرووها إلاّ دم المظلوم

فأصبحت مورقة الأشجار ... يانعة زاكية الثمار

أقعد كلّ قائم بنهضته ... حتّى أقام الدّين بعد كبوته

قامت به قواعد التوحيد ... مذ لجأت بركنها الشديد

وأصبحت قويّة البنيان ... بعزمه عزائم القرآن

316

معـاهـد الـسُّـنَّـة والـكـتاب	غدت بـه سـاميـة الـقـباب
مـاء الـحياة وهـو ظـمـآن صـادي	أفـاض كـالحيا عـلـى الـوراد
ريُّ الـورى والله يقـضي مـا يـشا	وكـضه الـظما وفي طـيِّ الحشا
فـأمطرت سـحائب القـدس دمـا	والـتهبت أحـشاؤه مـن الظما
بـيض الـسّيوف والرمـاح الـسَّمر	وقـد بـكته والـدموع حـمر
تفـتـر الـعـزم ولا تثـلـما	تفطر الـقلب مـن الظما ومـا
يـندكُّ طـود عـزمه مـن الـبلا	ومـن يـدك نـوره الطور فـلا
ومـن تجـوَّلاته الأفـلاك	تعجب مـن ثـباته الأمـلاك
قد ارتقى في المجد خير مرتقى	لا غـرو أنَّـه ابن بجدة اللقـا
لا بـل كـأنَّ الـغاب فـي اهابـه	شبل علي وهـو ليث غابـه
تكـوَّر الـليل عـلـى الـنَّار	كـرَّاته فـي ذلـك المـضمار
على بـقايا بـدر والأحـزاب	وعـضبه صـاعقة الـعذاب
بـالدم حتَّـى بـلغ الـسَّيل الزبى	سطا بـسيفه فـفاضت الربى
لـجمع شمل الـدِّين والـكمال	فـرَّق جمع الـكفر والـضلال
وفـي ومـيضه رمـوز الصدق	أنـار بـالبارق وجـه الـحق
يـشكر فـعله لـسان حـاله	حتَّى تـجلَّى الـدِّين فـي جمالـه
مـا لـيس يـعطى مـثله سـواه	قـام بـحق الـسَّيف بـل أعطاه
بـل القضا في حـدّ ذاك المنتضى	كـأن منتـضاه مـحتوم القضا
يـقـضى عـلى صـفوفهم رفيفه	كأنَّـه طـير الـفنا رهـيفه

أو صرصر في يوم نحس مستمر   كأنّهم أعجاز نخل منقعر

أو بصريره كريح عاتية   كأنّهم أعجاز نخلٍ خاوية

وفي المعالي حقّها لما علا   على العوالي كالخطيب في الملا

يتلو كتاب الله والحقايق   تشهد أنّه الكتاب النّاطق

قد ورث العروج في الكمال   من جدّه لكن على العوالي

هي العوالي وهي المعالي   والخير كلّ الخير في المثال

هو الذبيح في منى الطفوف   لكنّه ضريبة السّيوف

هو الخليل المُبتلى بالنّار   والفرق كالنّار على المنار

نوح ولكن أين من طوفانه   طوفانه فليس من أقرانه

تالله ما ابتلى نبيُ أو ولي   في سالف الدهر بمثل ما ابتلي

له مصائف تكلّ الألسن   عنها فكيف شاهدتها الأعين

أعظمها رزءاً على الإسلام   سبي ذراري سيّد الأنام

ضلالة لا مثلها ضلالة   سبي بنات الوحي والرسالة

وسَوقها من بلد إلى بلد   بين الملا أشنع ظلم وأشد

وأفظع الخطوب والدواهي   دخولها في مجلس الملاهي

ولدغ حيّة لها بريقها   دون وقوفها لدى طليقها

ويسلب اللب حديث السّلب   يا ساعد الله بنات الحجب

تحمَّلت أميّة أوزارها   وعارها مذ سلبت إزارها

وكيف يرجى الخير من خمارها   تبّت يد مُدّت إلى خمارها

318

وفـي ذراريــه قضت أوتارهـا	وأدركت مـن الـنّبيّ ثارهـا
مـن أهل بـدر بالبـدور النيّـرة	وآ عجبـاً يـدرك ثـار الكفـرة
بـما جـنـت بـه يـد الأعـادي	فـيا لـثارات الـنّبي الـهادي
أعـزّه الله بـفتح وظـفـر	ومَـن لـها إلّا الإمام المنتظـر

للحجّة آية الله المجاهد الشيخ محمّد جواد البلاغي :

لـيتني دونـك نـهباً للـسّيوفِ	يـا تريب الخد في رمضا الطفوفِ
وحمـى الـجـار إذا عـزّ المجيـر	يـا نـصير الـدّين إذ عزّ النّـصير
وثمال الـرفد فـي العـام العسوف	وشـديد الـبأس واليـوم عـسير
وابـن خيـر المرسلين المـصطفى	كـيف يـا خامس أصحاب الكسا
وشـفيع الخلق فـي اليـوم المخوف	وابن ساقي الحوض في يوم الظما
وخـضيب الـشيب مـن فـيض الوريد	يـا صـريعاً ثـاويـاً فـوق الـصعيد
ظـامئاً تـسقى بكاسـات الحتـوف	كـيف تقضي بـين أجنـاد يزيد
دامـيـاً تـنـهل مـنك الماضيـات	كـيف تقضي ظامئـا حـول الفرات
عـافـر الجـسم لقى بـين الطفـوف	وعـلى جـسمك تجري الـصافنات

نظم هذه القصيدة لأجل الموكب الذي سعى به ليلة عاشوراء ويومها في كربلاء ، في السّنة التي قُتل فيها السيد حسن ابن آية الله السيد أبو الحسن الاصفهاني وببركاته اتسع إلى هذه السنة فكان موكب النجفيين ليلة عاشوراء في كربلا يضم العلماء وأهل الفضل والمقدسين من أرباب المهن ، كل ذلك من انفاس هذا الشيخ الجليل المناضل دون الدين الحنيف وتوفي في الليلة الثانية والعشرين من شعبان سنة ١٣٥٢هـ وترجمته مفصلة في (شعراء الغرى ٢ / ٤٣٦) .

319

يـا مريـع المـوت فـي يـوم الطِّعـان لا خـطا نـحوك بـالر مـح سـنان
لا ولا شـمر دنـا مـنك فـكان مـا أمـاد الأرض هـولا بـالرجوف

سـيّدي أبـكيك للـشيب الخـضيب سـيّدي أبـكيك لـلوجه التريـب
سـيّدي أبـكيك للـجسم الـسليب مـن حـشا حـران بالـدمع الـذروف

سـيّدي إن مـنعوا عنـك الفـرات وسـقوا مـنك ظـماء المرهفـات
فسنـسقي كـربلا بـالعبرات وكـفا مـن عـلق القلـب الأسـوف

سـيّدي أبـكيك منهـوب الرحـال سـيّدي أبـكيك مـسبي الـعيال
بـين أعـداك عـلى عجـف الجمـال فـي الفيـافي بعـد هاتيـك الـسّجوف

سـيّدي إن نقـض دهـراً فـي بكـاك مـا قضـينا البـعض مـن فـرض ولاك
أو عـكفنا عمـرنا حـول ثـراك مـا شـفى غـلّتنا ذاك العكـوف

لـهف نفـسي لنـساك المعـولات والـيتامى إذ عـدت بـين الطغـاة
بـاكيات شـاكيات صـارخات ولـهاً حـولك تـسعى وتطـوف

يـا حـمانا مَـن لـنا بعـد حمـاك ومَـن الـمفزع مـن أسـر عـداك
ولِـمَن نـلجأ إنْ طـال نـواك ودهـتنا بـدواهيها الـصروف

يـا حـمانا مـن لأيـتام صـغار ومذاعـير تـعادي بـالفرار
راعـها الـمزعج مـن سـلب ونـار حـيث لا مـلجا ولا حـامٍ رؤوف

لـست أنـساها وقـد مالـت إلـى صـفوة الأنصـار صـرعى فـي الفـلا
أشـرقت مـنها محـاني كـربلا كـشموس غـالها ريـب الكـسوف

هاتـفات بـهم مستـصرخات بـاكيات نادبـات عاتبـات
صـارخات أيـن عنّـا يـا حمـاة يـا بـدور الـتمّ مـا هـذا الخسـوف

يـا رجـال البـأس فـي يـوم الكفـاح يـا ليـوث الحـرب فـي غـاب الرمـاح
كـيف آذنـتم جـميعاً بـالرواح ورحـلتم رحـلة القـوم الـضيوف

مـا لـكم لا غـالكم صـرف الـردى لا ولا أدركـتم بـيض الـظبى
أفتـرضون لنـا ذلّ الـسّبا وعنـاء الأسـر مـا بـين الألـوف

أفنُـسبى بـعدكم سـبي الـعبيد ثـمَّ نُـهدى مـن عـنيد لعنيـد
لا وقـفنا فـي الـسّبا عنـد يزيـد حـبّذا الـموت ولا ذاك الوقـوف

320

للعلّامة الحُجّة الشيخ محمّد حسين بن حمد الحلّي (أعلى الله مقامه) :

خـلـيـلـيَّ هـل مـن وقـفـة لكـمـا مـعـي عـلى جـدث أسـقيه صيب أدمعي

لـيـروي الـثـرى منـه بفيض مدامعي فإنَّ الـحـيا الوكاف لَـم يكُ مقنعي
لأنَّ الـحـيا يـهـمي ويـقـلـع تـارة وإنّـي لـعـظـم الـخطـب مـا جـفَّ مـدمعي
خـلـيـلَيَّ هـبـا فـالـرقـاد مـحـرَّم على كـلّ ذي قـلب مـن الوجـد موجـعِ
هـلـمَّا مـعـي نـعـقـر هـنـاك قـلوبنـا إذا الـوجـد أبـقـاهـا ولَـم تـتـقطّع
هـلـمَّا نـقـم بـالـغـاضـريَّـة مـأتـمـاً لـخـير كـريم بـالـسّـيوف مـوزّع
فـتـىً أدركـت فـيـه عـلوج أمـيّـة مـرامـاً فأردتـه بـبـيـداء بـلـقـع
غـداة أرادت أن تـرى الـسّـبـط ضـارعـاً ولَـم يكُ ذا خـدٍّ مـن الـضيم أضـرع
وكيف يـسام الضيم مـن جـدّه ارتـقى إلى الـعرش حتّى حـلّ أشرف موضـع
فـتـىً حـلّـقـت فـيـه قـوادم عـزِّه لأعـلى ذرى الـمـجد الأثيل وأرفـع
ولـمّـا دعـتـه لـلـكـفـاح أجـابها بـأبـيض مـشحوذ وأسمـر مـشرع
وآسـاد حـرب غـابها أجـمَ الـقنا وكـلّ كـميٍّ رابـط الـجـأش أروع
يـصول بـمـاضي الحـدّ غـير مكهم وفـي غـير درع الـصـبر لَـم يتـدرع
إذا ألـقـح الـهـيـجـاء حـتـفأ بـرمحه فمـاضي الـشبا منـه يقول لها ضعي
وإن أبـطأت عـنـه الـنّفـوس إجـابة فحـدّ سـنان الرمح قـال لها أسرع
فـلَـم تـزل الأرواح قـبـض أكـفّهم وتـسقط هـامات بـقـولهم قعي
إلـى أن دعـاهـم ربّـهـم لـلـقـائه فكانوا إلـى لقياه أسـرع مـن دعي
وخـرّوا لـوجـه الله تـلقى وجـوههم فمـن سُـجَّد فـوق الـصعيد وركّـع
وكـم ذات خـدر سـجفتهـا بـسمر قنـا خطـيّة وبـلَّـع
أماطـت يـد الأعـداء عنهـا سجـافها فأضحت بـلا سجف وكهف ممنع
لـقـد نـهبـت كـف الـمصاب فؤادهـا وأبـدى عـداها كـلّ بـرد وبرقـع
فـلم تـسـتطـع عـن نـاطـريهـا تـسـتـراً بغـير زنـود قـاصرات وأذرع
وقـد فـزعـت مـذراعـها الخطـب دهشة وأوهـى الـقـوي منهـا إلى خير مفزع
فـلـمَّا رأتـه بـالـعـراء مـجـدّلاً عـفيراً عـلى الـبوغـاء غـير مـشيع
دنـت مـنـه والأحـزان تمـضغ قلبهـا وحـنّـت حـنين الـوالـه الـمتفجّع
تـقول وظـفـر الـوجـد يـدمي فؤادهـا عـليَّ عـزيزٌ أن أراك مـوذّعي
عـليَّ عـزيزٌ أن تـموت عـلى ظمـا وتـشرب في كـأس مـن الحتـف متـرع
أخـيَّ ذا شمـر مـذلّتي فـأركبني مـن فـوق أدبـر أظلـع
وذا الـعـلـج زجـر أرغـم الله أنـفـه بـقـرع الـقنا والأصـبحيَّة مـوجعي

للعلّامة الشيخ محمّد تقي ابن الحُجّة المرحوم الشيخ عبد الرسول آل صاحب الجواهر :

مـا بـال فِـهـر أغـفلت أوتارهـا هـلا تـثير وغـى فتـدرك ثارهـا

321

أغفت على الـضيم الجفـون وضيّعت يـا لـلحميّة عـزّها وفخارها
عـجباً لـها هـدأت وتـلك أميّـة قـتلت سـراة قبيلها وخيارها
عـجباً لـها هـدأت وتلك نساؤها بالطفّ قد هَتك العـدى أستارها
مـن كـلٍّ ثاكلة تـناهب قلبها كفّ الأسـى ويد العدوّ خمارها
لـهفي لـها بعد التحجّب أصبحت حسرى تـقاسي ذلّـها وصغارها
تـدعو أمـير الـمؤمنين بمهجة فيها الـرزيّة أنـشبت أظفارها

أبتـاه يـا مـردي الفـوارس فـي الـوغى ومبيد جحفلها ومخمد نارها
قـم وانظر ابنـك فـي العراء وجسمه جعلته خـيل أمـيّة مضمارها
ثـاوٍ تغسّله الـدمـاء بفيضها عـارٍ تـكفّنه الـرياح غبارها
وخيـول حـرب منـه رضّت أضلعاً فـيها الـنبوة أودعـت أسـرارها
وبيوت قـدس مـن جلالـة قـدرها كانـت ملائكـة السّـما زوّارها
يقف الأمـينُ بـبابها مـستأذناً ومقبّـلاً أعتـابها وجدارها
أضحت عليها آل حـرب عنـوة فـي يـوم عاشـورا تـشنّ مغارها
كـم طـفلة ذعـرت وكم محجوبـة بـرزت وقـد سـلب العـدوّ إزارها
ويتيمة صاغ القطيع لهـا سِـوا راً عنـدما بـزّ الـعدوّ سِوارها
أيـن الكمـاة الـصيد مـن عمـرو العـلا عنهـا فتـرخص دونهـا أعمارها
أيـن الكمـاة الـصيد مـن عمـرو العـلا لِتثير لـلحرب العـوان غبارها

فأيّ حـشى لَـم يمس قبراً لجسمه وفـي أيّ قـلب مـا أُقيمت مآتمُـه؟
وهب دم يحيى قـد غـلا قبل فـي الثرى فإنَّ حسيناً فـي القلوب غلا دمُـه
وإن قـرّ مُـذ دعـا بـخت نـصر بـثارات يحـيى واسترّدت مظالمُـه
فليست دماء الـسّبط تهـدأ قبل أن يقوم بـإذن الله لـلثأر قائمُـه
أبـا صالـح يـا مُـدرك الثـار كـم تـرى وغـيظك وار غـير أنّـك كـاظمُـه
وهـل يـملك الموتور صبـراً وحوله يـروح ويغدو أمـن الـسّرب غارمُـه
أتنسى أبـي الـضيم فـي الطفّ مفرداً تـحوم عليه لـلوداع فـواطمُـه
أتنسـاه فـوق الـترب منفطر الحشا تـناهبه سمر الـردى وصوارمُـه
ورُبَّ رضيـع أرضـعته قسيهم مـن الـنّبل ثـدياً درّه الثـر فاطمُـه
فـلهفي لـه مُـذ طـوّق الـسّهم جيده كمـا زيّـنته قبل ذاك تـمائمُـه
ولـهفي لـه لـمّا أحـسّ بحـرّه وناغاه مـن طـير الـمنيّة حائمُـه
هفا لـعناق الـسّبط مبتسم اللمـى وداعـاً وهـي غـير العنـاق يلائمُـه
ولـهفي علـى أُمّ الرضيع وقد دَجى علـيها الـدُجى والـدوح ناحت حمائمُـه
تـسلل فـي الـظلماء ترتـاد طفلها وقـد نـجمت بـين الضحايا علائمُـه
فمـذ لاح سـهم النّحـر ودّت لَـو أنهـا تـشاطره سهم الـردى وتساهمُـه
أقلتـه بـالكفين تـرشف ثغـره وتـلثم نـحراً قَـبلَها الـسّهم لاثمُـه
وأدنتـه لـلثّهدين ولـهى فتـارة تناغيه الـطافاً وأخـرى تـكالمُـه
بُنَيّ أفق مـن سكرة الموت وارتضع بـثديك علَّ القـلب يـهدأ هائمُـه
بُـنَيّ فـقد درّا وقـد كـضك الظمـا فعلّك يُـطفي مـن غليلك ضارمُـه

بُنَيَّ لـقد كـنت الأنيس لِوحشتي وسلواي إذْ يـسطو مـن الهـمّ غاشمُه

مراثي الإمام الحسين من عيون الشعر العربي

أبو البحر صفوان بن إدريس بن إبراهيم النجيبي المرسي (٥٦١ - ٥٩٨هـ) ثم يذكر
واحدة من رثائياته التي يقول فيها:

سـلامٌ كأزهـارِ الربـى يتنـسـمُ	علــى منزلـةِ الهـدى يـتعلمُ
علـى مـصرع للفاطميين غيبـت	لا وجههــم فيـه بـدور وأنجـم
على مـشهد لـو كنت حاضر أهلـه	لعاينـت أعضاء النبـي تقسم
على كـربلاء لا أخلف الغيـث كـربلا	وإلا فـأن الـدمع أنـدى وأكـرم
مـصارع ضجت يثـرب لمـصابها	ونـاح علـيهن الحطـيم وزمـزم
ومكـة والأسـتار والـركن والـصفا	ومـوقـف حـج والمقـام المعظـم
لـو أن رسـول الله يحيـى بعيدهم	رأى أبـن زيـاد أمـه كيـف تعقـم
وأقبلـت الزهـراء قـدس تربهـا	تنـادي اباهـا والمـدامع تـسجم
تقول: أبـي هـم غـادروا أبنـي نهبة	كمـا صـاغة قـيس ومـامج أرقـم
وهـم قطعـوا رأس الحسين بكـربلا	كـأنهم قـد أحسنوا حـين أجرمـوا
فخـذ منـهم ثـأري وسـكن جوانحـاً	وأجفـان عـين تـستطير وتـسجم
أبـي وأنتـصر للـسبط وأذكـر مصابه	وغلتـه والنهـر ريـان مفعـم
فيـا أيهـا المغرور والله غاضـب	لبنـت رسـول الله أيـن تـيمم؟
ألا طـرب يقلـى ألا حـزن يـصطفى	ألا أدمـع تجـري ألا قـلب يـضرم
قفوا سـاعدونا بالـدموع فأنهـا	لتـصغر فـي حـق الحـسين ويعظم

323

| ومهما سمعتم في الحسين مراثيا | تعبر عن محض الأسى وتترجم |
| فمدوا أكفاً مسعدين بدعوة | وصلوا على جد الحسين وسلموا |

ومن شعراء الأندلس الذين اشتهروا برثاء الحسين)عليه السلام(أبو البقاء الرندي صاحب المرثية الأندلسية الشهيرة:

| لكل شيء أذا ما تم نقصان | فلا يغر بطيب العيش إنسان |

يقول في مرثية له للحسين عليه السلام:

| أبيت فلا يساعدني عزاء | إذا ذُكر الحسينُ وكربلاءُ |
| فخل الوجد يفعل ما يشاء | لمثل اليوم يدخر البكاء |

عفا من آل فاطمة الحواء

| بعينك يا رسول الله ما بي | دموعي في انهمال وانسكاب |
| وقلبي في أنتهاب والتهاب | على دار مكرمة الجناب |

عفتها الريح بعدك والسماء

| بكيت منازل الصبر السؤاة | بمكة والمدينة والفرات |
| معالم للعلا والمكرمات | عفت أثارها وكذاك يأتي |

على آثار من ذهب العفاء

شعر عقبة بن عمرو السهمي في رثاء الحسين عليه السلام :

أول شعر رثي به الحسين عليه السلام: جاء في مجالس المفيد و أمالي الطوسي عن المفيد ، عن محمد بن عمران ، عن محمد بن إبراهيم ، عن عبد الله ابن أبي سعد ، عن مسعود بن عمرو ، عن إبراهيم بن داحة قال :أول شعر رثي به الحسين بن علي عليه السلام قول عقبة بن عمرو السهمي من بني سهم بن عوف بن غالب :

إذا العين فرَّت في الحياة وأنتم	تخافون في الدُنيا فأظلم نـورها
مـررت على قبر الحسين بكربلا	ففاض عليه مـن دمـوعي غزيرهـا
فما زلت أرثيـه وأبكي لـشجوه	ويـسعد عينـي دمعهـا وزفيرهـا
وبكيت مـن بعد الحسين عصائب	أطافت بـه مـن جانبيها قبـورها
سلام على أهل القبـور بكربـلا	وقل لها منّي سلام يـزورها
سـلام بآصال العشي وبالضّحى	تـؤديه نكبـاء الرِّيـاح ومـورها
ولا بـرح الوفّـاد زوار قبـره	يفـوح عليهـم مسكها وعبيـرها

***

أضحكني الدهـر وأبكـانـي	والـدهر ذو صـروفٍ والـوانِ
لتسعةٍ بـالطفّ قـد غـودروا	صاروا جميعـا رهـن أكفانِ
وستة لا يتجـازى بهـم	بنـو عقيل خير فـرسان
ثـم عـلي الخير مولاهـم	ذكـرهم هيـج أحزانـي

ومن شعر لدعبل الخزاعي زمن الرضا عليه السلام غريب طوس:

يقول دعبل : دخلت على سيدي ومولاي علي بن موسى الرضا عليه السلام في مثل هذه الأيام فرأيته جالسا جلسة الحزين الكئيب ، وأصحابه من حوله ، فلما رآني مقبلا قال لي : مرحبا بك يا دعبل مرحبا بناصرنا بيده ولسانه ، ثم إنه وسع لي في مجلسه وأجلسني إلى جانبه. ثم قال لي : يا دعبل احب أن تنشدني شعرا فان هذه الأيام أيام حزن كانت علينا أهل البيت ، وأيام سرور كانت على أعدائنا خصوصا بني أمية ، يا دعبل من بكى

325

وأبكى على مصابنا ولو واحدا كان أجره على الله يا دعبل من ذرفت عيناه على مصابنا وبكى لما أصابنا من أعدائنا حشره الله معنا في زمرتنا ، يا دعبل من بكى على مصاب جدي الحسين، غفر الله له ذنوبه البتة .

ثم إنه عليه السلام نهض ، وضرب سترا بيننا وبين حرمه ، وأجلس أهل بيته من وراء الستر ليبكوا على مصاب جدهم الحسين عليه السلام ثم التفت إلي وقال لي: يا دعبل ارث الحسين، فأنت ناصرنا ومادحنا مادمت حيا ، فلا تقصر عن نصرنا ما استطعت.

عن أبي الصلت الهروي، قال: دخل دعبل بن علي الخزاعي على الرضا عليه السّلام بمرو فقال له: يابن رسول الله، إني قد قلت فيكم قصيدة و آليت على نفسي أن لا أنشدها أحدا قبلك. فقال الرضا عليه السّلام: هاتها. فأنشد:

نوائحُ عُجمُ اللفظِ و النطقاتِ	تجاوبنَ بالأرنانِ و الزفراتِ
أسارى هوىً ماضٍ و آخرَ آتِ	يُخبرنَ بالأنفاسِ عن سرِ أنفسِ
سلامٌ شجٍ صبّ على العرصاتِ	على العرصاتِ الخالياتِ من المها
من العطراتِ البيضِ و الخَفِراتِ	فعهدي بها خضرُ المعاهد مألفا
و يعدي تدانينا على العزباتِ	ليالي يعدين الوصال على القِلى
يسترن بالأيدي على الوجناتِ	و إذ هُنَّ يلحظنَ العيون سوافرا
يبيت بها قلبي على نشواتِ	و إذ كل يوم لي بلحظي نشوة
وقوفي يوم الجمع من عرفاتِ	فكم حسرات هاجها بمحسر
على الناس من نقضٍ و طول شتاتِ	ألم ترَ للأيام ما جرّ جورها
بهم طالبا للنور في الظلماتِ	و من دول المستهزئين و من غدا
إلى الله بعد الصوم و الصلواتِ	فيكف و من أنّى بطالب زلفة
و بغض بني الزرقاء و العبلاتِ	سوى حب أبناء و رهطه
أولوا الكفر في الإسلام و الفجراتِ	و هند و ما أدّت سمية و ابنها

326

و محكمـه بـالزور و الـشبهات	هـم نقضوا عهد الكتـاب و فرضه
بدعوى ضلال مـن هـن و هنـات	و لـم تـك إلا محنـة كـشفتهم
و حكم بـلا شـورى بغيـر هداة	تـراث بـلا قربى و ملك بـلا هدى
وردت أجاجـا طعـم كـل فـرات	رزايا أرتنـا خـضرة الأفـق حمـرة
علـى النـاس إلا بيعـة الفلتـات	و مـا سـهلت تلـك المـذاهب فيهم
بـدعوى تـراث فـي الـضلال نتـات	و مـا قيل أصحاب الـسقيفة جهـرة
لزمـت بمـأمون علـى العثـرات	و لـو قلّـدوا الموصـى إليـه أمورهـا
و مفتـرس الأبطـال فـي الغمـرات	أخي خـاتم الرسل المصفى من القذى
و بـدر و أحـد شـامخ الهـضبات	فـإن جحـدوا كـان الغدير شهيده
و إيثـاره بـالقوت فـي اللزبـات	و آي مـن القـرآن تتلـى بفـضله
مناقـب كانـت فيـه مؤتنفـات	و عـز خـلال أدركتـه بـسبقها
بـشيء سـوى حـد القنـا الـذربات	مناقب لـم تـدرك بخير و لـم تنـل
عكـوف علـى العـزى معـا و منات	نجـي لجبريـل الأمـين و أنـتم
و أذريـت دمـع العـين بـالعبرات	بكيت لرسـم الـدار مـن عرفـات
رسـوم ديـار قـد عفـت و عـرات	و بـان عـرى صبري و هاجت صبابتي
و منـزل وحـي مقفـر العرصـات	مـدارس آيـات خلـت مـن تـلاوة
و للـسيد الـداعي إلـى الـصلوات	لآل رسـول الله بـالخيف مـن منـى
و حمـزة و الـسجاد ذي الثفنـات	ديـار علـي و الحـسين و جعفـر
نجيّ رسول الله فـي الخلـوات	ديـار لعبـد الله و الفـضل صنـوه

و وارث عِلـــم اللهِ و الـــحـــسـنات	و سِبطي رسولِ اللهِ و ابني وصِيـه
على أحمد المذكورِ في الـصـلواتِ	منــازلُ وحـــي اللهِ يــنــزِل بينهـــا
فيؤمنَ مــنهم زلّـةَ العـثـراتِ	منــازلُ قـوم يهتــدي بهــداهم
و للــصوم و التطهيرِ و الـحـسناتِ	منــازلُ كانــت للــصلاةِ و للتقى
و لا ابن صهاكٍ فاتكُ الحرماتِ	منــازلُ لا تــيم يحــلّ بربعِهـــا
و لـــم تعـف للأيــام و الـسنواتِ	ديارُ عفاها جــورُ كــلِّ منابـذ
متــى عهــدها بالـصوم و الـصلواتِ؟	قفا نسأل الدار التي خفّ أهلها:
أفـانينٌ فـي الأقطارِ مفتـرقـاتِ	و أين الأولى شَطّت بهم غربةُ النوى؟
و هــم خيرُ سادات و خيرُ حُمـاةِ	هـم أهلُ ميراثِ النبيِّ إذا اعتـزوا
بأسـمائهم، لـــم يقبــلِ الــصلوات	إذا لـــم ننــاجِ اللهَ فـي صلواتنا
لقـد شرّفوا بالفضلِ و البركـاتِ	مطاعيمُ للأعسارِ في كـل مـشهد
و مــضطغن ذو إحنــة و تـراتِ	و مــا النــاس إلا غاصبٌ و مكــذّب
و يــوم حنــين أسبلوا العبراتِ	إذا ذكروا قتلـى ببــدرٍ و خيبـر
و هــم تركـوا أحشاءهم و غرات؟	فكيـف يحبــون النبيَّ و رهطـه
قلوبــا علــى الأحقــاد منطويـاتِ	لقـد لا ينــوه في المقالِ و أضمروا
فهاشمُ أولــى مــن هــن و هنات	فـإن لـــم يكــن إلا بقربـى محمـد
فقـد حــلّ فيه الأمنُ بالبركـاتِ	سقى اللهُ قبـرا بالمدينةِ غيثـه
و بلّــغ عنـا روحـه التحفـاتِ	نبـي الهـدى صلى عليـه مليكـه
و لاحــت نجـوم الليـل مبتـدرات	و صلى عليه اللهُ مـا ذرَّ شارِق

328

و قـد مـاتَ عطشانـاً بـشـطِ فـراتِ	أفاطمُ لـو خلتِ الحسينَ مجدلاً
و أجريتِ دمعَ العينِ في الوجنات	إذا للطمـتِ الخــدَّ فـاطمُ عنـدَهُ
نجـوم سمـاوات بـأرض فـلات	أفاطم قـومي يابنـة الخير و انـدبي
و أخـرى بفـخ نالهـا صلـواتي	قبـور بكوفـان و أخـرى بطيبـة
و قبر ببـاخمرى لـدى الغربـات	و أخـرى بـأرض الجوزجـان محلها
تـضمَنها الـرحمن في الغربـات	و قبـر ببغـداد لـنفس زكيـة
ألَحَّت على الأحشاء بـالزفراتِ	و قبر بطوس، يـا لهـا مـن مصيبة
يفـرَج عنـا الغـم و الكربـات	إلـى الحشر حتـى يبعث الله قائمـاً
و صلـى عليـه أفضل الصلوات	علي بـن موسـى أرشـد الله أمـره
مبالغهـا منـي بكنـه صفـات	فأمـا الممضات التي لـست بالغـا
معرَسـهم منهـا بـشط فـرات	قبـور ببطن النهر مـن جنب كربلاء
توقّيت فيهم قبـل حـين وفـاتي	توفّـوا عطاشـا بـالفرات فليتـني
سـقتني بكـأس الثكـل و الفظعات	إلى الله أشكو لوعـة عند ذكـرهم
مصارعهم بـالجزع فـالنخلات	أخـاف بـأن ازدارهـم فتشـوقني
لهـم عقـرة مغـشية الحجـرات	تغشّـاهم ريـب المنـون فمـا تـرى
مدينين أنـضاء مـن اللزبـات	خـلا أن مـنهم بالمدينـة عصبة
مـن الضبـع و العقبـان و الرخمـات	قليلـة زوار سـوى أن زورا
ثـوت في نـواحي الأرض مفترقات	لهـم كـل يـوم تربـة بمضاجع
و لا تـصطليهم جمـرة الجمـرات	تنكّبـت لأواء الـسنين جـوارهم

مغاوير نجَّارون في الأزمات	و قد كان منهم بالحجاز و أرضها
تضيء لدى الأستار و الظلمات	حمى لم تزره المذنبات و أوجه
مساعير حرب أقحموا الغمرات	إذا وردوا خيلا بسمر من القنا
و جبريل و الفرقان و السورات	فإن فخروا يوما أتوا بمحمد
و فاطمة الزهراء خير بنات	و عدّوا عليا ذا المناقب و العلى
و جعفرا الطيار في الحجبات	و حمزة و العباس ذا الهدي و التقى
سمية من نوكى و من قذرات	أولئك لا ملقوح هند و حزبها
و بيعتهم من أفجر الفجرات	ستسأل تيم عنهم وعديها
و هم تركوا الأبناء رهن شتات	هم منعوا الآباء عن أخذ حقهم
فبيعتهم جاءت عن الغدرات	و هم عدلوها عن وصي محمد
أبو الحسن الفرّاج للغمرات	وليهم صنو النبي محمد
أحبّاي ما داموا و أهل ثقاتي	ملامك في آل النبي فإنهم
على كل حال خيرة الخيرات	تخيّرتهم رشدا لنفسي إنهم
و سلّمت نفسي طائعا لولاتي	نبذت إليهم بالمودة صادقا
وزد حبهم يا رب في حسناتي	فيا رب زدني في هواي بصيرة
و ما ناح قمريّ على الشجرات	سأبكيهم ما حجّ لله راكب
و إني لمحزون بطول حياتي	و إني لمولاهم و قال عدوهم
لفكّ عتاة أو لحمل ديات	بنفسي أنتم من كهول وفتية
فأطلقتم منهن بالذربات	و للخيل لما قيّد الموت خطوها

أحب قصي الرحم من أجل حبكم | و أهجـر فيكم زوجتي و بناتي
و أكـتـم حبـيكم مخافـة كاشـح | عنيـد لأهـل الحـق غير مـوات
فيـا عيـن بكـيهم وجـودي بعبـرة | فقـد آن للتـسكاب و الهـمـلات
لقد خفت في الـدنيا و أيام سعيها | و إني لأرجـوا لأمـن بعـد وفـاتي
ألـم تراني مـذ ثلاثين حجـة | أروح و أغـدو دائـم الحـسرات؟
أرى فيئهم في غيرهم متقسّما | و أيـديهم مـن فيئهم صـفرات
و كيف أداوي من جوى بي و الجوى | أميـة أهـل الكفـر و اللعنـات
و آل زيـاد في الحريـر مـصونة | و آل رسـول الله منهتكـات
سـأبكيهم مـا ذرّ في الأفـق شارق | و نـادى منـاد الخير بالـصلوات
و مـا طلعت شمس و حـان غروبهـا | وبالليـل أبكـيهم و بالغـدوات
ديـار رسـول الله أصبحن بلقعـا | و آل زيـاد تـسكن الحجـرات
و آل رسـول الله تـدمي نحـورهم | و آل زيـاد ربـة الحجـلات
و آل رسـول الله يـسبى حـريمهم | و آل زيـاد آمنـوا الـسربات
وآل زيـاد في الحصون منيعـة | وآل رسـول الله فـي الفلـوات
وآل رسـول الله نحـف جسومهم | وآل زيـاد غـلظ القـصرات
إذا و تـروا مـدّوا إلـى واتريهم | أكفّـا عـن الأوتـار منقبـضات
فلـولا الـذي أرجـوه في اليوم أو غـد | تقطّـع نفسـي إثـرهم حـسرات
خـروج إمـام لا محالـة خـارج | يقـوم علـى إسـم الله و البركـات
يميـز فينـا كـل حـق و باطـل | و يجـزي على النعمـاء و النقمات

فيا نفس طيبي ثم يا نفس فابشري   فغير بعيد كل ما هو آت

و لا تجزعي من مدة الجور إنني   أرى قوتي قد آذنت بثبات

فيا رب عجّل ما أعمّل فيهم   لأشفي نفسي من أسى المحنات

فإن قرب الرحمان من تلك مدتي   و أخّر من عمري و وقت وفاتي

شفيت و لم أترك لنفسي غصة   و رويت منهم منصلي و قناتي

فإني من الرحمن أرجو بحبهم   حياة لدى الفردوس غير تباتي

عسى الله أن يرتاح للخلق إنه   إلى كل قوم دائم اللحظات

فإن قلت عرفا أنكروه بمنكر   و غطّوا على التحقيق بالشبهات

سأقصر نفسي جاهدا عن جدالهم   كفاني ما ألقى من العبرات

أحاول نقل الصم عن مستقرها   و إسماع أحجار من الصلدات

فحسبي منهم أن أبوء بغصة   تردّد في صدري و في لهواتي

فمن عارف لم ينتفع و معاند   تميل به الأهواء للشهوات

كأنك بالأضلاع قد ضاق ذرعها   لما حملت من شدة الزفرات

فلما وصل إلى قوله: «و قبرٍ ببغداد»، قال عليه السّلام له: أفلا ألحقُ لكَ بهذا الموضع بيتين بهما تمامُ صيدتك؟ قال: بلى يابن رسول الله. فقال: «و قبر بطوس» و الذي يليه. قال دُعبل: يابن رسول الله! لمَن هذا القبر بطوس؟ فقال: قبري، و لا ينقضي الأيام و السنون حتى تصير طوس معي في درجتي كان من زارني في غربتي كان معي في درجتي يوم القيامة، مغفورا له. و نهض الرضا عليه السّلام و قال: لا تبرح، و أنفذ إليَّ صرّة فيها مائة دينار ...

المصادر: ١. بحار الأنوار: ج ٤٩ ص ٢٤٥ ح ١٣، عن كشف الغمة. ٢. العدد القوية: ص ٢٨٨ ح ١٥، بزيادة فيه. ٣. رجال الكشي: ص ٤٢٦، شطرا منه و زيادة في آخره. ٤. الأغاني: ج ٢٠ ص ٦٩، على ما في العدد. ٥. كشف الغمة: ج ٢ ص ٣١٨. ٦. حلية الأبرار: ج ٤ ص ٣١٩ المنهج التاسع الباب الثامن. ٧. حلية الأبرار: ج ٤ ص ٤١٥ المنهج التاسع الباب التاسع. ٨. عيون الأخبار: ج ٢ ص ٢٦٧ ح ٣٤، شطرا من

الحديث. ٩. عيون الأخبار: ج ٢ ص ١٤١ ح ٨، شطرا قليلا منه.

ولدعبل الخزاعي أكثر من قصيدة في رثاء الحسين عليه السلام منها:

منازل بين أكناف الغري	إلى وادي المياه إلى الطوي
لقد شغل الدموع عن الغواني	مصاب الاكرمين بني علي
أتا أسفي على هفوات دهر	تضاءل فيه أولاد الزكي
ألم تقف البكاء على حسين	وذكرك مصرع الحبر التقي
ألم يحزنك أن بني زياد	أصابوا بالتراث بني النبي
وأن بني الحصان يمر فيهم	علانية سيوف بني البغي

ومنها أيضا:

جاؤا من الشام المشومة أهلها	للشوم يقدم جندهم إبليس
لعنوا وقد لعنوا بقتل إمامهم	تركوه وهو مبضع مخموس
وسبوا فواحزني بنات محمد	عبرى حواسر مالهن لبوس
تبا لكم يا ويلكم أرضيتم	بالنار ذل هنالك المحبوس
بعتم بدنيا غيركم جهلا ب	كم عز الحياة وإنه لنفيس
أخسر بها من بيعة أموية	لُعِنَتْ، وحظُ البائعينَ خسيسُ
بؤسا لمن بايعتم وكأنني	بإمامكم وسط الجحيم حبيس
يا آل أحمد ما لقيتم بعده من	عصبة هم في القياس مجوس
كم عبرة فاضت لكم وتقطعت	يوم الطفوف على الحسين نفوس
صبرا موالينا فسوف نديلكم	يوما على آل اللعين عبوس

333

مازلــت متبعــا لكــم ولأمــركم   وعليــه نفـسي مـا حييـت أسـوس

شعر خالد بن معدان في رثاء الحسين عليه السلام:

جــاءوا برأسـك يـا ابـن بنـت   محمــد متــرملا بدمائــه تــرميلا

قتلـوك عطـشانا ولـم يترقبـوا   فـي قتـلك التنزيـل والتأويـلا

وكأنمــا بـك يـابن بنـت محمــد   قتلــوا جهـارا عامـدين رسـولا

ويكبــرون بـأن قتلـت وإنمـا   قتلــوا بـك التـكبير والتهلـيلا

شعر الشريف المرتضى في رثاء الإمام الحسين عليه السلام:

لقـد كسرت للـدين فـي يـوم كربـلا   كسائـر لا تؤسـى ولا هـي تجبـر

فـإما سبـي بالرمـاح مـسوق   وإمــا قتيـل بالتـراب معفـر

وجرحى كمـا اختـارت رمـاح وأنـصل   وصـرعى كماشـات ضبـاع وأنـسر

ومن شعر له أيضا:

إن يـوم الطـلف يومـا كـان للـدين عـصيبا
لـم يـدع للقلـب منـي فـي المـسرات نـصيبا
لعـن الله رجـالا أترعـوا الـدنيا غـصوبا
سالموا عجـزا فلمـا قـدروا شنـوا الحروبا
طبلـوا أوتـار بـدر عنـدنا ظلمـا وحوبا

ومن شعر الشريف الرضي:

كـربلا لازلـت كربـا وبـلا   مـا لقـى عنـدك آل المـصطفى

كـم علـى تربـك لمـا صـرعوا   مـن دم سـال ومـن دمـع جـرى

334

نزلــوا فيهـا علــى غيـر قــرى	وضيــوف لفــلاة قفــرة
بحدي الســيف علــى ورد الــردى	لـم يـذوقوا المـاء حتى اجتمعـوا
لا تدانيهــا عــلوا وضيـا	تكسف الشمس شموس منـهم
أرجــل الــسبق وأيمـان النـدا	وتنــوش الوحش مـن أجسـادهم
قمـر غــاب ومـن نـجم هـوى	ووجوهـا كالمـصابيح فمـن
جائــر الحكـم عليهـن البلـى	غيرتهـن الليالـي وغـدا
وهـم مـا بيـن قتـل وسبـا	يـا رسـول الله لـو عاينتـهم
عاطش يسـقى أنابيـب القنـا	مـن رميـض يمنـع الظل ومـن
محمــول علــى غيـر وطـا	ومسـوق عاثـر يسـعى بـه خلـف
ثـم ساقوا أهلـه سوق الامـا	جزروا جـزر الأضـاحي نسـله
خامــس أصحــاب الكـسا	قتلـوه بعـد علـم منهـم أنـه
وأبــوها وعلـي ذو العـلا	ميـت تبـكي لـه فاطمة

شعر الصاحب بن عباد في رثاء الحسين عليه السلام:

لمـا صـح عنـدي مـن قبيـح غذائهم	برئـت مـن الأرجـاس رهـط أميـة
لكفرهـم المعـدود فـي شردائهم	ولعنهـم خيـر الوصـيين جهـرة
وسـبيهم عـن جـرأة لنسـائهم	وقـتلهم السـادات مـن آل هاشـم
حسين العـلا بـالكرب فـي كـربلائهم	وذبحهـم خيـر الرجـال أرومـة
لمـا ورثـوا مـن بغضـه فـي قنائهم	وتـشتيتهم شـمل النبـي محمـد
أديلـت وهـم أنصارهـا لـشقائهم	ومـا غـضبت إلا لأصنامها التـي

أيــا رب جنبنــي المكــاره واعـف | عن ذنـوبي لمـا أخلصتـه مـن ولائهــم
أيـا رب أعـدائي كثيـر فزدهـم | غيظهـــم لا يظفـــروا بابتغائهـــم
أيـا رب مـن كــان النبــي وأه | لــه وسـائله لـم يخـش مـن غلـوائهم
حسين توصـل لـي إلـى الله إنني | بليـت بهـم فـادفع عظيم بلائهـم
فكـم قـد دعـوني رافـضيا لحبكـم | فلـم ينثنـي عنكم طويـل عوائهـم

شـعر عقيلـة بنـي هاشـم الحـوراء زينـب فـي رثـاء أخيهـا الحسين عليـه السلام :

تمـسك بالكتـاب ومـن تــلاه | فأهـل البيـت هـم أهـل الكتـاب
بهـم نـزل الكتـاب وهـم تلـوه | وهـم كـانوا الهـداة إلـى الـصواب
إمامي وحـد الـرحمن طفـلا | وآمـن قبـل تـشديد الخطـاب
علـى كـل صديـق البرايـا | علــي كـان فـاروق العـذاب
شفيعي فـي القيامـة عنـد ربـي | نبـي والوصـي أبـو تـراب
وفاطمـة البتـول ، وسـيدا مـن | يخلـد فـي الجنـان مـع الـشباب
علـى الطـف الـسلام وسـاكنيه | وروح الله فـي تلـك القبـاب
نفوسـا قدسـت فـي الأرض قـدما | وقـد خلـصت مـن النطـف العـذاب
فـضاجع فتيـة عبـدوا فنامـوا | هجـودا فـي الفدافـد والـشعاب
علـتهم فـي مـضاجعهم كعـاب | بـأوراق منعمـة رطـاب
وصـيرت القبـور لهـم قـصورا | مناخـا ذات أفنيـة رحـاب
لئـن وارتهـم أطبـاق أرض كمـا | أغمـدت سـيفا فـي قـراب
كأقمـار إذا جاسـوا رواض | وآسـاد إذا ركبـوا غـضاب

336

من العافين والهلكى السغاب	لقد كانوا البحار لمن أتاهم
وقد عيضوا النعيم من العقاب	فقد نقلوا إلى جنات عدن
يسقن مع الاسارى والنهاب	بنات محمد أضحت سبايا
كسبي الروم دامية الكعاب	مغبرة الذيول مكشفات
فهن من التعفف في حجاب	لئن ابرزن كرها من حجاب
وقد أضحى مباحا للكلاب	أيبخل في الفرات على حسين
ولي جفن عليه ذو انسكاب	فلي قلب عليه ذو التهاب

قصيدة الشاعر جعفر الحلّي:

لم يجري في الأرض حتى أوقف الفلكا	الله أي دم في كربلاء سفكا
على حريم رسول الله فانتهكا	واي خيل ضلال بالطفوف عدت
له حمية دين الله اذ تركا	يوم بحامية الأسلام قد نهضت
والرشد لم تدر قوم اية سلكا	رأى بأن سبيل الحق متبع
كأن من شرع الأسلام قد افكا	والناس قد عادت اليهم جاهليتهم
يمسي ويصبح بالفحشاء منهمكا	وقد تحكم بالأسلام طاغية
وكيف صار يزيد بينهم ملكا	لم أدر أين رجال المسلمون مضوا
ومن خساسة طبع يعصر الودكا	العاصر الخمر من لؤم بنعصره
ما نزهت حمله هند عن الشركا؟	هل كيف يسلم من شرك ووالده
فسيفه بسوى التوحيد ما فتكا	لئن جرت لفظة التوحيد من فمه
وما الى أحد غير الحسين شكا	قد أصبح الدين منه يشتكي سقما

فمـا رأى الـسبط للـدين الحنيـف شفـا
الا اذا دمـه فـي كـربلاء سـفكا

ومـا سـمعنا عليـلا لاعـلاج لـه
الا بـنفس مداويـة اذا هلكـا

بقتلـه فـاح للأسـلام نـشر هـدى
فكلمـا ذكرتـه المـسلمون ذكـا

وصان ستر الهدى مـن كل خائنـة
سـتر الفواطم يـوم الطف اذ هتكـا

نفـسي الفـداء لفـاد شـرع والـده
بنفـسه وأهليـه ومـا ملكـا

وشبها بـذباب الـسيف ثـائرة
شـعواء قـد أوردت أعـداءه الـدركا

وأنجـم الظهـر للأعـداء قـد ظهـرت
نـصب العيـون وغطـى النقـع وجـه دكا

أحـال أرض العـدى نقعـا بحملتـه
وللـسماء سـما مـن قـسطل سـمكا

فـأنقص الارضـين الـسبع واحـدة
منهـا وزاد الـى أفلاكهـا فلكـا

كـسا النهار ثيـاب النقـع حالكـة
لكـن محيـاه يجلـو ذلـك الحلكـا

فـي فتيـة كـصقور الجـو تحملهـا
امثالهـا تـنقض الاشـراك والـشبكا

لـو اطلقوهـا وراء البـرق آونـة
ليمـسكوه اتـت والبـرق قـد مـسكا

الـصائدون سباع الـصيد ان عنـدت
ومـا سـوى سـمرهم مدوا لهـا شـركا

لـم تمـسي اعـدائهم الا عـلى درك
وجـارهم يـأمن الأهـوال والـدركا

ضاق الفضاء على حرب بحـربهم
حتـى رأت كـل رحـب ضيـق ضنكا

يا ويح دهر جرى بـالطف بـين بنـي
محمـد وبنـي سـفيان معتـركا

حشا بنـي فـاطم مـا القـوم كفـؤهم
شـجاعة لا ولا جـواد ولا نـسكا

لكنهـا وقعـة كانـت مؤسـسة
مـن الألـى غـصبوا مـن فـاطم فدكا

مـا يـنقم النـاس مـنهم غير انهم
ينهـون ان تعبـد الأوثـان والـشركا

338

شل الآله يدا شمر غداة على ... صدر ابن فاطمة بالسيف قد بركا

فكأن ما طبق الأنوار قاطبة ... من يومه للتلاقي مأتما وبكا

ولم يغادر جمادا "لا ولا بشرا" ... الا بكاه ولا جنا" ولا ملكا

فأن تجد ضحكا "منا فلا عجبا" ... فربما بسم المغبون او ضحكا

في كل عام لنا بالعشر واعية ... تطبق الدور والارجاء والسككا

وكل مسلمة ترمي بزينتها ... حتى السماء رمت عن وجهها الحبكا

يا ميتا" ترك الألباب حائرة" ... وبالعراء ثلاثا" جسمه تركا

تأتي الوحوش له ليلا" مسلمة ... والقوم تجري نهارا" فوقه الرمكا

ويل لهم ما اهتدوا منه بموعظة ... كالدر منتظما" والتبر منسبكا

لم ينقطع قط من ارسال خطبته ... حتى بها رأسه فوق السنان حكا

وا لهفتاه لزين العابدين لقى ... من طول علته والسقم قد نهكا

كانت عبادته منه سياطهم ... وفي كعوب القنا قالوا البقاء لكا

جروه فانتبهوا النطع المعد له ... وأوطأوا جسمه السعدان والحسكا

ومن شعر للحاج عبد الحسين الأزري:

عِشْ في زمانك ما استطعتَ نبيلا ... واترك حديثَك للرَواة جميلا

ولعزك استرخص حياتك إنه ... أغلى وإلا غادرتكَ ذليلا

تعطي الحياةُ قيادَها لك كلَّما ... صَيَّرتها للمكرُمات ذلولا

العزُ مقياسُ الحياة وظل مَن ... قد عدَّ مقياسَ الحياة الطُّولا

قل كيف عاشَ ولا تقل كم عاش ... من جَعلَ الحياةَ إلى علاه سبيلا

كـثرت مـحاسنُه وعـاشَ قـليلا	مـا غـرَ إن طَـوَتِ المنيـة ماجـداً
بـطلٌ تـوسَّد فـي الطُّفـوفِ قتـيلا	مـا كـان لـلأحرار إلا قـدوةً
لا تـقـبل الـتفـسيرَ والـتَّأويلا	بـعـثته اسفـارُ الـحقائـق آيـة
مـن عَـل ضـيماً واستكان خمـولا	يَـدوي صداها في المسامِع زاجـراً
فـي شَـأنها ويـزيدُها تَـرتيلا	لا زالَ يـقـرَؤها الـزَّمانُ مـعظماً
مـن عـل ضـيما واسـتكان خمـولا	يدوي صداها في المسامع زاجرا:
آله فـي حـفـظ الـذمار كفيلا	أفـديك معتصما بـسيفك لـم تجد
والـعرش لـولاك اسـتقام طـويلا	خـشيت أميـة أن تزعـزع عرشـها
المـستأجرون بمـا ادعـوا تـضليلا	بـثوا دعـايتهم لحربـك وافتـرى
حـسبتك سـيفا فوقهـا مـسلولا	مـن أيـن تـأمن منـك اروُس معـشر
يـدها شبـاتك وانتـضتك صقـيلا	طـبعتك اهـداف الـنبي وذربـت
واذا انـتـميت رأوك منـه سـليلا	فـاذا خطبـت رأوك عنـه معبـرا
وجـدوا بـه لـك منـشأ ومقـيلا	أو قمـت عـن بيـت النبوة معربـا
مـن كـل فـج عـصبة وقبـيلا	قطعـوا الطريـق لـذا عليـك والبوا
أو ذلـة فـأبيت الا الاولـى	وهـناك آل الامـر امـا سـلة
أزمعـت عـن هـذي الحيـاة رحيـلا	ومـشيت مـشية مطمـئن حينمـا
وفـد يـؤمل مـن نـداك منـيلا	تـستقبل البـيض الـصفاح كأنهـا
كـأنك قـد بعثـت رسـولا	فـكأن مـوقفك الابـي رسـالة وبـها
لـهم مـثالا فـي الحيـاة نبـيلا	نـهج الابـاة علـى هـداك ولـم تـزل

340

وتعشق الاحرار سنتك التي لـــم تـبـق عـذرا للـشجا مقبـولا

قـتلوك لـلدنيا ولـكن لـم تـدم لـبني أمـية بـعد قـتلك جـيـلا

ولرب نـصر عـاد شـر هزيمـة تـــركت بـيوت الظـالمين طلـولا

حملـت (بصفين) الكتاب رماحهم لـيكون رأسـك بـعده محمـولا

يـدعون بـاسم (محمد) وبكربلا دمـه غـدا بـــسيوفهم مـــطلولا

لـو لـم تـبت لنـصالهم نهبـا لما اجـترأ (الـوليد) فمـزق التنـزيلا

تمضي الـدهور ولا تـرى الاك فـي الـدنيا شـهيد المكرمـات جلـيلا

وكـفاك تـعظيما لـشأوك موقـف أمـسى عـليك مـدى الحيـاة دلـيلا

مـا أبـخس الـدنيا اذا لـم تـستطع أن تـوجد الـدنيا الـيك مثـيلا

بـسمائك الـشعراء مهمـا حلقـوا لـم يـبلغوا مـن ألـف ميل مـيلا

المصدر :منتديات شيعة علي عليه السلام وفاطمة الزهراء عليها السلام

رثاء الإمام الحسين عليه السلام:

يـا شـهيداً أبكـى العيـون جميعـاً وقتـيلا عطـشان جنب الفـراتِ

استضافوه أهـل كوفـان غـدراً ثـم حـدوا لقتلـه الـشفراتِ

يـا حسين المظلـوم أقرح جفنـي مـا توالـت عليـك مـن نكبـات

دمعـت فيـك عـين كـل نبـي ووصـي وأعـين الـسادات

يـا لـك مـن شـهيد عفير تركتـه الأعـداء فـي الفلـوات

داست الخيل صدره عـن عنـاد فعفـت منـه شـامخات الـسمات

جـردوه عـن الملابـس نهبـا فـسكته الرمـال بالـسافيات

341

وبــــه توجـــوا رؤوس القنــــاة	قطعـــوا رأســـه الشـــريف ضـــلالا
حيـــث أحنـــت لله فـــي الســجدات	كسـروا منـه جبهـة قـد تعالـت
طبـع المصطفى بهـا قبلات	ضـرب الرجـس بالقضيب شفاها
الــذل ثكلـى بلوعـة باكيـات	وسبـوا منـه نسـوة فـي أسـار
معـولات مـن الأسـى نادبـات	راكبـات علـى نياق هـزال

قال رزق الله بن عبد الوهاب بن عبد العزيز الحنبلي :

اجتمعت بمُلحدة المعرة ـ يعني أبا العلاء المعري ـ فقال لي : سمعت في مراثي الحسين بن علي رضي الله عنهما مرثية تكتب ، فقلت : قد قال بعض فلاحي بلادنا أبياتا تعجز عنها شيوخ تنوخ ، فقال : ما هي قلت قوله :

للمسـلمين علـى قنـاة يرفـعُ	رأس ابن بنت محمـد ووصيـه
لا جازع منهم ولا متفجـع	والمسلمون بمنظـر وبمسمع
وأنمـت عينـا لـم تكـن بـك تهجـع	أيقظت أجفانـا وكنـت لهـا كـرى
وأصـم نعيـك كـل أذن تسـمع	كحلت بمصرعك العيون عمايـة
لـك مضجع ولخط قبـرك موضـع	مـا روضـة الا تمنـت أنهـا

فقال المعري : ما سمعت أرق من هذه (١)

١ ـ تمام المتون في شرح رسالة ابن زيدون ص ٢٠٨ ورواها ابن الاثير في الكامل وقد تقدمت هذه الابيات في الجزء الاول / ٣٠٥ وأنها من شعر دعبل الخزاعي كما رواها الحموي في معجم الادباء.

أورد ابن عساكر في تاريخ دمشق لبعض الشعراء قوله في الحسين عليه السلام :

وتلـك الرزايـا والخطـوب عظـام	لقـد هـد جسمي رزء آل محمـد
لآل النبـي المصطفى وعظـام	وأبكـت جفـوني بـالفرات مصارع

عظـام بأكنـاف الفـرات زكيـة | لهـن علينـا حرمـة وذمـام

فكـم حـرة مـسبية فاطميـة | وكـم مـن كـريم قـد عـلاه حـسام

لآل رسـول الله صـلـت عليـهم | ملائكـة بـيض الوجـوه كـرام

أفاطم أشـجاني قتيـل ذوي العـلا | فـشبت وانـي صـادق لغـلام

وأصبحت لا ألتـذ طيب معيـشة | كـأن علـي الطيبـات حـرام

يقولـون لـي صبرا جميلا وسلوة | ومـا لـي الـى الـصبر الجميل مـرام

فكيـف اصطباري بعـد آل محمـد | وفـي القلـب منهم لوعـة وسقام؟

عثمان الهيتي:

وأكـره أن أشـاهدها أمـامي | تركـت الخيزرانـة مـن يمينـي

بهـا نكتـت ثنايـا ابـن الامـام | أأحمـل عـودة مـن خيـزرانِ

من نظم عثمان الهيتي كاتب الوالي داوود باشا في بغداد في حوالي سنة ١٢٤٠.

جاء في كتاب (شعراء بغداد وكتابها في أيام وزارة داود باشا والي بغداد) ذلك في حدود سنة ١٢٠٠ الى سنة ١٢٤٦ للهجرة ، والكتاب تـأليف عبدالقادر أفنـدي الخطيب الشهرابانـي. ان عثمان بيك كان والدا لوالي الموصل وهو محمد أمين باشا وان عثمان بيك كان عمره ثمانين عاما. وفي بعض الكتب ينسب هذا الشعر للشاعر عمر رمضان والله أعلم.

علي السيد سلمان:

أرى هممـا مكنونـة لا يقلهـا | فـضا هـذه الاولـى اتـساعا ولا الاخـرا

تقطـع أمعـاء الزمـان بحملهـا | اذا ذكـرت عنـدي خطـوب بنـي الزهـرا

بهـا طالبـا وتـرا مـن الـدهر لا أرى | شـفاء لـه مـا لا أزيـل لـه الـدهرا

أدك بهـا شـم الجبـال الـى الثـرى | وأبنـي لنـا فيهـا علـى زحـل قـصرا

343

ستدري الليـالي مـن أنـا ولطالمـا
تجـاهلن بـي علمـا وأنكرنني خبرا

بهـا لسـت أرضـى أن قيـصر خـادم
لـدي ولا أرضـى بـذلك مـن كـسرى

بـسطوة مـن جبريـل تحـت لوائـه
وقـد جـل ذا قـدرا ومـا زاده قـدرا

وصـاحب موسـى والمـسيح وحولـه
ملائكـة الافـلاك تنتظـر الامـرا

اذا مـا رنـا نحـو الـسماء بطرفـه
تمـور بمـن فيهـا الـسماء لـه ذعـرا

ولـو شـاء نـسفا للجبـال لاصبحت
ولا شـيء منهـا حيـث شـاء ولا قـدر

امـام تـولى كـل آيـة مرسـل
مـن الله منـا فهـو آيتـه الكبـرى

امـام يعيـد الله شـرعة جـده
بـه غـضة ايـام دولتـه الغـرا

كـأن عليـه التـاج رصـع وشـيه
بـضوء سنى المريخ نـورا وبالـشعرى

اذا مـا رأى الرائـي بـه الهـدي والهـدى
رأى مـن عظيـم الامـر مـا يدهش الفكـرا

بـه الـدهر مبيـض هـدى واستنارة
على أهلـه والارض مـشحونة ذكـرا

متـى يطرب الاسمـاع صـوت بـشيره
وأنـى لـسمعي قولـه لكـم البـشرى

متـى تقبـل الرايـات مـن أرض مكـة
أمـامهم نـور يحيـل الـدجى فجـرا

وأهتـف مـا بـين الكتائـب معلنـا
بيـال أبـي آبـاؤكم قتلـوا صبـرا

دمـاؤكم طلـت لـديهم كـدينكم
وفيئكم نهـب ونـسوتكم أسـرى

وآلكـم مـن عهـد احمـد بينهم
قلـوبهم قرحـى وأعينـهم عبـرى

وهـم تركونـا مطعمـا لـسيوفهم
وهـم غـصبونا فـي آبائنـا قهـرا

الـى م التمـادي يـا بـن أكـرم مرسـل
وحتـام فيهـا أنـت متخـذ سـترا

ألـم تـر أن الظلـم أسـدل ليلـه
على الافـق والاقطـار قـد ملئت كفـرا

344

فمـن مقلـة عبـرا ومـن كبـد حـرا	فمـا الـصبر والبلـوى تفـاقم أمرهـا
بمرئ أما كنت المحيط بها خبرا	أمـا كـان فعـل القـوم منـك بكربـلا
لـدى كربـلا تـذكارها يصـدع الصخرا	أفـي كـل يـوم فجعـة بعـد فجعـة
لهـا عبـرة الا ألمـت بنـا أخـرى	الى كم لنا بـألطف شنعاء مـا رقت
علينـا ولـم تبقـي لـسابقة ذكـرى	ومـا فجعـة بـألطف الا تفاقمـت
وهـذي وقـاك الله مـسلوبة خـدرا	فهـا كربـلا هـذا ذبيـح كمـا تـرى
فـأين سـواها المـستجار ومـن أحـرى	اذا لـم يغـث فـي سوحكم مستجيرها
ألـوف ومـا عـدى وأنـت بهـا أدرى	يطـل لـديها مـن دمـاء ولاتكـم
وكـم مـن دم يجرى وكم حـرة حـسرى	وكـم مـن مصونات عفـات تروعت
مـن القـوم ممـا لـم يـدع بعـده صبـرا	وانـت خبيـر بالرزايـا ومـا جـرى
عواديـه لا تخـشى أثامـا ولا وزرا	أجل ربما في الشرق والغرب من عما
علينـا وأن لا مـستجار لنـا ــ شـمرا	مـصائب أنـستها بكـر طرادهـا ــ
نعاني الرزايـا مـن غـوائلهم غـدرا	ألـم ترنـا كـشاف كـل ملمـة
فمـا أضيـق الغبـرا ومـا أبعـد الخضـرا	أحـاطوا بنـا مـن كـل فـج وأرهبـوا

يظهر من مجرى هذه الابيات ان القصيدة نظمت على اثر غارة الوهابيين سنة ١٢١٦ على كربلاء وانتهاكهم لقدسية حرم سيد الشهداء أبي عبد الله الحسين عليه السلام وسفك دماء الابرياء من رجال ونساء، فثارت حمية هذا العلوي الغيور فاندفع مستجيرا بصاحب العصر الامام الغائب حجة آل محمد صلوات الله عليه.

السيد علي آل السيد سلمان النجفي كان حيا سنة ١٢٣٣. كذا ذكره صاحب الحصون ج ٢ ص ٤٥٣ فقال : كان فاضلا كاملا شاعرا بليغا أديبا معاصرا للشيخ محمد حسين ابن الشيخ محمد علي الاعسم ، وكانا خليطين وبينهما مراسلات ومكاتبات ومن شعره يشكو دهره قوله :

345

عقــــار ولكـــن قـــد تخيـــل شــاربه	وقائلــة خفــظ عليــك فمــا الهــوى
يــرى فيــه أنــواع التقلــب صاحبه	ومــا الــدهر الا منجنونــا بأهلـه
يسالمه طـورا وطـورا يحاربـه	وما من فتى في الدهر الا وقد غدا
كمــا ســيف عمــرو لـم تخنــه مضاربه	فكن رجلا ما خانه الصبر في الردى
سـفهت فـأي النـاس تـصفو مـشاربه؟	وان كنت منه طالبا صفو مشرب
يجــاوبني فيهــا الــصدى وأجاوبـه	ديـار بهـا لا انس لـي غير أنني
يجــاذبني عنـه العنـا وأجاذبـه	هجرت الحمى لا عن ملال وانما

الشيخ صافي الطريحي (توفي حدود ١٢٥٥):

ورزء بنـي الهـادي الـى الحـشر يمتد	الاكـل رزء فـي الانـام لــه حـد
ورزؤهـم غـض متـى ذكـره يبـدو	فـلا زالـت الارزاء تـأتي وتنتهـي
مـوال لـه فـي القلب قـد أخلـص الـود	وكيف مصاب السبط يسلوه مؤمن
رسـائل غـدر لـيس يحصرها عـد	أنـساه اذ وافتـه بـالزور كتبهـا
وكـل فتـى منـا لنـصرك معتـد	ان اقـدم الينـا فـالجميع مـساعد
كـأن لـم يكن مـنهم لـه سبق الوعـد	فلمـا أتـاهم ضـيعوا الحـق بينـهم
يـسير بجـد حـين لا ينفـع الجـد	تجنـب عنـهم اذ بـدا الغدر مـنهم
بـه فـرس مـا كـان أتعبـه جهـد	الى أن أتى أرض الطفوف فلم يسر

عبد المحسن الملهوف المتوفى ١٢٦٠:

وتمـــزق البيـــداء بالآســـاد	دعهـا تجـدد عهـدها بـالوادي
قـد وكلـت بالـذرع والتعـداد	بـل تـذرع الفلـوات تحـسب أنهـا

قطـع المفـاوز مـن ربـى ووهـاد	زيافـة تهـوى الـذميل وشـأنها
تهـوى شمـوس هجيرهـا الوقـاد	لا تـستطيب الظـل الا انهـا
المـاء البـرود تهـش فـي الـوراد	لا تهتـوي المرعى الخصيب ولا الـى
تعطي المفـاوز مـن وراهـا الحـادي	مـا وكلـت بـالنجم الا واغتـدت
عسـرا ولا آلـت مـن التبعـادي	مـا أنكـرت قفـرا أتتـه ولا ادعـت
أمنـت بمـسراها علـى الاجيـاد	ولعـت بقطـع البيـد حتـى أنهـا
وتجـاف للاغـوار والانجـاد	دعهـا العـراق تـؤم لا تـشأم بهـا
هـي كعبـة العـافين والوفـاد	فهنـاك مـأوى الآملـين بمربـع
والزكيـة والوصـي الهـادي	ربـع بـه جدث الحسين ونفس أحمد
مـن كـل قـرم أشـوس ذواد	مـن حولـه فئـة تقاسـمت الـردى
فيـاض مكرمـة وغـوث منـاد	مـن كـل مـن رضـعت لـه العليـا فمن
يرقـى رقـى مـن فـوق سـبع شـداد	أو كـل عـالي همـة لـو شـاء أن
لجـلاء نازلـة عـدوا بعـوادي	أسـد ضراغمـة متـى مـا استصرخوا
البتـار يـوم الـروع بالميـاد	خطبـوا الوغى مهر النفوس وزوجوا
ركـضوا بأكبـاد اليـه صـوادي	قـوم متـى وجـدوا فخـارا فـي الـردى
البلـوى وفـي الاقـدام كالآسـاد	فـي الجـو كـالانوا وكـالاطواد فـي
تـروى لنـا متـواتر الاسنـاد	حـدث ولا حـرج عليـك فانمـا
فـازوا بهـا مـن واهـب جـواد	فوبيعـة وفـوا لهـا وبنعمـة
لـم يتركـوا وغـدا مـن الاوغـاد	لـو أنهـم شـاءوا البقـاء بهـذه

347

نظـــرا ورد بدهـــشة الارعــاد	ولـو أنهـم شــاؤا القـضا مـدوا لـه
الاكـدار وارتاحـت الـى الانـداد	لكـن تجــردت النفـوس وعافـت
متقـــدما وأخيـــــرهم للبـــــادي	أفمـا علمـت استـشهدوا وتغـابطوا
بالـــسبق للجنـــــات والاخـــلاد	هـذا بقـرب العهـد للمـولى وذا
طـرأ كـــأنهم علـــى ميعـــاد	كـانوا فـرادى فـي الملا فاستـشهدوا
أنـــى وهـــم مـــن أنجبـالاولاد	فبكـــتهم العليـا بـــدمع ثاكـل
كـــل الابـــتلا لاسـنة وحــداد	وبقـى الـصبور علـى البـلا وحمـول
بـأحر أفئـــدة مـــن الحقـــاد	بالنبـل يرمـي والرمـاح وبالظبـا
بيـضا علـى هـام مـن الاشـهاد	وانـصاع يخطـب فـي الـوغى بمحجة
لـــدن ومنبـره سـنام جـواد	ورداه مــسرود الحديـــد بكفـــه
كالـسيل صـادفه غـشاء الـوادي	مـا زجـه فـي الجـيش الا واغتـدى
فـي حالـــة الاصـــدار والايـراد	ومهنـد أدنـى مواهبـه الـردى
الا بـــساحة مهجـــة وفـــؤاد	ومثقـف لـدن ولـيس مقـره
يـم خـــضم مـد بالازبـادي	يتـدفع الجـيش اللهـام كأنـه
بـل أيـن موسـى منـه يـوم جـلاد	فكأنـه موسـى ومخذمـه العـصى
هـام الكمـاة وخلـسة الاكبـاد	بطـل تولـع فـي النـزال بنهبـه
محـو المهنـدس فاسـد الاعـداد	يمحـو لـدائرة الـصفوف بـسيفه
فـوق الـتلال وفـي خفيـض وهـاد	حتـى غـدوا كالعـصف تنـسفه الـصبا
منـــه الحيـــاة وآذنـــت بنفـــاد	مـا زال هـذا دأبـه حتـى انقـضت

جلـت معانيــه عـن الاطـواد	فانهار كـالطود الاشـم علـى الثـرى
اذ مـال عـن ظهـر الجـواد العـادي	عـدم النظيـر فمـا يمثـل حالـه
أو قلـت يحيـى فاقـه بجهـاد	ان قلت موسـى حيـن خـر سمـاله
لمـا أفـاق بليـت ظـل ينـاد	هـذا اسـتكن بدوحـة حـذرا وذا
فرضـا هـوى شكـرا بغيـر تمـادي	لكنـه متبتـل لمـا قـضى
عزرائيـل يقبـض طينـة الاجسـاد	يـوم ثـوى فيـه الحـسين ويـوم
وبحـار غـوري وأذنـي بنفـاد	فـدعوت مـورى يـا جبـال تصدعي
وعليـه يـا بـدر ادرع بحـداد	يا شمس فانخفضي ويا شهـب اقلعي
هـد العمـاد وعلـة الايجـاد	وعليـه يـا سبـع الـشداد تهيلي
لا انبعثـت صـواعق عـاد	لـولا بقيتـه وخـازن علمـه السجاد
الخفـرات بعـد كفـيلهن بـواد	واسـمع بشاويـة الـضلوع مصيبة
وقعـت بوسـط حبالـة الـصياد	أضـحت كمرتـاع القطـا مـن بعدما
تهمـي الـدموع دمـا كسيـل غـوادي	قـد المصاب قلوبهـا أو مـا تـرى
ومـلاذ هيبتهـا وخيـر سنـاد	فقـدت أعزتهـا وجـل مراتهـا
لكنهـا مـن صـفرة وسـواد	لبـست مـن الارزاء أبهـى حلـة
مسجورة الاحشـاء بالايقـاد	بـأبي وبـي أم الرزايـا زينبـا
مهمـا دعـت نفثـت كسقط زنـاد	تطوي الضلوع على لظـى حراتها
يـا كـافلي قـدح المـصاب فـؤادي	تـدعو الحـسين ومـا لهـا مـن منعم
أيـن التجلـد والفقيـد عمـادي	أوهـى قـوى جلـدي فبـان تجلـدي

مـــن يـــم أحزانـــي وريـــح نكـاد	سـفن اصـطباري قـد غـرقن بزاخـر
عظمـــى تمـزق قلـب كـل جمـاد	وتعـج تهتـف فـي الـذميل بعولـة
خـف القطـين وجـف زرع الـوادي	أمؤمـل الجـدوى بـساحة ربعهـم
فاشـدد رحالـك واحـتفظ بـالزاد	يـا ضيف بيت الجـود أقفـر ربعـه
مـــن عـاكف فيهـا ولا مـن بـادي	قـد كـان كعبـة أنعـم واليـوم لا
خجـلا وخـوف شـماتة الحـساد	وترقـرق الـدمع الهتـون تـصونه
كـي تبـصر القتلـى علـى الابعـاد	فكأنهـــا نظـــرت وراء زجاجـــة
صـونا لرفـع الـصوت بالانـشاد	وتخـط فـي وجـه الفـلا ببنانهـا
عـزت عـن الاشـباه والاضـداد	يـا راكبـا كومـا تهـش الـى الـسرى
سـرالوجود ومظهـــر الارشـاد	عـرج لطيبـة قاصـدا جـدثا بـه
مـدثر بـــردى الفخـار البـادي	وقـل الـسلام عليـك مـن مزمـل
ان الحـسين رمـي بـسهم عنـاد	يـا مظهـر الاسلام جئتـك مخبـرا
وضـريبة بـل حلبـة لطـراد	خلفتـه غرضـا هنـاك ومركـزا
أمـست غنيمـة غـادر ومعـادي	والطيبـات اللائـي كنـت تحوطهـا
مـن دمعهـا والوجـد أطيـب زاد	غرثـى وعطـشى غيـر أن شـرابها
كـي تبـصر القتلـى علـى الابعـاد	فكأنهـا نظـرت وراء زجاجـة

الشيخ صالح التميمي المتوفى ١٢٦١:

وقد اقترح عليه نظم هذه القصيدة الوزير علي رضا باشا على أن تتضمن قصة مقتل الحسين (عليه السلام).

وتنزيه نفسي عن غوي وآثم	أما ان تركى موبقات الجرائم
بها لي خلاص من ذنوب عظائم	وأجعل لله العظيم وسيلة
يذود بها عقبى ندامة نادم	وأختم أيامي بتوبة تائب
فلم تغنه يوما ملامة لائم	ومن لم يلم يوما على السوء نفسه
من العفو يهمي عن غزير المكارم	على أنني مستمطر غزر صيب
منيبا ومنقاد الى خير راحم	فكم بين منقاد الى شر ظالم
ولا لطريق الرشد يوما بشائم	وان كنت ممن لا يفيء لتوبة
صحائف قد سودتها بالمحارم	سأمحو بدمعي في قتيل محرم
جديد على الايام سامي المعالم	قتيل تعفى كل رزء ورزؤه
(علي) واجرى من دم دمع (فاطم)	قتيل بكاه المصطفى وابن عمه
عبيطا فما قدر الدموع السواجم	وقل بقتيل قد بكته السما دما
حنين تحاكيه رعود الغمائم	وناحت عليه الجن حتى بدا لها
معاهد كوفان بنوء المرازم	اذا ما سقى الله البلاد فلا سقى
وما رقمت الا بسم الاراقم	أتت كتبهم في طيهن كتائب
له نكبات أقعدت كل قائم	لخير امام قام في الامر فانبرت
بياض مشيب قبل شد التمائم	اذا ذكرت للطفل حل برأسه
على قدم نم عربها والاعاجم	أن أقدم الينا يا بن أكرم من مشى

351

رجـالا كرامـا فـوق خيــل كـرائم	فكـم لـك أنـصار لـدينا وشـيعة
متـون المراسـيل الهجـان الرواسـم	فـودع مـأمون الرسـالة وامتطـي
مـصاليت حـرب مـن ذوابـة (هاشـم)	وجـشمها (نجـد) العـراق تحفـه
تكفلــن أرزاق النــسور القـشاعم	قـساورة يـوم القـراع رمـاحهم
لـدى الـروع أمـضى مـن حـدود الصـوارم	مقلــدة عـن عزمهـا بـصوارم
وأجـرى نـوالا مـن بحـور خـضارم	أشـد نـزالا مـن ليـوث ضـراغم
وأوفـى ذمامـا مـن وفـي الـذمائم	وأزهـي وجوهـا مـن بـدور كوامـل
كمــا انـه للــسلم غيـر مـسالم	يلبـون مـن للحـرب غيـر محـارب
عليـــه ابـاء الـضيم ضـربة لازم	كمـي ينحيـه عـن الـضيم معطـس
ولاحـت بهـا للغـدر بعـض الملائـم	ومد أخذت في) نينوى) منهم النوى
سـرورا ومـا ثغـر المنـون ببـاسم	غـدا ضـاحكا هـذا وذا متبـسما
الـى المـوت تعلـوه مـسرة قـادم	ومـا سـمعت أذنـي مـن النـاس ذاهبا
هنالـك شـغل شـاغل بالجمـاجم	كـأنهم يـوم) الطفـوف) وللـضبا
أشـد انقـضاضا مـن نجـوم رواجـم	أجـادل عاثـت بالبغـاث وانهـا
علـى رغبـة مـنهم حقـوق المكـارم	لقـد صـبروا صـبر الكـرام وقـد قـضوا
كأشـلاء قـيس بـين تبنـا وجاسـم	الـى أن غـدت أشـلاؤهم فـي عراصها
فريـدا وحيـدا فـي وطـيس الملاحـم	فلهفـي لمـولاي الحـسين وقـد غـدا
تجلبـبن جلبـاب البكـا والمـآتم	يـرى قومـه صـرعى وينظـر نـسوة
وأوفـى ذمامـا مـن وفـى الـذمائم	هنـاك انتـضى عضبا مـن الحزم قاطعا

352

أبـوه علـي أثبـت النـاس فـي اللقـا | كمـا انـه للسـلم غيـر مسـالم

يكـر عليـهم مثلمـا كـر حيـدر | عليـه ابـاء الـضيم ضـربة لازم

ولمـا أراد الله انفـاذ أمـره | ولاحـت بهـا للغـدر بعـض الملائـم

أتـيح لـه سـهم تبـوأ نحـره | سـرورا ومـا ثغـر المنـون بباسـم

فـلا زال قبـر بـين تبنـى وجاسـم | عليـه مـن الوسـمي جـود ووابـل

ينحن كمـا نـاح الحمـام وبالبكـا | لا غـزر شـجوا مـن نـواح الحمائـم

فيا وقعـة كـم كـدرت مـن مشـارب | لنـا مثل مـا قـد رنقـت مـن مطاعم

بني المصطفى ما عشت أو دمت سالما | فـصبري علـى مـا نـابكم غيـر سالـم

لكـي لا تـزول الارض عـن مستقرها | والا فـأنتم فـوق هـام النعـائم

فلـو أن لـي حـظ عظـيم تقـدمت | حيـاتي بعـصر سـالف متقـادم

وصـلت علـى أعـدائكم بفـوارس | أشـداء فـي الهيجـاء مـن آل (دارم)

وان فات نـصر السـيف سـوف أعينكم | بـنظم كبـا مـن دونـه نظـم نـاظم

ومـا صـالح ان لـم تعينـوه صـالح | ومـا عـد الا مـن بغـاة المظـالم

علـيكم سـلام الله مـا هبـت الـصبا | ومـا حـرك الاغـصان مـر النسـائم

وللشيخ صالح التميمي :

مـا بـال جفنـي مغـرم بـسهاده | وغزيـر دمعـي لـم أفـز بنفـاده

لا فـي سعاد صبا فـؤادي فـي الـصبا | فـأقول قلبـي قـد لهـا بـسعاده

كـلا ولا أطـلال برقـة منشـد | برقـت مـدى الايـام فـي انشـاده

353

سلبت بسيف الحزن طيب رقاده	لكن مصارع فتية في كربلا
أسد سعى للموت في آساده	قتلى وفيهم من دؤابة (هاشم)
قدما وريع الدين في أطواده	يا للرجال لطود) أحمد) مذ ثوى
أبنائها والطهر في أولاده	يا للرجال لنكبة(الزهراء) في
يندبنه ويلذن في(سجاده)	أبكي القتيل أم النساء حواسرا
والبر قد غص الفضا بصعاده	أم أندب) العباس) لما أن مضى
بيض كساها فيلق بسواده	يبغي الوصول الى الفرات ودونها
همم سمت للمجد فوق مراده	فأتى دوين الماء فاعتاق الردى
ضمأ ونار الوجد ملء فؤاده	أبكي لمقطوع اليدين وقد قضى
يا عمتا كهفي هوى بعماده	ألذاك أبكي أم) سكينة) اذ دعت
عزمت له ما سل من أبراده	هذا أبي ملقى وأذيال الصبا
متحكم والهم من أوتاده	يا آل بيت محمد حزني لكم
بقبول ما قصرت في انشاده	أنا (صالح) ان أنتم أنعمتم

وله أيضا :

نهضت لشكر هم بعد القعود	ألا من مبلغ الشهداء أني
صبا لطلاق كاعبة النهود	رجال طلقوا الدنيا ومن ذا
غداة الطف من طعم الخلود	رأوا خمر الفناء الذ طعما
يشيب لذكره رأس الوليد	دعاهم نجل فاطمة بيوم
لظى من دونها ذات الوقود	دعاهم دعوة والحرب شبت

354

عراة الـذات مـن شـيم العبيد	فقـل مـن سـيد نـادى عبيـدا
رمـت ظفـرا ونابـا بالاسـود	أسـود بالهيـاج اذا المنايـا
لـصدق الطعـن أوفـوا بـالعقود	كـأن رمـاحهم تتلـو اليـهم
كمـا يـصبى الـى هـز القـدود	اذا مـا هـز عـسال تـصابوا
تجنـب حـزمهم نقـض العهـود	بنفـسي والـورى أفـدي كرامـا
مجـزرة علـى حـر الـصعيد	بنفـسي والـورى أفـدي جـسوما
تـشال علـى الرمـاح الـى (يزيـد)	بنفـسي والـورى أفـدي رؤوسـا
وريـح المـوت يلعـب بـالبنود	كـأني يـابن) عوسـجة) ينـادي
ولا كعنـاقكم بـيض الخـدود	هلمـوا عـانقوا بـيض المواضـي
فتـى يهـوى مـصافحة الحديـد	فلـيس يـصافح الحـوراء الا
ففـازوا منـه فـي يـوم سـعيد	رأوا فـي كـربلا يومـا مـشوما
لهـم عقبـاه فـي عـيش رغيـد	وكـدر عيـشهم حـرب فجـادت
نفـي عـن نـاظري طيـب الهجـود	ألا يـا سـادتي حزنـي علـيكم
فكـان جوابهـا هـل مـن مزيـد	أحـاذر أن يقـال هـل امتلأتـي
لـه شـفعاء فـي يـوم الخلـود	أعيـذوا (صالحا) منهـا وكونـوا
وفـزتم بالهنـا وقـت الـورود	منعـتم مـن ورد المـاء قـسرا

*****

ابو سعيد الشيخ صالح بن درويش بن علي بن محمد حسين ابن زين العابدين الكاظمي النجفي الحلي البغدادي المعروف بالشيخ صالح التميمي، الشاعر المشهور، ولد في

355

الكاظمية سنة ١٢١٨ وتوفي ببغداد لاربع عشرة ليلة بقيت من شعبان بعد الظهر سنة ١٢٦١ ودفن في الكاظمية . كان من بيت علم وأدب، ربي في حجر جده الشيخ علي الزيني الشهير في مطارحاته مع السيد بحر العلوم وغيره في النجف. انتقل مع جده من الكاظمية الى النجف فأقام برهة ثم سكن الحلة وبقي بها مدة حتى استقدمه والي بغداد داود باشا. أقول : هو في عصره كأبي تمام في عصره. وقد تولى رئاسة ديوان الانشاء في بغداد سنة ١٢٣٥ ، وله شعر كثير مدح به الامراء والاعيان والزعماء وله مؤلفات ذكرت بأسمائها وفي ديوانه المطبوع عدة مراسلات ومساجلات ، ورثاه العالم الشيخ ابراهيم صادق العاملي والشيخ عبد الحسين محي الدين وعبد الباقي العمري وأعقب ولدين : محمد سعيد ومحمد كاظم. وكتب عنه الدكتور محمد مهدي البصير في (نهضة العراق الادبية في القرن التاسع عشر) وجمع له مساجلاته ونوادره.

وقال عنه : أما صفاته فانها من أجمل ما وأفضل ما يتحلى به انسان ـ كان رحمه‌الله خفيف الطبع عذب الروح حلو المعاشرة حاضر النكتة غزير الحفظ واسع الرواية قيل له : كم تحفظ من بدائع الشعر وروائعه فأجاب : لو لا أن شيخي أبا تمام جمع محاسن الجاهليين والاسلاميين في حماسته المشهورة لجمعت أنا لكم من حفظي هذه الحماسة. وكان يجل أبا تمام كثيرا ويعجب به اعجابا شديدا ويعده اماما له ، والغريب انه رثاه على بعد ما بينهما من الزمن بقصيدة بليغة يقول فيها:

لـم يتـرك الوخـد لهـا مـن سـنام	يـا راكبـا وجنـاء عيديـة
وأبلـغ أبـا تمـام عنـي السـلام	ان جئت للحدباء قـف لـي بها
سـام القـوافي الغـر مـن نسـل سـام	وقـل لـه بـشراك يـا خيـر مـن
بالخلـد هاتيـك العظـام العظـام	فـضلك أحيـاك كـأن لـم تبـت

ومن غرر الشعر قصيدته في الامام أمير المؤمنين علي عليه السلام وهذا المقطع الاول منها :

ليـت شعـري مـا تـصنع الـشعراء	غايـة المـدح فـي علاك ابتـداء
وأميـر ان عـدت الامـراء	يـا أخـا المصطفى وخير ابـن عـم
ومعاليـك مـا لهـن انتهـاء	مـا نـرى مـا استطال الا تنـاهى
مـن نواحيـه أشـرقت أجـزاء	فلـك دائـر اذا غـاب جـزء
مـن غمـام الا عـراه انجـلاء	أو كبـدر مـا يعتريـه خفـاء

356

يحذر البحر صولة الجزر لكن   غارة المد غارة شعواء

ربما عالج من الرمل يحصى   لم يضق في رماله الاحصاء

يا صراطا الى الهدى مستقيما   وبه جاء للصدور الشفاء

بني الدين فاستقام ولولا   ضرب ماضيك ما استقام البناء

أنت للحق سلم ما لراق   يتأتى بغيره الارتقاء

معدن الناس كلها الارض لكن   أنت من جوهر وهم حصباء

شبه الشكل ليس يقضي التساوي   انما في الحقائق الاستواء

شرف الله فيك صلبا فصلبا   أزكياء نمتهم أزكياء

فكأن الاصلاب كانت بروجا   ومن الشمس عمهن البهاء

لم تلد هاشمية هاشميا   كعلي وكلهم نجباء

وضعته ببطن أول بيت   ذاك بيت بفخره الاكتفاء

أمر الناس بالمودة لكن   منهم أحسنوا ومنهم أساؤا

يا ابن عم النبي ليس ودادي   بوداد يكون فيه الرياء

فالورى فيك بين غال وقال   وموال وذو الصواب الولاء

وولائي ان بحت فيه بشيء   فبنفسي تخلفت أشياء

أتقي ملحدا وأخشى عدوا   يتمارى ومذهبي الاتقاء

وفرارا من نسبة لغلو   انما الكفر والغلو سواء

ذا مبيت الفراش يوم قريش   كفراش وانت فيه ضياء

فكأني أرى الصناديد منهم   وبايديهم سيوف ظماء

ء طهـــور لـــو غيرتـــه الـــدماء	صاديات الــى دم هــو للمـــا
ولديــه احرارهـــا ادعيـــاء	دم مــن ســاد فــي الانـــام جميعـــا
ولـــديهم قـــد اســتبان الخطـــاء	قصـرت مـذرأوك مـنهم خطـاهم
قصرت عـن بلوغـه الاتقيـاء	شـكر الله منـك سـعيا عظيمـا
وبــذات الفقـــار زال العمـــاء	عميت أعيـن عـن الرشـد مـنهم
منــك قـد حـل فـي يغـوث القضاء	يستغيثون فــي يغـوث الــى ان
فيــه طـول وريحـه نكبـاء	لـك طـول علـى قـريش بيـوم
أشـنع الاسـر أنهـم طلقـاء	كـم رجـال اطلقـتهم بعـد أسـر
بعـد بـدر لوقـال هـذا ادعـاء	يـردع الخـصم شـاهدان حنـين
هـو فـي الـدهر رايـة ولـواء	ان يـوم النفيـر والعيـر يـوم
لفنـاء عـدا عليـه الفنـاء	سـل وليـدا وعتبـة مـا دعـاهم

*****

السيد صدر الدين العاملي المتوفي ١٢٦٣ :

قال بمناسبة مولد الامام الحسين عليه السلام في الثالث من شهر شعبان :

فمـن بينهـا يمنـه الاشـهر	فـدت شـهر شـعبانها الاشـهر
أيــاد لعمـرك لا تنكـر	لثالثـه فـي رقـاب الانـام
ذنـوب العبـاد بـه تغفـر	وبـاب النجـاة الامـام الـذي
جنـي هـدايتها يثمـر	وغـصن الامامـة فيـه سـما

358

سني ومـن نـوره مزهر	وروض النبـوة مـن نـوره
لهـم طـاب فـي حبـه عنصر	لـتهن بمـيلاده شـيعة
فمـا زال عـن ريهـا يـصدر	غـذاه النبـي بابهامـه
مقامـا بـه فـي الـسما يـذكر	بـه الله رد علـى (فطـرس)
شـفيع الخلايـق اذ تحـشر	أكـان مـن النصف مثل الحـسين
ثلاثـا علـى التـرب لا يقبر	ومـن هـو ريحـان قلب النبي
بأسـيافهم جهـرة ينحـر	تعـادى عليـه جمـوع ابـن هند
وفـي قتلـه حـرب تستبـشر	بمـيلاده بـشر المـصطفى
وكـان بتـسكيته يـأمر	ومـا زال يؤلمـه ان بكـى
وفـي التـرب خديـه قـد عفـروا	فكيـف اذا مـا رآه لقـى
ويـدعو النصـير فـلا ينـصر	بنفسـي الـذي يـستغيث العـداة

السيد محمد ابن السيد صالح بن ابراهيم بن زين العابدين الموسوي ، المعروف بصدر الدين العاملي والمشتهر بهذا اللقب. عالم كبير وشاعر أديب. ولد في قرية جبشيت ٢١ ذي القعدة الحرام ١١٩٣ وجاء مع ابيه للعراق عام ١١٩٧ فعنى بتربيته ، والذكاء طافح عليه فقد كتب حاشية القطر وعمره سبع سنوات كذا ذكر البحاثة الطهراني في (الكرام البررة). وذكره صاحب الحصون ج ٩ ص ٣٣٦ فقال :

كان فاضلا عالما فقيها اصوليا محدثا متكلما ، له اليد الطولى في العلوم العقلية والنقلية حسن التقرير والتعبير ، اديبا شاعرا ، هاجر مع ابيه من جبل عامل في واقعة احمد باشا الجزار الى العراق وسكن النجف وتلمذ وتخرج على يد الشيخ جعفر كاشف الغطاء ، وصار صهره على ابنته ، ثم هاجر بعد موت استاذه الى أصفهان ومكث فيها برهة من الزمان ثم رجع الى النجف. وتوفي بالنجف ليلة الجمعة رابع عشر شهر المحرم سنة ١٢٦٣ ودفن في حجرة من حجر الصحن الشريف مما يلي الرأس يمين القبلة وخلف ثلاثة أولاد وعدة بنات وله جملة من المؤلفات منها كتاب كبير في الفقه ، وكتاب القسطاس المستقيم في الاصول ، وكتاب المستطرفات ، ومنظومة لـه في الرضاع ، وكتاب في النحو ورسالة في حجية الظن ورسالة في مسألة ذي الرأسين ، ورسالة في

شرح مقبولة عمر بن حنظلة وله شعر كثير في العرفانيات ومدائح اهل البيت صلوات الله عليهم ومراثيهم فمن ذلك قوله في الامام امير المؤمنين :

علــي بـشطر صفـات الالــه	حبيـــت وفيــك يـدور الفلــك
فلـــولا الغلــو لكنـت اقـول	جميـــع صـفـات المهـيمن لــك
ولمــا أراد الآلــــه المثـــال	لنفــي المثيـــل لـــه مثلــك
فمـن عــالم الـذر قبل الوجـود	لقــول بلـــى الله قـد أهلـك
وقـد كنـت علـة خلـق الـورى	مـن الجـن والانـس حتـى الملـك
وعلمـت جبريـل رد الجـواب	ولــولاك فـــي بحــر قهــر هلـك

وذكره النقدي في (الروض النضير) فقال : كان من أعاظم علماء اواسط القرن الثالث عشر ، وكانت له الجامعية في علوم شتى والنصيب الوافر في الادب وله شعر لطيف ، وذكره الشيخ الطهراني في (الكرام البررة) نقلا عن (التكملة) للسيد الصدر فقال : كان من اعيان الفقهاء والمجتهدين تلميذ الشيخ الاكبر وصهره ، ووالده السيد صالح كان صهر الشيخ علي ابن الشيخ محي الدين بن علي بن محمد بن الحسن بن زين الدين الشهيد الثاني ، رزقه الله من بنت الشيخ علي ، صاحب الترجمة واخيه السيد محمد علي. وذكره الحجة كاشف الغطاء محمد الحسين فقال : كان السيد الصدر جامعا لجميع الكمالات خصوصا كمال الادب الذي هو من اللازمات ، وقد كانت له فيها القدم الراسخة والنخوة الشامخة والسليقة العربية والنكات العجمية. ترجم له صاحب شعراء الغري وقال : له شعر كثير ولكنه تلف.

واليك قوله من قصيدته يمدح بها الامام امير المؤمنين علي بن ابي طالب:

جـاءت تجـوب البيــد سيارة	تهـــوي هـوي المرمـل الـصارخ
الـى علـي وزعيـم العلـى	يـوم الـوغى والعلـم الـشامخ
الـى الـسراة الانجبيـن الاولـى	أحصوا فنـون الـشرف البـاذخ
أولـى المزايـا الغـر أعباؤهـا	ينــوء فيهـا قلـم الناسـخ
قـد أيقنـوا منـه بجـزل الخطـى	ان عليـا لـيس بالراضـخ

السيد حيدر العطار المتوفى ١٢٦٥:

أمـيـم ذريـنـي والبـكـاء فـانني / عـن العـيـد واللـبس الجـديـد بمعـزل

أمـيـم أقلـي عـن ملامـك واتركـي / مقالـة لا تهـلـك أسـى وتجمـل

لان سـرك العـيـد الـذي فيه زينـة / لـبعض انـاس مـن ثيـاب ومـن حلـي

فقد عـاد لـي العـيـد الحـداد بعـودة / ألا فاعـذريـني يـا أمـيـم أو اعـذلـي

يـذكرني فعـل ابن هنـد وحزبـه / يزيد وقد أنسى الـورى فعـل هـر قـل

فكـم قـد أطلـوا مـن دم بمحـرم / وكـم حللـوا مـا لـم يكـن بمحـلل

ولـم يقتنعوا حتى أصابوا ابن فـاطم / بسهم أصاب الـدين فـانقض مـن عـل

وخـر علـى حـر الثـرى متبتـلا / الـى ربـه أفديـه مـن متبتـل

ومـذ كـان للايجـاد في الخلـق علـة / بكتـه البرايـا آخـرا بعـد أول

وخـضبت السـبع السمـوات وجهها / بقاني دم مـن نحـره المتسلسل

وذا العالـم العلـوي زلـزل اذا قـضى / كمـا العـالـم السـفلي أي تزلـزل

بنفسي وبي ملقى ثلاثا على الثرى / تهـب عليـه مـن جنـوب وشمـال

أبـى رأسـه الا العـلـى فـسما علـى / ذرى ذابـل يسمو علـى هـام يـذبل

بنفسـي أبـاة الـضيم مـن آل هاشـم / تـؤم الـوغى مـا بـين لـدن وفيصل

أداروا على قطب الفنـاء رحى القضا / فخاضـوا المنايـا أمـثلا اثـر أمثل

فبـين طـريح في الـصعيد مجـدل / وبـين ذبـيـح بالـدماء مزمـل

ونادبـة تـدعو أبـا الفـضل تـارة / وأخـرى حسينا نـدب ولهاء معـول

أخـي يـا حسينا كنت غوثـا وعصمة / كمـا كنـت غيثـا ثـر في كـل ممحـل

361

كمـــا كنــت للـوراد أعـذب منهـــل	أخـي كنـت للـرواد أخصـب مربـع
قفـا نبـك مـن ذكـرى حبيـب ومنـزل	خليلــي بيـت الـوحي شـط حبيبـه
وليـس لهـا الا أبـو حـسن علـي	ومـا قـد جـرى فـي كـربلاء قـضية

السيد حيدر ابن السيد ابراهيم العطار الحسني آية من آيات الدهر ومفخرة من مفاخر العصـر ، عـالم محقـق ، وفقيـه بـارع ، لـسان الحكمـاء والمتكلمين وصفوة الفقهاء والاصوليين ، وهو على جانب عظيم من الـورع والتقـوى والزهد والعبادة ورسوخ الايمان وطهارة القلب.

خلف آثارا قيمة وكتب عنه الكثير وأثنى عليه العلماء أحسن الثناء ، وممن ذكره شيخنا المحقق الطهراني في كتابه (سعداء النفوس) فقال : كان سيدا عالما فقيها جليلا مرجعا للخاص والعام ، غيورا في ذات الله مناظرا مع المبدعين والمخالفين.
وهو أعلى الله مقامه جد الاسرة الحيدرية واليه تنتسب هذه السلالة العلويـة ، ولـد رحمه‌الله سنة ١٢٠٥ هـ وأقام في الكاظمية ردحا من الزمن ، ثم هاجر الى عاصمة العلم ـ النجف الاشرف ـ

وتتلمذ على أعلام زمانه وجهابذة عصره حتى حصل على رتبة عاليـة ودرجـة رفيعـة في العلم والاجتهاد كما استفاد منه جملة من أعلام الفضل ، أما مؤلفاته فهي آية في التحقيق والتدقيق وكلها تنطق بعلمه وكماله نذكر منها ما يلي:

١ ـ البارقة الحيدرية في نقض ما أبرمته الكشفية.
٢ ـ العقائد الحيدرية في الحكمة النبوية.
٣ ـ المجالس الحيدرية في النهضة الحسينية كتبه بخطه سنة ١٢٦٠ هجرية)١.(
٤ ـ الصحيفـة الحيدريـة فـي الادعيـة والاسـرار ، صنفها بطلـب مـن محمد علـي شـاه القاجاري سلطان ايران.
٥ ـ النفخ القدسية في بعض المسائل الكلامية ، صنفها تلبية لطلب (هولاكوا ميرزا) حفيد فتح علي شاه القاجاري.
٦ ـ النفخة القدسية الثانية وهي في مباحث كلامية.
٧ ـ مجموعة في الحكم والنوادر.
٨ ـ رسالة في أصول الفقه.
٩ ـ كتاب في المنطق.
١٠ ـ حاشية على كتاب التحقيق في الفقه والاصول لعمـه آيـة الله الكبرى السيد أحمد البغدادي الشهير بالعطار.

---

١ ـ مخطوط في حيازة الدكتور حسين محفوظ نسخة منه.

١١ـ تعليقه على منظومة في الرجال لعمه أيضا. وكل هذه المؤلفات مخطوطة وتوجد متفرقة عند ذريته.

١٢ـ عمدة الزائر في الادعية والزيارات ، وقد طبع مرتين في النجف الاشرف.

توفي أعلى الله مقامه سنة ١٢٦٥ هـ وقيل أنه أخبر بأجله قبل حلوله. ودفن في رواق الحرم الكاظمي الشريف وأعقب سبعة من الاولاد كلهم علماء صلحاء أبرار أتقياء. ومن شعره في الامام الحسين:

ولا بوركـت أيـام عـشرك فـي الـدهر	محـرم لا أهـلا بوجهـك مـن شـهر
خطوبـا ورامـيهم بقاصـمة الظهـر	لانت المشوم المستطير على الورى
بـه غـرق الاسـلام فـي لجـة الكفـر	ولا سـيما عاشـور مـن عشرك الـذي
تذوق الـردى ظلمـا بحـرب بنـي صخـر	غـداة رجـال الله آل محمـد
وحيدا وقـد دارت بـه عـصبة الغدر	فان أنـسى لا أنـسى الحسين بكربلا
تطـاير أفـراخ البغـاث مـن الـصقر	فمـا شـد نحـو القـوم ألا تطـايروا
فخـر صـريعا لليـدين وللنحـر	فوافـاه سـهم خـارق فـي فـؤاده
على الله واستهزا بـشأن أولـي الامـر	ولا عجـب مـن مثـل شمر اذا اجترى
ولا سـيما كعـب بـن مـرة والنـضر	ومـيز رأسـا سـاد للعـرب مفخـرا
وقـد قتـل التكبير مـن حيـث لا يـدري	وشـال بـه فـوق الـسنان مكبـرا
بنـي أحمـد مـا ذنـب أحمـد مـن صخـر	عذيري من صخر بن حرب وحربهم
لمكـة فـي أهليـه بالقتـل والاسـر	جـزوه علـى اطلاقهـم يـوم فتحـه
سـوافر مـن فـوق الجمـال بـلا ستر	عـن الـسبي للنـسوان يبكـين حـسرا
أأنـت علـيم اننـا اليـوم فـي الاسـر	ينـادين يـا جـداه يـا خير مرسـل
تريبـا خـضيبا شيبه بـدم النحـر	لقـد تركـوا سبط النبي على الثـرى

363

فـــإذا رأســـه فـــوق الـــسنان كأنـــه   ســنا الـبـدر أو أبهــى ســناء مــن الـبـدر

السيد جعفر القزويني المتوفى ١٢٦٥:

السيد جعفر بن الباقر بن احمد بن محمد الحسيني القزويني من مشاهير شعراء وأدباء عصره. ولد في النجف الاشرف ونشأ بها نشأة عالية وأخذ معلوماته عن مشاهير عصره وما اجتاز العقد الثاني حتى أصبح علما يشار اليه بالبنان ، ذكر صاحب الحصون ج ٢ / ٥٥٧ فقال : كان فاضلا كاملا أديبا لبيبا بليغا شاعرا ماهرا جوادا سخيا ذا همة عالية تخصص للنظم والمسلاجلات الادبية الى أن نبا به الدهر الخؤون وتراكمت عليه الديون فلم يسعه المكث في النجف ـ مسقط رأسه ـ فارتحل الى (مسقط) عاصمة عمان، وكان معه عبده المسمى (نصيب)، فأدركته منيته هناك فمات فيها سنة ١٢٦٥ هـ فحملت جنازته الى النجف مع عبده نصيب فدفن مع آبائه في مقبرتهم مقابل مقبرة آل الجواهر فرثاه فريق من الشعراء منهم السيد حيدر الحلي بقصيدة مطلعها:

وتــدفن رضـــوى بـــبطن اللحـــود   كـــذا يلــج المــوت غــاب الاســود

وممن رثاه وأرخ وفاته الشيخ ابراهيم قفطان.

قال السيد الامين في الاعيان: رأينا في مجلة الحضارة نقلا عن بعض مجاميع الفاضل الشبيبي انه كان أديبا نابها من أدباء العراق رحل الى مسقط وتوفي هناك بعيدا عن وطنه ، ولرحلته قصة مثيرة وقد استوحاها كل من رثاه ثم ذكر أن من مراثيه قصيدة من بحر يسمى المحدث وانها رويت في بعض مجاميع النجف للشيخ ابراهيم قفطان وفي بعضها للشيخ محسن آل الشيخ خضر ، وهذا ما وجد منها :

فـي الــدار فلـم أعـرف أثـرا	صـــوبت وصـــعدت النظـــرا
أمـــست عبـــرا لمـــن اعتبـــرا	ولميـــة أطـــلال درســـت
نـالوا دهـرا منهـا وطـرا	أبكـــي وأناشـــدها عمـــن
فتجيـب قطينـك أيـن سـرى	يـا دار قطينـك أيـن سـرى
الا الارزاء بهـا زمـرا	خـشعت للبـين فلـست تـرى
ألــوى وتحققـت الخبـرا	فعلمـــت بـــأن مؤملهـــا
وهيـت قـوى وفـصمت عـرى	يـا مـرتحلا عنـي ولكـم

364

ولـيس يــرى مــنهم أثــرا	ومدير الطرف الــى أهليــه
داء فـي أحشـاك اسـتعرا	يـا مسعر دائـي مـن داوى
ولـو اثاقلت لمـا ظفـرا	أجـل نـاداك لمـسقطه
لـم لا سـليتك مفتكـرا	لـم لا واسـيتك مـضطهدا
منصدعا للغربة منكسـرا	لـم لا جـاورت أنينــك
لـم لا شـاهدتك محتـضرا	لـم لا عالجتـك معتـلا
وحساما فـي الهيجا ذكـرا	وامامـا فـاق بلاغتـه
يبـث مراثيـك الغـررا	لك عهد فـي عنقي مـا عشت
عقيقــا أحمــر أو دررا	وثـراك ترصعـه عينـاي

ولم يعقب سوى ولده السيد علي وابنته زوجة الميرزا جعفر القزويني وذكر صاحب الحصون جملة من شعره كما ذكره الشيخ المصلح الشيخ محمد حسين كاشف الغطاء في (العبقات العنبرية في شعراء الجعفرية).

ويحق أن أستشهد بالشعر المنسوب للامام زين العابدين علي ابن الحسين ابن علي بن أبي طالب عليهمالسلام حيث يقول:

أكابـد همـا بؤسـه لـيس ينجلي	عتبت علـى الـدنيا فقلت الـى متى
يكون عليـه الـرزق غير محلل	أكل شـريف مـن علـي نجـاره
بسهم عنـاد يـوم طلقنـي علي	فقالت نعـم يـا بن الحسـين رميتكم

محمد الصحاف: كان حيا سنة ١٢٧٠:

وطرس بـه من حسن أوصافكم سطر	بمـدحكم الاقـلام تفـرح والحبـر
تفوز بكـم اذ كان منكم لـها فخر	يفـوز سـواكم بـالقوافي وانهـا

365

لانــي اذا أحييتهــا يرفـع القــدر	فليلــة قــدر ليلتــي بمــديحكم
سليل حسيـن زانـه منكـم النجـر	أنـا ألقـن آل الرسـول محمـد
بـدا فـي ريـاض زاد نوارهـا القطـر	عليكم صـلاة الله مـا نـار نيـر

السيد محمد بن علي المعروف بالصحاف. ذكره المحقق الطهراني في (الكرام البررة) فقال : نزيل سوق الشيوخ ، كان أديبا فاضلا شاعرا ، رأيت تقريضه اللطيف البليغ نظما ونثرا على ارجوزة (تحفة النساك) من نظم الشيخ طاهر الحجامي المتوفى بسوق الشيوخ سنة ١٢٧٩ هـ وأولاده الى اليوم في سوق الشيوخ.

عبد العزيز الجشي: وفاته ١٢٧٠:

وهل للــدموع الجاريــات جمودُ؟	ألا هــل لاجفــان سهرن هجــودُ؟
فأوحشني بعــد الفــراق يعــود	وهل راحل شطت بـه غربة النـوى
عشاء وأنتـم بالهنـاء رقـود	أسهر ليلـي أرقـب النـجم فـيكم
مقامـا بــه سـبط النبـي فريـد	وذكرنـي يـوم انفـرادي بينـهم
فـديت ولـو بالعالميـن أجـود	ألا بـأبي أفديـه فـردا وقـل مـا
وللــسمر منــه صــادر وورود	فوالهـف نفسـي للقتيـل علـى ظما
سـموت بهــم فليهـنكن سـعود	فيا عرصـات الطـف أي أماجـد
فـأنتن فـيكن الحسـين شهيد	لـئن شـرفت أم القـرى بـالتي حـوت
ففـيكن أبنـاء وتلـك جـدود	وان طـاولتكن المدينـة مفخـرا
تـساوى قريـب عنـدها وبعيـد	فيا راكبا عيديـة شـأت الـصبا
زرودا وان ألـوت هنـاك زرود	عـداك البـلا ، عـج هكـذا متنكبـا
علـى الـرغم رايـات لكـم وبنـود	بنـي هاشـم يـا للحفيظـة نكست

366

ففر طليق بعدها وطريد	رمتكم كما شاء القضاء أمية
من الرعب أوغاد لها وحقود	وثارت عليكم بعد أن طال مكثها
فقد عز موجود وعز وجود	ودع عنك نجوى أهل مكة وارتحل
مشيحا ففيها عدة وعديد	ووجه لتلقاء المدينة وجهها
حسين عن الورد المباح مذود	ولذ بضريح المصطفى قائلا له
وآلـك في أرض الطفوف رقود	ألا يا رسول الله ما لك راقدا
تكاد لها شم الرعان تميد	فخذها كما شاء الحزين شكاية
العليل فأودى بالعليل قيود	عشية ساقوهن أسرى وقيدوا
فأعواده حيث التنشق عود	وقبل ثرى أعواد أحمد وارتحل
لذا سيرها الوجاف فهي صمود	ودعها على علاتها مستطيرة
على جدث فيه الوصي وصيد	لعلي أراها بالغري مناخة
اذا اقترعت تحت العجاجة صيد	أبا حسن أنت المثير عجاجها
على الدين حتى بات وهو عميد	أغارت بقايا عبد شمس ونوفل
ضواربه يوم القراع جنود	فيا هل تراها ان سيفك فللت
ببدر وأحد عتبة ووليد	وان الفتى القراض حطم صدره
رأت كيف تبدي حكمها وتعيد	فلو كنت حيا يوم وقعة كربلا
وسايدها صلد بها وصعيد	عشية باتت من بنيك عصابة
على بلذات التنعم عيد	لقى كأضاحي العيد لا عاد بعدهم
يلاحظها حسرى القناع يزيد	أترضى وانت الثاقب العزم غيرة

367

| بمعشـار عـشر الفعـل منـك ثمـود | أميـة كـم هـذا الغـرور فمـا أتـى |
| الرضيـع فايعـاد بـه ووعيـد | وراءكـم يـوم يـشيب لهولـه |

قال صاحب أنوار البدرين : الشيخ عبد العزيز الجشي من شعراء القطيف الاديب الشاعر الشيخ عبد العزيز بن الحاج مهدي بن حسن بن يوسف بن محمد الجشي قدسـسره البحراني القطيفي. كان له رحمه الله تعالى من الادب الحظ الوافر ومن الشعر والمعرفة النصيب الكامل له قصائد جيدة منها في رثاء الحسين (ع) تقرأ في المجالس الحسينية وله منظومة في الرد على النصارى ذكر فيها ما ذكره الشيخ سليمان آل عبد الجبار ومتضمنة للادلة التي ذكرها في الرد على النصارى جيدة حسنة وقد اشتغل في العلوم الا ان الشعر والتجارة غلبا عليه فكان بهما موسوما ولم أعلم بتاريخ وفاته ضاعف الله حسناته. انتهى. ويقول الشيخ علي منصور في شعراء القطيف : كانت وفاته سنة ١٢٧٠.

أقول وترجم له الشيخ الطهراني في (الكرام البررة في القرن الثالث بعد العشرة) وسماه بـ (السيد عبدالعزيز) وهو خطأ مطبعي.

السيد محمد ابو الفلفل

لهـم علـى الجيـش اللهـام زئيـر	وذوو المـروة والوفـا أنصـاره
فعناصـر طابـت لهـم وحجـور	طهـرت نفوسـهم لطيـب أصـولها
للنفـع لكـن أمـضي المقـدور	عشقوا العنا للدفـع لا عشقوا الغنا
لـو لا تمثلـت القصـور ــ قصور	فتمثلـت لهـم القصـور ومـا بهـم ــ
رحمـن لا ولـدانها والحـور	مـا شـاقهم للمـوت الا دعـوة الـ
والخيـل تـردى والعجـاج يثـور	بـذلوا النفـوس لنصره حتـى قضوا
ر الحـروب وعزمـه مـسجور	فغـدا ربيب المكرمـات يـشق تيا
غيـر الارامـل والعليـل نـصير	يـدعو ألا أيـن النـصير ومـا لـه
وعقائـل ومقاتـل وعفيـر	والكـل يـدعو يـا حسين فصبية

368

قال البحاثة المعاصر الشيخ علي منصور المرهون في كتابه (شعراء القطيف) السيد محمد الفلفل المتوفى سنة ١٢٦١ تقريبا. هو السيد الشريف السيد محمد بن السيد مال الله ابن السيد محمد المعروف بـ) الفلفل) أحد أهالي قرية (التوبي) من القطيف ، نزيل كربلاء من المعاصرين للسيد كاظم الرشتي ومن المقربين اليه ، ذكره صاحب الدمعة الساكبة وأثبت له القصيدة الهائية التي أولها (خلها تدمي من السير يداها) .

من شعر السيد محمد بن مال الله الملقب بالفلفل المتوفى ١٢٦١ ويقول صاحب الذريعة ان وفاته سنة ١٢٧٧ .

ذهب الشباب وأنتِ لم تتورع	يا نفس عن فعل الخطايا فاقلعي
غرت سواك بخدعة وتصنع	لا تخدعنك زينة الدنيا فقد
وبذكر قيصر ذي الجنود وتبع	أو ما سمعت بذكر كسرى في الورى
قذفتهم الدنيا بقبح الموضع	أين القرون وعادها وثمودها
وتمنعوا في كل حصن أمنع	أين الذين تمتعوا بنعيمها
بالظلم عن نهج الرشاد الاوسع	أين الطواغيت الذين تنكبوا
لم يستطع رد الجواب ولا يعي	كم ظالم تحت التراب وهالك
فعن القبايح والخطايا فاقلعي	يا نفس ان شئت السلامة في غد
وبآله فهم الرجا في المفزع	وتوسلي عند الاله باحمد
ان الحسين سليل فاطمة نعي	يا نفس من هذا الرقاد تنبهي
وتلهفي وتأسفي وتفجعي	فتولعي وجدا له وتوجعي
في الدين أكبر فتة لم تنزع	آه لها من وقعة قد أوقعت
بمصائب تبقى ليوم المجمع	آه لها من نكبة قد أردفت
حزنا عليه ويا جبال تصدع	قتل الحسين فيا سما ابكي دما

369

منعوه شرب المـاء لا شـربوا غدا	مـن كـف والـده البطـين الانـزع
مـذ جائهـا يبـدي الـصهيل جـواده	يـشكو الظليمـة سـاكبا للادمـع
يـا أيهـا المهـر المخضـب بالـدما	لا تقـصدن خـيم النـساء الـضيع
يـا مهـره قـف لا تحـم حـول الخبا	رفقـا بنـسوته الكـرام الهلـع
انـي أخـاف بـأن تـروع قلوبهـا	وهـي التـي مـا عـودت بتـروع
لهفـي لتلـك النـاظرات حماتهـا	فـوق الجنـادل كـالنجوم الطلـع
والـريح سـافية علـى أبـدانهم	فمقطـع ثـاو بجنـب مبـضع
ولزينـب نوحـا لفقـد شـقيقها	وتقـول يـا ابـن الزاكيـات الركـع
اليـوم أصبـغ فـي عـزاك ملابـسي	سـودا وأسـكب هـاطلات الادمـع
اليـوم شبـوا نـارهم فـي منزلـي	وتنـاهبوا مـا فيـه حتـى مقنعـى
اليـوم سـاقوني بقيـدي يـا أخـي	والـضرب آلمنـي وأطفـالي معـي
لا راحـم أشـكو اليـه أذيتـي	لـم ألـف الا ظالمـا لـم يخـشع
حـال الـردى بينـي وبينـك يـا أخـي	لـو كنـت فـي الأحيـاء هالـك موضعي
مـسلوبة مـضروبة مـسحوبة	منهوبـة حتـى الخمـار وبرقعـي
وهلـم خطـب يـوم قـوض ضعنهـا	مـن كـربلا فـي نـسوة تبـدي النعـي
مـروا بهـا لتـرى أعـزة قومهـا	صـرعى تكفـنهم ريـاح الزوبـع
فـرأت أخاهـا جثـة مـن غيـر مـا	رأس فألقـت نفـسها بتلـوع
فـوق الحسين السـبط حاضنـة لـه	فنعتـه نعـي الفاقـدات الـضيع
وتقـول حـان فراق شخصك يـا أخـي	مـن ذا لثاكلـة وطفـل مرضـع

370

قلبـي وتطفـي لوعـة فـي أضـلعي	يـا كـافلي هـل نظـرة أشـفي بهـا
غسـل ويهنـى بعـد فقـدك مضجعي	أتبيـت فـي الرمـضا بـلا كفـن ولا
وذخيرتـي فـي النايبـات ومفزعـي	حاشـا وكـلا يـا كفيـل أراملـي
بـي عنـك يـا غـوثي وغـوث المربـع	يـا واحـدي عزمـوا علـى أن يرحلـوا
أجـرا دمـوعي مثـل سحـب الهمـع	ودعتـك الـرحمن يـا مـن فقـده
وعليـك تـسليمي ليـوم المرجـع	لا عـن مـلال ان رحلـت ولا قـلا
قـف بـالطفوف ولـو كنعـسة هجـع	بـالله يـا حـادي الـضعون معجـلا
أسـفا بقـان مـن غزيـر الادمـع	لأبـث أحزانـي وأكتـم مـا جـرى
قـف ساعـة ان كنـت ذا اذن تعـي	يـا سائـرا يطـوي القفـار ميممـا
لجنـاب أحمـد ذي المقـام الارفـع	وأحمـل رسالة من أضـر بـه الجـوى
بهـم الـديار بكـل واد أشـنع	قـل يـا رسـول الله آلـك قـد نـأت
وأبنتـه للنـاس فيهم مـا رعـي	مـذ غبـت والحـق الـذي أظهرتـه
مـع صحبه قـد ذبحـوا فـي موضـع	وحبيبـك الـسبط الحـسين ونـسله
وضريبة للمرهفـات اللمعـي	قـد صيـروهم للـسهام رميـة
مـسبية تـسبى كـسبي الزيلـع	وبنـات بنتـك فـي القيـود أذلـة
يـا فـاطم بمصاب نـسلك فاسمعي	واعمـد الـى قبـر البتـول ونادهـا
قـتلاك بـين مبـضع ومقطـع	قومي انزلي أرض الطفوف وشاهدي
ورؤوسـهم تهـدى لـرجس ألكـع	ثاويـن حـول حبيـب قلبـك بـالعزى
منهـا الوجـوه مـن النكـال المفضـع	ونـساءك الحـور الحـسان تغيـرت

أطواقهـا قيـد العـدى وشـرابها   مـن دمعهـا والاكـل تـرداد النعـي

واقصد أخاه فـي البقيـع وقـل لـه   ذبـح الحـسين أخـاك يـا ابن الاروع

وبنيـك والاخـوان جمعـا صـرعوا   مـن حولـه بالـذابلات الـشرع

واذا قـضيت رسـالتي مـن يثـرب   فاقـصد بـسيرك للغـري واسـرع

وأطـل وقوفـك عنـد قبـر المرتضى   والـثم ثـراه علـى وقار واخـضع

قـل يـا أميـر المـؤمنين شكاية   فاسـمع لهـا يـا شافعي ومـشفعي

هذا الحسين لقى بعرصـة نينـوى   أكفانـه مـور الريـاح الاربـع

مـن غيـر دفـن والخيـول تدوسـه   بنعالهـا فـي صـدره والاضـلع

والـريح قـد لعبـت بـشيبته وقـد   صبغت بقـان فـوق رمـح أرفـع

ونـساءه مقرونـة بقيودهـا   محمولـة فـوق الجمـال الظلـع

وأذيـة الاطفـال أعظـم محنـة   مـن جوعهـا ومن الـسرى لـم تهجع

ان حـن طفـل ساعدته ثواكـل   لـم تلـف غيـر مروعـة ومروع

والعابـد الـسجاد فـي أقيـاده   لهفـي لـه مـن ناحـل متوجـع

يـا وقعـة راعت قلـوب اولي النهـى   جلـت ونحـن بمثلها لـم نـسمع

قـد جـاءكم ذو المخزيـات محمـد   لـم يلـف غيركم لـه مـن مفزع

فتعطفـوا وترفقـوا وتلطفـوا   بمحـبكم عنـد الحـساب اذا دعـي

وعلـيكم صـلى وسلـم ربكـم   مـا نـاح ذو وجـد بقلـب موجـع

ومن شعره قصيدته التي أولها:

تعزي فـلا شـيء مـن العيش راجع   وهـل فـي صـروف الـدهر ينفع نـافع؟

372

السيد محمد معصوم المتوفى ١٢٧١:

السيد محمد بن مال الله بن معصوم القطيفي النجفي المتوفى بالحائر الحسيني سنة ١٢٧١. شطر مقصورة ابن دريد وجعلها في رثاء الحسين عليه السلام بما يقرب من أربعمائة وخمسين بيتا مدرجة في ديوانه وأولها:

مـــا لـك لا تبكـــين ســبط المـصطفى	يـا ظبيـة أشـبه شـيء بالمهـا
رايقـة بـين الغـويـر واللـوى	تمـضين بعـد مـا دعـاك ضـاميا
بـيض مواضـينا بحومـات الـوغى	أمـا تـرى رأسـي حـاكى لونـه
طـرة صـبح تحـت أذيـال الـدجى	تلـوح فـي ليـل الـوغى كأنهـا

هو السيد محمد ابن السيد مال الله آل السيد معصوم القطيفي النجفي الحائري ، خطيب معروف ، وشاعر رقيق. يظهر من سيرته أنه ولد بالقطيف وهاجر منها وهو يافع والتحق بالنجف فاتصل بأعلامه من زعماء الدين وبعد أخذه المقدمات انصرف الى سرد قصة الامام الحسين (ع). ذكره الشيخ النوري فقال : كان جليل القدر ، عظيم الشأن ، وكان شيخنا الاستاذ العلامة الشيخ عبدالحسين الطهراني كثيرا ما يذكره بخير ويثني عليه ثناء بليغا ، وقال : كان تقيا صالحا ، شاعرا مجيدا ، وأديبا قاريا غريقا في بحار محبة آل البيت (ع) وكان أكثر ذكره وفكره فيهم ، حتى انه كان كثيرا ما نلقاه في الصحن الشريف فنسأله عن مسألة أدبية فيجيبنا عنها ويستشهد في كلامه ببيت أنشأه هو أو غيره في المراثي فينقلب حاله ويشرع في ذكر مصيبتهم على أحسن ما ينبغي فيتحول المجلس الى مجلس آخر وله حكايتان طريفتان ذكرهما النوري في كتابه دار السلام.

ذكره الشيخ ابراهيم صادق العاملي في مجموعته معربا عن اعجابه بتقريظه لموشح السيد صالح القزويني البغدادي فقال : وممن لمح ذلك الموشح بطرف غير كليل ، وسبح في تيار لجته فاستخرج منها دررا هي لتاج الادب اكليل وأي اكليل ، الراغم بفضله وأدبه عرين الملك الضليل والشامخ بحسبه ونسبه على كل ذي حسب زكي ونسب جليل ، قرة عين الفضائل والعلوم ، جناب السيد السند السيد محمد نجل المرحوم السيد معصوم فقرظ عليه بهذا الموشح المحلى بفرائد الدر المنظوم ، المطوق بأسنى قلائد تزري محاسنها بدراري النجوم.

وذكره صاحب الحصون في ج ٥ ص ٥٨٢ فقال : كان مجاورا في الحائر الحسيني ، وكان تقيا صالحا ، وشاعرا مجيدا ، وأديبا وقارئا ذاكرا لعزاء الحسين ، جليل القدر عظيم الشأن ، غريقا في بحار محبة آل البيت وأكثر ذكره وفكره فيهم وكان اذا هل ربيع

الاول ينشر قصائد في مدح الرسول (ص) في المجالس ويصفق بيده أثناء الانشاد ، توفي في حدود ١٢٦٩ هـ.

وذكره النقدي في الروض النضير ص ٣٦٦ فقال : من فضلاء القرن الماضي ، وكان له في التقوى والصلاح أسمى مكان، وكان من المعمرين.

وذكره المحقق الطهراني في كتابه الكرام البررة ص ٣٦٨ فقال القطيفي الحائري المتوفى ١٢٧١ هـ كان تلميذ السيد عبدالله شبر وكتب في ترجمة أستاذه هذا رسالة مستقلة.

وذكره السيد حسن الصدر في التكملة فقال : له رسالة أسماها نوافح المسك لم أقف عليها ، وله ديوان كبير عند الشيخ محمد السماوي فيه رثاء الشيخ احمد الاحسائي والسيد كاظم الرشتي والشيخ موسى بن جعفر كاشف الغطاء والشيخ محسن خنفر الذي توفي ١٢٧٠ هـ وهذا آخر زمن رثى به.

توفي المترجم له في حدود ١٢٧١ هـ وله شعر كثير أشهره اللامية المكسورة من حروف الرجز المسماة بزهر الربيع. وديوان شعره

مخطوط اشتمل على جميع الحروف. وله روضة في رثاء الحسين. انتهى

وفي الذريعة ـ قسم الديوان قال : ديوان السيد محمد بن مال الله ابن معصوم الموسوي القطيفي الخطي الحائري المتوفى ١٢٧١ هو من تلاميذ السيد عبدالله شبر وكتب رسالة في ترجمة أستاذه. رأيت ديوانه في مكتبة السماوي كل ما فيه قصائده في المراثي ، مرتبة على الحروف ، وكتب له بعض أصحابه مقدمة. وقال السيد حسن الامين في الاعيان ج ١٦ ص ٦٩ ان الشاعر السيد محمد القطيفي المقيم في الحائر أطرى شعره وفضله على شعر غيره خصوصا مراثيه في الامام الحسين وكان في دار آل الشيخ جعفر آل الشيخ خضر الجناجي النجفي واستدل على مدعاه بقوله في الامام عليه السلام:

| وسـود الحتـوف أسـى والقطـار | بكتك الـضيوف وبـيض السـيوف |
| وضـاع المـشيرون والمستـشار | وخـاب الملمـون والوافـدون |

فقال له الشيخ جعفر وهو يومئذ حدث السنان المشير والمستشار واحد واعترضه في غير هذا البيت أيضا بأن فيه من الزحاف الكف وهو حذاف السابع الساكن من مفاعيل وهو قبيح في بحر الطويل كما ان القبض في مفاعيلن في عروض الطويل واجب ، وقد أتى القطيفي به في قصيدته غير مقبوض فانتقده بمثل هذه القواعد العروضية حتى أفحمه .

ونشر البحاثة الشيخ محمد السماوي في مجلة الغري النجفية السنة السابعة تحت عنوان (ندوة بلاغة بلاغية) قال : للعالم الفاضل الاديب السيد محمد بن السيد مال الله السيد معصوم القطيفي النجفي الحائري ديوان شعر كبير مشتمل على الحروف ، ولقد كان معمرا ومن المكثرين والمجيدين في رثاء الامام الحسين (ع) وكانت وفاته سنة ١٢٦٩

هـ وله كذلك روضة عامرة في رثاء الامام الحسين (ع). وله يمدح الامامين الجوادين عليهماالسلام وهي من أواسط شعره:

لا تعقهـــا فلقـــد شـــق مـــداها	خلهـا تـدمي مـن السـير يـداها
تلتقـي الحصبا كمـا تفلـي فلاهـا	مـا هـوت فـي الـدو الا وانثنـت
فـانبرت تحمـد بالشـوق ضنـاها	هزهـا الشـوق فأبراهـا الضنا
رضـيت متلفـة السـير غـذاها	رضـيت حـر الهـوى مـاءا كمـا
عـن هـداها وهـداها فـي عماهـا	عميت عـن كـل مـا يـشغلها
رتـه فـالتف دجاهـا بـضحاها	عكـرت رحـب الفـضا ممـا أثـا
غمـر النـاس يـدا بعـض نـداها	قـصدها الكـاظم موسـى والـذي
حيـث تحبيهـا سـلاما مـن فنـاها	قـف فدتـك النـفس واغـنم أجرهـا
طالبـا للنـفس مـا فيـه هـداها	مبلغـا جـل سـلامي لهمـا
ولمن مـن جـوده نـال عصاهـا	قـل لمـن كلـم موسـى باسـمه
زورة تطغـي عـن النـفس لظاهـا	أشـهيدي جانـب الـزوراء هـل
جـدثي قدسـكما تجلـو جلاهـا	أم لعينـي نظـرة ممـن رأى
للـشهادات فـأنتم شـهداها	لـم يـر الله أناسـا غيـركم
مثـل مـا نلـتم فـأنتم غرباهـا	بـل ولا نـال اغترابـا غيـركم
فحـسوتم بعـده كأسـا حـساها	جـدكم أعظـم قـدرا وأذى
عطر القـرآن مـن عطـر شـذاها	وسـقاكم ثـدي أخـلاق بهـا
ذي العـرش الـورى والبـدء طاهـا	يـا ذواتـا أكمـلت علـة ايجـاد
كيـف والراجـي الميـامين فتاها	مـا رجـا راج بكـم الا نجـا

375

ثـم عـج يـا مرشـد الـنفس الـى ... أرض (سـامراء (ننـشق مـن ثراهـا

واعطهـا مقودهـا حتـى تـرى ... قبـة فيهـا رجاهـا ومناهـا

فعلـى نـوري عـلا حـلا بهـا ... مـن صلـوة الله والخلـق رضـاها

والـق عنهـا حلـس وعثـاء الـسرى ... وقـل البـشرى فقـد زال عناهـا

واطلـب الحاجـات تحظـى بـالا ... جابـة فـي حـال بقاهـا وفناهـا

ثـم انهـضني فـلا قـوة لـي ... مـن همـوم أبهـضتني مـن عـداها

نحـو سرداب حـوى خـوف العـدى ... عـصمة العـالم والمعطـي رجاهـا

وامش بـي رسـلا فمـا تـدري عسـى ... الله لبـى دعـوة فـي مـشتكاها

وادخلـن بـي خاضعـا مستـشفعا ... لـي بـأن اسعد يومـا بلقاهـا

نقـرأ التـسليم منـا عـد مـا ... خلـق الله الـى يـوم جزاهـا

يـا ولـي الله والمعطـي مـدى ... أمـد الايـام اقليـد عطاهـا

والنـضير الـشاهد الحـاكم فـي الـ ... ـخلق والموصـي لـه مـن نظراهـا

قـم علـى اسـم الله أثبـت مـا بقـي ... مـن رسـوم فالعـدى رامـوا محاهـا

طهـر الارض بأجنـاد أبـت ... أن يـرى مبـدؤها أو منتهاهـا

وابـسط العـدل بعيـسى الـروح و ... الخـضر محفوفـا بـأملاك سمـاها

ان دوحـات الرجـا قـد أذنـت ... بانحـسار فمتـى خـضرا نراهـا

جـرد الـسيف لثـارات بنـي ... امـك الزهـراء واجهـد فـي رضاهـا

تلتقـي جيـش العـدى ضاحكة ... والمواضـي مـن دم طـال بكاهـا

ابلغـوا للـدفع عـن حاميـة الـ ... ـدين يوصـي الكـل كـلا بحماهـا

376

لـم يزالـوا فـي الـوغى حتـى جرى	مـن يـد الاقـدار مـا حـم قصاها

وله يرثي السيد عبد الله شبر الكاظمي المتوفى ١٢٤٢ هـ ويعزى الشيخ محمد حسن صاحب الجواهر بفقده :

أروح وفـي القلـب منـي شـجن	وأغـدو وفـي القلـب منـي احـن
ولـم يـشجني فقـد عـيش الـشباب	وليـل الـصبا ولذيـذ الوسـن
ولا هـاجني منـزل بـالحمى	ولا ذكـر غانيـة أو أغـن
ولكـن شـجتني صـروف الزمـان	بأهـل الرشـاد ولاة الـزمن
بموسـى الكلـيم بـدت بـالردى	وكـم فيـه رد الـردى والمحـن
وثنـت بمـن لـم يكـن غيـره	امامـا لـدينا يقـيم الـسنن
فـأخنى الزمـان بنجـل الرضـا	وألبـسني منـه ثـوب الحـزن
وناعيـه لمـا نعـاه الـي	أذاب الفـؤاد وأفنـى البـدن
نعـى العـالم الهاشـمي التقـي	نعـى مـن لـه الفـضل فـي كـل فـن
فـلا غـرو أن بكـت المكرمـات	بـدمع جـرى فيـضه للقنـن
علـى مـن سـرى ذكـره فـي البـلاد	وشـاع بـذكر جميـل حـسن
فيـا طـود فـضل هـوى فـي الثـرى	وغيـب فـي بطنـه أو بطـن
ويـا راحـلا عـن ديـار الغـرور	فـذكر جميلـك فينـا قطـن
قـضيت الـذي كـان منـك يـراد	لتجـزى بـذلك مـن ذي المنـن
نـصبت الهـدى ونـشرت العلـوم	وغيـب لفقـدك كـل حـزن
ولا سـيما النـدب فـرد الزمـان	خـدين المعـالي بهـذا الـزمن

وحيــد الفـضائل فـي عـصره | ورب التقـــى والحجـــى والفطـــن
حميــد الفعـال كـريم الطبـاع | لــه الفـضل فـي سـر أو فـي علـن
وعلامــة الـدهر هادي الانـام | لـسبل الرشـاد محمـد حـس
أقـام عـزاء سـليل النبـي | وأفـضل مـن مـن مـن غيـر مـن
لفاتحــة فـي عـزاء تفـوق | كمـا فـاق فينـا علـى كـل فـن
وان أبـا حـسن قـد مـضى | لخلـد الجنـان وفيهـا سـكن
فـصبرا بنيـه وأرحامـه | فـصبر الفتـى مـا لـه مـن ثمـن
ولا زال يغـشى ضـريحا حـواه | سـلام مـن الله مـا الليـل جـن

وللسيد محمد معصوم القطيفي النجفي يرثي الامام الحسين (ع) :

أسـف لربـات الحجـا | ل بـرزن لا يـأوين كنـا
تبكـي أخـا كـرم شـمردل | طالمـا أغنـى وأقنـى
شـيخ العـشيرة ذا حمـى | مـا مـس منـه الـضيم ركنـا
والمـستغاث اذا الخطـوب | تراكمـت كالليـل دجنـا
أو لـم تكـن أنـت الـذي | بأمورنـا فـي الـدهر تعنـى
أو لـم ترانـا بعـد حفظـك | فـي يـد الاسـواء ضـعنا
وتعـج تهتـف والـشجى | يبـدي خفايـا مـا اسـتكنا
أمجـشما فـج الفـلا | مـا لا يعـد الحـزن حزنـا
عـرج بطيبـة مبلغـا | بعـض الـذي بـألطف نلنـا
مـأوى الـشجاعة والـسماح | وكـل معـروف وحـسنى

378

| فهـــم أحـــر القـــوم طعنـــا | قـــوم اذا حمـــي الطعــــان |

وللسيد محمد ابن السيد معصوم من روضته قصائد هذه اوائلها :

لـــه الارضـــون رجـــت أي رج	١ ـ أرزء مثـل رزء الـسبط مشج
وهـل لاسير حزنـك مـن بـراح	٢ ـ ألا يـا ليل هـل لـك مـن صباح
بـين الفـؤاد الـى القيامـة راسخ	٣ ـ حزني على سبط النبي محمـد
كـل يـوم مـن الاسـى بازديـاد	٤ ـ يـا فـؤادي ويـا لهيـب فـؤادي
لـديهم وعـن الـدنيا لقـد رغبـوا	٥ ـ روحي الفداء لمن هانت حياتهم

الشيخ حسن الصفواني، توفي سنة ١٢٧١ تقريبا:

جاء في شعراء القطيف : هو الاديب الاريب الشيخ حسن بن صالح الصفواني القطيفي من شعراء القرن الثالث عشر. ولم أتحصل على من يتعرف على هذا الشاعر فيمدني بمعلومات حياته غير اني تتبعت كثيرا من ديوانه قراءة فلمست منه انه ذلك التقي الورع الصالح في الرعيل الاول من رجالات الدين وشعراء أهل البيت (ع) وان ديوانه المرتب على حروف المعجم ليعطينا صورة عن كثير من حياته الفذة. توفي رحمه الله تعالى في التاريخ المذكور على حد التقريب. ومبلغ العلم انه موجود سنة ١٢٤٤ معاصر للفاضل الجشي الذي سبق ذكره.

نقتطف من ديوان المترجم هذه القصيد العامرة نظرا لاشتمالها على اسمه الكامل وهي التي دلتنا عليه ، لذا رجحنا ذكرها على غيرها من خرائده تغمده الله برحمته.

قوله في رثاء الحسين عليه السلام :

غـدوت أنـشد أشعـاري بأفنان	لمـا علـى الـدوح صـاحت ذات افنـان
أن لا أفـارق أشـجاني وأحزانـي	واستأصل الحزن قلبي وانطويت على
لـم تـألف الغمـض طول الليل أجفاني	وبـت مثـل سليم مـضه ألـم
فقل بـصبر عليل مؤسـر عانـي	حليـف وجـد نحيـل مـدنف قلـق

وذاك لا لــضعون زم ســائقها | يـوم الرحيـل ولا قـاص ولا دانـي
ولا لفقـد أنيـس قـد أنسـت بـه | ولا لتــذكار اخــوان وخـلان
ولا لتــذكار وادي الحــرتين ولا | دار خلـت مـن أخلانـي وجيرانـي
ولا لـدار خلـت مـن أهلهـا وغـدت | سـكنى الفراعـل مـن سيد وسـرحان
ولا فـراق نـديم كـان مـصطحبي | فـي العـل والنهـل عنـد الشـرب نـدماني
ولا لمانسـة الاعطـاف كاملـة الا | وصـاف ان خطـرت تـزري علـى البـان
لكن أسفت علـى مـن جـل مـصرعه | وأفجـع الخلـق مـن انـس ومـن جـان
أعنـي الحسين أبـا الاسباط أكرم من | نـاجى المهـيمن فـي سـر واعـلان
سـبط النبـي وفـرخ الطهـر فاطمـة | نجل الوصـي حـسين الفرقـد الثـاني
لـهفي لـه حـين وافـى كـربلا وبهـا | حـط المضـارب مـن صحب واخـوان
مستنـشقا لثراهـا خاطبـا بهـم | وهـو البليـغ بايـضاح وتبيـان
هـذي ديـاري وفيهـا مـدفني وبهـا | محـط قبـري ، بهـذا الجـد أنبـاني
فمـا ابن صـالح يرجـو غير فـضلكم | وانــه حـسن يـدعى بـصفوان
والوالـدين ومـن يقـرأ لمرثيتـي | والـسامعين ومـن يبكـي بـأحزان
ثـم الـسلام عليكـم مـا همـا مطـر | يومـا ومـا صـدحت ورق بأغـصان

الحاج سليمان العاملي المتوفى ١٢٧٢ :
هـل المحـرم فاسـتهل مكـدرا | قـد أوجـع القلـب الحـزين وحيـرا
وذكـرت فيـه مـصاب آل محمـد | فـي كـربلا فسلبت مـن عينـي الكـرى

380

وانهد مــن أركانهـا عـالي الـذرى	يـوم مبـاني الـدين فيـه تزلزلـت
لبـست ثيـاب حـدادها أم القـرى	وارتجت الارضون مـن جزع وقد
والـشمس والقمـر المنيـر تكـورا	خطـب لــه تبكـي ملائكـة الـسما
أضحى بـأرض ألطف شلـوا بـالعرى	مــن مبلــغ المختـار أن سـليله

الحاج سليمان بن الشيخ علي بن الحاج زين العاملي والد الشيخ محمد والشيخ أبو خليل الزين ولد سنة ١٢٢٧ وتوفي سنة ١٢٧٢ هـ. قال السيد الامين في الاعيان : كان من أهل الخير والصلاح والمبرات الكثيرة وكان يقوم بنفقات أكثر الطلاب في مدرسة الشيخ عبدالله نعمة في) جبع (وله شعر لا بأس به وجدناه بخطه في بعض المجاميع. وروى له رحمه‌الله شعرا وقال : انه قاله سنة ١٢٧٦ و ١٢٧٧ أي بعد وفاته بخمس سنين. وقد جاء ذلك سهوا.

السيد أحمد الفحام ت ١٢٧٤ :

قوله في الحسين (ع) :

قـاني الـدموع وحاربـت غفواتهـا؟	مـا بـال عينـي أسبلت عبراتهـا؟
أمست خـلاء مـن مهـى خفراتهـا	الـذكر دار شطـر جرعـاء الحمـى
تطـوي علـى الـصعداء مـن زفراتهـا	أم فتيـة شـط فغـادرت الحـشى
يـوم الطفـوف فأسبلت عبراتهـا	لا بـل تـذكرت الطفـوف ومـاجرى
بـالضرب تقطـر مـن دمـاء هداتها	يومـا بـه أضحـت سـيوف أميـة
نفوسـها زهقـا علـى صـعداتها	يومـا بـه أضحـت أسنتها تـسيل
فقضت علـى ظمـأ دويـن فراتهـا	سقيت أنابيب الوشيج علـى الـصدى
أسـرى بنـي الزرقـاء فـي فلواتهـا	وعقائـل الهـادي تقـاد ذليلـة
الا التقنـع فـي سـياط طغاتهـا	فـي أي جـد تـستغيث فـلا تـرى

381

عصفت بـه بـألطف ريـح شتاتها	أتـرى درى خيـر البريـة شمـله
قـد أدركـت فـي آلـه ثاراتهـا	أتـرى درى المختـار أن أميـة
سقطت بكـف يزيـد مـن هالاتها	تلـك البـدور تجللـت خسفا وقـد
فلـك المعـالي فـي أكـف بُغاتهـا	أبـدت غروبـا فـي الطفـوف يـديرها
رعيـت حمايتهـا بقتـل حماتهـا	تلـك السـتور تهتكـت قسـرا ومـا
ثاراتهـا أشــفت بــه أحناتهـا	نـسل العبيـد بـآل أحمـد أدركـت
خيـر الـورى فـي قتلهـا سـاداتها	ويـل لهـا أرضـت يزيـد وأغـضبت
مرعوبـة تبكـي لفقـد كفاتهـا	لهفي لزينـب وهـي مـا بـين العـدى
أنـضى النفـوس وزاد فـي حـسراتها	بعـدا ليومـك يـابن أمـي انـه
بـالطف شمـل بنيـك رهـن شتاتها	يـا جـد ان أميـة قـد غـادرت
وعـر الـصخور لقـى علـى عرصـاتها	هـذا الحـسين بكـربلا متوسـدا
بيـد الهـوان يـدار فـوق قناتهـا	تحـت السـنابك جسمه وكريمـه
تتقطـع الاكبـاد فـي خطراتهـا	الله أكبـر انهـا لمـصيبة
ئكهـا وآل الله فــي فلواتهـا	أبنـاء حـرب فـي القـصور علـى أرا
تمـشي نـشاوى سـكبها راحاتهـا	يمـسون قتلـى كـربلا وأميـة
س تقال يـوم الحـشر مـن عثراتهـا	يـا سـادتي يـا مـن بحـبهم النفـو
وافـى جميـل الـذكر مـن آياتهـا	مـاذا أقـول بمـدحكم وبمـدحكم
وضـح الـصباح وقـد جلـت ظلماتهـا	صلى الالـه عليـكم مـا ان بـدت

* * *

جاء في شعراء الغري : السيد أحمد ابن السيد صادق الفحام الاعرجي ذكره السيد الامين في الاعيان فقال : كان أديبا فاضلا وليس لدينا علم بشيء من أحواله كما ذكره صاحب (الحصون (وأثبت له من الشعر قوله:

اليك وحاجاتي اليك كما هيا	سأقضي بقرب الدار نحبي على أسى
وجمعته من طارفي وتلاديا	أرى حارما مالي وما ملكت يدي
مسجى على يأس الرجا من حياتيا	لقا بأعالي الرمل من حصن سامة
بحالي وتبكي رحمة لشبابيا	تقلبني أيدي العوائد رأفة
على مدرج الريح استقرت مكانيا	وشف الهوى جسمي فلا قمت واقفا
نأى السرب عنها ساعة الركب ماضيا	وما أم رسلان ببطن مفازة
فألفته محصوص الجناحين طاويا	ولما تناءى الركب عنها انثنت له
حبالي وقد كنت الخليط المصافيا	بأوجد مني يوم أصبحت صارما

وقوله :

ورابعها ايضا تضمن في الكتب	ثلاثة أشياء: فروح مضاعة
وعشق بلا وصل ، وبعد بلا قرب	فدين بلا عقل ، ومال بلا ندى

صالح حجي الكبير ت ١٢٧٥:

قال يرثي أبا الفضل العباس شهيد الطف :

فعلى ناظري الكرى محظور	هلّ لا هلّ بالهنا عاشور
الله واندك بيته المعمور	ذاك شهر به تزلزل عرش
علي حسامها المشهور	ذاك شهر به تفلل من آل

383

ذاك شهر به انطوى من بني عبد	مناف لواؤها المنشور
يوم فيه قد غال بدر المعالي	الخسف والشمس سامها التكوير
يوم أخنى على أبي الفضل فيه	قدر قبل آدم مقدور
وغدا بعده فريد بني الفضل	فريدا بناظريه يدير
قائلا أين من لصوني معد	ولنصري من والدي مذخور
أين حامي الحقيقة المتحامي	أين كبش الكتيبة المنصور
أين عني خواض بحر المنايا	وهو بالبيض والقنا مسجور
وأتاني بالماء رغما على الاعداء	والماء بالردى مغمور
وأبت نفسه الورود ونفسي	من أوام يشب فيها السعير
يا حميا غداة قل المحامي	ونصيرا غداة عز النصير
من لهذي الاطفال بعدك حام	ولهذي العيال بعدك سور
فبحر بي تظاهرت آل حرب	يوم ظهري خلا وأودى الظهير
بأبي من بكى الحسين عليه	ونعاه التهليل والتكبير
لست أنساه في الوغى يتهادى	باسم الثغر والعجاج يثور
قد تجلى على العراق مطلا	بسرايا منها الشئام تمور
كر في الحرب والجسوم تهاوى	بظبا الشوس والرؤوس تطير
يتلقى الجم الغفير بعزم	ما لديه الجم الغفير غفير
لم يزل يحصد الاسود الى أن	خر من بينها الهزبر الهصور
ذاك طور الهدى تجلى له النو	ر فلا غرو أن يدك الطور

أو امــا ليــت الفـرات يغــور	وبـشاطي الفـرات يقـضي أبـو الفـضل
نـــاهلا والمثقــف المطــرور	يـصدر المرهـف المهنـد عنــه
نــه والثــرى لــه كــافور	دمــه غـسله ونـسج الـصبا أكفـا
الــى الحـشر بالـدما ممطـور	يـا لهـا وقعـة بهـا نـاظر الـدين
ينجلــي فــي شـروقه الـديجور	لا يجلــى ديجورهـا غيــر بــدر
عنــا بــه وتـشفى الـصدور	رحمــة الله والــذي يكـشف الغمــاء
ـحق مـشكاة نــوره والنــور	علــة الكائنــات قطـب مـدار الـ

* * *

صالح بن قاسم بن محمد بن احمد بن حجي الطائي الحويزي الزابي النجفي. شاعر معروف وأديب فاضل. ذكره صاحب الحصون المنيعة ج ١ ص ٤١١ فقال : وآل حجي أسرة نجفية معروفة تنحدر من عشيرة الزابية وهي فخذ من قبيلة طي كان مسكنهم على شط الفرات ، وأول من رحل منهم الى النجف لتحصيل العلم الشيخ قاسم والد المترجم له فحضر على علماء عصره وانكب على التحصيل والتفوق في دراسة الفقه والاصول حتى حاز على مرتبة المجتهدين العظام ، ثم بعد رحل الى بلاد فارس ووصل الى خراسان فخلف هذا المترجم له ، ولم يكن في أول أمره مشغولا بالادب والشعر لكن عندما كف بصره جعل الشعر سلوة له فأكثر في النظم.

أقول وجاء ذكره في الحصون اكثر من مرة وفي عدة أجزاء منها. وجاء في (الطليعة) انه من العلماء الصلحاء والاجلاء الاتقياء ، له شعر كثير ومطارحات مع شعراء عصره وعلماء زمانه.

وترجم لـه في (طبقات أعلام الشيعة) فقال : هو الشيخ صالح ابن الشيخ قاسم ابن الحاج محمد الطرفي الحويزي النجفي ، من أعلام الادب في عصره ومن حفاظ القرآن. (آل حاجي) من بيوت النجف المعروفة بالفضل والادب ، قطنت النجف في القرن الثاني عشر ، وهم من قبيلة (بني طرف) الحويزيين ، وأول من هاجر منهم الى النجف الشيخ قاسم والد المترجم لـه وسكن محلـة (الحويش) ، ولحق جدهم محمدا لقب (الحاج) وبقي ملازما لاولاده وأحفاده.

وقال صاحب طبقات الشيعة : وقد ضاع معظم شعر المترجم له وتلف مع سائر آثار أسرته من جراء حوادث الطاعون الذي قضى عليهم وطمس آثارهم الا ما حفظته المجاميع النجفية المخطوطة ، وقد رأيت من شعره قصيدة في رثاء الشيخ محمد حسن صاحب (الجواهر) وأخرى في رثاء الشيخ محمد بن علي ابن جعفر كاشف الغطاء ، وثالثة في رثاء السيد شريف زوين أخ السيد صالح القزويني لأمه ، ورابعة في رثاء الشيخ حسن بن جعفر كاشف الغطاء ، وخامسة في رثاء السيد حسن بن علي الخرسان وقد أثبتها السيد جعفر الخرسان في مجموعته ، وقد خلف ولدين : الشيخ جواد والشيخ مهدي وكلاهما من أهل الفضل والادب.

من شعره قصيدته التي قرض بها موشحة السيد صالح القزويني البغدادي التي مدح بها الشيخ طالب البلاغي :

صاغ من جوهر النظام عقودا	راق كالدر سمطها منضودا
شهدت بالعلى له وأقامت	لعلاها منه عليها شهودا
واستعارت منها الغواني ثنايا	ها الغوالي فنظمتها عقودا
وغدا ابن الاثير وهو أثير	بعلاه كأبن العميد عميدا
وجميلا أرتك غير جميل	واسترقت كأبن الوليد الوليدا
صرعت قبله صريع الغواني	بعد ما صيرت لبيدا لبيدا
كبرت آية لصالح لو شا	هدها قومه لخروا سجودا
فصلتها يدا حميد فأضحى	ذكرها مثل ذكره محمودا
ملك من بني النبي وجدنا	ما بآبانه به موجودا
حدد المكرمات كما وكيفا	بيد جودها تعدى الحدودا
مكرمات زواهر تقتفيها	عزمات تصدع الجلمودا
فهو أعلى من أن يقال مجيد	أو هل غيره يعد مجيدا
ولعمري لهو المعد ليوم	لم يكن غيره له معدودا

طاميـــــا لـــم يكـــن بـــه ممـــدودا	بحـر علـم طمـى فلـم تلـف بحـرا
وحـسام لـم ينـب ضـربا حـدودا	وجـواد لـم يكـب جريـا كـلالا
طـوق العـالمين جيـدا فجيـدا	يـا سـحابا بفـيض جـدواه فـضلا
كـل يـوم مـن الهنـا بـك عيـدا	لـم نـزل والـورى جميعـا نـوافي

الشيخ قاسم الهر المتوفى ١٢٧٦ :

لـدن الرمـاح عنـاق الخـرد الحـور	لله درهـم كـم عـانقوا طربـا
الحـرب العـوان بقلـب غيـر مـذعور	وصـافحوا المشرفيات الـصفاح لـدى
رواح والحـرب منـه ذات تـسعير	وكـم أشـم مجـد العـصب يختلـس الا
بحادثـــات المنايـــا والمقـــادير	يلقـى المواضـي وسـمر الخـط متشحا
سطو على الهضب والآكـام والقـور	تثنى لـسطوتهم شـم الجبـال اذا
كالـشهب مـا بـين مطعـون ومنحـور	مـا سـالموا للعـدى حتـى اذا انتـشروا
أسـماؤهم فـوق عـرش الله بـالنور	مـن للهـدى والنـدى بعـد الالـى كتبـت
جـرت لآل علـي بالمـصادير	الله أكبـر يـا لله مـن نـوب
وغيـر النـور منهـا أي تغييـر	فكـم بـدور هـدى فـي كـربلا محقـت
تحـت الثـرى بعـدما غيلـت بتكـدير	وكـم نجـوم لاربـاب العلـى حجبـت

أقول وأول هذه القصيدة الحسينية :

وبيـضة الـدين قـد شـيبت بتكـدير	فلّت مواضي الهدى في يوم عاشور
طعـم العواسـل والبيـض المبـاتير	يوم بنو الوحي والتنزيل فيه غدوا

387

الشيخ قاسم بن محمد علي بن احمد الحائري الشهير بالهر والبصير أخيرا ، ولد سنة ١٢١٦ والمصادف ١٨٠١ م وتوفي سنة ١٢٧٦ والمصادف ١٨٥٩ م وأضر في آخر عمره ، وفي الطليعة : كان أديبا شاعرا عابدا ناسكا ، فقد بصره وهو في ميعة شبابه وشرخ صباه ، وتلقى العلم في المعاهد الدينية بكربلاء المقدسة أورد بعض شعره في المجموع الرائق ، وأخيرا كتب عنه صديقنا الاستاذ السيد سلمان هادي الطعمة في كتابه (شعراء من كربلاء) وذكر من كتب عن حياة هذا الشاعر كالسيد الامين في الاعيان والشيخ آغا بزرك الطهراني وغيرهما. توفي المترجم له بكربلاء المقدسه ودفن في الصحن الحسيني المقدس مما يلي باب السدرة ومن أشهر شعره قوله في الامام الحسين عليه السلام:

قـد سـرنـي ذا وهـذا زادنـي أرقـا	يومـان لـم أر فـي الايـام مثلهمـا
يـوم شـمـر علـى صـدر الحـسين رقـا	يـوم الحسين رقـى صدر النبي بـه

وقوله في رثاه (ع) :

ووصـف كاسـات وسـاق وراح	مـا أنـت يـا قلـب وبـيض الملـاح
حديث مـن فـي رزئـه الجـن نـاح	هلـم يـا صـاح معـي نـستمع
بـين ظبـا البـيض وسـمر الرمـاح	لقـد قـضى ريحانـة المـصطفى
مـوزع الجـسم ببـيض الـصفاح	لهفـي عليـه مـذ هـوى ظاميـا
ورحلـه فيهـا غـدا مـستباح	ثـوى أبـي الـضيم فـي كـربلا
بكـل مقـدام بيـوم الكفـاح	هبـوا بنـي عمـرو العلـى للـوغى
كأنهـا بـالنوح ذات الجنـاح	نـساؤكم بـالطف بـين العـدى

وهناك جملة من القصائد الحسينية في المخطوطات النادرة رأيناها في تجوالنا عن أدب الطف.

الشيخ عباس الملا المتوفى ١٢٧٦:

وقد ارتجلها في الحائر الحسيني بكربلاء:

لـك قاصـدا يـا سـيد الـشهداء	يـا سيد الـشهداء جئت مـن الحمى
فـأذن اذا لحـوائجي بقـضاء	متوسـلا بـك فـي قضاء حـوائجي

* * *

الشيخ عباس بن الملا علي بن الملا ياسين البغدادي النجفي من أسرة آل السكافي ، أسرة معروفة في النجف تتعاطى التجارة ، وأبوه الملا علي من ذوي النسك والصلاح يتعاطى بيع (البز) في بغداد ، وفي سنة ١٢٤٧ هاجر الملا علي الى النجف رغبة منه في مجاورة مشهد الامام أمير المؤمنين ولولده المترجم له يومئذ من العمر ثلاث سنين ، اذ أن مولده كان سنة ١٢٤٤ ففتح عينيه على الجو الادبي الذي يمتاز به هذا البلد واتصل بأدبائه وعلمائه فأين ما اتجه رأى عالما أو محادثا أو مؤلفا وكان له الميل الكامل

لذلك الجو العلمي فبرع في العلم والادب ونظم القريض ونبغ فيه قبل بلوغ سن الرشد فأصبح من ذوي المكانة بين أدباء القرن الثالث عشر الهجري ولا أدل على ذلك من قول:

بـديع والعلـوم علـى فنـون	أحطـت مـن العلـوم بكـل فـن
ومـا جـاوزت شـطر الاربعـين	فهـا أنـا محـرز قصب المعالـي

وقوله:

بنـو العليـاء مـن قـاص ودان	كفـاني أننـي لعـلاي دانـت
أشـار النـاس نحـوي بالبنـان	وحـسبي أننـي مـن حيـث أبـدو

صرح البحاثة الشيخ آغا بزرك الطهراني في الذريعة بأنه تفقه على العلامة الشيخ محمد حسن صاحب الجواهر ، وله مساجلات ومطارحات مع أدباء عصره وفي مقدمتهم الشاعر عبد الباقي العمري الموصلي فقد كان من المعجبين به فقد راسله ومدحه بطائفة من القصائد والمفردات منها قولـه في قصيدته يمدحه فيها تناهز الـ ٥٠ بيتا مثبتة بديوانه المطبوع واليك شاهدا منها:

٣٨٩

وألـسنة الافصاح عنـه غـدت لكنـا	لـه الله مـن ذي منطـق أعجـز الـورى
مـن المجـد قبـل المهـد متخـذا حـضنا	ترعرع فـي حجـر النجابـة وانثنـى
بـديـع اذا وشـى ، غـريـض اذا غنـى	حبيب اذا أنشأ ، صـريـع اذا انتشـى
يعلـــم فـــي اعرابــه معبـد اللحنـا	ومفتقـر (مغنـى اللبيـب) للفظـه
وأكبـــرهم عقـــلا وأصـغـرهم سـنا	تـسامى علـى الاقـران فهـو أجلهـم
وأنفــذهم فكـــرا وأشــحـذهم ذهنـا	وأكثـــرهم فــضلا وأفـضلهم ذكـا
لـه الـدهر يعطـي حـين ينـشدها الاذنـا	مـــراث بنعــت الال آل محمـــد
ويـسـتصرخ الامــلاك والانـس والجنـا	ويـستوقف الافـلاك شـجو نـشيده
تـمــور ووجـــه الارض يملـؤه حـزن	فيبكـي الحيـا والجـو ينـدب والـسما

وذكره العلامة السماوي في (الطليعة) وأورد شواهد من شعره ثم نشر بقلمه في مجلة (الغري) السنة ٧ الصادر سنة ١٣٦٥ وخلاصة ما قال : العباس بن علي بن ياسين أبو الامين كـان فاضلا أديبا جميل الشكل حسن الصوت لطيف المعاشرة ، وكان أبوه تقيا هاجر من بغداد الى النجف وابنه رضيع وكان وقاد الذهن حاد الفهم وسيما ذا عارضة شديدة وهمة عالية مشاركا في العلوم على صغر سنه ، وصاهره الحسين بن الرضا الطباطبائي على شقيقته فهنأ السيد وهنأ نفسه بمصاهرة آل الرسول ، وعرف بالتقوى وامتاز بالورع فهو كان من مشاهير الشعراء كان كذلك من مشاهير الاتقياء. تـوفي في أواسط شهر رمضان سنة ١٢٧٦ وعمره ٣٢ سنة ودفن بالصحن الحيدري تجاه باب الرواق الكبير ، ويقال في سبب موته انه هوى ابنة أحد الاشراف وأخفى هواه حتى أنحله الى أن قضى نحبه. رثاه العلامة السيد حسين الطباطبائي آل بحر العلوم بقصيدة تفيض بالحسرات والآلام وهذا أكثرها.

وأمــــاد للاسـلام أي عمــاد	رزء كـسا العليـاء ثـوب حـداد
أركانــه بــالرغم أي بــداد	أصـمت فوادحـه الرشـاد فبـددت
زعقاتـه أم ذاك صرصـر عـاد	هل ذاك نفـخ الـصور قـد صرت بنا
ديــن النبــي ومعـشر الامجـاد	جلـل عـرا فرمت سـهام خطوبـه

390

هاتيـك غـر الاكرمين لوجـدها   تـذري المـدامع مـن دم الاكبـاد

ثكلى ومـن فـرط الجـوى أحشاؤها   أبـدا ليـوم الحـشر فـي ايقـاد

قـف بالـديار الدراسـات طلولهـا   وانـشد ربـاهـا عـن أهيـل ودادي

بـالبنين ان سـلبوا القلـوب فـانهم   خلعـوا علـى الاجـساد ثـوب سواد

تققوا النجائـب مـن جوى وجفونها   تهمـي متـى يحـدو بهـن الحـادي

لله رزء أجـجـــت نيرانــــه   قلـب الـورى مـن حاضـر أو بـاد

رزء الفتى السامي أبي الفضل الـذي   حـاز الفـضائل مـن لـدى المـيلاد

مـن فـاق أربـاب العلـى بمفـاخر   علـم وأخـلاق وبـسط أيـادي

ذات سـمت فحـوت مناقـب جمـة   أعيـت عـن الاحـصاء والتعـداد

قس البلاغـة في الورى بل لـم يقس   كـلا بـسحبان وقـس أيـاد

ومهـذب مـزج القلـوب بـوده   مـزج الالـه الـروح بالاجـساد

ذاك الـذي شـرك الانـام بمالـه   لكـن تفـرد فـي هـدى ورشـاد

فقـضى وأنفـس زاده التقـوى وهـل   للمتقـين سـوى التقـى مـن زاد

لـو يفتـدى لفديتـه طوعـا بمـا   ملكـت يـدي مـن طـارف وتـلاد

لكـن اذا نفـذ القضا فـلا تـرى   تجـدي هنالـك فديـة مـن فـاد

خنت الـذمام وحدت عن نهـج الوفا   ان ذقـت بعد نـواه طعـم رقـاد

وسلوت مجدي ان سلوت مـصابه   حتـى ألاقيـه بيـوم معـادي

هـل كيـف تـسكن لـوعتي فيـه وقـد   أمـسى رهـين جنـادل الالحـاد

لـي كانـت الايـام أعيـادا بـه   واليـوم عـاد مراثيـا انـشادي

كـــان الحـري ومجـده بـودادي	أصـفيته دون الانـام الـود اذ
ان العيـــون بليــــة الاكبـــاد	لمحتـه عينـي فابتلـت كبـدي بـه
اذ تعــرف الاشـياء بالاضــداد	وعرفـت قـدر عـلاه مـن حسـاده
تحـت الثـرى عـن أعـين الاشـهاد	ذخـرى ومـن حـذري عليـه كنزتـه
تحكـي الغـوادي أو سـيول الـوادي	أتبعتـه عنـد الرحيـل مـدامعا
وطـري وأبلـغ مـن عـلاه مـرادي	فقضى برغمـي قبـل أن اقضـي بـه
ومعـذب بلظـى الجحـيم فـؤادي	يرتـاح فـي روض الجنـان فـؤاده
ألقـاه محمـولا علـى الاعـواد	يـا ليتمـا لاقيـت حينـي قبـل مـا
هـي نفسـه ففـدى المفـدى الفـادي	فـدى بقيـة عمـره نفسـي التـي
عونـا علـى صـرف الزمـان العـادي	مـن بعد فقدك لا أرى فـي الدهر لـي
أم المعـالي بـالثبور تنـادي	لله نعـشك مـذ سـرى ووراءه
طـودا يفـوق عـلا علـى الاطـواد	لله قبـرك كيـف وارى لحـده
سـطعت سـنا كالكوكـب الوقـاد	لله رمسـك كيـف غـشى طلعـة
ذاك الزمـان الغـض لـي بمعـاد	ولقـد صفـا بـك عيـشنا زمنـا فهـل
نـوب تهـد الراسـيات شـداد	كـم ذا أقاسـي فيـك مـن وجـد ومـن
متوسـد وعـلاك شـوك قتـاد	أتقلـب الليـل الطويـل كـأنني
ورقـاء فـوق المـايس الميـادِ	أبكيـك يـا جـم المكـارم مـا شـدت
(انـي بـوادٍ والعـذولُ بـوادِ)	أبكـي ولـم أعبـأ بلومـة عـاذل
هـو فاقـد الامثـال والانـداد	أفهـل تـرى لـي سـلوة فـي فقـد مـن

مـن كـان فـي الكـرب الشـداد عتـادي	هيهـات لا أسلـو وان طـال المـدى
الـرواد بـل يـا كعبــة الوفـاد	يـا منهـل الـوراد بـل يـا روضـة
أيـدي الزمـان ضيـاء ذاك النـادي	بـك كـان نادينـا يضيء وقد محـت
لكـن ذا أدهـى شـجى لفـؤادي	كـم ذا دهتنـي الحادثـات بفادح
لـك كـم تجـور علـى بنـي الامجـاد	وحشدت يـا دهر الضغائن لـي فمـا
الـصادي أجـل فـالله بالمرصـاد	أوريـت نيـران الآسـي فـي مهجـة
أبـدا مـدى الزمـان صـوب عهـاد	وسقى ضـريحا ضـم خيـر معظـم

ذكر الشيخ آغا بزرك ان الشيخ اليعقوبي الخطيب كان قد ظفر بديوان المترجم لـه وقد استنسخ منه نسخة كاملة بـ ٣٣٠ صفحة وان النسخة فقدت في جملـة مـا فقد في سنة ١٣٣٥.

وهكذا انطوت حياة هذا العبقري ولا تزال قصة غرامه أحدوثه السمر في أندية الادب. ومن شعره يمدح الامام أمير المؤمنين عليا عليه السلام ويستجير به من الوباء:

مـن وبـاء أولـى فـؤادك رعبـا	أيهـا الخـائف المـروع قلبـا
الله خير الانـام عجمـا وعربـا	لـذ بـأمن المخـوف صنـو رسـول
حبـست عنـده بنـو الـدهر ركبـا	واحبس الركـب فـي حمـى خير حـام
خضوعـا لـه فبـورك تربـا	وتمـسك بقبـره والـثم التـرب
فـامتحن حبـه تـشاهده رحبـا	واذا مـا خـشيت يومـا مـضيقا
لـك سلمـا مـن بعد مـا كـان حربـا	واستثره علـى الزمـان تجـده
مـل والملتجـي لمـن خـاف خطبـا	فهـو كهـف اللاجـي ومنتجـع الآ
أمحـل العـام واشتكى النـاس جـدبا	مـن بـه تخصب البـلاد اذا مـا

393

أحـــــد غيـــره يفرج كربــا	وبـه تفـرج الكـروب وهـل مـن
مــا دعــاه الـصريخ الا ولبـى	يـا غياثـا لكـل داع وغوثـا
يـه فـأزرت بواكـف الغيـث سكبا	وغمامــا سحـت غــوادي أيــاد
وأنـــى والليـــث للـضيم يـأبى	وأبيـا يـأبى لـشيعته الـضيم
للـــردى مغتمـــا وللمـــوت نهبـا	كيـف تغـضي وذي مواليـك أضحت
أن يــروع الــردى لحزبـك سـربا	أو ترضـى مـولاي حاشـاك ترضـى
أخلـصتك الـولا وأصـفتك حبا	أو ينـال الزمـان بالـسوء قومـا
ـيـا أمانـا مـن الـردى ـ لـك حزبـا	حـاش لله أن تـرى الخطـب يفنـي
عـودتهم كفـاك فـي الجـدب خصبا	ثـم تغـضي ولا تجيـر أناسـا
ولــو أنـي قطعـت اربـا فاربـا	لـست أنحـو سـواه لا وعـلاه
أن مـن حـل جنبـه عـز جنبـا	فـي حمـاه أنخـت رحلـي علمـا
وبـه قـد وثقـت بعـدا وقربـا	لا ولا أختـشي هوانـا وضـيما
ان سـطا صـرفه وجـرد عـضبا	وبـه أنتـضي علـى الـدهر عـضبا
وان كنـت أعظـم النـاس ذنبـا	وبـه أرتجـي النجـاة مـن الـذنب
أن أراه ان مـسني الـدهر حـسبا	وهـو حـسبي مـن كـل سـوء وحسبي
ذ بـآل العبـا غـدا لـيس يعبا	لـست أعبـا بالحادثـات ومـن لا

وله البيتان المكتوبان في الايوان الذهبي الكاظمي يمدح الامامين موسى الكاظم وحفيده محمد الجواد عليهماالسلام:

والـــدهر عيـــشك نكـد	لـــذ ان دهتـك الرزايـا

بكـــاظم الغيـظ موســى	وبـــــالجواد محمــــد

محمد بن عبد الله حرز المتوفى ١٢٧٧ :

عج بـالطفوف وقل يـا ليث غابتهـا	واذر الـدموع ونـاجي الرسـم والتـزم
وانح الفرات وسل عن فتيـة نزلـوا	يـوم الطفوف علـى الرمضاء والـضرم
ونسوة بعد فقد الـصون بـارزة	بـين الطفـوف بفرط الحـزن لـم تـنم
مـا بـين باكيـة عبـرى ونادبــة	تـدعو أبـاهـا ربيـب البيت والحـرم
تحنـو علـى الـسبط شوقـا كـي تقبله	فلــم تجد ملثمــا فيــه لملتـثم

والقصيدة تحتوي على ٦٥ بيتا ومطلعها :

قف بالديار وسل عن جيرة الحرم	أهـل أقامـوا برضـوى أم بـذي سـلم
أم يممـوا الصعب قودوا نحو قارعة	ومحنـة رسمـت فـي اللـوح والقلم
أم قد غدا في لظى الرمضاء ركبهم	نحـو الـردى والهـدى لله مـن حكـم

* * *

جاء في معارف الرجال : الشيخ أبو المكارم محمد بن الشيخ عبدالله بن الشيخ حمد الله بن الشيخ محمود حرز الدين المسلمى النجفي ولد في النجف حدود سنة ١١٩٣ هـ ونشأ وقرأ مقدمات العلوم فيها. هو عالم علامة محقق لـه المآثر الجليلة والخصال الحميدة وكان فقيها أصوليا منطقيا أديبا شاعرا ، ومن مهرة العلماء في العربية والعروض ، حدثنا الفقيه الشيخ ابراهيم الغراوي المتوفى سنة ١٣٠٦ ان المترجم له من أصحاب الفقيه الاجل الشيخ محمد الزريجاوي النجفي والسيد أسد الله الاصفهاني ، سافر الشيخ الى ايران لزيارة الامام الرضا (ع) وفي رجوعه صير طريقه على اصفهان لملاقاة صديقه العالم السيد أسد الله الاصفهاني صاحب الكري في النجف المتوفي سنة ١٢٩٠ وحل ضيفا على السيد فأفضل في اكرامه وتبجيله ونوه باسمه واظهار فضيلته علانية في محافل أصفهان والتمس منه الاقامة في اصفهان على أن يكون مدرسا فلم يؤثر على النجف شيئا وأراه الجامع الذي أحدثه السيد والده بعد قدومه من الحج سنة ١٢٣٠ هـ.

تتلمذ في الفقه على الشيخ علي صاحب الخيارات المتوفى سنة ١٢٥٣ والشيخ محمد حسن صاحب الجواهر الفقه والاصول. والسيد مهدي القزويني المتوفى سنة ١٣٠٠ وحضر يسيرا درس الشيخ محمد حسين الكاظمي.

مؤلفاته :

كتاب الحج فقه استدلالي مبسوط جدا يوجد في مكتبتنا بخطه ، وكتاب الحاشية في المنطق على شرح الشمسية بخطه ، والمصباح وهو كتاب جامع في أعمال المساجد الاربعة المعظمة والاوراد والادعية المأثورة وكتاب في الحديث ومقتل يتضمن شهادة الامام الحسين (ع) وأصحابه في واقعة الطف وفيه بعض مرثياته ، ومجموع يشتمل على جملة من مراثيه ومراثي بعض معاصريه كالشيخ عبدالحسين محي الدين والشيخ عبد الحسين الاعسم وفيه عدة قصائد في الغزل والنسيب وكتاب شرح الحديث ـ هو شرح لكتاب أستاذه السيد القزويني شارحا ما نظمه خاله العلامة السيد بحر العلوم من مضمون الحديث ـ قال في المقدمة الحمد لله الذي هدانا الى السبيل بمعرفة البرهان الدليل .. أما بعد فيقول العبد الجاني طالب العفو من الكريم الودود محمد ابن عبدالله بن حمد الله بن محمود حرز الدين المسلمى ، قال في نظم الحديث :

يفـــتح منـــه أكثـــر الابـــواب   و مـــشي خيـــر الخلـــق بـــابن طـــاب

وذكر الشيخ في شرحه أربعين بابه بخطه ، وتتلمذ عليه جماعة منهم الشيخ ابراهيم السوداني كما حدثنا عنه السوداني.

توفي في النجف سنة ١٢٧٧ هـ بداره بمحلة المسيل قرب مقبرة الصفا غربي البلد ودفن في وادي السلام بمقبرة آل حرز الدين ولم يخلف سوى بنتين.

وله في رثاء مسلم بن عقيل (ع):

اللـــدار أبكـــي اذ تحمـــل أهلهـــا   أم الـــسيد الـــسجاد أم أبكـــي مـــسلما

همـــام عليـــه الكـــون ألـــوى عنانـــه   وخانـــت بـــه الاقـــدار لمـــا تقـــدما

تجمعـــت الاحـــزاب تطلـــب ذحلهـــا   عليـــه وفيهـــا العلـــج عـــدوا تحكمـــا

كـــأنى بـــه بـــين الجمـــاهير مفـــردا   يحطـــم فـــي الحامين لـــدنا ولهـــذما

وقال في تخميس أبيات الجزيني الكناني في مدح زيد بن علي (ع):

٣٩٦

أبـي يـرى ان المـصاليت والقنا   لـديها المعـالي فـي الكريهـة تجتنـى

تولـت حيـارى القـوم تطلـب مأمنـا   ولمـا تـردى بالحمائـل وانثنـى

يصول بأطراف القنا والذوابل

فتـى كـان لا يهفـو حـذارا جنانـه   وقـوع العـوالي فـي الكريهـة شـانه

ولمـا انثنـى للـشوس يعـدو حصانه   تبينـت الاعـداء ان سـنانه

يطيل حنين الامهات الثواكل

همـام اذا مـا القعـضبية فـي اللقـا   تحـوم تـراه فـي الكتيبـة فيلقـا

ولمـا عـلا ظهـر المطهـم وارتقـى   تبيـن منـه مبـسم العـز والتقـى

وليدا يفدى بين أيدي القوابل

وقال يرثي ولده جعفر وكان شابا بعدة قصائد منها :

علـي الـدهر بالنكبـات صـالا   وفـاجئني بنكبتـه اغتيـالا

وأوهـى جـانبي فـصار جـسمي   لمـا ألقـاه مـن زمنـي خـلالا

وألـم مـا لقيـت مـن الرزايـا   فـراق أحبـة خفـوا ارتحـالا

ومـن شـأن القـروح لهـا انـدمال   وقرحـة جعفـر تـأبى انـدمالا

أروم سـلوه فتقـول نفـسي   رويـدك لا تـسل منـي محـالا

أرانـي كلمـا أبـصرت شـيئا   تخيـل مقلتـي منـه خيـالا

علـي الـدهر بالنكبـات صـالا   وفـاجئني بنكبتـه اغتيـالا

وأوهـى جـانبي فـصار جـسمي   لمـا ألقـاه مـن زمنـي خـلالا

وألـم مـا لقيـت مـن الرزايـا	فـراق أحبــة خفـوا ارتحـالا
ومـن شـأن القـروح لهـا انـدمال	وقرحــة جعفــر تـأبى انـدمالا
أروم سـلوه فتقـول نفـسي	رويـدك لا تـسل منـي محـالا
أرانــي كلمــا أبــصرت شــيئا	تخيـل مقلتـي منــه خيــالا

وقد أثبتنا له عدة قصائد في الجزء الثاني من النوادر. انتهى أقول وأورد صاحب (شعراء الغري) ترجمته وذكر مراثيه لولده ، أما تتمة هذه القصيدة:

أري أقرانــه فتجـود عينـي	فازجرهـا فتــزداد انهمــالا
لـو أن الـدهر يقنـع فـي فـداء	لكـان فـداؤه نفـسا ومـالا
فـلا والله لا أنـساك حتــى	أوسـد نحـو مـضجعك الرمـالا

درويش علي البغدادي المتوفى ١٢٧٧:

عـين سـحي دمـا علــى الاطـلال	بربـوع عفـت لـصرف الليـالي
قـد تـولى سعـود أنـسي بـنحس	بعـد خـسف البـدور بعـد الكمـال
مـا لهـذا الزمـان يطلـب بالثـارات	مـا للزمـان عنـدي ومـالي
أيـن أهـل التقـى مهـابط وحـي الله	أيــن الهــداة أهـل المعـالي
آل بيـت الالــه خيـر البرايـا	خيـرة العـالمين هـم خيـر آلِ
جرعـوا مـن كـؤوس حتـف المنايـا	ورد بـيض الـضبا وسـمر العـوالي
ليـت شعـري ومـا أرى الـدهر يـوفي	بــذمام لـسادة ومـوالي
غيـر مجـد فـي ملتـي نـوح بـاك	لطلـول بمـدمع ذي انهمـال
بـل شجاني نـاع أصـاب فـؤادي	بـابن بنـت النبـي شمـس المعـالي

398

النبــي الرســول فــرع الكمــال	كوكـب النيـرين ريحانـة الهـادي
يقاسـي عظــائم الاهــوال	بـأبي سبط خـاتم الرسـل اذ صـار
هـل نصير لنـا وهـل مـن مـوالي	لـست أنساه وهـو فـرد ينـادي
بقنـا الخـط أو برشـق النبـال	لــم تجبــه عـصابة الكفـر الا
لــم يـدع حجــة لقيـل وقـال	وغـدى يظهـر الـدلائل حتـى
فسقاها مـن المواضـي الـصقال	وأتتـه تـشن غـارة غـدر
آيـة الـسيف يـوم وقـع النـزال	وهـو فـرد وهـم الـوف ولكـن
حكـم البـيض مـن رقـاب الرجال	بطـل يرهـب الاسـود اذا مـا
فبكـائي لفقـد غيـث النـوال	وقضـى بـالطفوف غـوث البرايـا
فهـي تبكـي بمـدمع هطـال	فالـسماوات أعولـت بنحيـبٍ
أن يـرى باكيـا لبـدر الكمـال	وبكـى البـدر فـي الـسماء وحـق
منـه يـسري علـى العـسال	فعزيـز علـى البتولـة تلقـى الـراس
أسارى مـن فـوق عجـف الجمال	وبنـات النبـي تهـدى الـى الـشام

وللشيخ درويش علي من قصيدة :

ودع تـذكر جيـران بـذي سـلم	عـج بـالطفوف وقبِّـل تربـةً الحـرم
أرست على بقـع فـي السهل والأكـم	يا عج وعجل الى أرض الطفوف فقد
كمـا بمـدح حـسين راق منتظمـي	راقـت وجـاوزت الجـوزاء منزلـة
قـد استنارت كـضوء النـار فـي الظلم	اخلاقـه وعطايـاه وطلعتـه

399

في هـل أتـى وسبا والنـون والقلم	يكفي حـسينا مـديح الله حيـث أتـى
فعـاد ينـذرنـا مـن بعـد بـالهرم	كـان الزمـان بـه غـضا شـبيبته

ورأيت في كتابه (قبسات الاشجان) كثيرا من شعره في رثاء الامام الحسين (ع) فمن قصيدة يقول في أولها :

طـول المـدى حيـث قـد قامـت نواعيـه	هـل المحـرم لا طالـت ليـاليـه
وأظلـم الكـون واسـودت نواحيـه	مـا للسـرور قـد انـسدت مذاهبـه
جـار يـروي ثـرى البوغـاء جاريـه	فمطلـق الـدمع لا ينفـك مطلقـه
جبريـل فـي المهـد قـد أضحى يناغيـه	يعـزز عليك رسـول الله مـصرع مـن

وله من قصيدة حسينية :

وجـسمي ذاب مـن فـرط النحـولِ	صـروف الـدهر شـبت فـي غليلي

عبد الله الذهبة المتوفى ١٢٧٧ :

مـا للعـلـى لـم تلـف مـنكم نبـا؟	أيـن الابـا هاشـم أيـن الابـا؟
أكلكـم عـن حملـه قـد أبـى	هـذا لـوى العليـا بـلا حامـل
كيـف رضـيتم بمقـام الربـى	بعـد مقـام فـي ذرى يـذبل
أن جـازت الجـوزا بكـم منـصبا	ولـم تـزل ترفـع فـيكم الـى
حاشـا علـى العليـاء أن تـذنبا	فمـا جنـت اذ هجـرت فـيكم
وحـق يـا هاشـم ان تغـضبا	قـد أصبحت غـضبى لمـا نـابكم
فكـم أنـال الطلـب المطلبـا	فالجـد الجـد لمرضـاتها
لـم تـرض أو ترضى القنـا والـضبا	القتـل القتـل فـان العلـى

400

لمبعـــث النـــاس لظاهـــا خبـــا	وأضــرموا نــار وغــى لـــم تقـل
مـنكم بـــأثر المقنـــب المقنبـا	وواصلوا حتـــى تبيـدوا العـدى
لا يغتـدي بـــين البرايـــا هبـــا	الله يــا هاشـــم فـــي مجـدكم
فقـد غـدا فـي النـاس ايـدي سبـا	الله يـــا هاشـــم فـــي شـملكم
نـاطح منـــه الاخمـص الكوكبـا	ايـن الفخـار المـشمخر الـذي
شـــائنكم شـــرق أو غربـــا	أيـن الاغـارات التـي أرغمـت
قبـل وبـــرق لـــم يكـن خلبـا	ايـــن غمـام لـــم يكـن قلبـا
كـادت علـى الافـلاك أن تركبـا	كيـف وهـت عـزائم مـنكم
تعـدو عليهـا فـي شـراها الظبـا	وكـم غـدت أسـادكم هاشـم
مـن نبـأ منـــه شـباكم نبـا	أمـا أتـاكم مـا علـى كـربلا
علـى الثريـا مجـدكم طنبـا	مـا جـاءكم ان العظـيم الـذي
دهـــر بأجنـاد الـبلا اجلبـا	وكاشـــف الارزاء عـنكم اذا
أضحـى بهـا مجـدكم مخـصبا	وذي الايـادي الهـامرات التـي
رحـب البـسيط الـشرق والمغربـا	أضحـى فريـدا فـي خميـس مـلا
اذ جـاوز الخطـب بـلاغ الزبـا	لـم يلـف مـنكم مـن ظهيـر لـه
فيـــه الظمـــا ســاعره الهبـا	يخـوض تيـار الـوغى ذا حـشى
الـى الغـوى عـن نهجهـا نكبـا	مجاهـدا عـن شـرعة الله مـن
بعـد لمـن عـن نـصره قـد أبـى	حتـى قـضى لـم يلـف مـن ناصـر
بـرغمكم خيـل العـدى شـزبا	مقطـــرا تعـدو بأشـــلائه

لــصفوة الــرحمن مــا أعجبـا	مـا أعجـب الاقـدار فيمـا أتـت
عـن نابــه كــشر أن يغلبـا	كيـف قـضت لغالـب المـوت مـن
روح البرايــا أنـــشب المخلبـا	فمـا بقـى الاكـوان والمـوت فـي
لنـصره الــرحمن قبـل اجتبـى	مـضى الـى الـرحمن فـي عـصبة
مـا الله لابـن المـصطفى أوجبـا	قـضوا كرامـا بعـد مـا ان قـضوا
فـي سـترها هـامي النحـور الظبـا	علـى العـرى عـارين قـد شـاركت
دون محــام للعـدى منهبـا	وخلفــوا عزائــز الله مـن
وخفـضها صـرف القـضى أعربـا	غرائبـا فـي هتـك أسـتارها
دمعـا كوكـاف الحيـا صـيبا	تـذري علـى فقـدان سـاداتها
تطـوي بـأثر السبـسب السبـسبا	تحملهـا العـيس علـى وخـدها
نـضو مـن الاعيـا بهـا قـد كبـا	تقـرعهن الاصـبحيات ان
أن الــى الاقـدار أن تغـضبا	يـا غـضبة الاقـدار هبـي فقـد
جبريـل حـسرى فـي وثـاق السبـا	ان التـي يـسدف أسـتارها
مـلاك يقفـو الموكـب الموكبـا	ومـن علـى أعتابهـا تخـضع الا
مـن ذلـة الاسـر لهـا مهربـا	خواضـع بـين العـدى لـم تجـد
تمـسي لابنـاء الخنـا منهبـا	عـز علـى الامـلاك والرسـل ان
لمـا عـن الرائـي لهـا غيبـا	تـود لـو أن الـدجى سـرمدا
يـا صـبح لا أهـلا ولا مرحبـا	وان بـدا الـصبح دعـت مـن أسى
لهـا جـلال الله قـد حجبـا	أبـديت يـا صـبح لنـا أوجهـا

402

عـــن شـأنها القـرآن قــد أعربـا	تـراك قـد هانـت عليـك التـي
جنيــت فــي حــرات آل العبـا	فمـا جنـى يـا شـمس جـان كمـا
أوجههـا مـن دجنـة الغيهبـا	الليـل يكـسوها حـذارا علـى
فمـن جنـى مثلـك أو أذنبـا	وأنـت تبـديها لنظارهــا
للبعـث لمــا آن أن تــسلبا	لـم لا تواريـت بحجـب الخفـا
الخطـب قـد أعضـل واعصوصبا	يـا هاشـم العليـا ولا هاشـما
مـن هـامر الاوداج ان تـشربا	مـا آن لا بعـدا لاسـيافكم
أراقــم المـران أو تعطبــا	لا عـذر أو تجتـاح أعـداءكم
رام علـى عليــاك أن يـشغبا	أو تنعـل الافـراس مـن هـم مـن
وواصـلي بـين الطـلا والـشبا	جـافي عـن الاسـياف اغمادهـا
الله فــي ثـارك أن يـذهبا	حتـى تبيـدي أو تبيـدي العـدى
أو يجمـع الـشمل الـذي شـعبا	ولا تملـي مـن قـراع الـردى
زينـب والهفـا علـى زينبـا	مـا صـد أسـماعكم عـن نـدى
لكـن حـداها الثكـل أن تنـدبا	وقـد درت أن لا ملـب لهـا
لنـسوةٍ لهـا الـسبا اذهبـا	تنـدب واقومـاه مـن هاشـم
كـل الـورى ملجـا ولا مهربـا	هـذي بنـات الـوحي لـم تلـف مـن

قال صاحب أنوار البدرين : ومن الشعراء البحرين الشاعر المطبوع الحاج عبد الله ابن المرحوم الحاج احمد الذهبة البحراني ، هو من أهل قرية (جد حفص) سكن مسقط ثم لنجة وهناك انتقل الى رحمة الله ورضوانه.

كان شاعرا ماهرا من شعراء أهل البيت عليهمالسلام ، راثيا ومادحا بارع في الشعر ، اجتمعت به في دارنا بالقطيف وكان قد جاء زائرا للمرحوم شيخنا الشيخ احمد ابن الشيخ صالح. له ديوان شعر رأينا منه مجلدين ضخمين ومن قصائده الغراء رائعته التي يقول في أولها :

أبى الدهر أن يصفو لحر مشاربه

ويقول في آخرها:

بلهفـي ولا يخبـو مـن الوجـد لاهبُـه	ولهفـي ولا يشفى الـذي في ضمـائري
لهـا دان أعجـام الـورى وأعاربُـه	لربـات خدر لـم تـر الـشمس وجهها

الشيخ حسن قفطان المتوفى ١٢٧٧ :

مـن كـربلاء جـرى عليـه مـا جـرا	لمن الخبا المضروب في ذاك العرى
آسـاد غيـل دونهـا أسـد الـشرى	مـا خلـت الا أنـه غـاب بـه
نـسبا مـن الـشمس المنيـرة أنـورا	فتيـان صـدق مـن ذوابـة هاشـم
نـاران : نـار وغـى، ونـار للقـرى	شبوا وشب بـسيفهم وأكفهـم
طربـا سـوابق ضـمرا أو أسـمرا	يتـذاكرون اذا خلـوا بـسميرهم
يجـد المنيـة فيـه طعمـا مـسكرا	تقتـادهم للعـز عزمـة أصـيد
نقـع العـوادي فـي الطـراد العنبـرا	يلقـى الكتائـب بأسـما ويـشم مـن
طـوع المـشيئة قبلمـا أن يـأمرا	ملـك ممالكـه العـوالم كلهـا
لا جرهمـا ، لا تبعـا ، لا حِميَـرا	أعظـم بـه سـلطان عـز شامـخ
أو بتـول لا حـديث يفتـرا	شـرف تفـرع عـن نبـي أو وصـي
زمـر تـرى المعـروف شيئا منكـرا	بعثـت اليـه زخارفـا بـصحائف

404

فأقـــام فـيهم منــذرا ومبـشرا | ومحــذرا فــي الله حتــى أعـذرا

حتـى اذا ازدلفـوا اليــه رأوا بــه | أسـدا يحـامي عـن شـاره غـضنفرا

بـدرا تحـف بـه كواكب كلمـا | عاينتهـا صــبحا مـسفرا

وغـدت تواسـيه المنـون عـصابة | طابـت عاينـت مآثرهـا وطابـت عنصرا

تكسوهم الحـرب العوان ملابـسا | مستـشعرين بهـا النجيـع الاحمـرا

يتـسلقون مطهمـا يستـصحبون | مثقفـا يتقلــدون مــذكرا

يتظلللــون أرائكـا مـضروبة | بيـد العواسـل أو غمامـا عثيـرا

نـسجت عـواملهم مثـال دروعهـم | زردا بأجـساد العـدى متـصورا

نـصروا ابن بنت نبيهم فتـسنموا | عـزا لهـم فـي النـشأتين ومفخـرا

بـذلوا نفوسـهم ظمـاءا لا تـرى | مـاء يبـاح ولا سـحابا ممطـرا

حتـى أبيـدوا والريـاح تكفلـت | بجهـازهم كفنـا حنوطـا أقبـرا

متلفعـين دم الـشهادة سندسـا | يـوم التغـابن أو حريـرا أخـضرا

لله يــوم ابــن البتــول فانــه | أشـجى البتولــة والنبـي وحيـدرا

يـوم ابـن حيـدر والخيـول محيطـة | بخبـاه يـدعو بالنـصير فـلا يـرى

الا أعـاد فـي عـواد فـي عـوار | فـي عـوال فـي نبـال تبتـرا

فهنـاك دمـدم طامنـا فـي جأشـه | بمهنـد يـسم العديـد الاكثـرا

متـصرفا فـي جمعهـم بعوامـل | عـادت بجمعهـم الـصحيح مكسـرا

بـأس وسـيف أخرسـا ضوضاءهم | لكـن أمـر الله كـان مقـدرا

فهوى على وجـه الثرى روحي الفدا | لـك أيهـا الثـاوي علـى وجـه الثرى

405

فــرآك مقطـوع الــوتين معفـرا	أحسين هـل وافـاك جـدك زائــرا
فــردا غريبـا ظاميـا أم مـا درى	أم هـل درى بـك حيـدر فـي كـربلا
عـار ثلاثـا بـالعرا لـن يقبـرا	مـن مبلـغ الزهــراء أن سـليلها
شـلت يـداه أكـان يعلـم مـا فـرا	وفراسـنان نحــره بـسنانه
تـسبى على عجـف المطايـا حـسرا	وبناتهـا يــوم الطفـوف سـليبة
صـانوا عـن الـسب المعنـف قيـصرا	فكأنــا مــن قيـصر ولربمـا
يـا كافـل الايتــام يـا غـوث الـورى	لـم أنـس زينـب وهـي تنـدب نـدبها
مـرت على أجفانهـا سنـة الكـرى	سـهدت عينـي ليتهـا عميـت اذا
يـا طـود عـز كـان لـي سـامي الـذرى	أثكلتنــي اسـلمتني اذللتنـي
أمـسى بـأرض الطـف محلـول العـرا	ورواق أمـن كنـت فـي الـدنيا لهـا
رمـضائها لا أسـتطيع تـصبرا	هـل أستطيع تـصبرا وأراك فـي
بالـذكر قـد جعـل العـوالي منبـرا	مـا كنـت أعـرف قبـل رأسـك واعظـا
بثنائــــه فمهــــلا ومكبــــرا	نـصبوه خفظـا وهـو رفـع وانثنـوا
مترنمـا متـــشمتا متجبــــرا	ويزيـد ينكتـه بمخـصرة لـه
حرمـي ويـا كهفـي اذا خطـب عـرا	لـم أدر مـن أنعـاه يومـك يـا حمى
الطيـار أم أنعـى علـى الاكبـرا	الأخــوة أنعـى أم أبنـي عمـك
الحـسن الزكـي أم الرضـيع الاصـغرا	أم مـسلما وبنـي عقيـل أم بنـي
سـقما وأقتـادا وقيـدا والـسرى	أم لابنـك الـسجاد وهـو معـالج
ويـرين فـي الخيـم الحريـق المـسعرا	أم للنـساء الخائفـات يلـذن بـي

406

الا تـــردد زفــــــرة وتحـــسرا	منـــع الوعيـــد نعيهـــا وبكاءهـــا
بـدم وكـــادت فيـــه أن تتفطـــرا	يـوم قليـــل فيـــه ان بكـت الـــسما
ونـرى لـــه فــي الغاضرية عـسكرا	حتـى نـرى المهـدي يأخذ ثــاره
شـــرفا تمنـــت بعــضه أم القــرى	يـا كـربلا طلـت الـسماء مراتبـا
منـــه جنان الحـــور مـسكا أذفـرا	أرج تـضوع فـي ثـراك تعطـرت
لـي فـي المعاد ولـم يخب مـن أذخرا	يـابن النبـي ذخـرت فيـك شفاعة
وافـاك ظهـــري بالخطايـا مـوقرا	انظـر الـــي برحمـــة فيـــه اذا
لرثـاي فيـك ومـن رواه ومـن قـرا	والوالـدي ومـن أصـاخ بـسمعه
أحـد وسـبح أو دعـى أو كبــرا	صلـى عليـك الله مـا صلـى لـه

* * *

الشيخ حسن بن علي بن عبد الحسين بن نجم السعدي الرباحي)١(الدجيلي الاصل
اللملومي المحتد ، النجفي المولد والمسكن والمدفن الشهير بقفطان ولد في النجف
الاشرف سنة ١١٩٩ وتوفي بـالنجف سنة ١٢٧٩ عن عمر يناهز الثمانين كما في
الطليعة ودفن في الصحن الشريف العلوي عند الايوان الكبير المتصل بمسجد عمران كان
فاضلا ناسكا تقيا محبا للأئمة الطاهرين وأكثر شعره فيهم درس الفقه على الشيخ علي
ابن الشيخ الاكبر الشيخ جعفر حتى نبغ فيه وعد من الاعلام الافاضل ، واختص أخيرا
بصاحب الجواهر وكان بعد من أجل تلامذته وأفاضلهم ، اتخذ الوراقة مهنة لـه وورث
ذلك عنه أبناؤه وأحفاده الا انه كان يمتاز عنهم باتقان الفقه واللغة والبراعة فيهما ،
وهذا ما حدا باستاذه أن يحيل اليه والى ولده الشيخ ابراهيم تصحيح الجواهر ومراقبته
حتى قيل انه لولاهما لما خرجت الجواهر ، لان خط المؤلف كان رديا وقد كتب النسخة
الاولى عن خط المؤلف ثم صارا يحترفان بكتابتها ويبيعها على العلماء وطلاب العلم
وأكثر النسخ المخطوطة بخطهما ، وهذا دليل على أن المترجم كان يعرف ما يكتب ،
وكان جيد الخط والضبط ، ويظهر من ترجمة سيدنا الصدر لـه انه كان جامعا مشاركا في
العلوم بأكثر من ذلك فقد قال في (التكملة) : كان في مقدمي فقهاء الطائفة مشاركا في
العلوم فقيها اصوليا حكيما الهيا وكذلك لـه التقدم والبروز في الادب وسبك القريض ولـه
شعر من الطبقة العليا. انتهى.

توفي سنة ١٢٧٥ كما في التكملة أو ٧٧ كما في (الطليعة) وقال : ودفن في الصحن العلوي الشريف عند الايوان الكبير المتصل بمسجد عمران ، وترك آثارا هامة منها (أمثال القاموس) و (الاضداد) و (طب القاموس) ورسالة في الافعال اللازمة المتعدية في الواحد. وخلف من الذكور : الشيخ ابراهيم والشيخ احمد والشيخ حسين والشيخ محمد والشيخ علي والشيخ مهدي وفي) الكرام البررة) ان الشيخ حسين توفي في حياة أبيه حدود سنة ١٢٥٥.

ومن شعره في الحسين عليه السلام :

خانـــــــت مواثقـــــه الرعيـــه	نفــــسي الفـــداء لـــــسيد
بالـــسلم لا عـــزت أميــــه	رامـــــت أميـــــه ذلـــــه
والركـــــون الـــــى الدنيــه	حاشـــاه مــن خـوف المنيـة
مختــارا علـــى الـــذل المنيه	فــأبى ابـــاء الاســـد
ــعة بــالعوالي الـــسمهريه	وحمـــوه أن يـرد الـــشري
آســاد غيـــل هاشـــميه	فهنـــاك صـــالت دونــه
أخـــا الزكــي ابـــن الزكيـــه	يـــا ابـن النبــي ابـن الوصــي
لــك شنـــشنات حيدريـــه	لله كـــم فــي كـــربلا
ومواقـــف ســرت وصــيه	بــأس يـــسر محمـــدا
ضـــي عـن مغامـدها عريــه	يــوم ابـــن حيـدر والمـــوا
ف بمهجـــة حـــرى ظميـــه	يطفـــو ويرســب فــي الالــو
لــده علـــى الرمـضا رميـــه	ويـــرى أخـاه وابـــن وا
والمــاء تحـــت القعـضبيه	ملــك الـــشريعة ســيفه
لـــم يثـنهـــا غيـر المـشيه	وشـئنا الـــسراة بعزمـــة
الا مكارمـــه الـــسنيه	ســلبت محاســنه القنـــا

408

عة والمعالي السرمديه	يا سادة ملكوا الشفا
في الحشر لم يصحب وليه	حسن وليكم ومن
وحبكم يمحو الخطيه	ان الخطايا أو بقته
كم على الناس التحيه	وعليكم ما دام فضل

وله في مدح أمير المؤمنين ورثاء ولده الحسين عليهماالسلام :

في علي للمادحين مقالا	لم تدع مدحة الاله تعالى
فاسألنها عنه تجبك السؤالا	هل أتى لغير ثناه
ـزاب هودا والكهف والانفالا	والحظن الاعراف والحج والاح
ها ويـسين عم والزلزالا	وطواسين والحواميم بل طا
وامام يفصل الاجمالا	والمثاني فيها علي حكيم
وبه الله يضرب الامثالا	كل ما في الوجود أحصي فيه
ـه أتى لا تستعجلوا استعجالا	هو أمر الله الذي نزلت فيـ
عنه في كل حادث لن يخالا	هو أمر الله الذي صدرت كن
ح بلاء العباد والآجالا	وهو اللوح والذي خط في اللو
ومبين الاشياء حالا فحالا	مظهر الكائنات في مبتداها
د حديث ولا تقولن غالى	وقديم آثاره كل موجو
حين لا صورة ولا تمثالا	علم الروح جبرئيل علوما
ـه به يوم وزنه الاعمالا	وهو ميزانه الذي قدر اللـ

409

وقسيم للنار من كان عادا   ه ومولي الجنان من كان والى

ولواء الحمد العظيم بكفيـ   ـه وساقي أهل الولا السلسالا

وإياب الخلق المعاد اليـه   وعليـه حسابهم لـن يـدالا

مبدأ الأمر منتهى الأمر يـوم الـ   ـعرض سبحان من له الأمر والى

وهو نفس النبي لمـا أتـاه   وفد نجران طالبين ابتهـالا

فـدعاه وبنتـه أم سبطيـ   ـه وسبطيه لا يـرى ابـدالا

فاستهل القسيس والأسقف الـوا   فـد رعبـا اذ استبانا الوبـالا

واستمالا رضـاه بالجزية العظ   ـمى عليهم مضروبة اذلالا

أنزل الله ذا اعتمـادا اليـه   آيـة تـزعج الـوغى أهـوالا

ما استطاعت جموعهم يـوم عرض   لكفـاح الا عليهـا استطالا

وطواهم طـي السجل وطـورا   لفهـم فيـه يمنـة وشمـالا

يغمـد السيف في الرقاب وأخرى   يتحـرى تقليـدها الاغـلالا

صالح الجيش أن تكـون لـه الار   واح والنـاس تغـنم الامـوالا

قاتـل النـاكثين والقاسطين الـ   ـبهم والمـارقين عنـه اعتـزالا

كـرع السيف في دمـاهم بمـا حا   دوا عـن الـدين نزغـة وانتحـالا

من بـرى مرحبا بكـف اقتـدار   أطعمتـه مـن ذي الفقار الزيـالا

يـوم سـام الجبـان مـن حيث ولى   رايـة الـدين ذلـة وانخـذالا

قلـع البـاب بعـدما هـي أعيـت   عنـد تحريكهـا اليـسير الرجـالا

ثـم مـد الرتـاج جسرا فمـا تـم   ولكـن بـيمن يمنـاه طـالا

ولــه فــي الاحــزاب فتــح عظيــم   اذ كفــى المــؤمنين فيــه القتــالا

حــين ســالت ســيل الرمــال بــاعلا   م مــن الــشرك خافقــات ضــلالا

فلــوى خافقاتهــا بيمــين   ولــواه الخفــاق يــذري الرمــالا

ودعــا للبــراز عمــرو بــن ود   يــوم فــي خنــدق المدينــة جــالا

فمــشى يرقــل اشــتياقا علــي   للقــاه بــسيفه ارقــالا

وجثى بعــد أن بــرى ســاق عمــرو   فــوق عمــرو تــضر مــا واغتيــالا

ثــم ثنــى بــرأس عمــرو فــأثنى   جبرئيــل مهــلا اجــلالا

فــانثنى بالفخــار مــن نــصرة الديــ   ـن علــى الــشرك باســمه مختــالا

وبأحــد اذ أســلم المــسلمون الــ   مــصطفى فيــه غــدرة وانخــزالا

فأحاطــت بــه أعاديــه وانثــا   لــت عليــه مــن الجهــات أنثيــالا

عجــب مــن عــصابة أخرتــه   بــسواه لغيهــا اســتبدالا

أخرتــه عــن منــصب أكمــل اللــ   ـه بــه الــدين يومــه اكمــالا

ضــرب الله فــوق قبــر علــي   عــن جميــل الــرواق منــه جمــالا

قبــة صــاغها القــدير لافــلا   ك الــسموات شــاهدا ومثــالا

أرخــت الــشمس فوقهــا حليــة النــو   ر بهــاء وهيبــة وجــلالا

شــعب مــن شــعاعها ارتــسمت فــي   فلــك النيــرات نــورا تلالــى

وضــريح بــه تنــال الامــاني   وبــه تــدرك العفــاة النــوالا

يــا أخــا المــصطفى الــذي قــال فيــه   يــوم خــم بمــشهد مــا قــالا

لــو بعينيــك تنظــر الــسبط يــوم الــط   ـف فــردا والجــيش يــدعو النــزالا

411

ضــاق فيــه رحــب الفضـاء مجـالا	حــاربوه بعــدة وعديــد
وســقوه أســنة ونبــالا	حلــوه عــن المبــاح ورودا
فتيــة ســامروا القنــا العســالا	فتحامــت لــه حميــة ديــن
م تــراهم عنــد الكفــاح جبــالا	ثبتــوا للــوغى فللــه أقــوا
مــن حديــد كانــت لهــم ســربالا	وأضــافوا علــى الــدروع قلوبــا
يرهــب الجيــش سطوه حيــث صالا	لــيس فــيهم الا أبــي كمــي
لنحــور عــانقن بيــضا صقــالا	عــانقوا الحــور فــي القصور جزاء
فــي عـدى كالكثيــب حيــث انهــالا	وغــدا واحــد الزمــان وحيــدا
وبعــين يرنــو الخبــا والعيــالا	مفــردا يلحــظ الاعــادي بعــين
فــي صــفوف كالــسيل لمــا ســالا	شــد فــيهم وهــم ثلاثــون ألفــا
ملــك المــوت حــده الآجــالا	ناصــراه مثقــف وحــسام
فوقــه مثــل مــا ضــربن وصــالا	ضــاربا مهــره أرائــك نقــع
العــرش والارض زلزلــت زلــزالا	وهــوى الأخــشب الاشــم فمــال
ذا عنــان مرخــى وسرج مــالا	ورأت زينــب الجــواد خليــا
أمــة بــالطفوف ســاءت فعــالا	معلنــا بالــصهيل ينعــى ويــشكو
ونــادت وآســيدا وآثمــالا	فأماطت خمارهـا مـن جـوى الثكـل
أيــن مــن كــان لــي عمــادا ظــلالا	يــا جــواد الحــسين أيــن حــسين
مــن تــسنمت فــي ذراه الــدلالا	أيــن حــامي حمــاي عقــد جمــاني
حيــث مالــت وينــجح الآمــالا	أيــن للــدين مــن يقيم قنــاه

412

واستغاثت بربها ثم جرت ... نحو أشلاء ندبها أذيالا

ثم أومت لجدها والرزايا ... أسدلت دون نطقها اسدالا

جد يا جد لو رأيت حسينا ... أي هيجاء من أمية صالى

مستغيثا هل راحم أو مجير ... يستقي لابنه الرضيع زلالا

فسقاه ابن كاهل وهو في حضـ ... ـن أبيه عن الزلال نصالا

لو ترى السبط في البسيطة دامي ... النحر شلوا مبددا أوصالا

عاريا بالعرى ثلاثا وتأبى الـ ... وحش من هيبة له أن تنالا

حنطته وكفنته السوافي ... غسلته دماؤه اغسالا

ورؤوسا على الرماح أمالتـ ... ـها رياح السما جنوبا شمالا

أضرموا النار في خبانا فتهنا ... معولات بين العدى أعوالا

ما لهذا الحادي المعنف بالاد ... لاج لا ضجرة ولا امهالا

فتشاكين حسرة والتياعا ... وتباكين بالزفير وجالا

ومن قصائده في الامام الحسين عليه السلام قصيدته التي مطلعها :

يا كربلاء فهل دريت بمن على ... أكناف أرض الغاضرية خيما

من كل أروع تنتمي أحسابه ... لوسيم مجد في مراتبه سما

وله يذكر أبا الفضل العباس بن أمير المؤمنين عليه السلام :

هيهات أن تجفو السهاد جفوني ... أو أن داعية الاسى تجفوني

وأرى الخوامس في الهواجر كلما ... حنت لورد فهو دون حنيني

413

عــن وكـرهن أنينهــا كـأنيني	كــلا ولا الورقــاء ريــع فراخهــا
جــذوات وجــد مــن لظــى سجين	أنـى ويـوم الطف أضـرم في الحشا
فتيـــات فاطـم مـن بنـي ياسين	يـوم أبـو الفضـل استفزت بأسـه
للــدين أول عــالم التكــوين	فــي خيــر انصار بــراهم ربهـم
أنجـبن فيــه نتـائج الميمــون	فرقــى علـى نهـد الجـزارة هيكـل
نقـش الاراقـم فـي خطـوط بطـون	متقلــدا عـضبا كــأن فرنـده
مــن مـاء مرصـود الوشيج معـين	وأغــاث صـبيته الظمـا بمـزادة
نفـسا بهـا لاخيــه غيـر ضـنين	مـا ذاقـه وأخــوه صـاد بـاذلا
بـسداد جـيش بـارز وكمـين	حتــى اذا قطعـوا عليــه طريقـه
مــن يــوم بـدر أشـحنت بـضغون	وكتائــب مـشحونة مـشحوذة
بنفوسـها سـلبا قريــر عيــون	فثنـى مكردسهـا نـواكص وانثنى
فـي مقفـر بنجيعهـا مـشحون	أقـرى السـباع لحومهـا وعظامهـا
رسـمت لــه فـي لوحهـا المكنـون	ودعتــه أسـرار القـضا لـشهادة
عمـد الحديــد فخـر خيـر طعـين	حسموا يديـه وهامـه ضـربوه في
الان ظهــري يـا أخـي ومعينـي	ومشى اليه السـبط ينعـاه كسرت
وسـري قـومي بـل أعـز حـصوني	عبـاس كـبش كتيبتـي وكنـانتي
أسـطو وسـيف حمـايتي بيمينـي	يـا سـاعدى فـي كـل معتـرك بـه
شـملي وفـي ضـنك الزحـام يقينـي	لمـن اللـوى اعطـى ومـن هـو جامـع
ورواق أخبيتـــي وبــاب شــؤوني	أمنــازل الاقــران حامـل رايتـي

لـك موقـف بـالطف أنـسى أهلـه — حـرب العـراق بملتقـى صـفين

فـرس كـشفت بهـا الـشريعة انهـا — عـادت الــي بـصفقة المغبـون

فمـضيت محمـود النقيبـة فـائزا — بحريـر سندسـها وحـور عـين

وتركتنـي بـين العـدى لا ناصـر — يحمـي حمـاي ولا يحـامي دونـي

رهـن المنيـة بـين آل أميـة — مـا حـال مفقـود العزيـز رهـين

عبـاس تـسمع زينبـا تـدعوك مـن — لـي يـا حمـاي اذا العـدى سـلبوني

أولـست تـسمع مـا تقـول سُكَينة: — عمـاه! يـوم الاسـر مـن يحميـني؟

كـان الرجـا بـك أن تحـل وثـاقهم — لـي بالحبـال المؤلمـات متـوني

وتجيرنـي في اليتم مـن ضيم العدى — اليـوم خابـت فـي رجـاك ظنـوني

عمـاه ان أدنــو لجـسمك ابتغـي — تقبيلــه بـسياطهم ضـربوني

عمـاه مـا صـبري وأنـت مجـدل — عـار بـلا غـسل ولا تكفـين

مـن مبلـغ أم البنـين رسـالة — عـن واللــه بـشجائه مرهـون

لا تـسأل الركبـان عـن أبنائهـا — فـي كـربلاء وهـم أعـز بنـين

تـأتي لارض الطـف تنظـر ولـدها — كـابين بـين مبـضع وطعـين

الشيخ الفتوني وفاته ١٢٧٨ قال في منظومته عن الحسين (ع):

وقـام بـالأمر أخـوه الاصـغر — وهـو الحـسين الـسيد المطهـر

وهـو يكنـى بـأبي عبـدالله — لقـب بالـشهيد فـي علـم الله

مـيلاده الخمـيس في الازمـانِ — لخمـسة خلـون مـن شـعبان

قـد حملتــه بـضعة الرسـول — سـتة أشـهر علـى المنقـول

415

تاريخــه المولــود مـن غيـر دنـس	فـي طيبـة ولادة الزاكـي النـفس
بـالطف وهـو الاكبـر العميد	وولـده علـي الـشهيد
وشـهر بانويــه أم ذا الولــد	ثـم علـي الامـام المعتمـد
وهـو الـشهيد مـع أبيـه طفـلا	ثـم علـي الاصـغر ابـن ليلـى
كـذاك عبـدالله نجـل الناعيـه	وجعفـر وأمـه قـضاعيه
فاطمـة مـن البنـات تحـسب	سـكينة بنـت الربـاب زينـب
وبابـه الرشـيد ذو المقـدار	أزواجـه خمـس عـدا السـراري
بـسيف شـمر المظهـر البغـضاء	وفاتـه مـن طـف كـربلاء
وجمعـة ، خـذ وسـط القـولين	وذاك فـي السـبت أو الاثنـين

١ ـ أقول مما توصلنا اليه في بحثنا ودراستنا ان اليوم الذي قتل فيه الحسين عليه السلام هو يوم الجمعة عاشر محرم الحرام ولنا على ذلك أكثر من دليل :

١ ـ ان الحسين عليه السلام نزل كربلاء يوم الثاني من المحرم ـ وكان يوم الخميس ـ كما نص عليه جل المؤرخين بل كلهم ، وقتل يوم العاشر فيكون يوم الجمعةهو يوم مقتله.

٢ ـ صرح المؤرخون ان الحسين قد خرج من مكة يوم الثلاثاء يوم الثامن من ذي الحجـة ، فيكون يوم الثلاثين هو يوم الاربعاء وهو اول يوم من المحرم لان شهر ذي الحجـة كـان ناقصا.

٣ ـ روى المفيد في الارشاد وسائر ارباب المقاتل ان عمر بن سعد نهض لحرب الحسين عشية يوم الخميس لتسع مضين من المحرم ونادى يا خيل الله اركبي وبالجنة ابشري ، والحسين جالس أمـام بيتـه محتبيا بـسيفه اذ خفق بـرأسـه علـى ركبتيـه ، فسمعت اختـه الضجة فدنت من أخيها فقالت : يا أخي أما تسمع الاصوات قد اقتربت الى ان طلب الحسين منهم تأجيله ليلة واحدة وهي ليلة الجمعة فيكون صباح الجمعة هو يوم الواقعة.

٤ ـ ذكر أرباب المقاتل ان ابن سعد كتب الى ابن زياد يوم الثامن من المحرم وهو يوم الاربعاء ، فعلى هذا يكون مقتله يوم الجمعة.

٥ ـ جاء في كثير من أخبار أهل البيت في ظهور مهدي آل محمد (انه يظهر يوم الجمعة يوم مقتل الحسين).

٦ ـ ذكر الخوارزمي في (مقتل الحسين) ج ٢ ص ٤٧ قال : وذكر السيد الامام أبو طالب ان الصحيح في يوم عاشوراء الذي قتل فيه الحسين وأصحابه رضي الله عنهم انه

416

كـان يوم الجمعـة سـنة احدى وستين ، وقال السيد الامـين في (لـواعج الاشجان) :
وأصبح ابن سعد في ذلك اليوم وهو يوم الجمعـة أو يوم السبت فعبأ أصحابه. وقال الشيخ
عباس القمي في (نفس المهموم) : (قتل الحسين يوم الجمعة العاشر من المحرم سنة
احدى وستين من الهجرة بعد صلاة الظهر منـه ، وسنه يومئذ ثمان وخمسون سنة ،
وقيل ان مقتله كان يوم السبت وقيل يوم الاثنين والاول أصح ، قال أبو الفرج : وأمـا مـا
تقولـه العامة انه قتل يوم الاثنين فباطل ، هو شيء قالوه بلا رواية ، وكان اول المحرم
الذي قتل فيه هو يوم الاربعاء ، أخرجنـا ذلك بالحساب الهندي من سائر المزيجات واذا
كان كذلك فليس يجوز ان يكون اليوم العاشر من المحرم يوم الاثنين وهذا دليل صحيح
واضح تنضاف اليه الرواية ـ الى اخر ما قال.

في يـوم عاشـورا مـضى محزونـا	وعمــره الثمــان والخمــسون
قتـل الشهيد السبط جسمي أنهكا	قـد جـاء فـي تاريخـه حـد البكـا
مرقـده الطـف مـع الانـصار	والـراس عنـد المرتـضى الكـرار

* * *

أقول الظاهر من قولـه : والرأس عند المرتضى الكرار. انـه يختـار روايـة دفن الرأس
الشريف عند أبيه أميرالمؤمنين عليه السلام مع ان الروايات في الرأس مختلفـة وأكثرهـا
معتبرة ، فقال جماعة انـه في النجف عند أبيه أميرالمؤمنين ، ذهب اليه بعض علمـاء
الشيعة استنادا الى أخبار وردت بذلك في الكافي والتهذيب وغيرهما من طرق الشيعة
عن الائمة عليهمالسلام وفي بعضها ان الامام الصادق (ع) قال لولده اسماعيل : انه لما
حمل الى الشام سرقه مولى لنا فدفنه بجنب أميرالمؤمنين ، وهذا القول مختص بالشيعة
، وعقد لـه في «الوسائل» بابا مستقلا عنوانه : باب استحباب زيارة رأس الحسين عند
قبر أمير المؤمنين واستحباب صلاة ركعتين لزيارة كل منهما. وفي الكافي عن ابان بن
تغلب قالت كنت مع أبي عبدالله)ع) فمر بظهر الكوفة فنزل فصلى ركعتين ثم تقدم قليلا
فصلى ركعتين ، ثم سار قليلا فنزل فصلى ركعتين ، ثم قال هذا موضع قبر أميرالمؤمنين
، قلت جعلت فداك والموضعين الذين صليت فيهما ، فقال موضع رأس الحسين وموضع
منزل القائم المائل. قال : ولعل موضع القائم المائل مسجد الحنانة قرب النجف.
وعن يونس بن ظبيان عن أبي عبد الله (ع) في حديث انـه ركب وركبت معه حتى نزل
الذكوات الحمر وتوضأ ثم دنى الى أكمة فصلى عندها وبكى ثم مال الى أكمـة دونها ففعل
مثل ذلك ثم قال : الموضع الذي صليت عنده أولا موضع أميرالمؤمنين والاخر موضع
رأس الحسين (ع).

القول الثاني ان الرأس الشريف دفن بالمدينة المنورة عند قبر أمـه فاطمـة عليهاالسلام
وأن يزيد أرسلـه الى عمرو بن سعيد بن العاص بالمدينة فدفن عند أمـه الزهراء ، حكاه
سبط بن الجوزي في تذكرة الخواص عن طبقات ابن سعد.

417

القول الثالث ان الرأس الشريف بالشام حكاه سبط ابن الجوزي في تذكرة الخواص عن ابن سعد في الطبقات انه بدمشق ، حكى ابن أبي الدنيا قال وجد رأس الحسين عليه السلام في خزانة يزيد بدمشق فكفنوه ودفنوه بباب الفراديس () عند البرج الثالث مما يلي المشرق ، وكأنه هو المعروف الان بمشهد رأس الحسين عليه السلام بجانب المسجد الاموي وهو مشهد مشيد معظم.

القول الرابع ان الرأس الشريف بمصر نقله الخلفاء الفاطميون من باب الفراديس الى عقلان 'ثم نقلوه الى القاهرة وله فيها مشهد معظم يزار والى جانبه مسجد عظيم والمصريون يتوافدون الى زيارته أفواجا رجالا ونساء ويدعون ويتضرعون عنده.

القول الخامس انه أعيد الى الجسد الشريف بكربلاء ، قال السيد ابن طاوس في الملهوف على قتلى الطفوف : وكان عمل الطائفة على هذا المعنى ، قال الشيخ المجلسي : المشهور بين علمائنا الامامية انه أعيد الى الجسد وعن المرتضى في بعض مسائله انه رد الى بدنه بكربلاء من الشام. وقال الطوسي : ومنه زيارة الاربعين. وهذا القول ذكره العامة والخاصة.

أقول وقد كتب في هذا الموضوع سيدنا البحاثة المعاصر السيد محمد علي القاضي سلمه الله وأشبع البحث دراسة وتحقيقا بكتاب ضخم طبع مستقلا.

وجاء في كتاب(الحسين) لمؤلفه على جلال الحسيني ما نصه : وفي الجملة ففي أي مكان كان رأسه فهو ساكن في القلوب والضمائر قاطن في الاسرار والخواطر ، أنشدنا بعض أشياخنا :

لا تطلبـــوا المـــولى الحـــسين	بـــشرق أرض أو بغـــربِ
ودعـــوا الجميـــع وعرجـــوا	نحـــوي فمـــشهده بقلبـــي

قال السيد المقرم من معاصرينا في كتابه (مقتل الحسين) : البيتان لابي بكر الالوسي، وقد سئل عن موضع رأس الحسين فأجاب بهما.

أقول وللحاج مهدي الفلوجي بهذا المعنى:

لا تطلبـــوا رأس الحـــسين فانـــه	لا فـــي حمـــى ثـــاو ولا فـــي واد
لكنمـــا صفو الـــولاء يـــدلكم	فـــي أنـــه المقبـــور وسـط فـؤادي

ويطيب لي أن أذكر بيتين قيلتا في رأس نصب على رأس رمح وهما :

الـــشهب ومــا نالهـا هبــوبُ الرياح	هامـــة فـــي الحيـــاة طاولـت
لهــا مـــسكنا رؤوسَ الرمـــاح	أنفـت بعـد موتهـا التـرب فاختـارت

* * *

الشيخ حسين الفتوني هو العالم الاديب الشاعر حسين بن علي بن محمد بن علي بن محمد التقي بن بهاء الدين العاملي الحائري.

كان أحد الاعلام المبرزين بمعرفة الادب والنحو وكان شاعرا مجيدا جليل القدر كثير الاطلاع ، ذكره أصحاب السير والتراجم منهم شيخنا العلامة صاحب الذريعة أعلى الله مقامه بقوله : ولد في كربلاء ونشأ بها وله آثار منها (الدوحة المهدية) في تواريخ الأئمة المعصومين عليهم‌السلام وهي ارجوزة عدتها تاريخ نظمها وهي (١٢٨٧) بيتا نظمها بنفس السنة رأيتها في مكتبة الشيخ محمد السماوي في النجف كما ذكرناه في الذريعة ج ٨ ص ٢٧٤ ـ ٢٧٥ والمظنون ان جده التقي بن بهاء الدين شقيق الشيخ مهدي بن بهاء الدين الفتوني شيخ السيد مهدي بحر العلوم وظاهر أن وفاة المترجم بعد هذا التاريخ.

وذكره صاحب كتاب) ماضي النجف وحاضرها) قال :

كان حائري الولادة والمسكن وهو من الادباء الفضلاء ومن أشهر رجال هذه الاسرة وهو صاحب المنظومة المشهورة في تواريخ الأئمة وولاداتهم ووفياتهم وتعداد أزواجهم وأولادهم رتبها على مقدمة وأربعة عشر بابا وخاتمة تشتمل على ألف ومائتين وثمانية وسبعين بيتا قال في أولها:

الحمـــــــد لله العلـــيم الاحـــد	القــادر الحــي القـديم الابـدي
العلــم والقـدرة عــين ذاتـــه	والـــصدق والادراك مـــن صـــفاته

وقال في آخرها :

مـــن بعـد ســبعين مـع الثمـانِ	أبياتهـــا ألــــف ومائتـانِ

419

فرغ منها يوم الجمعة في الثاني والعشرين من المحرم سنة ١٢٧٩ هـ وله بند مشهور في مدح امامنا الهادي وبنيه وآبائه عليهم‌السلام يقول في أوله :

أيها المدلج يطوي مهمه البيد على متن نجيب أحدب الظهر متى جئت ربوع المجد والفخر وشاهدت بيوت العز والنصر فنادي داعيا بالحمد والشكر ، وبالتقديس والتهليل والتسبيح والذكر ، مرارا خاضعا مستوهبا الاذن من الحجاب ان رمت مزارا فاذا فزت باذن من عطاياهم فقد نلت من السعد وسامرت بني المجد فلجها بخضوع وخشوع صافي القصد تجد لاهوت قدس قد تردى بردة المجد وأثواب عفاف قد غشاها العلم بالزهد أنيطت بلحام الحلم والرشد وخيطت بخيوط الفضل فضلا وقارا بل تجد حبرا تقيا وشهاما هاشميا ورؤوفا فاطميا طاب فرعا ونجارا حاكم الشرع كريم الخلق والطبع حميد الاصل والفرع فذاك الكوكب الهادي الى الحاضر والبادي هو العالم والعامل والعادل والشاكر والحامد والخاضع والطالع سرا وجهارا والد البر الامين العسكري الحسن الدر الثمين ... الخ.

ولا تزال أسرة آل الفتوني تقطن كربلاء ومنها اليوم الحاج سلمان بن الشيخ مهدي بن الشيخ علي بن الشيخ حسين الفتوني من خدمة المخيم. وان كانت الفيحاء قد خلفت عبر تاريخها الادبي بند ابن الخلفة فان بند ابن الفتوني لا يقل عنه جمالا وروعة.

الشيخ ابراهيم قفطان ١٢٧٩

وسؤال رسم دارس مستعجم	سفه وقوفك بين تلك الارسم
قد كنت للوفاد محشد موسم	يا ربع مالك موحشا من بعد ما
غلبتك زفرة حسرة لم تكتم	أفكلما بالغت في كتم الهوى
صحب ابن فاطمة بشهر محرم	هلا وفيت بأن قضيت كما وفى
يعزى علا ولآل غالب ينتمي	من كل وضاح الفخار لهاشم
(ما بين سافع مهره أو ملجم)	واذا هم سمعوا الصريخ تواثبوا
ري العطاش بجنب نهر العلقمي	نفر قضوا عطشا ومن ايمانهم
بيد الضبا وغدت سهام الاسهم	أسفي على تلك الجسوم تقسمت
عن أن يحيط به فم المتكلم	قد جل بأس ابن النبي لدى الوغى

420

وأقـام مـائلهم بكـل مقـوم	اذ هـد ركـنهم بكـل مهنـد
متهلـل عنـد اللقـا متبسـم	يغشى الـوطيس بباس أروع باسل
حمـر تنـافر مـن زنيـر الـضيغم	ينحـو العـدى فتفـر عنـه كـأنهم
صـبحا تـبلج تحـت ليـل مظلـم	ويسـل أبـيض فـي الهيـاج تخالـه
فـي كـل سـطر بالأسـنة معجـم	واذا العـداة تنظمـت فرسـانها
مـسحا بكـل مقـوم ومـصمم	وافـاهم فمحـا صـحائف خطهـم
قـد خـط فـي لـوح القـضا المحكـم	قـد كـاد يفنى جمعهـم لـولا الـذي
سـهم بـه كبـد الهدايـة قـد رمـي	سـهم رمـى أحشاك يا ابن المصطفى
يـا قـوم مـا فـي جمعكم مـن مـسلم	لـم أنـس زينـب وهـي تـدعو بينـهم
ومخـدرات بنـي الحطـيم وزمـزم	انـا بنـات المـصطفى ووصـيه
منـي رداي ولا جـرى بتـوهمي	مـا دار فـي خلـدي مجاذبـة العـدى

* * *

الشيخ ابراهيم بن الشيخ حسن الرباحي من آل رباح والمشهور بقفطان ولد في النجف سنة ١١٩٩ وتوفي سنة ١٢٧٩ بالنجف عن ثمانين سنة ودفن في الصحن الشريف عند باب الطوسي مع أبيه وأخيه. وآل قفطان من بيوت العلم والفضل القديمة في النجف والمترجم له نشأ في النجف الاشرف وقرأ فيها وهو عالم عامل فاضل كامل أديب شاعر من مشاهير شعراء عصره ومن تلامذة الشيخ جعفر صاحب كاشف الغطاء. وله مراجعات ومطارحات مع شعراء عصره كعبد الباقي العمري وغيره ، ومن آثاره (أقل الواجبات) في حج التمتع ذكر فيه انه اختصره من مناسك شيخه المؤتمن الشيخ محمد حسن يعني مؤلف (الجواهر) ثم عرضه على شيخه الانصاري فكتب على هامشه ما هو طبق فتاواه وجعل رمزه (تضى) ، ومن تصانيفه أيضا رسالة توجد بخطه عند الخطيب الشيخ طاهر السماوي ألفها في اثبات حلية المتعة جوابا عن سؤالات بعض العامة ودفعا لشبهاته كتبها بأمر شيخه مؤلف (الجواهر) وفرغ منها في ١٥ صفر ١٢٦٤.

قال الشيخ آغا بزرك الطهراني في الجزء الثاني من (طبقات أعلام الشيعة) ويأتي ذكر أبيه الشيخ حسن واخوته : الشيخ احمد والشيخ محمد والشيخ علي والشيخ مهدي والشيخ حسين. أقول وللشيخ ابراهيم قصائد في رثاء الحسين عليه السلام مثبتة في

المخطوط الذي كتبته بخطي والمسمى بـ (سوانح الافكار في منتخب الاشعار) منها قصيدة أولها :

أنيخـت لهـم عنـد الطفـوف ركـابُ	ونـاداهم داعـي القـضا فأجـابوا

وأخرى مطلعها :

هـي كـربلا فاسـفح دموعـك فيهـا	ان لـم يكـن ودق الحيـا يـسقيها

عبد الباقي العمري وفاته ١٢٧٩

ومما قاله عبد الباقي العمري الموصلي البغدادي من ملحمته الشهيرة :

كنـي فـيهم وبهـم تلقبـا	طـه أبـو الغـر الميـامين الـذي
فـيهن والارض ومـن فيهـا ربـى	علـة ايجـاد الـسموات ومـن
ولا نبـي مرسـل قـد ركبـا	علـى البـراق لا نجـى مثلـه
أقـصى معـارج المعـالي رتبـا	سـرى بجسمه مـع الـروح الـى
مـن قـاب قوسـين اليـه أقربـا	أدنـاه منـه ربـه حتـى غـدا
أنجـد أو أتهـم عنـه معربـا	قـرب بعيـد الفـوز لـم يدركـه مـن
يـزدد يقينـا عنـده منـه نبـا	الا الـذي لـو كـشف الغطـاء لـم
بهـا كتـاب النـشأتين بوبـا	وبـاب هاتيـك المدينـة التـي
آثـر فـي طعامـه مـن سـغبا	أبوالحـواميم ومـن فـي هـل أتـى
سـواه للغـر الميـامين أبـا	أبـى الـه الخلـق أن يكـون مـن
وعـرض مـدحي لنجـاتي سـببا	جعلـت حبـي ومـوالاتي لهـم
تلـوح شـرعا وتبـدو هـضبا	سـفن النجـا معاقـل للالتجـا

422

مــن ســقم قــد أعجــز المطببـا	جـربتهم لقمـع كــل معضــل
خـل الطبيــب، واسـأل المجربـا	فقـل لمـن أعيـا الطبيـب داؤه
طـابوا نجــارا وتزكـوا حسـبا	عتـرة أشـرف النبيـين الاولـى
كفـوا كريمـا ونجيـا منجبـا	فكانـت الزهـرا كمـا كـان لهـا
مـن جـل عـن صـاحبة أن يصحبـا	زوجهـا فـوق السـموات بــه
النبـي والوصـي وابنيهـا حبـا	سـيدة النسـا لهـا الكسـا مـع
مثـل أبيــه خطــة الـضيم أبـى	أم الحسـين السـبط مـن بجـده
وسـال حتـى بلـغ السـيل الزبـى	حتـى جـرى بكـربلاء مـا جـرى
وانهالـت الاطـواد فيـه كثبـا	ومـادت الارض ومـادت السـما
أنفاسـها ودمعهـا تـصوبا	يـوم بـه الزهـراء قـد تـصعدت
فاختـار مـن حـوض أبيـه مـشربا	صـدوه عـن مـاء الفـرات صـاديا
عــذرا اذا عــاتبهم وانبـا	مـاذا يقولـون غـدا لجـده
للانبيـا والاوصـيا قـد نـصبا	كـان أبـوه سـيدا كجـده
رحمتــه الـذي بـه تقربـا	ذبـح عظيـم أبعـد الـرحمن عـن
أبـو الميامين النبـي المجتبـى	تغـر شـريف طالمـا قبلـه
الـى أبـي أبـي يزيـد نسـبا	سـل الـدعي ابـن زيـاد الـذي
لمـن غـدوا جـدا وأمـا وأبـا	والمـصطفى وابنتـه وصـهره
يـا آل حـرب مـنكم واحربـا	واحربـا يـا آل حـرب مـنكم
كـلا ولا أميــة المطلبـا	لا عبـد شمـسكم يـساوي هاشمـا

423

مـا لـو شـرحنـاه فـضحنـا الكتبـا	لكــم ومــنكم وعلــيكم وبكــم
فـألعن الـذي لهـا قـد شـعبا	يزيـد غيظـي كلمـا ذكـرتهم
مـا ذكـر اللعـن انتمـى وانتـسبا	الـى يزيـد دون ابلـيس اذا
قـد قـال للغـراب لمـا نعبـا	نقطـع فـي تكفيـره اذ صـح مـا
ملكـا عـضوضا فلهـذا اسـتكلبا	خلافـة قـد أرجعوهـا بعـده
أبـان مـن بغـى ومـن قـد غصبا	وقتـل عمـار بـصفين لنـا
خلـع علـي القـدر لمـا خطبـا	وأغـروا الغـر أبـا موسـى علـى
قـد فـاز فـي دنيـاه مـن تجلببا	خلـع بـه لـبس وفـي جلبابـه
عـن سـوأة ابـن العـاص لمـا غلبـا	وليلـة الهريـر قـد تكـشفت
وعـف والعفـو شـعار النجبـا	فحـاد عنـه مغـضبا حيـدرة
تركيـب مزجـي كمعـدي كربـا	ولـو يـشا ركـب فيـه زجـه

عبد الباقي الفاروقي العمري

هو ابن سليمان بن احمد العمري الفاروقي الموصلي المتوفى ١٢٧٩ هـ شاعر مؤرخ ولد بالموصل سنة ١٢٠٤ هـ ١٧٩٠ م وولي على الموصل ثم ولي ببغداد أعمالا حكومية ، وتوفي ببغداد سنة ١٢٧٩ هـ ١٨٦٢ م له ديوان شعر يسمى بـ (الترياق الفاروقي) ونزهة الدهر في تراجم فضلاء العصر ، ونزهة الدنيا ، مخطوط ترجم فيه بعض رجال الموصل من معاصريه و (الباقيات الصالحات) قصائد في مدح أهل البيت و (أهله الافكار في مغاني الابتكار) من شعره ، وعني بشرح جملة من قصائده جماعة من العلماء والادباء منهم العلامة أبو الثناء الالوسي وطبعت مستقلة عن الديوان في ايران والهند والعراق ، وللعمري مكانـة مرموقـة فـي الاوسـاط العراقيـة أدبيـة وسياسية واجتماعية ، وفي منن الرحمن لمؤلفه الشيخ جعفر النقدي ان عبد الباقي ينتهي نسبه بستة وثلاثين واسطة الى عمر بن الخطاب وكان من أفضل أدباء بغداد في عصره ، ولد سنة ١٢٠٤ وتوفي ١٢٧٨ هـ وقد أرخوا وفاته بهذا البيت:

بلـــسان يوحـــــد الله أرخ	ذاق كــاس المنــون عبــد البـاقـي

انتهى.

وله القصيدة العينية في مدح أمير المؤمنين علي بن أبي طالب عليه السلام التي يقول في أولها :

بـبطن مكــة وسـط البيـت اذ وضـعا	أنـت العلـي الـذي فـوق العلـى رفعـا
البـرج السماوي عنـه خاسئـا رجعـا	وانـت حيـدرة الغـاب الـذي أسـد
بغيـر راحــة روح القـدس مـا قرعـا	وأنـت بـاب تعـالى شـأن حارسـه

شرحها العلامـة الالوسـي ، وذكر الشيخ محمود شكري الالوسي في كتابه (المسك الاذفر) انه توفي ليلة الاثنين سلخ جمادى الاولى ١٢٧٨ هـ وقد سقط قبل موته بليلة في الساعة السادسة من ليلة الاحد من (طارمة) حرمه وكان قد خرج للتوضؤ لصلاة العشاء. ودفن بباب (الازج) ببغداد قرب قبة الجيلي. وكانت ولادته سنة ١٢٠٣ هـ. كتب عنه الدكتور محمد مهدي البصير في كتابه (نهضة العراق الادبية في القرن التاسع عشر) وجاء بكثير من نوادره وروائعه.

فمن شعره كما في ديوانه :

عليـه العقـول العشـر تلطـم بالعشـر	قضى نحبه في يوم عاشور من غدت
فعطـر منهـا الكائنـات ثـرى القبـر	قضى نحبه في نينـوى وبهـا ثـوى
نجيـع كـسا الآفـاق بالحلـل الحمـر	قضى نحبه في الطف من فوقه طفا
ببحـر دم فانصـب بحـر علـى بحـر	قضى نحبه من راح للحرب خائضا
بهـا نطقـت في الطعن ألسنة السحر	قضى نحبه والبـيض تكتب أحرفـا
تحـرر بـالانوار سـورة والفجـر	قضى نحبـه والشـمس فـوق جبينـه
ويخدش منـه الوجـه بالسن والظفـر	قضى نحبـه والكـون يـدمي بنانـه
كمـا أحدقت في بـدرها هالـة البـدر	قضى نحبـه والحـور محدقـه بـه

425

الى الله يشكو ما عراه من الضر	قضى نحبه والدين أصبح بعده
الى الملأ الاعلى بأجنحة النسر	قضى نحبه طود به طار نعشه
وما قد وقتها آل صخر من الكسر	قضى نحبه من للقوارير قد وقى
ويجرع في الهيجاء مرا على مر	قضى نحبه من يتبع الظيم بالظما
ومرقده في كربلا موضع السر	قضى نحبه روح الوجود وسره
بما تقتضيه الحكم من عالم الامر	قضى نحبه والامر لله وحده
تفوح ليوم النشر طيبة النشر	قضى نحبه ريحانة المصطفى التي
أذاق الردى عمرا وأعرض عن عمر	قضى نحبه ابن الانزع البطل الذي
سليلة فخر الكائنات أبي الغر	قضى نحبه ابن الطهر سيدة النسا
بمأتمه نحبا قضى واجب الوتر	قضى نحبه الوتر الحسين فمن قضى
لاهل كسامنه اكتسى الفخر بالفخر	قضى نحبه الفرد الذي هو خامس
بوجه المنايا وهي فاغرة الثغر	قضى نحبه والثغر يفتر باسما
أبوه حريا في أخى اشدد به أزرى	قضى نحبه ابن الصنو حيدر من غدا
ومتكأ فيها على رفرف خضر	قضى نحبه في جنة الخلد ثاويا
تكرر في أنداء مأتمه شعرى	قضى نحبه أزكى السلام عليه ما

ويقول عبد الباقي في مدح الرسول الاعظم صلى الله عليه وآله و سلم :

ولولاك آدم لم يخلق	تخيرك الله من آدم
كما ضاء تاج على مفرق	بجبهته كنت نورا تضيء

426

سجودا لـه بعـد طـرد شقى	لـذلك ابلـيس لمـا أبـى
نجـا وبمـن فيـه لـم يغـرق	ومـع نـوح اذ كنـت فـي فلكـه
فبـات وبالنـار لـم يحـرق	وخلـل نـورك صلـب الخليـل
بـه الـذكر أفـصح بـالمنطق	ومنـك التقلـب فـي الـساجدين
مـن النطـف الغـر لـم تعلـق	بمثلـك أرحامهـا الطـاهراتُ
مـع الـروح والجـسم لـم يلتقـى	سـواك مـع الرسـل فـي ايليـاء
لـك العهـد مـنهم علـى موثـق	فجئـت مـن الله فـي أخـذه
علـى غيـر رأسـك لـم يخفـق	وفـي الحـشر للحمـد ذاك اللـواء
لـدى قـاب قوسـين لـم تمـرق	وعـن غـرض القـرب منـك الـسهام
وفـي غيـر نـورك لـم ترمـق	لقـد رمقـت بـك عـين العمـاء
وصفـو المرايـا مـن الزئبـق	فكنـت لمرآتهـا زئبقـا
مـن العـدم المحـض فـي مطبـق	فلـولاك لا نظـم هـذا الوجـود
وجـود بعـرنين مستنـشق	ولا شـم رائحـة للوجـود
بحجـر العناصـر لـم يعبـق	ولـولاك طفـل مواليـده
ضـي لـك الله لـم يفتـق	ولـولاك رتـق الـسموات والارا
يـد الله فـسطاط اسـتبرق	ولـولاك مـا رفعـت فوقنـا
دنـانير فـي لوحهـا الازرق	ولا نثـرت كـف ذات البـروج
هـلال تقـوس كـالزورق	ولا طـاف مـن فـوق مـوج الـسماء
أيـدي الحيـا المغـدق	ولـولاك مـا كللـت وجنـة البـسيطة

427

مـــن اللؤلــؤ الرطــب فــي بخنــق	ولا كـست الـسحب طفـل النبـات
ولا راح يرفــل فـــي قرطــق	ولا أختـال نبـت ربـي فـي قبـا
وحــق أياديــك لـــم يـــورق	ولـــولاك غـصن نقـا المكرمـــات
على حــوزة الــدين لــم تنفـق	ولـــولاك سـوق عكـاظ الحفـاظ
لغير عروجـــك لـــم تخـــرق	وسـبع الـسماوات أجرامهــا
لموسـى بــن عمـران لـم يفلـق	ولـــولاك مثعنجــر بالعـصا
طرائـــق بـــالوهم لـــم تطــرق	وأسـرى بـك الله حتـى طرقـت
على رفـرف حـف بـالنمرق	ورقـاك مـولاك بعـد النـزول
ويـا سـابقا قـط لـم يلحـق	فيـا لاحقـا قـط لـم يـسبق
الـــى صـلب كـل تقـي نقـي	تـصوبت مـن صـاعد هابطـا
فـلا زلـت منحـدرا ترتقـي	فكـان هبوطـك عـين الـصعود

ومن شعر عبدالباقي العمري :

بغـدوة ورواحـــه المتعـــدد	ان الاثيـر علـى تقـادم عهـده
وبـدوره الايـام لـم تتجـدد	مـا كـرر الاعـوام فـي دورانـه
بـالطف مـأتم آل بيـت محمـد	الا ليـشهد عـشر كـل محـرم

وقال أيضا في شهر المحرم مخمسا لهذه الابيات :

قـد سـل نـصل محـرم مـن غمـده	يفـري قلـوب الطـاهرات بحـده
كيـف التجلـد والعـزا مـن بعـده	ان الاثيـر علـى تقـادم عهـده

بغدوه ورواحه المتعدد

428

رأس الحسين بدا برأس سنانه   لمـا رأى بـالعين مـن حدثانـه

مـا كـرر الاعـوام فـي دورانـه   والـشلو منـه مقطعـا بطعانـه

وبدوره الايام لم تتجدد

وبكـاؤه مـن رعـده لـم يـصرم   ودموعـه مـن عينـه لـم تـسجم

الا ليـشهد عـشر كـل محـرم   ولهيبـه مـن برقـه لـم يـضرم

بالطف مأتم آل بيت محمد

وقال عبدالباقي العمري ـ رواها الالوسي في شرح القصيدة العينية :

يـا عـاذل الـصب فـي بكـاه   بـالله ساـعفه فـي بكائـك

فانـه مـا بكـى وحيـدا   علـى بنـي المـصطفى أولئـك

بـل انمـا قـد بكـت علـيهم   الجـن والانـس والملائـك

يـا عـاذل الـصب فـي بكـاه   بـالله ساـعفه فـي بكائـك

فانـه مـا بكـى وحيـدا   علـى بنـي المـصطفى أولئـك

بـل انمـا قـد بكـت علـيهم   الجـن والانـس والملائـك

وقال :

لا تلمنـي ان قلـت للعـين سـحى   بـدموع علـى الحـسين وجـودي

كـل مـن فـي الوجـود يبكي علـى مـن   جـده كـان علـة للوجـود

وقال :

لــــي كــل يــوم عويــل   علـــى الحـــسين ومـــأتم

عليـــه حزنـــي طويـــل   أتـــم عمـــري ومـــا تـــم

وقال :

نحــن أنــاس اذا مـــــا   قـــد حـــل شـــهر المحـــرم

فكـــل شـــيء علينـــا   ســوى البكـــاء محـــرم

وقال في هلال المحرم متذكرا ما حل فيه من قتل أهل بيت النبي (ع):

هــل المحــر فاستــهل بعبـــرة   طرفــى علــى فقــدان أشـرف عتـرة

فتيقظـــت منـــي لـواعج حـسرة   وتنبهـــــت ذات الجنـــاح بـــسحرة

في الواديين فنبهت أشواقي

وأخــذت أنـشدها رثـاء ذوي المحـن   أخـــذت تـــردد بالغنـاء علــى فـنن

ورقـاء قـد أخـذت فنـون الحـزن عن   فبكـت معـي فقـد الحـسين أخـي الحـسن

يعقوب والالحان عن اسحاقٍ

مثلــي لتنـدب بـالطفوف عـصابة   هـي لــم تكـن ببنـي النبـي مـصابة

أنـى تبـاريني جـوى وصبابة   انـي اتخـذت رثـا الحـسين مثابـة

وكأبة وأسى وفيض مآق

وعلـى شهيد الطف حشو ضمائري   كمـــد أحـــاط ببـــاطني وبظـاهري

أو تــدرك الورقـاء كنـه سـرائري   وانـا الـذي أملـي الهـوى مـن خـاطري

وهي التي تملي من الاوراق

430

وقال وقد وقف على شاطيء الفرات متذكرا ما جرى على أبناء الرسول :

بعـدا لـشطك يـا فـرات فمـر لا تحلـو فانـك لا هنـي ولا مـري

أيسوغ لـي منـك الـورود وعنـك قد صـدر الامـام سليل سـاقي الكـوثر؟

وقال عند أول وقفة وقفها على أعتاب باب حضرة أبي تراب :

يـا أبـا الاوصياء أنـت لطاهـا صـهـره وابـن عمـه وأخـوه

ان لله فـي معانيـك سـرا أكثـر العـالمين مـا علمـوه

أنت ثاني الآباء في منتهى الـدور وآبـاؤه تعـد بنـوه

خلـق الله آدمـا مـن تـراب فهـو ابـن لـه وأنـت أبـوه

وقال في مدح الامام النازلة في رفعة قدره آية ويطعمون الطعام :

وسائل: هـل أتـى نـص بحـق علـي؟ أجبتـه هـل: أتـى نـص بحـق علـي؟!

فظننـي اذ غـدا منـي الجـواب لـه عين السـؤال صدى مـن صفحة الجبل:

ومـا درى لادرى جـدا ولا هـزلا انـي بـذاك أردت الجـد بـالهزلِ

وقال عندما جرت به السفينة في الفرات بقصد زيارة قبر أمير المؤمنين ويعسوب الدين في النجف الاشرف :

بنـا مـن بنـات المـاء للكوفـة الغـرا سبوح سرت ليلا فسبحان مـن أسرى

تمـد جناحـا مـن قوادمـه الـصبا تـروم بأكنـاف الغـري لهـا وكـرا

جرت فجرى كـل الـى خير موقـف يقـول لعينيـه قفـا نبـك مـن ذكـرى

وكـم غمـرة خـضنا اليـه وانمـا يخوض عباب البحر مـن يطلب الـدرا

تـؤم ضـريحا مـا الـضراح وان عـلا بـأرفع منـه لا وسـاكنه قـدرا

431

حـوى المرتضى سـيف القـضا   علي الـذرا، بــل زوج فاطمـة الزهـرا

مقـــام علـــي كــرم الله وجهـــه   مقــام علــي رد عـين العـلا حـسرا

وقال وهو سائر ليلا من كربلاء المقدسة للنجف الاشرف :

وليلــة حاولنـا زيــارة حيــدر   وبـدر دجاهـا مختـف تحـت أستار

بأدلاجنـا ضـل الطريـق دليلنـا   ومـن ضـل يـستهدي بـشعلة أنـوار

فلمـا تجلـت قبـة المرتـضى لنـا   وجدنا الهدى منها على النـور لا النـار

وقال يصف الصندوق العلوي والقفص الذي يمثل ضريح الامام عليه السلام :

الا ان صـندوقا أحـاط بحيـدر   وذي العرش قد أربى الى حضرة القدس

فـان لـم يكـن لله كرسـي عرشـه   فـان الـذي فـي ضـمنه آيـة الكرسـي

ومن قوله في أهل البيت عليهمالسلام :

أهـل العبـا كــم لهـم أيـاد   فاضـت علـى الكـون مـن يـديهم

فمـا احتوينـا ومـا اقتنينـا   ومـا لـدينا فمـن لـديهم

وحـق مـن قـال: (ربنـا ابعـث   فـيهم رسـولا يتلـو علـيهم)

انـي الـيهم أحـن شـوقا   أحـن شـوقا انـي الـيهم

وقال :

يـا آل مـن مـلأ الجهـات مفاخرا   وأتـى بكــم للكائنـات مظـاهرا

وهـم الـذي لكـم يعـد نظـائرا   ان الوجـود وان تعـدد ظـاهرا

وحياتكم ما فيه الا انتموا

432

أو مـا درى اذ راح يعلـن بالنـدا   ان الـذي هـو غيـركم رجـع الـصدا

فوجـدكم سـر الخليقـة أحمـدا   أنـتم حقيقـة كـل موجـود بـدا

وجميع ما في الكائنات توهم

وقال متضمنا آية" قل تعالوا ندع أبناءنا وأبناءكم ونساءنا ونساءكم" :

أهـل العبـا قـل تعالوا   علـى جميـع البرايـا

مـن بعـضها (قـل تعالوا)   وخصصـوا بمزايـا

وقال :

وجـدكم يـا آل احمـد اننـي   أعد لكـم حمـدي ومدحـي مـن الجـدِ

ومثلـي يراعـي منـه اذ شـاب مفرق   بحمـدكم سـميته شَـيبة الحمـدِ

وقال :

لا تعجبـوا ان نثـرت مـن كلمـي   فـي نعـت أبنـاء حيـدر دررا

لأننـي يـوم زرت حـضرته   ومنـه قبلـت بالـشفاه ثـرى

حـشا فمـي جـوهرا ففهـت بـه   منتظمـا تـارة ومنتثـرا

وقال :

أنـا فـي نعـت سـيد الرسـل طاهـا   وعلـي القـدر الرفيـع العمـاد

والحـسين الـشهيد بعـد أخيـه   الحـسن الـسبط والفتـى الـسجاد

وابنـه بـاقر العلـوم مـع الـصادق   والكـاظم العمـيم الايـادي

وعلـي الرضـا وقدوة أهل الارض   بحـر العطـا الامـام الجـواد

والمهـــــدي غـــوث العبـــاد	وعلــي النقي والعـسكري المنتقى
ملقيـا ســـمعه الـــى انــشادي	يسكت الـدهر ان نطقـت ويـصغي

وقال ـ وقد وقف بحضرة الامام موسى الكاظم عليه السلام :

علــي، ويـابن الطهـر سيدة النـسا	أيا ابن النبي المصطفى وابن صنوه
فأنـت الـــذي واديـه فيـه تقدسـا	لئن كـان موسى قد تقدس في طوى

وقال مرتجلا وقد وقف تجاه المرقد عائذا بأبي الرضا لائذا بجد الجواد :

كـرب وخفنـا نكبـة مـن حاسـدِ	نحـن اذا مـا عـم خطـب أو دجا
الـصادق بـن البـاقر بـن السـاجدِ	لـذنا بموسـى الكـاظم بـن جعفـر
طالـب بـن شــيبة المحامـدِ	ابـن الحـسين بـن علـي بـن أبـي

الشيخ حسين قفطان المتوفى بعد سنة ١٢٨٠
الشيخ حسين ابن الشيخ علي بن نجم الملقب بـ قفطان السعدي القفطاني توفي بعد سنة
١٢٨٠ بالنجف ودفن في الصحن الشريف في جهة باب الطوسي وقد تجاوز التسعين.
كان شاعرا وله قصائد في رثاء الحسين عليه السلام. انتهى عن الاعيان للسيد الامين.
أقول والاسرة مشهورة بالعلم والادب والشعر وجودة الخط يتوارثونه خلفا عن سلف ولا
عجب اذا برع في الشعر فالبيئة تحتم عليه ذلك أما شيخنا الشيخ آغا بزرك الطهراني فقد
ذكر في (الكرام البررة) ان الشيخ حسين توفي في حياة والده الشيخ علي وذلك في
حدود ١٢٥٥ هـ. وقال : توجد بعض أشعاره في مجموعة السيد يوسف بن محمد العلوي
الحسيني المكتوبة ١٣٠٢ رأيتها في مكتبة الملك بطهران. مرت بهذا الجزء ترجمة أخيه
الشيخ حسن وابن أخيه الشيخ ابراهيم وطائفة من أشعارهم.

الشيخ موسى محي الدين المتوفى ١٢٨١

وقف على قبر الحسين عليه السلام وقال :

بـه فـي كـل مـا أرجـو نجـاحي	أسبط المـصطفى المختـار يـا مـن
فتـى والاك مقـصوص الجنـاح	وحقـك لـم يكـن بحمـاك مثلـي

434

هـــزارك فـــي النـــواحي بـــالنواح	أرشـــني يـــا بـــن فاطمـــة فـــاني

* * *

الشيخ موسى ابن الشيخ شريف يوسف بن محمد بن يوسف آل محي الدين الحارثي الهمداني العاملي ، وتعرف أسرتهم قديما بآل أبي جامع ، وهو جدهم. لقب بذلك لانه بنى جامعا في (جبع) من لبنان في القرن العاشر واستوطنوا النجف منذ ثلاثة قرون أو أكثر ، ونبغ منهم عشرات الرجال من العلماء والادباء ومن مشاهيرهم في القرن الماضي الشيخ موسى المذكور وكان يختص بالشاعر عبدالباقي العمري وقد تكرر ذكره في ديوانه المطبوع كما كان يختص بالشاعر الشيخ عباس الملا علي وكانت وفاة الشيخ موسى سنة ١٢٨١ هـ وله ديوان شعر جمعه البحاثة الشيخ محمد السماوي بخطه وأضاف اليه ديوان ابن عمه الشيخ عبد الحسين محي الدين وجعلهما في مجلد واحد وشاعرنا المترجم له من شيوخ الادب في عصره وفرسان حلبات الادب. وساق السيد الامين في الاعيان نسبه الى أبي جامع الحارثي الهمداني فقال : الشيخ موسى ابن الشيخ شريف بن محمد بن يوسف بن علي بن جعفر بن علي بن حسن بن محي الدين بن عبد اللطيف بن علي بن احمد ابن أبي جامع الحارثي الهمداني العاملي النجفي. من أهل القرن الثالث عشر الهجري ذكره الشيخ جواد آل محي الدين العاملي النجفي في ملحق أمل الامل فقال : كان فاضلا كاملا شاعرا أديبا كاتبا ماهرا له ديوان شعر وقد خمس القصيدة المشهورة المقصورة لابن دريد وحولها الى مدح الحسنين وأبيهما أميرالمؤمنين عليهمالسلام. ذكرها السيد الامين وذكر جملة من شعره في مدح الشيخ محمد حسن صاحب الجواهر.

وجاء في (الحصون المنيعة) ج ٢ ص ٥٦٥ : كان فاضلا كاملا ، أديبا شاعرا كاتبا ماهرا له ديوان شعر. وقد خمس القصيدة الدريدية ، ومدحه الشيخ عباس الملا علي البغدادي بقصيدة عند قدومه من سفر ، مطلعها :

هـــلال علـــى غـــصن بـــان أنـــارا	تجلـــى فـــصير ليلـــي نهـــارا

كما راسله عبد الباقي العمري بقوله :

أرض الغري على باب الوصي علي	قـف بـالمطي اذا جئت العشي الـى
بـه لـك الخير يـا موسـى الكليم ولـي	وزر وصل وسلم وابك وادع وسل

435

وذكره السماوي في (الطليعة) بما يقارب هذا ، كما ذكره الشيخ الطهراني في) الكرام البررة). وله قصيدة تعرف بـ (الخالية) تتكون من ٣٢ بيتا آخر كل بيت منها كلمة (خال) وتعطي معنى غير الاخر ، وقد عارض بها قصيدة بطرس كرامة وقد تخلص في القصيدة لمدح العلامة الشيخ حسن آل كاشف الغطاء وأولها :

وأزهــر فـي أكنافــه الرنــد والخــال	سقى الخـال مـن نجد وسكانه الخـال

كما خمس القصيدة الخالية وبعث التخميس الى الآستانة الى ناظمها ، فلما وقف عليه قرضه فقال :

كالـشمس تـشرق بـين البـدو والحـضر	يا بن الشريف الذي أضحت فضائله
مطوقـا جيـدها عقـدا مـن الـدرر	خمـست بـالنظم ذات الخـال مكرمـة
أوتيـت سـؤلك يـا موسـى علـى قـدر	مـن البـديع ومـن سـحر البيـان لقد

ذكر الـدكتور عبدالرزاق محي الـدين في مؤلفـه (الحـالي والعاطل) المترجم لـه في معارضة قصيدة بطرس كرامة (الخالية) أما تخميسه للقصيدة الدريدية المذكورة في (الحـالي والعاطل) والتي نظمهـا ابن دريد في مدح ابني مكيال ـ كما هو معروف فقـد حولها شاعرنا المترجم لـه الى مدح الامامين الحسن والحسين عليهماالسلام بتخميسه للقصيدة وها نحن نروي جملة من هذا التخميس :

الحـسنين الاحـسنين عمــلا	همـا سـليلا احمـد خيـر المـلا
همـا اللـذان أثبتـا لـي أمـلا	همـا اللـذان انقعـالي غلـلا

قد وقف اليأس به على شفا

عاد بـه روض المنـى مـوردا	همـا اللـذان أورداني مـوردا
وأجريـا مـاء الحيـا لـي رغـدا	وأنـشناني بعـد مـا كنـت سدى

فاهتز غصني بعد ما كان ذوى

مـن خلتـه ألا يـرد طالبـا	كـم ردنـي بعـد الرجـاء خائبـا

هما الـلـذان عمـرا لـي جانبا	وحـين أصـبحت لــه مجانبا

من الرجاء كان قدما قد عفا

عـزاً بـه عـن درن الـدنيا اعتنت	وأولـيـاني مـا بــه الـنـفس اقتـنـت
وقلـداني منـة لــو قرنـت	وعـودانـي عـادة مـا امتهنـت

بشكر أهل الارض طراً ما وفى

اذ فـي ولاء المرتـضى قـد راشـني	أحمـد ربـي الله مـا أعاشـني
ان ابـن مكيـال الاميـر انتاشـني	فلـم أقـل وهـو بخيـر ناشـني

من بعد ما قد كنت كالشيء اللقى

وخـصني بمـا بـه قلبـي أمـن	ومـذ وفى لـي بالـذي لـه ضـمن
ومـد ضـبعي أبوالعبـاس مـن	قلـت أبـو السبطين بالوفـا قمـن

بعد انقباض الذرع والباع الوزي

وصنـو طـه المرتـضى خيـر المـلا	ذاك علـي المرتـضى عقـد الـولا
ذاك الــذي لا زال يــسمو للعـلا	ذاك الــذي رام المعـالي فعـلا

بفعله حتى علا فوق العلا

لــو كـان يرقـى أحـد بجـوده	ومـذ عـلا بـالرغم مـن حـسوده
بجـوده المـوفى علـى وفـوده	قلـت وحـق القـول مـن ودوده

ومجده الى السماء لارتقى

تـأمن فـي مـدحهما مـن الـزمن	فعـد الـى مـدح الحسين والحسن
نفـسي الفـداء لأميـري ومـن	وقـل اذا مـا فـزت منهمـا بمـن

437

وقال يمدح الامام (ع) :

يلــف الوعـوث علـى السـجسج	أقـول لمقتعـد الــيعملات
وفـي بـاب حيـدرة عـرج	أنخهـا علـى ذكـوات الغـري
مغيـث الـسغاب سـرور الـشجى	علـى أسـد الغـاب بحـر الرغـاب
ومعطـي الـسؤل الـى المرتجـي	وصي الرسـول وزوج البتـول
اذا العـام ضـاق ولـم يفـرج	أبـي الحـسنين وطلـق اليـدين
ويـا وجهـه فـي الظـلال الـدجي	وقـل يـا يـد الله فـي الكائنـات
مـن الخطـب والكـرب لـم يفـرج	سـلام عليـك بـصوت رقيـق
لأنـك أنـت حمـى الملتجـي	أتيتـك ملتجـأ منهمـا
طريـدين عنـي مهمـا أجـي	وجئـت وايقنـت أن يـصدرا
وألحـب فـي أعينـي منهجـي	فمثلـك مـن كـف عنـي الهمـوم

الحاج جواد بدقت المتوفى ١٢٨١

الحاج جواد بدقت قال في الحسين (ع) :

رسـوم بـأعلا الـرقمتين دوائـر	بواعـث انـي للغـرام مـؤازر
اذا انفـك عنهـا للجديـدين صـادر	يعاقـب فيهـا للجديـدين وارد
بـه كـل آن طـارق الـشوق خـاطر	ذكـرت بهـا الـشوق القـديم بخـاطر
فمـا لـك فـي دعـوى الـوداد أواخـر	وان لـم تـراع للـوداد أوائـلا
لمـا أنبـأت أن اللحـاظ سـواحر	وتلـك التـي لـو لـم تهـم بمهجتـي

438

لحـاظ كألحـاظ المهــى أن أتيتهـا	فواتـــك الا أن تلـك فــواتر
وجيد يريـك الظبـي عنـد التفاتهـا	هـي الظبـي مـا بـين الكثيبين نـافر
تحملـت حتـى ضـاق ذرعـا تحملـي	ومـل اصطبـاري عظـم مـا أنـا صابر
عدمتك فاقلـع عـن ملائمـة الهـوى	ألـم يعتبــر بـالأولين الاواخـر
أهـل جـاء أن ذو صـبوة نـال طـائلا	وان جـاء فـاعلم ان تلـك نـوادر
فان شئت ان تـوري بقلبـك جـذوة	يـصاعدها مـا بـين جنبيـك سـاجر
فبـادر علـى رغـم المـسرة فادحـا	عظيمـا لـه قلـب الوجـودين ذاعـر
غداة أبـو السـجاد والمـوت باسـط	مـوارد لا تلفـى لهـن مـصادر
أطـل علـى وجـه العراق بفتيـة	تناهـت بهـم للفرقـدين الاواصـر
فطـاف بهـم والجـيش تأكلـه القنـا	وتعبـث فيـه الماضـيات البـواتر
علـى معـرك قـد زلـزل الكـون هولـه	وأحجمـن عنـه الـضاريات الخـوادر
يزلـزلن أعـلام المنايـا بمثلهـا	فتقـضي بهـول الاولـين الاواخـر
وينقـض أركـان المقـادير بالقنـا	امـام علـى نقـض المقـادير قـادر
أمستنزل الاقـدار مـن ملكوتهـا	فكيـف جـرت فيمـا لقيـت المقـادر
وان اضطرابي كيـف يـصرعك القضا	وان القـضا انفـاذ مـا أنـت آمـر
أطـل علـى وجـه المعالـم مـوهن	وبـادر أرجـاء العـوالم بـادر
بـأن ابن بنت الوحي قـد أجهزت بـه	معاشـر تنميهـا الامـاء العـواهر
فمـا كان يرسو الدهر في خلدي بـأن	تـدور علـى قطـب النظـام الـدوائر
وتلـك الرفيعـات الحجـاب عـواثر	بأذيالهـا بـل انمـا الـدهر عـاثر

تجلى بها نور الجلال الى الورى	على هيئة لا أنهن حواسر
يطوف على وجه البراقع نورها	فيحسب راء أنهن سوافر
وهب انها مزوية عن حجابها	وقاهرها عن لطمة الخدر قاهر
فماذا يهيهن البدر وهو بأفقه	بأن الورى كل الى البدر ناظر
ولكن عناها حين وافت حميها	رأته صريعا فوقه النقع ثائر
فطورا تواريه العوادي وتارة	تشاكل فيه الماضيات البواتر
فيا محكم الكونين أو هي احتكامها	بأنك ما بين الفريقين عافر
وانك للجرد الضوامير حلبة	الا عقرت من دون ذاك الضوامر
ألست الذي أوردتها مورد الردى	فيا ليتها ضاقت عليها المصادر
فيا ليت صدري دون صدرك موطأ	ويا ليت خدي دون خدك عافر

*****

الشيخ كاظم الازري المسماة بـ (الازرية) عدد أبياتها ١٢٦٥ بيتا. أقول ويحتفظ بنسخة منها آل الرشتي بكربلاء ومطلعها :

هي الشمس في سماء علاها	أخذت كل وجهة بسناها

ومن شعره في رثاء الامام الحسين (ع):

شجتك الضغائن لا الاربع	وسال فؤادك لا الادمع
ولو لم يذب قلبك الاشتياق	فمن أين يسترسل المدمع
توسمتها دمنة بلقعا	فما أنت والدمنة البلقع
تعاتبها وهي لا ترعوي	وتسألها وهي لا تسمع

440

وسهمك طاش به المنزع	فعدت تروم سبيل السلو
فقد عاد في سلوة يطمع	خذوه بألسنة العاذلين
علام قد انضمت الاضلع	تجاهلت حين طلب السلو
فأمسيت من صابها تجرع	هل ارتعت من وقفة الاجرعين
يحط له الفلك الارفع	فأينك من موقف بالطفوف
وطاش بها البطل الانزع	بملمومة حار فيها القضاء
فيا ليتها الدهر لا تقلع	فما اقلعت دون قتل الحسين
أيجمعها للعلا مجمع؟	اذا ميز الشمر رأس الحسين
والا فليس لها مشرع	فيا ابن الذي شرع المكرمات
وفي نشر آلائكم يصدع	بكم أنزل الله ام الكتاب
وصدرك فيه القنا تشرع	أوجهك يخضبه المشرفي
وعلم الاله به مودع	وتعدو على صدرك الصافنات
وان غليلك لا ينقع	وينقع منك غليل السيوف
وكيف القضا بالردى يصرع	ويقضي عليك الردى مصرعا
وأحرزها دونك المصرع	بنفسي ويا ليتها قدمت
وأيسر ما كان لو يقنع	ويا ليته استبدل الخافقين
عزيز على الدين ما أوقعوا	لقد أوقعوا بك يابن النبي
تلقفها بعده مربعُ	وخوص متى نسفت مربعا
فهل بعدها جلل أسفع	لقد أوقروها بنات النبي

441

خـريم يغـار عليهـا الالــه   بمــن أرقلــوا وبمــن جعجعــوا

أتـدري حـدات مطياتهـا   وأملاكــه عنـدها تخـضع

يلاحظهـا فـي الـسبا أغلـف   ويحـدو بهـا فـي الـسرى أكـوع

يطـارحن بـالنوح ورق الحَمـامُ   فهـذي تنـوح وذي تـسجعُ

لـسهم الزفيـر بأكبادهـا   الـى أن تكـاد بـه تنـزع

تـسير وتخفـي لفـرط الحيـا   جواهـا ويعربـه المـدمع

وللحاج جواد بذكت:

فـوق الحمولـة لؤلـؤ مكنـونُ   زعـم العـواذل انهـن ضعونُ

لـم لقبوهـا بـالظعون وانهـا   غـرف الجنـان بهـن حـور عـين

يـا ايهـا الرشـأ الـذي سـميته   قمـر الـسماء وانـه لقمـين

انـي بمـن أهـواه مفتـون وذاك   بـأن يؤنـب بـالهوى مفتـون

مهمـا نظـرت وانـت مـرآة الهـوى   بـك بـان لـي مـا لا يكـاد يبـين

لـم تجـر ذكـرى نيـر وصفـاته   الا ذكرتـك والحـديث شـجونُ

ومنها :

يـا قلـب مـا هـذي شـعار متـيم؟   ولعـل حـال بنـي الغـرام فنـونُ

خفـض فخطبـك غيـر طارقـة الهـوى   ان الهـوى عمـا لقيـت يهـونُ

مـا برحـت بـك غيـر ذكـرى كـربلا   فـاذا قـضيت بهـا فـذاك يقـين

ورد ابـن فاطمـة المنـون علـى ظمـا   ان كنـت تأسـف فلتـردك منـون

ودع الحنـين فانهـا العظمـى فـلا   تـأتي عليهـا حـسرة وحنـين

442

ظهرت لها في كل شيء آية	كبرى فكاد بها الفناء يحين
بكت السماء دما ولم تبرد به	كبد ولو ان النجوم عيون
ندبت لها الرسل الكرام وندبها	عن ذي المعارج فيهم مسنون
فبعين نوح سال ما اربى على	ماسار فيه فلكه المشحون
وبقلب ابراهيم ما بردت له ـ	ما سجر النمرود وهو كمين
ولقد هوى صعقا لذكر حديثها	موسى وهون ما لقى هارون
واختار يحيى ان يطاف برأسه	وله التأسي بالحسين يكون
وأشد مما ناب كل مكون	من قال قلب محمد محزون
فحراك تيم بالضلالة بعده	للحشر لا يأتي عليه سكون
عقدت بيثرب بيعة قضيت بها	للشرك منه بعد ذاك ديون
برقي منبره رقي في كربلا	صدر وضرج بالدماء جبين
لولا سقوط جنين فاطمة لما	أودى لها في كربلاء جنين
وبكسر ذاك الضلع رُضّت أضلع	في طيها سر الاله مصون
وكذا على قوده بنجاده	فله علي بالوثاق قرين
وكما لفاطم رنة من خلفه	لبناتها خلف العليل رنين
ويزجرها بسياط قنفذ وشحت	بالطف من زجر لهن متون
وبقطعهم تلك الاراكة دونها	قطعت يد في كربلا ووتين
لكنما حمل الرؤوس على القنا	أدهى وان سبقت به صفين
كل كتاب الله لكن صامت	هذا وهذا ناطق ومبين

443

الشيخ صالح بن طعان المتوفى ١٢٨١

وغــير مجــد علــى مافــات، وانــدمي	فــآه وانــدمى مــن فــوت نــصرتِه
صــوت الجــواد أتاهــا قاصــد الخـيم	والظاهرات مـن الاستار حـين وعـت
اذا بــه مــن علــى ظهــر الجـواد رمــي	توجهــت نحــوه تلقــاء ســيدها
مــن الــصباح فلمــا ان رآه عمــي	فــصرن كــالمتمنى اذ يــرى فلقـا
مــا بــين رجــس وأفــاك ومغتــشم	لهفـي لهـن مـن الاستار بـارزة
ريـب ولا سـحبت فـي مـسحب أثـم	عــواثرا فــي ذيــول مــا تطرقهـا
كالــدر مــا بــين منثــور ومنتـظم	تخـال فـي صـفحات الخـد أدمعهـا
لـوذ القطـا خـوف بـأس الباشـق الضخم	كـل تلــوذ بــأخرى خـوف آسـرها
ركـبن فـوق ظهــور الانيــق الرسـم	حتـى اذا صـرن فـي أسـر العداة وقد
مــا بــين منعفــر فـي جنـب مـصطلم	مـروا بهـن علـى القتلـى مطرحـة
البوغـا خـضيبا بـدم النحــر واللمـم	فمـذ رأت زينـب جسم الحسـين على
الانفـاس فـي جنـدل كـالجمر مـضطرم	عـار اللبـاس قطيـع الـراس منخمـد
جـسم الـشهيد كطـود خـر منهـدم	ألقت ردى الصبر وانهارت هناك على
الاخـرى وتـدعوه يـا سـؤلي ومعتـصمي	وقد لــوت فوقـه احـدى اليدين على
يـسلوك قلبـي ولا يقلـو نعـاك فمـي	أخـي فقـدتك فقـدان الربيـع فـلا
بـشر وانـت رهـين التـرب والـرجم	هل كيف يجمل لي صبري ويهتف بي
قلب خفـوق ودمـع فـي الخـدود ودهمـي	وتــارة تـستغيث المـصطفى ولهـا

444

قـد اسـتحلوا دمـاه واحتـووا حرمـي	يـا جـد هـذا أخـي مـا بيـن طائفـة
بيـن العـدى مـن ظلـوم لـي ومهتضـم	يـا جـد أصبحت نهبـا للنوائـب مـا
ولا أخ لـي بقـى أرجـوه ذو رحـم	لا والـد لـي ولا عـم ألـوذ بـه
ضـاق الفسـيح وأطفـالي بغيـر حمـي	أخـي ذبيـح ورحلـي قـد أبيـح وبـي
والسـقم أبـراه بـري السـيف للقلـم	وابن الحسين كساه البين ثوب أسى
بيـد الفـلا مـدلجا بالسـير لـم ينـم	بـالله يـا راكـب الوجنـا يخـد بهـا
بقـرب قبـر علـي سـيد الحـرم	ان جزت بـالنجف الاعـلا فقـف كرمـا
واقـرى السـلام لخيـر الخلـق واحتـرم	وابـد الخضوع ولـذ بـالقبر ملتزمـا
وقـل لـه يـا امـام العـرب والعجـم	وانـع الحسين لـه واقصص مصيبته
نالـت ذراريـك أهـل المجـد والكـرم	هل أنـت تعلـم مـا نـال الحسين ومـا
بجانـب النهـر لهفـان الفـؤاد ظمـي	أمـا الحسين فقـد ذاق الـردى وقضـى
أمـسوا سـبايا كـسبي التـرك والخـدم	وصحبه أصبحوا صـرعى ونسـوته

* * *

الشيخ صالح بن طعان بن ناصر بن علي السـتري البحرانـي البركويانـي المتوفى بالطاعون في مكة سنة ١٢٨١ لـه ديوان في المراثي لأهل البيت مطبوع في بمبي. كذا ذكر البحاثة الطهراني في الذريعة وقال :

رأيت رثاءه للشيخ سليمان بن أحمد بن عبد الجبار المتوفى سنة ١٢٦٢ بخط صاحب أنوار البدرين وولده الشيخ احمد بن صالح المولود سنة ١٢٥١ وله ايضا ديوان مطبوع بمبي ، وتوفي سنة ١٣١٥ ذكره لنا ولده الشيخ محمد صالح بن احمد بن صالح ابن طعان المذكور قبل وفاته ١٣٣٣. وجاء في (الكرام البررة في القرن الثالث بعد العشرة) للشيخ الطهراني :الشيخ صالح بن طعان عالم فاضل وفقيه بارع ، وقال : أثنى صاحب (انوار البدرين في أحوال علماء الاحساء والقطيف والبحرين) على علمه وصلاحه ،

وكان من العلماء العاملين الورعين ، وله آثار كثيرة منها (تسلية الحزين) وله (ديوان المراثي) طبع.

الشيخ محمد علي كمونة المتوفى ١٢٨٢
الشيخ محمد علي كمونة مفخرة الامجاد وسلالة الاسخياء الاجواد نشأ في بيت الزعامة والرئاسة والوجاهة كان ولم يزل هذا البيت محط رحال الوفاد ومنتدى العلم والادب وله الشرف والرفعة والمكانة السامية لدى أهالي كربلاء وكانت بيدهم سدانة الحرم المطهر الحسيني من ذي قبل. نشأ شاعرنا نشأة علمية دينية أدبية ، نظم فأجاد وبرع حتى فاق أقرانه ولانه يتحدر من الاسرة العربية الشهيرة وهم بنو أسد الذين نالوا الشرف بمواراة جسد الحسين عليه السلام فهو لازال يفتخر بهم ولأن عددا غير قليل منهم نالوا السعادة وحصلوا الشهادة يوم عاشوراء بين يدي أبي عبدالله الحسين سيد شباب أهل الجنة فهو يتمنى أن يكون معهم ويغبطهم على هذه المنزلة فيقول :

قتــيلا ولـم أبلـغ هنـاك مـأربي	فـواحزني ان لـم أكـن يـوم كـربلا
مهجنـــة مـــن يعمــلات نجائــب	أعدها أخـا المـسرى لقطع السباسب
بنـو أسـد أسـد الهيـاج أقـاربي	فان غبت عن يـوم الحسين فلم تغب

وقد جمع بعض أحفاده شعره في مجموعة سماها (اللئالئ المكنونة في منظومات ابن كمونة) ويقع في خمسة آلاف بيت.

جاء في (الحصون المنيعة) للشيخ علي كاشف الغطاء ما نصه : الحاج محمد علي الشهير بكمونة كـان شـاعرا بليغـا أديبا لبيبا فصيحا آنست النـاس أشعاره الرائقة وأسكرتهم بمعانيها ومبانيها الفائقة ، درة صدف الادب والمعالي والعاقمة عن مثله أمهات الليالي ، قد شاهدته أيام صباي في كربلاء زمن توقفي فيها واجتمعت معه كثيرا واقتطفت من ثمار افاداته يسيرا وقد نـاهز عمره الثمانين من السنين ، وعرضت أول نظمي عليه ، وكان رجلا طوالا ذا شيبة بيضاء مهيبا شهما غيورا وكان قليل النظم وأكثر شعره في مدح الامام أمير المؤمنين عليه السلام ، وكان معاونا لأخويه الحاج مهدي والشيخ محمد حسن في تولية خدمة مرقد أبي عبدالله الحسين وسدانة هذه العتبـة المقدسة. توفي في شهر جمادي الاخرة ليلة الاحد سنة ١٢٨٢ بمرض الوباء في كربلاء ودفن مع أخيه الحاج مهدي في مقبرتهم المعدة لهم في الحائر الحسيني تجاه قبور الشهداء. أقول وفي سنة ١٣٦٧ هـ ١٩٤٨ م قام الاديب المعاصر محمد كاظم الطريحي بجمع ديوانه والتعليق عليه ونشره بمطبعة دار النشر والتأليف بالنجف الاشرف.

جاء في احدى قصائده الحسينية :

فغـــادر كـــل حـــشى مـــستطارا	متـــى فلـــك الحادثـــات اسـتدارا

446

كيــوم الـحسـين ونـار الــوغـى	تـــصـعد لـلفـرقـدين الــشـرارا
فــلــم تـــر الا شــهـابـا ورى	وشــهـما بفـيـض الـنجيـع تـوارى
فعـاد ابن أزكـى الـورى محـتـدا	وأمنـع كـل البرايـا جـوارا
تجـول علـى جـسـمه الـصـافنـات	وتكسـوه مـن نقعـها مـا اسـتأثارا

وقال رحمه الله في رأس الامام الحسين يوم طيف به على رمح :

رأس وقد بان عن جسم وطاف على	رمـح وترتيلــه القـرآن مـا بانـا
رأس تـرى طلعـة الـهادي البشـير بـه	كأنمـا رفعـوه عنــه عنوانـا
تنبـي البريـة سـيماه وبهجتـه	بـأن خيـر البرايـا هكـذا كانـا
يـسري ومـن خلفـه الاقتـاب مـوقرة	أسـرى يجـاب بهـا سـهلا وأحزانـا

وله رائعة غراء في سيدنا أبي الفضل العباس بن أمير المؤمنين علي بن أبي طالب أولها:

نبـت بالـذي رام المعـالي صـوارمه	اذا مـا حكتهـا بالفـضاء عزائمــه

وله القصيدة الشهيرة التي يصف فيها بطولة شهداء كربلاء ومنها :

أراه وأمـواج الهيـاج تلاطمــت	يعـوم بهـا مستأنـسا باسـما ثغـرا
ولـو لـم يكفكفـه عـن الفتـك حلمـه	لعفى ديـار الـشرك واستأصـل الكفـرا
ولمـا تجلـى الله جـل جلالــه	لــه خـر تعظيمـا لـه ساجدا شكـرا
هوى وهو طـود والمواضي كأنهـا	نـسور أبـت الا مناكبـه وكــرا
هـوى هيكـل التوحيـد فالـشرك بعـده	طغـى غمـره والنـاس في غمـرة سكـرى

447

وأعظم بخطب زعزع العرش وانحنى   لـه الفلـك الـدوار محـدودبا ظهـرا

غـداة أراق الـشمر مـن نحـره دمـا   لـه انبجست عـين السـما أدمعـا جمـرا

وان أنـس لا أنـسى العـوادي عواديـا   ترض القرى من مصدر العلم والصدرا

ولـم أنـس فتيانـا تنـادوا لنـصره   وللـذب عنـه عـانقوا البيض والسمرا

رجـال تواصلوا حيث طابت أصولهم   وأنفـسهم بالـصبر حتـى قـضوا صبرا

ومـا كنت أدري قبـل حمـل رؤوسـهم   بـأن العـوالي تحمـل الانجـم الزهـرا

حمـاة حمـوا خـدرا أبـى الله هتكـه   فعظمـه شـأنا وشـرفه قـدرا

فأصـبح نهبـا للمغـاوير بعـدهم   ومنـه بنـات المصطفى أبـرزت حسرا

يقنعهـا بالـسوط شـمر فـان شكت   يؤنبهـا زجـر ويوسـعها زجـرا

نـوائح الا أنهـن ثواكـل   عـواطش الا أن أعينهـا عبـرى

يصون بيمناهـا الحيـا مـاء وجههـا   ويسترها ان أعـوز السـتر باليسرى

والشاعر كمونة لم تقتصر براعته وشاعريته على الرثاء فقط وانما طرق أبواب الشعر من غزل ونسيب وفخر وحماسة فكم له من روائع عرفانية ووجدانية تنم عن ملكة أدبية ونوادر شعرية فمن ظرفه قوله في قصيدة :

نسيم الـصبا هيجت لاعـج أشـواقي   وألحقـت بالماضـي مـن الرمـق البـاقي

فيا صاحبي نجواي عوجا على الحمى   لعـل بـه رقيـا لمـا أعجـز الراقـي

فكـم لـي عهـدا بـالحمى متقادمـا   ذوى غـصن جـسمي هـو ينمـو بـايراق

ويـا عـاذلي فـي حب ليلى ومـا عسى   تـروم وميثـاقي علـى الحـب ميثـاقي

وله بمدح الامام أبي السبطين الحسن والحسين :

وصيره في شرب كوثره الساقي على جبهة العرش المعظم والساق فخلد في كفار قوم وفُسَّاق اذا وردوها من حميم وغساق

ألام على من خصه الله في العلى وزين فيه العرش فانتقش اسمه وأودع من عاداه نار جهنم لهم من ضريع مطعم وموارد

ومن نوادره قوله :

دهتني الليالي بالمشيب وبالكبر خلقت كبيرا ثم عدت الى الصغر

عصيت هوى نفسي صغير افعند ما أطعت الهوى عكس القضية ليتني

الشيخ حمادي الكواز المتوفى ١٢٨٣

فأزال رسمك أيها الطلل شوقي علمت فراعك العذل أبلت قشيبك بعدما احتملوا ربما اشتفى بك واله يسل مني نحول الجسم تنتحل أنبته كيف النار تشتعل تروي صداك وعندي الغلل ـن السحائب كيف تنهمل مطرا اليك سحابه المقل ما أنت من عشافهم عطل

أدهاك ما بي عندما رحلوا أم أنت يوم عواذلي جهلوا لا بل أراك دهتك عاصفة لو كنت تنطق أيها الطلل وكأنما ورباك ناحلة فتعير قلبي منك نار جوى ومن العجائب أن لي ديما علمت أجفاني البكاء فعلم ساق الهوى وحنيني الزجل ومن الأحبة أن تكن عطلا

449

لعبــا فجــد وجـده هـــزل	ومؤنــب ظــن الغـرام بــه
رحـــل العـزا عنـي مـــذ ارتحلـوا	وأتــى يــروم بــي العـزاء وقــد
فــي الخطـوب لمعـشر عـذلوا	ومـن الجـوى لــم تبـق باقيـة
صـبر يـــصاحبني ولا مهــل	مهـلا هـذيم فلـيس لـي أبـدا
أبنـــاء فاطمـــة بهـــا قتلـوا	قتـل الاسـى صبري بمعـضلة
بــين البريــة يـضرب المثـل	بأماثـل القـوم الـذين بهـم
نكـــد ولا بـــسيوفهم كل	ومهــذبين فمـا بجــودهم
وبحزمـــه فـي الحـرب معتقـل	مـن كـل مـشتمل بعزمتـه
كهـم الـضبا وتقـصف الأسـل	يمضي اذا ازدحـم الكمـاة وقـد
فكأنمــا هـي بـارد علـل	ويخـوض نـار الحـرب مـضرمة
غاياتـــه ولأحمــد يـــصل	وشمـر دل وصـل الثنـاء بـه
غيثــان منبعـث ومنهمـل	بــسحاب صـعدته وراحتـه
أسـد هزبـر وعـارض هطـل	وبيــوم معركـة ومكرمـة
مــن آل أحمـد فتيـة نبـل	وسرت تحـوط فتـى عـشيرتها
شـهد الحـسام بأنـه بطـل	وتحـف مـن أشـرافها بطـلا
نـسب بحبـل العـرش متـصل	وأشـم خلـق للعـلاء بـه
وجـل وقلـب عـدوه وجـل	ذوالمجد لـيس يحـل سـاحته
ظمـأ ولا لغزيرهـا وشـل	وأخـو المكـارم لا بـواردهـا
كـلا ولا الراجـي لـه خجـل	أبـدا فـلا اللاجـي بـه وجـل

450

راك وهــــي لعــزه ذلـــل	والمـستقاد لـه جبابرة الاشـر
مـسراهم المعـروف مرتحـل	ومقوضـين تحملــوا وعلــى
للمـوت فـيهم سـايق عجـل	ركبـوا الــى العـز الـردى وحـدا
ابـل المنايـا الـسود لا الابـل	وبهـم ترامـت للعلــى شـرفا
أقـصى المطالـب وانتهـى الامـل	حتــى اذا بـل المــسير بهــم
والـى الجنـان عـشية رحلـوا	نزلـوا بأكنـاف الطفـوف ضـحى
وبحـــبهم أرواحهـــم بـــذلوا	بأماجـد مـن دونهـم وقفـوا
حـرى كـأن لهـا الـضبا نهـل	وعلـى الظمـا وردوا بأفئـدة
ويـزل مـن زلزالـه الجبـل	فـي موكـب تكبـوا الاسـود بـه
وحمـى الـوطيس وسـمرهم ظلـل	فـاض النجيـع وخـيلهم سـفن
مـن قـضبهم ووجـوههم شـعل	وعجاجـة كالليـل يـصدعها
ـدنيا ورام نـداهم الاجـل	حتــى اذا رامـت بقـاءهم الـ
وعلـى الـردى جـادوا بمـا بخلـوا	بخلـوا علـى الـدنيا بأنفـسهم
أجـسامهم شـبح القنـا جعلـوا	وعـن ابـن فـاطم للعـدى كرمـا
مـن آل طـه الفـارس البطـل	ولآل حـرب ثـار بعـدهم
قتـل الحـسين يـسوقها الجهـل	جـاءت وقائـدها العمـى والـى
وأخيرهـا بالـشام متـصل	بجحافـل بـالطف أولهـا
جنـد وملـؤ صـدورهم ذحـل	ملـؤ القفـار علـى ابـن فاطمـة
أرض وفـوقهم الـسما ذبـل	طـم الفـلا فالخيـل تحـتهم

للـــشهم عـــن حالاتــــه حـــول	وأتت تحاولـــه الهـــوان وهـــل
يقـضي عليــه ذهابـــه الزجـــل	فـسطا وكـاد الكــون حـين سـطا
بـين الكتائـب هزهـا وهــل	والارض لمــا هــز أســمره
ل الالــه لهـم بمـا عملـوا	فاعجب لتـأخير العـذاب وامهـا
ديــن النبـي لغـيهم عـدلوا	مـالوا الــى الـشرك القـديم وعـن
الله مـن نـصروا ومـن خـذلوا	نـصروا يزيـد وأحمـدا خـذلوا
نهـب الـصوارم وهـو منجـدل	حتـى اغتـدى بـالترب بيـنهم
لأوام غلـــة صـــدره بلـــل	تـروي الأسنة مـن دمـاه ومـا
علمـوا هنـاك عظـيم مـا عملـوا	عجبا لهـم أمنـوا العـذاب وقـد
والكــون لــيس يحلــه الاجـــل	أيمــوت سـر الكـون بيـنهم
أودى بهـن الفـادح الجلـــل	وشـوامخ العليـاء مـن مـضر
وسمت لهـن علـى القنـا قلـل	فهـوت لهـن علـى الثـرى هـضب
ينـدك منهـا الـسهل والجبـل	والارض راكـدة الجوانــب لا
نـاءت بهـا العـسالة الـذبل	ورؤوس أوتـاد الـبلاد ضـحى
بـسماء مجـد افقهـا الاسـل	لا كالأهلـة بـل شموس عـلا
ببنــات فـاطم أنيـق بـزل	والـى ابـن آكلـة الكبـود سـرت
عـز الحمـا ودموعهـا بلـل	أسـرى علـى تلـك الجمـال وقـد
قـد أوقفتهـا المعـشر الـسفل	وعلـى يزيـد ضـحى بمجلـسه
نـدب ولا مـن هاشـم بطـل	لا مـن بنـي عـدنان يلحظهـا

452

كــــف المــصاب وجـــسمه العلـــل	الا فتـــى نهبــت حـــشاشته
بالخيزرانــــة أكـــوع رذل	وشــفاه رأس المجـــد ينكتهــا
فــي الغـي مــا لــم تركــب الاول	فاعجــب لآخــر أمــة ركبــت
أرجــاس عــاد بعــض مــا فعلــوا	هــذي فعـــالهم ومــا فعلــت
يعطـــي المـــراد ويبلـــغ الامـــل	أبنــي النبــي ومــن بحــبهم
أضــعاف مـا وهبـوا اذا ســئلوا	يـا مــن اذا لــم يســألوا وهبـوا
والعــاملون بكــل مــا عملــوا	والعـــاملون بكـل مـــا علمـــوا

* * *

جاء فـي البابليـات : اذا قـرأت ترجمـة الشاعـر الغامـر « الخبـز أرزي » وقرأت خبـر « الخبــاز البلـدي » فانـك واجـد فيهـا الموهبـة الشعرية بـارزة متجليـة : والعبقريـة لامعـة واضحة تعرف كل ذلك اذا علمت انهما كانا (أميين) لم يعرفا من التهجي حرفا ولا من الكتابة شكلا ومع ذلك فقد كانا ينظمان من الشعر مـا رق وراق وملأ الصحف والاوراق سيما وان الاول منهما كـان يبيع خبز الارز في دكان لـه فـي البصرة ينتابـه أهل الادب لاستماع شعره وطرائف نوادره. كما يروي لنـا ابن خلكان وغيره ، واذا نظرنـا بعين الحقيقة فلا نرى محلا للتعجب ولا مجالا للاستغراب فان هذا وأشباهه انما نشأوا و عاشوا في عصر هو أزهي العصور وأقربها عهدا للعربية « القرن الثالث للهجرة » عصر العلم والآداب والعروض والاعراب ، عصر الشعر والخطابة والانشاء والكتابة ، عصر الانديـة والمجالس والمعاهد والمدارس ، عصر الاحتفاء بالعلماء والاحتفال بالشعراء نعم العجب كل العجب ممن نبغ بعد أولئك بـألف عـام في عصر اندمجت فيه لغة القرآن باللغات الاجنبية التي تسيطر أهلها لا بـالعراق وحده بل على جميـع الشعوب العربية الاسلامية فطورا تحت سلطة التاتار والمغول وتارة تحت رحمة الاتراك والاعاجم فهل تأمل بعد هذا كله أن تسمع للعربية حسا أو لآدابها صوتا أو ترى في أحلامك لخيالها شبحا مـاثلا : كلا : ثم كلا ، أليس من الغريب المدهش أن ينجم في أمثال هذه العصور القاتمة شعراء فحول يضاهون من تقدمهم من شعراء تلك العصور الزاهيـة ان لم نقل يزيدون عليهم وفي طليعة هؤلاء الذين نشير اليهم هو المرحوم الشيخ حمادي الكواز فانـي لا أحسبك تصدقني من الدهشة والحيرة اذا قلت لك ان شاعرنا هذا الذي نريد أن نسرد عليك وجيزا من حياته ونثبت لك بعضا من مقاطيعه وأبياته كان أميا لم يقرأ ولم يكتب كما تسالم أهل بلاده على نقله وكان لا يعرف نحوا ولا صرفا ولا لغة ولا عروضا بل ينظم نحتا من قلبه جريـا على الذوق والسليقة واستنادا على مـا توحيـه اليه القريحـة من دون تغاير في

453

الاساليب أو اختلاف في التراكيب فاذا اعترض عليه أحد بزلة لحن في العربية يقول « راجعوا قواعدكم فالقول قولي » فيجدون الامر كما قال « بعد المراجعة « أليس هذا من الغرابة بمكان فاذا ضممت الى ذلك انه رحمه‌الله نشأ وعاش في الحلة كوازا حتى لقب هو وأخوه بذلك وانه لم يمتهن سوى بيع الكيزان والاواني الخزفية في حانوت له ينتابه الادباء والاشراف لاستماع شعره وهو مع ذلك يتضجر من الحياة وآلامها ويضج من نكد الدنيا وجور ايامها وقد أعرب عن نفسه بقوله :

الـــي أحـــداثها بالـــشر والـــشرر	أمـــسي وأصـــبح والايـــام جالبـــة
ولـــست اعـــرف غير الـــضر والـــضرر	تـــأتي فتمـــضي الـــى غيـــري منافعهـــا
اذا فمـــاذا أرى فـــي أرذل العمـــر	وفي الـــشبيبة قـــد قاسيت كـــل عنـــا
أعـــوذ بـــالله مـــن أيـــامي الأخـــر	ان كـــان آخـــر أيـــامي كأولهـــا

فهل يسعك بعد وقوفك على هذه الغرائب الا أن تؤمن به وتعتقد انه معجزة الدهر لا نابغة العصر الذي هو فيه فقد كان رحمه‌الله سريع البديهة حسن الروية كثير الارتجال فقد قرأت في احدى مجاميع البحاثة الاديب علي بن الحسين العوضي الحلي وهو من معاصري الكواز ما هذا نصه وقد نقلت ذلك من خطه قال : تذاكرت يوما أنا والكواز المذكور فيما كان يرتجله الشعراء الاقدمون من الاراجيز والقصائد فقال لي لا تعجب واكتب ما أملي عليك اذا شئت ثم ارتجل مقطوعة رقيقة لم يحضرني منها سوى قوله :

شـــوق المبـــرح فأشـــربا	أخـــوي هـــذي كـــؤس ال
ممـــا دهـــاني فانحبـــا	واذا انتحبـــت صـــبابة
ومـــن المـــلام تعجبـــا	لا تعجـــب مـــن صـــبوتي
م ولـــست أول مـــن صـــبا	مـــا كنـــت بـــدعا فـــي الغـــرا

وقال العوضي أيضا : كان هو وأخوه الشيخ صالح يمشيان معي فتذاكرنا من أنواع البديع تشبيه الشيء بشيئين فقلت في ذلك :

شـــفق المغيـــب ووجنـــة المحبـــوب	عاطيتـــه صـــرفا كـــأن شعـــاعها

وكان يوما في احدى أندية بغداد فسأله الحاضرون وفيهم العلامة السيد ميرزا جعفر القزويني والشاعر الشهير عبدالباقي الفاروقي العمري وأمين أفندي آل الواعظ وطلبوا منه تخميس البيتين المنسوبين لابن الفارض فقال على البديهة :

ز عـــم اللائــم المطيــل بعـــذلي	مثلــــه يـــستزل بـــاللوم مثلــــي

يـا نــديمي علــى الغــرام وخلـي	غـــن لـــي باســم مــن أحــب وخلـي

كل من في الوجود يرمي بسهمه

أيـــن حبـــي اذا أطعـــت الاعـــادي	بحبيــب هـــواه اقـــصى مـــرادي

فوحــق الـــوداد يـــا بـــن ودادي	لا أبـــالي ولـــو أصـــاب فـــؤادي

انه لا يضر شيء مع اسمه

أقول وقد نسب الدكتور مهدي البصير هذين البيتين للشيخ صالح الكواز وهو الاخ الاكبر للشاعر المترجم له.

وربما يشتبه غالبا في كثير من مجاميع المراثي الحسينية فينسب بعض قصائد المترجم لسميه ومعاصره الشيخ حمادي نوح أو لأخيه الشيخ صالح الكواز ـ وبالعكس ـ وها نحن نثبت مطالع قصائده في أهل البيت خاصة تمييزا لها عن سواها من مراثي غيره فمنها النونية التي مطلعها :

والـــى م تنتظـــر الرمـــاح طعانهـــا	حتـــى م تـــألف بيـــضكم أجفانهـــا

والحائية التي يستهلها بقوله :

أمـــسيت طـــوع يـــد اللـــواحي	حـــسبتك مـــن بعـــد الجمـــاح

والعينية التي أولها :

أمـا الأحبـة مـا لهـم رجـع	ألفـوا النـوى وتأبـد الربـع

455

ومن نفائسها قوله :

فكــأن مــا أوصــى بــه القطــع	أوصــى النبــي بوصــل عترتــه
فيــض الــدما ويلفهــا النقــع	هــذي رجــالهم يغـــسلها
ولآلــــه عــــن ورده دفــــع	والمــاء يـــشربه الــورى دفعــا
فغــدا لهــن علــى القنــا (رفــع)	وأبــت هنــاك(الخفــض) أرؤوسها

واللامية في رثاء أبي الفضل العباس بن علي (ع) :

مــن حملــوا العــبء الثقــيلا	أرأيــت يــوم دعــوا رحــيلا

أقول ورأيت ديوان الشاعر عند السادة آل القزويني في قضاء الهندية في خط جيد وفيه كل شعره ونقلت منه بعض القصائد ومنها هذه الرائعة الرقيقة في الامام الحسين (ع):

يكلــــف جفنــي بتـــسكابه	ألا مــا لقلبــي ممــا بـــه
أم هاجــه ذكــر أحبابــه	أهــل راعــه فقــد عصر الـشباب
لعهــد العــذيب وأترابـــه	نعــم كــان يـصبو زمان الـصبا
ويـــشنى الغــداف لتنعابـه	يعيـــر مـــسامعه للغنــا
ولا حـــب ميــة مــن دابـه	فأصــبح لا الـشوق مـن شأنه
مـــصاب الحـــسين وأصـــحابه	ولكــن شـجاه بــأرض الطفــوف
رماهــا الـــضلال بأحزابـه	عـشية بــالطف حــزب الالــه
تنقـــاد طوعــا لأذنابــه	أراد ابــن هنــد رؤوس الفخــار
ومـــن يـــدفع الليــث عن غابـه	ورام مــن العــز دفــع الأبــي

456

الا علــــى نيـــــل أرابـــــه	فنبــــه للحــرب مــــن لا ينــام
علــى الكــون طــراً باحــسابه	أخــا الــشرف البــاذخ المــستطيل
اذا عــضه الــدهر فــي نابـه	وملتجــأ الخــائف المــستجير
المنيـــة ســـهلا لطلابـــه	رأى الصعب في طلــب العــز فــي
بــأزكى الانـــام وأطيابـــه	فقـــارع أخبـــث كـــل الانـــام
دا فـــرد الخمـــيس لاعقابــــه	ومـــذ فقـــدوا اســتقبل القوم فــر
لكـــان القـــدير بأذهابـــه	ولــو شـــاء يــذهب مــن فــي الوجــود
ســجية ذي الــشرف النابــه	ولكـــن دعتـــه لـــورد الــردى
وجرعــه الحتـــف مـــن صــابه	فجانـــب للعــز ورد الحيـــاة
(محمـــد) كـــان المعــزى بـــه	فلـــو كـــان حيـــا نبـــي الهــدى
ســلب العـــدو لاثوابـــه	ولــو كنـــت فاطمـــة تنظــرين
كـــساك المـــصاب بجلبابـــه	خلعــــت فـــؤادك للحـــزن أو
فـــي الـــدهر غوثــا لمنتابــه	فمــا خلــت مـــن قـــد بـــراه الالــه
ويمـــضي بـــه حـــد أنيابـــه	بـــه الخطـــب ينـــشب أظفــاره
وشـــهب الــسما دون أطنابـــه	وبيـــت ســما رفعـــة فاغتــدى
وتهـــوي الملائـــك فـــي بابــه	تخــر الملــوك لـــه ســجدا
وتـــستاف تربـــة أعتابـــه	تطيـــل الوقـــوف بأبوابـــه
ولــم تـــرع حرمـــة أربابـــه	تـــضيع فيـــه حقـــوق الالــه
أميـــة فـــي قتـــل أوابـــه	وتـــدرك ثـــارات أوثانهـــا

وتهتك منـه الحجـاب الـذي   ملائكـه بعـض حجابـه

وتسبى كرائمه جهـرة   الـى أشـر الغـي كذابـه

فليت الوصـي يراهـن فـي   يـد الـشرك أسـرى لمرتابه

تجوب بهـا البر عجف النياق   فيقـذفهن لأسـهابه

وكافلهـا ناحـل يـشتكي   مـع الاسـر مـن ضـر أوصابه

يـصابرها محنـا لـم تـدع   مـن الحلـم شـيئا لأربابـه

يـشاهد أرؤوس سـمر العـدا   تمـيس بـأرؤوس أحبابـه

وفـي التـرب أجـسامهم صـرعا   بقـضب الـضلال وأحزابـه

ويرعـى نـساه ويرعينـه   بمنـسجم الـدمع منـسابه

يـراهن أسـرى وينظرنـه   بأسـر الـضلال ونـصابه

فينحـب شجوا علـى مـا بهـا   وتنحـب شجوا علـى مـا بـه

الـى أن تحـل بـأرض الـشئام   عـداها الغمـام بتـسكابه

الشيخ ابراهيم صادق العاملي المتوفى ١٢٨٤
قال في رثاء الحسين (ع) :

هل في الوقوف على ربى يبرين   بـرء لـداء فـي الفـؤاد دفـين

وهل الوقوف على الاماكن منقع   غلـلا وقـد بقيـت بغيـر مكـين

حتـام تتبـع لحـظ طرفك مجري الـ   ـعبرات اثـر ركائـب وظعـون

والام تنفـث مؤصـدا الزفرات عـن   جمـر بأخبيـة الحـشى مكمـون

تخفي الأسى وغريب شأنك في الأسى   بـاد يفـسره غـروب شـئون

في الخطب صبر لا يزال قريني	ولقد بلوت الحادثات وكان لي
لردى يريد الغمز ملمس لين	وتجلدي ما في كعوب قناته
جلت وان قطع الزمان وتيني	ورزين حلمي لا يطيش لمحنة
الا الذل شامل في الدين	وغزير دمعي لا يزال مصونه
أركان دين الله كل حصين	وخطوب آل محمد ضعفن من
حقا ، وعيبة علمه المخزون	هم خيرة الباري ومهبط وحيه
أبدا وموضع سره المكنون	هم نور حكمته وباب نجاته
في خلقه أبناء خير أمين	أمناؤه في أرضه خلفاؤه
من كل هول في المعاد يقيني	وهم الألى عين اليقين ولا هم
في النشأتين وحبهم يكفيني	ما لي من الاعمال الا حبهم
بدر الولا لرثائهم يدعوني	مهما أسأت وقد نسأت رثاءهم
نهضت جميع جوارحي تهجوني	واذا تقاعد منطقي عن مدحهم
رزء الاطانب من بني ياسين	أو ما درت تلك الجوارح شفها
دمعا به انبجست عيون عيوني	وحديث فاجعة الطفوف أذالها
مني بأذكى من لظى سجين	اني متى مثلتها سعر الجوى
جعلت أراجيف الاسى تعروني	ومتى أطف بالطف من ذاك العرى
ما زال يغري بالشمال يميني	وذكرت ما لم أنسه من حادث
زمر الضلالة وهو كالمسجون	حيث ابن فاطمة هناك تحوطه
عقدا لبيعته بكل يمين	وهم الألى قد عاهدوه وأوثقوا

459

حتــى أنــاخ بهــم بمــا يحويــه مــن ... آل وأمـــوال وخيـــر بنيـــن

غدروا بــه والغــدر ديــدن كــل ذي ... احـــن بكـــل دنيـــة مفتـــون

ورمـوه ـ لا عرفـوا السـداد ـ بأسـهم ... مــن كــف كفـر عـن قسـي ضغون

ولديــه مــن آســاد غالــب أشـبل ... يخـشى سـطاها ليـث كـل عـرين

وأماثـــل شـــربوا بأقـــداح الـــولا ... صـافي المـودة مـن عيـون يقـين

ســبقوا بجــدهم الوجــود وآدم ... مـا بيـن مـاء فـي الوجـود وطين

وهـم الألـى ذخـر الالـه لنـصره ... فــي كـربلا مـن مبـدأ التكـوين

لا عيـب فيهم غيـر أنهـم لـدى الــ ... ـهيجـاء لا يخـشون ريـب منـون

وعديـدهم نـزر القليـل وفـي الـوغى ... كـل يعـد اذا عـدا بمئيـن

والكـل ان حمـي الـوطيس يـرى بـه ... قـبض اللـوا فرضـا على التعيـين

مـا رنـة الاوتـار فـي نغماتهـا ... أشـهى لديـهم مـن صليـل ظبـين

كــلا ولا ألحـان معبـد عنـدهم ... في الـروع أطرب مـن صهيل صفون

ثـاروا كمـا شـاء الهـدى وتسـنموا ... صهوات قـب أياطـل وبطـون

وعدوا لقصدلو جـرت ريـح الصبا ... معهـم بـه وقفت وقـوف حـرون

واذا الهجـان جـرت لقصد أدركـت ... قـصبا يقـصر عنـه جـري هجـين

حتـى اذا مـا غـادروا مهـج العـدى ... نهبـا لكـل مهنـد مـسنون

وفـد الـردى يبغـي قـراه وكلهـم ... حـب القـرى بـالنفس غيـر ضنين

فلذاك قد سقطوا على وجـه الثـرى ... مـا بيـن مـذبوح وبيـن طعـين

وشـروا مفـاخرهم بـأنفس أنفـس ... يـنحط عنهـا قـدر كـل ثمـين

460

رجعوا هناك بصفقة المغبون	طوبى لهم ربحوا وقد خسر الألى
من بعدهم قالوا له المحزون	وغدا عميد المكرمات عميدهم
قوم حموا عنه ورود معين	ظامي الفؤاد ولا معين له على
شحنت مراصدها بكل كمين	يرنو ثغور البيد وهي فسيحة
وكأنها قطع الجبال الجون	ويرى كراديس الضلال تراكمت
كر الوصي أبيه في صفين	ويكر في تلك الصفوف مجاهدا
أزكى بنات للهدى وبنين	ويعود نحو سرادق ضربت على
فغدت فواقد هدأة وسكون	وكرائم عبث الأسى بقلوبها
يجدي ذوات لواعج وشجون	يسدي لها الوعظ الجميل وذاك لا
منها تسيخ مناكب الراهون	ونوائب عن حمل أيسر نكبة
بأغر وجه مشرق وجبين	ثم انثنى يلقى الصوارم والقنا
بثبات عزمته أبر يمين	قسما بثابت عزمه ــ واليتي
طرأ لأضحت ثم طعم منون	لو شاء اقراء الردى مهج العدى
قسرا لأومئ للمنايا كوني	أو شاء افناء العوالم كلها
ما بين كاف خطابه والنون	أنى ومحتوم المنايا كامن
سبقت بغامض علمه المخزون	لكن لسر في الغيوب وحكمة
كر المبين غدا بغير مبين	وخبا ضياء المسلمين ومحم الذ
دهش المصاب بعولة ورنين	وبنات خير المرسلين برزن من
ألف سوى التخدير والتحصين	من كل زاكية حصان الذيل ما

من هيبـــة البـاري منيـع حصون	ولـصونها أيـدي النبـوة شـيدت
فيـــه أجـب الظهـر والعـرنين	وأجـل يـوم راح مفخـر هاشـم
أسـرى تلـف أباطحـا بحـزون	يـوم بـه تلـك الفـواطم سـيرت
في السـير صعب القـود غير أمون	من فـوق غـارب كـل أعجف عـاثر
كـدموعها مـن لؤلـؤ مكنـون	وتقول للحـامي الحمى ومقالهـا
عطفـا علـي تغـض طرفـك دوني	عطـا علـي ولا أخالـك ان أقـل
خـدري وهدمت الطغـاء حصوني	أو لـست تنظرنـي وقد هتـك العـدى
مـا بـين مـذبوح وبـين طعـين	من بعد أن تركوا بنيـك على الثرى
مـن غيـر تغـسيل ولا تكفـين	عـارين منبـوذين فـي كنف العـرا
بـدم الفـؤاد كمـا أشـبن قرونـي	تلـك الرزايـا قـد أشـبن مـدامعي
جسم الحسين أراه نـصب عيـوني	أيمس عينـي الكرى وعلـى الثرى
في قلـب كـل موحـد مـدفون	مـن غير دفـن وهـو أفضل ميت

الشيخ ابراهيم بن صادق بن ابراهيم بن يحيى بن محمد بن سليمان بن نجم المخزومي العاملي الطيبي. ولد في قرية الطيبة من قرى جبل عامل سنة ١٢٢١ وتوفي بها سنة ١٢٨٤.

كان من العلماء الافاضل ، خفيف الروح درس في النجف الاشرف وكان سفره اليها سنة ١٢٥٢ ـ أقام بالنجف سبعا وعشرين سنة وبضعة أشهر قرأ على الشيخ حسن بن الشيخ جعفر صاحب كاشف الغطاء وأخيه الشيخ مهدي وعلي الشيخ مرتضى الانصاري ويروي عنهم بالاجازة ـ له منظومة في الفقه تزيد على الف وخمسمائة بيت وله قصائد عامرة في مدح أمير المؤمنين علي بن أبي طالب وقد كتب بعضها في الحرم العلوي المطهر وكان شاعرا وناثرا. ومما روى عنه قوله : وقلت أمدح سيدي ومولاي أمير المؤمنين صلوات الله عليه وعلى أبنائه الائمة الميامين ، وقد كتبت جملة من هذه القصيدة على دور ضريحه المقدس من الجوانب الاربع في ٢٠ رجب سنة ١٢٧١ ، ذكره سيدنا الحسن الصدر في (التكملة) فوصفه بالعالم الفاضل المحقق والاديب الشاعر المفلق. وكتب الاديب المعاصر السيد حسن الامين عن شاعرية الشيخ ابراهيم صادق تحت

462

عنوان (علائق شعرية عراقية عاملية) في مجلة البلاغ الكاظمية العدد السادس السنة الثانية وترجم له شيخنا الطهراني في (الكرام البررة في القرن الثالث بعد العشرة) قال : وآل صادق من أشرف بيوت العلم في جبل عامل وأعرقها في الفضل والادب نبغ فيهم أعلام في الفقه والشعر لم تزل آثارهم غرة ناصعة في جبين الدهر ولا سيما شعراؤهم الافذاذ الذين طار صيتهم في الآفاق ، وكانوا يعرفون قبل الشيخ صادق بآل يحيى نسبة الى جدهم الذي كان من صدور علماء عصره وأدبائه. أقول وسبق أن ترجمنا في هذه الموسوعة لجده الكبير الشيخ ابراهيم بن يحيى.

قال مستجيرا بالامام الحسين (ع):

فـــرض وطاعتـــه اطاعـــة جـــده	يـا سـيد الـشهداء يـا مـن حبـه
سـر الالــه مبـين مـنهج حمـده	وابن الامـام المرتضى علم الهدى
غـر الوجـوه لنـور بـاذخ مجده	وابن المطهـرة البتـول ومـن عنت
نـور الهـدى مـن نـور غـرة سعده	واخـا الزكي المجتبى الحسن الذي
وامـام كـل موحـد مـن بعـده	وأبـا علـي خيـر أربـاب العلـى
منـك الحبـا ورضـاك غايـة قـصده	وافـاك عبـدك راجيـا ومـؤملا
ــ يا خير مقصود ــ شرارة زنـده	فـاعطف عليـه بنظـرة تـوري بهـا
مـن لطـف بـاريه بجنـة خلـده	وأنلـه منـك شـفاعة يمـسي بهـا
أخنـى عليـه بجـده وبجهـده	وأقلـه سطوة حـادث الـزمن الـذي
فـــرض وطاعتـــه اطاعـــة جـــده	فلأنـت أكـرم مـن همـت أنـواؤه

وله يمدح الامام أمير المؤمنين (ع) وهي تزيد على ١٥٠ بيتا :

ولعـزه هـام الثريـا يخـضع	هـذا ثـرى حـط الاثيـر لقـدره
وجلالـه خفـض الـضراح الارفـع	وضـريح قـدس دون غايـة مجـده
مكنونـه ســر المهـيمن مـودع	أنـى يقـاس بـه الـضراح علا وفي

463

ومن الرضا واللطف نور يسطع	جدث عليه من الاله سرادق
بالبدر من حصبائه تترصع	ودت دراري الكواكب أنها
لو أنه لثرى علي مضجع	والسبعة الافلاك ود عليها
للمرتضى مولى البرية مربع	عجبا تمنى كل ربع أنه
في عالم الامكان منه موضع	ووجوده وسع الوجود وهل خلا
بعزائم منها القضا يروع	كشاف داجية القضاء عن الورى
من عزمه صبح المنايا يطلع	هزام أحزاب الضلال بصارم
فيها السواري وهي شهب تطلع	سباق غايات الفخار بحلبة
ضاقت بأيده الجهات الاربع	عم الوجود بسابغ الجود الذي
جدوى نداه كل غيث يهمع	أنى تساجله الغيوث ندى ومن
هي من ندى أمداده تتدفع	أم هل تقاس به البحار وانما
ألقى العصا بفنائه لا يفزع	فافزع اليه من الخطوب فان من
وشهدت أنوار التجلي تلمع	واذا حللت بطور سينا مجده
لجلال هيبته فؤادك يخلع	فأخلع اذا نعليك انك في طوى
عمن تمسك بالولا لا يمنع	وقل السلام عليك يا من فضله
عبد له بجميل عفوك مطمع	مولاي جد بجميلك الاوفى على
فضلا فأنت لكل فضل منبع	يرجوك احسانا ويأملك الرضا
ويهوله يوم القيامة مطلع	هيهات ان يخشى وليك من لظى
من كل ذنب لا محالة تشفع	ويهوله ذنب وأنت له غدا

لذوي الـولا مـن سلسبيل مترع	ويخاف مـن ظمـأ وحوضك فـي غد
ولديـه اعمـال الخلايـق ترفـع	يـا مـن اليـه الامـر يرجـع فـي غد
يعطـي العطـاء لمـن يشـاء ويمنـع	ولـه مـآل ثوابهـا وعقابهـا
يثنـي بمـدحتك البليـغ المـصقع	أعيت فضائلك العقول فمـا عـسى
قد أخطـأوا معنـى علاك وضيعوا	وأرى الألـى لـصفات ذاتـك حـدودا
يتـدبروا وحديث قدسـك لـم يعـوا	ولآي مجـدك يـا عظيم المجد لـم
والمـاء مـن صـم الـصفا لـك ينبـع	عجبي ولا عجب يلـين لـك الـصفا
لـدعاك مـن أقصى السباسب يـسرع	ولـك الفـلا يطـوى ويعفـور الفـلا
والـشمس بعـد مغيبهـا لـك ترجـع	ولـك الرمـام تهـب مـن أجداثها
بالـسر منـك وصـي موسـى يوشـع	والـشمس بعـد مغيبهـا ان ردهـا
مـن بـدء فطرتهـا تغيب وتطلـع	فهي التي بـك كـل يـوم لـم تـزل
تحصى وهـل تحصى النجـوم الطلـع	ولـك المناقـب كالكواكـب لـم تكـن
وكذا القـضا لـك مـن يمينـك أطـوع	فالـدهر عبـد طـايع لـك لـم يـزل
ضـربا فموسـى والعـصا لـك أطـوع	ولئن أطـاع البحـر موسـى بالعـصا
فلقـد نجـت بـك رسـل ربـك أجمـع	ولـئن نجـت بالرسـل قبلـك أمـه
أدنـى علاهـا كـل مـدح يـصنع	وصفاتك الحـسنى يقـصر عـن مـدى

ولـه ايضا فـي مدحه عليه السلام :

ومـن نـسمات كاظمـة شـذاها	أشـاقك مـن ربـي نجـد هواهـا
تـألق فـي العـشية مـن ربـاها	ونبـه وجـدك المكنـون بـرق

465

يحدث عن شذا وادي قراها	نعم وألم بي سحرا نسيم
بعامل لا عدا السقيا ثراها	فألمني وذكرني عهودا
ولي صحب كرام في حماها	بلاد لي بساحتها أناس
حنين مروعة ثكلت فتاها	أحن لجانب الشرقي منها
كما لعبت براياها صباها	وتلعب بي لذكراها شجون
عليه راح مزرورا خباها	واشتاق (الخيام)وثم صحبا
برغم الحلم تمرح في غواها	نعمت بقربها زمنا ونفسي
تمج الكاس عذبا من لماها	فكم من كاعب ألفت فبانت
بسوق اللهو طارحة عصاها	وكم هرعت لتلك وكم أقامت
لعمر العز عذب مجتناها	وكم قطعت هنالك من ثمار
غوافل راح مأمونا قضايا	بحيث العيش صفو والليالي
وان العمر أجمله تناهى	ولما أن رأيت الجهل عارا
الى الشهوات فاغرة لهاها	وان النفس لا تنفك تسعى
وألوت عن كثير من شقاها	رددت جماحها فارتد قسرا
عزائم قد أبت الا قلاها	وحركني الى الترحال عنها
تلف الارض لفا في سراها	فهبت بي لما أبغي عصوب
بفري مفاوز ناء مداها	معودة على أن لا تبالي
وتدآب السرى عنقا براها	كستها عزمة الرائي شحوبا
تثير النقع من طرب يداها	اذا ما هجهج الحادي وأضحت

466

تغافـــل وهـــي نافحـــة بـراهــا	وأمســت بعــد ارقـــال وخــب
يـسارع فـي المـسيل الـى وراهـا	يخيـــل لـــي بـــأن البـــر بحــر
رغاهـا تـشتكي نـصبا عراهـا	الـى أن مـست الاعتـاب أبـدت
يـرد الطـرف عـن بـادي سـناها	وقـد لاحـت لعينيهـا قبـاب
ونالـت بالـسرى أقـصى مناهـا	هنالـك قـرت الوجنـاء عينـا
يجاذبهـا لمـا تبغـي هواهـا	وأنحـت جانـب الغـروي شـوقا
يـضاهي النيـرين سـنا حـصاها	فوافـت بعـد جـد خيـر أرض
وأرسـت فـي ذرى حـامي حماهـا	فألقـت فـي مفاوزهـا عـصاها
وأكـرم مـن وطاهـا بعـد طاهـا	أبـي الحـسنين خيـر الخلـق طـرا
وأشـرف مـن بـه الـرحمن بـاهى	وأعظـم مـن نحتـه النيـب قـدرا
وأقـدم مفخـرا وأتـم جاهـا	وأطيـب مـن بنـي الـدنيا نجـارا
وأبـصرها اذا عميـت هـداها	وأصبرها علـى مـضض الليـالي
تطيـش لهـا حلـوم ذوي نهاهـا	وأحلمهـا اذا دهمـت خطـوب
اذا عـن نيلهـا قـصرت خطاهـا	وأنهـضها بأعبـاء المعـالي
يـرد الـدارعين الـى وراهـا	وأشـجعها اذا مـا نـاب أمـر
أحـال الـى لظاهـا مـن وراهـا	وان هـم أوقـدوا للحـرب نـارا
وارزم فـي مرابعهـا رجاهـا	وان طرقـت حماهـا مـشكلات
الـى قدسـي حضرتـه تنـاهى	جلاهـا مـن لعمـري كـل فـضل
وأولاه عـلاء لـن يـضاهى	أمـام هـدى حبـاه الله مجـدا

467

وبحـر نـدى سمـا الافـلاك قـدرا	فـدون مقامـه دارت رحاهـا
وبـدر عـلا لابنـاء الليـالي	سـناه كـل داجيـة محاهـا
متـى ودقـت مرابعهـا غيـوث	فمـن تيـار راحتـه سـخاها
أو اجتـازت مسـامعها علـوم	فزاخـر فـيض لجتـه غثاهـا
وان نهجـت سبيل الرشد يومـا	فمـن أنـوار غرتـه اهتـداها
وثـم مناقـب لعـلاه أمـست	يـد الاحصاء تقـصر عـن مـداها
وانـى لـي بحصر صفـات مـولى	لـه الاشـياء خالقهـا بـراهـا
ومـا مـدحي وآيـات المثـاني	علـى عليـاه مقـصور ثناهـا
أخـا المختـار خـذ بيـدي فـاني	غريـق جـرائم داج قـذاهـا
وعـدل فـي غـد أودي لأنـي	وقفـت مـن الجحـيم علـى شـفاها
وكـف بفـضلك الاسـواء عنـي	فقـد أخـنى علـى جلـدي أذاهـا
وباعـد بـين مـا أبغـي ودهـر	أبـت أحداثـه الا سـفاها
فأنـت أجـل مـن يـدعى اذا مـا	تفاقمـت الحـوادث لانجـلاهـا
فزعـت الـى حمـاك ونار شـوقي	للـثم ثـراك مسـعور لظاهـا
وبـت لـديك والآمـال تجـري	علـى خلـدي وظلـك منتهاهـا

السيد عبد الرحمن الالوسي ١٢٨٤

في مخطوطة بمكتبة الاوقاف العامة ببغداد ، عدد ٢٥٣٢٧ ما يلي : هذه الابيات قالها الفقير الى الله السيد عبد الرحمن الالوسي رثاء في حق جده سيد الشهداء وذلك في عاشر محرم ١٢٨٠ هـ :

هو الطف فاجعل فضة الدمع عسجدا	وضـع لـك فـولاذ الغرام مهنـدا

468

حديثا لجيران الطفوف مجددا	ورد منهل الاحزان صرفا وكررن
ودعها فداء السبط ، روحي له الفدا	وما القلب الا مضغة جد بقطعها
غدا جده المختار للناس سيدا	أترضى حياة بعد ما مات سيد
وجفن التقى والدين قد بات أرمدا	أترضى اكتحال الجفن بعد مصابه
الى الفوز واجعل صهوة الحزن مقعدا	خذ النوح في ذاك المصاب عزيمة
ألم تره من دمعه قد توردا	بكت رزءه الاملاك والافق شاهد
فما بعده نلقى ضياءا وفرقدا	فيا فرقدا ضاء الوجوه بنوره
بها عبثت أيدي الطغاء تعمدا	وريحانة طاب الوجود بنشرها
تمانعها الاوغاد منعا مجردا	ودرة علم قد أضاءت فأصبحت
ويا طال ما قد بات في حجر أحمدا	بروحي منها منظرا بات في الثرى
وهذا يزيد بالقضيب له غدا	وثغرا فم المختار مص رضابه
له فغدا في الترب ظلما موسدا	ورأسا يد الزهراء كانت وسادة
سيعلم أهل الظلم منزلهم غدا	لئن أفسدوا دنياك يا بن محمد
لكل امرء من نفسه ما تعودا	لنام أتوا بالظلم طبعا وانما
لأن الورى والخلق لم يخلقوا سدى	وحقك ما هذا المصاب بضائر
وألبسهم خزيا يدوم مدى المدا	فألبسك الرحمن ثوب شهادة
بأن لكم مجدا طويلا مخلدا	لبستم كساء المجد وهو اشارة
وقرر كل المسلمين وأشهدا	وطهركم رب العلى في كتابه
بأول قبح منك يا غادر بدا	أتنكر هذا يا يزيد وليس ذا

469

بني المصطفى عبد لكم وده صفا	فأضحى غـذاء للقلـوب ومـوردا
غريب عـن الاوطان نـاء فـؤاده	تـضرم مـن نـار الاسـى وتوقدا
ألـم بـه خطب مـن الـدهر مظلـم	تحمـل مـن أكـداره وتقلـدا
نـضى سيفه فـي وجهـه متعمدا	وجـرده عـن حقـه فتجـردا
ببـاكم ألقـى العـصا وحـريمكم	أمـان اذا دهـر طغـى وتمـردا
أتـاكم صريخا مـن ذنـوب تـواترت	على ظهره فـي اليـوم مثنـى ومفردا
أتـاكم ليـستجدي النـوال لأنكـم	كـرام نـداكم يـسبق الغيـث والنـدا
أتـاكم ليحمـي مـن أذى الـدهر نفسه	وأنـتم حمـاة الجـار ان طـارق بـدا
أتـاكم أتـاكم يـا سـلالة حيـدر	كـسيرا ينـاديكم وقـد أعلـن النـدا
حـسين أقلنـي مـن زمـان شـرابه	حمـيم وغـسلين اذا مـا صـفا صـدا
علـى جـدك المختـار صلـى الهنـا	وسـلم مـا حـاد الـى أرضـه حـدا

السيد عبد الرحمن الالوسي مفخرة من مفاخر العلم والادب وواعظ شهير قضى أكثر عمره في التدريس ، والارشاد وكان درسه ووعظه في جامع الشيخ صندل بالكرخ ببغداد ، ملم بالتفسير والفقه والحديث. أخذ العلم عن شقيقه الاكبر العلامة النحرير أبي الثناء السيد محمود شهاب الدين الالوسي ويتحلى بأخلاق فاضلة ونفس طاهرة ، محترما لدى الوزراء موقرا عند الامراء ولا سيما عند صاحب الدولة نامق باشا حين كان واليا ومشيرا على العراق حيث كان المترجم لـه حلو المفاكهة لطيف المسامرة ، ترجم لـه السيد محمود شكري الالوسي في الجزء الاول من (المسك الاذفر) المطبوع بمطبعة الآداب ببغداد سنة ١٣٤٨.

توفي يوم الثلاثاء ثالث عشر شهر ربيع الثاني من شهور السنة الرابعة والثمان بعد المائتين والالف من الهجرة ودفن قرب مرقد أخيه العلامة الشهير وعمره يقارب الستين عاما ورثاه جملة من الادباء منهم محمد سعيد النجفي فقد أنشد قصيدة غراء في مجلس العزاء وأولها :

مـن لـوى مـن بنـي لـويً ـ لواها	وطـوى طـود عزهـا وعلاهـا

470

الى أن يقول :

باسـم عبـد الـرحمن كـان نعاهـا	ان أم العلــوم تنعــى ولكــن
حادثــات الـردى فـشلت يـداها	علـم مـن بنـي لـوي لوتـه
مـن تـرى بعـد فقـده مقتـداها	كـان للنـاس مقتـدى وامامـا
حيـث مـات النـدب الـذي أحياهـا	ندبتـه مـدارس العلـم شجوا

الشيخ عبد الحسين شكر المتوفى ١٢٨٥ يرثي الحسين عليه السلام :

بـل سـقاك الـرذاذ والهطـال	تربـة الطـف لاعـدتك الـسجال
الـصبح والعـصر جـائلا يختـال	وتمشى النـسيم فـي روضـتيك
ء علـى سـبط أحمـد تنهـال	طـاولي الـسبعة الـشداد ببوغـا
مـن سـنا ضـوئه استمد الـهلال	انمـا أنـت مطلـع لهـلال
وعـروج جبريلهـا ميكـال	مهبط الـوحي عنـده فـي هبـوط
لهـم عنـك بالأسـى اشـغال	انمـا أنـت مجمـع الرسـل لكـن
وعلــي وفـاطم والآل	فيـك قـد حـل سـيد الرسـل طـه
فيـك جـذت يمينهـا والـشمال	وسـرايا بنـي نـزار ولكـن
عثـرت أي عثـرة لاتقـال	يـوم فـي عثـير الـضلال أمـي
عـصبا قادهـا العمـى والـضلال	واسـتفزت لحـرب آل علـي
ورد مـاء الفـرات وهـو الحـلال	وعـليهم قـد حرمـت يـالقومي
ترجـف الارض مـنهم والجبـال	فاسـتثارت لنـصرة الـدين أسـد

471

علــــوا لكنهــــا قــــسطال	وأقــاموا مربــا مــست النــجم
م وللــشزب الجــسوم نعــال	حيــث ســمر الرمــاح عمتهـا الهـا
كنجــوم الــسما زهيــر هــلال	فامتطــت للغــوى العتــاق رجــل
شــحذوا المرهفــات وهــي صــقال	افرغــوا الــسابغات وهــي دلاص
ولأيــــديهم خلقــــن النــــصال	بــأكف مــا اســتنجدت غير نــصل
وهــي مــن حملهـا القلـوب ثقـال	طعنــوا بالقنــا الخفــاف فعــادت
ودعــاهم داعــي القــضا فانثــالوا	صافحتهم أيــدي الــصفاح المواضي
ناصــراه الهنــدي والعــسال	فانثنى ليــث أجمــة المجــد فــردا
كتبــت فــي فرنــده الآجــال	فــصا مــن البــاس عــضبا
فيــه للحــشر تــضرب الامثــال	فــرأت منــه آل سفيان يومــا
يــرمحتهم دون اليمــين الــشمال	وأبيــه لــولا القــضا والمقــاد
حــشاه ســمر القنــا والنبــال	لكــن الله شــاء أن يتنــاهين
مــر امــام مــن شــأنه الامتثــال	حــين شــام الحــسام وامتثــل الا
الطــود لله كيــف تهــوي الجبـال	وهــوى ســاجدا علــى التــرب ذاك
وعلــى مثلـه يحـق الــزوال	كــادت الارض والــسما أن تــزولا
تــرع يومــا لاحمــد أثقــال	يــالقومي لمعــشر بيــنهم لــم
وليــتم لــم تــرحم الاطفـال	لــم تــوقر شيــوخه لمـشيب
فــصالا لــه الــسهام فــصال	ورضــيع يــال البريــة لــم يبلــغ
لــم تــصنها خـدورها والحجـال	ونــساء عــن ســلبها وســباها

472

اسدل النور حجبـــه والجــلال	ابرزوهـا حـسرى ولكـن عليهـا
وتـــداعين والـــدموع تـــذال	فتعـادين والقلـــوب حــرار
نفحـــت فيـك للـسرى مرقـــال	أيهـا الراكـب المجـد اذا مـا
مـــن شذاها طابـت صبا وشمال	عـج علـى طيبـة ففيهـا قبـور
تنتمـي البيـض والقنـا والنـزال	ان فـي طيهـا اسـودا اليهـا
مـــن لـــوي نـــساؤها والرجال	فـاذا اسـتقبلتك تـسأل عنـا
ظنـي تخفـى علـى نـزار الحـال	فاشـرح الحـال بالمقـال ومـا
قـد تنـــاهبنكم حـداد صـقال	نـاد مـا بينهـا : بنـي المـوت هبـوا
لـم يبـل الـشفاه منهـا الـزلال	تلـك أشيـاخك علـى الارض صـرعى
ارجـل الخيـل كفنتهـا الرمـال	غـسلتها دماؤهـا قلبتهـا
ركـبن النيـاق وهـي هـزال	ونـساء عودتموهـا المقاصـير
بفنـا دارهـا تحـط الرحـال	هـذه زينـب ومـن قبـل كانـت
هـق تلقـي عـصيها الـسؤال	والتـي لـم تـزل علـى بابهـا الشا
يـال قـومي تـصدق الانـذال	أمـست اليـوم واليتـامى عليهـا
مـن علـى جـوده الوجـود عيـال	مـا بقـي مـن رجالهـا الغلـب الا
وسـير الهـزال والاغـلال	وهـو يـا للرجـال قـد شفـه السقم
مغـدق الـودق والحيـا الهطـال	آل سـفيان لا سـقى لـك ربعـا
قطعـت مـن أبنائـه الاوصـال	أي جـرم لاحمـد كـان حتـى
سد فلليـث فـي الـشرى اشبـال	فالحـذار الحـذار مـن وثبـة الا

473

ت ومـــن لـــم يكـن اليـــه المئـــال	انمـا يعجـل الـذي يختـشى الفـو

*****

الشيخ عبد الحسين بن الشيخ احمد بن شكر النجفي بن الشيخ أحمد بن الحسن بن محمد بن شكر الجبـاوي النجفي. تـوفي بطهران سنة ١٢٨٥ وكان والده الشيخ احمد مـن العلماء المصنفين. رثى أهل البيت عليهم السلام بقصائد كثيرة تزيد على الخمسين منها روضة مرتبة على الحروف ، وشعره يرويه رجال المنبر الحسيني في المحافل الحسينية ، وقد تصدى الخطيب الشهير الشيخ محمد علي اليعقوبي لجمع ما نظمه الشاعر في أهل البيت عليهم السلام من القصائد والمقاطيع من مديح ورثاء فنشره في كراسـة تناهز المائة صفحة طبعت على نفقة الوجيه الحاج عبد الله شكر الصراف بالمطبعة العلمية بالنجف الاشرف عام ١٣٧٤ هـ ولأجله. وممن ترجم للشاعر المذكور شيخنا البحاثة الشيخ السماوي في (الطليعة) والعلامة الجليل الشيخ علي آل كاشف الغطاء في (الحصون المنيعة. (وآل شكر أسرة قديمة من الاسر العربية الشهيرة بالنجف عرفت باسم (شـكر) أحد أجدادها الاقدمين وأصلهم مـن عرب الحجاز. واليكم بعض قصائده الحسينية:

قـد جـذ ـ عـرنينكم فـي صـارم الغلـب	هبوا بني مضر الحمرا على النجب
قادت بها الـصعب مـنكم بـل وكل أبـي	سلت أمـي ـ حـدادا مـن مغامـدها
لأسـهم غيـر قلـب الـدين لـم يـصب	ومعرك غادر ابن المصطفى غرضا
لـم يحتملهـا نبـي أو وصـي نبـي	لله أعبـاء صـبر قـد تحملهـا
كـريم يحيـى على طـشت مـن الـذهب	فان تكـن آل اسـرائيل قـد حملـت
رأس ابن فاطمـة فـوق القنـا الـسلب	فـآل سفيان يـوم الطـف قـد حملـت
كزينـــب ويتاماهـا علـى القتـب	وهـل حملـن ليحيـى فـي الـسبا حـرم
شربوا عليه؟ هل قرعوه الثغر بالقضب	هـل سيروا الرأس فوق الرمح؟ هل
منهـا المقـانع بعـد الخـدر والحجـب	هـل قنعـت آلـه الاسـواط هـل سلبوا
أيـن الـسرايا سـرايا اخـوتي وأبـي	كـل تنـادي ولا غـوث يجيـب نـدا

474

جثمانه الحوت في قفر الفضا الرحب	وان يكن يونس آساه مذ نبذت
نبت الأسنة في جثمانه الترب	فابن النبي عن اليقطين ظلله
أبى ابن أحمد الا أشرف الرتب	وان يكن يفد بالكبش الذبيح فقد
بالنفس والاهل والابناء والصحب	حتى فدى الخلق حرصا في نجاتهم
على الخليل سلاما من أذى اللهب	ونار نمرود ان كانت حرارتها
ان تلق كل الرواسي بعضها تذب	ففي الطفوف رأى ابن المرتضى حرقا
أودى بأحشاه حر السمر والقضب	حر الحديد هجير الشمس حر ظمأ
ما بين ظام ومطوي الحشا سغب	وأعظم الكل وقدا حال صبيته
كأنها هضب سألت على الهضب	ونصب عينيه من أبنائه جثث
يا عين سحي دما يا أدمع انسكبي	يا نفس ذوبي أسى يا قلب مت كمدا
لآل يعقوب من حزن ومن كرب	هذي المصائب لا ما كان في قدم
في الحزن يعقوب في بدء وفي عقب	أنى يضاهي ابن طه أو يماثله
عيناه في مدمع والرأس ان يشب	ان حدبت ظهره الاحزان أو ذهبت
أن الفراق دهى أحشاه بالعطب	فان يوسف في الاحياء كان سوى
وانه لنبي كان وابن نبي	هذا ويحضره من ولده فنة
شبيه أحمد في خلق وفي خطب	فكيف حال ابن بنت الوحي حين رأى
بضربة رأسه ملقى على الكثب	مقطعا جسمه بالبيض منفلقا
يكفكف الدمع اذ ينهل كالسحب	هناك نادى على الدنيا العفا وغدا

وله أيضا :

لـم لا تثير نـزار الـحـرب والرهجا
وعـضب حـرب فـرى اكبادهـا ووجـا

هـلا امتطت مـن بنـات البرق شـزبها
وأفرغـت مالهـا داود قـد نـسجـا

واعتمت البيـض سـودا مـن عمائمها
واسـتلت البيـض كيمـا تـدرك الفلجا

هـل بعدما نهبـت بـالطف مهجتها
تـرجـو حيـاة وتسـتبقي لـهـا مهجـا

عهدي بها وهي دون الظيم مـا برحت
خواضـة مـن دمـا أعـدائها لجـجـا

فمـا لـها اليوم فـي الغابـات رابـضة
ومـن حـسين فـرت أعـداؤها ودجـا

تستمرئ المـاء من بعد الحسين ومن
حـر الظمـا قلبـه فـي كـربلا نـضجـا

وتـستظل وحاشـا فهـر أخبيـة
والـشمس قد ضـوعت من جسمه الأرجا

فلتـنـض اكفانهـا ان ابـن فاطمـة
مـر الـشمال لـه الاكفـان قـد نـسجا

ولتبـد فـي بـرد الهيجـا كواكبهـا
فشمـسها اتخـذت وجـه الثرى برجـا

ورأسـه فـوق ميـاد أقيـم ومـن
ثقـل الامامـة أبـصرنا بـه عوجـا

بـدر ولكـن ببـرج الـذابح انخـسفت
انـواره فكـست حمـر الدماسبجا

تـرى النصارى المسيح اليوم مرتفـعا
والمـسلمون تخـال المـصطفى عرجـا

وانمـا هـم لـسان الله قـد رفعـوا
فلـم يـزل ناطقـا فـي وحيـه لهجـا

لله مـن قمـر حفـت بـه شـهب
والكـل منهـا لعمـر الله بـدر دجـى

مـا للنهـار تجلـى بعـد أوجههـا؟
والليـل مـن بعد هاتيك الجعود سجا؟

لكـن أشجى مصاب شج مـن مضر
هاماتهـا ومـلا صـدر الفضاء شـجى

ولا أرى بعـده لا والأبـاء عـلى
الاجداث ان لفظت أجسادها حرجا

476

مـذاب أكبادهـا فـي دمعهـا امتزجـا — سبي الفواطم يـال الله حاسـرة

الافـرى رمـح زجـر قلبهـا ووجـا — أتلـك زينـب لـم تهطل مـدامعها

احشائها بـين بحـري دمعها مزجـا — بحران في مقلتيها غير ان لظى

هـزل عـوار سـرى الحـادي بهـا دلجـا — أولئـك الخـزر أم آل النبـي علـى

رأت بهـا الرحـب أمسـى ضيقا حرجـا — ضـاقت بهـا الارض أنـى وجهت نظرا

نـساءها لا ولا الطفـل الرضيـع نجـا — لـم ينجح أشـياخها سـن ولا حجـب

قلـب ابـن هنـد بمـا قـد نالهـا ثلجـا — أمـسى بهـا قلـب طـه لاعجـا وغـدا

وله أيضا :

وغـادر جفـن المعـالي قريحـا — دهـى الكون خطـب فسد الفسيحـا

فـأزهق مـنهن روحـا فروحـا — ورزء عـرا المجـد والمكرمـات

فأشـجى الكليـم وأبكـى المـسيحا — أطلـت علـى الرسـل أشـجانه

وجلبـب بالثكـل والنـوح نوحـا — وأوقـد بـالحزن نـار الخليـل

فوادحـه عرشـها والـصفيحا — وغيـر عجيـب اذا زلزلـت

ففـي الطف أضـى حسـين طريحـا — حقيـق قوائمـه أن تميـد

وقـد غيـرت منـه وجهـا صبيحـا — وان لا نـرى الـشمس بعد الطفوف

بمـرأى مـن النـاس كـم رد يوحـا — أتصهره الـشمس وهـو ابن مـن

فدتـه اذ الكـبش يفـدي الـذبيحا — ذبـيح فياليتمـا الكائنـات

من العـدو جسم ابن طـه جريحـا — عقـرن جيـاد بهـا قـد غـدا

وكـسرن للـدين جـسما صـحيحا — فقـد سـودت أوجـه العاديـات

بـرغم بنـي هاشـم هـشمت جوارحــه فاســتحالت جروحــا

تهـشم أنـوار قـدس هـوت وفـي غـرة العـرش كانـت شبوحـا

تـروح وتغـدو عـلى ماجـد لأحمـد قـد كـان روحـا وروحـا

بـرغم نـزار غـدا رقهـم لـسبي حرائــرهم مـستبيحا

فواقـد ثكلـى تـروم المنـاح فتمنـع بالـضرب مـن أن تنوحـا

وزينـب تـدعو وفـي قلبهـا أسـى تـرك الجفـن منهـا قريحـا

أغثنـي أبـي يـا غيـاث الـصريخ ومـن فـي الحـروب أبـان الفتوحـا

وقـم يـا هزبـر الـوغى منقـذا حرائـر طـه وشـق الـضريحا

تكتـم مـن خيفـة شـجوها فتـستمطر العـين دمعـا سـفوحا

صـبرت وكيـف عـلى فـادح بـرى الاصـطبار وسـد الفـسيحا

ألـم تـدر حاشـا وأنـت العلـيم الـى قلبـك الـوحي لا زال يـوحى

بـأن سـنانا بـراس الـسنان مـن الـسبط عـلا محيـا صبيحا

عـلى منبـر الـسمر يتلـو الكتـاب فيخـرس فيـه الخطيـب الفـصيحا

وان ابـن سـعد عليـه اجـال مـن الـسابحات سبوحـا سـبوحا

فيـا لرزايـا لقـد طبقـت غياهبهـا أرضـها والـصفيحا

أبـت تنجلـي بـسوى صـارم بنـصر مـن الله يبـدي الفتوحـا

بكـف امـام اذا مـا بـدا تـرى الخـضر حاجبـه والمـسيحا

يثيـر لتـدمير آل الـضلال كـصرصر عـاد مـن الحتـف ريحـا

وله في رثاء الحسين عليه السلام وهي من أشهر قصائده :

قــد فنيـتم مـا بـين بـيض الـشفار	البــدار البــدار آل نـــزار
نقبـوا بالقتـام وجـه النهـار	قومـوا الـسمر كـسروا كـل غمـد
واتركوهـا تـشق بيـد القفـار	سـوموا الخيـل أطلقوهـا عرابـا
فلقـوا الهـام بالـضبا البتـار	طـرزوا البـيض مـن دمـاء الاعـادي
ذاهـــب بــرقهن بالابــصار	افـرغـوا الـسابغات وهـي دلاص
وارفعـوا للـسما سـماء غبـار	واسطحوا مـن دم على الارض أرضا
وامتطـوا للنـزال قـب المهـار	خـالفوا الـسمر بـين بـيض المواضي
وسـمت أنـف مجـدكم بالـصغار	وابعثوهـا ضـوابحا فـأمي
ألبـستكم ذلا مـدى الاعمـار	سـلبتكم بـالرغم أي نفـوس
مـن بنـي غالـب وكـل يـسار	يـوم جـذت بـالطف كـل يمـين
ان تـــركتم أميــة بقـرار	لا تلــد هاشــمية علويــا
تركتهـا العـدى بـلا أشـفار	مـا لأسـد الـشرى وغمـض جفـون
رفعـوه فـوق القنـا الخطـار	طـاطؤ الـروس ان رأس حـسين
بعـد ظـام قـضى بحـد الغـرار	لا تـذوقوا المعـين واقـضوا ظمايـا
ان فـي الـشمس مهجـة المختـار	لا تمـدوا لكـم عـن الـشمس ظـلا
فحـسين علـى البـسيطة عـار	أنـزار نـضوا بـرود التهـاني
هـذه زينـب علـى الاكـوار	حـق أن لا تكفنـوا هاشـميا
سـاتر دون محـصنات نـزار	لا تـشقوا لآل فهـر قبـورا

كدن يغرقن بالدموع الجواري	هتكوا عن نسائكم كل خدر
عن بكا بالعشي والابكار	هل خبا بعد محصنات حسين
قصمت من لوي كل فقار	باكيات لولا لهيب جواها
د ليوث الوغى حماة الذمار	شأنها النوح ليس تهدأ آنا
هذه زينب على الاكوار	نادبات فلو وعتها لوي
ساتر دون محصنات نزار	أين من أهلها بنو شيبة الحم
السير كلا ولا الهزال العواري	أين هم عن عقائل ما عرفن
يتشاكين عن قلوب حرار	أين هم عن حرائر بأنين
وليهبوا طرا لاخذ الثار	فليسدوا رحب الفضا بالعوادي
بأيادي في الطعن غير قصار	وليقلوا الاعلام تخفق سودا
أسد الله حيدر الكرار	وليؤموا الى زعيم لوي
ولينادوا بذلة وانكسار	وليضجوا بعولة وانتحاب
فهم في الطفوف نهب الغرار	عظم الله في بنيك لك الاجر
قد غدا مرتعا لبيض الشفار	قم أثر نقعها فان حسينا
وبأحشاك أي جذوة نار	حاش لله أن تغض جفونا
حدبت من قراك أي فقار	لا ولكنما رزايا حسين

السيد راضي القزويني المتوفى ١٢٨٥ قال في أبي الفضل العباس عليه السلام :

أبى الفضل الا أن تكون له أبا	أبا الفضل يا من أسس الفضل والابا
وما كل ساع بالغ ما تطلبا	تطلبت أسباب العلى فبلغتها

480

ودون احتمال الـضيم عـز ومنعـة   تخيـرت أطـراف الأسـنة مركبـا

وفيت بعهد المـشرفية فـي الـوغى   ضـرابا وما أبقيـت للـسيف مـضربا

لقـد خـضت تيـار المنايـا بموقـف   تخـال بـه بـرق الأسـنة خلبـا

اذا لفظت حرفـا سيوفك مهمـلا   تتـرجمـه سـمر العوامـل معربـا

ولمـا أبـت أن يـشرب المـاء طيبـا   أميـة لا ذاقـت مـن المـاء طيبـا

جـلا ابـن جـلا ليـل القتـام كأنـه   صبـاح هـدى جلـى مـن الشرك غيهبا

وليـث وغـي يـأبى سـوى شـجر القنا   لـدى الـروع غابـا والمهنـد مخلبا

يـذكرهم بـأس الوصـي فكلمـا   رمـى موكبا بـالعزم صـادم موكبا

وتحـسب فـي أفـق القتـام حـسامه   لـرجم شـياطين الفـوارس كوكبـا

وقفـت بمـستن النـزال ولـم تجـد   سوى الموت في الهيجا من الضيم مهربا

الـى أن وردت المـوت والمـوت عـادة   لكـم عرفـت تحـت الأسـنة والـضبا

ولا عيب فـي الحر الكريم اذا قـضى   بحـر الـضبا حـرا كريمـا مهـذبا

رعـى الله جـسما بالـسيوف موزعـا   وقلبـا علـى حـر الظمـا متقلبـا

ورأس فخار سيم خفضا فمـا ارتضى   سوى الرفـع فـوق السـمهرية منصبا

بنفسي الـذي واسـى أخـاه بنفسه   وقـام بمـا سـن الأخـاء وأوجبـا

رنـا ظاميـا والمـاء يلمـع طاميـا   وصـعد أنفاسـا بهـا الـدمع صـوبا

ومـا همـه الا تعطـش صـبية   الـى المـاء أوراهـا الاوام تلهبـا

على قربـه منـه تنـائى وصـوله   وأبعـد مـا ترجـو الـذي كـان أقربـا

ولـم أنـسه والمـاء مـلء مـزاده   وأعـداه مـلء الارض شـرقا ومغربا

ولكــــن رأى طعـــم المنيــة أعـذبا	ومــا ذاق طعـم المــاء وهـو بقـربـه
وتعدو على جثمانـه الخيـل شـزبا	تـصافحه البيـض الـصفـاح دواميـا
لـديها العقـول العـشر تقـضي تعجبا	مضت بالهدى في يـوم عاشـور نكبة
يـرى زينبــا والقـوم تـسلب زينبا	فليـت علـي المرتـضى يـوم كـربلا
وقـد شـرق الحـادي بهـن وغربـا	وللخفـــرات الفاطميـــات عولـــة
مـصابا بـأن تـسبي عيانـا وتـسلبا	حواسـر بعـد الـسلب تـسبى وحسبها
فلــم تــر لا جـدا لـديها ولا أبــا	لهــا الله اذ تـدعوا أباهـا وجـدها

* * *

السيد راضي بن السيد صالح بن السيد مهدي الحسيني القزويني النجفي البغدادي شاعر موهوب. ولد في النجف الاشرف عام ١٢٣٥ ونشأ بها ودرس على والده مبادئ العلوم والاصول والادب واستمد من مجالس النجف ومن أعلام الادب روحا أدبية عالية ، ساجل فحول الشعراء وباراهم ، ولما انتقل أبوه الى بغداد انتقل معه عام ١٢٥٩ وسافر الى ايران أكثر من مرة واتصل بالشاه ناصر الدين القاجاري وكانت له منزلة في نفس الشاه ومكانة سامية ، كما كانت له صلات مع أمراء العراق في عهد الدولة العثمانية وتجد في ديوانه كثيرا من التقاريظ والموشحات لشعر عبد الباقي العمري والسيد حيدر الحلي وغيرهما توفي بتبريز في شهر المحرم عام ١٢٨٥ هـ والمصادف ١٨٦٨ م ونقل جثمانه الى النجف فدفن تحت الميزاب الذهبي في الصحن الحيدري وخلف ولدين هما : الشاعر السيد احمد والسيد محمود ، ورثاه فريق من الشعراء منهم أبوه السيد صالح الشاعر الشهير والآتية ترجمته. جمع ديوانه أخوه السيد حسون بن السيد صالح وفرغ من جمعه له في ١٥ شعبان ١٣٤١ هـ ، وقد ترجم له البحاثة علي الخاقاني في شعراء الغري وقال : ذكره صاحب الحصون المنيعة في ج ٩ ص ٢٠٦ وقال عنه : كان أديبا وشاعرا بارعا مفلقا ، جيد النظم رقيق الغزل حسن الانسجام ماهرا في التشطير والتخميس لا يكاد يعثر على مقطوعة أو (دو بيت) وقد استحسنهما الا خمسهما. وتوفي بعده والده المعمر عالم بغداد الجليل في وقته والمعاصر للعلامة الشيخ محمد حسن آل ياسين في سنة ١٣٠٥ هـ.

محمد عبد الصمد الاصفهاني المتوفى ١٢٨٧

ذكره صاحب روضات الجنات من جملة أساتيده الذين تلقى عنهم العلم فقال : ومنهم السيد السند ، النبيل المعتمد والفقيه الاوحد الامير سيد محمد بن السيد عبد الصمد وهو السيد النسيب الحسيني الاصبهاني المنتهى اليه رياسة التدريس والفتوى في هذا الزمان بأصبهان ، لم نر أحدا يدانيه في وصف الاشتغال بأمر العلم والتعليم ، كان معظم تلمذه وقرائته على المرحوم الحاج محمد ابراهيم ، وعلى الفاضل العلاني الكربلائي سيد محمد بن الامير سيد علي الطباطباني.

وكتب سلمه الله في الفقه والاصول كثيرا منها شرحه الشريف الموسوم بـ (أنوار الرياض) على الشرح الكبير المسمى بـ (رياض المسائل) ومنها كتاب سماه (العروة الوثقى) في الفقه وآخر سماه (الغاية القصوى) في الاصول. ومنها منظومته الفقهية التي لم يكتب مثلها في الاستدلال المنظوم. ونظمه رائق فائق جدا لفظا ومعنى ، وأنشد كثيرا بالعربية في مراثي أبي عبدالله الحسين (ع). وهو الان متجاوز ببناء عمره السعيد حدود السبعين. انتهى)١(توفي بأصفهان سنة ١٢٨٧.

السيد مهدي داود الحلي المتوفى ١٢٨٩
قال في الحسين عليه السلام:

وجــرت مقلتــي كــصوب العهـــاد	بــين البــين لــوعتي وسـهادي
عـــن ســـراكم ســويعة لفـؤادي	أيهـــا المــدلجون بــالله ريــضوا
نقـضوا للحـسين حــق الــوداد	أنقـضتم عهــود ودي كمــا قــد
غيــر صــحب بــسيرة الاعــداد	مفــردا لــم يجــد لــه مــن نـصير
نــابهم فــي الهيــاج ســمر الـصعاد	هـم أســود العــرين فــي الحـرب لكـن
تـسبق الـريح فـي مجـاري الطـراد	قــد ثنــوا خــيلهم شــوازب تعـدو
لا يــرى فيـه غيـر ومـض الحـداد	وعـلا فـي هيـاجهم ليـل نقـع
جثمــا عــن متــون تلـك الجيـاد	فـدنا مـنهم القـضا فتهـاووا
بــين أهــل الـضلال والالحـاد	وبقـى ثابـت الجـلاد وحيـدا
غيـر رمـح وصـارم وجـواد	مـستغيثا ولـم يجـد مـن مغيـث
البـيض لــف الاجنـاد بالاجنـاد	جـزر الكفر حطـم الـسمر فـل

483

ثيـاب الاسـى ليـوم المعـاد	يـا لقـومي لفـادح ألبـس الـدين
لـديها كموسـم الاعيـاد	كـم نفـوس أبيـة رأت المـوت
فأسـيلت على الظبـا والـصعاد	هـي عـزت عـن أن تـسام بـضيم
أضــحت مغـارة للجيـاد	وصدور حـوت علـوم رسـول الله

أبو داود العالم الاديب السيد مهدي بن داود بن سليمان الكبير ، ميلاده في الحلة سنة ١٢٢٢ ونشأ بها نشأة صالحة على أخيـه السيد سليمان الصغير وجد واجتهد ودرس اللغة وآدابها واستقصى دواوين العرب وتواريخهم وأيامهم حتى أصبح مرجعا ومنهلا يستقي منه رواد الادب ، ونهض بأعباء الزعامة الدينية والادبية التي كان يقوم بها أعلام أسرته من قبله ، ودرس الفقه على العلامة صاحب (أنوار الفقاهة) ابن الشيخ جعفر كاشف الغطاء ـ يوم كان مقيما بالحلة ـ ثم هاجر الى النجف فحضر في الدروس الفقهية على الشيخ صاحب (الجواهر) وقد رثى أستاذيه المذكورين بقصيدتين كلتاهما في ديوانه المخطوط.

جاء في (البابليات) عند ترجمته ما يلي :

كان من النسك والورع والتقى على جانب عظيم بحيث يأتم بصلاته كثير من الصلحاء في مسجد خاص ملاصق لداره في الحلة يعرف بمسجد « أبو حواض » لوجود حوض مـاء كبير فيه وكان هذا المسجد كمدرسة أدبية لتلاميذه الذين يستفيدون منه وهم جماعة من مشاهير أدباء الفيحاء وهم بين من عاصرناهم أو قاربنا عصرهم كالشيخ حسن مصبح والشيخ حمـادي الكواز والشيخ حسون بن عبدالله والشيخ علي عوض والشيخ محمد الملا والشيخ علي بن قاسم والشيخ حمـادي نـوح الـذي طالمـا عبر عنه في ديوانـه المخطوط بقوله : ـ سيدنا الاستاذ الاعظم ـ وقد وجه المترجم أكبر عنايته في التهذيب دون هؤلاء لابن أخيه وربيب حجره الشاعر المفلق السيد حيدر فانه مات أبوه وهو طفل صغير فكفله هذا العم العطوف فكان له أبا ومهذبا كما صرح بذلك في قصيدته التي رثاه فيها وقلما يوجد مثلها في مراثيه ومطلعها :

ذهـب الزمـان بعـدتي وعديـدي	أظبى الـردى انصلتي وهـاك وريدي

ومنها :

والـدهر يرمقنـي بعـين حـسود	وأنـا الفـداء لمـن نـشأت بظلـه

مـا زلـت وهـو علـى أحنـى مـن أبـي	بـألـذ عـيـش فـي حمــاه رغيــد
مـا لـي وللايــام قـوض صـرفهـا	عنـي عمـاد رواقـي المـمــدود

وقال في كلمات نثرية صدر فيها تخميسه لقصيدة عمه الدالية في (العقد المفصل) ولا
غرو ان حذوت مثاله وشابهت أقوالي أقواله فان من حياضه مشربي ومن أدبه كان ادبي
فترانا حر يين بقول المؤمل بن أميل الكوفي :

وجئــت وراءه تجـري حثيثــا	ومـا بـك حيـث تجري مـن فتـور
وان بلـغ الـصغير مـدى كبيــر	فقـد خلـق الـصغير مـن الكبيــر

له مصنفات في الادب واللغة والتاريخ أحسنها على مـا قيل «مصباح الادب الزاهر»
وهو الذي يروي عنه ابن أخيه السيد حيدر في كتاب (العقد المفصل) ـ ولا وجود لـه
اليوم ـ ولـه مختارات من شعر شعراء العرب في جزئين ضخمين سلك فيهما طريقة أبـي
تمام في ديوان الحماسة وقد استفدنا منهما كثيرا يوم كنا في الحلة وكتاب في أنواع
البديع وكتاب في تراجم الشعراء المتقدمين ونوادرهم وكأنه لخص فيه تراجم جماعة من
شعراء اليتيمة ووفيات ابن خلكان وغيرهما ، رأيت قطعة كبيرة منه بخط الخطيب الاديب
القاسم بن محمد الملا نقلها عن نسخة الاصل وديوان شعره الذي لم يكن مجموعا فـي
حياته بل كان في أوراق متفرقة أكثرها بقلم ابن أخيه حيدر وقد جمعها حفيد المترجم
السيد عبد المطلب بن داود بن المهدي وكلف بنسخها الشيخ مهدي اليعقوبي وجعلـه في
جزئين مرتبين على الحروف ، الاول في مديح ورثاء جماعة من علمـاء عصـره فـي
النجف والحلة ، كآل بحر العلوم وآل كاشف الغطاء وآل القزويني وآل كبه في بغداد ، وقـد
أورد ابن أخيه كثيرا منه في العقد المفصل و «دمية القصر ـ خ ـ» والثاني في مدح
ورثاء أجداده الطاهرين (ع) ويقع في «١٢٨» صفحة وقد نظم هذا القسم في أيام كبره
وألتف ما قاله من الشعر في أواسط حياته في بعض الناس وقد رأيت له مقطوعة يتأسف
فيها على ما فرط به من مديح ورثاء لغير آل الرسول (ص) ممن لا يضاهيه في السؤدد
ولا يساويه في شرف المحتد ، منها قوله :

فوا خجلتي منكم أفي الشيب مذودي	لغيـركم جيـد المـدايح لافـت
أمـدح مـن دونـي ومجـدي مجـده	مـن الارض حيـث الفرقدين التفاوت
وفرعي مـن أعلـى أرومـة هاشـم	علـى شـرف المجـد المؤثـل نابـت

والى ما قاله في أهل البيت (ع) أشار ابن أخيه في العقد المفصل حيث قال عن عمه المذكور ما لفظه : أوصى الي في بعض قصائد كان نظمها في مدح جده وعترته أن أجعلها معه في كفنه ا هـ وألمح الى ذلك في مرثيته لعمه بقوله :

| وجريـــت فـــي أمـــد اليـــه بعيـــد | وأرى القريض وان ملكـت زمامـه |
| من مــدح جـدك طائرا فـي الجيـد | لـم تـرض منـه غيـر مـا ألزمتـه |

وفيه تلميح الى قوله تعالى : « وكل انسان ألزمناه طائره في عنقه » وقد أثبت بعض مراثيه الحسينية سيدنا العلامة الامين في) الدر النضيد .(وهذه نماذج من شعره :
قال من قصيدة في مدح المرحوم الحاج محمد صالح كبه :

فهـل سـرت مجتـازا علـى دمنتـي هنـد	نسيم الصبا استنشقت منك شذا الند
ليـال سـرقناها مـن الـدهر فـي جعد	فـذكرتني نجـدا ومـا كنت نـاسيا
يمـد بعمـري فهـو غايـة مـا عنـدي	ليـال قـصيرات ويـا ليت عمرهـا
ظلامـان مـن ليـل ومـن فـاحم بعـد	بها طلعت شمس النهار فلفهـا
أرتنـي لهيـب النـار فـي جنـة الخلـد	قـد اختلـست منهـا عيـوني نظـرة
أمـن دم قلبـي لونهـا أم مـن الـورد	وفـي وجنتيهـا حمـرة شـك نـاظري
لآلاه نظمـــن مـــن ذلـك العقـد	وفـي نحـرهـا عقـد توهمـت ثغرهـا
عرفت مذاق الـراح مـن ريقهـا الشهد	ومـا كنـت أدري مـا المـدام وانمـا
وقبـل حسام اللحـظ مـا الصارم الهنـدي	وقبـل اهتـزاز القـد مـا هـزة القنـا
صحوت بها يـا مـي مـن سكـرة البعـد	ومـن قربهـا مالـت برأسـي نـشوة
فـلا طـب حتـى يـدفع الـضد بالـضد	وان زال سكر البعد من سكر قربهـا
وهمـا عرتـه رعـشة الـرأس والقـد	تعـشقتها طفـلا وكهـلا وأشيبـا

486

وقلبـي مـن نـار الـصبابة فـي وقـد	ولـم تـدر ليلـى أننـي كلـف بهـا
جفـوني ولا قلبـي لمـن ذاب فـي الوجـد	ومـا علمـت مـن كتـم حبـي لمـن بكـت
وأدفـع فـي هنـد وميـة عـن دعـد	فـأذكر سـعدى والغـرام بزينـب
أو المنحنـى فـاعلم حننـت علـى نجـد	وان قلـت شـوقي بـاللوى فبحـاجر
ذكـرت ولكـن تعلمـا لـنفس مـا قـصدي	ومـا ولعـت نفـسي بـشيء مـن الـذي
تناقلـه الافـواه للحـر والعبـد	وليس الفتـى ذوالحـزم مـن راح سـره

وله يهنيء الحاج محمد صالح كبة في عرس ولده المصطفى :

ونـشر الخزامـي فـي الغلائـل يعبـق	أتتك ومنها الشمس في الوجه تشرق
حشا صبها عـن قـوس حاجب ترشـق	رشـيقة قـد فـي سـهام لحاظهـا
وأنـى ومنهـا قـد ميـة أرشـق	ولـم تـشبه الاغـصان قامـة قـدها
كمـن هـو مـن مـاء الـشبيبة مـورق	وليس التي بالمـاء يـورق غصنها
وان هـي فـي عينيـه تـدنو وترمـق	لقد فضحت في عينها جؤذر النقا
على وفـق قرطيها مـن الـشوق يخفـق	تمـيس وقرطاهـا قليقـان والحـشا

وله :

فأضـحى وعـن علائـه النـسر يقـصر	وكـم ذي معـال بـات يخفـض نفـسه
ويكبـر قـدر المـرء مـن حيـث يـصغر	تـصاغر حتـى عـاد يكبـر قـدره

وله :

أتعـيش فـي أمـل الـى الـرمس	اقطـع هـديت علائـق الـنفس

تمسي وتأمل في الصباح ترى	خيرا فتصبح مثلما تمسي

وله :

كم تقي للخلق يظهر نسكا	ولباري النفوس في السر عاصٍ
فهو في نسكه تظن أبا ذرٍ	وعند التحقيق فابن العاصى

أجاب المترجم له داعي ربه في الرابع من محرم الحرام أول سنة ١٢٨٩ هـ في الحلة ونقل الى النجف الاشرف كما أرخ ذلك تلميذه الشيخ محمد الملا في آخر مرثية له بقوله:

وحين مضى جاء تاريخه	مضى عجلا لجنان النعيم

ومن هنا يتحقق ان ما نشرناه في « العرفان » وما نقله عنه الزركلي في » الاعلام « من ان وفاته سنة ١٢٨٧ كان سهوا. والى وفاته في المحرم يشير ابن أخيه السيد حيدر في مرثيته له :

فكأنما أضلاع هاشم لم يكن	أبدا لها عهد بقلب جليد
لم تقض ثكل عميدها بمحرم	الا وأردفها بثكل عميد
يبكي عليه الدين بالعين التي	بكت الحسين أباه خير شهيد
ان يختلط رزءاهما فكلاهما	قصما قرى الايمان والتوحيد
أبه نعى الناعي لها عمرو العلى	أم شيبة الحمد انطوى بصعيد

ورثاه عامة شعراء الحلة الذين شهدوا يومه بعدة قصائد أشهرها قصيدة الشاعر المجيد المتوفى بعده بعام واحد الشيخ صالح الكواز حيث يقول :

تعاليت قدرا أن تكون لك الفدا	نفوس الورى طرا مسودا وسيدا
وكيف تفدى في زمان ولم يكن	لدينا به الذبح العظيم فتفتدى

488

وتلبس ثوبـا للمصيبة أسـودا	فقـل لقريش تخلع الصبر دهشة
وتغضي علـى الاقـذاء طرفـا مسهدا	وتـصفق جـذا الـراحتين بمثلهـا
عليهـا بمـا خـص النبـي محمـدا	لقد عمها الرزء الذي جدد الاسى
وكـان الـذي ينتاشنـا مـن يـد الـردى	فـان أبـا داود عاجلـه الـردى
فوطـد مـن فـوق الاسـاس وشيدا	حذا حذو آبـاه الألى أسسوا العلى
لعمري منهـا شـذ مـا قـد تجـردا	اذا لـبس الـدنيا الرجـال فانـه
ولـو شـاء مـن أي النـواحي لهـا اهتدى	فـوالله مـا ضـلت عليـه طريقهـا
ومـا ملكـت منـه الدنيـة مقـودا	فمـا مالـت الايـام فيـه بـشهوة
أقلهـم مـالا وأكثـرهم نـدى	اذا مـا توسمت الرجـال رأيتـه
ولله ذاك النـور مـن كـان أخمـدا	فللـه ذاك الطـود مـاذا أزالـه

وجاء في شعراء الحلة للخاقاني السيد مهدي بن السيد داود بن السيد سلمان الكبير الحلي. أشهر مشاهير شعراء عصره ، نشأ على أخيه السيد سلمان الصغير المتوفى ١٢٤٧. له آثار قيمة توجد في الحلة عند حفيده السيد هادي بن السيد حمزة ومن بينها ديوانه ويقع في جزئين ، ونسخة أخرى من ديوانه عند الخطيب الشيخ مهدي الشيخ يعقوب جمعة سنة ١٣٢٩ رأيته بخطه.

قوله في رثاء سيد الشهداء الحسين بن علي (ع) :

أميـــة فـي قـضبها كـربلاءا	سـقت مـن رقـاب لـوى دمـاءا
نجومـا ففاقت بهـن الـسماءا	وفي أرضـها نثـرت مـنهم
أماجـد مـن حـزبهم نجبـاءا	وفـي الطـف فـي بيضها جدلت

489

وترجم له السيد الامين في أعيان الشيعة وسماه بـ (السيد داود الحسيني الحلي) ، وقال في جزء ٣٠ من الاعيان : هو من الطائفة التي منها السيد حيدر الحلي الشاعر المشهور ، ولم يمكننا الان تحقيق ذلك ولا معرفة شيء من أحواله سوى أنه أديب شاعر ، وعثرنا من شعره على قصيدة في رثاء الحسين عليه السلام من جملتها :

فـــي كـــربلا ظلمـــا قتامــه	مـــا ان أثـــار لحربـــه

ثم استدرك في جزء ٣١ فقال : وعلمنا بعد ذلك انه عم السيد حيدر الحلي ، فاذا هو السيد داود بن سليمان بن داود بن حيدر. أقول والصحيح كما ذكرنا سابقاً فهو السيد مهدي بن السيد داود بن سليمان الكبير. وديوانه يضم مختلف ألوان الشعر وعدة قصائد في الامام الحسين (ع) فمنها ما وسعنا تدوينها :

وانحــب أســى بـــدم ذروف	قـف بـين أجـراع الطفوف
طمـة غـدا نهـب الحتـوف	في عرصـة فيهـا ابـن فـا
ذوي الـــشرف المنيـــف	في ثلـة مـن آل عـدنان
قبـابهم لقـرى الـضيوف	الـضاربين علـى الطريـق
بالقـضب فـي اليـوم المخـوف	والمـــانعين ذمـــارهم
ـرهم علـى القمـرين مـوفي	وبـدور مجـد نـور فخـ
حمـر الأسـنة والـسيوف	بـيض الوجـوه وفـي الـوغى
جـزر الكتائـب والـصفوف	مـن دأبهـم يـوم اللقـا
بـة هاشـم شـم الانـوف	بـأبي كرامـا مـن ذؤا
قـوم علـى العـزى عكوف	عكفـوا بقـضبهم علـى
ضـي بيضة الـدين الحنيـف	وحمـوا ببـيض ظبـا المـوا
الـسبط كاسـات الحتـوف	شـربوا علـى ظمـأ دويـن

490

وبقــــى حليــف المجــد غيــ...   ...ـر العضب لـم يـر من حليف

يلقـــى الــصفوف كملتقـا   ه بـاســمـا زمــر الــضيوف

فتــرى الــسيوف بــه تطيــر   مـع الــسواعد والكفــوف

حتــى اذا حـــم القــضا   فهـوى وغـودر بالخــسوف

وغــدت هنالــك زينــب   تــدعوه عــن كبــد لهيـف

ومن مراثيه :

بـأبي مـن بكـت عليـه الـسماءُ   ونعتــــه الامــــلاك والانبيــاءُ

واستثارت في الكون حين هـوى   فــي التــرب ريــح لاجلـه سوداءُ

يـا لحـى الله عـصبة قـد أريقت   بظباهــا مــن آل طــه دمــاءُ

مـا وفت عهـد خاتم الرسل فيهم   كيــف يرجــى مــن اللئام الوفـاء

هـي مـن يـوم حـرب بـدر وأحد   زرعــت فــي قلوبهــا الــشحناء

فقضى ظاميا لـدى الماء حتـى   ود مــن أجلــه يغــور المــاء

حولــه مــن بنـي أبيـه ومـن أصـ...   ...ـحابه الغـر معـشر نجبـاء

بـذلوا دونـه نفوسـا عزيـزات   بيــوم قـد عـز فيـه الفـداء

بـأبي أنفـسا على الـسمر سالت   حـــذرا أن يـسؤهن قمـاء

ووجوهـا تعفـرت بثـرى الغبـ...   ...ـرا وكانـت تجلى بهـا الغمـاء

وأكفـا تقطعت وهـي يـوم الـ...   ...ـمحل للخلـق ديمـة وطفـاء

وصـدورا عـدت عليها العـوادي   وهـي للعلـم عيبـة ووعـاء

يـا لهـا وقعـة لهـا رجت الغبـ...   ...ـرا ومالـت من عظمهـا الخضراء

491

ليس تسلى بيدى الزمان كـأن فـي كـل يـوم يمـر عاشـوراء

يـا بـن بنـت النبـي أنتـم رجـاني يـوم نـشر الـورى ونعـم الرجـاء

فاشـفعوا لـي انـي مسيء وأنتـم لمـواليكم غـدا شـفعاء

وعـلـيكم مـن الالـه صـلاة وسـلام مـا حنـت الورقـاء

ونكتفي عن ذكر البقية من قصائده الحسينية بذكر مطالعها :

١ ـ خطب دهى مضر الحمرا وهاشمها وفـل فـي مرهفـات المـوت صـارمها

٢ ـ سلب الردى من رأس فهر تاجها قـسرا وأطفـأ فـي الطفـوف سـراجها

عباس القصاب كان حيا عام ١٢٨٩

ترجم له الاديب المعاصر السيد سلمان هادي الطعمة في شعراء كربلاء ، قال : وكان يعمل قصابا ومن انتباهه تاريخ نظمه في خزان ماء الروضة الحسينية بأمر من والدة السلطان عبدالمجيد خان العثماني عام ١٢٨٢ هـ ويقع في الجهة الجنوبية الشرقية من الصحن الحسيني الشريف. قال:

سلـسبيل قـد أتـى تاريخـه اشـرب المـاء ولا تـنس الحـسين

أقول : سبق وأن ترجمنا في هذه الموسوعة لأبي الحسين الجزار المتوفى ٦٧٢ هـ وهذا هو الجزار الثاني الذي فجر قريحته بالشعر حب الامام الحسين عليه السلام ولا عجب فالحسين بنهضته المباركة ألهب العواطف وشحذ القرائح فأنارت بالشعر والادب.

الشيخ صالح الكواز المتوفى ١٢٩٠

باسـم الحـسين دعـا نعـاء نعـاء فنعـى الحيـاة لـسائر الاحيـاء

وقضى الهـلاك على النفوس وانمـا بقيـت ليبقـى الحـزن فـي الاحشـاء

يـوم بـه الاحـزان مازجـت الحـشا مثـل امتـزاج المـاء بالـصهباء

لـم أنـس اذ تـرك المدينـة واردا لا مـاء مـدين بـل نجيـع دمـاء

٤٩٢

جاءتــه ماشــية علــى اسـتحياء	قــد كـان موسـى والمنيـة اذ دنـت
فـي طــور وادي الطـف لا سـيناء	ولــه تجلــى الله جــل جلالــه
منــه الكلــيم مكلـم الاحـشاء	وهنـاك خـر وكـل عضو قـد غدا
ابنــاك منــى أعظـم الانبـاء	يـا أيهـا النبـأ العظـيم اليـك فـي
الارمـاح فـي صـفين بالهيجـاء	ان اللــذين تــسرعا يقيانـك
عمـا أمامـك مـن عظـيم بـلاء	فأخــذت فـي عـضديهما تثنيهمـا
فـي كــربلاء مقطـع الاعـضاء	ذا قــاذف كبـدأ لــه قطعـا وذا
فـي فتيـة بـيض الوجـوه وضـاء	ملقـى علـى وجـه الـصعيد مجـردا
الاقمــار تـسبح فـي غـدير دمـاء	تلـك الوجـوه المـشرقات كأنهـا
وغفـت جفـونهم بـلا اغفـاء	رقـدوا ومـا مـرت بهـم سنة الكـرى
متمهــدين حـرارة الرمـضاء	متوسـدين مـن الـصعيد صـخوره
مــزملين علــى الربـا بـدماء	مـدثرين بكـربلا سـلب القنـا
بــدم مــن الاوداج لا الحنـا	خـضبوا ومأشـابوا وكـان خـضابهم
شـوقا الــى الهيجـاء لا الحـسناء	اطفـالهم بلغـوا الحلـوم بقـربهم
عبـرات ثكلـى حـرة الاحـشاء	ومغـسلين ولا ميـاه لهـم سـوى
ينــدبن قــتلاهن بالأيمـاء	أصـواتها بحـت وهـن نـوائح
مــن نهـب أبيــات وسـلب رداء	أنـى التفـتن رأيـن مـا يـدمي الحـشا
مغـض ومـا فيـه مـن الاغـضاء	تـشكو الهـوان لنـدبها وكأنـه
يجـدي عتـاب مـوزع الاشـلاء	وتقـول عاتبـة عليـه ومـا عـسى

493

قـد كنت للبعـداء أقـرب منجـد	واليـــوم أبعـــدهم عـن القربـــاء
أدعـوك مـن كثب فلـم أجـد الـدعا	الا كمــا نــاديــت للمتنــائي
قـد كنت فـي الحـرم المنيـع خبيئـة	فـاليوم نقـع الـيعملات خبـائي
أسبى ومثلـك مـن يحـوط سـرادقي	هــذا لعمـري أعظـم البرحـاء
مـاذا أقـول اذا التقيـت بـشامت	انـي سـبيت واخـوتي بـأزائي
حكـم المنـون عليكم أن تعرضـوا	عنـي وان طـرق الهـوان فنـائي
هـذي يتامـاكم تلـوذ ببعـضها	ولكـم نـساء تلتجـي بنـساءِ
مـا كنت أحـسب ان يهـون عليكم	ذلـي وتـسييري الـى الاعـداء
عجبـا لقلبـي وهـو يـألف حـبكم	لـم لا يـذوب بحرقـة الارزاء
وعجبت مـن عينـي وقد نظرت الـى	مـاء الفـرات ولـم تـسل فـي المـاء
وألـوم نفـسي فـي امتـداد بقائهـا	اذ لـيس تفنـى قبـل يـوم فنـائي
مـا عـذر مـن ذكر الطفوف فلـم يمت	حزنـا بـذكر الطـاء قبـل الفنـاء

الشيخ صالح الكواز :

كـأن جسمك موسـى مـذ هوى صعقا	وأن رأسـك روح الله مـــذ رفعـا

ان المحافل الحسينية ترتـاح وتطرب لشعر الكواز ولـه المكانـة المرموقة في الاوسـاط الادبيـة والدينيـة لمـا أودع فيـه من الفن والصناعـة والوقائع التاريخيـة الـذي قل من جـاراه فيهـا من أدبـاء عصره مضافا الـى مـا فيـه من رصانـة التركيب والنظم العجيب والرقـة والسلاسـة والدقـة في المعانـي والابداع في التصوير واليك بعض الشواهد علـى ذلك مـن قصائده المتفرقة :

لـي حـزن يعقـوب لا ينفـك ذا لهـب	لـصرع نـصب عينـي لا الـدم الكـذب

494

وتحتوي هذه القصيدة على ٤٠ بيتا ولم يخل بيت واحد منها من اشارة الى قصة تاريخية أو نكتة بديعية أو صناعة بيانية أو أدبية. ويقول في أخرى :

سليمان مـن فـوق البنـاء المحلـق	وهـل تـؤمن الـدنيا التـي هـي أنزلـت
طريـق الـردى يومـا ولا رد مـا لقـى	ولا سـد فيهـا السـد عمـن أقامـه
كوجـه (قـصير(شـانه جـذع منـشق	مضى مـن (قصي (مـن غدت لمضيه

ومن أخرى في شهداء كربلاء :

لمصعب في الهيجا ظهور المصاعب	تأسـى بهـم آل الزبيـر فـذللت
لـدى واسـط مـوت الابـي المحـارب	ولـولاهم آل المهلـب لـم تمـت
لآبائـه الغـر الكـرام الاطائـب	وزيـد وقـد كـان الابـاء سـجية
تـشكل فيـه شـبه عيـسى لـصالب	كـأن عليـه ألقـي الـشبح الـذي

وقوله في قصيدة ثالثة :

لمـا نالـت النمـران منـه منالهـا	ولـو لـم تنـم أجفـان عمـرو بـن كاهـل

وقوله من مرثية في أهل البيت عليهمالسلام :

(خلـصوا نجيـا(بعـد مـا تركـوني	وقفـوا معـي حتـى اذا مـا استيأسـوا
وكـأنني بـصراعه اتهمـوني	فكـأن يوسـف فـي الـديار محكـم

وفيها يقول :

كالنون ينبـذ فـي العـرا (ذا النـون)	نبـذتهم الهيجـاء فـوق تلاعهـا
شـجر القنـا بـدلا عـن اليقطيـن	فتخـال كـلا ثـم يـونس فوقـه

من رثائه للإمام الحسين (ع) ويذكر في آخرها الشهيد زيد ابن علي بن الحسين بن علي بن أبي طالب عليهم السلام :

عـذرتكم لــم تـهمكـم بجفــوة	ولا ساورتكم غفلـة فـي النوائب
وباكيـة حـرى الفـؤاد دموعهـا	تـصعد عـن قلـب مـن الوجـد ذائب
تـصك يـديها فـي الترائـب لوعـة	فتلهـب نـارا مـن وراء الترائـب
شكت وأرعوت اذلم تجد من يجيبها	ومـا في الحشا مـا في الحشا غير ذاهب
ومـدت الـى نحـو الغـريين طرفهـا	ونـادت أبـاهـا خيـر مـاش وراكـب
أبـا حـسن ان الـذين نمـاهم	أبـو طالـب بـالطف ثـار لطالـب
تعاوت عليهم من بنـي صخر عصبة	لثـارات يـوم الفتح حـرى الجوانـب
فـساموهم امـا الحيـاة بذلـة	أو المـوت فاختـاروا أعـز المراتـب
فهـاهم على الغبـراء مالت رقـابهم	ولمـا تمـل مـن ذلـة فـي الـشواغب
سـجود علـى وجـه الـصعيد كأنمـا	لهـا فـي محـاني الطف بعض المحـارب
معارضـهـا مخـضوبة فكأنهـا	ملاغـم أسـد بـالـدماء خواضـب
تفجر مـن أجسامها الـسمر أعينـا	وتـشتق منهـا أنهـر بالقواضـب
ومـما عليك اليـوم هـون مـا جـرى	ثـووا لا كمثـوى خـائف المـوت ناكـب
أصـيبوا ولكـن مقبلـين دمـاؤهم	تـسيل علـى الاقـدام دون العراقـب
ممزقـة الادراع تلقـا صـدورها	ومحفوظـة مـا كـان بـين المناكـب
تأسـى بهـم آل الزبيـر فـذللت	لمصعب في الهيجا ظهـور المصاعب
ولـو لاهـم آل المهلـب لـم تمـت	لـدى واسـط مـوت الأبـي المحـارب
وزيد وقـد كـان الابـاء سجية	لأبـائـه الغـر الكـرام الاطائـب

كأن عليـه ألقـي الـشبح الـذي — تـشكل فيـه شـبـه عيـسى لـصالب

فقل للذي أخفى عن العين قبره — متى خفيت شمس الضحى بالغياهب

وهل يختفي قبر امرئ مكرماته — بزغن نجومـا كـالنجوم الثواقب

ولو لم تنم ـ القوم فيه الى العدى — لنمـت عليـه واضحات المناقب

كأن الـسما والارض فيـه تنافسا — فنال الفضا عفوا سني الرغائب

لـئن ضاق بطن الارض فيه فانه — لمن ضاق في آلائه كل راحب

عجبت وما احدى العجائب فاجأت — بمقتـل زيد بـل جميـع العجائب

أتطرد قربى أحمد عن مكانه — بنو الوزع المطرود طرد الغرائب

وتحكم في الدين الحنيف وانها — لأنصب للاسلام من كل ناصب

ومن مراثيه :

لي حزن يعقوب لا ينفك ذا لهب — لصرع نصب عيني لا الدم الكذب

وغلمة من بني عدنان أرسلها — للجد والدها في الحرب لا اللعب

ومعشر روادتهم عن نفوسهم — بيض الضبا غير بيض الخرد العرب

فأنعموا بنفوس لا عديل لها — حتى أسيلت على الخرصان والقضب

فانظر لاجسادهم قد قدَ ـ من قبل — اعضاؤها لا الى القمصان والأهب

كل رأى ضر أيوب فما ركضت — رجل له غير حوض الكوثر العذب

قامت لهم رحمة الباري تمرضهم — جرحى فلم تدعهم للحلف والغضب

وآنسين من الهيجاء نار وغى — في جانب الطف ترمي الشهب بالشهب

ومــا لهــم غيـر نـصر الله مـن ارب	فيمموهـا وفـي الايمـان بـيض ضبا
هـش الكلـيم علـى الاغنـام للعـشب	تهـش فيهـا علـى آسـاد معركـة
فالهـام سـاجدة منهـا علـى التـرب	اذا انتـضوها بجمـع مـن عـدوهم
ليـل العجاجـة يـوم الـروع والرهـب	ومـولجين نهـار المـشرفية فـي
مـن كـل شـلو مـن الاعـداء مقتـضب	ورازقـي الطيـر ماشـاءت قواضبهم
مـن الـشهادة غيـر البعـد والحجـب	ومبتلـين بنهـر مـا لطاعمـه
منــه غليـل فـؤاد بالظمـا عطـب	فلـن تبـل ـ ولا فـي غرفـة أبـدا
سـكينة وسـط تـابوت مـن الكثـب	حتـى قـضوا فغـدا كـل بمـصرعه
قـد نـال داود فيـه أعظـم الغلـب	فاليبـك طـالوت حزنـا للبقيـة مـن
مقيـدا فـوق مهـزول بـلا قتـب	أضـحى وكانـت لـه الامـلاك حاملـة
اضـلاعهن علـى جمـر مـن النـوب	يرنـو الـى الناشـرات الـدمع طاويـة
والموريـات زنـاد الحـزن فـي لهـب	والعاديـات مـن الفـسطاط ضـابحة
والنازعـات بـرودا فـي يـد الـسلب	والمرسـلات مـن الاجفـان عبرتهـا
حزنـا لكـل صـريع بـالعرى تـرب	والـذاريات ترابـا فـوق أرؤوسـها
رضيعها فاحص الـرجلين فـي التـرب	ورب مـن ضـعة مـنهن قـد نظـرت
مـن حالـه وظماهـا أعظـم الكـرب	تـشوط عنـه وتأتيـه مكابـدة
متـى تـشط عنـه مـن بحـر الظمـا تـؤب	فقـل بهـاجر اسـماعيل احزنهـا
غـداة فـي الـيم القتـه مـن الطلـب	ومـا حكتهـا ولا أم الكلـيم أسـى
وهـذه قـد سـقي بالبـارد العـذب	هـذي اليهـا ابنهـا قـد عـاد مرتـضعا

498

فـأين هاتـان ممـن قـد قضـى عطشا رضيعها ونـأى عنهـا ولـم يـؤب

شـاركنها في عمـوم الجنس وانفردت عنهن فيمـا يخص النـوع مـن نـسب

بـل آب مـذاب مقتـولا ومنـتهلا مـن نحـره بـدم كالغيـث منـسكب

كانـت ترجـي عـزاء فيـه بعـد أب لــه فلـم تحـظ بـابن لا ولا بـأب

فأصـبحت بنهـار لا ذكـاء لــه وأمسـت الليـل فـي جـو بـلا شـهب

وصبية مـن بنـي الزهـرا مربقـة بالحبـل بـين بنـي حمالـة الحطـب

كـأن كـل فـؤاد مـن عـدوهم صخـر بـن حـرب غدا يفريه بـالحرب

ليت الألـى أطعمـو المسكين قوتهم وتاليـه وهـم فـي غايـة السـغب

حتى أتى هل أتى في مدح فضلهم مـن الالـه لهـم فـي أشـرف الكتـب

يـرون بـالطف ايتامـا لهـم اسرت يستـصرخون مـن الآبـاء كـل أبـي

وأروس سـائرات بالرمـاح رمـى مـسيرها علمـاء النـجم بالعطـب

تـرى نجومـا لـدى الآفـاق سـائرة غيـر التي عهدت بالسبعة الشـهب

لم تدر والسمر مذ ناءت بها اضطربت مـن شدة الخوف أم مـن شدة الطرب

كواكـب فـي سـما الهيجـاء ثابتـة سـارت ولكـن بـأطراف القنـا السلب

وله :

مـا ضـاق دهـرك الا صـدرك اتـسعا فهـل طربـت لوقـع الخطـب مـذوقعا

تـزداد بـشرا اذا زادت نوائبــه كالبـدر ان غـشيته ظلمـة سـطعا

وكلمـا عثـرت رجـل الزمان عمى أخـذت فـي يـده رفقـا وقلت لعـا

وكـم رحمـت الليـالي وهـي ظالمـة ومـا شكوت لهـا فعـلا وان فـضعا

499

على فتى ببني المختار قد فجعا	وكيف تعظم في الاقدار حادثة
بعد الشتات وشمل الدين منصدعا	ايام اصبح شمل الشرك مجتمعا
أمامها وثنت حربا لهم تبعا	ساقت عدي بني تيم لظلمهم
لو لا ... لنهج الغصب قد شُرِّعا	ما كان أوعر من يوم الحسين لهم
وناولاها يزيدا بنسما صنعا	سلا ضبا الظلم من أغماد حقدهما
ببيض قضب هما قدما لها طبعا	وقام ممتثلا بالطف أمرهما
عصفن في يذبل لانهار مقتلعا	يا ثابتا في مقام لو حوادثه
للجاهلية في أحشائها زرعا	لله أنت فكم وتر طلبت به
حتى اذا أمنوا نار الوغى فرعا	قد كان غرسا خفيا في صدورهم
مثل السلاحف فيما اضمرت طمعا	واطلعت بعد طول الخوف أرؤوسها
وأظهرت ثار من في الدار قد صرعا	واستأصلت ثأر بدر في بواطنها
على قلوبهم الشيطان قد طبعا	وتلكم شبهة قامت بها عصب
والنقع أظلم والهندي قد لمعا	ومذ أجالوا بأرض الطف خيلهم
الا وصارمك الماضي له شفعا	لم يطلب الموت روحا من جسومهم
أسيافكم لهم في الموت متسعا	حتى اذا ما بهم ضاق الفضا جعلت
فم الردى بعد مضغ الحرب مبتلعا	وغص فيهم فم الغبرا فكان لهم
يد القضا لا زال الشرك وانقشعا	ضربت بالسيف ضربا لو تساعده
قد كان غير الذي تهواه ما صنعا	بل لو يشاء القضا أن لا يكون كما
فحكمه ورضاكم يجريان معا	لكنكم شئتم ما شاء بارئكم

لـه نفوسكم شوقا لمـا فـضعا	ومـا قهرتم بـشيء غير مـا رضيت
فمـا أمـات لكم وحيـا ولا قطعا	لا تـشمتن ـ رزايـاكم عـدوكم
فخيب الله مـن فـي ذلكـم طمعـا	تتبعـوكم ورامـوا محـو فـضلكم
لـدى التـشهد للتوحيـد قـد شفعـا	أنـى وفـي الـصلوات الخمس ذكركم
بـه لـك الله جـم الفضل قـد جمعـا	فمـا أعابـك قتـل كنـت ترقبـه
الميـاد منـك محيـا للـدجى صدعا	ومـا عليـك هـوان أن يـشال علـى
وأن رأسـك روح الله مـذ رفعـا	كـأن جسمك موسـى مـذ هـوى صعقا
لـه النبيـون قـدما قبـل أن يقعـا	كفـى بيومـك حزنـا أنـه بكيت
وكنـت نورا بـساق العرش قـد سطعا	بكـاك آدم حزنـا يـوم توبتـه
يبكـي بـدمع حكـى طوفانـه دفعـا	ونـوح أبكيتـه شجوا وقـل ـ بـأن
نيـران نمـرود عنـه الله قـد دفعـا	ونـار فقـدك فـي قلـب الخليـل بهـا
عينـاه دمعـا دمـا كالغيـث منهمعـا	كلمـت قلـب كلـيم الله فانبجـست
عيسـى لمـا اختـار أن ينجـو ويرتفعـا	ولـو رآك بـأرض الطف منفـردا
ولا أراد بغيـر الطـف مـضطجعا	ولا أحـب حيـاة بعـد فقـدكم
يطـوي أديـم الفيـافي كلمـا ذرعـا	يـا راكبا شـذ قميا فـي قوائمـه
لـو جـازه الطير فـي رمضائه وقعـا	يجتـاز متقـد الرمـضاء مـستعرا
فـي القفـر شخصا وأذنيـه اذا سـمعا	فـردا يكـذب عينيـه اذا نظـرت
بـصرخة تمـلأ الـدنيا بهـا جزعـا	عج بالمدينـة واصرخ فـي شوارعها
لبـوه قبـل صدى مـن صوتـه رجعـا	نـاد الـذين اذا نـادى الـصريخ بهـم

يكـاد ينفـد قبـل القصـد فعلهـم
بنـصر مـن لهـم مـستنجدا فزعـا

مـن كـل آخـر للهيجـاء أهبتهـا
تلقـاه معـتقلا بـالرمح مـدرعا

لا خيلـه عرفـت يومـا مرابطهـا
ولا علـى الارض يومـا جنبـه وضعـا

يصغي الى كل صوت عل مصطرخا
للأخـذ فـي حقـه مـن ظالميـه دعـا

قـل يـا بنـي شيبة الحمـد الـذين بهـم
قامـت دعـائم ديـن الله وارتفعـا

قومـوا فقد عصفت بـالطف عاصفة
مالـت بأرجـاء طـود العـز فانـصدعا

ان لـم تـسدو الفضا نقعا فلم تجدوا
الـى العـلا لكـم مـن مـنهج شـرعا

لا أنـتم أنـتم ان لـم تقـم لكـم
شـعواء مرهوبـة مـرأى ومـستمعا

نهارهـا أسـود بـالنقع مـرتكم
وليلها أبـيض بالقضب قـد نـصعا

فلتلطم الخيل خـد الارض عاديـة
فخـد عليـا نـزار للثـرى ضرعـا

ولتملأ الارض نعيـا مـن صواركم
فـان نـاعي حسـين في الـسماء نعـى

ولتـذهل اليـوم مـنكم كـل مرضعة
فطفلـه مـن دمـا أوادجـه رضعـا

لئن ثـوى جسمه فـي كـربلاء لقى
فرأسـه لنـساه فـي الـسباء رعـى

نـسيتم أم تناسـيتم كـرائمكم
بعـد الكـرام عليهـا الـذل قـد وقعـا

اتهجعون وهـم أسـرى وجدهم
لعمـه ليـل بـدر قـط مـا هجعـا

فليـت شـعري مـن العبـاس أرقـه
أنينـه كيـف لـو أصواتهم سـمعا

وهادر الـدم مـن هبـار سـاعة اذ
بالرمح هـودج مـن تنمـى لـه قرعـا

مـا كـان يفعل مـذ شـيلت هوادجها
قسرا على كل صعب في السرى ضلعا

بنـي علـي وانتم للنجـا سـببي
فـي يـوم لا سـبب الا وقـد قطعـا

502

ويـوم لا نـسب يبقـى سـوى نـسب | لجـدكم وأبـيكم راح مرتجعـا
لومـا أنهنـه وجـدي فـي محبتكم | قـذفت قـلبـي لمـا قـد نـالني قطعـا
فانهـا النعمـة العظمـى التـي رجحت | وزنـا فـلـو وزنـت بالـدهر لارتفعـا
مـن حـاز مـن نعـم البـاري ولا يـتكم | فـلا يبـالي بـشيء ضـر أو نفعـا
مـن لـي بـنفس علـى التقـوى موطنـة | لا تحفلـن بـدهر ضـاق أو وسـعا

وقال :

أمـا فـي بيـاض الـشيب حلـم لأحمـق | بـه يتلافـى مـن ليـاليـه مـا بـقي
ومـا بـالأولى بـانوا نـذير لـسامع | فـان منـاديهم ينـادي الحـق الحـق
وان امـرءا سـرن الليـالي بظعنـه | لاسـرع ممـن سـار مـن فـوق أينـق
وسيان عند الموت من كان مصحرا | ومـن كـان مـن خلـف الخبـاء المـسردق
وهـل تـؤمن الـدنيا التـي هـي أنزلـت | سـليمان مـن فـوق البنـاء المحلـق
ولا سـد فيهـا(الـسد) عمـن أقامـه | طريـق الـردى يومـا ولا رد مـالقي
واعظـم مـا يلقـى مـن الـدهر فـادح | رمـى شمـل آل المـصطفى بـالتفرق
فمـن بـين مـسموم وبـين مـشرد | وبـين قتيـل بـالـدماء مخلـق
غـداة بنـي عبـد المنـاف انـوفهم | أبـت أن يـساف الـضيم منهـا بمنـشق
سـرت لـم تنكـب عـن طريـق لغيـره | حـذار العـدى بـل بـالطريق المطرق
الـى أن اتـت أرض الطفـوف فخيمـت | بـاعلا سـنام للعـلاء ومفـرق
وأخلفهـا مـن قـد دعـاهم فلـم تجد | سوى السيف مهما يعطها الوعد يصدق

503

فمــالت الـى ارماحهـا وسـيوفها   وأكــرم بهـا انـصار صـدق وأخلـق

تعاطت على الجرد العتـاق دم الطلا   ولا كمعاطـاة المـدام المعتــق

فمـا برحـت تلقـى الحديـد بمثلـه   قلوبـا فتثنـي فيلقـا فـوق فيلـق

الـى أن تكـسرن العواسـل والظبـا   ومزقـت الادراع كـل ممـزق

لـو ان رسـول الله يبعـث نظـرة   لـردت الـى انسان عـين مـؤرق

وهـان عليـه يـوم حمـزة عمـه   بيـوم حـسين وهـو أعظـم مـا لقي

ونـال شجى مـن زينـب لـم ينلـه من   صـفية اذ جـائـت بـدمع مرقـرق

فكم بـين مـن للخـدر عـادت مصونة   ومـن سـيروها فـي السـبايا لجلـق

وليت الـذي أحنى علـى ولـد جعفـر   برقـة أحـشاء ودمـع مـدفق

يرى بـين أيدي القـوم أبنـاء سبطه   سبايا تهـادى مـن شـقي الـى شـقي

وريانـة الاجفـان حرانـة الحـشى   ففـي محـرق قامـت تنـوح ومغـرق

فقـل للنجـوم المـشرقات ألا اغربـي   ولا تـرغبـي بعـد الحـسين بمـشرق

وقـل للبحـار الزاخـرات ألا انـضبي   مـضى مـن نـداه مـدها بالتـدفق

وقال : وهي من روائعه ، وأولها :

هـل بعـد موقفنـا علـى يبـرين   أحيـا بطـرف بالـدموع ضـنين؟

ومنها :

قـال الحـداة وقـد حبـست مطيهم   مـن بعـد مـا أطلقـت مـاء شئـوني

مـاذا وقوفـك فـي ملاعـب خـرد   جـد العفـا بربعهـا المـسكون

504

وقفـوا معـي حتـى اذا مـا استيأسـوا   خلـصوا نجيـا بعـد مـا تركـوني

فكـأن يوسـف فـي الديـار محكـم   وكـأنني بـصواعه اتهمـوني

الى أن يقول :

قلبـي يقـل مـن الهمـوم جبالهـا   وتسيخ عـن حمـل الـرداء متـوني

وأنـا الـذي لـم أجـزع لرزيـة   لـو لا رزايـاكم بنـي ياسـينِ

تلـك الرزايـا الباعثـات لمهجتـي   مـا ليـس يبعثـه لظـى سـجينِ

كيـف العـزاء لهـا وكـل عـشية   دمكـم بحمرتهـا السـماء ترينـي

والبـرق يـذكرني وميـض صـوارم   أردتكـم فـي كـف كـل لعـين

والرعـد يعـرب عـن حنيـن نـسائكم   فـي كـل لحـن للـشجون مبـين

ينـدبن قومـا مـا هـتفن بـذكرهم   الا تضعـضع كـل ليـث عـرين

السـالبين النـفس أول ضـربة   والملبـسين المـوت كـل طعـين

لا عيـب فـيهم غيـر قبـضهم اللـوى   عنـد اشتباك السـمر قـبض ضنين

سـلكوا بحـارا مـن دمـاء أميـة   بظهـور خيـل لا بطـون سـفين

لـو كـل طعنـة فـارس بـأكفهم   لـم يخلـق المـسبار للمطعـون

حتـى اذا التقمـتهم حـوت القـضا   وهـي الامـاني دون كـل أمـين

نبـذتهم الهيجـاء فـوق تلاعهـا   كـالنون ينبـذ بـالعرى ذا النـون

فتخـال كـلا ثـم يـونس فوقـه   شـجر القنـا بـدلا عـن اليقطـين

خـذ فـي ثنائهـم الجميـل مقرضـا   فـالقوم قـد جلـوا عـن التـأبين

هـم أفضـل الـشهداء والقتلـى الاولى   مـدحوا بـوحي فـي الكتـاب مبـين

505

ليـت المواكـب والوصـي زعيمهـا   وقفـوا كمـوقفهم علـى صـفين

بـالطف كـي يـروا الاولـى فـوق القنـا   رفعـت مـصاحفها اتقـاء منـون

جعلـت رؤوس بنـي النبـى مكانهـا   وشـفت قـديم لـواعـج وضغـون

وتتبعـت أشـقى ثمـود وتبـع   وبنـت علـى تأسـيس كـل لعـين

الـواثبين لظلـم آل محمـد   ومحمـد ملقـى بـلا تكفـين

والقائلين لفـاطـم آذيتنـا   فـي طـول نـوح دائـم وحنـين

والقـاطعين أراكـة كيمـا تقيـل   بظـل أوراق لهـا وغـصون

ومجمعي حطب علـى البيـت الـذي   لـم يجتمـع لـولاه شمـل الـدين

والقائـدين امـامهم بنجـاده   والطهـر تـدعو خلفهـم بـرنين

خلـوا ابـن عمـي أولا كـشف للـدعا   رأسـي وأشـكو للالـه شـجوني

مـا كـان ناقـة صالـح وفـصيلها   بالفـضل عنـد الله الا دونـي

ورنـت الـى القبـر الـشريف بمقلةٍ   عبـرى وقلـب مكمـد محـزون

قالـت وأظفـار المـصاب بقلبهـا: أبتـاه! قَـلَّ علـى العـداة معينـي

أبتـــاه هــــذا...   تبعـا ومـال النـاس عـن هـرون

أي الرزايـا أتقـى بتجلـد   هـو فـي النوائـب مـا حييـت قرينـي

أم أخـذهم ارثـي وفاضـل نحلتـي   أم جهلهـم قـدري وقـد عرفـوني

قهروا يتيميـك الحـسين وصنـوه   وسـئلتهم حقـي وقـد نهرونـي

بـاعوا بـضائع مكرهم وبـزعمهم   ربحـوا ومـا بـالقوم غيـر غبـين

واذا أضـل ــ الله قومـا أبـصروا   طـرق الهدايـة ضـلة فـي الـدين

506

والدمع مـن ذكـر الفـراق يـسيل	فأتتـه زينـب بـالجواد تقـوده
حزنـا فيـا ليـت الجبـال تـزول	وتقـول قـد قطعت قلبـي يا أخي
صـرعى ومنهم لا يبـل غليـل	فلمن تنـادي والحمـاة علـى الثـرى
الا نـساء وآلـه وعليـل	مـا فـي الخيـام وقـد تفانـا أهلـها
فـرس المنـون ولا حمـى وكفيـل	أرأيـت أختـا قـدمت لـشقيقها
أختـاه صـبرا فالمـصاب جليـل	فتبـادرت منـه الـدموع وقـال يا
وعليـك مـا الـصبر الجميل جميـل	فبكت وقالت يا ابن أمي لـيس لـي
مـن للنـساء الـضائعات دليـل	يا نـور عينـي يـا حشاشة مهجتي
عظمـى تـصب الـدمع وهـي تقول	ورنـت الـى نحـو الخيـام بعولـة
بجـواده ان الفـراق طويـل	قومـوا الـى التوديـع ان أخـي دعـا
وغـدا لهـا حـول الحسـين عويـل	فخـرجن ربـات الخـدور عـواثرا
تلـك المـدامع للـوداع تـسيل	الله مـا حـال العليـل وقـد رأى
وعـراه مـن ذكـر الـوداع نحـول	فيقـوم طـورا ثـم يكبـو تـارة
هـل للوصـول الـى الحسـين سبيل	فغـدا ينـادي والـدموع بـوادر
يـا ليتنـي دون الابـي قتيـل	هـذا أبـي الـضيم ينعـي نفـسه
حزنـا وانـي بعـدكم لـذليل	أبتـاه انـي بعـد فقـدك هالـك

* * *

507

الشيخ محمد بن الشيخ علي بن ابراهيم آل نصار الشيباني أو الشبامي اللملومي النجفي المعروف بالشيخ محمد بن نصار.

توفي في جمادى الاولى سنة ١٢٩٢ في النجف الاشرف ودفن في الصحن الشريف عند الرأس وهو من أسرة أدب وعلم ، أصلهم من لملوم سكنوا النجف لطلب العلم وتوفي منهم في طاعون سنة ١٢٤٧ ما يقرب من أربعين رجلا طالبا للعلم وهم غير أسرة آل نصار المعروفين في النجف الذين منهم الشيخ راضي رحمه‌الله يسكنون محلة العمارة.

والمترجم له فاضل أديب له شعر باللغتين الفصحى والدارجة وقل ما ينعقد مجلس عزاء للحسين عليه السلام فلا يقرأ شعره الدارج. ولعل السر أن الناظم كان من أهل التقوى ، ولشدة حبه لاهل البيت سمى كل أولاده باسم علي وجعل التمييز بينهم في الكنية فواحد يكنى بأبي الحسن والثاني بأبي الحسين وهكذا.

أقول وأطلعني السيد ضاحي آل سيد هادي السيد موسى على مخطوطة بخطه ومن تأليفه المسمى (لملوم قديما وحديثا) ان الشيخ علي والد الشيخ محمد نصار قد أقام في ناحية الشنافية. ومن قوله في رثاء الامام الحسين (ع):

الظلمـــــاء بكــــرا مقحمـا	يـا مـدلجا فـي حنـدس
المـــولى فعـــرج عنـدما	ان شـمت لمعـة قبـة
خـضعت لادناهـا الـسما	واخـضع فثمـة بقعـة
وقـل: أيـا حـامي الحمـى	واحـث التـراب علـى الخـدو
لهـب الـوطيس اذا حمـى	يـا مخمـدا يـوم الـوغى
ان سـل أبـيض مخـذما	ومفلقـا هـام العـدى
ان هـز أسـمر لهـذما	ومنظمـا صـيد الـورى
طريـدة لبنـي الامـا	قـم فالحـسين بكـربلاء
رحـب البـسيطة أظلمـا	قـد أمـه جـيش بـه
كـل أجـرد أدهمـا	مقتـادة شـعث النواصـي
والمواضـي معنمـا	فتقاسـمتها الـسمهرية
الا القنـا والمخـذما	وغـدا ابـن احمـد لا يـرى

508

فهنالكم أم العدى	بطل البسالة معلما

وقال في العقيلة زينب الكبرى :

هاج وجدي لزينب اذ عراها	فادح في الطفوف هد قواها
يوم أضحت رجالها غرضا للنب	ل والسمر فيه هاج وغاها
ونعت بين نسوة ثاكلات	تصدع الهضب في حنين بكاها
آه والهفتاه ماذا تقاسي	من خطوب تربو على ما سواها
ولمن تسكب المدامع من عين	جفا جفنها لذيذ كراها
ألنهب الخيام أم لعليل	ناحل الجسم أم على قتلاها
أم لاجسامهم على كثب الغب	راء مخضوبة بفيض دماها
أم لرفع الرؤوس فوق عوالي ال	سمر أم رض صدر حامي حماها
أم لاطفالها تقاسى سياق ال	موت أم عظم سيرها وسراها
أم لسير النساء بين الاعادي	ثاكلات يندبن: يا آل طه
وهي ما بينهن تندب من قد	ندبته الاملاك فوق سماها

أحمد ققطان المتوفى ١٢٩٣ قال من قصيدة في الحسين (ع) :

لم يشجني طلل الديار الأبكم	كلا ولا رسما بها أتوسم
أنى يجاذبني هوى آرامها	وانا الجموح لهن لا أستسلم
لو لا المحرم ما سفكت مدامعا	لسوى المحرم سفكهن محرم
يوم الحسين بكربلاء وصحبه	ضربوا القباب على البلاء وخيموا

509

حلـق الـدروع علـى القلـوب وأقـدموا	فتقلـدوا بـيض الـسـيوف وأفرغـوا
أو قطبـت صـيد الـوغى يتبـسـمُ	مـن كـل خـواض المنايـا عـابس
ووقـاه بـالارواح كـل مـنهُم	حفظـوا وصـية احمـد فـي سبطه

فقـم فالـضبا سـئمت غمـدها	أميـة قـد جـاوزت حـدها
تجـور ولـم نـستطع ردهـا	الـى م النـوى وعلينـا العـدى
تحمـل أيـسـره هـدها	تحملنـا مـا لـو أن الجبـال
علـى رغـم آنافنـا قـصدها	تباغـت علينـا وقـد أدركـت
نكابـد طـول المـدى وجـدها	رمتنـا بفادحـة لـم نـزل
ولا موقـع مثلهـا بعـدها	فمـا أوقـع الـدهر مـن قبلهـا
سـقت مـن دمـائكم حـدها	غـداة ظـوامي الـضبا فـي الطفوف
على صـدره جعلـت وردهـا	وجـدك مـا بينهـا والخيـول
ينـسـج ريـح الـصبا بردهـا	وأسـرته حولـه بـالعرى
لهـا الله مـا ضـمنت لحـدها	ثـوت كالاضـاحي بحـر الهجير
نـساؤكم غورهـا نجـدها	وفـوق المهـازل تطـوي القفـار
أبـاهـا وآونـة جـدها	أسـارى تبـث الجـوى تـارة
تنـوح ولاطمـة خـدها	فمـا بـين لا دمـة صـدرها
يـؤلم قـارعـة زنـدها	يـذيب الجـوى قلبهـا والـسياط

وزينـــب تـدعـو أسـى والخطـوب	باحــــشائهـا قـدحت زنـدها
بنـــي غالـب سـومـوا الـصافنات	وانتـــدبوا للـــوغى أسـدها
بهـــن مواجيـف طلـيـق العنان	تقفـــوا ســلاحبها جردهـــا
قعدتم وأعـداؤكم فـي الطلـوف	شـــفت مـن أعـزتكم حقـدها
فـلا عـذر حتـى نـرى بيـضكم	رقـــاب أعـــاديكم غمـــدها
لان ضـــاع وتـــر بنـــي هاشـم	اذا عـدمت هاشـــم مجـدها

* * *

توفي الحاج سالم بن محمد علي الطريحي النجفي الرماحي في النجف في حدود سنة
١٢٩٣ كان فاضلا شاعرا يعاني حرفة التجارة ، قاسم ماله بعض اخوانه لوجهه تعالى ،
وقد ترجم لـه الكثير من الباحثين منهم العلامة الكبير الشيخ علي كاشف الغطاء في
(الحصون) والشيخ محمد السماوي في (الطليعة) وآل طريح من أقدم الاسر العربيـة
التي استوطنت النجف الاشرف منذ أكثر من أربعة قرون ، ومن مشاهيرهم في القرن
الحادي عشر الشيخ فخر الدين بن الشيخ محمد علي وهو الجد الخامس لشاعرنا
المترجم له ابي محمد الحاج سالم بن محمد علي بن سعد الدين ابن جلال الدين بن شمس
الدين بن الشيخ الاجل فخر الدين.

ولد في النجف سنة ١٢٢٤ هـ ونشأ وشب على حب الكسب وتعاطي التجارة حتى أصبح
في أواسط حياته من ذوي الثروة والجاه وسعة الحال وهو الى جنب ذلك يحمل ثروة
أدبية لا تقل عن ثروته المادية. وفي سنة ١٢٧٥ هـ وفقه الله لحج بيت الله الحرام فنظم
ارجوزة ذكر فيها ما اتفق له في طريق الحج وما شاهده في الحجاز ونجد ، توجد نسخة
منها عند أحد المشايخ من أبناء عمه ، ووالده شاعرا وقارئـا ذاكرا تخرج عليه جماعة
من الخطباءمنهم الخطيب الشيخ كاظم سبتى.

وهذه روائع من قصائده الحسينية :

عرجـا بـي علـى عـراص الطفـوف	أبـك فيهـا أسـى بـدمع ذروف
يـا عراص الطفـوف كـم فيـك بدر	غالـه حـادث الـردى بخـسوف
وهزبـر قـضى طلـيـق محيـا	بين سمر القنا وبيض السيوف
يـوم هاجت عصائب الشرك للهيـ	جاء تقفـوا الصفوف اثـر الصفوف

511

حاولت أن يضام وهو الأبي الـضـ ... ـيم كهـف الطريـد مـأوى الخـوف

شـد فيها وكـم لطيـر المنايـا ... مـن خفـوق على العـدى ورفيـف

يحسب البيض في الكريهة بيضا ... ووشـيج القنـا معـاطف هيـف

مـن لـؤي بـيض الوجـوه أبـاة الـضـ ... ـيم أسـد العـرين شـم الانـوف

عـانقوا المرهفـات حتـى تهـاووا ... صـرعا فـي الثـرى بحـر الـصيوف

وبقـى ابـن النبـي لـم يرعونـا ... فـي الـوغى غير ذابـل ورهيـف

فـانثنى للنـزال يكتـال آجـا ... لا فـوفى بالـسيف كـل طفيـف

كـم جيـوش يفلهـا عـن جيـوش ... وزحــوف يلفهــا بزحــوف

كلمـا هـم أن يـصول عليـهم ... همـت الارض خيفـة برجيـف

لـم يـزل يـورد المواضي نجيعـا ... مـن رقـاب العـدى بقلـب لهـوف

فـدعاه داعـي القضـاء فـألوى ... عـن هـوان لـدار عـز وريـف

وهوى ثاويـا على التـرب مـا بـ ... ـين الاعـادي ضـريبة للـسيوف

فبكتــه الـسـماء وارتجـت الار ... ضـون والـشمس آذنـت بكـسوف

يـا قتـيلا تقـل سـمر العـوالي ... منـه رأسـا على سنا الشمس مـوف

وتـسوق العـدى نـساه أسـارى ... فـوق عجف المطـى بـسير عنيف

أعلى النيب تنتحي البيد أيـن النـ ... يـب والبيـد مـن بنـات الـسجوف

تلـك تـدعو بمهجة شفها الوجـ ... ـد احتراقـا وذي بـدمع ذروف

ايـن اسـد العـرين شـم العرانيـ ... ـن حمـاة الـورى أمـان المخـوف

سـومـوهـا يـا آل غالـب جـردا ... تخـبط الارض مـنكم بوجيـف

512

وأبعثوهــا صــواهلا عابـسـات   يمــلأ الجـــو نقعهــا بــسدوف

لتــروا نــسوة لكــم حاسـرات   جـشمتها الاعـداء كـل تنـوف

ولكــم أوقفــوا بـدار ابن هنـد   مــن تــرى المــوت دون ذل الوقـوف

وقال من قصيدة :

أيــا مــدلجا بالــذميل العنيـف   خفافــا شـأت بالمـسير الرياحـا

تجــوف الفــلا سبـسبا سبـسبا   وتقطعهـــن بطاحـــا بطاحـــا

أنخهــا مريحـا بـوادي الغـري   مثيــرا لديــه بكــا ونواحــا

وقـل يـا مبـدد شمـل الـصفوف   اذا ازدحمــت يــوم حـرب كفاحـا

لعلـك لــم تـدر يــوم الطفـوف   غــداة غــدى دمكـم مـستباحا

وأعظـم مـا يقـرح المقلتـين   ويدمي الفــؤاد شـجى وانقراحـا

مجـال الخيـول علـى ابـن النبـي   تــرض قــراه غــدوا رواحـا

وعترتــه حولــه كــالنجوم   ينبعـث الليـل منهـا صـباحا

وقتـه الـردى فتيـة فـي النـزال   تـصافح دون الحسين الـصفاحا

تـرى البيـض بيـضا وسمـر الـصعاد   قــدودا وكــأس المنيــة راحــا

وراحـت تخـوض غمـار الـردى   وتحـسب جـد المنايـا مزاحـا

تلقـى الـسهام ببـيض الوجـوه   بيــوم بــه صـائح المـوت صـاحا

ومنها :

ولــرب قائلــة ومــن عبراتهـا   ثقلـت جـوى قطـع الـسحاب الجـون

513

ورمـت بأكنـاف اللـوى وحجـون	الجيـرة تبـدي الجـوى أم أربـع
ذهبـت بحلمـك صفقـة المغبـون	وآهـا عليـك فمـا ربحـت وانمـا
يـوم علـى الاسـلام يـوم شـجون	فاليـك عنهـا معرضـا وعليـك فـي
والبـيض يرشـح حدهـا بمنـون	يـوم ابـن فاطـم والرمـاح شـوارع
غـص الفضـاء بجيـشه المشـحون	والخيـل عابـسة الوجـوه بمعـرك
يمنـاه غيـر الـسيف والميمـون	يثنـي مكردسـها بـأروع لـم تـرم
بـالنفس يـوم المـوت غير ضـنين	ضـنت بـصارمه يـداه وانـه
ضخم الدسـيعة شامخ العـرنين	وأشـم عبـل الـساعدين شمـردل
الايـدي مناجيـب القـرون قـرين	فـي معشـر بـيض الوجـوه سـوابغ
ذكـرت أميـة ملتقـى صـفين	تغشى الـصفوف بملتقى مـن هولـه
فيهـا يـرون العـين رأي يقـين	حتـى دعـوا لحـضيرة القـدس التـي
مـا بـين منحـور الـى مطعـون	فتنـاثروا مثـل النجـوم علـى الثـرى
نـار الـوغى فـردا بغيـر معـين	وبقـى ابـن أم المـوت ثمـة موقـدا
شـاء تنـافر مـن ليـوث عـرين	يـسطو فتنثـال الجيـوش كأنمـا
فـي الحـرب حـد الـصارم المسنون	ظـام يـروي مـن دمـاء رقابهـا
فقـدان أكـرم معـشر وبنـين	حتـى اذا سـئم الحيـاة ونابـه
فأصـاب قبـل حشـاه قلـب الـدين	وافـاه سـهم كـان مرمـاه الحشـا
حزنـا عليـه برنـة وحنـين	فهـوى فـضجت في ملائكهـا الـسما
يومـا لحفرتـه ولا مـدفون	وثـوى علـى الرمـضاء لا بمـشيع

ملقــى بــلا غــسل ولا تكفــين	الله أكبر كيف يبقى فـي الثـرى
مـن كـل نافـذة المغـار صـفون	ويـروح للاعـداء تـورد صـدره
الـسامي وموضـع سـره المكنـون	مـا راقبـت غـضب الالـه لجنبـه
بغيـا وعيبـة علمـه المخـزون	رضـت خـزائن وحيـه بخيولهـا
الراهون ضعضع جانـب الراهـون	وأمـض داء فـي الحـشا لـو لامـس
فـي دار أخبـث عنـصر ملعـون	سبي الفـواطم حـسرا ووقوفهـا
ولهانـة تـدعو بـصوت حـزين	وقفت بمـر أى مـن يزيـد ومـسمع
العـافي وكنـز البـائس المـسكين	أحسين يـا غـوث الـصريخ وملجـأ
تـسود مـن ضـرب الـسياط متـوني	أحسين يـا عـزي يعـز عليـك أن
ذهبت بحلمـك صـفقة المغبـون	وآهـا عليـك فمـا ربحـت وانمـا
يـوم علـى الاسـلام يـوم شـجون	فاليـك عنهـا معرضـا وعليـك فـي
والبـيض يرشـح حـدها بمنـون	يـوم ابـن فـاطم والرمـاح شـوارع

وقال :

فهمـت وشـبت باحـشاك نـار	أهاجتـك مـن ذي النخيـل الـديار
فبـادرن منـك الـدموع الغـزار	أم البـرق أومـض مـن بـارق
لهـا مـن مـذاب حـشك انهمـار	أراك وقـد غالبتـك الـدموع
عـداك الحجـا ان شـجتك الـديار	لعلـك ممـن شـجته الـديار
أهاجـت جواهـا الرسـوم الـدثار	فـدعها ولا تـك ذا مهجـة
وأظلـم حزنـا عليـه النهـار	وقـم باكيـا مـن بكتـه الـسماء

يكفنــــــه العثيـــــر المـــستثار	غـداة غـدى ثاويـا بـالعرى
عـوادي المهـار عقـرن المهـار	أيــا ثاويــا وزعـت شـلوه
على صـدره أي صـدر يغـار	لهـا الويـل هـل علمت فـي المغار
لهـا يـا بـن طـه عليـك مغار	فوالهفــة الـدين حتـى الخيـول
دمــا مثلمــا يــستهل القطــار	حقيـق علـى العـين أن تـستهل
ورأسـك فــوق الـصعاد يـدارُ	أترضـى وجـسمك فـوق الـصعيد
تـشق ولا نعـش فيـه يـسارُ	وتبقـى علـى التـرب لا حفـرة
لهــا فـي حنايـا ضـلوعي أوار	وأعظـم مفجعـة فـي الطفـوف
أسـرى تقـاذف فيهـا القفـار	ركـوب بناتـك فـوق الـصعاب
لهــن بغيـر الاكـف اسـتتار	حواسـر لـيس عـن الناضرين

وله أيضا :

ودهى فجب مـن الهدايـة غاربـا	خطـب أمـاد مـن المعـالي جانبـا
أشـجى الانـام مـشارقا ومغاربـا	خطـب أطـل علـى الانـام بفـادح
بأسـا فـصب علـى نـزار مـصائبا	وأصـاب مـن عليـا نـزار أسـدها
عـصب تؤلـب للكفـاح كتائبـا	يـوم بـه جائـت يغـص بهـا الفضا
للحـرب فيهـا شـزبا وسـلاهبا	يقتادهـا عمـر بـن سعد مجلبـا
فـأبى الابـي فـأب منهـا خائبـا	حـسب الابـي يـروح منهـا ضـارعا
أسـدا تـصول علـى العـداء غواضبا	وغـدا أبـي الـضيم يبعـث للـوغى

516

حسبت حمام الموت سجع حمائم	فيها ومطرد الكعوب كواعبا
وغدت تحطم في الصدور عواسلا	منها وتثلم في النحور قواضبا
حيت بها بيض الظبا فكأنما	حيت من البيض الظباء ترائبا
حتى هوت صرعى فتحسب أنها	أقمار تم في الطفوف غواربا
وبقي ابن أم الموت لم ير صاحبا	بين العدى الا المهند صاحبا
فغدا يمزق سحبها عدوا كما	مزقن أنفاس الشمال سحائبا
ما زال يخطف بالحسام نفوسها	حتى أراها في النزال عجائبا
فهناك حم به القضاء مفوقا	سهما بأوتار المنية صائبا
فهوى فدكدكت الجبال وكورت	شمس الضحى وغدا النهار غياهبا

السيد أحمد الرشتي المتوفى ١٢٩٥

رزء له الاسلام ضجا	والدين والايمان رجا
رزء له الاملاك تنزل	للعزا فوجا ففوجا
رزء له البيت الحرام بكا	ومن لبى وحجا
رزء له رأس الفخار	بسيف أهل البغي شجا
يا يوم عاشوراء يوم	فيه عرش الله عجا
يوم به سبط النبي	على الثرى ملقا مسجا
لهفي لزينب اذ دعت	يا كافلي أنت المرجا
أدعوك مالك لا تجيب	وليس لي الاك ملجا
طيب الرقاد هجرته	اذ عذب عيشي صار مجا

517

وأضــحكت كلبــا وعلجــا	أبكــت رزيتــك الكــرام
فأخترت فــوق الــرمح برجا	قــد كنت شمس هدايــة
ومــاج بحــر الهــم موجــا	ســفن اصطباري قــد غرقن
الــدنيا فلــم أر قــط نهجا	ضــاقت علــي فدافــد
يســج فــي الادلاج ســجا	يا راكبــا كــور النيــاق
وعرضــن فجــا ففجــا	عــرج الــى أرض الغــري
مــن بــه للنــاس منحــا	والــثم ثــرى أعتــاب حيــدر
الطفــوف بقــى مــسجا	قــل يــا علــي حســين فــي أرض
عصائب فوجــا ففوجــا	طافــت بــه فــي كــربلاء
يرجــو بيــوم الحــشر منجا	يــدعو الاهــل راحــم

* * *

السيد أحمد الحسيني الرشتى المقتول سنة ١٢٩٥ ، نشأ في بيئـة أدبيـة علميـة وتلقى الشـعر والادب على أبيه السيد كاظم بن السيد قاسم الحسيني الرشتى ، وكانت الزعامـة الدينيـة بهذا البيت وورثها السيد احمد عن أبيه وأصبح ديوانـه حافلا بالادباء والشعراء. جاء في) الكرام البررة (ما نصه : السيد احمد بن السيد كاظم بن السيد قاسم الحسيني الرشتي الحائري عالـم أديب ، كان والده أرشد تلامذة الشيخ احمد الاحسائي قام بعده برئاسـة الفرقـة الشيخية الى أن توفي بكربلاء عام ١٢٥٩ فقام مقامه ولده المترجم لـه تلميذ أبيـه وانتهت اليه مرجعية قومـه الى أن قتل غيلة ليلة الاثنين ١٧ جمـادى الاولى ١٢٩٥ وقام مقامه ولده قاسم سمي جده.

للشاعر قصائد متفرقة قالها في أغراض شتى وقد تناول في شعره مدح ورثاء أهل البيت صلوات الله عليهم كما رثى الامراء والعلمـاء ، ولشعره أثر كبير في الغزو الوهابي فقد عبر عن هذا الحادث المروع بحسرة ولوعة اذ أهينت حرمة كربلاء وانتهكت قدسيتها سنة ١٢١٦ وقتل عشرات الالوف من الابرياء. لذا اندفع السيد احمد يهنئ مدحت باشا قائد الجيش العثماني والذي فتح نجد فقال :

فطبــق وجــه الارض بالعــدل والــنجح	بــدا نــور ظــل الله يــشرق كالصبح

518

مليك على العرش استوى ولعزه | جميع ملوك الارض تعلـن بالمـدح
ارادتــه العظمـى بنافـذ أمـره | لقـد صدرت كـي يبـدل الغي بالصلح
الى مدحة المولى الوزير الذي غدا | لـسيده مـا اختار شيئا سوى النصح
من افتض بكر الفكر في طلب العلى | فجاءتـه سعيا غيـر طاويـة الكشح
وزيـر على متن الـوزارة قـد رقـى | أحاط بها خيـرا فمـا احتـاج للشرح
قد اقتطفت أهل القطيف ثمارهـا | تأملـه فـي دوحـة العـدل والصفح
ومـذ فتحت نجد دعا السعد ارخوا | لقـد جـاء نـصر الله يزهـر بـالفتح

ومن شعره قوله أثناء رحيله الى الحج :

اسائل أهل الحـي والـدمع سائل | أهـل فـي حمـاكم للوصـول وسائل؟
منازل كانـت بـالطفوف عهـدتها | تقاصـر عنهـا فـي السمـاك منـازل
أصـعد أنفاسـا لـذكر أحبتـي | وأنـى ودونـي أبحـر وجنـادل
فقلبـي كـالرابور والطرف مـاؤه | فواعجبـا للمـاء فيـه مـشاعل
فكـم بـابلي اللحـظ تـاه بحسنه | وهاروت نادى سحري اليـوم باطل
أنا البحر فوق البحر والغيث فوقنـا | ثـلاث بحـور مـا لهـن سواحل
جليسـي كتـاب والاكـارم حولنـا | أجالـسهم طـورا وطـورا أساجل
ومـن روض أزهار الاحاديث أجتنـي | ورودا بأكمـام يحييـه وابـل
وفخـر بنـي فهـر بنـا وبجـدنا | فـان كنت في شك تجبك القبائل
فمـا وصف الطائي بعد ظهورنـا | ولا ذكـرت بكـر ولا قيـل وائـل

519

تعبــت فــان البــدر لا يتنــازل	فقــل للــذي رام النجــوم بــشأونا
فعيــر قــسا بالفهاهــة بــاقل	فــان عيرتنـا فـي علانـا عـصابة
وقــال الــسهى للــصبح لونــك حائل	وقـال الـدجى للـشمس أنـت خفيـة
تفـيض عليهـا أبحـر وجـداول	وكـم بللـت مـن فـيض بحـر أكفنـا
أراعـي حقوقـا للعلـى وأواصـل	يراعـي أراع النـاس طـرا واننـي
لآت بمـا لـم تـستطعه الاوائـل	وانـي وان كنـت الاخيـر زمانـه
شـواهد فيمـا أدعـي ودلائـل	فكـم قـد أقيمـت فـي ثبـوت مـأثري
وكوكـب أعـدائي بنـوري آفـل	شموس سعودي أشرقت من بروجها

الشيخ حمزة البصير المتوفى ١٢٩٧

الشيخ حمزة بن ناصر الحلي الشهير بالبصير ، شاعر مقبول وأديب نابه ، ذكره الشيخ النقدي في الروض النضير فقال : كان شاعرا أديبا أخذ عنه العلم جماعة من شعراء الحلة وتأدب عليه قسم كبير منهم ، وقد ذهب بصره على الكبر ، يقضي أكثر أوقاته في قرى العذار ، وله شعر في مدح أهل البيت عليهم السلام ورثائهم جاء في مجموعة صديقه الشيخ محمد الملا الحلي بعض أشعاره ، منه في رثاء الصديقة فاطمة الزهراء عليها السلام وله بمدح أهل البيت من قصيدة قالها عام ١٢٧٩ :

منـاقبهم لـن يحـصهن معـدد	هـم حجـج الـرحمن آل محمـد
صنـايع والـرحمن للكـل موجـد	صنـايع بـاريهم وكـل الـورى لهـم
وطـه وذوالقربـى وايـاك نعبـد	بهـم نزلـت والمرسـلات وهـل أتى
ورشـدهم لـم يلـف فـي الارض ملحـد	ولـو يهتـدي كـل الـورى بهـداهم
بيـوم بـه تـشقى الانـام وتـسعد	سيـسأل مـن عـاداهم وأحـبهم

520

وله مراث لاهل البيت بأوزان مختلفة يلحنها النواحون. أما قصيدته في الزهراء فاطمة فقد ذكر الشيخ اليعقوبي قسما منها كما ذكر الخاقاني في كتابه (شعراء الحلة) هذا القسم.

الشيخ مهدي حجي المتوفى ١٢٩٨

لا تلمنـي علـى البكـا والعويــل	لمصاب بكتـه عيـن الرسـول
لـست أنسـى ركائبـا لنـزار	صاح فيهـا حادي القضا بالرحيل
فامتطـت للـوغى متـون عـراب	أرسـلتها ضـوابحا فـي الخيـول
وانتضت للكفـاح بيـض صفـاح	صاقلات تفـل حـد الصقيـل
وغـدت تحصـد الـرؤوس لـوي	مـن بنـي حـرب فـي القراع المهـول
ودعاهـا القضـا فلبـت وخـرت	سـجدا كـالنجوم فـوق الرمـول
لهف نفسي لهم على الترب صرعى	مـن شـيوخ لهاشـم وكهـول
وقتيـل لآل فهـر خـضيب	بـدماه نفـسي الفـدا للقتيـل

الشيخ مهدي بن الشيخ صالح بن الشيخ قاسم بن الحاج محمد ابن أحمد الشهير بحجي الطائي الحويزي الزابي النجفي. شاعر فاضل وأديب كامل. وآل حجي أسرة علمية أدبية ، وقد سبقت ترجمة والده الشيخ صالح الكبير ، كتب عنه البحاثة علي الخاقاني في (شعراء الغري) ونقل عن الشيخ محمد رضا الغراوي انه كتب ديوانه الذي جمعه ولده الشيخ صالح وهو يقرب من خمسة آلاف بيتا. ولكنه فقد ولم يبق لـه أثر ، وروى لـه كثيرا من أدبه الفصيح ولونا من أدبه الشعبي من (الموال) و (القصيد) و (البوذية).

السيد موسى الطالقاني المتوفى ١٢٩٨

أنـخ الركـاب فانمـا هـي بقعـة	فيهـا لأحمـد قـد أنـبخ ركـاب
واعقل قلوصك انما هـو مربـع	ضـربت لآل الله فيـه قبـاب
يـا نـازلين بكـربلا كـم مهجـة	فـيكم بفادحـة الكـروب تـصاب

521

ما فيكم الا عميد سرية	في الروع لا نكل ولا هياب
ومعانق سمر الرماح كأنها	تحت العجاج كواعب أتراب
بطل ينكره الغبار وعابد	ما أنكرته الحرب والمحراب
شهب بضيء بها المحارب في الدجى	وهموا لابطال الحروب شهاب
كم موقف لهم به خرس الردى	رعبا وضاقت بالكماة رحاب
وجثوا لشارعة الرماح بمعرك	كادت تزول به ربى وهضاب
عثرت بأشراك المنية منهم	شيب يزينها النهى وشباب
وثووا ثلاثا لا ضريح موسد	لهم يشق ولا يهال تراب
وسط الهزبر ففر جند ضلالها	من بأسه وتفرق الاحزاب
أسد يفر الموت خيفة بطشه	وله الأسنة في الكريهة غاب
ريان أفئدة الصوارم قد قضى	ظمآن يرنو الماء وهو عباب
شاء الاله بآن يراه مجدلا	وعليه من فيض الدما جلباب
ثاو على الرمضاء غير موسد	تحنو عليه قواضب وحراب
وبنات وحي الله ما بين العدى	تطوى بهن فدافد وشعاب
أسرى تساق على النياق حواسرا	ولهن من حلل العفاف حجاب
نهب قفار البيد ناحل جسمها	بالسير واستلب القلوب مصاب
ومروعة تدعو الكفيل وما لها	الا بقارعة السياط جواب

* * *

هو السيد موسى بن السيد جعفر بن السيد علي بن السيد حسين الطالقاني النجفي. ولد في النجف سنة ١٢٥٠ هـ وكانت وفاته سنة ١٢٩٨ ودفن بالنجف.

522

معروف بالفضل والادب وله ديوان يحتوي على شعره بمختلف المناسبات. ومن شعره قصيدة رائية يمدح بها الميرزا باقر بن الميرزا خليل الرازي النجفي ويهنئه بزفاف ولديه الشيخ صادق والميرزا كاظم ومن شعره أيضا قوله :

علـــي وأظلـــم غـــرب وشـــرق	أحبـاي قـد ضـاق رحب الفضا
تيقنـــت أن القيامـــة حـــق	ومـذ راعنـي هـول ليـل النـوى
وللـــريح حـولي رفيـف وخفـق	فكـم ليلـــة بتهـا سـاهرا
وطبـــل الرعيـــد بعنـف يـدق	وقد جـال فـي الجو جيش الغمـام
ويـــسكب جفنـــي اذا لاح بـرق	فيخفـــق قلبـي لخفـق الريـاح
ونحـت وغنـت علـى الـدوح ورق	سهرت وقد نـام جفـن الخليـل
وانـــي بـالنوح منهـــا أحـق	وحـــق لهـا دون قلبـي العنـا
ولا هـاجهن الـــى الكـوخ شأوق	فمـا غـاب عـن عينهـا الفهـا

وطبع أخيرا ديوانه بمطابع النجف ، وأعقب الشاعر الاديب السيد محمد تقي المتوفى سنة ١٣٥٤ وتأتي بعون الله في الجزء الآتي تراجم لأسرة آل الطالقاني.

السيد ميرزا جعفر القزويني المتوفى ١٢٩٨

وأطلـــب فـــوق الـــسماكين دارا	سأمضي لنيل المعـالي بـدارا
وأن لا أقــر بــدار قــرارا	يطـالبني حـــسبي بـــالنهوض
مسير همـام عـن الـضيم سـارا	تقول لـي النفس شمـر وسـر
تظمـــى مـرارا وتـروى مـرارا	فمـا أنـت بـاغ بهـذا القعـود
وأدمـــي الاكـف دمـاء غـزارا	فقلـت سـأخلع تـوب الهـوان
يـؤجج فـي دارة الحـرب نـارا	وأجلبهـا كـل طلـق اليـدين
اذا مـا تنـادى الرجـال الفـرارا	وأنـصب نفسي مرمـى الحتـوف

تثيــــــر بـــأرجلهن الغبــــارا	كيـــوم ابــن أحمـــد والعاديـــات
وبحـــر المنايـــا عليــــه اسـتدارا	غـدات حـسين بـأرض الطفـوف
حـــرب بخيـــل مــلأن القفــارا	أتـت نحـوه مثـل مجـرى الـسيول
ويـــأبى لـــه الـسيف الا الفخــارا	تحاولــه الـضيم فـي حكمهـا
أولا يـــرى للأعـــادي ديـــارا	فأقـــسم امـــا لقــاء الحمــام
تعـرف يــوم الهيــاج الحــذارا	بآسـاد ملحمـــة لا تكـــاد
أبــاحوا رقــاب الاعــادي الـشفارا	وغلـب اذا مـا انتفـضوا للـوغى
علـى صـفحتي سـيفه حيـث سـارا	بكـل كمـي تـسير النفـوس
اذا سـعر الحـرب كاسـا عقـارا	وذي عزمـــات يخـال الـردى
حمـــام العـدو اذا النقـــع ثــارا	فـدى لـسراة بنـي غالـب
اذا صـوح العـام أرضـا بـوارا	حمـاة النزيـل كـرام القبيـل
فـانتثروا فـي الـصعيد انتثـارا	تـداعوا صـباحا لـورد المنـون
وكـان يمـد نـداها البحـارا	بنفـسي بحـور نـدى غيـضت
ومنهـا هـلال الـسماء اسـتنارا	بنفـسي بـدور هـدى غيبـت
ثـلاث ليـال غـدت لا تـوارى	بنفـسي جـسوما بحـر الهجيـر
يطـاف بهـن يمينـا يـسارا	بنفـسي رؤوسـا بـسمر القنـا
وآخـر يلقـى المواضـي حـرارا	وطفـلا يكابـد حـر الأوام
فتعـرب عمـا أسـرت جهـارا	وحـسرى تـصعد أنفاسـها
فينهمـر الـدمع منهـا انهمـارا	تـرى قومهـا جثمـا فـي العـراء

طـوت قطـع البيـد دارا فـدارا	فيـا راكبـا ظهـر غيداقـة
فتقـدح كالزنـد منهـا شـرارا	بأخفافهـا تترامـى الحصـى
ونـاد حمـاة المعالـي نـزارا	أنخهـا صباحـا بجنـب البقيـع
أطلـت لـدى آل حـرب جبـارا	بـأن دمـاء بنـي الـوحي قـد
تبـل سنانـا وتـروي غـرارا	وان ابـن أحمـد منـه العـدى
تحملهـن الاعـادي أسـارى	ونسـوته فـوق عجـف النيـاق
ويقطعـن فيهـا ديـارا ديـارا	يطفـن بهـا فدفـدا فدفـدا
جسـوما لاكفائهـا لا تـوارى	تقـول وقـد خلفـت فـي الثـرى
ذمـارا وأزكـى البرايـا نجـارا	ألا أيـن هاشـم أحمـى الـورى
فتعـدو علـى آل حـرب غيـارى	لتنظـر مـا نـال منـا العـدى
عـداها وتطلـب بالثـار ثـارا	وتـروي صـدى بيضهـا مـن دمـا
يغـاث الانـام اذا الـدهر جـارا	ألا يـا بنـي الطهـر يـا مـن بهـم
بديعـة فكـر بكـم لا تجـارى	اليكم بنـي الـوحي مـن (جعفـر)
وان هـي قـد أصبحت لا تبـارى	تبـاري النجـوم بألفاظهـا
مـا فلـك الكائنـات اسـتدارا	وصلـى عليكم الـه السـماء

جاء في(البابليات) هو أبو موسى جعفر بن معز الدين المهدي ابن الحسن بن أحمد الحسيني القزويني، الحلي مولدا ومنشأ ومسكنا. قال عنه معاصره شيخنا الاجل العلامـة الشيخ علي آل كاشف الغطاء « ره » في « الحصون » : (كان عالمـا فقيهـا أصوليـا منشئا بليغـا رئيسا جليلا مهابا مطاعا لـدى أهالي الحلة مسموع الكلمة عند حكامها وأمرائها. ولما هاجر أبوه الى النجف في أواخر حياتـه استقل هو بأعباء الرئاسـة في الحلة وأطرافها ، فكان فيها مرجع الفقراء وموئل الضعفاء تأوي الى داره الالوف من

الضيوف من أهل الحضارة والبادية التي مرجعها لواء الحلة لاجل حوائجهم وهو يقضيها لدى الحكام وولاة بغداد غير باخل بجاهه ، وكان ثبت الجنان طلق اللسان يتكلم باللغات الثلاث : العربية والتركية والفارسية ودرس العلوم اللسانية في الحلة وحضر مدة مكثه في النجف على خاله الشيخ مهدي بن الشيخ علي في بحوثه الفقهية وفي الاصول على الشيخ مرتضى الانصاري والملا محمد الايرواني وبعد رجوعه الى الحلة حضر عند والده كما حضر عنده جماعة من فضلاء الحلة. وله من المؤلفات « التلويحات الغروية » في الاصول و » الاشراقات » في المنطق وغيرهما وكان أغلب اشتغاله في حسم الخصومات وقضاء حوائج الناس مما ترك ألسن الخاصة والعامة تلهج بالثناء عليه الى اليوم وكانت الدنيا زاهرة في أيامه وعيون أحبابه قريرة في حياته) اه.

وقد ذكره خاتمة المحدثين الشيخ النوري في « دار السلام » بعبارات تدل على علو مقامه. وأنبأنا سيدنا الاستاذ الاعظم شقيقه السيد محمد عن عمر أخيه المترجم له يوم وفاته كان خمسا وأربعين سنة فيكون مولده سنة ١٢٥٣ وهي السنة التي توفي فيها جده لأمه الشيخ علي بن الشيخ جعفر ومن هنا يظهر لك السهو الذي ورد في ترجمته في » أعيان الشيعة » من كونه « تخرج بخاله الشيخ علي » لان الشيخ علي جد المترجم لا خاله. وولادته سنة وفاة جده ، فكيف يكون تخرج عليه ، والصحيح انه تخرج بخاله الشيخ مهدي بن الشيخ علي كما ذكرنا آنفا ، ومما يؤكد لدينا أن مولده كان في الحلة قوله في فقرات نثرية من رسالة طويلة بعث بها الى خاله وأستاذه المهدي يخبره بوصوله الى الحلة عائدا اليها من زيارة النجف ويصف استقبال الحليين له : « وطلعت علينا هوادي الخيل وجرت الينا أبناء الفيحاء مثل مجرى السيل فأمطنا بتلك الارض نقاب التعب وشققنا بها قميص النصب ثم دخلنا بابل وحللنا تلك المنازل :

بلاد بها حل الشباب تمائمي	وأول أرض مس جلدي ترابها

أجاب داعي داعي ربه أول المحرم سنة ١٢٩٨ في الحلة وحمل نعشه على الرؤوس والاعناق الى النجف وما مروا فيه بمكان الا واستقبل مشيعا بالبكاء والعويل ودفن في رأس الساباط مما يلي « التكية » من الصحن الحيدري. وقد حدثنا الوالد رحمه الله عما شاهده في النجف يوم ورود جثمانه اليها مما لم يتفق مثله لعظيم مات قبله وخرج الناس لتغسيله في بحيرة النجف في الموضع المعروف بـ) البركة (ولما رجعوا به للصلاة عليه في الصحن الحيدري تقدم والده المهدي وأم الناس للصلاة فانصدعت الجماهير أيما انصداع وارتفعت الاصوات بالنحيب من كل جانب فعندها تقدم العالم الرباني الشيخ جعفر الشوشتري وأم الجماعة ليسكن هيجان الناس وصلى أبوه عليه مأموما بصلاة الشيخ والى ذلك أشار الشيخ حمادي نوح في مرثيته له :

لو لا الامام صدوق النسك يقدمنا	سوى أبيك اماما قط ما اعتبروا
في (جعفر) الصادق الهادي اقتدت أمم	صلت عليك وأملاك السما أمروا

526

ورغب الشيخ المذكور أن يكون قبره قريبا منه فعمر له قبرا من حجرات الصحن مقابلا له وبينهما الطريق ودفن السيد حيدر الحلي بينهما بعد ست سنوات. وأقيمت له المآتم في كل مكان ورثته شعراء النجف والحلة وغيرهما حتى أن السيد حيدر جمع مراثيه ورتبها وجعل لها مقدمة شجية سماها : « الاحزان في خير انسان » تقع في ٩٥ صحيفة واليك أسماء الشعراء الذين أبدعوا في تأبينه ورثائه « ١ » أخوه السيد ميرزا صالح « ٢ » أخوه السيد محمد « ٣ » أخوه السيد حسين « ٤ » السيد حيدر الحلي « ٥ » السيد محمد سعيد الحبوبي « ٦ » السيد ابراهيم الطباطبائي « ٧ » الشيخ حمادي نوح « ٨ » الشيخ محسن الخضري « ٩ » السيد جعفر الحلي « ١٠ » الحاج حسن القيم « ١١ » السيد عبد المطلب الحلي « ١٢ » الحسين ابن السيد حيدر « ١٣ » الشيخ عباس الاعسم « ١٤ » السيد جعفر زوين « ١٥ » الشيخ حسين الدجيلي « ١٦ » الشيخ علي عوض « ١٧ » الشيخ حسون الحلي « ١٨ » الشيخ محمد التبريزي « ١٩ » الشيخ حسن مصبح « ٢٠ » الشيخ درويش الحلي « ٢١ » الشيخ عباس العذاري « ٢٢ » الشيخ محمد الملا. وربما رثاه بعضهم بقصيدتين أو ثلاث.

حياته العلمية والادبية :

أما حظه من العلم والعرفان فهو البحر الذي لا ينزف وقد أجيز بالاجتهاد والفتوى من والده ومشاهير علماء عصره وقد اجتمعت في ذاته الكريمة المتناقضات فانه جمع الى عظيم الهيبة والعزة ونظافة البزة وترف العيش ، تواضع جده النبي وزهد والده الوصي وكان مع شغله الدائم بادراة شؤون الاسرة والبلد واهتمامه بكل صغير وكبير من أمور الناس وابتلائه بمخالطة الحكام وأولي الامر وما أودع الله له من المحبة في قلوبهم والهيبة في عيونهم لا يفوته ورد من أوراده ولا ذكر من أذكاره ولا نافلة من صلاته وما ظنك بمن أصبح موضع الثقة عند والده بحيث ينوب عنه في صلاته وفي كل ما يتعلق به من مهماته. وأما طول باعه في النظم والنثر فحدث ولا حرج. ولولا خوف الاطالة وخشية الملل لذكرنا نماذج من رسائله التي كاتب بها جماعة من العلماء والادباء كخاليه الشيخ مهدي والشيخ عباس والسيد جعفر الخرسان والسيد نعمان الالوسي وآل جميل وغيرهم وكلها تدل على تضلعه في الحكمة والفلسفة والادب والتاريخ واللغة. وقد أثبت سيدنا الامين في « الاعيان » كثيرا من رسائله وقليلا من مراثيه الحسينية ومقاطيعه الشعرية ، وكتب في صدر رسالة الى خاله العباس بن علي بن جعفر كاشف الغطاء :

له الشفا ولا تسليه الرقى	أبقيتم مضنى لكم لا يرتجى
منه الدمع حزنا لا رقا	لو يحمد الدمع على غير بني أحمد
شهب السنين جمعا وفرقا	القاتلين المحل ان تتابعت
رعبا وسكان البسيط رهقا	والقائدين الجيش يملأ الفضا
لاجلها ما في الوجود خلقا	والباذلين في الاله أنفسا

527

لمـا جـرى يـوم الطفـوف غرقـا	انسان عيني فـي بحـار أدمعـي
لـو مـد منـه البحـر مـا تدفقـا	وبحـر أحزانـي مديـد وافـر
تكـاد نفـسي حزنـا أن تزهقـا	اذا ذكـرت كـرب يـوم كـربلا
يـأتي وأنـسى كـل رزء سبقـا	جـل فهـان كـل رزء بعـده
حـرب رمـت حربـا يـشيب المفرقـا	وعـصبة مـن شيبة الحمـد لـها
جـاش قـديم كفرهـا واتفقـا	قـادت لـها الجيـش اللهـام عنـدما
ساق لمـا منهـا رأت فـي الملتقـى	وقامـت الحـرب تحيبهـا علـى
الثغـر بعـزم ثابـت عنـد اللقـا	فاسـتقبلت فرسـانها باسـمة
رأس رئـيس وأبانـت مرفقـا	واستنهـضت قواطعـا كـم قطعـت
الا جـلا فجـر سـناها الغـسقا	مـا أغـسقت ظلمـة ليـل نقعهـا
ن وغـى للـسمع منهـا اسـترقا	فأحرقت شهب ظباهـا كـل شـيطا
صـحيح جمـع القـوم قـد تفرقـا	كـم مفـرد لا ينثنـي حتـى يـرى
لـه دمـا طـرز فيـه الافقـا	لله يـومهم وقـد أبكـى الـسما
بـأس العـدا ولا تولـوا فرقـا	مـا سئمـوا ورد الـردى ولا اتقـوا
فيـه التقـى الـدين الحنيـف والتقـى	حتـى تفانـوا والأسـى فـي مـصرع
كـان بهـم وجـه الزمـان مـشرقا	غـص بهـم فـم الـردى مـن بعد مـا
بنـار الحـرب نمـرود الـشقا	فكـم خليـل مـن بنـي أحمـد ألقـاه
يـرى الفنـا فـي ربـه عـين البقـا	وكـم ذبـيح مـن بنـي فاطمـة
أنـواره مـذ خـر يهـوى صعقـا	وكـم كلـيم قـد تجلـت للـورى

528

يا خائضا أمواج تيار الفلا	كأنه البرق اذا تألقا
من فوق مفتول الذراع سابح	قد عز شان شأوه أن يلحقا
يكاد أن يخرج من اهابه	اذا تولى مغربا أو مشرقا
لوكان لا يهوى الانيس في السرى	رأيته لظله قد سبقا
وطائر الخيال لو رام بأن	يجري على منواله لحلقا
عج بالبقيع ناعيا لأهله	مهابط الوحي وأعلام التقى
قل يا بني فهر الألى سيوفهم	أوهت قوى الضلال حين استوسقا
والمرغمين يوم بدر بالظبى	معاطس الشرك وآناف الشقا
والفاتحين يوم فتح مكة	بقضبهم للدين بابا مغلقا
حي على الحرب فقد القحها	بالطف أبناء العتاة الطلقا
عادت بها هدرا دماؤكم لدى	رجس عن الدين القويم مرقا
ورأس سبط أحمد يهدى لمن	يوما بشرع أحمد ما صدقا
والطاهرات من بنات فاطم	لم تبق منها النائبات رمقا
لا عذب الماء الفرات لامرئ	على ولا آل النبي خلقا
ولا سقى الرحمن صوب عفوه	من منه أبناء النبي ما سقى
وآعجبا يقضي الحسين ظاميا	وماؤه القراح ما ترنقا
وللسماء كيف لم تهو على الغبر	اوقد هوى الحسين صعقا
والارض ما ساخت بأهليها وقد	ثوى عليها عاري الجسم لقى
يا لك من رزء به قلب الهدى	شجوا بنيران الهموم احترقا

دمـــا بــه جيـــد الاثيـــر طوقــا	وفــادح أبكــى الســموات العلـــى
يومــا لقــاؤه يــشيب المفرقــا	عــسى يديـل الله مـــن أميــــة
ينجــي ولا فــي الارض تلقــى نفقــا	بحيـث لــم تلـف لهـا مـن ملجـأ

الشيخ صادق أطيمش المتوفى ١٢٩٨
قال يرثي الحسين (ع):

فقــد أمـــسى بــه الاسـلام نهبــا	أرق بـالطف وكـف الـدمع سكبا
وآل أميـــة بــالطف حربـــا	غـداة أقامـت الهيجـاء حـرب
علـيهم مـن بنـي الطلقـاء حزبـا	رمـت حـزب الالـه بـه وقـادت
وأوسـعهم بهـا طعنـا وضـربا	سطت فسطا أبـو الاشـبال فـردا
وأظلـم يومـــه شـرقا وغربـا	الـى أن خـر فـي البيـدا صريعا
وعـدنان الاولـى ولـوي عتبــا	ألا أبلـغ سـراة المجـد كعبـا
سـقته مـن نجيـع النحـر شـربا	أتعلـم بـابن فاطمـة ذبيحـا
تجـوب بهـن صعـب العيـس سـهبا	وهـل تـدري كرائمـه أسـارى
وقـد هتـك العـداة لهـن حجبـا	وأن سـتورها عنهـا أميطـت

* * *

الشيخ صادق بن الشيخ احمد أحد أعلام الفضل ورجال الادب ، وهو أشهر رجال هذه الاسرة وأول من اشتهر منها بالعلم هاجر الى النجف على عهد والده فاشتغل بطلب العلم ودرس على علماء عصره فأصبح أحد أعلام النجف علما وفضلا وأدبا ثم كر راجعا الى بلاده بعد أن حاز رتبة الاجتهاد ونزل في الارض العائدة الى جده فأخذ بمجامع القلوب وأقبلت عليه الوجوه والاعيان من تلك الانحاء فصار من المراجع في القضاء والفتيا وكان شهما هماما سخيا كريما مرجعا لامراء المنتفك يرجعون اليه ويأخذون برأيه ، جلب قلوب الناس بتقواه وسماحته وكرم أخلاقه ولما امتاز به من أمهات الغرائز علا

530

شأنه وارتفع ذكره فقصده أهل الفضل من ذوي الحاجات والمعوزين قال معالي الشبيبي عنه : كان فقيها كبيرا وأديبا ضليعا وصارت اليه الرئاسة والامامة في تلك الديار (ديار المنتفك) وله بها ضياع ومزارع معروفة الى اليوم وهو جد الشبيبي الكبير لأمه وهو الذي قام بتربيته وكان كثير الرعاية له والعناية به حريصا على تربيته وتهذيبه.

وكان شاعرا مجيدا شعره سلس اللفظ فخم المعنى خفيف على السمع.

توفي سنة ١٢٩٩ في الغراف ونقل الى النجف ودفن فيها وخلف عدة أولاد أكبرهم وأشهرهم الشيخ باقر وهو ممن هاجر الى النجف واشتغل بتحصيل العلم حتى صار من أهل الفضل وكان والد المترجم له الشيخ احمد هو أول من هاجر الى النجف وغرس بذرة العلم في هذه الاسرة على عهد الشيخ الكبير صاحب كشف الغطاء وكان من أهل العلم.

أقول ومقبرته المدفون بها تقع في محلة البراق احدى محال النجف ، ورأيت في كتب النسب سلسلة نسبه فهو صادق بن محمد ابن احمد بن اطيمش الربعي نسبة الى ربيعة القبيلة العربية الشهيرة في التاريخ ورأيت في بعض المخطوطات مراسلات ومكاتبات كثيرة وله مراث في الائمة الطاهرين عليهم‌السلام كما روى السماوي في (الطليعة) ذلك.

ناصر بن نصر الله المتوفى ١٢٩٩:

حتـى لذيـذ الغمـض مقلتـى جفـا	أرقنـى رزء لآل المـصطفى
خيـر بنـي حـوا عـلا وشرفا	رزء الحسـين السـبط سـبط احمـد
يشق منـه صفـصفا فصفـصفا	لـه أنسـه يجـوب كـل فدفـد
ورأسـه في الرمـح يتلـو المصحفا	وأبـأبي معفـرا علـى الثـرى
أملاكهـا تبكـي عليـه أسـفا	أفلاكهـا تعطلـت لفقـده
عميـدها مربعـة لقـد عفـا	أنديـة العلـم ألا فاندرسـي

العالم الشيخ ناصر بن احمد بن نصر الله أبو السعود القطيفي ، له شعر كثير في مراثي الامام الحسين)ع(وله منظومـة في الاصول الخمسة. وآل نصر الله وآل أبي السـعود قبيلتـان عريقتـان في النسب لهم الزعامة ولمع منهم أدباء وشعراء وصلحاء ومنهم المترجم لـه ، قـال فـي) أنوار البدرين (: هو من المعاصرين وقد قرأ علي كثيرا من شعره توفي سنة ١٢٩٩ وتاريخ وفاته (تبكي المدارس فقد ناصرها).

وللمترجم له ولد اسمه الشيخ عبدالله بن الشيخ ناصر ، ذكره صاحب انوار البدرين بعد ترجمة أبيه فقال : وله ولد صالح فاضل عالم اسمه الشيخ عبد الله سلمه الله له شعر كثير

في الرثاء على سيد الشهداء وله منظومة في صاحب العصر والزمان وله قصيدتان في رثاء شيخنا العلامة الصالح الرباني وكان ممن قرأ عليه وحضر لديه. انتهى.

السيد مهدي القزويني المتوفى ١٣٠٠

وان طالـت الايـام واتصـل العمـر	حـرام لعينـي أن يجـف لهـا قطـر
همـولا وقلـب لا يـذوب جـوى عـذر	ومـا لعيـون لا تجـود دموعهـا
وان مـدها مـن كـل جارحـة بحـر	على أن طول الوجد لـم يبـق عبرة
ويصبح كالخنساء مـن قلبـه صخـر	كـذا فليجـل الخطب وليفدح الاسى
وناحت عليـه الـشمس والانجم الزهر	لفقـد امـام طبـق الكـون رزؤه
لـه الـشامخات الـشم وانخسف البدر	وماجت لـه السبع الطبـاق ودكدكت
وضجت علـى الافـلاك املاكهـا الغـر	ورجت لـه الارضون حزنـا وزلزلـت
عليـه ثيـاب الحـزن وانهتـك الـستر	وقـد لبـست أكنـاف مكـة والـصفا
متـى كـر فـي أوسـاط دارتهـم فـروا	يـصول عليـهم صـولة حيدريـة
الـى المـوت لا يلـوي لـديهم اذا كـروا	بغلـب رقـاب مـن لـوي تـدفعوا
وعيـن الـردى فيهـا نواظرهـا شـزر	أطـل عليـهم والمنايـا شـواخص
لـه وعليـه ان سـطا النهـي والامـر	ومـا المـوت الا طـوع كـف يمينـه
بـرود تقـي مـن تحتهـا الحمـد والـشكر	الـى أن ثـوى تحـت العجـاج تلفـه
وغيثـا لراجيـه اذا مـسه الـضر	فتـى كـان للاجـي مغيثـا ومنعـة
فـأكرم بـه صـدرا لـه فـي العلـى الصدر	فتـى رضت الجرد المضامير صدره

* * *

أبو جعفر معز الدين محمد بن الحسن المدعو بالسيد مهدي الحسيني الشهر بالقزويني

532

من أشهر مراجع الامامية وزعمائها العظام الذين نهضوا بزعامة التقليد والمرجعية العامة في أواخر القرن الثالث عشر بعد وفاة شيخ الطائفة الشيخ مرتضى الانصاري - ره - ـ وانما قدمنا ذكر ولده السيد ميرزا جعفر على ذكره لانه سبق أباه في الوفاة بعامين.

جاء في) البابليات) : ولد المترجم -ره- سنة ١٢٢٢ هـ في النجف الاشرف وبها حصل ما حصل من العلوم العقلية والنقلية وقد أخذ عن فطاحل أساتذة عصره فمنهم العلامة الفقيه الشيخ موسى وأخوه الشيخ علي والشيخ حسن أنجال الاستاذ الاكبر الشيخ جعفر كاشف الغطاء ، وعمه السيد باقر والسيد علي والسيد تقي آل القزويني ، ونال مرتبة الاجتهاد بشهادات واجازات ممن ذكرناهم وهو ابن ١٨ سنة.

وقال سيدنا الحجة المؤتمن أبو محمد محمد الحسن بن الهادي آل صدر الدين الكاظمي في تكملة أمل الامل ـ فلما بلغ المترجم تسع عشرة سنة أجازه العلامة السيد محمد تقي القزويني تلميذ السيد محمد المجاهد الطباطبائي وكتب له اجازة مبسوطة رأيتها مجلدة تاريخها ١٨ محرم سنة ١٢٤١ وقد أثنى عليه ثناء حسنا. ١ هـ.

وابتدأ من ذلك العهد بالتصنيف ولم يزل حتى بعد كبر سنه وشيخوخته مكبا على البحث والتدريس والمذاكرة والتأليف وهو مع ذلك في جميع حالاته محافظ على أوراده وعباداته في لياليه وخلواته مدئبا نفسه في مرضاة ربه وما يقر به الى الفوز بجواره وقربه لا يفتر عن اجابة المؤمنين في دعواتهم وقضاء حقوقهم وحاجاتهم وفصل خصوماتهم في منازعاتهم حتى انه في حال اشتغاله في التأليف ليوفي الجليس حقه والسائل مسألته والطالب دعوته ويسمع من المتخاصمين ويقضي بينهم بعد الوقوف على كلام الطرفين فما أولاه بما قال فيه الكواز الكبير من قصيدة :

يحـدث أصـحابا ويقـضي خـصومة   ويرســم منثــور العلــوم الغرائـب

وهاجر الى الحلة حوالي سنة ١٢٥٣ وقد تجاوز عمره الثلاثين وبقي الى أواخر العقد التاسع من القرن المذكور فأخذت قوافل الزائرين من مقلديه من ايران وغيرها تتردد الى الحلة لزيارته ـ بعد اداء مراسيم زيارة العتبات المقدسة ـ حتى تغص فيهم الدور والمساكن ، الامر الذي اضطره الى القفول الى النجف والاقامة فيها وأولاده في خدمته عدا السيد ميرزا جعفر فانه بقي في الحلة ليقوم مقام ابيه في المهمات والمراجعات حتى توفي بها في حياة والده.

وقد تعرض لذكر سيدنا المترجم العلامة الجليل الشيخ ميرزا حسين النوري في « دار السلام » و « جنة المأوى « و « النجم الثاقب » و « الكلمة الطيبة » و « المستدرك ». ونقل نص ما قاله عنه صاحب كتاب « المآثر والآثار » ـ بالفارسية ـ بعنوان « الحاج سيد محمد مهدي القزويني الاصل الحلي المسكن ». نقل المحدث القمي الشيخ عباس في « الكنى والالقاب « عن شيخه النوري ما نصه :

السيد الاجل السيد مهدي القزويني الحلي ذكره شيخنا صاحب المستدرك في مشايخ اجازته بالتعظيم والتجليل بعبارات رائقة ثم قال : وهو من العصابة الذين فازوا بلقاء من الى لقائه تمد الاعناق صلوات الله عليه ، ثلاث مرات وشاهد الآيات البينات والمعجزات

الباهرات ثم ذكر انه ورث العلم والعمل عن عمه الاجل الاكمل السيد باقر صاحب سر خاله بحر العلوم وكان عمه أدبه ورباه وأطلعه على أسراره وذكر انه لما هاجر الى الحلة صار ببركة دعوته من داخل الحلة وأطرافها من طوائف الاعراب قريبا من مائة الف نفس اماميا مواليا لاوليا الله ثم ذكر كمالاته النفسية ومجاهداته وتصانيفه في الدين وغير ذلك قال : وكنت معه في طريق الحج ذهابا وايابا وصلينا معه في مسجد «الغدير» و «الجحفة» وتوفي ـ ره ـ في ١٢ ع ١ سنة ١٣٠٠ قبل الوصول الى السماوة بخمسة فراسخ تقريبا وظهر منه حينئذ كرامة باهرة بمحضر جماعة من الموافق والمخالف. انتهى ملخصا. وقال المؤرخ السيد حسون البراقي في آخر كتاب «الدرة الغروية» عند ذكر وفيات جماعة من علماء عصره : ومنهم السيد الهمام والحبر القمقام صاحب العلوم العجيبة والتصانيف الغريبة السيد مهدي القزويني فانه توفي عند رجوعه من بيت الله الحرام على بعد فرسخين من السماوة في طريق «السلمان» وجاءوا به عصر يوم الاحد الـ ٢٥ من ربيع الاول وكانت وفاته عصر الثلاثاء الـ ١٣ من الشهر المذكور من سنة ١٣٠٠ ودفن قرب عمه السيد باقر القزويني.

رثاه السيد حيدر الحلي بقصيدته الرنانة التي استهلها بقوله :

فهـــل طـــرق الــدنيا فنــاء يزيلهـــا   أرى الارض قـد مـارت لامـر يهولها

ومنهم العلامة السيد محمد سعيد الحبوبي بقصيدته العصماء التي مطلعها :

وآب ولا حــاد لهــم غيــر ناعيـــه   ســرى وحـداء الركـب حمـد أياديـه

آثاره ومؤلفاته :

المترجم له تصانيف جمة في الفقه وأصوله والرياضيات والطبيعيات والتفسير وغير ذلك ما بين كتب ورسائل ، فمنها في الفقه ، بصائر المجتهدين في شرح تبصرة المتعلمين للعلامة الحلي وهو كتاب شافي وافي مبسوط في الاستدلال كثير الفروع غزير الاحاطة لا سيما في المعاملات استوفى فيه تمام الفقه في ضمن خمسة عشر مجلدا من أول الطهارة الى آخر الديات عدا الحج. ومختصر هذا الكتاب : وقد اختصره في ضمن ثلاث مجلدات وهو على اختصاره كثير النفع لا يكاد يشذ عنه فرع مع الاشارة الى الدليل ، مواهب الافهام في شرح شرائع الاسلام : في سبع مجلدات وهو كتاب في الاستدلال مبسوط لا يكاد يشذ عنه فرع مع الاشارة الى الدليل ، مواهب الافهام في شرح شرائع الاسلام : في سبع مجلدات وهو كتاب في الاستدلال مبسوط لا يكاد يوجد في كتب المتأخرين أبسط منه جمع فيه بين طريقة الاستدلال والتفريع وما يقتضي له التعرض من أحوال رجال الحديث. نفائس الاحكام برز منه أكثر العبادات والمعاملات وهو حسن التأليف واسع الدائرة لا ينفك عن الاشارة الى أدلة الاحكام مع ما اشتملت عليه مقدمته من المسائل الاصولية ، واليه يشير السيد حيدر الحلي في احدى قصائده :

وغيثـا لراجيـه اذا مسـه الضـر   والبحـر يبـرز عنـه أنفـس الـدرر

منه لما رغبت عنه الى الصدر	فأكرم به صدرا له في العلى الصدر
والبحر يبرز عنه أنفس الدرر	له «نفائس» علم كلها درر
منه لما رغبت عنه الى الصدر	لو أصبحت علماء الارض واردة

القواعد الكلية الفقهية : حسن الترتيب جاعلا للقواعد كلا في بابه للسهولة على طلابه ، فلك النجاة في أحكام الهداة ، وافية بتمام العبادات ، وسيلة المقلدين الى احكام الدين برز منها كتاب الطهارة والصلاة والصوم والاعتكاف حسنة الاختصار ، رسالة في المواريث بتمام أحكامه جيدة التفريع ، رسالة في الرضاع وتسمى اللمعات البغدادية في الاحكام الرضاعية ، رسالة تشتمل على بيان أحوال الانسان في عوالمه وما يكون فيه سببا في تكليف غيره من الاحكام الشرعية الفقهية وهي آخر تأليفاته وتصنيفاته وعليها جف قلمه الشريف كتبها في مكة المشرفة ، منسك في أحكام الحج كبير ، منظومة في الفقه برز منها تمام العبادات ، شرح اللمعة الدمشقية برز منه أكثر العبادات على اختصار ولم يتمه.

وأما كتبه الاصولية فمنها : الفرائد : برز منه من أول الاصول الى آخر النواهي خمس مجلدات ضخام مبسوطة جدا على طريقة المتأخرين ، الودائع : واف بتمام المسائل الاصولية سلك فيها مسلك القدماء في التأليف ، المهذب : جمع في كلمات التوحيد الآغا البهبهاني مرتبا لها من أول علم الاصول الى آخر التعادل والتراجيح مع تهذيب منه وتنقيح واختيارات وزيادات ، الموارد : هو متن حسن الاختصار تام ، شرح قوانين الميرزا القمي برز منه جملة من الادلة العقلية وبعض التعريف واشتمل على فوائد جليلة ، رسالة في حجية خبر الواحد ، منظومة وافية بتمام علم الاصول حسنة السبك جيدة النظم سماها السبائك المذهبة ، رسالة في آيات الاصول مبتكرة في بابها فيها كل آيه يمكن ان يستدل بها على مطلب أصولي من أول المبادئ اللغوية الى آخر التعادل والتراجيح والكثير منها لم يذكره الاصوليون بكتبهم ، رسالة في شرح الحديث المشهور بحديث ابن طاب المروي عن الامام الصادق)ع(وقد أشار الى هذا الحديث السيد بحر العلوم في منظومته حيث يقول :

يفتح منه أكثر الابواب	ومشي خير الخلق بابن طاب

وحيث أن الكثرة في لسان الشرع تحمل على الثمانين استنبط منه ـ ره ـ ثمانين بابا أربعين في الاصول وأربعين في الفقه.
وله كتب ورسائل في علوم متفرقة منها : مضامير الامتحان في علم الكلام والميزان برز منه علم الميزان وتمام الامور العامة وأكثر الجواهر والاعراض ، آيات المتوسمين في أصول الدين في ضمن مجلدين ، قلائد الخرائد في أصول العقائد)، القلائد الحلية في العقائد الدينية ، رسالة في أبطال الكلام النفسي.

وله في التفسير : رسالة في تفسير الفاتحة ، تفسير سورة القدر ، تفسير سورة الاخلاص ، رسالة في شرح الحديث المشهور : حب علي حسنة لا تضر معها سيئة ، رسالة في شرح كلمات أمير المؤمنين (ع) من خطبة من نهج البلاغة وهو قوله (ع) : لم تحط بها الاوهام بل تجلى لها بها وبها امتنع عنها واليها حاكمها ، مشارق الانوار في حل مشكلات الاخبار ، شرح جملة من الاحاديث المشكلة كحديث : من عرف نفسه فقد عرف ربه ، وغيره وليته أتمه ، الصوارم الماضية في تحقيق الفرقة الناجية واليه يشير السيد حيدر الحلي في قصيدة يمدحه فيها :

فعــل الـــسيوف ثكلــت أغمادهـــا   فاســـتلها صـــوارما فـــواعلا

رسالة في أجوبة المسائل البحرانية ، رسالة في أسماء قبائل العرب مرتبة على الحروف الهجائية ، كتاب الاقفال وهو متن في علم النحو في غاية الاختصار. قال ولده العلامة السيد حسين فيما كتبه عنه من ترجمة حياته وبيان مؤلفاته : ـ هذا ما وقفنا عليه من تصانيفه الموجودة المحفوظة واما ما لم نقف عليه مما عرض له التلف لكونه تداولته أيدي المشتغلين للمطالعة والمراجعة فمن ذلك الفوائد الغروية في المسائل الاصولية. وكتاب معارج النفس الى محل القدس في الاخلاق والطريقة. ومنظومة تسمى مسارب الارواح في علم الحكمة ، وكتاب معارج الصعود في علم الطريقة والسلوك ، وكتاب مختصر للامور العامة والجواهر والاعراض في علم الكلام. وشرح منظومة تجريد العقائد. وكتاب قوانين الحساب ، في علم الحساب. ومنها شرح ألفية ابن مالك في النحو. ومنها كتاب المفاتيح في شرح الاقفال في النحو ايضا وحاشية على المطول للتفتازاني. وحاشية على شرح التفتازاني في الصرف وجميعها لم تقف منها على رسم ولا سمعنا منها سوى الاسم تلف جلها بسبب تفرق أوراقها عند المشتغلين واضمحلالهم في الطاعون. ١ هـ.
وقد كتب العلامة الحجة السيد حسين القزويني المتوفى ١٣٢٥ ترجمة لوالده سيدنا المترجم له في رسالة خاصة تتضمن مراحل حياته أطلعني عليها الشاب الباحثة السيد جودت السيد كاظم القزويني. وقد رأيت له جملة قصائد في رثاء الامام الحسين (ع) منها قصيدة مطلعها :

أهاشـم لا للبـيض أنـت ولا السـمر   ولا أنـت للقـود الهجـان ولا المهـر

وأخرى أولها :

مـصاب يعيد الحـزن غـضا كمـا بـدا   قـضى أن يكـون النـوح للنـاس سـرمدا

ومـا أنتجـت أم الرزايـا بفـادح   بمثـل الـذي في كـربلا قـد تولـدا

لطف الله بن يحيى بن عبدالله بن راشد بن علي بن عبد علي ابن محمد الحكيم الخطي. كان فاضلا تقيا ورعا له أياد بيضاء أوجبت محبته في القلوب ، له مراث كثيرة في أهل البيت ، فمن شعره هذه المرثية :

حيـا الحيـا سـاحاته مـن منـزل	ألغيـر كاظمـة يـروق تغزلـي
غـض وصبغة صبوتي لـم تنصل	واذا كلفـت بــه وغـصن شـبيبتي
وصـلا فتعمـل حيلـة المتوصـل	وظبـاه كـن أوانـسا لـي تبتغـي
ـبح الـشيب فـوق مفارقي كالمشعل	حتـى انجلى ليل الـشباب وبـان صـ
والمنحنــى وربيــع دارة جلجـل	فنـسيت بعـدهم العقيـق ولعلعـا
(سـقط اللـوى بـين الـذحولِ فحومـلِ)	وجذبت مـن يـد صـاحبي كفي علـى
لرضـاه فـي حـالي وفـي مـستقبلي	وطلبـت مـن كـرم الكـريم وسيلـة
بـاب النجـاة ونجحـة المتوسـل	حتـى اهتـديت لخيـر كـل وسيلة
الابـرار خيـر مكبـر ومهلـل	المـصطفى والمرتـضى وبنوهمـا
والـشهادة والمقـام الاكمـل	أهـل النبـوة والامامـة والكرامـة
فيهـا مـن الـرزء العظيـم المهـول	وسمعت واعيـة الطفوف ومـا جرى
قتلـوا علـى ظمـأ دويـن المنهـل	أبكـي الحـسين وآلـه فـي كـربلا
الا بطعنـة ذابـلٍ أو منـصل	مـاتو ومـا بلـوا حـرارات الحـشا
ذكـراك أحزننـي وسـاق الكـرب لـي	يـا كـربلا مـا أنـت الا كربـة
قطـع الغمـام وجنـح ليـل أليـل	مـذ أقبـل الجيـش اللهـام كأنـه
كالـشهب تزهـو فـي ظـلام القسطـل	بـأبي وبـي أنـصاره مـن حولـه

537

يدعوهم بلطيف ذاك المقول	أفديه وهو مخاطب أنصاره
السير قبل الصبح وليترحل	يا قوم من يرد السلامة فليجد
والعيش بعدك يا ربيع الممحل	فالكل قال له على الدنيا العفا
لا بد منه لمسرع أو ممهل	أنفر عنك مخافة الموت الذي
حلو كطعم السلسبيل السلسل	والله طعم الموت دونك عندنا
هيا سراعا للرحيل الاول	فجزاهم خيرا وقال ألا انهضوا
البيض الرقاق بسمر خط ذبل	فتوطنوا الجرد العتاق وجردوا
جنح الظلام يزينه النسب العلى	من كل صوام النهار وقائم
صافي الطلاء مطهم ومحجل	من فوق كل أمون عثرات الخطى
تبة العليا صدر الجيش صدر المحفل	ما زال صدر الدست صدر الـر
حمر فتنفر كالنعام الجفل	يتطاولون كأنهم أسد على
ومسبح ومقدس ومهل	ومضوا على اسم الله بين مكبر
سيم العطاش الى ورود المنهل	يتسابقون الى المنون تسابق الهـ
فوق الوهاد كشهب أفق أفل	حتى قضوا فرض الجهاد وصرعوا
وسقى ثراهم صوب كل مجلجل	صلى الاله عليهم وسلامه

ايضاح: سبق وان ترجمنا في الجزء الخامس للشيخ لطف الله بن محمد بن عبد المهدي بن لطف الله بن علي البحراني الجد حفصي ونسبنا القصيدة المذكورة له ، ثم ترجمنا في الجزء الخامس ايضا لحفيده : الشيخ لطف الله بن علي بن لطف الله ، والان يأتي دور سميهما والمتأخر عنهما في الزمن.

الشيخ محسن الخضري المتوفى ١٣٠٢ من شعره في الحسين (ع) :

538

ملكتم بني سفيان في الارض أشهرا	فأبكيتم عـين الفواطم أعصرا
أفخرا عـلى قـوم أبـوه استرقكم	لـدى الـروع اذ كنتم اذل وأحقرا
فأطلق عفـوا والطليـق أبـوكم	فـأهون بـه اذ ذاك عبـدا تحـررا
تعدون أقصى الفخر فخر أبـيكم	فهـلا عـددتم يـوم صفين مفخـرا
وهـلا استطالت يـوم بـدر رمـاحكم	قصرن ويـوم الفتح قـد كـن أقصرا
فيا لـشهيد مثلـت فيـه هنـدكم	فجـاءت بمـالا تعـرف النـاس منكـرا
بغيض رسـول الله اذ هـي نظمـت	قلادتهـا أنفـا وشنفـا وبنصـرا
ومـا مـر فـي الايام أغيظ موقـف	كموقفـه اذ سـاءه ذاك منظـرا
سننتم بني صخـر بن حرب قطيعة	لهـا كـاد صـم الـصخر أن يتفطـرا
فمـا كـان مـنكم عتبـة ووليـده	كحمـزتهم لا فـي قـراع ولا قـرى
لان شـمخت بـالطف عـوج انـوفكم	فبـا لجـدع قـد كانت أحـق وأجـدرا
فقل لابن هند حين ثـوب شامتـا	بأهليـه ان كـانوا أعـق وأكفـرا
أفخـرا بيـوم الطف اذ هـم عصابة	حشدتم عليهـا مـا خـلا الجـن عسكـرا
سلوا ذلـك الجيـش اللهـام تـشله	ميـامين يتلونـا الكتـاب المطهـرا
يـشلونه ضـربا وطعنـا وصرخة	تـذكرهم فـي يـوم صفين حيـدرا
فمـا نـازلوهم فـي الكفـاح وانمـا	يـسيلون جـري الـسيل عدوا اذا جـرى
فمنهـا الـذي جلى على (ابن حوية)	بزبرتـه عـن ساعديه مـشمرا
فمـا كلـت الهيجـاء الا أعادهـا	أغـر اذا مـا استقبل الجيش غبـرا
اذا اقـتحم الـصف المقدم لفـه	بـآخر مـن خلف الـصفوف تـأخرا

539

من الخط يمحو للكتيبة أسطرا	ويطعن وخزا في الصدور بأسمر
ميامين يتلونا الكتاب المطهرا	سلوا ذلك الجيش اللهام تشله
فخيل مليك الرعد في الجوز مجرا	وصاح بهم والموت أهون صيحة
يهل تصهالا وجبريل كبرا	وخاض غمار العلقمي جواده
فهل كان طعم الماء في فيه ممقرا	فروى وما أروى غليل فؤاده
ويطوي حشى من مائها لن تقطرا	وجاء بها مملوءة يستلذها
اليك تسامى الفضل عزا ومفخرا	أبا الفضل قبل الفضل أنت وبعده
أخاك ومقطوع الذراعين جعفرا	فواسيت طعانا أباك وصابرا
عمود حديد ظل يرديك للثرى	وزدت عليه اليوم فرقا يشقه
تباع بها نفس الكريم وتشترى	فلا قام للهيجاء سوق حفيظة

* * *

الشيخ محسن الخضري هو ابن الشيخ محمد الخضري المولود سنة ١٢٤٥ والمتوفى سنة ١٣٠٢ هـ ينتهي نسبه الى مالك الاشتر والجناجي الاصل، النجفي المولد والمنشأ والمسكن والمدفن. عالما فاضلا كاملا أديبا لبيبا سريع البديهة في نظم الشعر، درس على الشيخ مهدي كاشف الغطاء وعلى الشيخ مرتضى الانصاري والسيد الشيرازي والسيد ميرزا محمد حسن. كتب عنه الدكتور مهدي البصير وانه نظم الشعر وهو ابن اثني عشر عاما، ومن هنا يتبين انه رجل كلام وفقه علاوة على انه رجل أدب، وهذا ديوانه المطبوع بجهود ابن أخيه الاستاذ الشيخ عبد الغني الخضري يجمع الغزل والوصف والرثاء والمديح وغيرها وفيه قصائد عامرة في أهل البيت عليهم السلام، وخصوصا في يوم الحسين سبط رسول الله وجهاده بكربلاء، فواحدة يقول في أولها:

مذيلا من العين قلبا مذابا	على المازمين حبست الركابا
اذا الذاريات كستها الثيابا	وما أنا ممن شجته الديار

بلــى ذللـــت أدمعــي نكبــة	بهــا اشتعل الــرأس شيبا فــشابا
غداة طغى في عـراص الطفوف	دم أوجس الكــون منــه انقلابــا
دم حرمــت سـفكه الـصابئون	ولكــن أباحتــه حــرب الحرابــا
بيـــوم تألبـــت الـصافنات	تقـل الــى الـروع أسـدا غـضابا
اذا انبعثـــت يـسبكر القتــام	فتنـــسج للـــشمس منهـا نقابـا

وفي أخرى أولها :

آلـت تهامــة أن تجـوس خلالهـا	فحمــت عليــك ســهولها وجبالهـا

ويأتي الى شهداء الطف فيقول :

متربـصين تـلاع كـل ثنيــة	كالأسد ترصد في الـشرى أشبالها
متسربلين على الحديـد بـأنفس	أوحـى لهـا الـرحمن مـا أوحـى لهـا
زهر كأمثـال الكواكـب في الـوغى	مستنهــضين زهيرهـا وهلالهـا

الشيخ علي سبيتي المتوفى ١٣٠٣ قال يذكر أبا الفضل العباس بن علي عليهما السلام :

ضمائر فيهـا البيـن والهـم نافث	تهيجهــا للحادثـــات حــوادث
وقـائع في أثنـا وقـائع لا يعـي	لهـا غـابر حتـى يوافيـه حـادث
وأعظمها وقعا لذي اللب في الحشى	اذا ضـاع مـوروث وأعـوز وارث
سـأرمي بهـا دوا يـضح فجاجه	ولـم يمـش فيـه للـسحاب نوافـث
اليك أبا الفضل الرضا زمت العلا	حـدائجها والامــر للامـر كـارث
أأنساك يـوم الطـف والخيـل تـدعي	فيــنحط عريـد ويرعـد لاهـث

541

صليت لظاها دونك الشوس تدعي	بأيامها والخطب للخطب عائث
ويوم دعتك الهاشميات والحشى	تلاعب فيه نافخ الحر عابث
ونادى مناديها هل اليوم فارس	عصته العوالي والسيوف النوافث
وكل جسور يولد الموت صوته	اذا صاح لبته المنايا الغوارث
فأخمدت من هيجائها كل مرجل	يقر لك الجمعان انك حارث
ورثت من القوم الذين وصاتهم	اذا أمحل العامان غوث وغائث
ترى حلمهم تحت الظبا غير طائش	وخطوهم بين القنا متماكث

* * *

الشيخ علي السبيتي هو ابن الشيخ محمد بن احمد بن ابراهيم ابن علي بن يوسف العاملي الكفراوي. والكفراوي نسبة الى كفري بفتح الكاف وسكون الفاء بعدها راء مهملة مقصورة ـ من قرى جبل عامل وعمل صور. ولد في كفرى في الخامس والعشرين من ذي الحجة سنة ١٢٣٦ وتوفي بها ليلة الجمعة مستهل رجب سنة ١٣٠٣ ، عالم فاضل ثبت صالح زاهد ، نحوي بياني لغوي ، شاعر كاتب مؤرخ ، مصارح بالحق غير مداهن. قال السيد الامين في الاعيان ج ٤٢ / ١٩ رأيناه فشاهدنا فيه الزهد والتقوى والصلاح والمجاهرة بالحق وكان حسن النادرة ظريف المعاشرة ، قرأ على علماء جبل عامل وكان مشهورا بعلم اللغة والبيان والنحو والتاريخ. ذكره صاحب جواهر الحكم فقال:

كان شيخا ورعا بارا تقيا صدوقا يحب الخير ويفعله الى آخر ما قال. له من المؤلفات (الجوهر المجرد في شرح قصيدة علي بك الاسعد). يحتوي على كثير من تاريخ جبل عامل وترجمة جملة من علمائه المتأخرين ، سمعنا به ولم نره ، وكتاب شرح ميمية أبي فراس ، ورسالة في رد فتوى الشيخ نوح الذي حلل فيها دماء الشيعة وأموالهم ، وكتاب الكنوز في النحو لم يتم واليواقيت في البيان ، وكتاب الرد على البطريرك مكسيموس ، ورسالة في الرد على رسالة أبي حيان التوحيدي رواها أبو حامد أحمد بن بشر المروزي عنه كما نقله ابن أبي الحديد في شرح النهج فرغ منها سنة ١٢٧٣ بقرية كفرى ، ورسالة في فضل أمير المؤمنين)ع(الى غير ذلك من الرسائل ، قال صاحب جواهر الحكم : والجميع نسجت العناكب عليها.

أقول: وروى السيد له جملة من شعره في الفخر والحماسة وفي مناسبات كانت في زمانه ، وقال من قصيدة :

ولـيلتنـا يـوم ذات الاثـل	رعـى الله أيامنـا بـالنقى
ويـشكر فيهـا المـساء الاصل	ليـالي تحمـد ظلماؤهـا
ويـومي رطيـب بظـل أظل	ليـالي بـيض بوصـل الحـسان

السيد الكاظم الأمين المتوفى ١٣٠٣

السيد كاظم الامين بن السيد احمد بن السيد محمد الامين ابن السيد أبي الحسن موسى ولد سنة ١٢٣١ وتوفي في بغداد في ٢٧ ربيع الثاني سنة ١٣٠٣ ونقل الى النجف الاشرف ودفن في حجرة آل كبة في الصحن الشريف قرب باب الطوسي ، كان عالما فاضلا حافظا متقنا مؤرخا واحد زمانه في الاحاطة والضبط وحفظ التواريخ والآثار ودقائق العربية وكان شاعرا مطبوعا منشأ بليغا وواعظا زاهدا عابدا ، هاجر من جبل عامل الى النجف الاشرف لطلب العلم في حياة والده السيد احمد وكان عمره قريب خمس عشرة سنة مع ابن عمه السيد محسن بن السيد علي بن السيد محمد أمين. وقرأ على الفقيه الشيخ مشكور الحولاوي وتزوج ابنته وبقي مكبا على طلب العلم حتى فاق أقرانه بعلوم كثيرة منها اللغة والتاريخ ، وترك بخطه من فرائد التفسير واللغة والتأريخ ودقائقها شينا كثيرا وجل شعره في المواعظ والنصائح والآداب والحكم والمراسلات ، ذكر أكثر شعره صاحب الاعيان. ومن شعره ـ وهو يشكو من الزمان ويذكر مصائب أهل البيت عليهم‌السلام ـ ومصيبة الحسين خاصة وقد أرسلها الى ابن عمه السيد محمد الامين :

ولا ذو حجـى حـر بـه عيشـه يهنـو	لعمـرك مـا للـدهر عهـد ولا أمـن
وأحداثـه فـي كـل يـوم لهـا لـون	وهـل مـن أمان للزمـان ووده
ترحـل عنـه الاب والأم والابـن	وكيف يطيب العيش فيها الـذي نهى
لميـت وان لـم يعلـه التـرب واللبن	وان امـرءا أصـلاه ماتـا ، وفرعـه
مـن العمـر في الدنيا يـروق لـه حسن	وهل بعد عد المرء خمـسين حجـة
بلـوغ المنـى والعظـم قـد نابـه وهن	وبعد اشتعال الرأس بالشيب ينبغي
فهـل انـت الا فـي تـضاعيفها شن	فهب انك نـاهزت الثمانين سالما
فقـل وهت الاحشاء واستوهن المتن	وان نازعتك النفس يومـا لـشهوة

543

وقد أزف الترحال واقترب الظعن	أتأمل في الدنيا القرار سفاهة
اذا ما ذوى غصن ذوى بعده غصن	وأنا بني حواء أغصان روضة
أو البدن ما تدري متى يومها البدن	وهل نحن الا كالاضاحي تتابعت
ونلهو اذا ولت وما جاءنا أمن	نراع اذا ما طالعتنا جنازة
فلما مضى عادت لمرتعها الضأن	كثلة ضأن راعها الذئب رتعا
وعين شعوب نحونا أبدا ترنو	نروح ونغدو في شعوب من المنى
ونعشو عن الاخرى وهذا هو الغبن	نحوم على الدنيا ونبصر بطشها
غدا كل حر وهو عبد لها قن	وأعجب شيء وهي ألئم جارة
لما اعتادنا غمض ولا ضمنا ركن	ولو أننا نخشى المعاد حقيقة
تحول بنا عن نيله ظلل دجن	ولكننا عن مطلب الخير في عمى
وفي طلب الدنيا لنا الحزم والذهن	لنا الوهن والاغفال في طلب التقى
بغي لها في كل آونة خدن	وتخدعنا الدنيا ونعلم أنها
على أنها في عين أهل النهى سجن	ونهوى بها طول المقام جهالة
بقفر فلما أسفرت سافر الظعن	وانا بها كالضعن عرس ليلة
ولا بطل يخشى بوادره قرن	وهيهات لا يبقى جواد مؤمل
ولا ملك يوقيه جيش ولا خزن	ولا سوقه من سائق الموت هارب
ومن طوف الدنيا وقامت به المدن	فأين أنو شروان كسرى وقيصر
قرون وكم من بعده قد مضى قرن	تبين بذي القرنين كم قبله انطوت
ودوخت الدنيا جيوشهم الرعن	وأين الذين استخلفوا من أمية

بلاقـع بـالزوراء أرسـى بهـا الـدمن	وأين بنـو العبـاس تلـك ديـارهم
غـداة اليـه قـوض الابيـض الجـون	وفـي التـاج منهـا عبـرة وعجيبـة
وأعـلاه مـن أدنـاه فأعجـب لـصما افتنـوا	فـأحكم أس التـاج مـن شـرفاته
يرنحـه مـن صـوت عـذب اللمـى لحـن	عفا وكـأن لـم يـصطبح فيـه متـرف
حمـام الـى أقـصى خراسـان والبـين	وهارون من قصر السلام رمى بـه الـ
يبابـا مغانيهـا لـوحش الفـلا وطـن	وتلـك بـسامرا مـواطنهم غـدت
وللبـوم والغربـان آطامهـا وكـن	فآكامهـا للعفـر والعـصم موئـل
رسـول بأشـخاص النفـوس لـه الاذن	تخطـى الـيهم فـي معاقـل عـزهم
والا تكـن مـن لا يقـام لـه وزن	فـذا هـادم اللـذات لا تـنس ذكـره
قـد انطرفـت عـين وسكـت بـه اذن	مـنغص شـهوات الانـام فكـم بـه
وفـي البـيض مـن أنيابهـا الـسم مكـتن	فـلا يـأمن الـدنيا امـرء فهـي أيـم
لـك الباقيـات الـصالحات هـي الـسفن	ومـا هـي الا لجـة فلـتكن بهـا
معاشـر لا تـصغي لـداع ولا تـدنو	فقـصر فمـا طـول الـدعاء بنـافع
عوائـده حتـى يواريـه الـدفن	تعـودت الـسوءى ومـا المـرء تاركـا
وفـي وعظ مـن لا يـرعوي تخـرس اللـسن	فكـم عظـة مـرت ولـم ننتفـع بهـا
فلـيس بمـوروع وان علـت الـسن	ومـن لـم يرعـه لبـه وحيـاؤه
فجانبـه هـين لـصاحبه لـين	ولله فـي بعـض العبـاد عنايـة
ولا وجـوده يومـا يكـدره مـن	صـروف الليـالي لا تكـدر وده
ولا هـو للـساعي اليـه بهـم اذن	حميـد الـسجايا لا يـشاكس قومـه

اخـو كـرم يـولي الجميـل صديقه   وفـي نفـسه ان الـصديق لـه المـن

لعمـر أبـي والنـاس شتى طباعهم   فمـنهن زيـن والكثيـر لهـم شيـن

ومـن عجب فرخـا نقـاب الـى أب   وأم وفـي الاخـلاق بينهمـا بـون

وكـم مـن بعيد وده لـك صـادق   قريـب ودان وده شـاحط مـين

ورب أخ أولاك دهـرا صـفاءه   فطابـت بـه نفس وقرت بـه عيـن

جـرى طلقـا حتـى اذا قيل سـابق   تداركـه عـرق ولـيس بـه ايـن

فبـات على رغـم المكارم والعلى   يغض على الاقـذاء مـن عينـه جفـن

ويـزعم ان الـسيل قـد بلـغ الزبى   لـذاك وان قـد ثـل مـن عرشـه ركـن

فيـا نائيـا والرحـل منـه قريبـة   وذا شـرف فـي القـوم أخلاقـه خشـن

أمثـل شقيق المرء يـسلى اخـاؤه   لـك الخير لـولا رغبـة النفس والـضن

ومثـل عميـد القوم ينـسى ظهيـره   على المجد وهو الناقد الجهبذ القرن

ويجهـل مسعى مـن أغذ مهـاجرا   الـى بلـد فـي جـوه العلـم واليمـن

وأشـرف دار جنـة الخلد صحنها الـ   ـمقدس والفردوس مـا ضمـه الصحـن

ضـريح ثـوى فيـه الوصـي ، وآدم   ضجيع لـه والـشيخ نـوح لـه ضمـن

وثـم ضريح للـشهيد بكـربلا   ثـراه شفـاء للـورى ولهـم أمـن

ومـشهد موسـى والجـواد محمـد   تنـال بـه الحاجـات والنائـل الهتـن

وللسادة الهـادين في سر مـن رأى   معاهـد يستـسقى بمـن حلهـا المـزن

حضائر قـدس جارهـا فـي كرامـة   مـن الله ترعـاه العنايـة والـصون

أقـام بهـا والـصبر مـلء اهابـه   يقدمـه فـن ويعلـو بـه فـن

يزينك بين القوم فهو لنا زين	ألست ترى يا ابن الاكارم انما
بلبنان يثرى بالعقار وما أقنو	وقد كان لي لو شئت أفسح منزل
اليهم فمن كعب بن مامة أو معن	لدى معشر تعزى المروءة والندى
حفاظا وهبوا للنضال ولم يثنوا	وان ضام عاد جارهم غضبوا له
وحتف العدى ان قيل يوم الوغى ادنوا	من القوم اخدان الوفا لذوي الولا
لديها مثار النقع ان غضبت هين	يخوضون تتيار المنايا بأنفس
بفوها فيها يذهب الزيت والقطن	فان ضربوا قدوا وان طعنوا أتوا
يشد الى أمثالها الماجد الفطن	ولكنني وجهت وجهي الى التي
غناه ولا الحرمان والله لي عون	ولم أختش الاعسار والله واسع
وذا عزمة والوهم يثنيه والظن	فيا علما يرجى لكل كريمة
عطاء مليك كل يوم له شأن	نشدتك انظر سفح لبنان راجيا
على العلم والاقوام كالعلم لم يجنوا	فكم من بيوت للعلى رفعت به
فمشربه للناس مزدحم لزن	له مورد عذب المذاقة سائغ
أحل به منك التهاون والوهن	وبيتك بيت المجدو العلم والتقى
اليه أما تهفو عليه اما تحنو	اما انبعثت من قلبك الشهم نخوة
وتنهل من عين العلى أدمع هتن	على أهل ذاك البيت فليفدح الأسى
يدا والى غير الفضائل ما حنوا	كرام الى غير المكارم ما ثنوا
فراحت وفي أعلى الجنان لهم عدن	سقى الله أرواحا لهم زانها التقى
له العلم يعزى والرياسة واللسن	وياواحد السادات مجدا وفرع من

كمـا أنـنـي معنـى بـه واثـق طمـن	وخيـر ابـن عـم لا فقدت اعتنـاءه
صحيح الهـوى مـا فـي دخيلتـه ضغـن	شـهدت لان وافـاك نعـي مهـذب
لهـا الـذل أو يـودي بـه الـضرب والطعن	حريص علـى عـز العشيرة كـاره
أجـل وعلـى أمثالـه يقـرع السـن	قرعت عليـه السـن منـك ندامـة
ومـا فيـه من شيء سوى النصح يعتن	واشـهد ربـي ان قـولي نـصيحة
علـي اذا الـوى بـه خلـق خـشن	وذلـك حـق فـي أخ أو قرابـة
لمـن شأنه الازراء في النـاس والطعن	وقـد علـم الاقـوام أنـي لـشانئ
لامـارة بالـسوء لـي كـسبها غـبن	علـى أننـي والله لـست مبرئـا
فعينـي علـى مـا نـابني دمعهـا سـخن	لقد وقفت بـي من ذنـوبي على شفا
بخدمـه مـن غـر الجبـاه لـه تعنـو	فغفرانـك اللهـم ذنـب مقـصر
لرضـوان فيهـا يـذهب الغـم والحـزن	فأسـألك الرضـوان ربـي ونظـرة
بهـم قامـت الاشـياء وانتظم الكـون	بأسـمائك الحـسنى أجـب وعـصابة
حمى المتـوالي في الاراجيف والحصن	نبـي الهـدى والغـر مـن أهل بيتـه
جميـع الـورى مـا ضلـت الانـس والجـن	وأعـلام حـق لـو تنـور ضـوءها
بخـسف ولاوارى سنـاها ضحـى مـزن	ولـو بـذراها لاذت الـشمس لـم تـشن
يهجنـهم بـين المـلا معـشر هجـن	فأين رسـول الله عـن أهـل بيتـه
بـه غص من ذاك الفضا السهل والحزن	ويعـدو عليـهم مـن أميـة جحفـل
وقـد هتكـت عنهـا البراقـع والسـدن	وتغدو بـأرض الطف ثكلى نساؤهم
وحسرى تقي عن وجهها اليد والردن	فمـن حـرة عبـرى تلـوذ بمثلهـا

548

قضوا عطشا بالطف والماء حولهم   الى ورده اكباد صبيتهم ترنو

حمتها العدى ورد الشريعة ويلهم   اما فيهم من بالشريعة مستن

يسومونهم قتلا وأسرا كأنما   لهم بات ثار عند أحمد أو دين

تداعوا لهم في كربلاء وجعجعوا   بهم في العرا بغيا ليملكهم قين

هنالك ألفوا ليث غاب تحوطه   ليوث شرى غاباتها الاسل اللدن

تشد فينثالون عنها طريدة   وأسد الشرى تشقى بشداتها الاتن

فشبت لهم بالطف نار لدى الضحى   يجلل وجه الافق من نقعها دجن

على حين ما للمرء مرأى ومسمع   من النقع الا البيض تلمع والردن

وحيث فراخ الهام طارت بها الظبا   وظلت سواني نينوى من دم تسنو

وراحت حماة الدين تصطلم العدى   ولم يبرحوا حتى قضى الله أن يفنوا

ولم يبق الا السبط في حومة الوغى   ولا عون الا السيف والذابل اللدن

وأضرمها بالسيف نارا وقودها   جسوم الاعادي والقتام لها عثن

اذا كر فروا مجفلين كأنهم   قطأ راعها باز شديد القوى شثن

فكم بطل منهم براه بضربة   على النحر أو حيث الحيازم والحضن

وكم أورد الخطي فيهم فعله   بجائفة حيث الجناجن والضبن

قضى وطرا منهم ومذا برم القضا   مضى لم يشن علياه وهن ولا جبن

أرد يدا مني اذا ما ذكرتهم   على كبد حرى وقلب به شجن

اطائب يستسقى الحيا لوجوههم   لعمري وتنهل العيون اذا عنوا

عليهم سلام ما مر ذكرهم   وأحسن في اطرائهم بارع لسن

الحاج يوشع البحارنة المتوفى ١٣٠٣

الحاج يوشع بن حسين البحارنة كان من الاتقياء والاخيار والتجار المرموقين والمشهورين بالورع. وآل البحارنة أسرة كريمة عريقة في الحسب ويوجد اليوم منهم في القطيف والبحرين أفراد لهم مكانتهم المحترمة ، والمترجم له هو عقد القلادة ، ترجم له الشيخ علي المرهون في (شعراء القطيف) وقال : كانت وفاته سنة ١٣٠٣ هـ وذكر له قصيدة مطولة في رثاء سيد الشهداء أبي عبد الله الحسين سلام الله عليه ومطلعها :

| زارت بليل على جنح من السحر | فأرج الربع منها نفحة العطر |

وبعد التغزل على عادة الشعراء يتخلص للحسين (ع) فيقول :

| يوم الحسين الذي أبكى السماء دما | والارض حزنا وعين الشمس والقمر |

ويختمها بقوله :

سمعا ليوشع مولاكم مهذبة	يحلو على جيدها عقد من الدرر
ألبستها حلة من مدحكم فغدت	تختال حسنا ، وقد جاءت على قدر
سميتها الحرة العذرا وقلت لها	ألا اكمدي أنفس الحساد وافتخري
صلى الاله عليكم ما سرى فلك	أو سارت العيس في الابكار والسحر
أو عاقب الليل صبح يستضاء به	وما تغرد قمري على شجر

الشيخ عبد الرضا الخطي

الشيخ عبدالرضا ابن الشيخ حسن الخطى من شعراء القرن الثالث عشر

أمنزل الشوق جادت ربعك السحب	وحل رسمك طل ساقط صبب
وناشر فيك للازهار أردية	تهدى السرور وللاحزان تستلب
وزار تربك معتل النسيم سرى	للمسك والعنبر الفياح يصطحب

550

مــا عـن ذكـرك الا حـن لـي كبـد	مـروع ونبـار الوجـد ملتهـب
ولا مـررت بقلبـي خـاطرا أبـدا	الا انثـى دمـع عينـي وهـو منسكب
يـا منـزلا لـم أزل أشـتاق أربعـه	ومـالـه الشـوق لـو لا الخـرد العـرب
لـولا ظبـاك لمـا أصبحـت ذا شغـف	متيـم القلـب مـضنى شفـه الوصـب
ضعائـن ان سـرت حاطـت هوادجهـا	مــن المغـاوير أسـاد اذا وثبـوا
القاطنـون بقلبـي أينمـا قطنـوا	والـذاهبون بـصبري أيـن مـا ذهبـوا
مـا أنـصفوا الكمـد المـضنى ببينهم	ولا رعـوا مـن ذمـام الـصب مـا يجب
أغـروا بـه نائبـات الـدهر وارتحلـوا	وجرعـوه ذعـاف الهجـر واغتربـوا
حـسب النوائـب منـي أننـي دنـف	ضئيـل جـسم عـن الابـصار محتجـب
أعاتـب الـدهر لـو رقـت جوانبـه	لعاتـب قـد بـراه الوجـد والنصـب
أيـن الزمـان واسـعاف المحب بمـا	يهـوى وكيـف ترجـى عنـده الارب
والدهر حرب لأهل الفضل مـا برحت	صـروفه تنتحيهـم أيـن مـا ذهبـوا
أخنـى علـى عتـرة الهـادي ففرقهم	فأصبـح الـدين يبكـيهم وينتحـب
آل النبـي هـداة الخلـق مـن ضـربوا	فـي مفـرق المجـد بيتـا دونـه الشهب
جنـب الالـه وبـاب الله والحجـج	الهـادون أشـرف مـن سـارت بها النجب
سحـب النـدا وربـوع الجـود ممحلـة	أسـد الـشرى ولظـى الهيجـاء تلتهـب
الوافـدون لبيـت الله مـن وفـدوا	والـضاربون بـسيف الله مـن ضـربوا
ما فارقوا الحق في حال وان غضبـوا	كأنمـا مـرة فـي فـيهم الـضرب
يـرون مـن قربـوا مثـل الاولـى بعـدوا	عنهم ومـن بعدوا مثـل الاولـى قربـوا

ولا تمـر بهـا الادنـاس والريـب	لا ينـزل الـضيم أرضـا ينزلـون بهـا
أنـف حمـي وبـأس شـأنه الغلـب	يـأبى لهـم عن ورود الـذل ان ظمئـوا
نـور الهـدى وظـلام الجهل منتـصب	سفن النجـا وبحـور الغي مترعـة
سمت باسـماهم الاعـواد والخطـب	متوجـون بتـاج العـز ان ذكـروا
تـأتي الكـرام علـى مقدارها النـوب	جلـوا فجـل مـصاب حـل ساحتهم
جسومهم بحـدود البيـض واستلبوا	أغرى الـضلال بهـم أبنـاه فانتهبوا
وأدركـوا مـن حـسين ثـار مـا طلبـوا	غالوا الوصي وسموا المجتبى حسنا
والـشمس مـن عثيـر الهيجـاء تنتقـب	يـوم ابـن حيـدر والابطـال عابـسة
والبيـض مـن قمـم الاقـران تختـضب	والـسمر مـن طـرب تهتـز مائـسة
منـه وتحجـب بـدرا لـيس يحتجـب	رامـت اميـة ان تقتـاد ذا لبـد
بـصولة ريـع منهـا الجحفـل اللجب	فانـصاع كالـضيغم الكـرار مبتـدرا
بالمجـد متـزر بـالفخر محتقـب	أغـر مكتـسب للحمـد ذو شـيم
كـأنهم لنـدى كفيـه قـد طلبـوا	يلقـي الكمـاة بثغـر باسـم فرحـا
سقـي الرمـاح دماها بعـض مـا يجب	يقري الصوارم أشـلاء العدى ويرى
فخر وهـو يطيـل الـشكر محتـسب	وافتـه داعيـة الـرحمن مـسرعة
مـن صدره والمواضـي منـه تختـضب	نفـسي الفـداء لـه والـسمر واردة
حتـى قضـى وهو ظمآن الحـشى سغب	مـضرج الجـسم مـا بلـت لـه غلـل
علـى الثـرى ودم الاوداج ينـسكب	دامـي الجبـين تريـب الخـد منعفـر
ذاري الريـاح ووارتـه القنـا الـسلب	مغـسل بنجيـع الطعـن كفنـه

قضى كريما نقي الثوب من دنس   يزينه كل ما يأتي ويجتنب

يا قائدا جمع الاقدار طوع يد   كيف استقادك منها جامع درب

لئن رمتك صروف الدهر عن احن   وقارعتك مواضيه فلا عجب

كنت المجير لمن عادى فحق له   ان يطلب الثار لما أمكن الطلب

يا مخرس الموت ان سمتك نادبة   من النوادب كيف اغتالك الشجب

ياصارما فل ضرب الهمام مضربه   ولا تعاب اذا ما ثلت القضب

ان كورت منك كف الشرك شمس ضحى   فما على الشمس نقص حين تحتجب

لو تعلم البيض من أردت مضاربها   نبت وفل شباها الروع والرهب

ولو درت عاديات الخيل من وطأت   أشلاءه لاعتراها العقر والنقب

ما كنت أحسب والاقدار غالبة   بأن شمل الهدى الملتام ينشعب

ولا عهدت الثرى تطوي بحور ندى   ما حل ساحتها غور ولا نضب

بنو امية لا نامت عيونكم   ولا تجنبها الاقذاء والصبب

أبكيتموا جفن خير المرسلين دما   لكي يطيب لكلب منكم الطرب

لم يكفكم قتلكم سبط النبي ظما   عن سبي نسوته كالزنج تجتلب

راموا بمقتله قتل الهدى فجنوا   عارا تجدده الاعوام والحقب

لله أي دم للمصطفى سفكوا   وأي نفس زكت للمرتضى اغتصبوا

وكم عفيفة ذيل للبتول سرت   بها أضالع لم يشدد لها قتب

تطوي على جمرات الوجد أضلعها   وقد أضر بها الاظماء والسغب

حسرى مسلبة الاستار تسترها   من العفاف برود حين تستلب

لئـن تـشفى بنـو حـرب بمـا صنعوا | وأدركـوا مـا تمنـوا بالـذي ارتكبـوا
فـسوف يـصلون نـارا كلمـا نـضجت | منهـا جلـودهم عـادت لهـم اهب
يـا أقمـرا بعـراص الطـف آفلـة | أضحت بـرغم العلى قـد ضمها التـرب
سـقاك مـن صلـوات الله منـسجم | يـروى صـداك مـدى الازمـان منسكب
لا زال لـي كبـد تطـوى علـى كمـد | حزنـا عليـك ودمـع سـائل سرب
ومقـول بنظـيم الـدر منتثـر | مـزر بمـا ابتكـر المـداح واجتلبـوا
يقول شعري لمـن يبغـي مطـاولتي | لقـد حكيـت ولكـن فاتـك الـشنب
صلـى الالـه عليكم حيـث ذكـركم | بـاق تـزان بـه الآيـات والكتـب

الشيخ عبد الله المشهدي
قال في مطلع قصيدة في الامام الشهيد عليه السلام :

دعـني فمـا لاح الـسرور بخـاطري | كـلا ولا ألـف الـسهاد بنـاظري
كيـف التـصبر والحـسين بكـربلا | فتكـت بـه عـصب الـدعي الكـافر
وهـو الامـام أبـو الأئمـة أشـرف | الثقلـين سبط للنبـي الطـاهر
بحر النـدى علم الهدى مردي العدى | بالـسمهرية والحـسام البـاتر

وقال في أخرى في الامام عليه السلام :

دع العيد واذكر مـا جـرى بمحـرم | فمـا أسـفي مـن بعـده بمحـرم
غـداة حسين الطهـر أضـحى بكـربلا | وعترتـه مـن كـل شـهم وضيغم
ألا بـأبي ذاك الطريـد عـن الحمى | بأسـرته في الـسهل والحـزن يرتمي

554

الشيخ موسى الكاظمي الأسدي

الشيخ موسى بن جعفر بن محمود الكاظمي الاسدي من شعراء أهل البيت عليهمالسلام وشعره ذكره ولده الشيخ محمد علي في كتابه (حزن المؤمنين في مصائب آل ياسين) طبع بمبى ، ألفه للسلطان أمجد علي شاه ، وفرغ من تأليفه سنة ١٢٥٥ هـ ومما أورده من شعر أبيه قصيدة أولها :

وحزنــي عليهم مـستمر مـدى العمـر	مـصابي بـآل الله بــاق الـى الحـشر
مـصاب فتــى أودت بـه أسـهم الكفـر	وتـزداد أشـجاني بهـم متـذكرا
كـؤس المنايـا مـن صـوارمها البتـر	لقد جرعتـه بـالطفوف أميـة
ولا حرمـة الكـرار والبـضعة الطهـر	ولــم تـرع يـالله حرمـة احمـد

ومنها :

وأدمعهـا كالسيل مـن عينها تجري	وزينـب تبكـي ثـم تنـدب جـدها
ويتـرك شلـوا بـالعراء بـلا قبـرِ	أيقتل ظلمـا غوثنـا وملاذنـا

وقال في مطلع قصيدة أخرى في رثاء أبي الفضل العباس حامل راية الحسين (ع) :

عزيـز الـسبط مقطـوع اليمـينِ	على العبـاس يـا عـين اسعديني

السيد حسين بن الشمس الحسيني :

عالم فاضل وصفه الميرزا حسين النوري صاحب مستدركات الوسائل فيما علقه بخطه على هامش رجال أبي علي : بالسيد الحسيب النسيب ذي المجدين وقال : ان له ارجوزة في سني وفاة النبي (ص) والائمة عليهمالسلام وتاريخ ولادتهم وبيان موضع قبورهم أولها :

ولفظـه يخبـر عـن جنانـه	قـال أبـو هاشـم فـي بيانـه
بالمـصطفى والآل والقـرآن	الحمـد لله علـى الايمـان

555

لنظم تاريخ لـه أذيع	لقد حداني مـن لـه أطيع
وآلـه المطهرين الخلفا	فهاك تـاريخ النبي المصطفى
بمكـة والحـرم الجليـل	فمولـد النبـي عـام الفيـل
بكعبـة الله العلـي ذي الكـرم	ومولـد الوصي أيـضا فـي الحـرم

عبد الله القطيفي

العالم الكامل الشيخ عبدالله بن احمد بن عبدالله بن عمران قال الشيخ فرج القطيفي في كتابه (تحفة أهل الايمان في تراجم آل عمران) : كان من شعراء أهل البيت عليهم‌السلام وقفت له على قصيدة مقصورة في رثاء الحسين عليه السلام ، ذهب أكثرها ولا بأس بذكر الموجود منها ، قال قدس‌سره :

يـشبه المسك أريجـا وشـذى	بـين روض مونـق أنفاسـه
راتعـا بـين غـزال ومهـى	كم سـحبت الـذيل فيها مارحـا
أرقـب البـدر ولا نجـم السـهى	لـم أخـف واش ولا هجـرا ولا
قـوض الرحـل ولا خـل نـاي	لا ولا أجـزع للركـب اذا
وقعـة الطف ومـا فيهـا جـرى	غيـر أنـي بـت كالملسوع مـن
وأسـلت الـدمع حزنـا عنـدما	وأذبـت القلـب همـا وأسـى
زمـر الاعـدا وأولاد الخنـا	لا نـسيت السـبط اذ حفت بـه
نحـوهم يوضح طرقـا للهدى	بعـد أن قـد كـانبوه ونحـا

أقول وذكره البحاثة الشيخ آغا بزرك الطهراني في (الكرام البررة) في القرن الثالث بعد العشرة.

أبو طالب الجعفري محمد بن عبدالله بن الحسين بن عبدالله بن اسماعيل بن عبدالله بن جعفر بن أبي طالب. قال المرزباني في معجم الشعراء ص ٣٨٢ : شاعر مقل ، سكن

الكوفة فلما جرى بين الطالبيين والعباسيين بالكوفة ما جرى وطلب الطالبيون قال أبو طالب :

فينهض فـي عـصيانكم مـن تـأخرا	بنـي عمنـا لا تـذمرونا سفاهة
لطـاعتكم منـا نـصيبا مـوقرا	وان ترفعـوا عنايـد الظلـم تجتنـوا
ليوثـا تـرى ورد المنيـة أعـذرا	وان تركبونـا بالمذلـة تبعثـوا

وله :

وسـامنا الـدهر خـسفا	قـد ساسـنا الاهـل عـسفا
جـورا علينـا وحيفـا	وصـار عـدل أنـاس
بـرءا لـدائي أشـفى	والله لـولا انتظـاري
تكـون بـالنجح أوفـى	ورقبتـى وعـد وقـت
ألفـا وألفـا وألفـا	لـسقت جيـشا الـيهم
رحـى البليـة عطفـا	حتـى تـدور علـيهم

ورأيت في معجم شعراء الطالبيين مخطوط العلامة المعاصر السيد مهدي الخرسان : أبو طالب الجعفري : جده الحسين أخذه بكار الزبيري بالمدينة ايام ولايته عليها فضربه بالسوط ضربا مبرحا فمات. وأبوه عبدالله امتنع من لبس السواد وخرقه لما طولب بلبسه فحبس بسر من رأى حتى مات في الحبس ، وذلك في ايام المعتصم. وكان شاعرا ويلقب هو أبوه الحسين بـ كلب الجنة كما كان حفيده أبو العوام أحمد يلقب بذلك. وكان أخو المترجم له اسماعيل بن عبدالله ممن قتل بطبرستان فيمن قتل من وجوه الطالبيين.
أقول ومما رأيته في كتاب الاقتباس هذه الابيات في رثاء الامام الحسين (ع) بقوله ؛ وقال بعضهم :

كـان النبـي المعـزى	أيـا قتـيلا عليـك
كـأن فـي القلـب وخـزا	قـد أقـرح الحـزن قلبـي
ورأسـه يـوم حـزا	اذا ذكـرت حـسينا

557

سارت بـــه البـرد جمــزا	الـــى اللعـــين يزيــــد
ثغـــرا وينهـــز نهــزا	فظـــل ينكـــث منـــه
بـــه يـــدور ويخـــزى	فـــسوف يـــصلى ســعيرا

الشيخ حسن النح

الشيخ حسن النح ، شاعر قطيفي من علماء القرن الثامن الهجري ويعرف بابن النح رأيت له شعرا كثيرا في رثاء الامام الحسين عليه السلام كما رأيت له في المخطوطات القديمة شعرا جيدا في مدح النبي الاعظم صلى الله عليه وآله وسلم. وهذه احدى قصائده انتسخها من مخطوطة قديمة قال كاتبها : ومما قاله الاديب العالم الشيخ حسن بن علي النح عليه الرحمة :

أم ضـــوء فرقـك قـد بـدا أم فرقـد	أومـيض بـرق فـي الـدجا يتوقـد
يـــرمقن أم بـــيض حـــسان خـــرد	وضبا تجرد مـن جفونـك أم ضـبا
تهتــز عجبــا أم غــصون تـأود	ومعـــاطف عطفـــت دلالا أم قنـــا
وعليـه جعفـر مـدمعي لا يحمـد	يـا مـن بـه يحيـى غرامـي خالـد
فعسـاك تـصبح شافعي يـا احمـد	نعمـان خـدك مالـك لقلوبنـا
متـــواتر لقـديم وجـدك مــسند	لـي فـي هـواك حـديث وجـد لـم يـزل
يجـري وقلبـي نـاره لا تخمـد	ومـن العجائـب أن دمعـي لـم يـزل
يـستل أبـيض وهـو لحـظ أسـود	عجبـي لفـاتر طرفـه فـي فتكـه
سـيف الوصـي الطهـر حـين يجـرد	لا شيء أمـضى مـن مضاربه سوى
المقـدام ولليـث الهزبــر الامجـد	الفـارس البطـل الهمـام الاروع
العلـم الـولي الزاهـد المتعبـد	الحـاكم العـدل الرضـي العـالم
الـصادق المتـصدق المتهجـد	الماجـد النـدب الـشجاع المجتبى

558

عند اللقا منها يذوب الجلمد	خلق أرق من النسيم وعزمة
الهيجاء منصور اللواء مؤيد	هو أشرف الثقلين في حسب وفي
في غير هامات العدى لا يغمد	بمهند ماض الغرار كعزمه
عنهم بفعل من علاه يؤكد	حتى غدا نون الوقاية ساقطا
معناه والفخر الذي لا ينفد	يا من له الشرف الذي لا ينتهي
قدرا ومن رام المعالي يحسد	حسدوك لما أن علوت عليهم
يوم الطفوف وأي ظلم جددوا	مولاي لو شهادت ما فعل العدا
فعلا تكاد لها الجبال تأود	فعلوا بمولاي الحسين ورهطه
منهم وتضطرب السماء وترعد	والارض تخسف خشية مما جرى

والقصيدة تتكون من ١٠٣ بيت قال في آخر بيت منها :

حسن الجزاء وغيركم لا يقصد	مولاي نجل النح يرجو منكم

وللشيخ حسن النح في مدح النبي صلى الله عليه وآله وسلم:

مطالع أقمار بزغن على قضب	بمنعرج الجرعاء عن أيمن الهضب
نثرن دموع العين كاللؤلؤ الرطب	بها السفح من وادي العقيق جآذر
بروق ثغور حسنها للورى يسبى	وبين ثغور المنحنى دون بارق
فقلبي ودمعي بين صب ومنصب	أسرن فؤادي حين أطلقن أدمعي
وغاباتها سود المحاجر والهدب	ربارب لكن الاسود عرينها

559

أرقـن دمـي عمـدا وأنكـرن مـاجرى   وأصدق شيء في الهوى شاهد الحب

بحك قف ان شمت عن أيمن الحمى   سنا بـارق قـد لاح مـن ذلـك الـشعب

وسلعا اذا مـا جئت سل عن حبائبي   وان ملت من عجبي الى نحوهم عج بي

لعـل اذا مـر معتـل نـشرها   يـصح بـه جـسمي وحيـى بـه قلبـي

منازل عـرب خيمـوا حـين يممـوا   بقلبـي لا بـين الاكلـة والحجـب

هـم الطيبون الطاهرون ومـن هـم   اذا جار صرف الدهر دون الورى حسبي

هـم الحامدون الشاكرون لذي العلى   هـم الـصادقون الـصابرون لـدى الكرب

محمـد المختـار مـن سـائر الـورى   أبـوهم وحـسن الفرع عن أصـله ينبي

نبـى سـمى كـل النبيـين رفعـة   وقـد سـار حتـى صـار في حضرة الرب

دنـى فتـدلى قـاب قوسـين عنـدما   رقـى وحبـاه الله بـالانس والقـرب

وخاطبـه الـرحمن مـن فـوق عرشـه   خطـاب محـب هـام وجدا الـى حـب

تقـدم كـل الانبيـاء بأسـرها   وصـلى امامـا بالملائكـة النجـب

فيـا رتبـة لـو رام أن يلمـس الـسها   بهـا لـم يكـن مـا رام بـالموقف الـصعب

مـن العرب كل أعجموا عند وصفه   لـذلك يـدعى سـيد العجـم والعرب

كـريم يـد لـو قـيس بـالبحر جـوده   لـزاد علـى جـدواه بـالمورد العـذب

ولـو يحكـه قطر الغمـام لمـا غـدت   فجـاج الثرى تبغـي الامـان مـن الجـدب

محـا رسـم أهل الشرك قاطع عضبه   بحـد الـى ايجابـه نـسبة الـسلب

ناصر بن أحمد المتوج

لقد مرت ترجمة والده الشيخ احمد في الجزء الرابع من هذه الموسوعة وفاتنا أن نتبعها بترجمة الولد وهو الشيخ ناصر فهو الجدير بأن يذكر ، يقول صاحب أنوار البدرين : كان نادرة عصره ونسيج وحده وقبره بجنب قبر أبيه وقد زرتهما مرارا ومشهدهما من المشاهد المتبرك به ، انتهى كلام شيخنا الرباني الشيخ سليمان الماحوزي البحراني.

وقد ذكر هذا الشيخ الجليل كل من تأخر عنه كالمحدثين البحرانيين والحر في الامل وخريت هذه الصناعة الملا عبدالله أفندي في (رياض العلماء) والسيد المعاصر في (روضاته) والفاضل المعاصر في آخر المستدرك وأثنوا عليه بكل جميل ، وذكره تلميذه الفاضل السبعي الاحسائي شارح قواعد العلامة بما لا مزيد عليه وذكر ان له شروحا على مشكلات القواعد وله ايضا من المصنفات تفسير الكتاب المجيد وله رسالة الناسخ والمنسوخ وله أشعار كثيرة منها نظم مقتل الحسين (ع) رأيناه ومراثي كثيرة وله مدح حسن في أمير المؤمنين علي بن أبي طالب عليه السلام.

ومن تلامذته الشيخان الجليلان : الشيخ احمد بن فهد الحلي والشيخ احمد بن فهد المضري الاحسائي ولكل منها شرح على الارشاد فهو من غرائب الاتفاقات.

السيد هاشم الصياح الستري:

ففيــــه ردت رؤوس الآل للحفــر	قم جدد الحزن في العشرين من صَفَر
فيها خذوا تربها كحلا الى البصر	يا زائري بقعة أطفالهم ذبحت
الى مصارع قتلاهن والحفر	والهفتا لبنات الطهر يوم رنت
تلك القبور بصوت هائل ذعر	رمين بالنفس من فوق النياق على
منها الخدود ودمع العين كالمطر	فتلك تدعو حسينا وهي لاطمة
وتلك تصرخ وايتماه في الصغر	وتلك تصرخ واجداه وا أبتا
أرض المدينة ذاك المربع الخضر	يا راجعين السبايا قاصدين الى
وخاطبوا الجد هذي تحفة السفر	خذوا لكم من دم الاحباب تحفتكم

رَبَّنَا تَقَبَّلْ مِنَّا ، إنَّكَ أنْتَ السَمِيعُ العَلِيمُ

561

Made in the USA
San Bernardino, CA
27 December 2016